THE CHURCH
Its Changing Image Through
Twenty Centuries

THE CHURCH

Its Changing Image Through Twenty Centuries

ERIC G. JAY

John Knox Press
ATLANTA

First published in two volumes by SPCK, London, and copyright © 1977, 1978 by Eric G. Jay.

Library of Congress Cataloging in Publication Data

Jay, Eric George.
    The church.

    Bibliography: p.
    Includes index.
    1. Church—History of doctrines.   I.   Title.
BV598.J38   1980   262'.009   79-92070
ISBN 0-8042-0877-8
ISBN 0-8042-0878-6 (pbk.)

Printed in the United States of America by John Knox Press, Atlanta.

Acknowledgements

Thanks are due to the following for permission to quote from copyright sources:

A. & C. Black: *Early Christian Doctrines* by J. N. D. Kelly; *A History of the Church in England* by J. R. H. Moorman.

The Revd Walter M. Abbott, S. J. and the American Press: *The Documents of Vatican II*, edited by Walter M. Abbott, S. J.

George Allen & Unwin Ltd: *The Churches Survey Their Task*, An Oxford Conference Report; and *The Social Teaching of the Christian Churches* by Ernst Troeltsch, translated by Olive Wyon (by permission also of Barnes and Noble).

Cambridge University Press: *The Doctrine of the Church in the New Testament* by G. Johnston (by permission also of the Reverend Professor G. Johnston); and *The Protestant Tradition* by J. S. Whale (by permission also of Dr. J. S. Whale).

T. & T. Clark Ltd: *The Christian Faith* by Friedrich Schleiermacher, translated by H. R. Mackintosh and J. S. Stewart; and *Church Dogmatics* by Karl Barth, edited by G. W. Bromiley and T. F. Torrance.

Les Editions du Cerf: *L'Ecclésiologie du haut Moyen-Age*, and *L'Eglise de saint Augustin à l'époque moderne*, both by Yves Congar.

William Collins Sons & Co. Ltd. and John Knox Press: *The Humanity of God* by Karl Barth, © 1960 by C. D. Deans.

Doubleday & Company, Inc.: *The Suburban Captivity of Churches* by Gibson Winter. Copyright © 1961 by Gibson Winter.

Fortress Press: *Luther's Works*, vols. 39, 41, and 44.

Harper & Row, Publishers, Inc.: *On Religion: Speeches to its Cultured Despisers* by Friedrich Schleiermacher.

Institut Francais d'Etudes Byzantines: 'Conférence sur la Primauté du Papa à Constantinople en 1357' by J. Darrouzes, *Revue des Etudes Byzantines* 19, 1961 (Mélanges Raymond Janin).

Professor Nikos A. Nissiotis: Background Paper on the Lectures for the Seminar on Orthodox Worship and Theology, 5-18 April 1971, at the Ecumenical Institute, World Council of Churches.

Oxford University Press: *The New Temple* by R. J. McKelvey.

Paulist Press: *Ancient Christian Writers,* vol. 26, edited by R. P. Lawson.

Penguin Books Ltd: *Western Society and the Church in the Middle Ages* by R. W. Southern, 2 (1970), pp. 92-3, 100, © R. W. Southern 1970; and *The Orthodox Church* by Timothy Ware (1963), p. 35, © Timothy Ware 1963.

SCM Press Ltd and The Westminister Press: *Calvin: Institutes of the Christian Religion,* vols. xx and xxi, The Library of Christian Classics, edited by John T. McNeill and translated by Ford Lewis Battles. Published in the USA by The Westminster Press. Copyright © MCMLX, by W. L. Jenkins. *Letters and Papers from Prison* (revised enlarged edition) by Dietrich Bonhoeffer, copyright © 1953, 1967, 1971 by SCM Press Ltd; *The Secular City* by Harvey Cox, copyright © Harvey Cox 1965 (both by permission also of Macmillan Publishing Company); *The Kingdom of Christ* by F. D. Maurice, edited by Alec Vidler; *Dogmatics in Outline* by Karl Barth (by permission also of Harper & Row, Inc.).

Search Press Ltd: *The Church* by Hans Küng; and *Structures of The Church* by Hans Küng, copyright © 1974 by Thomas Nelson & Sons (by permission also of Thomas Nelson, Inc.).

Sheed & Ward Ltd: *The Church Against Itself* by Rosemary Radford Ruether; and *God The Future of Man* by Edward Schillebeeckx (USA publisher: Sheed, Andrews & McMeel).

The Society for Promoting Christian Knowledge: *The Ecumenical Advance: A History of the Ecumenical Movement, 1948-1968,* edited by Harold E. Fey; *Thomas Arnold: Principles of Church Reform,* edited by M. J. Jackson and J. Rogan; and *A History of the Ecumenical Movement,* 1517-1948, edited by R. Rouse and S. C. Neill.

The University of Chicago Press: *Systematic Theology* by Paul Tillich, copyright © The University of Chicago 1951.

The World Council of Churches: *The New Delhi Report: The Third Assembly of the World Council of Churches, 1961,* edited by W. A. Visser't Hooft.

Biblical quotations from the Revised Standard Version of the Bible, copyrighted 1946 and 1952 by the Division of Christian Education of the National Council of the Churches of Christ in the USA, are used by permission.

Preface

Since 1958 I have regularly taught a course on 'The Nature of the Church' to theological students representing various churches, and most of whom have been preparing for ordination. Bibliographies have been provided; students have been directed to certain authorities, ancient and modern, required to read selected passages from them, and encouraged to gain the good habits of wide reading and study in depth. But undergraduates have other courses to take, and there is a limit to the number of books they can be expected to read in a single term. There is need, it has seemed to me, for a single textbook which, in the hands of a student, would give him a review of this subject and help him to gain more from the lectures, and contribute more to the tutorials, during the term in which the course is offered.

This, then, is an attempt to provide for what I feel to be a need. I have chosen to do so by way of tracing the history of the idea of the Church, following the example of others who, some decades ago, produced historical studies of such doctrines as the Person of Christ and the Atonement (Sydney Cave), the Eucharist (Darwell Stone), and Penance (O. D. Watkins) which have proved of great help to students. While I recognize ruefully that it is impossible to overcome subjectivity in any historical survey, objectivity has been sought in allowing theologians to speak for themselves by an extensive use of quotation or by providing summaries of their thought as fairly as I can.

The book has been written with the theological student in mind, but also in the hope that it may find other readers in days when many are asking the questions 'What is the Church?' and 'What is the Church for?'

I owe a particular debt of gratitude to Mrs Kenneth Naylor of Montreal for typing the manuscript, and for many useful suggestions (including the wording of the title).

McGill University, Montreal   ERIC G. JAY

Contents

Abbreviations

Part 1

THE CHURCH IN
THE NEW TESTAMENT

1

The Word 'Church' in the New Testament

The word 'church' is the usual translation of the Greek word *ekklesia*. Its first occurrence as applied to a group of Christians is in the first verse of St Paul's First Epistle to the Thessalonians: 'Paul, Silvanus, and Timothy, to the church [*ekklesia*] of the Thessalonians in God the Father and the Lord Jesus Christ: Grace to you and peace.' First Thessalonians is the earliest extant Christian document, being written about A.D. 50,[1] some fifteen years before the earliest date which scholars are prepared to allot to St Mark's Gospel.

What is this church which Paul addresses in this letter? What can be learned about it from this document? If the Christian movement had been a short-lived phenomenon, and if 1 Thessalonians were the only documentary evidence for it, what could we know about the church? Relying on the internal evidence alone, we can make several assertions:

1   The church includes a group of people in Thessalonica, a town in Macedonia which Paul had visited some months before (2.1).

2   On this visit he had communicated to them 'the gospel of God' (2.2,9). This gospel was also the gospel of Christ (3.2). It declared that one named Jesus, whom Paul calls 'Christ' and 'Lord', is the Son whom God the Father has sent into the world to bring salvation to it (5.9). Jesus had suffered and died (2.15), but he rose again (1.10; 4.14) and will come again to 'establish' them before God (3.13) so that they may always be with their Lord (4.17).

3   This group in Thessalonica had accepted this gospel and had become believers (2.13). As a consequence they had received power and inspiration from the Holy Spirit (1.5–6; 5.19), and had become imitators of Jesus, of Paul and other apostles, and of other churches in Judaea, especially in the courageous enduring of suffering (1.6; 2.14). In their turn they had proclaimed and spread the same gospel to

others (1.8; 4.10). An outgoing love had become characteristic of their lives day by day (3.6,12; 4.9–10), motivated by the desire to please God (4.1), and they lived in the expectation of the coming of Jesus, their Lord, who would bring them to their final salvation (1.10; 5.1–11).

4 The group of people whom Paul addresses is a local church. It is the church of the Thessalonians. But it is not a self-contained group isolated from other Christian groups. It is actively in contact with 'all the believers in Macedonia and in Achaia' (1.7; 4.10). Paul conceives of them also as having an intimate relationship with 'the churches of God in Christ Jesus which are in Judaea', despite the difference in race (2.14). Paul himself and Timothy, who had recently paid them a second visit (3.2), provided their main links with the churches in the more distant places.

5 The group met together regularly. This is implied by the references to prayer (5.17), prophesying (5.20), and mutual encouragement (5.11), and by Paul's assumption that there would be opportunities for his greetings to be conveyed and his letter read to the brethren.

6 The church of the Thessalonians evidently regarded Paul as a person of authority. He himself, though he addressed them as 'brethren' (1.4), thought of himself as a father over them who not only had the duty of exhorting, encouraging, and charging them while he was with them (2.11), but also claimed the right to do so by letter when he was absent (5.12 ff). That this claim was recognized is shown by the content of the report which Timothy, after his second visit, had brought back to Paul (3.6–8). Nevertheless the community had its local leaders, 'those who labor among you and are over you [*proistamenoi humōn*, literally 'those who stand before you'] in the Lord and admonish you', whom Paul charges the Thessalonians to respect and esteem (5.12–13).

These six paragraphs summarize what we could learn about the Church if 1 Thessalonians were the only document at our disposal. The letter has much to tell us about what the members of this church believed and how they acted, but little about its nature and constitution. The argument from silence may not legitimately be used here. For example, because 1 Thessalonians contains no reference to an initiatory rite or a communal meal, it does not follow that Paul at the time of writing considered baptism and the Lord's supper unimportant or that they had no place in the life of the Thessalonian Christians. We do not pack into the letters we address to friends references to matters which are taken for granted among us. We should not expect Paul to do so.

But the Christian movement was not short-lived, and 1 Thessalonians is not our only documentary evidence for it. Within a few years the Church had been planted in many places, from Palestine and Syria westward to Italy. Within the next few decades a lively literature grew up to which Paul himself contributed several more letters. The most significant of these writings were collected together in what we now call the New Testament. Before turning to inquire what the New Testament as a whole has to tell us of the nature of the Church, it will be useful to examine the word *ekklesia*. The study of the root meaning of a word and its general usage often provides information about the nature of that to which it refers.

EKKLESIA

This word had a long history before Paul employed it. In Athens, the city from which Paul probably wrote 1 Thessalonians, it had for several centuries been used of the assembly of the whole body of citizens, met together to elect magistrates, to confirm political decisions, and to hear appeals arising from judicial decisions. Other Greek cities also had their *ekklesiai*, varying in the powers they enjoyed. After the subjugation of Macedonia and Greece by the Romans, completed about 150 B.C., Greek cities still had their *ekklesiai*, although they retained little political power.

In classical Greek literature, therefore, the word was used of an assembly of citizens, officially constituted to do such business as the laws of the city appointed for it. *Ekklesia* is closely connected with the Greek verb *kaleo*, 'call', in its compound form *ekkaleo*, 'call out'. This signifies that an *ekklesia* is a gathering of people who have been duly summoned, or called out. The Greeks had another word, *sullogos* (connected with the verb *sullego*, 'collect together'), for unofficial or chance gatherings. The two words were sometimes used interchangeably, but strictly *ekklesia* means an officially summoned body, and *sullogos* an unofficial gathering of the people.

The use of the word *ekklesia* in another body of literature, the Septuagint (LXX), is more significant for an understanding of the Christian use of it. This was the Greek version of the Hebrew Scriptures, produced in Alexandria during the second century B.C. Its name, the Greek word for 'seventy', derives from the tradition that seventy scholars were simultaneously engaged in the translation. The LXX was familiar to Hellenistic Jews, from among whom came many of the earliest converts to Christianity. The New Testament takes its Old Testament citations much more frequently from the LXX than from the Hebrew.

In the Hebrew Scriptures the two most common words for a gathering of people are *ĕdhah* and *qāhāl*.[2] The root of *ĕdhah*[3] means 'appoint', and that of *qāhāl* means 'call'. Although both words are used of gatherings of all kinds, they also appear very frequently in the phrases '*ĕdhah* (*qāhāl*) of Israel' and '*ĕdhah* (*qāhāl*) of Yahweh' (the congregation, or assembly, of Israel, or of Yahweh). The root meaning of the two words would indicate that Israel is here regarded as a people appointed or called by God. Thus used the words have a technical and theological meaning and designate a people, called into being by God, who from time to time are gathered together for such solemn religious occasions as the receiving of the Law (Deut. 5.22), the dedication of Solomon's Temple (1 Kings 18.14 ff), and the reading of the book of the Law by Ezra (Neh. 8.2).[4]

In the LXX *ĕdhah* is uniformly translated by *sunagōgē*, literally 'a gathering together' (connected with the Greek verb *sunago*, 'bring together'). *Qāhāl*, however, is translated by *sunagoge* in Genesis, Exodus, Leviticus, Numbers, and in the Prophets; but by *ekklesia* in Deuteronomy (with a single exception), the historical books from Judges to Nehemiah, and in the Psalter (with the exception of Ps. 40.10).[5]

It is probably an unprofitable task to seek for some special significance in the way in which the LXX translation of *qāhāl* is distributed between *sunagōgē* and *ekklesia*. It might be worth attempting if the LXX came from one hand or a single team of translators. But 'the Alexandrine Bible is not a single version, but a series of versions produced at various times and by translators whose ideals were not altogether alike'.[6] Moreover, texts were subject to the errors of scribes, their well-meant efforts to correct, and all the other hazards involved in textual transmission before the invention of printing. And, as K. L. Schmidt says,[7] *ekklesia* and *sunagōgē* in the LXX, like the Hebrew words behind them, have much the same meaning: 'Both words are used both technically and non-technically, as underlined by the fact that translation varies between "assembly", "company" and "congregation".'

It is more to our purpose to inquire why Paul, writing about A.D.

50, chose *ekklesia* rather than *sunagōgē* to designate the community of those who accepted Jesus as Lord. Schmidt says[8] that the Hellenistic Christians found *ekklesia* preferable, because this word was falling into disuse among Greek-speaking Jews, who at the same time were tending to give *sunagōgē* a purely local meaning. It is perhaps not so certain as Schmidt implies that the word *ekklesia* was falling into disuse by the Jews, but there does seem to have been a tendency to employ *sunagōgē* for the local Jewish community and for the building in which they met for worship.[9] It is probable that more than one reason determined the Christian choice of the word *ekklesia*: (a) founders of early Christian groups, like Paul, must have known that in the LXX *ekklesia* was more frequently used than *sunagōgē* to translate *qāhāl*, and that *qāhāl* and not *ʿedhah* was the word used to designate official gatherings of the people on certain especially significant occasions (see p. 6 above); (b) *qāhāl* and *ekklesia* both have the consonantal sounds k and l,[10] and both have the root meaning of 'call'; (c) *ekklesia*, with its continuing secular usage in the Hellenistic world to denote a gathering of citizens 'was not so distinctively Jewish as to be unsuitable for a society which quickly accepted Gentiles to membership on the profession of their faith in Christ as Lord';[11] (d) the frequent use of *sunagōgē* for the building in the town or village where Christians were increasingly unwelcome.

THE USE OF *EKKLESIA* IN THE NEW TESTAMENT

St Paul frequently uses *ekklesia* of gatherings of Christians in a particular place, such as a house. He speaks of 'the church in your house' (Philem. 2); he sends greetings 'to Nympha and the church in her house' (Col. 4.15).[12] He employs the word also of a group of Christians assembled for worship (1 Cor. 11.18; 14.19). Appeal is made to such texts as these by those who maintain that the Church is essentially the gathering together of believers in a local congregation for worship.

But Paul also uses *ekklesia* of all the Christians in a city. In Thessalonica, for instance, there were no doubt a number of house churches. He speaks of these together as 'the church of the Thessalonians' (1 Thess. 1.1; 2 Thes. 1.1). Consequently it is natural for him to use *ekklesia* in the plural when he wishes to refer to all the Christian communities in an area: 'the churches of God in Christ Jesus which are in Judaea' (1 Thess. 2.14); 'the churches of Galatia'

(Gal. 1.2); he assures Christians in Rome that 'all the churches of Christ greet you' (Rom. 16.16).

This language is not to be taken to imply that Paul thinks of Christ's faithful simply as a number of smaller or larger local groups. When he confesses, 'I persecuted the church of God' (Gal. 1.13), he means something more than that he harried a number of Christian congregations in Jerusalem and Judaea. He was conscious that his offence was against the whole body of believers, wherever they might be (and, indeed, against their Head), even though it was but a few local gatherings which seemed to be affected. These local gatherings were the Church, the new people of God, embodied in those localities. Some have seen, probably correctly, the same significance in Paul's wording of the address in his letters to the Corinthians: 'to the church of God which is at Corinth' (1 Cor. 1.2; 2 Cor. 1.1). The *ekklesia* in Corinth, itself consisting of a number of *ekklesiai* (house churches), was the whole Church expressed and concretized in that city. It is not that the *ekklesia* is divided into *ekklesiai*. It is not that the *ekklesiai* are added up to make the *ekklesia*. Rather, the *ekklesia* is to be found in the places named.[13]

In the Acts of the Apostles *ekklesia* is also used both of believers in a single locality and of believers everywhere. The usage in the course of the narrative describing the growth of the Christian movement is instructive. The *ekklesia* in Jerusalem was the local church in the city, but originally it was also the 'whole church' (Acts 5.11). As the gospel advances beyond Jerusalem and Judaea we find *ekklesia* used in two ways, of the whole brotherhood and of a local community. Acts 9.31 records that 'the church throughout all Judea and Galilee and Samaria had peace and was built up; and . . . was multiplied'. Here 'church'[14] is most naturally taken of the Church as a whole, even though particular areas are mentioned. It was *the* Church which was growing. In Acts 20.28 Paul is recorded as exhorting the elders of Ephesus 'to feed the church of the Lord which he obtained with his own blood'. It is the church in Ephesus in which these elders have pastoral responsibilities, but it is the Church as a whole which Christ 'obtained'. On the other hand, in 14.27 and 15.3, *ekklesia* is used of the local Christian community of Antioch, in 15.4 of Jerusalem (which was now no longer the whole Church), and in 18.22 of Caesarea.

In the four Gospels there are only two occurrences of the word *ekklesia*, both in Matthew. This is not surprising, since the evangelists were concerned with the significance of the person, words, and work of the one who called into being the new community of the people of God, the one without whose suffering, death, and resurrection it would never have been. Writing after several decades of Christian expansion, they were certainly aware that the word *ekklesia* had gained wide usage.[15] Their failure to use the word may simply be because they were also aware that in the lifetime of Jesus it, or an Aramaic equivalent, was not yet used of believers.

Little need be said here of the two occurrences in Matthew. Matthew 16.18, 'You are Peter, and on this rock I will build my church', is a text which later became crucial because of the claim that the primacy which it appears to give to Peter among the apostles devolves upon the bishop of Rome as the successor of Peter. If it is an authentic saying of Jesus, which many scholars have doubted, it was probably spoken in Aramaic, and Schmidt gives reasons[16] for holding that the word used was k^enishta which could be the equivalent either of qāhāl or of édhah. Matthew 18.17, which prescribes the role of the *ekklesia* in cases of dispute among the faithful, seems to use the word of the kind of local group of Christians which came into being after Pentecost. The saying has the stamp of a very early piece of ecclesiastical legislation, placed anachronistically by the evangelist within the teaching of Jesus.[17] The whole thrust of the New Testament is that the *ekklesia* is the fellowship *of the risen Christ*. This is neither to deny that its foundations were being laid upon the apostles in the lifetime of Jesus nor to assert that it had no continuity with ancient Israel.[18]

'CHURCH' IN OTHER LANGUAGES

Ecclesia, the Latin transliteration of the Greek *ekklesia*, became the technical term for the Church in the Latin-speaking West, rather than such possible translations as *convocatio, contio,* or *comitia.* From the Latin it has passed into the French *église* and the Spanish *iglesia.*

The English word 'church' is almost certainly derived from the Greek adjective *kuriakos*, 'the Lord's', 'belonging to the Lord'.[19] This adjective is found in the New Testament in the phrases 'the Lord's supper' (1 Cor. 11.20) and 'the Lord's day' (Rev. 1.10), but is not applied to the Christian community. Other forms of the word are the German *Kirche*, Swedish *kerke*, Gaelic *kirk*, Russian *cerkovi*. In all of these it will be observed that the same consonantal sounds are used, k, r, and k, the k sound being sometimes aspirated. It is not known certainly where the word first gained currency as a synonym for *ekklesia*, or when precisely it came into the languages of northern and western Europe.

2

The Doctrine of the Church
in the New Testament

Turning from our consideration of the word 'church' (*ekklesia*), we now inquire what the New Testament has to say about the *nature* of the Church. We find nothing in the way of a formal definition. The N.T. is not a textbook of dogmatic theology. Rather we find that certain broad themes like 'people of God' and 'fellowship of the Spirit' are employed in speaking of the relation of the believers to Christ and to one another, and that the various writers seek to sharpen the reader's understanding of the relationship by using striking images (some would prefer to say 'metaphors') such as body, bride, sheepfold, vine, house, temple. These themes and the more frequent images we must now examine.[1]

THE CHURCH AS THE PEOPLE OF GOD

In a discussion of the words which might have been adopted as the name for the Christian community, Professor George Johnston mentions *laos* (the Greek word for 'people'): 'It particularly denotes the people of Israel, God's chosen. But it was not generally adopted: national limitations probably caused its rejection.'[2] Hebrews 4.9 and 1 Peter 2.9–10 are the only N.T. instances of its application to the Christian community. Yet many N.T. writers use language which suggests that they thought of Christians as the continuance, renewal, and enlargement of God's chosen people, Israel. Paul, who has come to realize that 'neither circumcision counts for anything, nor uncircumcision, but a new creation', prays that 'peace and mercy be upon all who walk by this rule, upon the Israel of God' (Gal. 6.15–16). Those who belong to Christ are 'Abraham's offspring, heirs according to promise' (Gal. 3.29).[3] The Epistle of James is addressed to 'the twelve tribes in the dispersion', and 1 Peter to 'the exiles of the dispersion in Pontus, Galatia, Cappadocia, Asia and Bithynia'. In 1 Peter

2.9–10 we find several designations of the Church which are used in the O.T. of ancient Israel. With Peter's 'chosen race' compare Deuteronomy 7.6 and 10.15; with 'royal priesthood' and 'holy nation', Exodus 19.6; with 'God's own people' (A.V. 'peculiar people'), Deuteronomy 4.20, 7.6, and 14.2.

Paul's image of the olive tree from which some branches are broken off and into which others are grafted from a wild olive (Rom. 11.17–24) recalls Jeremiah 11.16. The discourse in John 15 in which Jesus speaks of himself as the vine, of the vine-dresser as the Father and of those who abide in him as the branches recalls the imagery of Israel as God's vine in Isaiah 5.1–7 and in Psalm 80.8 ff. Some of the other N.T. images of the Church which will be discussed below also have clear O.T. parallels. Moreover, themes like the new covenant (e.g. in Mark 14.24, 1 Cor. 11.25 and elsewhere in Paul, and frequently in Hebrews) and the messiahship of Jesus give strong support to the suggestion that N.T. writers conceived of the Christian community as the ancient people of God reconstituted, Israel renewed and revivified.

Many scholars have agreed with T. W. Manson[4] in his argument that the N.T. doctrine of the Church rests upon the O.T. theme that Israel is the elect people of God, bound by a covenant sealed with blood to remain faithful and to keep God's law. The O.T. frankly faces the fact of the apostasy of the majority in Israel, and the idea of the remnant emerges, the righteous few who survive the catastrophe which overtakes the nation because of its apostasy. In the thought of several O.T. writers the remnant idea seems to attach itself closely to Israel's expectation of the Messiah (e.g. Isa. 11.1, 10–11; Jer. 23.3–6; Mic. 5.2–9). There is much in the N.T. which suggests acceptance and further development of this interpretation of biblical history. The remnant is seen as narrowed down to Jesus alone, the one true representative of Israel, utterly faithful and obedient. The priests of the temple and the guardians of the law reject him; the multitudes who at first heard him gladly, melted away; in the end his most intimate disciples 'forsook him and fled' (Mark 14.50). Hoskyns and Davey[5] believe that the considerable use made by all four evangelists in their Passion narratives of Psalm 22, 'treating of the afflictions of the "afflicted"; his rejection by men, and apparent forsaking by God' is significant. It points to the climax of the history of Israel as God's people. Jesus in his own person is the remnant. He accepts for himself the catastrophe of death which must overtake the apostasy of the many. He accepts it actually at the hands of those many who have taken offence at his own firm obedience to God's will, and it is for these many that he accepts it as the one true representative of God's people. But the temporal finality of death was cancelled by the act of God in raising him from death. 'Strictly speaking,' writes G. Henton Davies,[6]

> the Resurrection of our Lord is the end of the remnant idea. Here he who is truly the righteous remnant 'survived' the ultimate catastrophe, 'death', by resurrection. In that 'survival' life was maintained and indeed made available by the act of God, and thereafter the Presence and Kingship of God are manifested in and bound up with the resurrected Lord.

Christians believed that, through repentance and faith, they shared in this life of the risen Christ, were conscious of this presence, and thought of themselves as the continuing people of God. Paul could speak of them still as 'a remnant chosen by grace' (Rom. 11.5). But in fact the shrinking process was now reversed: 'Henceforth it is the destiny of the Christian remnant not to dwindle but to expand',[7] and Luke, the earliest Church historian, marks the advance stage by stage.[8]

This *Heilsgeschichte*[9] of the diminishing and expanding remnant has been challenged as an arbitrary and unverifiable interpretation of certain events in Jewish history and of Christian origins. But it is undeniable that early Christian writers did view the events in this way. There is so much reference either directly or by allusion to the remnant idea, and to the Church as Israel which has emerged into new life through the gift of God in Jesus the Messiah, that it cannot be ignored as evidence of what these writers conceived the nature of the Church to be.

THE BODY OF CHRIST

The idea of the Church as the people of God is closer than may at first appear to what is usually thought to be the most prominent N.T. image of the Church, that of the body of Christ. What brings them together is the concept of Christ as the remnant implicit in the former, and the concept of Christ as a corporate personality implicit in the latter.

Paul has several very frequent phrases which describe the relationship of the believer to Christ.[10] These are 'in Christ', which first appears in 1 Thessalonians 1.1; 'with Christ', which is frequent in passages which speak of the Christian suffering and dying, rising and living with Christ (e.g. Rom. 6.1–11); 'into Christ', in passages which deal with the significance of baptism (e.g. Rom 6.3; Gal. 3.27). Christians thus brought 'into Christ' become 'members of Christ' (1 Cor. 6.15), a phrase which brings us close to the idea of the body of Christ.

Ernest Best writes:[11] 'Behind all these descriptions (i.e. of the Christian community as a body, a bride, etc.) and behind the descriptions of the Church as "in Christ" or "with Christ" there is a conception of Christ as a corporate or inclusive personality and of believers as solid with him'. The idea of Christ as corporate personality appears clearly in 1 Corinthians 15: 'For as in Adam all die, so also in Christ shall all be made alive' (v. 22), and 'The first man Adam became a living being; the last Adam became a life-giving spirit' (v. 45), and the following versus continue the argument. Romans 5.12–21 presents the same idea, which may be summed up in the words of verse 18: 'Then as one man's trespass led to condemnation for all men, so one man's act of righteousness leads to acquittal and life for all men'. As men are physically in racial solidarity with Adam, so the believer is in spiritual solidarity with Christ, and this is proleptically true of all mankind. In these Pauline passages the universalism is very marked.[12]

The solidarity of mankind is not a concept which is readily grasped by those who have not freed themselves from the 'rugged individualism' which was perhaps the nineteenth century's main legacy to the western world. But modern genetics in its doctrine of transmitted characteristics, and the modern psychology which emphasizes the significance of racial memory, have each made it clear that the concept cannot be dismissed as merely primitive mythology not to be taken seriously by twentieth-century scientific man. 'Solidarity', says J. A. T. Robinson, 'is the divinely ordained structure in which personal life is to be lived.'[13] St Paul's claim is that in Jesus Christ who died on the cross and overcame death by his resurrection an analogous solidarity is being created: 'If any one is in Christ, he is a new creation . . . the new has come' (2 Cor. 5.17).

First Corinthians 12.12–27 is the earliest passage in which Paul treats at length the idea of the Church as a body. On the surface it seems that he presents us with a simile—the Church is *like* a body. Comparison with the human body is worked out vividly, even humorously. The human body would be limited indeed if it were nothing but a seeing instrument: 'If the whole body were an eye, where would be the hearing?' Stress is equally laid on the necessary co-operation between the diverse members: 'The eye cannot say to the hand, "I have no need of you".' Even what appear to be less important members are indispensable (v. 23). Paul then goes on to speak of the varied ministries appointed by God in the Church.

But there are several indications here that Paul is doing more than suggest a simile. 'You are the body of Christ and individually members of it' (v. 27) says more than 'you are like a body' or 'you may usefully think of yourselves as a kind of body'. The language of verse 12 which opens the passage is instructive:

> For just as the body is one and has many members, and all the members of the body, though many, are one body, so it is with Christ.

Had Paul been employing simile, we should have expected the last phrase to be 'so it is with the Church'. But what Paul is saying is that *Christ* possesses many members, those who have been baptized into him and have received the Holy Spirit (v. 13). Christ is this body. The members, too, are the body of Christ, but only in him; without integration by faith, baptism, and the gift of the Spirit of God they could not be this kind of body, the body of Christ.

There have been many scholarly discussions about whether Paul was using the phrase 'body of Christ' in a simile, metaphorically or analogically, literally or ontologically. E. Best, who interprets the phrase as a metaphor, provides an example.[14] I am of the opinion that, whatever difficulties it presents to the modern mind, Paul is asserting that, in *reality*, Christ, now risen and glorified is, to use Best's own words, 'a corporate or inclusive personality',[15] into solidarity with whom God has already brought believers and wills to bring all men. What is 'a corporate or inclusive personality' but a body? Not, indeed, a body which corresponds to any body, animal, human, or societal, which can be empirically studied, for it is the body which God has willed before the foundation of the world, the body of the redeemed by and in his eternal Son.[16]

The Epistles to the Colossians and Ephesians develop the body of Christ theme further. That these came from the hand of Paul has been seriously disputed, but scholars who reject Pauline authorship are generally inclined to admit that the thought is Pauline.[17]

Colossians declares that God's purpose in the incarnation of his Son, 'the image of the invisible God' in whom and for whom all things were created (1.15–16), was the reconciliation with himself of all that is estranged (1.20). Jesus Christ has done the work of reconciliation in 'his body of flesh' (1.22). In his risen body 'he is the head of the body, the church; he is the beginning, the firstborn from the dead, that in everything he might be pre-eminent' (1.18). From this 'beginning', which is Christ, the body develops, but only as believers hold fast 'to the Head, from whom the whole body, nourished and knit together through its joints and ligaments, grows with a growth that is from God' (2.19).

Ephesians at greater length works out the theme of the 'mystery' of God's purpose now revealed in Christ and his Church. God's mighty act has brought it about that Christ, raised from the dead, has become 'the head over all things for the church, which is his body, the fulness of him who fills all in all' (1.22–3). This body is the body of those who are reconciled to God (2.16), of which Gentiles are now fellow members (3.6). It is a body which is to grow to maturity, the maturity of Christ the head, aided by gifts of the Holy Spirit which he has made available, by the work of the apostles, prophets, evangelists, pastors, and teachers whom he has called (4.11–12), living in unity and love (4.2–3, 15; 5.2). The thought of Colossians 2.19 is repeated:

> We are to grow up in every way into him who is the head, into Christ, from whom the whole body, joined and knit together by every joint with which it is supplied, when each part is working properly, makes bodily growth and upbuilds itself in love (4.15–16).

It has seemed to some that Ephesians 1.23 which speaks of the Church as the fulness of Christ, suggests that Christ is not complete without the Church. It is unlikely that the writer who speaks of Christ in 4.13 as already possessing the fulness to which the Church must attain can have meant this. The Christ is complete. There is fulness in him which Colossians 2.9 speaks of as 'the whole fulness of deity'. We cannot enter here into a full discussion of this admittedly difficult verse which is capable of various translations.[18] But three facts are to be borne in mind: (a) the Pauline epistles everywhere affirm the perfection, completeness, and sovereignty of Christ; (b) they express the conviction that within the body of Christ all will attain the measure of the stature of the fulness of Christ (Eph. 4.13; cf. 1 Cor. 15.27–8); (c) they recognize realistically that the Church is still far from attaining this fulness.

The whole passage, Ephesians 1.15–23, expresses the consciousness of Christians that in Christ victory has been accomplished (v. 20), but that its fruits are yet to be claimed (vv. 17–19). The

Church experiences a perplexing tension in its recognition that salvation and fulfilment belong to it *now* by the grace of God, but also are *not yet* fully manifested in its life. This tension appears at several points in Paul's thought, and we refer to it again below (p. 20). We shall therefore not be far wrong if we interpret Ephesians 1.22–3 as intended to convey the sense that the fulness of Christ, which is his even though the Church be small and sinful, is to be claimed by the Church, is in fact being continually imparted to it, and will be wholly experienced in the age to come.

THE EUCHARISTIC BODY OF CHRIST

Paul speaks also of the body of Christ in connection with the Lord's supper. His account of the institution of the eucharist in 1 Corinthians 11.24 records the words of Jesus in breaking the bread: 'This is my body which is for you.' In an earlier passage, where he exhorts the Corinthians to have nothing to do with pagan sacrifices, he writes:

> The cup of blessing which we bless, is it not a participation in the blood of Christ? The bread which we break, is it not a participation in the body of Christ? (1 Cor. 10.16).

The next verse makes clear the connection in his mind between the supper and the community:

> Because there is one loaf, we who are many are one body, for we all partake of the same loaf.

It perhaps goes further than the evidence warrants to say with A. E. J. Rawlinson[19] that the occurrence of the word 'body' in the words of institution and his grasp of the significance of the eucharist suggested to Paul the application of the term 'body of Christ' to the Church. What is clear, however, is that Paul sees the supper, instituted, according to the tradition which he had received, by Christ himself, as integral to the life of the Christian community. Paul's understanding of this is well elucidated by G. Johnston in the book which has already been cited several times:

> The Lord's Supper has a similar place (i.e. to baptism) in the life of the Church as the growing Body of Christ. It is distinctive from other fellowship meals (e.g. those of the mystery religions) because it is associated with the living Christ who has died to save the world. It must be the *Lord's* Supper or nothing (1 Cor. 11·20). Here the dying Christ is

recalled and the death proclaimed 'till he come', by the eating of the loaf and drinking the cup (1 Cor. 11.26). In the blood shed a new Covenant had been ratified; hence to drink this cup is to share the promise. Surely all who do so must be one in Christ! As the loaf was broken, so the mortal body of Christ had been slain. But in Him, the triumphant Saviour, all the redeemed became one spiritual body. It is in this capacity that they meet to celebrate the Supper. As they eat they all participate in Christ's death. Surely that should cement their unity! The Lord himself is in their midst, judging their attitude as they come to his table. That is why division here is so heinous.[20] Christ suffers in the suffering of His people. This mutual sharing in the dying Jesus is the very highest point of the Church's unity. Christ's spirit of sacrificial love is to be the ideal and inspiration of its corporate life. Only so can it really be the Body of Christ.[21]

The intimate connection of the eucharist with the very life of the Church has been stressed throughout the history of Christian thought. We shall find this in Ignatius of Antioch (p. 35 below) and St Augustine (pp. 84–5 below). It is implied in excommunication which was early introduced as a disciplinary measure against those whose lives were judged to belie their Christian membership. In the Confessions of the Churches of the Reformation the definition of the Church which is proffered invariably includes among its marks the administration of the sacraments of baptism and the supper according to Christ's ordinance. Both in the teaching and the practice of the Orthodox Churches of the East, which generally refrain from dogmatic definitions, the Church is regarded as essentially a eucharistic community.

Paul, as we have seen, can use the image of the body in a very practical way to assure each Christian, however humble, of the importance of his place and function within the whole membership. But for him this image primarily concerns the inward relationship of the faithful with Christ and with one another. 'Body of Christ' speaks of a fellowship more closely knit and deeply rooted than any other known to men, a fellowship in which the faithful enter into the experience of the Redeemer himself, dying with him, and living with him, feeding upon the nourishment and abounding in the energy which he gives. Each who truly enters into this Christ-centred experience is in unity and love with every other who shares it.

THE BRIDE OF CHRIST

In the Pauline writings the image of the Church as a bride appears in 2

Corinthians 11.2 and Ephesians 5.22–33.[22] Precedent for this exists in O.T. passages in which the relationship between God and Israel is likened to that between husband and wife (Hos. 1–3; Isa. 54.1–8). Certain elements in the tradition of the teaching of Jesus may also have suggested the Pauline use of the image, namely, Jesus' reference to himself as the bridegroom (Mark 2.18–20) and the parables of the marriage feast in Matthew 22 and the ten virgins in Matthew 25.

In 2 Cor. 11.2 Paul is referring to the local church in Corinth when he writes: 'I betrothed you to Christ to present you as a pure bride to her one husband.' But in Ephesians 5.22–33 the bridge is the whole Church. The context is one in which the mutual love and duties of husband and wife are discussed. The relationship between Christ and the Church is suggested as the perfect model:

> The husband is the head of the wife as Christ is the head of the church, his body, and is himself its Savior. As the church is subject to Christ, so let wives also be subject in everything to their husbands. Husbands, love your wives, as Christ loved the church and gave himself up for her, that he might sanctify her, having cleansed her by the washing of water with the word (Eph. 5.23–6).

The passage itself seems to recognize the inadequacy of the parallel. Christ is the Saviour of his Church, and that cannot be said in any ultimate sense of a husband in relation to his wife. A man, loving his wife, and knowing that she is utterly worthy of his love, may be ready to die for her. But Christ in his love for the Church dies for it, and *then* makes it worthy (vv. 25–6). His will is

> that the church might be presented before him in splendor, without spot or wrinkle or any such thing, that she might be holy and without blemish (v. 27).

It will be noted that in this passage the image of the head and body is interwoven with that of the husband and bride. This is an appropriate place to note that in each of these images an ambiguity is implicit.

The body and head may be thought of as two separate parts of an organism. The head has its own special function within the organism, and the body, considered as the trunk in distinction from the head, is a collection of members each having its own function. But while head and body can be thought of in this compartmental way, in reality they are an integrated unity within the living organism. Without the head, which is the governing member, the body, considered as trunk, is lifeless.

Similarly, husband and wife may be thought of as two individuals, each with obligations to the other which may or may not be fulfilled. But the will of God is that 'the two shall become one' (Eph. 5.31; cf. Gen. 2.24, 'one flesh') in a mutuality of love and responsibility. There is a sense, then, in which a man's love of his wife is a nourishing and cherishing of his own flesh (Eph. 5.28–9), that one flesh which he has become with his wife.

The ambiguity inherent in the relationship of head to body and of husband to wife remains when they are taken as images of the relationship between Christ and the Church. The two in principle have become an integrated unity, yet it is still possible, and even necessary, to think of them in distinction. Body and head are not identical; the bride is not the bridegroom; the Church is not the Christ. There is a tension of thought here: integrated unity, yet not identity. In its unity with Christ the Church shares in his glory and perfection. But thought of as one partner in a marriage, or as a body distinguishable from its head, the Church owes obedience to Christ which is nowhere and never completely rendered. It is far from glory and perfection. In the history of doctrine this tension of thought comes to the fore whenever the sense in which the word 'holy' may be attributed to the Church is discussed.[23] The same tension is experienced in the life of the individual believer, whose status Luther was to sum up in the phrase *simul justus et peccator*, 'justified, yet at the same time a sinner'. It is the tension between the 'now' of appropriating in faith the redemption that Christ has once for all won for man, and the 'not yet' of conscious unworthiness and the realization that life with its temptations lies ahead. The Church is holy; the Church is to become holy.

Paul, whose realism has already been mentioned, was well aware of this tension. He can turn immediately from the most exalted language about the Church to warnings against divisive and uncharitable behaviour. He had no illusions about the perfection of the members of the church in Corinth.

THE CHURCH AS GOD'S BUILDING

In the four Gospels, the Acts, the Pauline Epistles, 1 Peter, the Epistle to the Hebrews, and Revelation allusions to the people of God as a building, a house, a sanctuary, or temple abound.[24] The building image has roots in the O.T. The prophets frequently speak of God's people as 'the house of Israel' or of Jacob. Isaiah 28.16 and Psalm 118.22–3 introduce the idea of God's building containing a 'cornerstone'. The stone of Psalm 118 which is rejected by the builders as unsuitable but is reinstated by God as the chief cornerstone is most naturally taken to refer to some person in the community. The application of this to the person of Jesus Christ by the early Church (Matt. 21.42; Acts 4.11; 1 Peter 2.7) doubtless helped to suggest the image of the Church as a building whose principal stone is the rejected and crucified, but now risen, Lord.

Paul frequently speaks of 'building up' the Church in his letters to the Corinthians.[25] This is the work not only of apostles, but of every member. In Ephesians the idea of building up the Church is combined with the idea of the Church as a body: 'building up the body of Christ' (4.12); 'the whole body ... makes bodily growth and upbuilds itself in love' (4.16).

This language describes the *process* of building. Elsewhere the Church is spoken of as *a building*. Paul tells the Corinthians that they are God's building. He himself has laid a foundation, and that foundation is Jesus Christ (1 Cor. 3.9–15). The other main Pauline passage which speaks of the Church as a building is Ephesians 2.19–22:

> You are ... members of the household of God, built upon the foundations of the apostles and prophets, Christ Jesus himself being the chief cornerstone, in whom the whole structure is joined together and grows into a holy temple in the Lord; in whom you also are built into it for a dwelling place of God in the Spirit.

There is a division of opinion about the Greek word *akrogōniaios*, translated 'cornerstone'. Some[26] take it to be a stone connected with the foundations of a building; others[27] to be the important locking stone at the crown of the archway above the main entrance of a building. The first interpretation presents the picture of a number of foundation stones, the most important of which is Christ, the others being the apostles and prophets. The second identifies the apostles and prophets as the foundation, and likens Christ to a stone which is the last to be put into position, and which secures the whole building.

In either case the imagery is deficient. If the 'cornerstone' which is Christ is the last to be built in, it is suggested that the building of the Church originated in human enterprise. If the 'cornerstone' which is Christ is a foundation, the image fails to do justice to the concept of the continuing activity of the risen Christ in the life of the Church. But the basic defect of the image is that stones are lifeless things. The author of the Epistle is evidently aware of this, for by the use of the phrase 'grows into a holy temple' in verse 21 he alludes to the body image which he expounds elsewhere. 1 Peter, which also employs this imagery, attempts to overcome its inadequacy by speaking of Christ as the 'living stone' (2.4) and of Christians as 'living stones' (2.5).

We noted above that the images of the Church as the body of Christ and the bride of Christ both contain an ambiguity which reflects the tension in which the Church of Christ always exists. We spoke of it as the tension between the 'now' and the 'not yet'. The same ambiguity is found in the image of the Church as God's building. From one point of view the building is complete and perfect in Christ. From another it is incomplete: stones are continually being added, and the building will not be complete and perfect until the full number is built in. R. J. McKelvey's comment[28] on this ambiguity is helpful:

> The conception of the church as a building under construction, with no suggestion of when the work will be completed, and at the same time as a temple in which God is actually dwelling and worship is being offered, looks like a contradiction. What we have here, however, is a paradox which is basic to much New Testament thinking, the paradox of present possession and future hope. Like each of its members, the Church is called to become what it is, the dwelling-place of God in the Spirit. Recognition of this fact preserves the church from the twin evils of complacency and despair.

THE FELLOWSHIP OF THE SPIRIT

I have left to the end of this very selective treatment of the N.T. doctrine of the Church consideration of the theme which many believe to be the most significant, that of the Church as the fellowship of the Holy Spirit. The idea of the constitutive role of the Holy Spirit is, however, often present in the themes which I have already discussed: 'Do you not know', writes Paul to the Corinthians, 'that you are God's temple and that God's Spirit dwells in you?' (1 Cor. 3.16). The Church as the Lord's holy temple is 'a dwelling place of God in the Spirit' (Eph. 2.22). Listing the bonds of Christian unity and peace, Ephesians 4.3–7 places the 'one body' and the 'one Spirit' together. Christians are baptized into the one body by the one Spirit (1 Cor. 12.13), whose enabling gifts Paul discusses at length immediately following his first major treatment of the body image in 1 Cor. 12.12–27.

The idea of the Holy Spirit as the creator of the Church is already implicit here. A discussion of the relationship between Christ and the Spirit would lead us beyond our present task into the field of Trinitarian theology. But G. Johnston is clearly correct in affirming that in the thought of Paul 'God is the Father of the Lord Jesus Christ; God's Spirit therefore is Christ's Spirit'.[29] For Paul the Spirit of God and of Christ is active throughout and from the very beginning of the saving process. The Christian's confession that Jesus is Lord (1 Cor. 12.3) is prompted by the Spirit, and 'the graces of the Christian life are the fruit of the Spirit, since those who belong to Christ possess His Spirit and are temples of the Spirit of the living God. . . . To be in Christ is also to be in the Spirit.'[30] The Christian man is 'led by the Spirit of God' and by the same Spirit becomes aware of membership in the community of the sons of God (Rom. 8.14–17).

Consider the word 'fellowship'. Familiarity tends to obscure for us the extraordinary phenomenon of a body of ancient literature in which the idea of and the words for fellowship and sharing abound as they do in the N.T. Of frequent occurrence are the adjective *koinos*, 'shared in', 'held in common', and its cognates, the nouns *koinōnia*, 'sharing', 'fellowship', and *koinōnos*, 'sharer', 'partner', and the verb *koinōneo*, 'to have (or give) a share in'. Frequent synonyms for *koinōneo* are *metecho* and *metalambano*. The prefix *sun*, 'together with', is used with nouns far more frequently than in any other ancient writings, and we read of 'fellow-workers', 'fellow-prisoners', 'fellow-soldiers', 'fellow-servants', 'fellow-heirs', 'fellow-citizens'.

The N.T. speaks of Christians as sharing in the benefits which Christ has made available. They are partakers of grace (Phil. 1.7), of God's promise (Eph. 3.6), of glory to be revealed (1 Pet. 5.1), even of the divine nature (2 Pet. 1.4). They also share *with* Christ in his experience. Baptism signifies being united with Christ 'in a death like his' and 'united with him in a resurrection like his' (Rom. 6.5). This theme often recurs: 'You were buried with him in baptism, in which you were also raised with him through faith' (Col. 2.12; cf. 2 Cor. 4.10). The Christian can therefore recognize that personal adversity is to 'share his sufferings, becoming like him in his death' (Phil. 3.10).

There is also a fellowship and sharing of Christians with each other. Passages which teach the privilege and duty of brotherly love, sympathy, and forgiveness are numerous and to be found in almost every book.[31] Practical expressions of it are the experiment in the sharing of goods by Christians in Jerusalem (Acts 2.44; 4.32) and a collection which Paul organized among his Gentile converts for poor Christians in Jerusalem (Rom. 15.26; 2 Cor. 8.1 ff and 9.1 ff). The word which Paul uses for this collection is *koinōnia*, which in this context might be translated 'an expression of fellowship'.

All this describes the content which the New Testament Church gave to the word *koinōnia*, what Christians understood it to mean in their daily lives. The inspiration and motive power for it they ascribed to the Spirit of God and Christ. They believed themselves to be living in 'the fellowship (*koinōnia*) of the Spirit'.

What does the word 'of' mean in this phrase? The English 'of' can be as ambiguous as the Greek genitive case which it here represents. Does '*koinōnia* of the Spirit' mean 'participation in the Spirit' as in the R.S.V. translation of Philippians 2.1? Or does it mean 'fellowship which the Spirit bestows'? This would seem the better interpretation in 2 Corinthians 13.14 where Paul obviously has the divine prevenience in mind. It is not necessary to decide between these interpretations, for both are valid.[32] They complement each other. It is because the Holy Spirit bestows fellowship that participation in the Spirit and the gifts of the Spirit is made possible.

Again and again the N.T. insists on the prevenience of the Spirit in the life both of the individual believer and of the whole Church. The life of the believer originates with the Holy Spirit: 'God's love has been poured into our hearts through the Holy Spirit which has been given to us' (Rom. 5.5). In the baptism which opens the believer's heart to receive his continuing influence the Holy Spirit is already at work (1 Cor. 12.13). Of those who are truly in Christ it must be said that they are 'in the Spirit' (Rom 8.9–11), are 'led by the Spirit' (Rom 8.14; Gal. 5.18), and 'walk by the Spirit' (Gal. 5.16, 25) so that the 'fruit of the Spirit' is seen in their lives, 'love, joy, peace, patience, kindness, goodness, faithfulness, gentleness, self-control' (Gal. 5.22–3). The Holy Spirit is the creator and sustainer of the Christian's life.

The Holy Spirit is also the creator and sustainer of the Church's life. The account of Pentecost in Acts 2.1 ff, which is presented as the fulfilment of Christ's promise to clothe his disciples with power from on high (Luke 24.49; Acts 1.8)[33] testifies to the conviction that the Church's historical existence was empowered by the Holy Spirit. 'The Church is a creation through the act of God in Christ'; but it is 'at the same time a fellowship created by the Holy Spirit'.[34] The creator Spirit is also the Church's guide and sustainer. To his guidance are attributed decisions taken at certain crucial points in the Church's early history: the baptism of the first Gentile (Acts 14.44 ff); the first overseas mission (13.2); the admission of Gentiles without requiring their circumcision (15.28); the bringing of the gospel to Europe (16.6–10). It is the Spirit of God, too, who distributes the varieties of gifts and ministries which nourish the Church's life.

This self-understanding as 'the fellowship of the Spirit' is another indication that the early Church thought of itself as the people of God, renewed and living in the day of the Messiah. According to the prophets the messianic age was to see a renewed activity of the Spirit (Isa. 11.1–2; Ezek. 36.26–7, 37.1–14; Joel 2.28 ff). So the N.T. portrays it. The coming of Jesus the Messiah is by the power of the Spirit who is present at his conception (Luke 1.35), at his baptism (Mark 1.10), as he faces the implications of his vocation (Matt. 4.1; Mark 1.12; Luke 4.1) and as he opens his ministry (Luke 4.14, 18). The messianic kingdom is inaugurated. Joel's prophecy begins to be fulfilled (Acts 2.16) with the outpouring of the Spirit on the Messiah's first followers at Pentecost. To those who by faith and repentance subsequently enter the messianic community the Spirit comes and brings his gifts and graces of which the greatest (1 Cor. 13.13) is that love 'which binds everything together in perfect harmony' (Col. 3.14), the unity of the Spirit.

The Kingdom is *inaugurated*; it is yet to come to fulfilment. Consequently the Church in history is not identical with the Kingdom. The Kingdom, says G. Johnston,[35] 'is a realm in which God, Christ, and the Ecclesia are united in the Spirit. ... The Church is the sphere on earth of the incarnating of this Holy Spirit, a visible society with an invisible life, a divine-human phenomenon.' He prefers to speak of the *incarnating* rather than the *incarnation* of the Spirit. It is more true to the Church's experience of tension between the 'now' and the 'not yet' and to its consciousness of imperfection while it lives in hope of the gift of maturity in the body of Christ and in the unity of the Spirit.[36]

THE CHURCH AND THE INDIVIDUAL

The N.T. throughout lays great stress on the corporate nature of the Church. It is apparent in all the Church themes and images which we have studied: people of God, body, marriage relationship, fellowship of the Spirit; it is true even of the seemingly inanimate image of the building, for God's building is at once 'the household of God' (Eph. 2.19) and the temple of a worshipping community (Eph. 2.21). Whatever may be the validity of the concept of a private Christian withdrawn from membership of the community, the N.T. knows no such person. 'Church' does not mean the sum of individuals who have a private relationship with Christ and a private inspiration of the Holy Spirit. It is a community of believers incorporated into Christ's filial relationship with God by the adopting initiative of God himself who 'has sent the Spirit of his Son into our hearts' (Gal. 4.6). This is not to say that the individual is submerged. In the body all members have their necessary place (1 Cor. 12.14 ff); in the household and temple all have their priestly work (1 Pet. 2.5, 9; Rev. 1.6). 'Let every one lead the life which the Lord has assigned to him, and in which God has called him,' writes Paul (1 Cor. 7.17). And he is confident that in the consummation God will raise man's physical body into a spiritual body (1 Cor. 15.42–50). This resurrection body is 'none other than the Body of Christ in which we have a share'.[37] Man's destiny is the completion of his incorporation into the body of Christ which began at baptism, the fulfilment of solidarity with Christ's risen and glorious body. But this does not mean the loss of individuality. The teaching of Jesus contains a strong emphasis on the worth of the individual. Paul and other N.T. writers were doubtless too well aware of this, and of Jesus' own concern for persons, to suggest any eschatology of absorption.

Part 2

THE PATRISTIC PERIOD

3

From Clement of Rome
to Irenaeus

A quarter of a millennium elapsed from the birth of Jesus Christ before the first work dealing specifically with the nature of the Church was written. This was *On the Unity of the Church* by Cyprian, Bishop of Carthage, 248–58.[1] The first theological concern of the early Church was the doctrine of the Person of Christ in relation to the doctrine of God. But the articles of Christian faith, later to be drawn together in the creeds, are all integrally related. The doctrine of Christ's Person has direct implications for a doctrine of man and man's relationship to God. We find indications, therefore, in the earliest Christian Fathers, of how they thought about the Church, even though they do not address themselves to the nature of the Church as a particular theological problem.

Empirically the Church existed as a number of congregations scattered over the Mediterranean countries. In view of the distance which separated them they might easily have become self-contained groups, developing in idiosyncrasy and showing great variety in teaching, modes of worship, and customs. Variations there were, but in general we have a picture of remarkable unanimity in doctrine, worship, and, certainly by the end of the second century, in forms of ministry and general structure. This unanimity witnesses both to the faithfulness of the Church's early missionaries and their converts to the tradition they had received, and to the excellence of the means of communication and travel in the Roman Empire which made it possible. Congregations were reminded that the Church which expresses itself wholly in the worship and work of the local Christian community nevertheless transcends it. 'Wherever Jesus Christ is, there is the Catholic Church,' writes Ignatius of Antioch.[2] Polycarp, Bishop of Smyrna, is reported, in the account of his martyrdom written soon after the event (*c.* 155), to have prayed for 'the whole Catholic Church throughout the world'.[3] The word 'catholic' is used here in its literal sense of 'universal' or 'in its totality' (from the Greek *kath'holon*) in distinction from a local church. It is somewhat later that the word is used to distinguish the Church which adheres to accepted doctrine from groups judged to be heretical or schismatic.

From the beginning Christian writers used the N.T. themes and imagery of the Church. The following is a list of the most notable instances in the earliest Fathers:

THE CHURCH AS THE NEW ISRAEL

Clement of Rome (*c.* 94), *To the Corinthians* XXIX, 1–3, where the argument is that whereas in time past Israel was 'the portion of the Lord', God has now 'made us [Christians] the portion of his choice for himself'; The *Epistle of Barnabas* (*c.* 70–100) III, 6 and V, 7: the Church is 'the new people'; Justin Martyr (*c.* 150), *Dialogue with Trypho* XI, 5 and CXXIII; Irenaeus (*c.* 180), *Adversus Haereses* V, 32.2: 'Abraham's seed is the Church', and V, 34.1.

THE CHURCH AS THE BODY OF CHRIST

1 Clement XXXVII; Ignatius, *Smyrnaeans* I: the crucified body of Jesus is seen as a standard which rallies the faithful in 'the one body of his Church'; the preacher of the sermon which is erroneously called the Second Epistle of Clement (*c.* 140) says: 'I imagine that you are not ignorant that the living Church is the body of Christ' (2 Clem. XIV); Irenaeus, *Adversus Haereses* IV, 33.7: the Church is 'the great and glorious body of Christ'.

THE CHURCH AS THE BRIDE OF CHRIST

2 Clement XIV: 'The Scripture says "God made man male and female"; the male is Christ, the female is the Church'. In the context in which this passage occurs the preacher ties together, somewhat confusedly, the three biblical images of the Church as the body of Christ, the bride of Christ and the dwelling-place of the Spirit.

THE CHURCH AS GOD'S BUILDING

Ignatius, *Ephesians* IX, 1; *The Shepherd* of Hermas (*c.* 140–50), Vision III and Similitude IX, where this image of the Church is worked out in great detail.

THE CHURCH AS THE TEMPLE OF THE HOLY SPIRIT

Irenaeus, *Adv. Haer.* III, 24.1:

> Where the Church is, there is the Spirit of God; and where the Spirit of God is, there is the Church and all grace; and the Spirit is the truth. Those, therefore, who do not participate in the Spirit neither feed at their mother's breasts nor drink the bright fountain issuing from Christ's body.[4]

Several of these writers, however, introduce new ideas, or attempt a greater precision on matters concerning the nature of the Church of which there are only hints in the N.T.

1   CLEMENT OF ROME (*c.* 94)

Clement's letter to the church in Corinth[5] was prompted by a quarrel in that church which threatened its unity. Certain properly appointed and blameless presbyters had been deposed (XLIV). Clement exhorts the Corinthian Christians to restore them to their office and the church in Corinth to good order and amity. He draws instances from the O.T. to commend the virtues of brotherly love and patience and to demonstrate the dangers of the vices of hatred and envy. He cites the orderly movements of the heavenly bodies and the tranquil succession of the seasons and of night and day to inculcate the lessons of peacefulness and orderliness. Brotherliness and good order are essential to the Church.

APOSTOLIC SUCCESSION

Integral to his argument is what later came to be known as the doctrine of apostolic succession. This doctrine affirms that it is essential that the ministers of the Church be appointed in a succession from the apostles. Clement states (XLII and XLIV) that the apostles foresaw the possibility of discord about the exercise of rule (the Greek word is *episkope*) in the Church. They were therefore careful to appoint men to continue the work of the ministry in the places to which they had brought the gospel in their missionary journeys, and to make provision for a continuing succession of ministers. The Corinthians, therefore, have acted unjustly in deposing men who were appointed by apostles or by others whom the apostles had authorized to do so, and who had done nothing to deserve such treatment. This is a sin against the good order of the Church.

We have here, then, the first mention in Christian literature of the idea of apostolic succession. It is a passage which has been submitted to a good deal of scholarly scrutiny, but there are different opinions about its interpretation. It is clear, however, that in Clement the words 'bishop' (*episkopos*) and 'presbyter' (*presbuteros*) refer to the same order of ministry. The two words are synonymous, as they undoubtedly are in Acts and the Pastoral Epistles.[6] The term presbyter-bishop is usually employed to denote this identification. Some twenty years later in Ignatius of Antioch (see below, pp. 35–6) we find the word 'bishop' used of a single individual, distinct from the presbyters, in whom is invested the oversight (*episkope*) of the local church. For the bishop in this sense (which became universal towards the end of the second century) the term 'monarchical bishop'[7] is used.

The dispute about the interpretation of 1 Clement XLII and XLIV centres on the question of the ministerial *agent* of the succession. Does Clement mean that the succession is passed on by the presbyter-bishops in each community? Or does he mean that the apostles appointed men to a special ministry, comparable to that of the monarchical bishop, with the exclusive right to ordain? In other words, does he conceive of a presbyteral or an episcopal succession? To follow the arguments on either side, Clement's words must be studied:

> The Apostles ... preached from district to district, and from city to city, and they appointed their first converts, testing them by the Spirit, to be bishops and deacons of the future believers ... (XLII).

> Our Apostles also knew through our Lord Jesus Christ that there would be strife for the title of bishop. For this cause, therefore, since they had received perfect foreknowledge, they appointed those who have already been mentioned, and afterwards added the codicil that if they should fall asleep, other approved men should succeed to their ministry. We consider therefore that it is not just to remove from their ministry those who were appointed by them, or later on by other eminent men, with the consent of the whole Church, and have ministered to the flock of Christ without blame ... (XLIV).

Much depends upon whether 'other approved men' and 'other eminent men' refer to the same people. Those who would see here a doctrine of apostolic succession of the monarchical bishop hold that the 'other eminent men' are *not* to be identified with the 'other approved men'. They interpret Clement as saying that the apostles appointed presbyter-bishops to continue the work of the ministry in the places which they had evangelized, and that they also appointed other men to a distinct office, an important element in which was the ordaining of a continuing supply of presbyter-bishops.

Others take the 'other eminent men' to refer back to the 'other approved men'. Clement, they hold, means that the apostles appointed reliable Christians as presbyter-bishops, and arranged that, when it became necessary, these should appoint their own successors. This is to say that the passage envisages a succession of presbyter-bishops, the oversight of the local community together with authority to ordain being lodged in the presbyteral body as a whole.

While there is nothing in the passage, grammatically or in its general flow, to forbid the first of these interpretations, I, episcopalian though I am, incline to the second. Had the monarchical bishop existed in Rome or Corinth when the letter was written it is odd that it provides no clearer indication of it than the ambiguous wording of this passage. We should also have expected it to have been addressed to the bishop under whose authority the Corinthian Christians lived, bidding him exercise a firmer pastoral control.[8] Clement himself, moreover, nowhere claims to write as *the* bishop of Rome. It is true that some eighty years later in the list of bishops of Rome given by Irenaeus (*Adv. Haer.* III, iii.2) his name appears as the third after Peter and Paul. But all that can be certainly affirmed of this letter is that it is written in the name of the church of Rome. It is reasonable to suppose that Clement enjoyed a position of leadership among the Roman presbyter-bishops, and was their spokesman. This may well be a clue to the way in which the monarchical episcopate emerged during the second century.

THE CHURCH AS AN ARMY

As we have seen, Clement uses N.T. language about the Church as the New Israel and the body of Christ. But there is one short passage where the idea of the Church as Christ's army is employed. This is not a N.T. image, although Ephesians 6.10–7 and 2 Timothy 2.3–4 apply the military metaphor to the Christian individual. In XXXVII, however, Clement is probably simply using the example of the organization and discipline of the Roman army to bring home once more to his readers the advantages of good order:

> Let us then serve in our army, brethren, with all earnestness, following his faultless commands. Let us consider those who serve our generals, with

what good order, habitual readiness, and submissiveness they perform their commands. Not all are prefects, nor centurions, nor in charge of fifty men, or the like, but each carries out in his own rank the commands of the emperor and of the generals. The great cannot exist without the small, nor the small without the great.

Comparison of the Church with an army appears frequently in Christian thought: for example, in the directions for his monks of Pachomius (*c.* 363–424) who himself had been a Roman soldier; in the organization of the Society of Jesus (established in 1540) founded by Ignatius Loyola who had also been a soldier; and in the widely used phrase 'the Church militant'. The establishment of the Salvation Army (1865), which was a model for similar organizations within several denominational churches, and the popularity of S. Baring-Gould's hymn 'Onward, Christian soldiers', testify to the appeal of this concept of the Church, slight though its N.T. foundations may be.

THE LAITY OF THE CHURCH

It is noteworthy that as early as Clement a distinction is drawn between clergy and laity. In XL, impressing on his readers the importance of orderliness, Clement cites the regulations in Leviticus by which special responsibilities are assigned to the high priest, priests, and Levites,[9] adding that 'the layman (*laikos*) is bound by the ordinances for the laity'. Clement does not draw the distinction so sharply as to reduce the layman to the passive nonentity which he tended to become in the Middle Ages. Note the concluding words of the quotation from XXXVII above. Clement also says (XLI) that each member of the Church has his ministry with its own appointed rules. The early Fathers are as insistent as the N.T. that the baptized Christian is to be no mere nominal member. Even though he holds no office he has an active part in the worship and mission of the Church.

The word 'layman' (*laikos*) is the adjective of the Greek *laos* (people), the biblical word in the phrase 'people of God', by which is meant the whole people, those who hold office and those who do not. Strictly, therefore, the individual 'layman' in Clement's and the modern sense of the word represents the whole Church and bears responsibility for its total life (worship, order, mission), a truth which the idea of the priesthood of the laity preserves. And on the other hand, since office-bearers bear their responsibilities on behalf of and as representatives of the whole Church, the early Fathers carefully note that the whole Church, which includes the *laikos*, has a voice in their appointment.[10]

2   IGNATIUS OF ANTIOCH (died *c.* 115)

During a journey under guard to Rome from Antioch where he had been condemned to death by the Roman magistrates, Ignatius wrote seven letters, two to churches where he had stopped en route (Philadelphia and Smyrna), three to churches which had sent representatives to greet him when he stayed in Smyrna, one to the church in Rome, and one to Polycarp, Bishop of Smyrna, who had shown him much kindness. It is probable that Ignatius suffered martyrdom in Rome *c.* 115.

His letters have doctrinal importance in several ways, but especially for the early trends in Christology and for the doctrine of the Church. As we have seen, Ignatius uses the N.T. images of the Church, and shares Paul's understanding of the catholicity of the Church (*Smyrn.* VIII, 2). But his main concern, like Clement's, is for the Church's unity and good order, and for a similar reason: the occurrence of schism in the church in Philadelphia (*Phil.* III and VII) and its threat elsewhere (*Eph.* VII, *Magn.* VIII, *Trall.* VII).

A THREEFOLD MINISTRY

It is clear that in the churches in Syria and Asia Minor which Ignatius knew, a threefold ministry of bishop, priest, and deacon had emerged. A detailed study of the doctrine of the ministry is not the intention of this book, but the first appearance of the pattern of ministry which was to prevail in the Church from the second to the sixteenth century demands a brief discussion here. Moreover, Ignatius obviously sees the bishop's role as essential to the Church.

THE BISHOP

The bishop presides over the council of the local church[11] (*Magn.* VI). He presides also at the eucharist and at baptisms, though apparently he may depute these functions, and the holding of a love-feast (*agapē*), to others, presumably the presbyters:

> Let that be considered a valid eucharist which is celebrated by the bishop, or by one whom he appoints. Wherever the bishop appears let the congregation be present, just as wherever Jesus Christ is, there is the Catholic

Church. It is not lawful either to baptize or to hold an 'agape' without the bishop; but whatever he approve, this also is pleasing to God, that everything which you do may be secure and valid (*Smyrn.* VIII).

The bishop is also seen by Ignatius as the focus of the unity of the local church. Again and again he insists on the duty of obedient submission to the bishop.[12]

THE PRESBYTERS

Ignatius does not say how many presbyters there were in these churches. Since he frequently likens them to the apostles it is tempting to think that in each church there were twelve. If this number seems too large for what must have been quite small communities, it is to be remembered that they were not full-time salaried officers. At all events Ignatius' use of the collective noun *presbuterion* (presbytery) (*Magn.* XIII) and his description of them as a council (*Magn.* VI) suggest that there were more than one or two. The phrase 'aptly woven spiritual crown' (*Magn.* XIII) may imply that they sat in council with the bishop in a circle. In the council they would no doubt collaborate with the bishop in matters of church policy and discipline, and exercise the function which Ignatius says (*Trall.* XIII) is particularly fitting for presbyters, namely 'to cheer the soul of the bishop'.[13]

THE DEACONS

Ignatius frequently mentions deacons, but says little about their functions. From other early Christian writings[14] we learn that deacons were closely associated with the bishop, under whose authority they administered the alms of the congregation to provide for the physical needs of widows, orphans, sick, and poor. That they had these duties in the churches Ignatius knew is implied in *Trall.* II:

> And they also who are deacons of the mysteries of Jesus Christ must be in every way pleasing to all men. For they are not the ministers of food and drink, but servants of the Church of God; they must therefore guard against blame as against fire.

Ignatius is anxious to show that, although the deacons deal in mundane things like food and drink, their ministry is a spiritual one. They are, he says (*Magn.* VI), 'entrusted with the service (*diakonia*) of Jesus Christ'. In their office they represent the ministry of Christ and the whole Church to the needs and sufferings of men.

Ignatius sees this threefold ministry as patterned on the relationship between God the Father, Jesus Christ, and the apostles. Although he is not always consistent, he usually correlates the bishop with the Father, the presbyters with the apostles, and the deacons with Jesus Christ, as in *Magn.* vi:

> Be zealous to do all things in harmony with God, with the bishop presiding in the place[15] of God and the presbyters in the place of the Council of the Apostles, and the deacons, who are most dear to me, entrusted with the service of Jesus Christ.

And in *Trall.* iii:

> Likewise let all respect the deacons as Jesus Christ, even as the bishop is also a type of the Father, and the presbyters as the Council of God and the college of Apostles. Without these the name of 'Church' is not given.

Ignatius is silent on several matters about which we should like to know what he could have told us. How, for instance, were the bishop and presbyters chosen and commissioned? It is probable that all were chosen by the local church, but we should like to know whether the bishop was ordained by the presbytery (presbyteral consecration), or by other bishops from neighbouring places (episcopal consecration). And was the ordination of a presbyter at the hands of the presbyterate, or was ordination the prerogative of the bishop alone?

Ignatius does not invoke the principle of apostolic succession. On the other hand he strongly repudiates the suggestion that the pattern of ministry which he advocates is no more than a human invention to counteract schism:

> I cried out while I was with you, I spoke with a great voice—with God's own voice—'Give heed to the bishop, and to the presbytery and deacons.' But some suspected me of saying this because I had previous knowledge of the division of some persons: but he in whom I am bound is my witness that I had no knowledge of this from any human being, but the Spirit was preaching, and saying this, 'Do nothing without the bishop' . . . (*Phil.* vii).

And in *Eph.* iii he declares that 'the bishops, who have been appointed throughout the world,[16] are by the will of Jesus Christ'.

B. H. Streeter[17] interprets Ignatius' constant insistence on obedient submission to the bishop as evidence that monepiscopacy[18] was a recent development which he was over-anxious to bolster up. Streeter speaks of him as a neurotic with a 'will to power'. It is most probable that monepiscopacy was of recent development, but it may be doubted whether Streeter's estimate of Ignatius' character is consonant with the picture of him which emerges from these letters written on the way to martyrdom. It is important to note, too, that the bishop of whom Ignatius speaks is by no means an autocratic prelate. With him in the government of the local church is associated the council of presbyters. In most of the passages where the recipients are exhorted to be obedient to the bishop they are also called on to render obedience and respect to the presbyters and deacons. One who could write, 'Let not office exalt anyone, for faith and love is everything, and nothing has been preferred to them' (*Smyrn.* VI), can hardly have seen the bishop as a 'prelate'.

THE CHURCH OF ROME

The letter which Ignatius sent ahead to the church in Rome, imploring that no steps be taken to save him from death, presents a puzzle. In this letter alone there is no mention of the bishop. Is this because he assumed that the church which he describes in most congratulatory terms in the opening sentence must have had a paragon of a bishop and that the Roman Christians would surely be living in loving obedience to him, so that there was no need to insist on loyalty to the bishop as in the other six letters? But if so, why no greetings to the Bishop of Rome, no mention of him? Or is it because Ignatius knew that Rome had no bishop in the sense that he understood the term? We do not know. But we have noted that Clement's letter, written from Rome some twenty years before, provides no evidence that Rome had a monarchical bishop.

3 THE SHEPHERD OF HERMAS (c. 150)

This second-century 'Pilgrim's Progress' was written in Italy, probably in Rome. The Muratorian Fragment[19] informs us that Hermas was the brother of Pius who was the occupant of the *kathedra* (bishop's seat or throne) of the city of Rome, and implies that he wrote *The Shepherd* while his brother was bishop, c. 140–50.

The book recounts a series of visions, lays down a number of moral commandments (Mandates), and presents ten long and involved parables (Similitudes). Hermas is concerned throughout with the Church's holiness, and the moral purity of its members, and he advocates a rigorous exercise of discipline. He provides an early example of the ecclesiology[20] which in stressing holiness as an essential mark of the Church tends to neglect other important aspects of its nature.

THE CHURCH AS A PRIMAL CREATION OF GOD

We have already noted[21] that Hermas gives considerable elaboration to the N.T. image of the Church as God's building. In the 'Visions' he also introduces the idea of the Church as a primal creation of God which is not to be found in the N.T. unless Ephesians 1.4[22] be taken to imply it. Hermas records several visions of an old woman (Vis. I, ii; II, i, iv) who had encouraged and instructed him. A young man, appearing in a dream, asked Hermas who he thought the old woman was:

> I said, 'the Sybil'. 'You are wrong,' he said, 'she is not.' 'Who is she then?' I said. 'The Church,' he said. I said to him, 'Why then is she old?' 'Because', he said, 'she was created the first of all things. For this reason she is old; and for her sake was the world established' (Vis. II, iv).

In subsequent visions the old woman becomes progressively younger, until she is radiant with beauty (Vis. III, x-xiii).

The N.T. view of the Church as the renewal of the people of God provides a scriptural basis for the idea that it pre-dates the birth of Christ, but, apart from the possibility that Ephesians 1.4 implies it, the idea that it is the first of God's creations is new. It is one, however, which appears at much the same time in the sermon already mentioned on p. 30:

> Thus, brethren, if we do the will of our Father, God, we shall belong to the first Church, the spiritual one which was created before the sun and moon (2 Clem. XIV).

A tendency to allegorize the Scriptures in 2 Clement suggests that it emanates from Alexandria, where this hermeneutical method was prevalent. It is there that Clement of Alexandria towards the end of the second century, and Origen early in the third, were to expound a similar doctrine of the Church.[23]

THE MINISTRY

Most of Hermas's references to the ministry are vague. He speaks of 'elders [*presbuteroi*] who are in charge of the church' (Vis. II, iv). In two passages he mentions *episkopoi*, but as he does so in the plural it is impossible to say whether the word is a synonym for *presbuteroi* or not. In his vision of the Church as a building he tells us that the square stones which are firmly set are the apostles and *episkopoi* and teachers and deacons (Vis. III, v); and in Similitude IX, xxvii *episkopoi* are referred to as 'hospitable men who at all times received the servants of God into their houses gladly and ... sheltered the destitute and the widows'.

But there is one passage which strongly suggests the existence in Rome at this time of the monepiscopate in a form which in one respect at least recalls the Ignatian bishop. In Mandate XI, 1 Hermas describes a vision of a group of men seated on a bench, and another man who is sitting on a *kathedra* (throne).[24] The application of this to the monarchical bishop on his throne with his 'aptly woven spiritual crown' (Ignatius, Magn. XIII) sitting around him is tempting. Can Hermas here be referring to Pius whom Irenaeus lists as the ninth bishop of Rome and the Muratorian Fragment identifies as Hermas's brother? Whoever he was, Hermas did not approve of him. He goes on to denounce him as a false prophet who corrupts the minds of the servants of God.

It is appropriate here to cite the evidence of Justin Martyr (died *c.* 165) whose *Apology* must have been written soon after *The Shepherd.* Justin nowhere mentions the *episkopos.* In the well-known passages which describe the Paschal eucharist and the Sunday eucharist (*Apol.* LXV–LXVII) the celebrant is spoken of as the president (*prohestōs*).[25] The evidence of Hermas and Justin Martyr taken together strongly suggests that in the middle of the second century Rome had an ecclesiastic who occupied the *kathedra* and normally presided at the eucharist, but that he was not yet commonly known as *the* bishop (*episkopos*). That he was so designated later in the second century is well attested by the Muratorian Fragment, Irenaeus,[26] and *The Apostolic Tradition* of Hippolytus.[27]

4   THE EPISTLE TO DIOGNETUS

Although written in the form of a letter this work is really an apology, the intention of which is to commend the Christian way of life to a pagan inquirer. Of its authorship, date, place of origin, and the identity of Diognetus nothing is known with certainty. That scholars tend to date it in the middle of the second century[28] justifies our treating of it at this point. It presents a different concept of the Church from anything we have so far met. The writer does not use the word 'church', but speaks simply about 'Christians'. The Epistle presents a strong Christology of incarnation (VII–VIII) and a doctrine of Atonement which sees Christ's death as a ransom and his righteousness as that which justifies the believer (IX), but does not develop this into a doctrine of the Church as the body of Christ. Rather, on the analogy of the Platonic view of the relation of soul to body, the writer thinks of Christians as the soul of the world:

> What the soul is in the body, that the Christians are in the world. The soul is spread through all members of the body, and Christians throughout the cities of the world. The soul dwells in the body but is not of the body, and Christians dwell in the world, but are not of the world. The soul is invisible, and is guarded in a visible body, and Christians are recognized when they are in the world, but their religion remains invisible. . . . The soul has been shut up in the body but itself sustains the body; and Christians are confined in the world as in a prison, but themselves sustain the world (Diogn. VI).

The Epistle develops the Pauline idea that the Christian's true citizenship is in heaven (Phil. 3.20), and at the same time explains the meaning of the Church's universality. His designation of Christians as 'this new race' (Diogn. I) is elaborated in the following words:

> The distinction between Christians and other men, is neither in country nor language nor customs. . . . While living in Greek and barbarian cities, according as each obtained his lot, and following the local customs, both in clothing and food and in the rest of life, they show forth the wonderful and confessedly strange character of the constitution of their own citizenship. They dwell in their own fatherlands, but as if sojourners in them; they share all things as citizens, and suffer all things as strangers. Every foreign country is their fatherland, and every fatherland is a foreign country. . . . They pass their time upon the earth, but they have their citizenship in heaven. They obey the appointed laws, and they surpass the laws in their own lives. They love all men and are persecuted by all men . . . (Diogn. v).

It is an attractive account of the significance of Christian life in the world. Its limitation is that it does not free itself from the Platonic idea of the body as the prison of the soul, and consequently regards Christians as imprisoned by the world. While the writer, nevertheless, conceives of the world as invisibly sustained by the Church, he gives no more than a hint that it is the field of the Christian's service and the Church's mission. His ecclesiology is, however, more true to the

nature of the gospel than those which, with a more thoroughgoing
Platonism, view matter, and consequently the body, as inherently evil,
and see the true Christian as one who restricts the demands of the
body to the utmost possible degree, and the Church as a 'holiness
group' separated from the world and its concerns.

5   IRENAEUS (*c*. 130–200)

Irenaeus became Bishop of Lyons in Gaul in 177 in succession to
Pothinus, who was martyred in a persecution during the reign of the
Emperor Marcus Aurelius. His most important book, *The Refutation
of False Knowledge*, is usually known as *Adversus Haereses*.[29] It is
mainly a refutation of the teachings and claims of Gnostic teachers.

THE GNOSTIC THREAT

Gnosticism was a mode of thought which was being actively
promoted in the Graeco-Roman world of the second century. The
Gnostic teachers differed greatly in the details of their systems, but
each claimed to possess a secret knowledge (Greek, *gnosis*) about God
and the world which a man must acquire if he wished to be assured of
salvation. Gnosticism was a mixture of philosophy and religion which
drew elements from most of the philosophies and religions of the ancient Near East, including Judaism and Christianity. The main tenets,
common to most of the Gnostic teachers, are that the Supreme Being is
spiritual, transcendent, and unknowable; he cannot possibly have any
contact with matter; the world of matter therefore originates from
some other being or beings. Gnostic mythology predicates a series or
hierarchy of beings, sometimes called 'aeons', proceeding by emana-
tion from the Supreme Being, less spiritual, more foolish or mischievous the lower their place in the hierarchy.

At this point Gnostic imaginative fancy is brought into full play.
The numbers, names, and characters of the aeons differ in the various
systems. Saturninus spoke of seven (*Adv. Haer.* I, XXIV.1), Valentinus
of thirty (I, i.1–2).[30] The origin of matter, and therefore of the world,
is attributed either to an unfortunate accident caused by the
foolishness of the aeons, or to the deliberately mischievous action of
one of them, often called the Demiurge, and by some identified with
the God of the O.T. Matter and the human body are uniformly
regarded as inherently evil. But in some human beings there has been

implanted an element of spirit. For these, and only these, salvation is possible, but the spiritual element must be freed from its imprisoning matter.

Gnostics like Valentinus who incorporated Christian ideas to any large extent, spoke of Jesus as a saviour.[31] Salvation, however, is not won by his sacrificial life and death and appropriated through faith in him. It is a matter of having correct knowledge about the world, the aeons and their relation to the Supreme God, knowledge which will enable the spiritual man to overcome the dangers which will face him after death, and to pass safely to his destiny with the Supreme Absolute Spirit. Jesus imparted this knowledge to his apostles. Gnostic teachers claimed to have received it from them by a secret tradition, and thus to be able to make it available to their adherents.

This was the kind of teaching which was gaining a grip on intellectuals and unlearned alike. Clothed in a Christian dress though it often was, for example by Valentinus, Basilides, and Marcion, it denied fundamentals of Christian faith. It was dualistic, it had no place for the doctrine of the incarnation, and its view of the body as intrinsically evil was incompatible with the Christian estimate of man's dignity as God's creation.

THE CANON OF TRUTH

Irenaeus' refutation of Gnostic teaching brings him into the realm of ecclesiology at the point at which he deals with the Gnostic claim to possess a secret tradition derived from the apostles. It is the Church, he insists, which possesses the true apostolic tradition. It is not secret; it is enshrined in the Scriptures, and is contained also in what he calls the canon (or rule) of truth, taught openly to all who will in sincerity and humility learn from the Church's authoritative teachers. He summarizes this canon of truth as follows:

> The Church, though dispersed throughout the whole world, even to the ends of the earth, has received from the apostles and their disciples this faith: (She believes) in one God, the Father Almighty, Maker of heaven, and earth, and the sea, and all things that are in them; and in one Christ Jesus, the Son of God, who became incarnate for our salvation; and in the Holy Spirit, who proclaimed through the prophets the dispensations of God, and the advents, and the birth from a virgin, and the passion and the resurrection from the dead, and the ascension into heaven in the flesh of the beloved Christ Jesus, our Lord, and His (future) manifestation from heaven in the glory of the Father 'to gather all things in one' (Eph. 1.10)

and to raise up anew all flesh of the whole human race, in order that . . . He should execute just judgement towards all; that He may send . . . the angels who transgressed . . . together with the ungodly . . . among men, into everlasting fire; but may, in the exercise of his grace, confer immortality on the righteous and holy . . . and may surround them with everlasting glory (*Adv. Haer.* I, x.1).[32]

Irenaeus' argument may now be presented under four headings:

a   The universality of the canon of truth
He claims that these doctrines, summarized in the canon of truth, are taught everywhere in the Church:

> The Church, having received this preaching and this faith, although scattered throughout the whole world, yet, as if occupying but one house, carefully preserves it. ... Although the languages of the world are different, yet the import of the tradition is one and the same ... in Germany ... in Spain ... in Gaul ... in the East ... in Egypt ... in Libya (ibid.).

The claim can be verified by comparing Irenaeus' canon of truth with the passage in which his younger contemporary, Tertullian of Carthage, summarizes what he calls 'the canon of faith',[33] and the passage in which Origen of Alexandria, writing about 220, presents at rather greater length what he calls 'the teaching of the Church'.[34] The similarity in content is striking. Each might be a preliminary draft for the later and more succinct 'Apostles' Creed'. Here is evidence, within a period of about forty years, from places as far apart as Gaul, the Roman province of North Africa, and Alexandria, to support Irenaeus' contention that the Church 'believes these points just as if she had but one soul, and one and the same heart, and she proclaims them, and teaches them, and hands them down, with perfect harmony, as if she possessed only one mouth' (ibid.). This is in strong contrast with the widely differing systems of the Gnostic teachers. Irenaeus' point is the simple and compelling one that the unanimity of Christian teaching in so many different places is evidence that it is derived from one source and genuinely represents the original teaching.

b   The succession of bishops
Irenaeus claims that the substantial identity of the Church's canon of truth with the teaching of the apostles is further guaranteed by the unbroken succession in the various local churches of those who are the official guardians and teachers of this canon, the bishops:

It is within the power of all ... who may wish to see the truth, to con-
template clearly the tradition of the apostles manifested throughout the
whole world; and we are in a position to reckon up those who were by the
apostles instituted bishops in the churches, and (to demonstrate) the
successions of these men to our own times (*Adv. Haer.* III, iii.1).

He says that if the apostles had known of 'hidden mysteries', such as
the Gnostics claimed to be able to impart, they would surely have
transmitted them to the men to whom they were entrusting the
churches. It would be tedious, he goes on, to give the succession lists
of all the churches. He takes Rome as an example:

... the very great, the very ancient, and universally known church
founded and organized at Rome by the two most glorious apostles, Peter
and Paul.... For it is a matter of necessity that every church should agree
with this church, on account of its pre-eminent authority (*Adv. Haer.* III,
iii.2).[35]

Irenaeus goes on to give a list of the bishops of Rome, a list which, according to the early fourth-century historian, Eusebius of Caesarea,
Hegesippus had begun to compile some twenty-five years before (*c.*
155). The list is Linus, Anacletus, Clement (whom he identifies as the
writer of the letter to the Corinthian church), Euarestus, Alexander,
Sixtus, Telesphorus, Hyginus, Pius (mentioned in the Muratorian
Fragment: see p. 38 above), Anicetus, Soter, and Eleutherus who
'does now, in twelfth place from the apostles, hold the inheritance of
the episcopate' (*Adv. Haer.* III, iii.3).

Irenaeus then mentions Smyrna and Ephesus which similarly
provide witness to the true apostolic line, but without listing their
bishops. In both cases, however, the lists would have been shorter. At
Smyrna, Polycarp lived until *c.* 165, and Irenaeus accepts the tradition
that the apostle John presided over the church in Ephesus 'until the
times of Trajan', who was emperor between 98 and 117.

c Succession to a see

It is important to notice that Irenaeus traces the apostolic succession
through the previous holders of a see (*kathedra*), and not through
bishops who lay on hands in consecrating. He conceives of each of the
important Christian centres as having a *kathedra*, a teaching chair,
which must be occupied by one who will faithfully and responsibly
guard the canon of truth. When, through death or for other reasons,
the chair falls vacant, the Church must choose a suitable successor.
There can be no doubt that Irenaeus believed that a bishop must be

properly elected and consecrated, but he says nothing of these things. Nor does he speak of the bishop's pastoral and governing functions, or of the bishop as presiding at the eucharist. In his argument against the Gnostics he concentrates on the bishop's role as the official teacher of the local church, the guardian of the purity of the canon of truth, who has succeeded to this office in a particular church in direct line from the apostles.

d The Scriptures

Irenaeus believed that the true doctrine of Christ was not only transmitted by oral teaching, but was also committed to written documents. But it was not possible for him to use the Scriptures as a sole court of appeal. The Gnostics were adept in criticizing the Scriptures (III, ii.1) and in twisting their meaning to suit their own theories (I, xix.1–2). They were also zealous in producing 'Gospels' and 'Acts', strongly tinged with Gnostic ideas, and purporting to be the work of apostles (I, xx.1). Moreover, in Irenaeus' day the canon of the New Testament Scriptures had not yet been settled. There was uncertainty, for instance, about whether works like the Epistle of Clement to the Corinthians, and *The Shepherd* of Hermas should be included. In these circumstances Irenaeus was on stronger ground in his controversy with the Gnostics in putting the stress on the canon of truth as it was handed down by the succession of the Church's official teachers, the bishops. It is not that he undervalued those writings which he was fully assured were the work of apostles or apostolic men. For him the written tradition and the unwritten tradition protect and interpret each other. A passage in *Adv. Haer.* IV, xxxiii.8 makes clear his position on this matter. Here he lists the various elements which contribute to a knowledge of the truth. They include the tradition taught by the bishops, which he says is 'safeguarded without any written documents'. It is, in other words, self-authenticating. He obviously does not mean that there were no documents to which, if necessary, appeal could be made, for in the same sentence he includes the reading of the Scriptures and their regular and careful exposition.

In the same passage Irenaeus speaks also of the distinctive life of the Church as the body of Christ, and the 'special gift' of love, more precious than knowledge, more glorious than prophecy (an allusion to 1 Cor. 13). For all his insistence on the importance of the apostolic succession for the preservation of true doctrine, he well understood that there are other important elements in the idea of succession. The tradition of true doctrine would be barren if there were not with it a tradition of the love which the apostles had met in Jesus Christ and learned from him.

EPISCOPAL OR PRESBYTERAL SUCCESSION?

Before leaving Irenaeus' doctrine of apostolic succession, two points must be noted. First, although there is no doubt that Irenaeus uses the word bishop in the sense of the monarchical bishop, here and there he speaks of a succession of presbyters: '... that tradition which originates from the apostles, which is preserved by means of the successions of presbyters in the churches' (III, ii.2); 'it is incumbent to obey the presbyters who are in the church—those who, as I have shown, possess the succession of the episcopate, have received the certain gift of truth' (IV, xxvi.2). What are we to make of this?

We saw reason to believe that Clement of Rome was concerned with the apostolic succession of presbyters.[36] The above quotations strongly suggest that Irenaeus also thinks of the succession as basically presbyteral. In his time, in the face of dangers posed by erroneous teaching, in particular that of the Gnostics, the practice of appointing one of the presbyters to occupy the *kathedra* as the official teacher and guardian of the faith in the local Christian community had been adopted. The title of *episkopos*, originally an alternative for 'presbyter', is now applied to him exclusively. But he is still a presbyter, and Irenaeus can therefore speak both of a succession of bishops and of a succession of presbyters.

An ecclesiastical problem is raised here. How in the second century did the bishop enter upon his office? Doubtless he was believed to be called by God, and his commissioning was thought of as an act of God through the Church. But by whose hands was he set apart for his particular ministry, those of the presbytery or those of other bishops from neighbouring places? The former would imply that the episcopate was not a distinct order of ministry, but that presbyters appointed one of their number to perform the functions of the *episkopos* as their representative, while remaining a member of their order. On the basis of evidence up to the time of Irenaeus it is impossible to give a confident answer to the question. Our authors are silent on the matter. However, Hippolytus in his *Apostolic Tradition*, written early in the third century but purporting to describe liturgical procedures in Rome at an earlier date, insists that in the consecration of a bishop

bishops alone lay on hands.[37] This suggests strongly that bishops are
regarded as a distinct order of ministry. Yet, 200 years after Irenaeus,
Jerome (c. 342–420) recalls that originally it was not so, that churches
were governed by a presbytery, and that later, as a protection against
schism, one of the presbyters was chosen to preside.[38] But Irenaeus'
argument that the apostolicity of Christian teaching had been
protected by authorized teachers in a line of succession back to the
apostles is not weakened whether the *episkopos* was consecrated by
presbyters or by another bishop or other bishops. Whether Clement,
for example, whom Irenaeus placed third in his list of bishops of
Rome, was ordained to his office of leadership by the presbyters of
Rome or by somebody who already held the same office does not
affect the strength of the argument that the teaching of the Church
was in fact handed down by persons duly chosen, accredited, and ordained by others who were everywhere in the churches acknowledged
to possess the authority to do so.

THE GRACE OF ORDINATION

The second point arises in the sentence from *Adv. Haer.* IV, xxvi.2: 'the
presbyters who are in the church . . . who, together with the succession
of the episcopate, have received the certain gift of truth [Latin,
charisma veritatis certum]'. This is sometimes seen as an early
appearance of the idea of the transmission of grace through the
apostolic succession. In later centuries the notion was conceived that
Christ gave to his apostles a deposit of grace, a portion of which was
transmitted by the laying on of hands in the consecration of those who
followed the apostles in the episcopal succession. This doctrine (it is
usually known as the pipeline theory) is open to grave theological
objections: it conceives of grace as a material or quasi-material com-
modity, and it confines God to one method, and an indirect and
almost mechanical method, of imparting what is by definition his own
free gift. Such an idea, however, is not to be squeezed out of Irenaeus'
words in this sentence. Nothing he says is inconsistent with the
thought that grace for ministry is given directly by God to the man
who, having been duly elected and tested, is consecrated to the office
of bishop.

What Irenaeus does evidently hold is that the grace which the
bishop receives includes a 'certain' (the word means nothing less than
'infallible') grasp of theological truth. Unhappily the history of the

Church does not justify such confidence. There have been heretical bishops, an awkward fact which was to provide the Church with difficult problems.

THE MINISTRY AND THE NATURE OF THE CHURCH

As we have investigated the idea of the Church in these early Christian writers, questions relating to the ministry have constantly arisen. The Church, being a community of persons, must have its servants or ministers; it needs leadership. In the earliest book of the N.T. we read of those who worked among the communities and were leaders (1 Thess. 5.12), and elsewhere apostles, prophets, teachers, *episkopoi* or presbyters, deacons, and other ministers are mentioned. The authors we have studied in this chapter make it clear that the early Church quickly came to realize that its well-being, its unity and effectiveness had much to do not only with the quality of its ministers, but also with their recognition, by the Church as a whole, as being properly invested with authority. There cannot long be a healthy life in any community if there are no leaders and servants who are recognized as such by the community. Consequently, the possession of an ordered and recognized ministry is integral to the nature of the Church.

It is not the purpose of this book to present a theology of Christian ministry or a detailed history of its development. As we trace the development of the idea of the Church, however, we shall realize that convictions about the structure of the ministry frequently affect a writer's views on what the Church is. We shall see that some wish to go beyond the fundamental concept that an ordered and recognized ministry belongs to the nature of the Church, and insist that a *particular* detailed structure of ministry is essential. The seeds of such a claim are doubtless to be found in the writings of Ignatius of Antioch. We shall shortly find Cyprian of Carthage pressing this point of view; and it was largely taken for granted throughout the medieval period. In the twentieth century this is still perhaps the most formidable obstacle to the success of ecumenical endeavours to bring separated churches together.

4

The Early Third Century

In this chapter we discuss the ecclesiologies of two western theologians, Tertullian of Carthage and Hippolytus of Rome, who have much in common, and of the two earliest representatives of the theology, strongly influenced by Platonism, which was characteristic of Egypt, namely Clement of Alexandria and Origen.

1   TERTULLIAN (*c*. 160–*c*. 220)

Tertullian of Carthage, trained as a lawyer, the first theologian we know of who wrote in Latin, laid down guidelines and provided a terminology for western theology in several areas, especially in Trinitarian doctrine, Christology, atonement, and penitential theology. He was converted to Christianity about 193, but by 213 he had associated himself with the Montanists, a Christian sectarian movement of a pentecostal and rigoristic type. His later ecclesiology presents a strong contrast in many respects to that of his pre-Montanist days.

SCRIPTURAL CONCEPTS

We find Tertullian in his *Apologeticus* using the N.T. body imagery in a simple way in order to present to non-Christian readers an impression of the corporate life of the Church. It is a body united by a common profession, discipline, and hope. Christians meet together in a congregation that they may present their unanimous prayers to God. These include prayers for emperors and those in authority. Their corporate life is expressed both in their own discipline, and more outwardly in their charitable ministrations to the poor, orphans, aged, and prisoners.[1] He uses also the scriptural image of the bride of Christ[2] with the closely connected idea of the Church as the mother of the faithful. He speaks of 'our lady mother the Church'.[3]

THE APOSTOLIC TRADITION AND SUCCESSION

He follows Irenaeus in claiming that the Church's unity, indeed its very essence, consists in its possession of a tradition of doctrine, which he usually refers to as 'the canon of faith', everywhere received from the apostles through the succession of the bishops. Like Irenaeus, he employs this argument against the Gnostics:

> Jesus Christ our Lord ... did, whilst he lived on earth, Himself declare what He was ... what the Father's will was ... what the duty of man was ... to his disciples of whom he had chosen the twelve chief ones to be at his side. ... After first bearing witness to the faith in Jesus Christ throughout Judaea, and founding churches (there), they next went forth into the world and ... founded churches in every city, from which all the other churches, one after another, derived the tradition of the faith, and the seeds of doctrine. ... Therefore the churches, although they are so many and so great, comprise but the one primitive church (founded) by the apostles, from whom they all (spring). In this way all are primitive, and all are apostolic, whilst they are all proved to be one, in (unbroken) unity, by their peaceful communion, and title of brotherhood, and bond of hospitality—privileges which no other rule directs than the one tradition of the self-same mystery (*De Praescriptione* xx).[4]

> ... all doctrine which agrees with the apostolic churches [i.e. those which the apostles founded], those moulds and original sources of the faith, must be reckoned for truth, as undoubtedly containing that which the (said) churches received from the apostles, the apostles from Christ, Christ from God (ibid. xxi).

Tertullian, since the church in Carthage could not claim to have been founded by an apostle, is careful to 'tighten up' the doctrine of apostolic succession by claiming that recently founded churches, provided that they 'derived the tradition of the faith, and the seeds of doctrine' from churches founded by the apostles are themselves to be reckoned apostolic.[5] In such churches the substance of preaching and the canon of faith will agree with what is preached and taught in churches founded directly by apostles. This is the test to be applied to the churches which, Tertullian says, are being founded every day. If they hold the same faith as the churches founded by the apostles they are to be accounted no less apostolic than they. The churches of Africa, being founded from Rome, where the apostles Peter and Paul were martyred are, Tertullian asserts, rightly called apostolic.[6]

In answering the Gnostics' claim that their teachings have been handed down from the apostles, Tertullian gives rein to the pungent oratorical style which he had acquired in the law courts:

> Let them produce the original records of their churches; let them unfold the roll of their bishops, running down in due succession from the beginning in such a manner as that first bishop of theirs shall be able to show for his ordainer and predecessor some one of the apostles or of apostolic men (ibid. XXXII).

He is confident that the Gnostics have no such lists. Even if they should forge them it would be of no help to them, for their teachings are so contradictory among themselves, and so diverse from that of the apostles that they are evidently not of apostolic origin. The teaching of the apostles is well known. It is that 'canon of faith' which he summarized in *De Praescriptione* XIII,[7] and which we have already noted[8] as being identical in substance with the 'canon of truth' described by Irenaeus some twenty years earlier and 700 miles to the north, and the 'teaching of the Church' which Origen was to set out twenty years later some 900 miles to the east.

THE APOSTOLIC TRADITION AND THE SCRIPTURES

Nor, Tertullian argues, have the Gnostic heretics any rights in the Scriptures. He sets an imaginary scene in a law court where the question at issue is whether Marcion, Valentinus, and other Gnostics possess the right to use the Scriptures:

> It may be very fairly said to them, 'Who are you? When and whence did you come? As you are none of mine, what have you to do with that which is mine? ... This is my property. Why are you, the rest, sowing and feeding here at your own pleasure? This (I say) is my property. I have long possessed it before you. I hold sure title-deeds from the original owners themselves, to whom the estate belonged. I am the heir of the apostles. ... As for you, they have, it is certain, always held you as disinherited' (ibid. XXXVII).

Tertullian, as J. N. D. Kelly notes,[9] was well aware of 'the futility of arguing with heretics merely on the basis of Scripture'. They were masters in twisting it to their own use, and in producing specious reasons for their alterations and omissions.[10] Consequently Tertullian, like Irenaeus, takes the position that the Church in its possession of the 'canon of faith' has a key to the correct interpretation of Scripture. This canon is no more, nor less, authoritative than the written tradition. Neither Irenaeus nor Tertullian exalts it above Scripture. But it is, to use Tertullian's legal metaphor, a title-deed which enables the Catholic Christian to enter by right into the property of the Scriptures and to use them as they were meant to be used. There is no denigration of the Scriptures here. Both in his Catholic and in his Montanist writings Tertullian repeatedly appeals to the Scriptures for support.[11]

Tertullian's 'major premiss remained that of Irenaeus,' writes Kelly,

> viz. that the one divine revelation was contained in its fulness both in the Bible and in the Church's continuous public witness. If he stressed the latter medium even more than Irenaeus, elaborating the argument that it was inconceivable that the churches could have made any mistake in transmitting the pure apostolic doctrine, his reason was that in discussion with heretics it possessed certain tactical advantages.[12]

THE MONTANIST IDEA OF THE CHURCH

Thus far Tertullian reproduces in a more emphatic manner the ecclesiology of which we have traced the development from Clement of Rome and Ignatius of Antioch to Irenaeus, namely that the unity of the Church, indeed its very being, consists in agreement in that doctrine which is contained in Scripture and which is expressed in a 'canon' of truth, or faith, of which the official guardians and teachers are the bishops who occupy their sees in a succession traceable back to the apostles. But when Tertullian became a Montanist (c. 207) the eloquent defender of this ecclesiology became its equally articulate critic at several points.

Montanism arose in Phrygia about the middle of the second century, taking its name from Montanus. He and two women companions claimed to be instruments of the Holy Spirit and the recipients, during ecstatic trances, of divine revelations. These revelations were put into the form of brief epigrammatic oracles, to which their followers began to attach an authority higher than that of Scripture. The Montanist prophets taught a rigoristic discipline. They allowed no forgiveness for post-baptismal sin, inculcated a strict rule of fasting and other ascetic exercises, and taught that those who would be perfect should refrain from marriage and that martyrdom, while not to be sought, was to be welcomed as the one death by which Christ was most truly glorified.[13] Despite the non-fulfilment of their prophecy that Jerusalem would descend from heaven on a certain date near Pepuza, the movement won many adherents. The bishops of Asia Minor complained that the churches were being emptied.

At a time when laxity was creeping into the Church—and there is evidence that this was so in Rome and elsewhere—the Montanist insistence on a costly discipline and a courageous attitude towards persecution was doubtless attractive to stouter spirits in the Christian ranks. These were the aspects of Montanism which drew Tertullian. He was also impressed with the phenomenon of ecstatic speaking with tongues which the Montanists practised.[14] But it is doubtful whether he accepted the more extravagant claims put forward by some Montanists, for example that Montanus was a divine incarnation.

Tertullian now sees the Church in a different light, in which the ministry of inspired prophets overshadows that of the bishops, presbyters, and deacons, although the latter does not completely disappear from his view. He sees the Montanist movement which he calls the 'New Prophecy'[15] as the fulfilment of the prophecies in John 14–16 that the Paraclete will bear witness to Christ and reveal necessary truths:

> The integrity of His [i.e. the Paraclete's] preaching commands credit for these (revelations) albeit they be 'novel', inasmuch as they are now in course of revelation . . . (they are revelations) however of none other than Christ who said that He had withal 'other many things' which were to be fully taught by the Paraclete (*De Monogamia* II).

The era of Montanism, therefore, represents the Church's maturity:

> Righteousness . . . was first in a rudimentary state, having a natural fear of God: from that stage it advanced, through the Law and the Prophets, to infancy; from that stage it passed, through the Gospel, to the fervour of youth: now through the Paraclete, it is settling into maturity (*De Virginibus Velandis* I).

Tertullian now, therefore, defines the Church as a society of the Spirit, and its true members are spiritual men. In a tract in which he discusses authority to remit serious sins after baptism[16] he writes:

> The very Church itself is, properly and principally, the Spirit Himself, in whom is the Trinity of the One Divinity—Father, Son, and Holy Spirit. (The Spirit) combines[17] that Church which the Lord has made to consist in 'three'. And thus, from that time forward, every number (of persons) who may have combined together into this faith is accounted 'a church', from the Author and Consecrator (of the Church). And accordingly 'the Church', it is true, will forgive sins: but (it will be) the Church of the Spirit, by means of a spiritual man, not the Church which consists of a number of bishops (*De Pudicitia* XXI).

R. C. Moberly, in commenting on this passage, says[18] that 'while Tertullian's main positive is a truth immovable and of priceless value, his negative inference is an exaggeration and an untruth'. By the 'positive' he means the concept of the Church as the creation of God the Father through the Son in the power of the Holy Spirit to be the Body of the Spirit's presence. By 'negative inference' he means Tertullian's apparent conclusion that the ministerial structure of bishops, presbyters, and deacons has no place in the Church. Such an inference, Moberly rightly says, is so to affirm Spirit as to deny Body. Spirit must always express itself through bodily organisms.

But Moberly is wrong to conclude that Tertullian repudiates the episcopal system. It is as a Montanist that he appealed to the principle of apostolic succession against the teaching of Marcion.[19] In another Montanist work in which he stresses the priesthood of the whole Church, he nevertheless speaks of the distinction between the 'clergy' and the 'laity' as being established by the authority of the Church, and as marked with honour by the allotment of a 'special bench'— presumably in places of worship.[20] It is true that in the same passage he allows the right of all to 'offer' (i.e. to celebrate the eucharist) and baptize, but this is in cases of necessity in the absence of clergy. There is no outright denial of a proper, even a necessary, place within the Church for an ordained ministry. Tertullian, we may conclude, was protesting not so much against the idea of ministerial order as such as against the failure of bishops, whether by laxity or by officialism, to be what they should have been. Such protests have been needed, and that of Tertullian and the Montanists was the first of many.

2 HIPPOLYTUS (*c.* 170–236)

A contemporary of Tertullian in Rome, Hippolytus also attacked what he believed to be the lax discipline in the Church of his day. It is curious that, despite his forthright opposition to contemporary bishops of Rome, and although it seems (though the evidence is far from clear) that for a period he set himself up as an 'anti-pope', Hippolytus came to be canonized.

THE CHURCH AS THE HOLY SOCIETY OF THE RIGHTEOUS

Hitherto the sins of adultery, murder, and apostasy committed by baptized persons had been regarded as incapable of remission. Callistus, Bishop of Rome, 217–23, introduced a less rigorous discipline in restoring to communion after due penitence Christians who had committed the sin of adultery. According to Hippolytus (*Refutation of All Heresies* IX, xii.22 ff) he justified this from the parable of the tares among the wheat, and the account of unclean, as well as clean, beasts being received into Noah's ark. For Hippolytus, however, the Church is 'the holy society of those who live in righteousness' (*Commentary on Daniel* I, 17). He stands with Tertullian for the Church as a community of saints which must exclude sinners. It is an ecclesiology which, in different ways, was to be championed by the Novatianists thirty years later, by the Donatists in the fourth century, and was to reappear constantly in the history of the Church. Christian theology generally has resisted it. While acknowledging fully the Christian's vocation to saintliness, it has conceived of the Church as a 'school for sinners' which cannot exclude those who sincerely acknowledge their sins and will to amend their lives.

THE CHURCH'S HIERARCHY

Hippolytus compiled a 'Church Order' known as *The Apostolic Tradition*. It gives an account of the services of ordination, the testing and instruction of candidates for baptism, the baptismal ceremonies, the times of prayer, and of other liturgical and devotional practices. The book was part of Hippolytus' campaign of recalling the church of Rome from its laxity to the stricter discipline of his youth. It is therefore evidence, although the text is not always reliable, for practice in Rome in the last quarter of the second century.

In this work we have our earliest information about how a bishop was consecrated:[21]

> Let the bishop be ordained (being in all things without fault), chosen by all the people. And when he has been proposed and found acceptable to all, the people being assembled on the Lord's day together with the presbytery and such bishops as may attend, let (the choice) be generally approved.
>
> Let the bishops lay hands on him and the presbytery stand by in silence. And all shall keep silence, praying in their heart for the descent of the Spirit. After this one of the bishops present, at the request of all, laying his hand on him (who is ordained bishop), shall pray thus. . . . (*Apostolic Tradition* I, ii).

The prayer which follows asks:

> Now pour forth that Power which is from Thee of 'the princely Spirit'

which Thou didst deliver to Thy Beloved Child Jesus Christ, which He bestowed on Thy holy Apostles ... grant upon this Thy servant whom Thou hast chosen for the episcopate to feed Thy holy flock and serve as Thine high priest, that he may minister blamelessly by night and day, that he may unceasingly (behold and) propitiate Thy countenance and offer to Thee the gifts of Thy holy Church. And that by the high priestly Spirit he may have authority 'to forgive sins' according to Thy command.... (ibid. I, iii).

The newly consecrated bishop then celebrates the eucharist.

Two points need careful notice. First: while the bishop is to be chosen and ordained with the active consent of all the people of the local church, it is other bishops alone who lay hands on his head. The presbytery had no part in this action. This implies that, apart from questions of inward calling and the enabling grace of God, the authority to exercise a bishop's office must officially be imparted by those who already hold that office. This is the first clear evidence for this procedure, which rapidly became universal. As we have seen, evidence is lacking about the mode of appointment of the monarchical bishop up to this time.[22] Whatever the previous practice had been, Hippolytus insists that only a bishop possesses the authority to consecrate another bishop. Indeed, Hippolytus sees the bishop as alone having authority to ordain presbyters and deacons.

To be noted secondly is Hippolytus' equation of the bishop with the Aaronic high priest in respect of his functions of offering the 'gifts' of the Church and remitting sins. It is an equation which some, almost certainly incorrectly, have seen in 1 Clement.[23] Tertullian not infrequently speaks of the bishop as *summus sacerdos* or *sacerdos*,[24] as does Cyprian of Carthage thirty years later. The implication of this language is that the bishop's office is analogous with that of the Aaronic high priest. The bishop is the Church's principal liturgical officer. He is the chief celebrant of the eucharist, wherein the Church offers to God the sacrifice made available by Christ, together with its own offerings of alms, bread and wine, with thanksgiving and praise. He is also the principal penitential and disciplinary minister of the local church. There is, indeed, a certain analogy here with the functions of the Aaronic high priest as described in Leviticus 16. Whether or not this justified the use, which became increasingly common, of the terms 'high priest' and 'priest' for the bishop and presbyter may perhaps be considered a question which in itself raises no important theological issue. But it is otherwise with the application to the bishop of the Levitical conception of the high priest as one who propitiates God on behalf of the people.[25] This was to introduce a new idea of the Christian ministry, and one which endangered the teaching of the N.T. that the sacrifice of Christ alone is the sufficient redemptive act on man's behalf.[26] This view of the ministry, as it gained acceptance, doubtless aided by the common use of sacerdotal terminology,[27] inevitably led to a new ecclesiology which sees the Church as essentially a hierarchical body. The concept of the Church as the whole people of God lost ground, and the distinction between clergy and laity was highly sharpened as the latter were relegated to the role of passive dependants. This ecclesiology was to come under formidable attack in the sixteenth century.

Hippolytus' *Apostolic Tradition* presents the bishop as the sole ordaining officer. It is true that in the ordination of a presbyter the other presbyters present lay on hands (I, viii.1). We are told that this is 'because of the similar spirit (which is) common to (all) the clergy' (I, ix.6):

> For the presbyter has authority only for this one thing, to receive. But he has no authority to give holy orders. Wherefore he does not ordain (a man) to orders but (by laying on hands) at the ordination of a presbyter he (only) blesses while the bishop ordains (I, ix.7–8).

In the ordaining of a deacon, the bishop alone lays on hands (I, ix.1) because, says Hippolytus,

> he is not ordained for a priesthood, but for the service of the bishop that he may do (only) the things commanded by him. For he is not (appointed to be) the fellow-counsellor of the (whole) clergy but to take charge (of property) and to report to the bishop whatever is necessary (I, ix.2–3).[28]

The development of this ecclesiology, which places so much emphasis on the monarchical bishop as guarantor of the Church's continuity with the apostles and of the purity of the Church's teaching, as the focus of unity, the chief minister of the sacraments, and the sole ordainer, comes to its peak in Cyprian of Carthage. But we shall first take note of two eminent Alexandrians whose writing activity covered much the same period of time as that of Irenaeus, Tertullian, and Hippolytus.

3   CLEMENT OF ALEXANDRIA (*c.* 150–*c.* 215)

Clement of Alexandria taught at the catechetical school in Alexandria to the headship of which Origen was to succeed him in 203. Clement was a cultivated man who had a wide knowledge both of Greek literature and the Scriptures. He believed that Greek philosophy often supported the claims of Christianity. The strength of the Platonist influence upon him is revealed in his emphasis on the intellect: 'The perpetual exertion of the intellect is the essence of an intelligent being' (*Stromateis* IV, xxii). Against Gnostic claims he produces an apologetic very different from that of Irenaeus or Tertullian. His argument is that it is the Christian who is the true Gnostic. In his trilogy[29] he endeavours to show that the Word of God (the *Logos*), who brought enlightenment to ancient Israel and to the Greek philosophers, has now, in Jesus Christ, come in a new way to bring the saving knowledge of God to all men. He pleads with his readers to take Christ as their tutor. He will first exhort them. Then, after their conversion, he will train them with a salutary discipline, and lead them from the first rudiments of discipleship, through fear to hope, on to disinterested love and to knowledge which is now desired for its own sake, the knowledge of God.

THE EMPIRICAL CHURCH AND THE CHURCH ON HIGH

Clement's ecclesiology was undoubtedly influenced by Plato's doctrine of Forms, that is, the conception that each empirical thing has its perfect pattern and its true reality in the eternal world. He distinguishes between the Church on earth and 'the Church on high', between the historical and empirical Church and the Spiritual Church.

This is not to say that he denigrates the Church as an institution. On the contrary, he tells us[30] that he delights to think of it as at once 'virgin and mother—pure as a virgin, loving as a mother'. This mother has no milk, but nourishes her children with the Word, Jesus Christ, whose flesh and blood are given for their strengthening. There follows a discussion of the eucharist in which, with his usual intellectualizing tendency, he interprets the 'flesh and blood' of Christ as meaning the Spirit and the Word. Nevertheless Clement is here speaking of the Church as an institution, with its preaching, sacraments, and teaching. The same is true in the following passage:

> It is my opinion that the true Church, that which is really ancient, is one, and that in it those who according to God's purpose are just, are enrolled. ... [It is] an imitation of the one first principle. ... In substance and idea, in origin, in pre-eminence, we say that the ancient and Catholic Church is

alone, collecting as it does into the unity of the one faith . . . those already ordained, whom God predestinated, knowing before the foundation of the world that they would be righteous.

But the pre-eminence of the Church, as the principle of union, is in its oneness, in this surpassing all things else, and having nothing like or equal to itself (*Stromateis* VII, xvii).

This is the Church, he tells us, which heretics and schismatics try to tear asunder. Yet in the same book he can present the Church as a spiritual entity, 'the Church on high'. Its members are the true Gnostics who have given themselves to the unending contemplation of God, rising above earthly concerns. These are the true presbyters and deacons, whether or not they hold such office in the empirical Church (*Strom.* VI, xiii–xiv). 'The earthly Church is the image of the heavenly', and therefore Christians pray that God's will may be done on earth as it is in heaven (ibid. IV, viii). Clement's distinction is one way, and a natural way for one who shared the Platonic outlook, of interpreting the tension which we observed in the N.T. between the idea of the Church as complete and perfect and the Church as it exists in the process of growth and sanctification, having among its members many who have obviously not proceeded very far on the road to sanctity.

The distinction which Clement makes is to be distinguished from that of Tertullian between the Church of the Spirit and the Church of the worldly. Whereas for Tertullian the sign of the member of the spiritual Church is moral rectitude, for Clement it is intellectual apprehension of the truth which issues in the unceasing contemplation of God. Moreover, while Tertullian would have had grave doubts about the salvation of worldly Christians, Clement believed in the eventual salvation of all men (universalism). His ecclesiological distinction does not, therefore, point to an ultimate distinction between the redeemed and the damned. We shall discuss this matter further in connection with Origen who makes a distinction similar to that of Clement.

4   ORIGEN (c. 185–255)

Clement was succeeded by the more famous Origen as head of the catechetical school of Alexandria. Like his predecessor, Origen also distinguished what he spoke of as 'the true Church'[31] from the Church as an historical institution, of which, however, he remained a loyal member until his death which was hastened by sufferings undergone in prison during the persecution under the Emperor Decius.

THE CHURCH AS HISTORICAL INSTITUTION

His many works, theological, e.g. *De Principiis*; apologetic, e.g. *Contra Celsum*; commentaries on the Scriptures; and homilies (his sermons taken down and later published by disciples) contain numerous references to the organization of the Church, its ministry, and the responsibilities of all its members. This Church is the guardian of the teaching of the apostles which has been handed down through the apostolic succession:

> Let the Church's teaching, handed down from the apostles through the order of succession and which continues in the churches to the present day, be preserved (*De Prin.*, Preface 2).[32]

In the Preface to *De Principiis* he goes on to summarize this 'teaching of the Church', which as already noted[33] is strikingly similar in substance to the 'canon of truth' as given by Irenaeus and the 'canon of faith' of Tertullian, although Origen's version is greatly expanded.

THE MINISTRY

This Church is an organized community with a properly constituted ministry of priests, to whose appointment the local congregation must give consent, and at whose ordination 'the presence of the people is required, so that they may all know and be certain that the man elected to the priesthood stands out from all the people in learning, holiness, and eminence in every kind of virtue'.[34] Origen has much to say of the responsibilities of the Church's ministers. The bishops who like Peter have received the keys of the Kingdom, the disciplinary authority to bind and loose, must themselves be men of Peter's quality such that Christ may build the Church upon them.[35] Those pastors who are appointed to examine and instruct candidates for baptism have exacting responsibilities which Origen describes in more than one place.[36]

THE PRIESTHOOD OF THE WHOLE CHURCH

But every member of the Church has a priesthood. 'Do you not know', Origen writes, 'that the priesthood is given to you also, that is to the whole Church of God, the people who believe?' All, therefore, 'must offer to God sacrifices of praise, prayers, pity, purity, righteousness, and holiness'.[37] 'All, whoever have been anointed with the ointment of the holy chrism [i.e. the baptized] have been made priests.'[38]

THE SHORTCOMINGS OF THE EMPIRICAL CHURCH

Origen fully recognizes the defects of the Church and its members. Commenting on 'The Lord has opened his treasury and has brought forth vessels of his wrath' (Jer. 1.25 in the LXX version), he says:

> I can confidently say that the treasury of the Lord is his Church, and in that treasury ... there often lurk men who are vessels of wrath ... chaff with the grain, and fish which have to be thrown out and destroyed together with good fish which have all come into the net (*Homilies on Jeremiah* xx, 3).[39]

In another homily he uses the parable of the tares and wheat in a similar way: 'It is impossible for the Church to be entirely purified while it is on earth.' Open sinners may be excommunicated, but there remain those whose sins are secret.[40] More than once he declares that not all who have been baptized have been 'washed unto salvation'.[41]

THE TRUE CHURCH

Thus Origen was led to distinguish between the empirical Church and the spiritual. The latter is 'the true Church', which the Epistle to the Ephesians describes as 'without spot or wrinkle ... holy and without blemish'.[42] It is the assembly of the saints or perfect ones,[43] whereas the empirical Church is the 'assembly of believers'.[44] This 'true Church' is also 'the heavenly Church', and like Hermas, II Clement and Clement of Alexandria, Origen holds that it existed before the creation of the world. He argues that this is implicit in what is said about the Church in the Epistle to the Ephesians:

> You must please not think that she is called the Bride or the Church only from the time when the Saviour came in flesh: she is so called from the beginning of the human race and from the very foundation of the world—indeed, if I may look for the origin of the high mystery under Paul's guidance, even *before* the foundation of the world. For this is what he says: ... 'as He chose us in Christ before the foundation of the world, that we should be holy and unspotted in His sight' (Eph. 1.4) (*Commentary on the Song of Songs* ii, 8).[45]

Origen goes on to note that Paul (Eph. 2.20) says that the Church is built on the foundation of the prophets as well as the apostles. He interprets 'prophets' as meaning those of the O.T. among whom he includes Adam.[46] Moreover, Ephesians 5.25 ff also implies the pre-existence of the Church, for how could Christ have loved his Church if it did not already exist?

> Undoubtedly he loved her who did exist; she existed in all the saints who have been since time began. .... They themselves were the Church whom He loved to the intent that He might increase her in multitude and develop her in virtue and translate her through the love of perfectness from earth to heaven (ibid.).

The Platonic doctrine of Forms (that earthly entities and institutions are imperfect copies of heavenly realities) has undoubtedly influenced Origen's ecclesiology, but his appreciation of the importance which the O.T. and N.T. alike attach to human history has transformed that doctrine. The last sentence quoted above shows that his distinction between the Church on earth and the true or heavenly Church is not precisely the Platonic distinction. Rather he seems to envisage the Church on earth as the historic community in which men, by participation in Christ, become fitted to be members of the heavenly Church. The distinction is more akin to the popular medieval distinction between the Church Militant and the Church Triumphant. This statement, however, must be qualified, because there are passages in Origen which indicate his belief that within the membership of the visible Church there are some who must even now be accounted members of the true Church, those within the body

> who are called eyes, doubtless because they have the light of understanding and of knowledge, and others ears, to hear the word of teaching, and others hands to do good works and to discharge the function of religion (ibid. II, 7).

Nor must Origen's distinction be confused with that which we shall find in Augustine[47] and the sixteenth-century Reformers, between the visible Church which includes impenitent sinners who will be damned and an invisible Church which contains only the elect. Such a distinction could not have been the intention of Origen or of Clement, his predecessor. They were both universalists, and for them there could be no question of any contrast between actual and ideal, or between visible and invisible which suggests that any will fail to obtain final salvation.

PROBLEMS IN ORIGEN'S ECCLESIOLOGY

Origen's doctrine of the Church is, therefore, difficult to interpret. His universalism raises the question what more essential place the Church, and indeed the incarnation, can have in his theological system than as aids to hasten the recovery for some men of that state of unity with God which they lost in a pre-cosmic fall, a state which, in his view, all will in the end regain. Yet Origen clearly believes that the incarnation of the *Logos* in Jesus Christ and the life of the Church are integral to the divine plan for universal salvation. We must assume, though he himself is not explicit, that he held that the healing work of Christ in the Church proceeds in those 'aeons' (worlds, or stages) which he envisages beyond this life. When, therefore, he says 'let no man persuade and deceive himself: outside this house, that is, the Church, no man is saved'[48] he is not excluding from salvation those who in their earthly lives are outside the Church. In another sermon he likens these to the humbler household vessels of 2 Timothy 2.20. By God's mysterious and merciful dispensation they will yet have their place in 'the great house'.[49] The phrase 'outside the Church' is Origen's own, but he seems to see these 'humbler vessels' as members of the Church in a nascent sense. In yet another sermon, in commenting on the Pauline phrase 'body of Christ', he says that this body 'is all mankind—rather perhaps the totality of every created thing'. Referring to 1 Corinthians 15.28, he reminds his hearers that it may not properly be said that Christ is subjected to God so that God may be all in all, while any one of those who are Christ's members are not, because of their sin, themselves subjected to God.[50] But at the consummation all men will be subject to Christ, all creation restored through Christ to its primal unity, and God will be all and in all.[51]

5

Cyprian of Carthage

The ecclesiology of Cyprian (Bishop of Carthage 248–58) is the basis of the doctrine of the Church which prevailed in the West throughout the Middle Ages. Compared with the ecclesiology of his older contemporary, Origen, it shows the marks which are usually said to be characteristic of western theology generally. It was practical, legalistic, and logical. Cyprian, like Tertullian whom he spoke of as 'the master', had been trained in Roman law. Throughout his episcopate he was faced with urgent pastoral problems. In his ecclesiology there is tension between the rigorist disciple of Tertullian and the sensitive pastor.[1]

Shortly after Cyprian's election as Bishop of Carthage, the persecution of Christians inspired by the Emperior Decius occurred. Being terminated on Decius' death in 251 it was not of long duration, but it was prosecuted fiercely, especially in Rome and North Africa. Under threat of death many Christians had yielded to the demand to throw incense into braziers before the statues of the gods of Rome or of the Emperor (whose deification was claimed). When the persecution ceased, the question of readmitting the lapsed to communion was vigorously discussed. In the church in Carthage one party demanded their readmission with little or no discipline. Another party demanded the rigorous application of the ancient rule of the Church that apostates be and remain excommunicated. Cyprian ruled that the question should be decided by a council of North African bishops to be called as soon as possible. Meanwhile he admitted to communion penitents who were on the point of death and bade others give strict heed to their penitential exercises. The eventual decision was to judge each case on its merits and, after due discipline, to admit those who were sincerely penitent, although lapsed clergy were inhibited from exercising their ministry.

In Rome, a rigorist party opposed the bishop, Cornelius, who favoured a policy similar to that of Cyprian. It was led by a presbyter, Novatian, and went into schism when he was elected Bishop of Rome in opposition to Cornelius by his supporters who obtained his consecration at the hands of sympathizing bishops. The schism takes its name from Novatian. In Carthage likewise the rigorist party and the laxist party each set up a bishop in opposition to Cyprian. Carthage thus had three men, each claiming to be the legitimate holder of the see. It is not surprising that Cyprian's main theological concern was the unity of the visible Church.

When renewed persecution was threatened in 252 Cyprian permitted readmission to communion of all who were under discipline, that as communicant Christians they might prove their loyalty in the coming trial. This removed the *raison d'être* of the laxist party, but Novatianist opposition increased.

NOVATIANIST ECCLESIOLOGY

Upholding the full rigour of the Church's ancient disciplinary rule of no absolution for apostasy, the Novatianists argued that a church which included lapsed persons or was willing to receive them to communion ceased to be a church because it lacked the mark of holiness. Apostasy corrupts the Church to the point of extinction.

This ecclesiology, then, finds the essence of the Church in its holiness, and its holiness is determined by its members. The Church is seen as the 'Congregation of the Holy'. The vulnerability of such an ecclesiology lies in the difficulty of setting a standard of holiness. The Novatianists placed the emphasis on freedom from apostasy, and appeared to be unconscious of the seriousness of other forms of unholiness of which many of them were certainly guilty themselves: jealousy, ambition, intrigue, and lack of charity. Against them Cyprian and Cornelius used the same arguments by which Pope Callistus[2] had defended his moderating discipline towards adulterers: the appeal to the parable of the tares, etc. It is God who will separate the tares from the wheat. Novation is usurping God's prerogative of judgement.[3] And of the Novatianist schism, Cyprian says:

> This is a worse crime than that which the lapsed seem to have fallen into, who nevertheless, standing as penitents for their crime, beseech God with full satisfactions. In this case, the Church is sought after and entreated; in that case the Church is resisted ... on the one hand, he who has lapsed has only injured himself; on the other, he who has endeavoured to cause a

heresy or a schism has deceived many by drawing them with him ...
while the lapsed has sinned but once, he sins daily (*De Unitate Ecclesiae*
19).[4]

The Novatianist schism raised a new problem in connection with the
doctrine of the unity of the Church. The Novatianists who had wilfully
separated themselves from the Catholic Church were theologically
orthodox; they accepted the 'canon of faith'. It was no longer
sufficient, then, to insist that the basis of unity was the orthodox faith,
the teaching of the apostles. Cyprian now maintains that the principle
of unity is the episcopate.

But the Novatianists claimed to have the episcopate. Their bishops
had been consecrated by bishops who themselves had been validly
consecrated. Nevertheless it was Cyprian's contention that they were
not bishops. The bishop's throne in Carthage was not vacant when the
Novatianist Maximus was set up as a bishop in opposition. Nor was
that of Rome vacant when Novatian's consecration took place.
Cyprian himself and Cornelius respectively held these sees.[5] Neither
Novatian nor Maximus had succeeded to a vacant see, and consequently they were not bishops. It is to be noted that Cyprian is
working here with the concept that the succession of a bishop is to be
traced not through the bishops who consecrated him, but through his
predecessors in office. It is a concept which excludes the possibility of
a bishop who has no properly constituted see.

Having disposed of the Novationist claim to have bishops, Cyprian
insists that it is the possession of the episcopate which gives unity to
the Church:

> Our Lord ... describing the honour of a bishop and the order of His
> Church, speaks in the Gospel and says to Peter: I say unto thee, that thou
> art Peter; and upon this rock will I build my Church. ... Thence, through
> the changes of times and successions, the ordering of bishops and the plan
> of the Church flow onwards; so that the Church is founded upon the
> bishops, and every act of the Church is controlled by these same rulers
> (*Ep.* xxvi,1; [xxxiii]).[6]

> You ought to know that the bishop is in the Church, and the Church in
> the bishop; and if any one be not with the bishop, that he is not in the
> Church. ... The Church, which is Catholic and one, is not cut or divided
> but is indeed connected and bound together by the cement of priests

[*sacerdotes*, i.e. bishops][7] who cohere with one another (*Ep.* LXVIII, 8 [LXVI]).

From this clearly enunciated principle of 'No bishop, no Church' Cyprian drew the logical conclusion that the ecclesiastical acts of Novatianists had no validity whatever. A bishop alone has authority to ordain; he is the proper minister of the sacraments, and he alone can delegate their celebration to others. Consequently Novatianists, having no bishops, have no ordinations, baptisms, absolutions, eucharists. When Novatianists sought admission to the Catholic Church, Cyprian's practice was to baptize them, counting their Novatianist baptism as no baptism at all. Several of his letters deal with this subject. The following extracts summarize his position:

> Baptism is therefore one, because the Church is one, and there cannot be any baptism out of the Church. For since there cannot be two baptisms, if heretics truly baptize, they themselves have this baptism. . . . But we say that those who come thence are not re-baptized among us, but are baptized. For indeed they do not receive anything there, where there is nothing (*Ep.* LXX, 1 [LXXI]).

Novatianist orthodoxy, moreover, is quite irrelevant to this question:

> If any one objects, by way of saying that Novatian holds the same law which the Catholic Church holds, baptizes with the same symbol [i.e. creed] with which we baptize, knows the same God and Father, the same Christ the Son, the same Holy Spirit, and that for this reason he may claim the power of baptizing, namely that he seems not to differ from us in the baptismal interrogatory . . . they lie in their interrogatory, since they have not the Church (*Ep.* LXXV, 7 [LXIX]).

Cyprian thus meets the Novatianist claim that there is one true Church, namely the Church of the holy (interpreted as those who have no dealings with the lapsed) with the equally blunt claim that there is indeed one true Church, but it is the Church which does not depart from the bishops who have lawfully succeeded in the established sees. This is the Church of which he writes,[8] 'outside the Church there is no salvation'.

CYPRIAN AND STEPHEN, BISHOP OF ROME

On the subject of baptizing heretics and schismatics Cyprian found himself fighting on yet another front. Cornelius had been succeeded as

Bishop of Rome by Stephen in 254. Although he held heretics and schismatics to be outside the Church as strongly as did Cyprian, he opposed the latter's practice of baptizing converts who had already received baptism in schismatic churches. He held that baptism outside the Church was valid provided that it was administered with water in the name of the Trinity. Stephen tried to impose his views on the North African Church, and threatened excommunication.[9] A council of North African bishops gave Cyprian strong support, and a protest was sent to Stephen.[10] The severing of communion between Rome and Carthage was averted by Stephen's death in 257. His successor, Xystus, did not attempt to press the Roman practice outside his own sphere of authority.

In this controversy logic appears to have been on Cyprian's side, but the consensus of the Church has supported Stephen. Canon 8 of the representative (though not judged ecumenical) Council of Arles (314) laid down that members of heretical or schismatic bodies who seek reconciliation should be required to recite the creed. If they had already been baptized in the triune name they should be received by the laying on of hands. This principle, which was to be important for Augustine's ecclesiology, has been generally followed in the Church.[11]

CYPRIAN'S POSITIVE DOCTRINE

It is in *De Catholicae Ecclesiae Unitate*[12] that Cyprian presents his conception of the Church positively, and despite the rhetorical style, systematically. The argument is that the Church *is* one. When the 'enemy' deludes some to claim 'the title of the Christian name', and invents heresies and schisms to 'subvert the faith ... corrupt the truth ... divide the unity',[13] it is a question of discovering where the true Church is. Cyprian finds the substance of the answer in Matthew 16.18–19 and John 20.20–23:

> The Lord speaks to Peter, saying, 'I say unto thee, that thou art Peter; and upon this rock I will build by Church....' And although to all the apostles, after his resurrection, He gives an equal power, and says, 'As the Father hath sent me, even so send I you ...;' yet, that he might set forth unity, He arranged by His authority the origin of that unity, as beginning from one. Assuredly the rest of the apostles were also the same as was Peter, endowed with a like partnership both of honour and power; but the beginning proceeds from unity. ... Does he who does not hold this unity of the Church think that he holds the faith? Does he who strives against and rends the Church trust that he is in the Church ...? (*De Unitate* 4).[14]

Cyprian then alludes to Paul's witness to the oneness of the Church in Ephesians 4.4–6, and claims that this unity, first given to the Church in Peter and the apostles, is now manifested in the episcopate. As the apostles formed a college or corporate body, so also does the episcopate:

> *Episcopatus unus est, cuius a singulis in solidum pars tenetur.*[15]

The literal translation of the Latin is: 'The episcopate is one, of which a part is held by individual bishops in solidarity.' *In solidum* is a legal phrase used of joint ownership in a property in which each party is not regarded as possessing a *share*, but rather as possessing rights in the *whole*, and as accountable for the whole. Cyprian's concept, then, is of a corporation or college of bishops, with each in his own person and within his own sphere of jurisdiction exercising the whole authority of the episcopate. The concept appears frequently in Cyprian.[16] J. N. D. Kelly points out[17] that it is a rider to this doctrine 'that each bishop is entitled to hold his own views and to administer his own diocese accordingly, and that the principle of charitable respect for each other's opinions must be maintained'. In the letter to Stephen in which he explains his practice in the matter of baptizing schismatics, Cyprian writes:

> We neither do violence to, nor impose a law upon, any one, since each prelate has in the administration of the Church the exercise of his will free, as he shall give an account of his conduct to the Lord (*Ep.* LXXI, 3 [LXXII]).

In *De Unitate* Cyprian goes on to assert that whoever separates himself from the Church whose unity is thus constituted in the episcopal college, separates himself from the promises of Christ to the Church:

> He is a stranger; he is profane; he is an enemy. He can no longer have God for his Father, who has not the Church for his mother (*De Unitate* 6).

THE 'PAPAL' TEXT OF *DE UNITATE*

Another version of the fourth chapter is extant, known as the 'Papal' or 'Primacy' text. It asserts that the 'primacy is given to Peter', that Christ set up 'one throne', and asks whether 'he who deserts the throne of Peter, on which the Church is founded' is confident that he is in the Church. The two versions have occasioned much controversy.

Some have argued that the 'Papal' version is original and provides evidence that the primacy of the Bishop of Rome was acknowledged in the third century. Others have seen the 'Papal' version as the result of later insertions into the manuscripts in the interests of the papal theory. R. H. Bettenson, who gives a brief summary of the issue in his *Early Christian Fathers* says that the 'dominant view at present seems to be that the "Primacy Text" was altered by Cyprian to the *Textus Receptus* as a result of the controversy about baptism with Stephen, Bishop of Rome'.[18]

The 'Papal' text does not very explicitly assert that the Bishop of Rome has jurisdiction over all other bishops. Cyprian was, no doubt, prepared to accord the Bishop of Rome a primacy of honour, but his views on that bishop's right to control policy within the jurisdiction of other bishops may be judged from his resistance to Stephen on the baptismal question. Moreover, for Cyprian to have admitted that the Bishop of Rome had any such right would have contradicted what is clearly his main thrust—that the unity of the Church resides in the consensus of the collective episcopate.

THE PERSON AND OFFICE OF THE BISHOP

Cyprian has much to say about carefulness in the choice of bishops. Several of his letters deal with the subject. There must be a public election, and general consent must be sought. Writing to the church in Spain he says:

> You must diligently observe and keep the practice delivered from divine tradition and apostolic observance, which is also maintained among us, and almost throughout all the provinces; that for the proper celebration of ordinations all the neighbouring bishops of the same province should assemble with the people for which a prelate is ordained. And the bishop should be chosen in the presence of the people, who have most fully known the life of each one, and have looked into the doings of each one as respects his habitual conduct (*Ep.* LXVII, 5).

In a letter to Cornelius he speaks of the choice of a bishop as the result of 'the divine judgement, after the suffrage of the people, after the consent of the co-bishops'.[19] We are given no details of how elections were conducted. It appears that the choice was made by the bishops, but that the people had a definite power of veto. Presbyters seem to have had no more influential part in an election than the laity.

There are passages where Cyprian appears to suggest that once a bishop is consecrated he is without fault: 'To believe that they who are ordained are unworthy and unchaste, what else is it than to believe that his priests (*sacerdotes*) are not appointed in the Church by God, nor through God?'[20] But unhappily, unworthy and even immoral bishops are not unknown, and elsewhere Cyprian shows himself well aware of this. Of them he uses words which might have been used by a Novatianist: 'A people obedient to the Lord's precepts, and fearing God, ought to separate themselves from a sinful prelate, and not to associate themselves with the sacrifices of a sacrilegious priest (*sacerdos*), especially since they themselves have the power either of choosing worthy priests, or of rejecting unworthy ones'.[21] Cyprian's insistence on great care in episcopal elections is no doubt prompted by his realization that unworthy bishops exist.

Here is a weakness in an ecclesiology such as Cyprian's. What is the Christian's duty if his bishop, properly elected ard validly consecrated, lives a scandalous life which is tolerated by his brother bishops, and makes demands which are unreasonable and against conscience? In the course of the Church's existence many have felt that they must refuse obedience and form a separated Christian community. Christian disunity occurs not only when men depart from obedience to the college of bishops in the pride and obstinacy which was undoubtedly characteristic both of the Novatianist and laxist schismatics of Cyprian's day, but also when they do so for motives of high Christian principle. The problem of the Church's unity is a more difficult one than Cyprian saw, or perhaps could possibly see in his day.

Cyprian, as we have seen, frequently speaks of the bishop as *sacerdos*. Tertullian had done so before him, and both Tertullian and Hippolytus had also referred to the bishop as 'high priest'.[22] Cyprian consolidates this tendency to draw a close parallel between the Christian ministry and the hierarchical Aaronic priesthood and its sacrificial functions. While for Cyprian himself the pastoral function of the bishop is clearly of the utmost importance, the way is being prepared for a conception of the bishop's office in which his teaching and pastoral duties are overshadowed by his liturgical functions, the most important of which he performs as the chief celebrant of the eucharist which comes increasingly to be thought of in sacrificial terms.[23] Cyprian himself foreshadows later medieval teaching in a passage like the following:

> For if Jesus Christ, our Lord and God, is Himself the chief priest of God the Father, and has first offered Himself a sacrifice to the Father, and has

commanded this [i.e. the eucharist] to be done in commemoration of Himself, certainly that priest (*sacerdos*) truly discharges the office of Christ, who imitates that which Christ did, and he then offers a true and full sacrifice in the Church to God the Father, when he proceeds to offer it according to what he sees Christ himself to have offered (*Ep.* LXII, 14 [LXIII]).

SUMMARY

Cyprian's concept of the Church and its ministry is a fuller develop-ment of what we found in Ignatius of Antioch, Irenaeus, the earlier Tertullian, and Hippolytus. Although significant new emphases were to be introduced by Augustine, it is true to say that Cyprian's hierarchical and sacerdotal view of the Church was to dominate western Christianity for centuries.

Cyprian does not follow the Alexandrians into speculations about an ideal Church whose essence is conceived in an other-worldly sphere. It is the empirical, geographically extended Church which is his concern. In this domain its essential nature and unity must be realized and maintained. This unity is indeed fruitful of great variety, as he argues in *De Unitate*. He illustrates this by the sun and its many rays, the tree and its many boughs, the fountain and its many streams. The Church is also the fruitful mother of Christians.[24] But she is also 'the spouse of Christ (who) cannot be adulterous. She knows one home. . . . She appoints the sons whom she has borne for the kingdom . . . .'[25] The passage ends with the well-known words, previously quoted, 'He can no longer have God for his Father, who has not the Church for his mother.'

Cyprian also uses the Noah's ark image, but in a distinctly new way. The image had often been used to assert the mixed nature of the Church (the clean and unclean animals) against the doctrine of the Church as an exclusive society of the perfect. Cyprian however fastens on the thought that only those inside the ark were saved: 'If any one could escape who was outside the ark of Noah, then he also may es-cape who shall be outside of the Church.'[26]

His doctrine of the Church may be aptly summarized by the use he makes of the episode of Christ's seamless robe (John 19.23–4):

This sacrament of unity [i.e. the Church], this bond of a concord in-separately cohering, is set forth where in the Gospel the coat of the Lord Jesus Christ is not at all divided nor cut. . . . That coat bore with it a unity that came down from the top, that is . . . the Father, which was not to be at all rent by the receiver and the possessor.... By the sacrament and sign of His garment, He has declared the unity of the Church (*De Unitate* 7).

Thus, for Cyprian the Novatianists, the schismatic bodies of laxists or any other group which, for whatever reason, separates itself from the Church which coheres in the corporate episcopate, are not parts *of* the Church. They are outside the Church altogether and outside the possibility of salvation. A question mark has often been put against this stark doctrine.[27] There are, as we shall see, passages in Augustine where the shape of that question begins faintly to emerge.[28]

6

The Fourth and
Early Fifth Centuries

During the fourth century and the first half of the fifth theologians
were chiefly engaged upon the doctrines of the Trinity and of the Person of Christ. It was the period of the Arian, Apollinarian, Macedo-
nian, Nestorian, and Eutychian controversies. Yet important contributions to ecclesiology were made.

1 ORGANIZATION

First it should be noted that this was the period when the administrative structure of the Church took the shape which, apart from
the non-episcopal reformed churches, it retains today. It was
modelled, understandably enough in view of the Emperor Constantine's conversion, on the administrative structure of the Roman Empire. The major ecclesiastical regions were now made to coincide with
the civil provinces or 'eparchies'.[1] In the majority of cases the capital
city of the eparchy became the see city of the bishop who had primacy
over other bishops within the eparchy. Such a bishop was known as a
metropolitan (from the Greek mētēr, mother, and polis, city). The
primacy which the bishops of certain sees had long been accorded over an
area much larger than a single eparchy, notably the bishops of Rome,
Alexandria, and Antioch was, however, preserved.[2]

The canons of Church councils frequently dealt with matters of
jurisdiction. Canon 6 of the Council of Nicaea (325) ratified the
Bishop of Alexandria's jurisdiction over the bishops of Egypt, Libya,
and Pentapolis, and that of the Bishop of Antioch over the bishops of
neighbouring eparchies, and noted that there was a similar custom in
the case of the Bishop of Rome. The Council of Constantinople (381),
in Canon 3 enacted that 'the Bishop of Constantinople has seniority
of honour after the Bishop of Rome because Constantinople is new
Rome'. Constantinople, formerly the comparatively unimportant

Byzantium, had quickly grown in size and importance since Constantine designated it his imperial city in 326. A new see was created there, whose bishops began to claim jurisdiction over the churches in a wide area. This was resented by bishops of Alexandria, whose see hitherto had been regarded as the most influential of the East. The *status quo*, however, was maintained at the Council of Ephesus (431), apart from granting independence from the Bishop of Antioch to the bishops of Cyprus (Canon 8). But the Council of Chalcedon (451) in Canon 28 gave the Bishop of Constantinople jurisdiction over the Church in the civil dioceses or exarchies of Pontus, Asia,[3] and Thrace, 'rightly judging that the city which was honoured by the Imperial presence and the Senate and which enjoyed equal privileges with ancient imperial Rome, should also, like Rome, have greater importance in ecclesiastical matters, as being second to it'.

The Bishop of Jerusalem had always been accorded a precedence of honour, and was counted among the patriarchs (a title which came into use in the sixth century) with the bishops of Rome, Constantinople, Antioch, and Alexandria. The patriarchal powers included the right to consecrate the metropolitans within their sphere of jurisdiction, to try them if accused of misdemeanours, and to hear appeals against their decisions. The adoption of the hierarchical administrative system of the Roman Empire as a model was clearly a departure from that notion of a collegiate episcopate for which Cyprian had contended.

2 THE EAST

CYRIL, BISHOP OF JERUSALEM (c. 315–86)

In his *Catechetical Lectures* (*c.* 350), to candidates for baptism,[4] Cyril of Jerusalem devotes one section of Lecture XVIII to the doctrine of the Church. After his rejection by the Jews the Saviour 'built out of the Gentiles a second Holy Church, the Church of us "Christians". It is of this Church that he promised it would not fail' (*Cat.* XVIII, 25). He enlarges on the meaning of the word 'Catholic'. The Church is called 'Catholic' because

> it extends over all the world ... and because it teaches universally and completely one and all the doctrines which ought to come to men's knowledge ... and because it brings into subjection to godliness the whole race of mankind, governors and governed, learned and ignorant; and

because it universally treats and heals the whole class of sins ... and possesses in itself every form of virtue which is named, in deeds and words, and in every kind of spiritual gift (*Cat.* xviii, 23).[5]

The candidates are warned to mark the difference between the Catholic Church and sects which call themselves churches:

If ever thou art sojourning in cities, inquire ... not merely where the Church is, but where is the Catholic Church. For this is the peculiar name of this Holy Church, the mother of us all, the spouse of our Lord Jesus Christ (ibid. xviii, 26).

THE MYSTICAL BODY

Cyril's instructions on the meaning of the successive stages in Christian initiation serve to introduce a concept of the Church which is implicit in St Paul's teaching on baptism and the body of Christ,[6] and which was now to become basic to the understanding of the Church both East and West. This is the idea of the mystical body (*corpus mysticum*) of Christ. The word 'mystical' is derived from the Greek *mueomai*, 'to be initiated'. The reference is primarily to the initiatory ceremonies by which a person becomes a member of the Church. The elements of initiation, it is to be noted, are instruction, the renunciation of evil, the confession of the Church's faith in the words of the Creed, immersion in water, 'sealing' with the Holy Spirit (symbolized by anointing with oil), and receiving the body of Christ in the eucharist. That this is what is meant by Christian initiation, and not water baptism alone, is clear not only from Cyril, but also from the much earlier *Apostolic Tradition* of Hippolytus. The mystical body of Christ, therefore, is the company of those who have become his members by initiation. The reference is not to a Church of the intellectually or spiritually élite, nor to an invisible Church whose members are known to God alone, but to the visible Church on earth of the Christian congregations with their bishops, presbyters, and deacons, the Church of the Scriptures and the sacraments.

As he expounds the initiatory ceremonies Cyril teaches that those 'who have been found worthy of divine and life-giving Baptism'[7] have entered into union with Christ through the Holy Spirit. At the first anointing (before their immersion) they were 'made partakers of the good olive tree, Jesus Christ', for the oil symbolizes participation in Christ's richness.[8] After the immersion they were anointed again with chrism,[9] the symbol of the Holy Spirit, and were made christs, 'because you are images of Christ'. The chrism given to them is 'the anti-type of that wherewith Christ was anointed' when the Holy Spirit rested on him after his baptism in Jordan.[10] So they have been 'made partakers and fellows of Christ'.[11] They can now be called Christians, a title to which they had no real claim before.[12] The candidates' first participation in the eucharist, which immediately followed the anointing with chrism, is what makes them 'of the same body and blood with Christ':[13]

> For in the figure of Bread is given to thee His Body, and in the figure of Wine His Blood; that thou by partaking of the Body and Blood of Christ mayest be made of the same body and the same blood with Him. For thus we come to bear Christ in us, because His Body and Blood are distributed through our members; thus it is that, according to the blessed Peter, 'we become partakers of the divine nature' (*Cat.* xxii, 3).

This text (2 Peter 1.4) is the scriptural basis of a salvation doctrine which is typical of the eastern Fathers of this period. This is the doctrine of *theosis* ('deification') of the Christian in virtue of his participation in Christ: 'The Word was made man in order that we might be made divine',[14] words of Athanasius written early in the fourth century, are often quoted in illustration of it. The concept of the Church as Christ's mystical body is closely interwoven with it.

GREGORY OF NYSSA (c. 330–c. 395)

likewise speaks of the incarnation as a conjoining of the divine nature with human nature 'in order that our nature might ... itself become divine'.[15] This 'conjoining' is extended in the Church: 'All being conjoined to the one body of Christ by participation, we become his one body.' In the consummation, therefore, Christ will be subjected to the Father 'mingled with his own body which is the Church'.[16]

CYRIL OF ALEXANDRIA (d. 444)

The idea of the Church as the mystical body of Christ is presented in several passages by Cyril, Bishop of Alexandria. He does so at some length in his *Commentary on St John's Gospel* in a section which expounds John 17.21, 'that they may all be one, even as thou, Father, art in me, and I in thee'. The passage is given here at some length since it represents the doctrine of the Church which has predominated in the eastern Churches ever since. It will be noted that the idea of the Church as the fellowship of the Spirit is not neglected.

In the foregoing [an expounding of the doctrine of the Trinity] we said, and not without reason, that the mode of the divine unity, the identity of substance of the Holy Trinity and the complete coinherence (of the Three Persons) must be copied in the unity of believers through their unanimity of heart and mind. But now I want to show that there is what we might call a unity of nature by which we are bound to one another and are all bound to God. ...

The Mystery[17] which has to do with Christ is established, as it were, as a beginning and a way of our participating in the Holy Spirit and in union with God. ... The Only-begotten, through the wisdom which is his and through the counsel of the Father, found and wrought a means by which we might come into unity with God and with one another—even we ourselves, although by our differences we are separate individuals in soul and body. For by one body, and that his own he blesses those who believe in him by a mystical communion and makes them of one body with himself and one another. ... For if we all partake of the one loaf, we are all made one body; for it is not possible that Christ be divided. Therefore the Church is called 'Body of Christ' of which we are individually members, according to Paul's understanding. For we are all united to the one Christ through his holy body, inasmuch as we receive him who is one and undivided in our own bodies. ...

Now if we are all of one body with one another in Christ, and not only with one another but with him who assuredly is within us through his own flesh, clearly we are all one, both in one another and in Christ. For Christ, who is both God and man in one person, is the bond of unity.

With regard to union in the Spirit ... we shall say again that we have all received one and the same spirit, namely the Holy Spirit, and are, so to speak, mingled with one another and with God. For though Christ makes the Spirit of the Father who is also his own Spirit to dwell in each of us individually, many as we are, yet the Spirit is one and undivided; and in that individuality which is his by nature he holds together in unity those spirits which are separated from unity one with another, showing them all to be as one in himself. For as the power of the holy flesh makes those in whom it may come to dwell to be of one body, in the same way, I hold, the one indivisible Spirit dwells in them all and binds them all into spiritual unity (*Comm. in Joannem* xi, 10).

These Greek Fathers, then, present a doctrine of the Church as the mystical body of Christ, the faithful baptized in and with their Lord, nourished, vivified, and unified by and in his eucharistic body and by and in his Holy Spirit.

3 THE WEST

HILARY, BISHOP OF POITIERS (315–67)

It was the Donatist schism, beginning early in the fourth century, which caused the next wave of urgent concern with the doctrine of the Church's nature on the part of western theologians. But first the ecclesiology of Hilary of Poitiers, who was not directly concerned with the Donatist question, must be mentioned.

Hilary speaks of the Church as the fellowship of the faithful, the bride of Christ and his body. The Church is one in that it holds the apostolic and Nicene faith. This unity is much deeper than the holding of ideas in common. In his *De Trinitate* he argues against those who hold that the unity of the Church consists merely in being 'of one heart and soul' (Acts 4.32). The unity of the Church indeed comes through faith. But those who are one 'through faith' are one 'through the nature of faith', and thus have 'a natural unity'. This is given in baptism, by which those who acknowledge one God, one Lord, and one hope become 'one by regeneration into the same nature'.[18] Hilary thus begins to sketch a doctrine of the mystical body which becomes clearer when a little later he speaks of the Church's unity being manifested in the eucharist:

> Now how it is that we are in Him through the sacrament of the flesh and blood bestowed upon us, He Himself testifies, saying, '. . . because I live ye shall live also; because I am in My Father, and ye in Me, and I in you'. If He wished to indicate a mere unity of will, why did He set forth a kind of gradation and sequence[19] in the completion of the unity, unless it were that, since He was in the Father through the nature of Deity, and we on the contrary in Him through His birth in the body, He would have us believe that He is in us through the mystery of the sacraments? (*De Trinitate* VIII, 15).

Hilary proceeds to speak of the eucharist as 'the sacrament of this perfect unity', and concludes:

> I have dwelt upon these facts because the heretics [Arians] falsely main-tain that the union between Father and Son is one of will only, and make use of the example of our own union with God, as though we were united to the Son and through the Son to the Father by mere obedience and a devout will, and none of the natural verity of communion were vouchsafed us through the sacrament of the Body and Blood; although the glory of the Son bestowed upon us through the Son abiding in us after the flesh, while we are united in Him corporeally and inseparably, bids us preach the mystery of the true and natural unity (ibid. VIII, 17).

The idea of the mystical body of Christ was, then, being developed in the West while Athanasius and Cyril of Jerusalem were developing it in the East. This ecclesiology is characterized by its emphasis on the sacraments. The unity of the body is a mystical unity because men enter into it through baptism in which 'all were born again to innocence, to immortality, to the knowledge of God, to the faith of hope'.[20] Since there is but one God, one hope, and one baptism they enter into a unity of nature which finds its climax in the eucharist which, it is to be remembered, is integral to Christian initiation. Nothing is further from the minds of exponents of this ecclesiology than that a catechumen would participate in the baptismal eucharist and then cease to be a communicant. They see the Church as a eucharistic community whose life is maintained by continuing and faithful participation in the sacramental body and blood of Christ.

DONATISM

There are many points of similarity between Donatism and Novatianism. Both schisms originated in the aftermath of persecution, both denied that the Church should have any dealings with the lapsed, both stood for the idea of the Church as the Congregation of the Holy, and both flourished in North Africa.

One of the objects of the severe persecution initiated by the Emperor Diocletian in 303 was the destruction of Christian books. Under threat of death some bishops and others who had charge of copies of the Scriptures, service books, and other Christian writings had handed them over to the Roman authorities. They were known as *traditores*.[21] When the persecution ceased some Christians, like the Novatianists some sixty years before, insisted that the Church must dissociate itself from all *traditores*. In particular they objected to the consecration of Caecilian as bishop of Carthage (311) on the ground that one of his consecrators was a *traditor*. A *traditor* is unholy, they argued, and cannot be a member of the holy Church. Those who have dealings with a *traditor* themselves lose sanctity and cease to be members of the Church. Those who are thus outside the Church cannot perform ecclesiastical functions. If they claim to have the sacraments the claim is false, for the validity of the sacraments depends on the worthiness of the minister. Hence they held that Caecilian was not a bishop and set up a bishop of Carthage of their own, Majorinus, succeeded in 313 by Donatus, from whom the schism is named.

The Donatists baptized the converts they received from the Catholic Church. This was logical since, in their view, the Catholic Church by its recognition of Caecilian had ceased to be the Church and to possess the sacraments. It is to be noted that the Donatists did not teach an ecclesiology of the invisible Church. For them the empirical Church on earth must be holy. Their standard of holiness was that of having no dealings whatsoever with *traditores* as being apostates whose reconciliation was impossible. Donatism, like Novatianism, ignored other dimensions of holiness. It was 'a fanatical brand of puritanism'.[22]

The accusation against Caecilian's consecrator was proved to be unfounded after an exhaustive inquiry instituted by the Emperor Constantine. In 314 the western Council of Arles, summoned by Constantine to settle dissensions which had arisen from the persecution, enunciated the principle that ordination by an unworthy minister is not invalid (Canon 13). Nevertheless, the schism persisted, aided by the nationalist feeling of the native Berbers, whose opposition to any institution supported by imperial Rome could be counted on. During the fourth century Donatists gained possession of many North African churches, often by violence or its threat. Bishops were set up, and since these were consecrated by sympathizers among the episcopate, and in some cases installed in sees which were vacant, they could present a plausible claim to be in the apostolic succession. The Donatists also claimed the authority of Cyprian for one of their main positions, for Cyprian had taught that sacraments are invalid outside the one true Church.[23] The Donatist schism, therefore, raised unprecedented problems of ecclesiology which demanded new theological answers.

OPTATUS (fl. 370)

Optatus, Bishop of Milevis in North Africa, wrote seven books on the schism of the Donatists, directed against Parmenian, the Donatist Bishop of Carthage. His points were to be taken up and developed by St Augustine (see Chapter 7), and are therefore only summarized here with brief comments.

(1) The Church's sacraments derived their validity not from the worthiness of the minister but from God.

If this argument stood by itself it would appear to allow for the recognition of the sacraments of any dissident and separated group of

Christians, and to undermine any concept of Church order. It is, however, but one point in Optatus' chain of argument. It is a reminder to the Donatists that no man, however holy, gives the grace of the sacraments he administers. God is the giver, and as St Thomas Aquinas was to insist, the true minister of all the sacraments is Jesus Christ.[24] The principle enabled Optatus to meet the uncharitable intransigence of the Donatists' refusal to acknowledge sacraments outside their own body with an assurance of his readiness to recognize the validity of their sacraments.

(2) The holiness of the Church depends not on the moral character of its members, but on the endowments it has from God. These endowments include the Trinitarian creed, the chair of Peter, the faith of believers, Christ's teaching, and the sacraments. The parable of the tares shows that Christ wills to have sinners within his Church until the final judgement. It is impossible for man, who does not see with the eyes of God, to separate the good from the bad.

(3) Catholicity and unity are also important marks of the true Church. As for catholicity, taken in its geographical sense alone, the Donatists were confined to North Africa, but a small part of the world. The Church's unity was outwardly manifested by communion with the see of Rome, whose first occupant was Peter, the apostle whom Christ, for the sake of unity, placed before all the others.[25] But the Donatists did not have communion with the see of Rome. By their own act they had severed themselves from the Church, and like branches broken off from a tree they are cut off from the source of life.

7

Augustine and Jerome

When Augustine became Bishop of Hippo[1] in 396 his diocese had long been split by the Donatist schism. Both the practical and the theological implications of the schism claimed his attention as a bishop in this strife-torn part of the Church, and many of his writings deal with the nature of the Church and its unity. As a presbyter he had written *A Psalm Against the Donatists*, designed to give a simple explanation of their tenets. His major works on Donatism are *On Baptism, Against the Donatists* (in seven books, 400–401), *Against the Writings of Petilian the Donatist* (400–402), *A Letter to Catholics on the Unity of the Church* (402), *Against Cresconius the Donatist* (406), and *On One Baptism Against Petilian* (410). Many passages of his *Expositions on the Book of Psalms* and a number of his sermons and letters deal with the same issues.

THE MYSTICAL BODY

Basic to Augustine's ecclesiology is the idea of the Church as the mystical body of Christ. Scripture, he contends,[2] speaks of the one Christ with three points of reference: as the eternal Word, equal to the Father, as the Mediator between God and man, and as the Church. Among instances of the last he several times cites the words of Christ (Acts 9.4) to the persecutor of the Church: 'Saul, Saul, why do you persecute me?'[3] 'The head of the Church is Christ, and the Church is the body of Christ';[4] but also 'Head and body are one Christ: not because he is not whole without the body, but because he has also deigned to be whole with us, who even without us is whole and entire.'[5] In view of this integral unity of head and body Augustine speaks in various passages of the Church as 'the whole Christ', 'one man', 'entire man', 'one person', 'perfect man'.[6]

In one of his sermons Augustine in graphic language speaks of the eucharist as that which expresses the unity into which the Christian has entered through the ceremonies of initiation:

> If you wish to understand the body of Christ, hear what the Apostle says to the faithful: 'Now you are the body of Christ, and his members' (1 Cor. 12.27). Therefore if you are the body and members of Christ, it is your mystery which is set forth on the Lord's table, and which you receive. To that which you are you answer 'Amen',[7] and in so answering you declare your assent. You hear the words 'body of Christ', and you answer 'Amen'. Then *be* a member of the body of Christ, that your 'Amen' may be true. What then is the significance of the loaf? Let us bring to this question no answers of our own, but listen once more to the Apostle. When speaking of this sacrament he says 'we, the many, are one loaf, one body' (1 Cor. 10.17). . . . 'The many are one body.' Remember that a loaf is not made of one grain, but of many. When you were exorcized you were, so to speak, ground. When you were baptized you were, so to speak, moistened. When you received the fire of the Holy Spirit you were, so to speak, baked. Be what you see [upon the table] and receive what you *are*. This is what the Apostle meant about the loaf. . . . So also of the wine. There are many grapes hanging in the cluster, but their juice is mingled in a unity. Thus the Lord Christ has put his mark upon us, willed us to belong to him, and consecrated the mystery of our peace and unity upon his table (*Sermon* 272).[8]

THE FELLOWSHIP OF THE SPIRIT

In developing the image of the Church as the body of Christ, Augustine does not neglect the N.T. idea of the Church as the fellowship of the Holy Spirit. As the human body is indwelt and quickened by the soul so the Holy Spirit indwells and quickens the mystical body. 'The spirit by which every man lives is called the soul: you see what the soul does in the body. It gives life to all its members. . . . What the soul is to the body of a man, the Holy Spirit is to the body of Christ, the Church.'[9] Now it is fundamental to Augustine's theology that the Holy Spirit is the bond of love, both in the life of the Divine Being[10] and in human relationships. Therefore it must be said that the quickening principle of the Church is love. Here we have one of Augustine's firmest convictions. The Church is a fellowship of love, a fellowship created by the Spirit who is love and a fellowship of those who love both God and the sons of God in Christ:

> Nor can any love the Father except he love the Son . . . by loving he becomes himself a member, and comes through love to be in the frame of

the body of Christ, so there shall be one Christ, loving Himself. For when the members love one another, the body loves itself (*Homilies on 1 John* x, 3).

Thus Augustine holds closely together the ideas of the Church as the body of Christ and as the creation, the temple, and the fellowship of the Holy Spirit.

THE UNITY OF THE CHURCH

From this concept of the Church as the fellowship of the Holy Spirit of love, Augustine deduces the nature of the Church's unity. Those who do not love God or their fellow-Christians sever themselves from the one Church. For Augustine true unity and charity are synonymous, and consequently schism and lack of charity are closely linked. The schismatic actions of the Donatists, their antagonism to that body of which the love of God and man is the very soul, betray their failure in charity. And since the Holy Spirit is the giver of charity he concludes that the Donatists do not have the Holy Spirit:

> He who has the Holy Spirit is in the Church, which speaks with the tongues of all men. Whoever is outside this Church does not have the Holy Spirit. The Holy Spirit deigned to reveal himself in the languages of all nations precisely so that when a man is contained within the unity of the Church which speaks with all languages, he may know that he has the Holy Spirit (*Sermon* 268.2).[11]

Augustine was prepared to allow to the Donatists what Cyprian would not grant to the Novatianists, that their sacraments were valid. But he held that they could not be effective for salvation unless and until the recipient was received into the Catholic Church, when the Holy Spirit would make them efficacious and fruitful.

> If a member is cut off from the body it may still be recognized for what it is, finger, hand, arm, ear. Apart from the body it has form, but no life. It is the same with a man who is separated from the Church. You ask him about the sacrament? You find it there. Baptism? You find it. The Creed? You find it. But it is only the form. Unless you live inwardly by the Spirit, it is vain to boast outwardly about the form (ibid.).

The point is made more explicitly in the following:

> All things [i.e. the sacraments] were indeed theirs before, but profited them nothing, because they had no charity. For what truth is there in the profession of Christian charity by him who does not embrace Christian

unity? When, therefore, they come to the Catholic Church, they gain thereby not what they already possessed, but something which they had not before—namely that those things which they possessed begin then to be profitable to them. For in the Catholic Church they obtain the root of charity in the bond of peace and in the fellowship of unity (*Letters* LXI, 2).

Although he differs from Cyprian about the technical validity of the sacraments of schismatic bodies, Augustine agrees with him that there is no salvation outside the Church.[12] Schismatics have not the Holy Spirit, they are without love and outside the unity of the Church.

Yet some have discerned in Augustine a certain reluctance to draw the conclusion that the Donatists were in no sense with the Church. Cyprian had spoken of the seamless robe of Christ as incapable of being rent,[13] implying that the schismatics of his day had not torn the Church into pieces, but had departed from it, leaving it entire and undivided in itself. But Augustine speaks of the Donatist schism as a rending of the seamless robe and a tearing of Christ's body.[14] and this language implies, it is suggested, that though the Church is thereby divided, the sundered parts still belong to the Church.[15] His use of the seamless robe metaphor cannot be pressed too far, but Augustine's willingness to allow that Donatist sacraments were valid lends support to the suggestion that he was unwilling to regard the Donatists as utterly separated from the Church. Cyprian's position, that the Novatianists were outside the Church, was the more logical. For Augustine, perhaps we may say, pastoral concern overcame logic. He ardently desired to open a way for Donatists to enter into communion with the Catholics, and so to enter into the sphere of the spirit of charity in which alone, he believed, they could find salvation.

If Augustine's ecclesiology discloses some ambiguity, it also raises some formidable theological objections. A doctrine that the Holy Spirit is effectively active among men nowhere but within the boundaries of the visible Catholic Church seems forgetful of the biblical doctrine of the Spirit of God as the giver of life in all its dimensions. Augustine's argument seems also to imply that a separated body of Christians, and a member of a separated body, can express or experience *nothing* of the love of God, of Christ, and of neighbour.

The distinction which Augustine makes between the 'sacrament' and 'the effect or use of the sacrament'[16] is fraught with problems for sacramental theology. That a sacrament administered by a Donatist presbyter should lie dormant until, perhaps years later, the recipient is reconciled to the Catholic Church, when it will at last produce its fruits of grace, suggests a mechanical view of the sacraments. Optatus' declaration[17] that the sacraments belong to God implies a sacramental theology different from this.

Holy Scripture clearly supports the concept of a 'mixed' Church. But it also speaks of the Church as holy, 'without spot or wrinkle'. How could this be said of the Church of which Augustine was a member, which, as he well knew, included many unworthy men among its members? He found a solution of this difficulty in a distinction, which at first appears to have affinities with that made by Clement of Alexandria and Origen, between the empirical and the essential.[18] There are, he admits, within the Church 'the covetous, and defrauders, and robbers, and usurers, and drunkards, and the envious'. But the true members of the Church are 'the holy and just'. They are the 'garden enclosed, the fountain sealed, a well of living water, the orchard of pomegranates with pleasant fruits' of which the Song of Solomon speaks.[19] At this point Augustine's doctrine of predestination exerts its influence. The true members of the Church are 'the fixed number of the saints predestined before the foundation of the world'.[20] Among this number, Augustine says,

> there are some also who as yet live wickedly, or even lie in heresies or the superstitions of the Gentiles, and yet even then 'the Lord knoweth them that are His'. For, in that unspeakable foreknowledge of God, many who seem to be within yet really are without (*On Baptism* v, 27 (38)).

A distinction between the Church as inclusive of both worthy and unworthy members and the Church's righteous core has given way to a distinction between the visible Church and an invisible Church consisting of a fixed number of people, known to God alone and predestined by him for salvation from before their creation, a doctrine which, J. N. D. Kelly contends, means that 'the notion of the institutional Church ceases to have any validity'.[21]

Augustine did not imitate the Donatists in setting up a criterion by which true members of the Church might be distinguished. This was God's prerogative. Moreover, out of his own experience he knew that God's grace could effect conversions which confounded the judgement which one man might make about another's worthiness. And it was with the visible Church, its unity, its life and well-being, that he was chiefly occupied throughout his long episcopate, as the pastoral concern, so clearly documented in his sermons and letters, shows. He believed that those who were destined by God for salvation must before death find their way by baptism into the fold of the Catholic Church. For this he laboured, and this explains both his eventual reluctant agreement to the use of force by imperial officers to compel Donatists into the Church, and his opposition to the death penalty for those who refused.

THE CATHOLICITY OF THE CHURCH

In his controversy with the Donatists, Augustine uses the credal adjective 'catholic' in its geographical sense. How, he asks, can the party of Donatus claim to be the Church when it exists in North Africa alone?[22] Alluding to the accusation that communion between Catholics in North Africa and *traditores* contaminates the Catholic Church throughout the world, he speaks of the folly of 'pronouncing the whole world defiled by unknown crimes of Africans, and the heritage of Christ destroyed through the sins of these Africans by the maintenance of communion with them' (*Letters* LIII, 6). The catholicity of the Church consists in communion with the see of Rome and with the universal Church.[23] The Church is the *Ecclesia Catholica*, and Augustine, especially in his anti-Donatist writings, frequently designates it by the one word *Catholica*.

For Augustine, however, the universality of the Church is extended not only geographically, but also in time.[24] The body whose head is Christ is co-extensive with all who by grace live in righteousness, 'from Abel to the last elect person'.[25]

THE APOSTOLICITY OF THE CHURCH

Augustine takes from Irenaeus and from his North African predecessors, Tertullian and Cyprian, their doctrine that the apostolic faith and life of the Church is guaranteed by an unbroken succession of bishops in the sees founded by apostles, and in their daughter sees. He makes the point that it is futile for Donatists to claim apostolicity for their 'party' since there has never been a Donatist among the successive bishops of Rome which he regards as the outstanding example of an apostolic see. It appears, then, that he conceives of apostolic succession in the same way as his predecessors: a bishop succeeds to a vacant see, and traces his succession through his predecessors in that see. But Augustine's admission that Donatist bishops were validly bishops, who could therefore validly consecrate other bishops, points to another way of interpreting episcopal succession; namely, that a bishop traces his succession through his consecrators (of whom the Council of Nicaea had laid down that there should be at least three). This interpretation came increasingly to be taken for granted in later centuries. The consecrating bishops are seen as bringing the new bishop into the apostolic succession and providing authority for his sacramental ministry.

This interpretation of apostolic succession, if accepted, must be applied to others than the Donatist bishops whom Augustine hoped to reconcile to the Catholic Church. It means that any man who has received consecration at the hands of validly consecrated bishops must be regarded as capable of conferring orders even though he becomes a heretic or schismatic. It is an interpretation which has in fact ministered to great confusion, and to the proliferation of numerous splinter episcopal 'churches'.[26] The doctrine of apostolic succession relates to Church order, and if a particular interpretation leads to confusion it must be inadequate. The older doctrine which interprets the succession as that of those who have been chosen with the full concurrence of the Church, duly consecrated and installed in a recognized sphere of pastoral, sacramental, and juridical authority, has greater merit.

THE CHURCH AS MOTHER

Augustine frequently used the metaphor, previously employed by Tertullian and Cyprian, of the Church as the mother who gives birth and nourishment to Christians and provides a safe home for her children: 'You are safe who have God for your Father and His Church for your mother.'[27] She gives birth through baptism, and Augustine argues[28] that it is she who gives birth to Christians baptized in Donatist churches: 'It is the Church that gives birth to all, either within her pale ... or beyond it.'[29] This is because these schismatics have retained the sacraments which belong essentially to the Catholic Church alone. Therefore, 'the generation ... proceeds from the Church, whose sacraments are retained', not from the sect as such, which, if it were to abandon what it has 'retained of the essence of the Church' would 'lose the power of generation'.[30] In line with his doctrine of the Church as a 'mixed society' Augustine acknowledges that many of the children whom this mother brings forth prove to be sinners. Repentance is always possible, and reconciliation always offered ('we ought to despair of no man').[31] But there is no second baptism; the sinner 'is purged by faithful discipline and truthful confession'. He returns to his mother.

The concept of the Church as mother, bringing to birth, nursing, caring for, and agonizing over both her wayward and her exemplary children, has had a continuing attraction.[32] Its appropriateness, however, only becomes credible when the Church, through its pastors and people, in fact exercises this self-sacrificing care.[33] Augustine himself set a shining example.

In several passages[34] Augustine develops a saying of St Ambrose: 'Mary is the type of the Church.' He draws out the similarities and dissimilarities between Mary, the mother of Christ who is the Head, and the Church which gives birth to the members. In view of the mystical union between Head and members the Virgin Mary typifies the Church. Yet, sanctified and saved as she is through her Son, she is but one member among many, and the Church is greater than she.

THE CITY OF GOD AND THE CHURCH

Augustine's best known work, after his *Confessions*, is his *De Civitate Dei*, 'On the City of God'. It was written primarily to give an answer to the accusation that the calamity of the fall of Rome to the Goths (410) was caused by Rome's desertion of its old gods in favour of Christianity. In providing it Augustine found himself obliged to present what amounts to a history of the world interpreted as the progress of two 'cities', the heavenly City of God, and a city which revolts from God. The creation of the angels originates the City of God, and the angels form a large part of it. The foundation of the city which opposes God is laid by the wilful disobedience of the angels who fell. With the creation and fall of man the two cities became established in this world. History is interpreted as the intermingling, sometimes the co-operation, sometimes the enmity and always the tension between these two cities, the earthly and the heavenly, both constituted by love, the former 'by the love of self even to the contempt of God, the heavenly by the love of God, even to the contempt of self'.[35]

Augustine undoubtedly identifies the City of God with the Church:

What is the city of God, but the Holy Church? For men who love one another, and who love their God who dwelleth in them, constitute a city unto God. Because a city is held together by some law; their very law is Love; and that very Love is God; for openly it is written, 'God is Love'. He therefore who is full of Love is full of God; and many, full of Love, constitute a city full of God (*Expositions on the Psalms* xcviii, 4).[36]

But in what sense of the word 'Church' is this identification to be understood? To this question various answers have been given:[37] the empirical Catholic Church; the Church as the mystical body, or bride of Christ; the invisible Church of the elect. Identification of the City of God with the empirical Church is made difficult in that the latter is a 'mixed society' within which are some who are not predestined to salvation. Complete identification with the mystical body is made difficult in that angels are said to be the first citizens of the City of God[38] while Augustine never speaks of them as members of Christ's body. A probable conclusion is that the City of God is indeed the Church whose extent and membership are invisible to man, which in its celestial part 'is made up of the holy angels',[39] and in that part 'which wanders as a stranger on the earth'[40] consists of those members of the Catholic Church who are the 'congregation of the saints', persevering in faith and love and predestined at the consummation of all things to enter into the peace and blessedness of God's eternal city. It must not be forgotten that for Augustine membership of the Catholic Church by baptism is a *sine qua non* of final salvation.

Augustine's theological influence has been immense. R. W. Battenhouse has written:

> The civilization of medieval Christendom was to owe more to him than to any other of the Church Fathers. Gregory the Great turned to him for scriptural commentary and theology, Charlemagne for political theory, Bonaventura for mysticism, and Aquinas for elements of scholastic philosophy. Later, with the coming of the Reformation, Luther and Calvin became his disciples and, after them, Pascal—each gathering from the bishop of Hippo fresh stimulus for revitalizing Christian piety.[41]

In ecclesiology Augustine's doctrine of the mystical body governed the thinking of the medieval Church. His teaching that the unity of the Church is secured by communion with the see of Rome gave influential support to the mounting claims of that see to primacy and supremacy. His arguments against the Donatists provided a ready arsenal whenever a sect arose to insist that the Church must dissociate itself from sinners and to claim that it alone was the Church of the Holy. His doctrine of the Church as the invisible company of the elect was to be taken up again by Calvin in the sixteenth century.

JEROME (340–420)

We quote here two passages from Augustine's famous contemporary, Jerome, biblical scholar and translator, traveller, presbyter, and monk of Bethlehem. The first suggests an origin of episcopacy different from that which was generally accepted in his day:

> A presbyter, therefore, is the same as a bishop, and before ambition entered into religion by the devil's instigation and people began to say: 'I belong to Paul, I to Apollos, I to Cephas' (1 Cor. 1.12), the churches were governed by the council of the presbyters, acting together. But after each began to think that those whom he had baptized were his, not Christ's, it was unanimously decreed that one of the presbyters should be elected and preside over the others, and that the care of the Church should wholly belong to him, that the seeds of schism might thus be removed (*Commentary on the Epistle to Titus* I, 6–7).[42]

From the time of Irenaeus it had been generally assumed that the apostles appointed bishops, and that in each of the important centres of Christianity a succession of bishops could be traced back to apostles. Jerome suggests that in the earliest times oversight of the churches (*episkope*) was exercised by a college of presbyters, and that the practice later arose by which the presbyters delegated this oversight to one of their number, who then became known as *the* bishop (*episkopos*).

Jerome's jealousy for his reputation for orthodoxy is well known; he cannot have intended to write anything which could draw the accusation of unorthodoxy. As a biblical student he may have seen his theory as an implication of the N.T. passages which equate *episkopos* and *presbyteros*, some of which[43] he cites in the same commentary. This theory of the origin of the episcopate receives some support from evidence that in Alexandria until 230 *episkope* was regarded as residing in the college of presbyters. Alexandria certainly had bishops before this date, but they were elected and consecrated by the presbyters.[44] Jerome himself mentions this in *Epistle* CXLVI, 1. He travelled extensively (Gaul, Syria, Egypt, Italy, Palestine) and it is possible that he found local traditions elsewhere which supported his theory.

The second passage, from a letter to Pope Damasus who had sponsored his Latin version of the Bible (Vulgate), is one of the clearest declarations of the primacy of the Bishop of Rome made in the first four centuries:

Following no one as leader except Christ, I associate myself in communion with your Beatitude, that is, with the see of Peter. I know the Church was built on that rock. Whoever eats a lamb outside this house (Exodus 12.46) is profane. Any who is not in Noah's ark will perish when the flood prevails (*Epistle* xv).

The ecclesiology which declares not only the primacy of the bishop of Rome, but also his supremacy in all ecclesiastical affairs to be essential to the idea of the Church will be the major topic in the following chapter.

Part 3

THE MEDIEVAL PERIOD

8

The Church
as Papal Monarchy

Throughout the long and turbulent period known as the Middle Ages there was one, and only one continuing institution, the Christian Church. These centuries saw changing economic systems and social structures, political innovations, and new cultural expressions. The Church influenced all these movements, and was influenced by them, but itself, in the eyes of most, stood out above them as having made good the claim to everlastingness once claimed for ancient Rome.

The medieval Church of western Europe was a highly structured organization centred on the papacy, for which increasingly the claims of primacy and supremacy were made. We have already noted passages in some of the early Fathers which accord to the see of Rome a primacy of honour[1] and have been thought by some to acknowledge more than this. But it is extremely unlikely that even those who admit the most (Optatus, Jerome, Augustine) ever envisaged the total *magisterium* over all bishops which was soon to be claimed for the papacy, still less its temporal claims.

'The real framers and promoters of the theory of the Roman primacy were the popes themselves,' writes J. N. D. Kelly.[2] Men like Damasus (366–84), Siricius (384–99), Innocent I (402–17), and their successors not only strove to advance it on the practical plane, but sketched out the theology on which it was based.

LEO I

Pope Leo I, the author of the *Tome* which was accepted at the Council of Chalcedon, 451, as an orthodox expression of the doctrine of Christ's Person, drew together and systematized pronouncements of his predecessors, and provided what may be called a firm first draft for the doctrine of the papacy. The bases of the doctrine are:

    (1) that Christ chose one man, Peter, and gave him precedence

over all the apostles and all the Fathers of the Church, so that, although there are many bishops and pastors among the people of God, Peter properly rules all those whom Christ originally also rules (*Sermons* IV, 2).

(2) that the words of Christ in Matthew 16.18 ('upon this rock') refer to Peter himself, and not to his faith (ibid. IV, 3).

(3) that Peter was in fact the first Bishop of Rome, and that his precedence over the whole Church devolves upon the successive bishops of Rome, who are therefore 'vicars of Peter', and his heirs.

(4) that just as the authority given to Peter by Christ was conveyed to the other apostles through Peter,[3] so the authority of the bishops is derived, not immediately from Christ, but through the Bishop of Rome.

(5) that, therefore, the Bishop of Rome has the plenitude of power, *plenitudo potestatis*, in the Church, whilst other bishops have only a share in his responsibility, *pars sollicitudinis* (*Epistles* XIV, 1).[4]

Such claims are to be found in many of the extant sermons and letters of Leo. Their most systematic treatment is in *Sermon* IV and *Letter* XIV to which reference is made above.

GELASIUS, BISHOP OF ROME, 492–6

Towards the end of the fifth century, Pope Gelasius wrote a letter to the Emperor Anastasius which contained the following passage:

> There are two powers, august Emperor, by which this world is chiefly ruled, namely the sacred authority of priests and the power of kings. Of these, the responsibility of the priests is the heavier in that in the divine judgement they will have to give an account even for kings. For you know, most dear son, that you are permitted rightly to rule the human race, yet in things divine you devoutly bow your head before the principal clergy and ask of them the means of your salvation. . . . In these matters, as you know, you are dependent on their judgement, and you have no desire to compel them to do your will. And if it is proper that the hearts of the faithful be in submission to all priests everywhere who exercise their divine ministry aright, how much more is obedience to be given to the bishop of that see whom the Most High God willed to be pre-eminent over all other bishops? (*Ad Anastasium Imperatorem*).[5]

Apart from the reiteration of the papal claim to be the vicar of Peter, this statement on the surface seems to be no more than a reminder from an influential bishop to a Christian ruler of his Christian responsibilities. But it is pregnant with larger claims which were soon to be made explicit. Meanwhile the papal claim to be vicar of Peter was by no means generally admitted. The Church in the East was well aware that no General Council had ever granted the Bishop of Rome jurisdiction over other metropolitans, or over other bishops outside his own metropolitical sphere. And in the West explicit and universal admission of the papal claims was slow in coming.

GREGORY I, THE GREAT, BISHOP OF ROME, 590–604

But several factors contributed to the eventual recognition in the West of the pope's primacy in much more than an honorific sense. The centre of imperial administration had long been in Constantinople. In the West the Roman bishop gained in prestige. In a society increasingly under the attack of barbarian tribes, he represented an institution dedicated to peace and order. This prestige was enhanced by the character and energy of the popes themselves, many of whom were active in providing the protection and promoting the welfare services for the distressed which the emperors would not or could not give. Of particular importance was the work of Pope Gregory I.

His ecclesiology was predominantly Augustinian. He followed his predecessors in maintaining that the see of Rome is 'the Church of the blessed Peter', and that its bishops were the heirs of the 'prince of the apostles' from whom they had inherited the power to bind and loose. But he saw authority as to be exercised only in humility and service; and the more so, the greater the authority might be. He laboured incessantly to protect Rome from the invading Lombards; he fought plague and famine; he promoted missions for the conversion of the northern barbarians; and in all this displayed a high order of political wisdom, administrative ability, and pastoral concern. 'In such a man the might of the papacy stood more erect than any claims to Petrine singularity could ever have predicted.'[6] By the year 700, says R. W. Southern, 'no one in the West denied that the pope possessed all the authority of St Peter over the Church'.[7] This is not to say that the doctrine was everywhere vigorously promoted. For example, as Yves Congar notes,[8] the writings of the Venerable Bede (d. 735), whose ecclesiology is based on Augustine and Gregory the Great, contain no mention of a primacy of the pope. Yet he clearly shares the devotion to St Peter which was characteristic of the age. The theological arguments which linked papal primacy to the apostle Peter were often simply taken for granted.

'THE DONATION OF CONSTANTINE'

It is possible to read into the letter of Gelasius to the Emperor Anastasius[9] a hint of claims over temporal rulers which were not confined to matters ecclesiastical. Circumstances during the eighth century led to the venture of attempting to transform this hint into reality. The benefits of collaboration between the papacy and the ambitious Frankish chieftains became clear to both parties. Charles Martel and his son, Pepin the Short, were greatly impressed with the civilizing success amongst Germans east of the Rhine of the missionary work of Boniface, the emissary of Pope Gregory II (715–31). Pepin was named King of the Franks, and anointed by Boniface, now Archbishop of Mainz, in 751. His son, the able Charles the Great (Charlemagne), found it possible to promote the military and political ambition of the Franks, and Christian missions at the same time. According to his biographer,[10] St Augustine's *De Civitate Dei* was Charlemagne's favourite reading. It is possible that he believed himself called to establish the City of God on earth by a revival of the ancient Roman Empire, but if there was any connection in his mind between this and *De Civitate* he clearly mistook Augustine's intention. On Christmas Day 800, Charlemagne was crowned Emperor of the Romans by Pope Leo III in the basilica of St Peter in Rome. His biographer tells us that this was unexpected, and that he agreed with reluctance, but papal records represent it as a well-planned occasion. It is unlikely that Charlemagne and the Pope saw precisely the same significance in the ceremony.

The papal interpretation of this coronation was that it simply recognized the status and privileges of the Bishop of Rome as set forth in the 'Donation of Constantine'. This was a document of unknown authorship which appeared during this period, and probably in the late eighth century. It was one of those documents, of which history provides many examples, 'in which the theories of the present were represented as the facts of the past'.[11] It purports to be a letter from the Emperor Constantine to Sylvester I, Bishop of Rome (314–35). Its contents are conveniently summarized by R. W. Southern:[12]

> ... a long account of Constantine's conversion, baptism, and cure from leprosy at the intercession of Pope Sylvester. It then goes on to record the Emperor's gifts to the vicar of St Peter: the grant of pre-eminence over the patriarchal sees of Antioch, Alexandria, Jerusalem, and Constantinople, and all other churches; the gift of the imperial insignia, together with the

Lateran palace in Rome; and finally the transfer to the pope of the imperial power in Rome, Italy, and all the provinces of the West.

Thus the pope is seen, not only as supreme over the Church, but as supreme in the West in temporal affairs. The coronation of Charlemagne by the Pope was a recognition of this, not to be forgotten; but the endeavour to make the claim effective was to be the work of centuries.

THE CHURCH IN THE WESTERN WORLD

Effective government in the West was, however, short-lived. Such centrality of government as Charlemagne had achieved was soon to be broken in internecine struggles between powerful feudal lords, the dukes, some of whom would make good a claim to be 'king' over a certain territory, a few of whom aspired to, and were accorded, the title of Emperor of the Romans. The feudal system, into which were built elements from both the Germanic and Roman world, tended to exacerbate and prolong the conflicts. The system, by no means identical in all places, was hierarchical. Each man, from the serf working on an estate and the local lord of the manor to the more powerful dukes and the king, was a vassal, bound in allegiance to his overlord. Theoretically, the emperor was at the head of this hierarchy. Allegiance entailed payments in money, kind, or service, including military service when required. Each of the great lords could expect, for the lives and livelihood of their vassals depended on it, the provision of fighting men whenever they were engaged, as they frequently were, in struggle with a neighbour. These were not times in which popes, however able, could effectively exercise temporal lordship.

It was hardly less difficult for them to exercise the vicariate of Peter in the spiritual affairs of western Europe. It was impossible to convene general councils. Papal letters might or might not arrive at their destination; if they did, the pope had no means of enforcing his wishes.

The Church, perhaps inevitably, became part of the feudal system. Its leaders, the bishops and abbots, were overlords in respect of those who worked in their service, and vassals in respect of the dukes and kings from whom the Church received gifts of land. The writer of the Epistle to Diognetus[13] had spoken of Christians as sharing all things as citizens whilst knowing that their true citizenship is in heaven, and of obeying the established laws whilst outdoing those laws by their lives. It is possible to see the feudal period as one in which the Church was attempting to work out such a programme. An alternative might have been, ignoring the dominical 'ye are the salt of the earth', to attempt to withdraw from society, prepared to accept whatever might come, even though it be extinction. Its choice was, however, to live in the world, and that world was the feudal world. How successfully it manifested the ideal of the Epistle to Diognetus, and provided salt for the feudal world is a matter for debate.[14] On the one hand one notes the careers of such men as the warlike Odo, Bishop of Bayeux, who was devoted to the cause of William the Conqueror, and distinguished himself at the Battle of Hastings. On the other hand there is much evidence that many bishops and abbots strove to reduce warfare, to protect the weak, and to promote good husbandry on their estates.

In these confused times the bishop and the abbot in most places in the West were the two persons who were the leading representatives of the oldest existing institution, one which was acknowledged to have not only divine sanction, but also long experience in effective and beneficent administration. They, and their clergy and monks, were more often than not fully deserving of the confidence and affection which the common people gave to them. It is certain that the great feudal lords were alive to the advantages of co-operation with bishops and abbots. So important did they believe this to be that they claimed, and not infrequently exercised, the right to appoint bishops. Pope John XI in 921 protested sharply against its exercise by a local duke, while admitting 'the ancient custom' that a Christian king might present a bishop for consecration. Nevertheless the bishops and the abbots were to be the pope's men in the controversies with monarchs which were later to develop.

TRENDS IN ECCLESIOLOGY, NINTH AND TENTH CENTURIES

THE MYSTICAL BODY OF CHRIST

The basic emphasis remains the Augustinian concept of the mystical body. The incarnate body of Christ, the eucharistic body, and the body which is the Church are three realizations of the same mystery. The words of Haymo of Halberstadt (d. 891) are typical:

> Just as that flesh [which the Word of God assumed] is the body of Christ, so this bread becomes the body of Christ. Nor are there two bodies, but

one body ... and as that bread and blood [*sic*] become the body of Christ, so all those in the Church who worthily partake of it are one body of Christ. ... Yet that flesh which he assumed, and this bread, and the Church as a whole do not make three bodies of Christ, but one body (*Commentary on 1 Corinthians* x).[15]

PAPAL PRIMACY OR SUPREMACY?

Despite the now official interpretation at Rome of Matthew 16.18 as supporting papal supremacy, elsewhere the interpretation of Cyprian[16] who, taking the text in conjunction with Matthew 18.18 and John 20.22–3, read them as pointing to a collegial episcopate, persisted strongly. Bede (d. 735) and Paul the Deacon (d. *c.* 800) had so interpreted them in the eighth century; Haymo of Halberstadt and Rabanus Maurus (d. 856) followed suit in the ninth, and Rathier of Verona (d. 974), and Gerbert of Aurrilac who became Pope Sylvester II (d. 1003) in the tenth.[17] 'Everybody in the West acknowledged the Roman primacy, but not everybody did so in the sense that had been given to it at Rome since St Leo.'[18]

Hincmar, Archbishop of Rheims (845–82) in particular resisted the claims of successive popes to override metropolitan bishops by judging in the first instance matters concerning bishops. He maintained also that the college of bishops is more than merely a passive instrument under the absolute authority of the pope; it must play an active part in regulating the life of the Church. Hincmar recognized the primacy of Rome as of divine institution, but declared that papal decisions must be in accordance with the Scriptures and the canon law which derives from the acknowledged ecumenical councils. It is in such Catholic councils that the mind of the Church is expressed, and the episcopal college plays its rightful role therein. Only when a bishop, even a pope, judges or decides in accordance with canons derived from conciliar decisions, can he be sure that the whole Church judges and decides with him.[19]

THE CHURCH 'WHICH ESPECIALLY CONSISTS OF THE CLERGY'

In this period the distinction between clergy and laity was accentuated. Yves Congar writes:[20]

The faithful no longer understood Latin. From the end of the eighth century the Canon of the Mass was said in a low voice, the priest celebrated with his back to the people, the faithful no longer brought their offerings to the altar, private masses became frequent in the monasteries; at the beginning of the ninth century, instead of the simple phrase 'who offer to thee' (i.e. in the third person) we find 'for whom *we* offer to thee or who offer to thee' in the Canon. ... From this period one could begin making a list of passages which imply that the Church consists principally in the clergy.

He offers as examples: 'the Church which especially consists of the clergy' (Florus of Lyons, d. 860);[21] 'for the Church is nothing other than the faithful people, although the word particularly designates the clergy'(? John VIII, Pope 872–82).[22]

Here the idea of the Church as the congregation of the faithful is in danger of being lost, and the great majority of Church people in process of becoming passive nonentities.

TRENDS IN ECCLESIOLOGY, ELEVENTH AND TWELFTH CENTURIES

LEO IX, POPE 1049–54

R. W. Southern, in the book already cited several times, bids us pay attention, if we would understand the increased papal claims of the latter part of the eleventh century, to the activity of Leo IX. He mentions: 'the political alliance with the Normans; the exacerbation of relations with the Greeks;[23] the reform of papal administrative machinery; the beginning of a consistent plan of government through legates, councils, and a vastly increased correspondence'.[24] He gathered round him a group of able men, among them two monks: Hildebrand, and Humbert who was appointed cardinal-bishop of Silva Candida in 1049. Canon law, into which the Donation of Constantine was incorporated, was revised. The idea of the Church, first sketched by Leo I and briefly exemplified by Gregory the Great, was brought to the fore. The Church was seen as 'a unique kingdom under the papal monarchy in whose universal responsibility and power the bishops had only a partial share'.[25] The Roman Church is the see of Peter. In relation to the rest of the Church it is 'head', 'mother', 'hinge', 'fount', 'foundation'. It cannot err in the faith. Long-needed reforms were taken in hand, in particular against simony (the granting of ecclesiastical offices in consideration of bribes). Humbert wrote a treatise 'Against Simoniacs', in which he asserted that ordinations by simoniacal bishops were invalid.

GREGORY VII (HILDEBRAND), POPE 1073–85

Building on the success of this reactivation of the papal claims and of
the practical activities which supported them, Hildebrand, himself one
of Leo IX's most able advisers, when he became Pope Gregory VII
some twenty years later was ready to extend them both by words and
action. The words are to be found in brief notes, known as the *Dic-
tatus Papae* ('The Dictations of the Pope'). Whether they were actually dictated by Gregory is disputed. They appear among the collection
of his letters, and certainly belong to his pontificate.[26] There are
twenty-seven notes, but they may be summarized under four heads:

1 The Roman Church
The *Ecclesia Romana* was founded by God alone; its bishop is
rightly called universal. It has never erred and never will. Nobody is
a Catholic who does not agree with it.

2 Papal power over the Church
The Bishop of Rome can ordain anyone from any part of the
Church. He alone can depose, reinstate, or transfer bishops to
another see. A papal legate, even though of lesser ecclesiastical
rank, presides over bishops in council. The pope alone can make
new laws, create new episcopal sees or unite existing ones. He alone
can call a general council; actions of synods are not canonical
without his authority. His decrees can be annulled by no one, but he
can annul the decrees of anyone. All important ecclesiastical disputes must be referred to him.

3 Papal authority in relation to emperors and kings
The pope has the power to depose emperors. On appeal to the pope
no one shall be condemned in any other court. The pope may permit or command subjects to accuse their rulers, and may absolve
subjects from their oath of allegiance to wicked rulers.

4 The papal status
The pope alone may use the imperial insignia. All princes shall kiss
his foot alone. He can be judged by no one. A pope who has been
canonically ordained is made a saint by the merits of St Peter.

These words, describing the pope's all-embracing authority over the
whole of Christendom, emperors and kings and their affairs no less
than the officers of the Church and theirs, were dramatically
translated into action in 1076 when Gregory deposed and excom-

municated Henry IV of Germany, heir to the imperial throne. He conceived himself to be acting as vicar of Peter, to whom he addressed the deed of deposition and excommunication:[27]

> ... I now declare in the name of the omnipotent God, the Father, Son and Holy Spirit, that Henry, son of the Emperor Henry, is deprived of his Kingdom of Germany and Italy; I do this by thy authority and in defence of the honour of thy Church, because he has rebelled against it.'

Henry submitted, and did penance at Canossa in 1077, whereupon Gregory withdrew the deposition and lifted the excommunication.

The ecclesiology which is implied in all this is apparent. It may be described as a doctrine of the Church as a papal monarchy. The Bishop of Rome is supreme not only over ecclesiastics and ecclesiastical affairs, but over emperor and rulers and the affairs of civil government. The Church is seen as coterminous with the empire, a notion which in theory, and often in practice, denied the privileges of citizenship and even protection to those who were not in communion with the see of Rome, not only heretics and schismatics, but groups like the Jews. It is a doctrine of the Church which, for its implementation, demanded a tight structure of papal legates in every country, emissaries to the courts of every king, prince, or baron, and an elaborate court of political experts in Rome to keep a finger on the whole. Beneath this new hierarchy the authority of metropolitans and bishops in their own provinces and dioceses was often reduced to vanishing-point.

REACTION

There was no lack of protesting voices. Gregory was accused of treating the bishops as a large landowner treats his farmers.[28] The German bishops at a synod at Worms in 1076 charged him with pride and ambition. He had 'introduced worldliness into the Church'; 'the bishops have been deprived of their divine authority'; 'the Church of God is in danger of destruction' through Gregory's presumption.[29]

The papal claim to temporal supremacy met with opposition from every ruler powerful enough to make his influence felt. They received support from some theologians and canonists,[30] who took up again the dictum of Gelasius: 'There are two powers by which this world is chiefly ruled. . . .'[31] More radical opposition was also forthcoming. An unknown writer, the so-called 'Anonymous Norman' (*c.* 1000) contends that the Church is to be defined as 'the Christian people', 'the congregation of faithful Christians living together in the house of God in one faith, hope and love'. It is a royal and priestly people. Its only head is Christ. Priesthood is related to the temporary humiliation of the Word in the incarnation, while kingly rule derives from his divinity. Kings then are vicars of God, priests only of Christ in his humanity. From this it follows that kings have a sacred power of government in ecclesiastical matters, and authority over bishops, and that kings properly invest bishops with their authority.[32]

The first stages of the long-drawn-out struggle between popes and rulers were fought on the investiture issue. A compromise was reached between Callistus II (Pope 1119–24) and the Emperor Henry V at the Concordat of Worms in 1122. Elections of bishops were to be the free prerogative of the Church. Bishops would be invested with the ring and crozier, representing their spiritual authority, by the pope or his deputies, while the emperor would invest them with their temporal authority and possessions and receive their homage.

BERNARD OF CLAIRVAUX, 1090–1153

The founder and first abbot of the Cistercian monastery at Clairvaux was both a supporter and a critic of the papacy. His sermons on the Song of Solomon present a doctrine of the Church as the mystical body, and at once the spouse of Christ. The sense of the need for deep personal religion inspires his writing. The union in the mystical body is the spiritual union of souls with Christ in Love. He can use the phrase: 'The Church or the soul which loves God'.[33] The Church is the Saviour's spouse, but every soul also is the spouse of Christ insofar as it shares individually in the love for Christ of the one and only spouse.

Bernard preached the ideal of poverty, and was deeply critical of the imperial style of life which the papacy had assumed, and which was likely to present the pope to the world as the successor of Constantine rather than St Peter.[34] He warned Eugenius III (Pope 1145–53), his former pupil and a Cistercian monk, against involving himself in a continuous round of secular and litigious business.[35] While he did not doubt that the pope possessed *plenitudo potestatis*,[36] it was not appropriate that he should do all that he had the power to do.[37] If the Church is to be the Church of God, who according to Scripture is Love, not Honour or Dignity,[38] it must not confine itself within the structures of power and juridical authority.

TRENDS IN ECCLESIOLOGY, THIRTEENTH CENTURY

INNOCENT III, POPE 1198–1216

The high point of the papal claims and of the ability to translate them into action was reached in the pontificate of Innocent III, who was elected after a long campaign on his behalf by members of the influential Conti family from which he came.[39] His aim was to display the papal *plenitudo potestatis*, interpreted now not merely in relation to the *pars sollicitudinis* of other bishops, but as supremacy in all the affairs of men. He built up an efficient organization of legal and financial officers in Rome. His legates and other emissaries penetrated to every part of western Europe. His own knowledge of canon law, and the skill of the canonists whom he enlisted, enabled him to make effective use of the papal appeal court.

FOURTH LATERAN COUNCIL, 1215

Innocent was a competent theologian, and it was by his inspiration that the Fourth Lateran Council in its first canon set out a summary of Christian doctrine (the Trinity, the Incarnation, the Church, and the Sacraments). It defined the eucharistic presence of Christ in terms of transubstantiation, a doctrine to which the development of medieval theology had been leading.[40] The Council laid down rules for the administration and reception of the sacraments.[41] A programme of education of the faithful was proposed. The checking of abuses, such as the superstitious use of relics, was promised.[42] Plans were approved for a new crusade against the Saracens (never to be undertaken, although Innocent devoted much attention to its preparation during his last months).

The Council also forbade the creation of new monastic Orders, whose recent proliferation alarmed Innocent. It was perhaps reluctantly that he had sanctioned the rule of St Francis of Assisi. The two Orders of friars, Franciscan and Dominican, which had their beginnings during Innocent's pontificate, were, however, to prove strong pillars of papal power.

PAPAL AUTHORITY IN ACTION

Among the many ways in which Innocent demonstrated his authority over bishops was his restriction of their power to grant indulgences, which effectively diverted income to the papacy. He was the first to *require* bishops to grant benefices to his own nominees. The later growth of this practice was a chief cause of national resentment against the popes.

His exercise of temporal supremacy was illustrated by the episode of the excommunication of King John of England in 1209, of John's capitulation and the surrender of his territories 'to God, and to Saints Peter and Paul His apostles and to the Holy Roman Church our mother, and to our lord Pope Innocent III and his Catholic successors',[43] receiving them back as the Pope's vassal for the payment of 1,000 marks annually. In his dealings with the imperial throne, Innocent was less successful. At the beginning of his pontificate there were several claimants. After a long period of political activity, carefully documented in the papal registry of letters, Innocent was able to secure the election of the man of his choice, Otto IV. Otto, however, proved to be a broken reed, and in 1211 Innocent successfully promoted the election of his youthful ward, Frederick II. Frederick's extraordinary career was to provide manifold difficulties for Innocent's successors, and to make clear that the papal claim to temporal lordship was incapable of fulfilment.

THE VICAR OF CHRIST

Canon 1 of the Fourth Lateran Council, among its doctrinal statements, affirms simply that 'there is one universal Church of the faithful, outside of which there is absolutely no salvation'. How Innocent himself interpreted this is made clear in his letter to King John of England (1215). Jesus Christ who is both King of kings and eternal Priest has established both his kingdom and his priesthood in the Church. The Church, therefore, is both a priestly kingdom and a royal priesthood. Christ has set one, the Bishop of Rome, as his vicar on earth over all. As every knee should bow to Jesus, so obedience is required of his vicar. Consequently, unless kings venerate and serve this vicar they must doubt whether they are reigning properly. Kingdom and priesthood, for the benefit of each, are to be united in the person of the vicar of Christ.

'The vicar of Christ', not now the vicar of Peter. 'We are the successor of the Prince of the Apostles,' Innocent admitted, 'but we are not his vicar, nor the vicar of any man or Apostle, but the vicar of Jesus Christ himself.'[44] To be 'vicar of Peter', indicating merely authority over the successors of the apostles, was a title no longer adequate to indicate the temporal claims of the pope.

GREGORY IX (POPE 1227–41) AND INNOCENT IV (POPE 1243–54)

Innocent III's successors, although hindered by the defiance of the Emperor Frederick II until his death in 1250, hammered in a little more deeply some of the nails which he had placed. Gregory IX consolidated the canon law, and sponsored the School of Bologna as a centre for its study and dissemination. He initiated a practice designed to bring the Italian sees firmly under papal control, by appointing the very able but youthful Ottaviano degli Ubaldini as his agent, with the title of archdeacon, in the diocese of Bologna during a deliberately maintained interregnum. Innocent IV made Ottaviano a cardinal and appointed him his legate in northern Italy, equipped with practically full papal power. His influence, in fact, extended far beyond Italy. He became a kind of shadow pope, distrusted and feared by almost all. His relationship with the papal enemy, the excommunicated Frederick II, was ambiguous. Dante placed him (*il cardinale*) with the Emperor in hell.

BONIFACE VIII (POPE 1294–1303)

The beginning of the fourteenth century saw the publication, 1302, of Boniface's Bull, *Unam Sanctam*. It is an important document which gives classical expression to the papal concept of the Church as it was understood after eight and a half centuries of theoretical and practical development upon foundations laid by Leo I. It must be quoted at some length:[45]

> ... There is one holy Catholic apostolic Church ... outside of her there is no salvation or remission of sins, as the Bridegroom says in the Song of Solomon: 'My dove, my undefiled is but one....' (Song 6.9); which represents the one mystical body, whose head is Christ.... In the time of the flood there was only one ark, that of Noah, prefiguring the one Church ... all things on the earth outside of this ark were destroyed. This Church we venerate as the only one, since the Lord said by the prophet: 'Deliver my soul from the sword; my darling from the power of the dog' (Ps. 22.20). He prayed for his soul, that is, for himself, the head; and at the same time for the body; and he named his body, that is, the one church, because there is but one Bridegroom,[46] and because of the unity of the faith, of the sacraments, and of his love for the church. This is the seamless robe of the Lord which was not rent but parted by lot (John 19.23). Therefore there is one body of the one and only church, and one head, not two heads, as if the church were a monster. And this head is Christ and his vicar, Peter and his successor; for the Lord himself said to

Peter: 'Feed my sheep' (John 21.16). And he said 'my sheep', in general, not these or those sheep in particular; from which it is clear that all were committed to him. If therefore Greeks or anyone else say that they are not subject to Peter and his successors, they thereby necessarily confess that they are not of the sheep of Christ. For ... there is one fold and only one shepherd (John 10.16). By the words of the Gospel we are taught that the two swords, namely the spiritual authority and the temporal are in the power of the church.[47] For when the apostle said 'Here are two swords' (Luke 22.38)—that is in the church, since it was the apostles who were speaking—the Lord did not answer 'It is too much', but 'It is enough'. Whoever denies that the temporal sword is in the power of Peter does not properly understand the word of the Lord when he said: 'Put up thy sword into the sheath' (John 18.11).[48] Both swords, therefore, the spiritual and the temporal, are in the power of the church. The former is to be used by the Church, the latter for the church; the one by the hand of the priest, the other by the hand of kings and knights, but at the command and permission of the priest.

Boniface goes on to show why the temporal must be subject to the spiritual authority. He quotes Romans 13.1 which declares that all existing powers are ordained by God, and takes 'ordained' in the sense of 'arranged in order'. He then calls to his aid the authority of Dionysius the Areopagite[49] to support the proposition that a hierarchical order of things is of divine origin, and that it is a law of the universe that the lower is given its due order, and thereby enhanced, by the higher. He adds that it is necessarily to be admitted that the spiritual power surpasses any earthly power, and with some naivety claims that the truth of this is evident from the fact that men pay tithes to and receive benediction from the spiritual power:

Thus the prophecy of Jeremiah concerning the church and the ecclesiastical power is fulfilled: 'See, I have this day set thee over the nations and over the kingdoms, to root out, and to pull down, and to destroy, and to throw down, to build and to plant (Jer. 1.10).

First Corinthians 2.15 is then quoted to show that the spiritual power will rightly judge the temporal, itself being subject to the judgement of no man, but of God only. The familiar Matthew 16.18–19 is used to show that

this authority, although it is given to man and exercised through man, is not human, but divine. For it was given by the word of the Lord to Peter, and the rock was made firm to him and his successors, in Christ himself whom he had confessed.

Finally, Boniface alludes to Romans 13.2: 'Therefore he who resists the authorities resists what God has appointed, and those who resist will incur judgement.' He ignores the plural 'authorities', and assumes that the authority of which St Paul speaks is that of the Bishop of Rome:

> We therefore declare, say, and affirm that submission on the part of every man to the bishop of Rome is altogether necessary for his salvation.

It should be noted how the papal doctrine of the Church is impressed upon the old scriptural and patristic images of the Church, many of which are present in this document: the bride, the dove of Solomon's Song, the ark, the body, the seamless robe. To be noted too is the ingenious combination of symbolic and literal interpretation of the Scriptures. It is a document which Innocent III could have signed, although he would probably have eliminated its ambiguities[50] and exegetical infelicities. Leo I would probably have applauded it—and marvelled that the time should have come when such a document could be published. One can only guess that Clement I in 96 would have been thoroughly puzzled by it. Does its ecclesiology represent a legitimate or divinely ordered development? The events of the fourteenth century were strongly to suggest a negative answer.

In the year after the publication of the Bull, Boniface died. His Bull *Clericis Laicos* of 1298, which forbade secular rulers to impose any taxes whatsoever upon clerics without papal permission, and threatened the excommunication of rulers who exacted or clerics who paid such unauthorized taxes, thoroughly antagonized Edward I of England and Philip IV of France. The latter sent an expedition of French soldiers to attack the papal palace at Anagoni, and Boniface died as a result of the violence and insults he received. So ended a period of cordial relationship between the papacy and kings of France which had lasted nearly 200 years. In 1309 Pope Clement V moved to Avignon. The minor scandal of the removal of the centre of government of the successor of Peter from the city of which the apostle had been the first bishop and where he was martyred was ended sixty-nine years later when Gregory XI returned to Rome, only to be succeeded by the greater scandal of the 'Great Schism'. Between 1378 and 1449 there were only seventeen years when there were not at least two popes claiming to have been duly elected by the cardinals. Secular rulers were not slow to take advantage of a situation in which the first half of a *divide et impera* policy was actually provided for them. To play one pope off against another was as easy as it was obvious. The number of acts designed to limit papal temporal jurisdiction multiplied in the statute books of many countries. Voices of protest from churchmen, appeals for reform and for new definitions of the order and function of the Church, though they had not been lacking in the thirteenth century, now became more frequent and persistent. We shall consider these in Chapter 10.

9

The Ecclesiology
of the Schoolmen

The thirteenth century has been described as the golden age of scholasticism, that is the theology of the scholars (scholastics or schoolmen) who taught at the universities. The universities arose during the twelfth century. Their beginnings were in the schools of learning established by monastic Orders and, in the thirteenth century by the Franciscans and Dominicans, in the larger cities of Europe. Anselm, Archbishop of Canterbury (d. 1109) is often called 'the Father of the Schoolmen', but perhaps Peter Lombard (1100–1160), who taught at the School of Notre Dame in Paris, has a better claim to the title, for his *Sentences* became a standard textbook of theology, and commentaries on them were written by most of the later schoolmen of consequence, including Albertus Magnus, Thomas Aquinas, and Bonaventure.

The schoolmen in their commentaries on the *Sentences*, and their *Summae*, treated the whole range of theology. Yves Congar notes[1] that 'none of the great scholastics undertook a special treatise on the Church'. Professor Hans Küng[2] also remarks that the medieval period produced much less writing on the theology of the Church than canonical material on questions of ecclesiastical constitution and authority. The ecclesiology of these writers is for the most part to be found in the context of their Christology and their doctrines of grace and the sacraments. Perhaps the fullest treatment of the doctrine of the Church is that of Thomas Aquinas in his *Expositio super Symbolo Apostolorum* ('An Exposition on the Apostles' Creed').

The scholastic theologians of the twelfth and thirteenth centuries employ the biblical and patristic images and symbols of the Church, and in the main follow the lines of St Augustine. As we look briefly at the ecclesiology of some of them we shall, however, note a new development in a tendency to make a certain distinction between 'Church' and 'mystical body of Christ'.

HUGH OF ST VICTOR, 1096–1141

Hugh taught at the school of the abbey of St Victor in Paris. The Church, he maintained, is the body of Christ. Its principle of unity is faith, confirmed by the baptism by which we are incorporated into Christ.[3] The Church is at once the body of Christ and the creation of the Holy Spirit: 'Just as the spirit of a man comes down by the mediation of his head to give life to all his members, so the Holy Spirit comes to Christians through Christ.'[4] 'When you become a Christian, you become a member of Christ, participating in the Spirit of Christ.'[5]

Congar notes[6] that in the twelfth century the 'birthday' of the Church is less frequently identified with Pentecost, than with the flowing of water and blood from the side of Christ on the cross (John 19.34). This notion occurs several times in Hugh. The reference to the sacraments of baptism and the eucharist is clear. The Church is seen as the sphere where the sacramental grace which flows from Christ's humanity operates. There is a tendency here, which will be more pronounced in the thirteenth century, towards a doctrine of the Church which is 'essentially Christological, not pneumatological'.[7]

ALEXANDER OF HALES, 1170–1245

Alexander of Hales, a Franciscan who studied and taught in Paris, the author of a commentary on Peter Lombard's *Sentences* and a *Summa*, presents two points of interest. The first is reminiscent of Jerome's equation of the presbyter with the bishop.[8] The ecclesiastical orders may be considered either from the point of view of sacramental power, or of power in relationship to the Church. In the first case, the order of the priesthood, which has the power to celebrate the eucharist, stands at the head of the hierarchy. But from the point of view of the total needs of the Church, which include the ordination of priests and pastors, the episcopate must be added.[9]

Secondly, in Alexander we find a distinction between the members of the Church and the members of Christ. For membership in the Church faith[10] is sufficient, but for membership in 'the body of the Church' or the mystical body of Christ charity, or faith which has been formed (*fides formata*), is necessary. By receiving the sacrament of faith (baptism) one can be a member of the Church in point of number (*numero*), i.e. as merely one of a number. But by faith which has been formed one is not only a member of the Church, but a member of Christ,[11] and this in point of merit (*merito*), i.e. deservedly.

BONAVENTURE, 1221–74

Bonaventure, a Franciscan who taught in Paris and a commentator on the *Sentences*, whose doctrine of the Church is basically Augustinian, makes a distinction similar to that of Alexander, whose pupil he was. Here and there he identifies 'Church' and 'mystical body', but introduces a distinction when he considers the status of sinners. Unrepentant sinners are 'within the Church',[12] even members of the Church. But they are not members of the mystical body, unless one can say that they are 'dead and rotten members'.[13] Congar sums up Bonaventure's position thus: 'It is clear that for him "Church" denotes the body in and by which salvation is at work, and one can be a member of it merely as one of a number (*numero*); while the "mystical body" implies union with Christ by charity and living fellowship. Its members are those who are members of the Church deservedly (*merito*).'[14]

Bonaventure was a strong supporter of the concept of the papal monarchy, but expressed himself cautiously on the question of the political power of the pope. But he has no doubt that the pope possesses plenitude of power over the Church. It is a 'triple' power, because (a) 'he alone has the whole plenitude of authority which Christ conferred upon the Church'; (b) 'he possesses it everywhere in the churches'; and (c) 'all authority flows from him throughout the Church to all the lower ranks'.[15] 'If everything in the Church were destroyed, and he alone remained, he could restore it all.'[16] The pope's authority is both juridical and doctrinal: 'It is recognized that at the time when truth and grace were revealed the plenitude of power was conferred upon the vicar of Christ, and consequently it must be said that to assert anything in a matter of faith or morals which is contrary to what he has defined is an evil in no way to be tolerated.'[17] This is close to an assertion of papal infallibility.

ALBERTUS MAGNUS, 1206–80

The Dominican, Albertus Magnus,[18] who also taught in Paris, writes frequently of the mystical body. He treats it in close relationship with the eucharist. Incorporation with the mystical body is through the eucharistic body which he thinks of as the extending to all of the union which the Word of God effected with human nature in the incarnation. Yet for him the Holy Spirit is the principle of unity of the body of

Christ, and the sanctifier of the Church.[19] His pupil, Thomas Aquinas, was to develop this pneumatological aspect of the Church, which was not prominent among the scholastics.

Albert, like Alexander of Hales and Bonaventure, distinguishes between the 'Church' and the 'mystical body'. The mystical body means something more than 'the congregation of faithful people'—charity is necessary. Yves Congar remarks that 'Albert says the same about the Church, which strictly would lead to the unacceptable idea of a Church composed only of saints.'[20] But elsewhere he makes a distinction between belonging to the communion of grace and belonging to the society of the means of grace, between being a member of the Church *merito* and a member *numero*.[21]

The pope's plenitude of power is acknowledged;[22] jurisdiction descends from the pope. But Albert ascribes to him neither absolute monarchy nor infallibility. He speaks of indefectibility (based on Luke 22.32, 'that thy faith fail not') rather than infallibility, and he refers it to the 'see of Peter and his successor', not to the pope personally.[23]

THOMAS AQUINAS, 1225–74

The life span of St Thomas Aquinas fell between the pontificates of Innocent III and Boniface VIII, and thus coincided with the period when popes and canonists were mounting their largest claims for papal supremacy, both spiritual and temporal. Thomas, an Italian of noble family, was a Dominican friar, a pupil of Albertus Magnus, and taught in Paris.

THE MYSTICAL BODY

The ecclesiology of Augustine dominates Thomas's doctrine of the Church. It is the mystical body of which Christ is the head. He draws an analogy with the human body of which the head is the centre of order, perfection, and power (all the senses are centred there). The analogy, however, he warns must not be pressed; it is a question of resemblance rather than exact correspondence.[24] The analogy is inadequate in that the members of a human body are all joined together at one time, but 'the members of the mystical body are not all together ... since the body of the Church is made up of the men who have been from the beginning of the world until its end.'[25] In the same passage (in which he is commenting on 1 Timothy 4.10: 'the Saviour of all men, especially of those who believe') he says that Christ is the Head of all mankind, but not of all men in the same way:

> First and principally, He is Head of such as are united to Him by glory; secondly, of those who are actually united to Him by charity; thirdly, of those who are actually united to Him by faith; fourthly, of those who are united to Him merely in potentiality, which is not yet reduced to act, yet will be reduced to act according to Divine predestination; fifthly, of those who are united to Him in potentiality, which will never be reduced to act; such are those men existing in the world, who are not predestined, who, however, on their departure from this world, wholly cease to be members of Christ, as being no longer in potentiality to be united to Christ.

Thomas's strong doctrine of predestination brings him close here to a doctrine of the invisible Church.

THE CHURCH AS THE CREATION OF THE HOLY SPIRIT

Thomas takes up again[26] the theme that the Church on earth derives its existence from Christ's passion: 'From the side of Christ, sleeping on the cross, the sacraments flowed—namely, blood and water—on which the Church was established.'[27] This is in line with the Christologically centred doctrine of the Church which is typical of western medieval theology. Yet he acknowledges the constitutive activity of the Holy Spirit in the life of the Church:

> As in one single human being there is one soul and one body but many members, so the Catholic Church has one body but many members. The soul animating this body is the Holy Ghost.[28] Hence the Creed, after bidding us believe in the Holy Ghost, adds, 'the Holy Catholic Church' (*Exposition on the Apostles' Creed* 9).[29]

It is the Holy Spirit who anoints the Church, just as the faithful Christian receives an anointing for his sanctification,[30] and who is the ultimate principle of its unity.[31] But, as Congar says:[32] 'It must be admitted that Thomas has hardly gone into detail in this regard. His theology of habitual grace[33] led him to think chiefly of Christ as the communicator of grace.'

THE CHURCH A MIXED SOCIETY

Although he frequently speaks of the Church as *societas sanctorum* (a society of saints), he clearly does not conceive of it as a society of the perfect. Quoting Ephesians 5.27, 'a glorious Church, not having spot or wrinkle', he says that this must be understood of the goal to be achieved through Christ's passion, that is, 'in heaven, and not on earth, in which "if we say that we have no sin, we deceive ourselves" (1 John 1.8).'[34]

THE CONGREGATION OF THE FAITHFUL

In one section on the Church in his *Exposition on the Apostles' Creed* Thomas says that 'church' means 'congregation', and defines Holy Church as 'the congregation of believers of which each Christian is a member', citing Ecclesiasticus 51.23: 'Draw near to me, ye unlearned; and gather yourselves together into the house of discipline.' Here again, the Church is seen as a mixed society, the school of sinners and the ignorant, rather than a society of the perfect. Hans Küng[35] draws special attention to the frequency with which Thomas speaks of the Church as the *congregatio fidelium*. This definition, or description of the Church, seemingly at variance with the tendency of medieval ecclesiology to emphasize the hierarchy, was never quite submerged. It was not forgotten even by the canonists,[36] whose concern for the most part was to support the idea of the Church as a hierarchy under the papal monarchy, and it was to be the basis of the conciliarists' argument for the superiority of a general council over the pope.[37]

The *Exposition* goes on to comment on the four credal marks of the Church. The tone is devotional, rather than dogmatic.

One

The Church is one. The Song of Solomon 6.9, 'My dove, my perfect one, is only one', supplies Thomas's text.[38] This unity has a triple cause in the agreement of faith, hope, and charity: of faith, because all who belong to the body of Christ hold the same truths; of hope, because they have the same confidence of receiving eternal life; of charity, because all are bound together in the love of God and one another. He recognizes that this is not always so (again the admission that the Church is a mixed society) in the words which follow: 'The genuineness of this love is shown when the members of the Church care for one another and are compassionate together.'

In this context of the unity of the Church he employs the ancient image of the ark of Noah, but not with the polemical and exclusive intent we have noted in others.[39] That the Church is like Noah's ark 'outside of which nobody can be saved' is a reason for gentle treat-

ment of weaker brethren: 'Nobody should be despised, nobody should
be treated as an outcast.'

Holy

The Church is holy. Here he uses the biblical image of the temple: 'Ye
are the temple of God' (1 Cor. 3.16). When a sacred building is consecrated it is washed and anointed. So the members of the Church
have been washed by the blood of Christ and have received the anointing of the Holy Spirit for their sanctification. The Church, therefore,
is holy. 'Moreover, the Church is holy by the indwelling of the Blessed
Trinity.' Neither here nor elsewhere does he work out the possibilities
of this pregnant theological assertion.[40] That members of the Church
are not always holy he recognizes in adding: 'Let us guard against
defiling our souls with sin: "for if any man violate the temple of God,
him shall God destroy" (1 Cor. 3.17).'

Catholic

The Church is catholic, or universal, in three ways. First, with regard
to place. It extends to every nation as it obeys the commission to go
into the whole world and preach the gospel to all men (Mark 16.15).
Moreover, it extends to heaven and to purgatory, where saints and
waiting souls are its members.[41] Second, with regard to human beings.
No one is rejected, from whatever race, class, or sex (Gal. 3.28).
Third, it is universal in time. It began with Abel, and will endure to the
end of the world, 'and even after, for the Church remains in heaven'.[42]

Apostolic

The principal foundation of the Church is Christ; secondary foundations are the apostles and their teaching. This is why the Church is
called apostolic. With such foundations the Church stands firm. Peter,
the Rock, represents this strength. The Church will never be
overthrown, despite persecutions, errors, and other attacks of the
devil. While there are regions where the faith has been lost or greatly
weakened, the Church of Peter, 'to whose lot fell all Italy when the disciples were sent out to preach', has always stood firm, and 'still
flourishes in faith and free from heresy'. This is not surprising, for
Christ said to Peter: 'I have prayed for thee that thy faith fail not'
(Luke 22.32).

The Papacy

Thomas, therefore, accepts the papal interpretation of St Peter's confession of faith at Caesarea Philippi and of Christ's commission to

Peter (John 21.15 ff). Peter was made supreme pontiff, and the pope
succeeds him. He accords to the pope plenitude of power over the
Church in spiritual matters, but this power is not to be used
capriciously. He may dispense from ecclesiastical regulations in
matters of human law, but 'in matters of the Natural Law, the articles
of faith, and the sacraments, he cannot dispense, and any claim to
such power is not authentic, but a pretence'.[43] Thomas also declares
the pope to have a supreme teaching authority in matters of faith, even
to the extent of publishing a new creed:

> A new edition of the symbol [i.e. creed] becomes necessary in order to set
> aside the errors that may arise. Consequently to publish a new edition of
> the symbol belongs to that authority which is empowered to decide
> matters of faith finally, so that they may be held by all with unshaken
> faith. Now this belongs to the authority of the Sovereign Pontiff: 'I have
> prayed for thee, Peter, that thy faith fail not, and thou, being once con-
> verted, confirm thy brethren.' The reason for this is that there should be
> but one faith of the whole Church . . . this could not be secured unless any
> question of faith that may arise be decided by him who presides over the
> whole Church, so that the whole Church may hold firmly to his decision.
> Consequently it belongs to the sole authority of the Sovereign Pontiff to
> publish a new edition of the symbol, as do all other matters which concern
> the whole Church, such as to convoke a general council (*Summa* IIa–IIae,
> 1, 10).

It is to be noted that Thomas asserts that the pope alone has power
to summon a general council. This assumption, understandable in the
heyday of the success of papal claims, was to be challenged by the
conciliarists.[44]

Thomas, however, gave no support to the papal claim to supreme
temporal authority:

> Spiritual power and secular power both derive from divine power.
> Consequently the secular power is subject to the spiritual power only to
> the extent that it is so subordinated by God, namely, in matters relating to
> the soul's salvation, where the spiritual power is to be obeyed before the
> secular. In matters of political welfare, however, the temporal power
> should be obeyed before the spiritual: 'Render to Caesar the things that
> are Caesar's.' That is the rule, unless historically it happens that secular
> power is joined to spiritual power, as in the Pope, who occupies the peak
> of both powers, according to the dispensation of Christ, who is both priest
> and king (IV *Sentences* XLIV, iii. 4).[45]

Of the apparent exception to the rule in favour of the pope, Gilby justly remarks[46] that the reference is probably to the pope's power within the papal estates. It does not mean that Thomas shared the political view of thirteenth-century canonists.

In matters of faith, however, Thomas evidently regarded the pope as possessing the authority which in earlier centuries was thought to reside in a general council. Cyprian's teaching that the unity of the Church in the apostles' faith is guaranteed by the whole episcopate acting as a collegiate body is left far behind.

10

Opposition to the
Papal Concept of the Church

THE ALBIGENSIANS

The most overt opposition to the papacy and the hierarchy came from a sect, known as the Albigensians, which appeared in the Albigeois region of Aquitaine during the twelfth century. Its strongholds were the cities of Albi and Toulouse. They are also known as the Cathari (the Pure Ones), a term used also, however, for similar sectarian groups in other parts of Europe. The Albigensians taught a Manichaean dualism and an exaggerated asceticism set within a semi-Christian framework.[1] From the Manichaean premiss that there are two gods, they concluded that there were two churches: that of the good God, the Father of greatness and the source of all light, founded by Jesus Christ, which they identified with their own community; and that of the evil god, or Satan, identified with the Church of Rome which they described in such terms as 'the mother of fornication', 'Babylon the Great', 'sanctuary of the devil', 'synagogue of Satan'. In keeping with the Manichaean doctrine of matter as evil, their Christology was docetic, and the ceremonies which they substituted for the Catholic sacraments were given a purely spiritual interpretation. There were two classes of adherents, the 'perfect', from whom their ministers were chosen, and 'believers' who were regarded as not yet capable of perfection. A rigid asceticism was demanded. Marriage was forbidden to the 'perfect'; all were required to refrain from eating flesh, cheese, milk, and eggs. The taking of oaths was forbidden. The requiring of oaths and the application of sanctions against the nonconformists by secular powers were regarded as wicked. The endurance of suffering and persecution even to death was demanded.

The Albigensians drew numerous converts from those who were affronted by the wealth and laxity of the Church and were attracted and challenged by the demand for 'spiritual' perfection. The majority were peasants who cannot have understood that the basic dualism of the Albigensian teaching undermined the foundations of Christian faith. The papacy, however, saw clearly that here was heresy; and heretics must be made to recant or be extirpated. Pope Innocent III first tried to convert them by missions, but in 1209 launched a crusade against them under the leadership of Simon IV de Montfort. The conflict was lengthy and had disastrous and long-lasting results for the economy of a large area of southern France. Pope Gregory IX (1227–41) set up a tribunal (the Inquisition) under the Dominican friars with wide powers to root out the heretics, and by the middle of the thirteenth century the task was completed. This ruthless harrying of misguided peasants is one of the greatest blots in the history of the medieval Church.

THE WALDENSIANS

Simultaneously with the rise of the Albigensians another protest movement developed. The Waldensians took their name from Peter Waldo (c. 1140–1217), a wealthy merchant of Lyons who relinquished his riches and gave himself to a life of preaching in 1173. Waldo and his followers in their early days accepted Catholic doctrine and order, and believed themselves to be loyal members of the Church. They renounced worldly goods and preached a gospel of poverty. Waldo called his disciples 'the Poor Ones of Lyons'. Catholic opposition, however, was aroused by their preaching without ecclesiastical licence and their use of unauthorized vernacular translations of the Scriptures. Their asceticism linked them in Catholic minds with the Cathari, with whom they were often confused, despite the documented fact that the Waldensians regarded the Cathari as Manichaean heretics. They received the same treatment as the Albigensians. Eighty were burned at the stake in Strasbourg. The survivors began to scatter to other parts, and also to move to an independent position in ecclesiology and sacramental doctrine which anticipated the sixteenth-century reformers. A Waldensian catechism of disputed date[2] has these questions and answers on the Church:

Q. Do you believe in the holy Church?
A. No, for it is a creature, but I believe that it exists.
Q. What do you believe regarding the holy Church?
A. I say that the Church must be thought of in two ways; one in terms of its substance or nature, the other in terms of the ministry. As for its sub-

stance, the holy Catholic Church is made up of all God's elect, from the beginning to the end who have, according to the grace of God by the merits of Christ, been gathered together by the Holy Spirit and previously ordained to eternal life, their number and names being known only to the one having chosen them. ... But the Church with regard to the ministry comprises the ministers of Christ with the people submitted to them, profiting from the ministry of faith, hope, and charity.[3]

Here is the idea of the invisible Church of the elect who are known only to God. Yet the Church as a visible institution is not rejected as a mere human contrivance. Faithful ministry within the institution builds people up in faith, hope, and charity. Preaching, sacraments, and prayer help to deepen the Communion of Saints. The Waldensian communities appointed their own ministers, of whom an exemplary life was required. Their duties were to preach the gospel and to administer properly the sacraments of baptism and the eucharist. The improper administration of the sacraments is described as

... when the priests do not understand the mind of Christ and, not knowing his purpose in the sacraments, say that grace and truth are bound up with external ceremonies alone, thus leading men to receive these same sacraments without the truth of faith, hope, and charity (ibid.).

Although this catechism is to be dated later than originally thought, there is no doubt that the early Waldensians protested against the idea of the mechanical operation of the sacraments which was popularly held in the medieval Church. Their prohibition of anything in Christian worship, discipline, and life which was not enjoined in the Scriptures was a protest against the multiplication of ecclesiastical observances, ceremonies, and devotions in the medieval Church.

In the sixteenth century there were Waldensian communities in north-west Italy and the neighbouring parts of France. Friendly contacts were made with Reformation leaders. In recent years the Waldensians in Italy have increased in numbers, and have become active in missionary work.

ROBERT GROSSETESTE, BISHOP OF LINCOLN, *c.* 1175–1253

There were also individual clerics (and we have noted that Bernard of Clairvaux was among them) who, while remaining loyal to the papacy, could also be outspoken in their criticism. Such was the forthright Robert Grosseteste, Bishop of Lincoln (1235–53), during the pontificates of Gregory IX and Innocent IV. From the beginning of his episcopate he vigorously undertook the reformation of his own diocese, the largest in England. To the consternation of the lax he travelled round the archdeaconries and rural deaneries, calling the clergy together to meet him. He initiated a programme of evangelism through the agency of the Franciscans. He defined the duties of archdeacons and rural deans, arranged for the periodic visitation of monasteries and parish churches and provided an exhaustive question-naire for use on these occasions. He was not a man who laid himself open to the criticism he levelled against others.

In a memorandum[4] he wrote of the evils of the times, widespread unbelief, the state of schism in the Church, the prevalence of heresy and vice. Avaricious and immoral clergy have, he admits, a good deal to do with this. But, although he declares he fears to say it, the primary cause is in the papacy. The occupant of the holy see is peculiarly the representative and vicar of Christ, pledged to work for the coming of the Kingdom of God; yet the Roman court does little to combat the evils.

Grosseteste particularly attacked papal 'dispensations', by which acts or states of life were permitted which were strictly against canon law, and papal 'provisions', by which the pope or his legates secured, over the head of legitimate patrons and bishops, benefices for their own nominees. These were usually foreigners who had little sense of the pastoral needs of their flocks. As often as not, these 'provided' rec-tors were absentees who secured a priest to perform the minimal duties for a pittance. But it is not enough to provide a priest to ad-minister the sacraments and to recite the daily offices—and even these things, he says, are rarely done by these 'mercenaries'. Pastoral care consists also of teaching the truth of God, rebuking vice and punishing it when necessary, things which absentee rectors cannot, and their ill-paid deputies dare not do. Pastoral care includes also ministering to the hungry, clothing the naked, giving hospitality, visiting the sick and prisoners, things again which absentee incumbents cannot do and poorly paid 'hirelings' have not the resources to do. Grosseteste clear-ly sees the papal practice of 'provision' as the direct cause of the deterioration in the life of many parishes. He goes on:

> Those who preside in this see (of Rome) are in a special degree the
> representatives of Christ, and to that extent are entitled to be obeyed in

all things. If, however, through favouritism or on other grounds they command what is opposed to the precepts and will of Christ, they separate themselves from Christ and from the conception of what a Pope should be, they are guilty of apostasy themselves and a cause of apostasy in others. God forbid that such should be the case in this see! Let its occupants, therefore, take heed lest they do or enjoin anything which is at variance with the will of Christ.

These are strong words. Whether or not the memorandum from which they are quoted ever came to the notice of the Pope, it was made clear in Rome that Grosseteste had strong opinions about what a pope might do in 1253 when he refused Innocent IV's demand that a canonry in Lincoln cathedral be given to his nephew.

JOHN OF PARIS, b. 1240–64(?), d. 1306

During the latter part of the thirteenth century and in the fourteenth, criticism of the papal view of the Church, and especially the claim to all-inclusive temporal power, grew steadily.

John of Paris, a Dominican friar, in his *On the Power of Kings and Popes*[5] argues that while the spiritual or priestly power excels the temporal or kingly power in that it is directed towards man's ultimate end, it is not greater in all respects. The temporal power is not derived from the spiritual. Each is derived from a higher power, the divine. Temporal power, therefore, has its own autonomous sphere, namely in temporal affairs. Even so, since the spiritual power is greater than the temporal, it must be conceded that in an absolute sense the priest is greater than the prince.

In his definition of the spiritual power, John of Paris anticipates the later conciliarists. Authority in the Church is derived from God and rests in the whole Church, the body of Christ. The authority of bishops and pope, while it comes from God, comes also indirectly from the Church, through its electing and consecrating representatives. The pope, then, is not an absolute monarch, but essentially 'servant of the servants of God', a title which Pope Gregory VII had used. Christ is the head of the Church; the pope may only be so described in the sense that he is the first among its ministers. The faith, moreover, is the faith of the Church, and the pope cannot define it without a general council. A general council represents the authority of the Church more fully, and its convoking is necessary in the event of papal heresy of maladministration. The possibility of the deposition of a pope is envisaged.

MEISTER JOHN ECKHART, c. 1260–1327

The teachings of John Eckhart,[6] known as the *Meister* (Master), a German Dominican, imply a different kind of criticism of the highly institutionalized Church of the later Middle Ages. Eckhart ardently desired for himself and his readers and hearers a consciousness of the presence of God and union with him. This is not an end to be attained necessarily by living as a hermit or monk, or by busying oneself with ecclesiastical practices and devotions. It is a question rather of an inward poverty and solitude. Man's only part is to attain a state of sheer nothingness. This opens the soul to God, and God then fills it as he wills. When this happens a man knows God everywhere, in the streets as much as in church or in a monastic cell; he has learned to penetrate things where they are and find God, for God is everywhere.

Out of their context some of Eckhart's words suggest that the outward practice of religion lacks all value. So he was understood by many, and this was among the reasons for the condemnation of his teaching, shortly after his death, by Pope John XXII (1329). He seemed to be undermining the Church as a papal and hierarchical institution by inculcating an individual search for God in the ordinary walks of life.

DANTE ALIGHIERI, 1265–1321

In his *De Monarchia*, written probably between 1309 and 1317, Dante takes up the arguments of John of Paris, sharpening them on his sense of outrage at ecclesiastical politics of which he had first-hand experience during his early political life in Florence. He was appalled that the papal powers were so often used to promote the careers and fortunes of members of the pope's family.

Dante declares that papal and imperial power are each derived immediately from God, the one that men may be led to eternal life, the other that men may be led to the temporal beatitude which can minister to spiritual welfare. Emperors and kings do not hold their authority from the pope. They have their own responsible sphere in the temporal which they are charged to administer for the spiritual blessedness of their subjects. He grants that the pope's spiritual authority does extend over much of man's temporal life, since mortal felicity is to be subordinated to immortal felicity. There is a sense, then, in which the Roman prince is subject to the Roman pontiff, and Caesar should pay to Peter the reverence due from a son to a father. But what is most needed is the collaboration of the spiritual and temporal powers, and in this lies the hope of human peace and happiness which Dante so greatly desired.

Dante always remained a loyal and orthodox Christian, but he ceased to trust the leadership of popes. In the *Divina Commedia* Boniface VIII, together with his predecessor and successor are placed in the *inferno* among those guilty of simony: 'You have made a god of gold and silver for yourselves: wherein do you differ from the idolater?'

MARSILIUS OF PADUA, c. 1275–1342

Far more radical is Marsilius of Padua, who in his *Defensor Fidei* ('The Defender of the Faith')[7] presents a scheme which may fairly be described as a thoroughgoing Erastianism.[8] The book ends with forty-two 'Conclusions',[9] which may be summarized as follows.

There can be only one supreme ruling authority in a state. This is the 'legislator', that is the whole body of citizens, its majority, or the prince who rules by its expressed will. The legislator (the whole body or the elected prince) has jurisdiction over all individuals and groups, lay and clerical, and over their possessions within the state. The legislator, as defined (who is assumed to be a Christian), alone has power to determine the number of churches, and of the clergy to serve them; to control the qualifications for ordination and to promote to orders; to remove from ecclesiastical office; to use ecclesiastical property after the needs of the clergy, the poor, and the expenses of divine worship have been met; to permit or forbid the establishment of religious Orders and houses; to condemn and punish heretics; to permit marriages forbidden by 'human law' (but not those forbidden by the New Testament); to legitimatize children of an illegitimate union; to release from oaths. Excommunication must be authorized by the legislator. He alone can confer or take away 'separable'[10] ecclesiastical offices including those of bishop and archbishop. And only the legislator may convoke a general or local council.

Within the Church a general council is the supreme authority, as representing the whole body of faithful people. It consists of bishops, priests, and laymen and, he says elsewhere, must include those learned in divine law. They are to be chosen from each state, and the legislator has the chief voice in their appointment with coercive power over reluctant appointees. The primary function of a general council is to define ambiguous passages in the Scriptures and decide what articles of faith are necessary to salvation: 'No partial council or single person of any position has the authority to decide these questions.' Its other functions include arrangements of divine worship, the creation of metropolitan churches and bishops, the canonization of saints, the making of disciplinary rules, for example about the marriage of clergy, and dispensation from them. He adds that the council or the legislator alone may prohibit practices, trades, or teachings which divine law permits.

There are some ambiguities here which make it difficult to understand Marsilius' conception of the relation between the 'legislator' and the general council in all respects. For instance, Conclusion 42 gives to the general council alone the power to create a metropolitan bishop; by his definition, this is a 'separable' ecclesiastical office to be 'conferred or taken away only by the authority of the "legislator"', according to Conclusion 23. Nevertheless the general picture is of a very definite subordination of the spiritual to the temporal power.

The Church, for Marsilius, is the totality of the faithful who believe and call upon the name of Christ. Bishops and priests are essentially equal; differences between them are by the appointment of temporal rulers. He denies the primacy of the papacy:

> All bishops derive their authority in equal measure immediately from Christ, and it cannot be proved from the divine law that one bishop should be over or under another, in temporal or spiritual matters.
>
> The other bishops, singly or in a body, have the same right by divine authority to excommunicate or otherwise exercise authority over the bishop of Rome, having obtained the consent of the 'legislator', as the bishop of Rome has to excommunicate or control them.[11]

It is not surprising that a number of propositions from his teaching were condemned by Pope John XXII (1327) and that Marsilius was declared heretical.

WILLIAM OF OCKHAM, *c.* 1290–1349

Marsilius' younger contemporary, the English Franciscan William of

Ockham, was equally critical of the Church of his day. Martin Luther was frequently to declare his indebtedness to him. Ockham defines the Church as the congregation or community of the faithful: 'the whole congregation of the faithful living at the same time in this mortal life'.[12] The idea of the mystical body plays little part in his ecclesiology. He lays great stress on faith as constitutive of the Church. The Church is essentially a community of 'true and real persons'[13] who profess one faith. Yves Congar writes:[14]

> The great concern of Ockham is to defend the liberty of persons. In this are brought into play at the same time his English outlook with its emphasis on the individual, his philosophy of the concrete individual sub-ject (i.e. nominalism) and finally his Franciscan evangelism which expresses itself in an original affirmation of the liberty of the gospel: 'the liberty of the law of the gospel'. As few rules as possible! It is the first time that a theologian of stature applies this great concept effectively to ecclesiology. Christians are no longer under the old law. There is here, in Ockham, a positive Christian element which is very remarkable. He is an initiator of a new world. ... He had inaugurated for the believer, in place of a world of natures, institutions, and laws, a world of persons and of liberty in the faith.

Ockham's *On the Authority of Emperors and Popes*[15] is his main work in criticism of the papal claims. Christ, he argues, gave no plenitude of power to Peter in temporal matters. Luke 22.25 ('The kings of the Gentiles exercise lordship. ... But not so with you.') and its parallels prove this. Nor did he give plenitude of power in spiritual matters, for this must have included power to impose heavier burdens than those of the old law, which Peter himself said 'neither our fathers nor we have been able to bear' (Acts 15.10). Such a plenitude of power would be contrary to 'the liberty of the law of the gospel'. Consequently neither Peter nor his successors possessed plenitude of power, temporal or spiritual. In particular, for the pope to intervene in temporal affairs is 'to put his sickle into another's harvest'.[16]

In his *Dialogue* Ockham discusses whether a pope who is heretical may be deposed, and if so how. The rule that a general council may not be called without the authority of the pope is normally to be observed. But it is to be interpreted 'sensibly'. A general council may be necessary at a time when it either will not or cannot be called by the pope, namely when the pope is heretical, and when during a vacancy the cardinals have failed to elect. He goes into some detail about the composition of a general council. His suggestion is that representatives be sent from parishes or local communities either to an episcopal council or to the parliament of a secular power, which should then elect its representatives to the general council. Thus the whole of Christendom would be represented.

Ockham was excommunicated by Pope John XXII in 1328, but sought reconciliation towards the end of his life.

JOHN WYCLIF, *c.* 1328–84

Equally radical was the criticism of the papal conception of the Church of John Wyclif, a secular priest,[17] the pioneer of translation of the Scriptures into English. He spent most of his life at Oxford, first as student, and then as lecturer, engaging fully in the theological debates which were a feature of university life in the later medieval period. He was very influential at the University of Oxford, whose authorities tried to protect him when, towards the end of his life, certain theses from his writings were condemned by a synod at Blackfriars, London. He had a powerful supporter in John of Gaunt, the heir apparent to the throne, who saw in Wyclif's teachings a strong weapon against the Avignon popes, and justification of the removal of obstreperous clerics. John of Gaunt presented him to the rectory of Lutterworth where he spent his last years.

Wyclif produced the works which made him famous[18] in the last eight or nine years of his life. It was a time when the proponents of the papal idea of the Church were greatly embarrassed by events. Gregory XI had restored the papal court to Rome from Avignon. His death in 1378 signalled the beginning of the 'Great Schism' which was to last for decades. Gregory's successor, Urban VI, within a few months alienated the cardinals, and the French members of that body declared his election invalid and set up an anti-pope at Avignon.

TRUE LORDSHIP

Central to Wyclif's ecclesiology is the doctrine of 'true lordship'. This depends, not on any right received from an overlord, temporal or spiritual, but is held from God and belongs to those who keep God's law and receive and live by his grace. Lordship over persons and property is forfeited by those who break God's law. In the contemporary Church, Wyclif held, there was no true lordship, and confiscation of church property was justifiable. It was in this kind of teaching that John of Gaunt saw interesting possibilities. Opponents were not slow to attack Wyclif as an anarchist. He would not have agreed that the application of his doctrine of the 'dominion of grace' would produce anarchy. While the temporal *dominium* of the papacy and the hierarchy ought to be abandoned, the authority of the Bible would replace it. The way would be opened for a return to the simple organization and the poverty of the early Church. The magnificence of the papal court and the wealth of cardinals, bishops, and abbots were in scandalous contrast with the Christianity of the New Testament. It was a 'religion of fat cows'. The pope's claim to be the vicar of Christ was to be measured by his imitation of Christ who thrust away worldly lordship.

THE INVISIBLE CHURCH

Wyclif's ecclesiology draws much from Augustine, especially the idea of the invisible Church as the whole body of the predestined. Unlike Augustine, however, he makes a definite identification of the mystical body of Christ with the invisible Church of the elect: 'The Church is truly called the mystical body of Christ because, by the eternal words of predestination, it is joined with Christ its spouse.'[19] This Church is to be distinguished from the Church of 'prelates and priests'. Wyclif, therefore, offers an entirely new interpretation of the mystical body.

THE CHURCH TRIUMPHANT, EXPECTANT, AND MILITANT

In his *On the Church and Its Members* he shows something of a conservative strain, reproducing the accepted threefold partition of the Church as triumphant, expectant, and militant.[20] The first part consists of angels and saints in the bliss of heaven, the second of those who are purging their sins in purgatory (to pray for whom is, however, a cause of many errors), and the third is that of good Christians who will be among the saved. These are they who are 'of the Church'. Others, sinners not predestined to salvation, may be 'in the Church'. In the Church militant we do not know whether we are members of 'holy Church', although the strength of a man's hope may give him grounds for supposing that he is. Thus Wyclif is able to accept the idea of the Church on earth as a mixed society of good and bad, and a great deal of his writing is aimed at its purification and reformation. In such passages it is clear that he does not entirely sweep aside the 'Church of prelates and priests'; but he would have the clergy realize that their office is a ministry, not a lordship.

On the other hand, there is also much to suggest that he did think of the 'Church of prelates and priests' as an altogether different Church from the mystical body. He constantly draws a strong contrast between God's law and canon law; he expresses the opinion that it was the failure of priests which led to the foundation of monasteries, the covetousness of monks which occasioned the rise of the semi-monastic canons, and the laxity of these which made way for the coming of the friars, whose existence in the Church, he suggests, has no divine sanction; and he designates the pope as 'Antichrist' and the 'head vicar of the fiend'. A picture of an anti-church is cumulatively built up. Yet, despite the fulminations, the impression is given that Wyclif would willingly recognize any pope, prelate, priest, monk, or friar who truly exercised the lordship of grace as a sound member of the Church militant. The truth is, as Professor Geddes Macgregor suggests,[21] that Wyclif's ecclesiology is not fully worked out, and leaves some untidy ends.

CHRIST THE HEAD OF THE CHURCH

On one thing Wyclif makes himself perfectly clear. He constantly insists that Christ is the only Head of the Church. Here he applies the Chalcedonian doctrine of the two natures of the one Person of Christ in a novel and over-subtle way. In his *On the Church* he argues that the Church cannot have two heads like a monster. Nevertheless there is a mysterious sense in which it does have two heads. For Christ has two natures. In virtue of his divine nature he has what Wyclif calls 'extrinsic headship' over all men and things, and therefore over the Church and its members. In virtue of the human nature which Christ assumed for man's salvation he has headship over the Church in a second way which is *intrinsic* to the Church, a way in which he forms a living body with his members, continually present with and activating them. Thus the two natures of Christ may be said to give him a twofold headship over the Church, although in view of the unity of his Person there is but one head, the one Christ. This is a forceful expression of the idea of the Church as the mystical body founded in the humanity of the incarnate Christ.[22] It must not be forgotten, however, that for Wyclif the mystical body is the invisible Church of the elect, known to God alone.

Later in *On the Church*,[23] and also in *On the Office of the King*,[24] Wyclif draws another conclusion from the doctrine of the two natures of Christ. Since by his divine nature Christ has headship over all men and things, the authority of secular rulers answers to the divine nature. The authority of the Church corresponds to the human nature. The king is the vicar of Christ's divinity; and since divinity is more glorious and powerful than humanity, the conclusion that the king has supreme authority within his state in much the way that Marsilius of Padua conceived the authority of the 'legislator' can hardly be avoided.

Some of Wyclif's propositions were condemned by Pope Gregory XI in 1377, and by a synod at Blackfriars in 1382, but Wyclif was not excommunicated.

JOHN HUS, *c*. 1369–1415

Wyclif's doctrines were to prove a greater threat to the papacy in Bohemia than in England. There were good communications between the two countries, and especially between the universities of Oxford and Prague. John Hus, a priest and member of the University of Prague, of which he was chancellor in 1409, and other academics, themselves engaged in an attack on the corruption of the Church, adopted much of Wyclif's teaching. Hus translated Wyclif's *Trialogus* into Czech, and incorporated much of Wyclif's material into his own *De Ecclesia*. Professor Matthew Spinka has shown[25] that Hus was by no means Wyclif's slavish imitator, but his ecclesiology was undoubtedly greatly indebted to the English reformer, and we shall not consider it separately here.

The reforming movement in Bohemia coincided with the rise of national spirit among the Czechs. Hus was a leader both in the nationalist and in the reforming movement. He preached and wrote against the corruption of the clergy, and the simoniacal practices of the papacy. He advocated the restoration of the chalice to the laity and a vernacular liturgy. The Archbishop of Prague secured from the pope an order to destroy Wycliffite books in 1410, and the excommunication of Hus in 1411. But Hussite teaching continued to gain acceptance and the movement spread rapidly. When the Council of Constance gathered late in 1414, both anti-papalists like Gerson and d'Ailly,[26] and conservatives, were determined to stamp it out. Hus was summoned before the Council, being promised safe conduct by the Emperor Sigismund. Hus, who had expected a theological debate on his views, was, however, arrested. He was tried, condemned as a heretic, and handed over to the secular authorities for burning. The Council now condemned 267 propositions in Wyclif's works, ordered all copies to be burned, and his body to be removed from consecrated ground.

THE CONCILIARISTS

Mention of the Council of Constance necessitates some account of the 'conciliarists'. Several writers already mentioned in this chapter present the idea that authority in the Church is given to the congregation, or whole body, of the faithful (*congregatio*, or *universitas fidelium*), and that this authority can be expressed through a general council. The medieval Church never entirely lost sight of this concept of authority in the Church. Even the 'decretists', the lawyers who worked upon the body of canon law, and did so mainly in the interests of papal authority, did not reject the concept of the Church as the *universitas fidelium*. The idea persisted in the canon law itself, alongside the idea of the Church as a hierarchical body of clerics with the pope as its head. One of the decretists, Huguccio, Bishop of Pisa, in his *Summa* (*c.* 1190) asserted that it was to the Church in the sense of *universitas fidelium* that preservation from error was promised. The decretists discussed such questions as the relation of the pope to a general council and the necessary procedures if a pope fell into heresy, which Gratian in his *Decretum* (*c.* 1150) maintained was possible. But these were as yet hypothetical questions, learnedly discussed with a view to reconciling discrepancies in the rapidly increasing *corpus* of canon law.[27]

The state of the Church during the Avignon papacy and the subsequent 'Great Schism' led to an open demand for a general council. The term 'conciliarists' denotes the canonists and others who worked for this end during the latter part of the fourteenth century and in the early fifteenth. Among the most influential were Conrad of Gelnhausen (*c.* 1320–90), Henry of Langenstein (1340–97), Francis Zabarella (1360–1417), Dietrich of Niem (*c.* 1340–1418), Pierre d'Ailly (1350–1420), Jean Gerson (1363–1429), Nicholas of Clémanges (1367–1437) and Nicholas of Cusa (*c.* 1400–1464).

These men approached the question of authority in the Church from different angles, 'so that there is no body of conciliarist doctrine that might be set down as common to them all'.[28] But they agreed that a distinction, which in no way necessarily diminishes the *proper* authority of the papacy, must be drawn between the Church as *congregatio fidelium* and the Church understood as personified in the pope who possesses *all* the authority of the Church and exercises it through the papal curia.

They argue that authority resides in the whole body of the faithful. For the most part they do not dispute that it may be given to one man, the pope, but they hold that if so given it is not irrevocably given. If it is abused it can be withdrawn. There are occasions (and they include papal heresy and a disputed papacy) when the *congregatio fidelium* must resume the exercise of its inherent authority. This was to be done through a general council, and some argued that such a council possessed an authority superior to that of a pope, being more broadly representative of the Church than a single person.

PIERRE D'AILLY (1350–1420)

The notion that the body of the Church has the authority to take action on behalf of its unity and welfare through a general council without convocation by a pope can be well illustrated by summarizing the principles drawn up by Pierre d'Ailly shortly before the Council of Pisa in 1409. The document is known as *Propositiones Utiles*, from its first words: 'Useful propositions for ending the present schism by a general council'.[29]

Because 'Christ is the head of the Church' and 'we are all one body in Christ', the unity of the mystical body of the Church depends completely on the unity of Christ. The pope may 'in a certain way' be called head of the Church, but its unity does not depend on or originate from him. It remains even when there is no pope. The Church has its authority immediately from Christ, and with it the power to assemble, or to call a general council to represent it, especially to protect its unity. Christ promised his presence where two or three are gathered in his name, not in the name of Peter or the pope. This power of the Church is supported also by natural law, because every natural body summons up all its members and powers to resist partition.

D'Ailly notes that James and not Peter presided at the Council of Jerusalem (Acts 15.13). Canon law had restricted the calling of councils to the pope, partly to honour the apostolic see, and partly to prevent heretics and schismatics from persuading secular rulers to convoke councils in support of their errors. But positive laws cannot completely remove from the Church what belongs to it by divine and natural laws. The positive law of those canons which give the pope authority to convoke councils was introduced for the good of the Church; but there are circumstances in which this law can harm the Church, namely the occurrence of heresy or persecution during a papal vacancy, if there should be a mad or heretical pope, and (as in 1409) if there should be rival popes.

The canon law on this point must, therefore, be interpreted sensibly (*civiliter*, literally, in a civilized manner).[30] The document finally asserts that the present crisis of the Church justifies the calling of a council without the pope's authority, either by the cardinals or by any faithful Christian who is influential enough to secure it.

THE COUNCILS OF THE FIFTEENTH CENTURY

What the conciliarists had worked for came to pass with the convoking of the Council of Pisa in 1409, the first of a series held during the next forty years. The details of their successes and failures do not concern us here. Hopes were considerably higher than achievement. At the conclusion of the Council of Pisa there were three instead of two rival claimants to the papacy, and not until 1449 could it be said that there was an undisputed bishop of Rome. The 'Great Schism' was, however, formally brought to a close by the Council of Constance (1414–18), which received the resignation of one of the three claimants to the papacy, deposed the others, and elected Martin V. Hopes for the healing of the schism between Constantinople and Rome mounted during the Council of Florence (1438–45),[31] but came to nothing.[32]

Special mention must be made of the Council of Constance of which d'Ailly and Gerson were influential members. On its legitimacy and that of its procedure in the matter of the three claimants to the see of Rome, Hans Küng says that 'the legitimacy of Martin V (1417–31) and all other subsequent popes up to the present day depends'.[33] Its decree *Sacrosancta* (1415) declared that the Council was legitimately convoked, represented the Church militant, and held its authority directly from Christ. The decree *Frequens* gave directions about the frequency of future councils: the first should be held five years from the conclusion of Constance, another seven years after the close of the first, and 'for ever thereafter one shall be held every ten years'. The decree *Sacrosancta* declares:

This holy synod of Constance, being a general council, and legally assembled in the Holy Spirit for the praise of God and for the ending of the present schism, and for the union and reformation of the Church of God ... ordains, declares, and decrees as follows: And first it declares that this synod, legally assembled, represents the Catholic Church militant and has its authority direct from Christ; and everybody, of whatever rank or dignity, including also the pope, is bound to obey this council in those things which pertain to the faith, to the ending of this schism, and to a general reformation of the Church in its head and members. Likewise it declares that if anyone ... including also the pope, shall refuse to obey the commands ... of this holy council, or of any other holy council properly assembled, in regard to the ending of the schism and to the reformation of the Church, he shall be subject to the proper punishment.[34]

JOHANNES DE TURRECREMATA, 1388–1468

Despite this affirmation of the conciliar idea of the Church, the papal curia worked so successfully for the restoration of the papal authority that by 1460, Pope Pius II could venture to publish the Bull *Execrabilis* which forbade an appeal from the pope to a general council. By this time the papacy had entered into the period of the so-called Renaissance popes, some of whom were more concerned for their literary style than for the welfare of the Church, and the days were closing in towards the more radical and activist protest which was the sixteenth-century reformation. At this point we must take note of a book written in support of the papal idea of the Church in the light of the conciliar activity of the early fifteenth century.

This was the *Summa de Ecclesia* of Cardinal Johannes de Turrecremata (or Juan de Torquemada), a Spanish Dominican, published posthumously in 1489. Early in the work he examines the word *ecclesia*, discovering in it fifteen meanings. The Church is the *congregatio fidelium* considered as a whole, or as gathered for public worship, or meeting in a house for prayer. *Ecclesia* may also mean the local church, the elect, the clergy, or hierarchy. Geddes Macgregor makes the comment[35] that Turrecremata does not explain how these meanings are related to each other: 'He treats them as aspects of the same thing. He finds himself able to consider the aspect of the Church as the company of Christ's faithful side by side with the aspect of the Church as the hierarchically organized institution whose head is the Pope.' The idea of the Church as the *congregatio fidelium* is, however, well to the fore in Turrecremata's ecclesiology, and this is another reminder that the sixteenth-century reformers in using it were not reintroducing an ecclesiology which had been entirely neglected in the medieval period. We have already met it in the conciliarists, in Thomas Aquinas, and even in the twelfth-century decretists. These, however, had seen it as providing one important insight, amongst others, into the nature of the Church. The reformers were to use it much more exclusively as a definition of the Church.

Christ is the efficient cause of the Church and its unifying principle. The Christian must put his faith in Christ, not in the apostles or the Church; nevertheless the Church is Christ's and there is no salvation outside it.[36] Turrecremata's treatment of the Church as the mystical body[37] is Augustinian. Christ unites the faithful to himself by the indwelling of the Holy Spirit and in unity of will. Turrecremata follows Augustine in other respects: his treatment of the four credal notes of the Church; his use of the image of the net to explain why the Church on earth is a society which contains both bad and good; and his argument that Abel was the first member of the Church.[38] He rejects the view of a contemporary (Augustin Favaroni) that Christ became Head of his body, the Church, only by the incarnation.

Turrecremata is in no doubt that the hierarchical structure of the Church is divinely ordained. The distinctions between clergy and laity, and between bishop, priest, and deacon are biblically rooted and intended by Christ. So also was the papacy, which is one of the strongest bonds of the Church's unity. It distinguishes the Church from separated gatherings of heretics and schismatics.[39] Books II and III of the *Summa de Ecclesia* deal with the papacy and councils. The pope is head of the Church not merely in the sense that authority is vested in him by the body of the Church as a whole. He is the vicar of Christ whose power comes immediately from Christ. In this he is the successor of Peter who alone was made a bishop immediately by Christ.[40] The following passage reveals the argument:

> When Peter is said to have received power for all, and more than all, we must not understand that he received it in the way a single agent may receive some gift in the name of certain others ... but in the way that we say the sun received light from God more than all the stars and for them all. 'More than all', because in greater plenitude than the other stars. 'For them all', because it was so that light might fall upon the rest of the stars from the sun as from a fountain. ...[41] So it is with Peter who was not merely endowed with authority more than all others, but was made head and the ruler whose influence extends to all others in the body of the Church (*Summa de Ecclesia* II, 22).

Consequently, all jurisdiction within the Church is derived from the pope.[42]

Yet, as Hans Küng points out, Turrecremata was 'in no way espoused to a papal absolutism in everything'.[43] He admits the possibility of an heretical or schismatic pope, and the necessity of a general council in such cases. With regard to heresy he declares that 'by heresy a pope ceases to be pope'.[44] The rock on which the Church is built is faith in Christ,[45] and one who falls away from the faith ceases to be a member of the Church, and cannot be its head. This being so, the council does not depose the pope; rather it declares that he is judged by God not to be pope. On the possibility of a schismatic pope, he says that schism is not only to be understood as separation from the pope. Basically it is separation from Christ, and it is possible for a pope, although he is Christ's representative, to separate himself from Christ by disobedience. In such a case, too, it must not be thought that the council causes the pope to lose office. The judgement of God upon an unfaithful pope causes this; the council declares it and makes it effective. This interpretation of the function of a general council in relationship to an offending pope (which is supported by present-day Roman Catholic canonists)[46] rebuts the claim of the more radical conciliarists that a general council is superior to the pope.

Aside from the situations described above, Turrecremata assigns to the council a definitely subordinate role. It is little more than an advisory body. The pope must consult with men of wisdom, by whom he undoubtedly means the cardinals, on matters of divine law, and it will be sufficient if he has such men at hand in Rome.[47] He does, however, say that in a matter of faith which has not yet been defined the opinion of a general council is to be preferred to that of the pope.[48]

For Turrecremata, therefore, the institutional Church as it existed in the mid-fifteenth century was a development in accordance with the will of God. He recognizes that there may be abuse of power within it, as his discussion of the possibility of an unfaithful pope reveals, but he is strangely silent about many of the matters which not only radical protesters like Wyclif and Hus, but also moderate conciliarists had regarded as abuses. His *Summa de Ecclesia* is important for two reasons in particular. First, it was from this that all subsequent defenders of papal primacy, including Bellarmine, up to the First Vatican Council (1870), drew their arguments. Second, it sets out clearly, close to the beginning of the Reformation, the papal idea of the Church which a large part of Europe was emphatically to reject.

11

Ecclesia in Eastern Orthodoxy

Relations between East and West

Relations between the Church in western and eastern Europe worsened slowly throughout the medieval period. It is not our object to tell the story of this deterioration, but reference to some of the events must be made since they help towards an understanding of the different emphases in ecclesiology.[1]

By the year 700 the expansion of Islam had overtaken the territories of the patriarchs of Alexandria, Antioch, and Jerusalem. Those patriarchates survived, but with little communication with the Church elsewhere. Of the four eastern patriarchates Constantinople alone, the most recent of them, now had any effective voice in the affairs of the Church. Constantinople had no desire to challenge the primacy of the see of Rome, but steadily resisted western attempts to translate primacy into a supremacy over the whole Church. On this issue Constantinople firmly took its stand on those canons of the early general councils which dealt with ecclesiastical jurisdiction.[2] These councils allowed a primacy of honour to the see of Rome. They ratified a certain jurisdiction of the bishop of Rome over other ecclesiastical dioceses in the West, but they did the same for Constantinople, and indeed for Alexandria and Antioch in the East. There was nothing here to justify Rome's claim to jurisdiction over the whole Church.

In the seventh and eighth centuries, despite tensions both of a political and an ecclesiastical nature, there was no question of a split between Eastern and Western Christendom. Indeed there were many expressions of unity and good will. Greek Christian refugees from the Islamic invasions were received hospitably in Rome; papal legates were sent to councils in the East; the Pope himself visited Constantinople in 710. Patriarchs of Constantinople called on the support of Rome against the encroachments of Byzantine emperors into the sphere of doctrine, especially during the long-drawn-out iconoclastic controversy. Iconoclasm (Greek *eikon*, image or picture; *klasma*, smashing), became imperial policy under the Emperor Leo III who in 726 issued an edict for the destruction of icons in all churches. He deposed and replaced Germanus, Patriarch of Constantinople, who resisted the order. Iconoclasm made considerable headway in the East. A council at Hieria (attended neither by the Pope nor by any eastern patriarch) condemned the cult of the icons in 754. In the West a strong resistance was maintained. Pope Gregory III condemned iconoclasm at two synods held at Rome in 731 and excommunicated all iconoclasts. The first phase of the controversy ended in 787 after the death of Leo III's grandson. His orthodox widow, Irene, made possible the convoking of the second Council of Nicaea (the seventh Ecumenical Council), to which Pope Hadrian I sent delegates. It restored icons to the churches and defined the sense in which veneration might be shown to them. The campaign against icons was renewed in 815 by the Emperor Leo V, but, again under an empress, Theodora, the icons were restored in 842.

For the West, the repercussions of this controversy had political consequences. In retaliation for the opposition of the Pope, the Emperor Leo III annexed the papal lands in southern Italy and Sicily. This, in addition to the fact that for decades the Byzantine emperors' interest in the West had been largely financial and that no assistance was forthcoming from them against the encroachment of the Lombards into Italy, led the popes to look towards the Frankish rulers for an alliance. The coronation of Charlemagne as Emperor of the Romans by Pope Leo III in St Peter's, Rome (800), signalled the fact of a politically divided Europe in which for centuries the 'Emperor of the Romans' and western kings and princes were to be engaged in a continual struggle for power, and the Greek (Byzantine) emperor was left to face the still expanding power of Islam.

The ecclesiastical division of Europe still lay in the future. But divisive influences were at work: the difference in language; a growing diversity in ecclesiastical customs; and a mounting contempt, in the West for the effete and dilettante Byzantines, and in the East for the barbarian westerner. Doctrinal difference became an issue over the western addition of 'and the Son' (*filioque*) after the phrase 'the Holy Spirit ... who proceedeth from the Father' in the Nicene Creed. This unauthorized addition seems to have originated in Spain in the seventh century. Its use spread to France; Charlemagne tried to enforce its universal use. The popes long resisted the innovation, but it was in use in Rome with papal approval by 1030. The Greeks, with good reason, objected to this unilateral insertion into an ecumenical creed. They also objected to the theology of the added phrase. Had an addition been permissible, it should have been 'through the Son'. To say that the Holy Spirit proceeds from the Father *and* the Son implied that there were two sources of being in the godhead. Western theologians denied that it had this intention. But apart from the question of theological adequacy, the Church of the West was not justified in adding to the creed of an ecumenical council.

In the ninth century relations were seriously strained in the pontificate (858–67) of Nicholas I, which occurred during a period when the patriarchate of Constantinople was in dispute between Ignatius and Photius. Nicholas, the most energetic of ninth-century popes in asserting papal supremacy, intervened in the dispute and demanded that the deposed Ignatius and Photius who had replaced him should submit to his arbitration. Photius refused, and was declared deposed by Nicholas at a council held in Rome in 863. Affronted also by western manoeuvring to bring Bulgarian Christians within the jurisdiction of Rome, Photius retaliated in 867 by an encyclical which condemned the Latin intrusion into Bulgaria, denounced the *filioque* clause, and designated those who used it as heretics. In the same year a council at Constantinople declared Nicholas I deposed and excommunicated. A reversal of fortune for Photius and the reinstatement of Ignatius shortly afterwards led to another council at Constantinople in 869 which withdrew the decisions of the previous council. In the West this was reckoned as the eighth ecumenical council. In the East it is usually known as 'the anti-Photian Council'. Photius, however, was restored to the patriarchate on the death of Ignatius in 877. Better relations with Rome were established. Pope John VIII (872–82), much more irenic than Nicholas, recognized Photius as legitimate patriarch of Constantinople. The uneasy peace was not much disturbed during the tenth century which was a period of degeneracy and enfeeblement for the papacy which was in no position to enforce its claims in the East.

It was in the eleventh century at a time which seemed propitious for strengthened relations that the decisive break occurred. The papacy and the Byzantine emperor had a common enemy in the Normans. Pope Leo IX (1048–54) had suffered military defeat at their hands, and they were threatening southern Italy, still part of the Greek emperor's territory. The pope prepared to open negotiations with the

Byzantine emperor. At this time a letter written by the Greek metropolitan of Bulgaria which was highly critical of western ecclesiastical customs, came into the hands of the pope. The papal legates who in 1054 carried Leo IX's proposals for a mutually beneficial alliance to the Greek emperor, also carried letters to the patriarch of Constantinople, Michael Cerularius. They portrayed the Church of Rome as above human judgement, unswervingly orthodox, the Mother whose spouse is God. Constantinople was a disobedient, pleasure-loving, and insolent daughter from whom complete obedience was demanded. The papal point of view was presented in the strongest language. Any nation which disagreed with Rome was 'a confabulation of heretics, a conventicle of schismatics, a synagogue of Satan'.[3] Cardinal Humbert,[4] one of the legates charged with this mission of reconciliation, has been suspected of influencing the language of these letters, if not of composing them himself (Pope Leo IX was a prisoner of the Normans at the time of their dispatch). Further controversy ensued in Constantinople, and the outcome was that the legates placed a Bull on the altar of the Church of St Sophia, excommunicating 'Michael and his followers'. Among the reasons which the document gives for this action is that the Greeks had *omitted* the *filioque* from the creed! The patriarch responded by excommunicating the authors of the 'impious document'. To what extent these excommunications were intended to include the patriarchate of Constantinople and the Church of the West respectively as a whole is a matter of debate. The excommunications were lifted over nine centuries later, simultaneously in Rome and Istanbul in 1965, 'by a courageous act of Christian reconciliation on the part of Pope Paul VI and the Patriarch Athenagoras, who mutually asked each other's forgiveness'.[5]

The breach, however, was not complete. The earlier crusaders were offered and received the sacraments from Orthodox bishops and priests in the countries where they campaigned. There were attempts to effect reconciliation by means of what R. W. Southern[6] calls 'the political package deal'. An example of this in all its simplicity is provided in a letter of Pope Clement IV to the Byzantine Emperor Michael VIII, Palaeologus, in 1267. Its gist is: you attack the Moslems on one side, and the western crusaders will attack them on the other. If you are afraid that the Latins will attack you, 'the answer is simple: return to the unity of the Roman Church and all fears of this kind can be put aside for ever'.[7] Such a fear was not an unnatural one for the Greeks to entertain. In 1204 one of the most disgraceful episodes in ecclesiastical history had occurred when soldiers of the Fourth Crusade attacked Constantinople, sacked the city, and plundered the churches. The 'package deal' was attempted a few years later at the Council of Lyons (1274). The envoys of the Emperor Michael VIII agreed to all the Roman conditions, and reunion was proclaimed. But the Emperor was completely unsuccessful in persuading the clergy and people of Constantinople to accept the agreement, which quickly became a dead letter.

The subsequent century and a half is not without signs of a guilty conscience on the part of Latin Christians for the western share of responsibility for the continuance of the schism. On the Greek side also some appreciation of the value of western theology and respect for Latin concepts of order and discipline were replacing the traditional Greek disdain for the intellectually inferior West. Unhappily the Western Church did not reciprocate with any attempt to understand the theology and life of the Eastern Church. 'This attitude', writes R. W. Southern, 'has run through western history with astonishing consistency.'[8]

We have already noted the demand for a general council which arose in the West at the end of the fourteenth century. Several of the conciliarists, Jean Gerson in particular, and, somewhat later, Nicholas of Cusa, hoped that a general council would end the schism between Rome and Constantinople. The Council of Constance (1414–18) did not reach this subject on its agenda. It had a prominent place on the agenda of the Council of Basle, convoked in 1431. Some years previously the Byzantine Emperor Manuel Palaeologus had appealed to the Pope for help against the Ottoman Turks who were now threatening Constantinople, and received from Pope Martin V in 1422 the now stereotyped reply: military aid was possible only at the price of 'full agreement' with the Church of Rome. Conciliarists like Nicholas of Cusa, however, had the higher and more realistic hope that the unity of Christians might be achieved at a council, representative of Latins, Greeks, and Bohemians (Hussites) in a spirit of dialogue rather than by dictation. But these hopes were to be dashed. Pope Eugenius IV succeeded Martin V, whose views about papal supremacy he fully shared, in 1431, shortly after the Council had begun its work at Basle. He tried unsuccessfully to dissolve it, but nevertheless succeeded in forestalling the desires of the more enlightened canonists and conciliarists. He transferred the Council to Ferrara in 1438 and then to Florence where in 1439 the reunion of

Rome and Constantinople was declared. The size of the Greek delegation had greatly diminished since 1431, and there were few
theologians among them. Persuaded by the Byzantine Emperor John
VIII to whom assistance against the Turks was all-important, the
delegation signed the decree with the single exception of Mark,
Metropolitan of Ephesus, whom Professor John Meyendorff
describes[9] as the only spokesman for the true Byzantine theology of
the time. The decree declared that the *filioque* had been legitimately
added to the Nicene Creed, and set forth the papal claims to govern
the universal Church although it contained a face-saving clause for the
Byzantines: 'without prejudice to the privileges and rights of the
patriarchs of the East'.

The agreement at once met with strong opposition from the clergy
and people in Constantinople. It was not until December 1452 that it
was proclaimed in the church of St Sophia, and then only through the
emperor's pressure on a complaisant patriarch. Like the agreement at
the Council of Lyons, it became a dead letter almost at once. On 29
May 1453, Constantinople fell to the Turks, the last of the Byzantine
emperors having died during the siege. Pope Pius II's offer to the conqueror, Mahomet II, to make him emperor of the Greeks if he would
but be baptized, was ignored. Then began the long history of the
patriarchate of Constantinople under Turkish rule.

The clear lesson from this melancholy history is that the schisms of
the Church are unlikely to be healed under political pressure, or over
the heads of the great body of clergy and people.

THE CHURCH IN EASTERN ORTHODOXY

That the ecclesiology of eastern Orthodoxy is treated no earlier than
in Chapter 11, may betray my western stance. In the early chapters of
this work, however, I was dealing in fact with the ecclesiology of the
Church of the East. It is in the Scriptures and in what the ecumenical
councils and creeds and the early Fathers have to say about the
Church that Orthodoxy finds sufficient material to guide and govern
the life of the Church, whose existence it holds to be a mystery. The
Church is a mystery, a fact which is given by God. Yves Congar,
speaking of ecclesiology in the early medieval period, says:[10]

There is no more a 'dogma' of the Church in the East than in the West:
less indeed, if that is possible. St John Damascene,[11] for example, has no

chapter on the Church in his *On the Orthodox Faith*; only an occasional mention, which suffices, however, to show that for him the Church is the reality which envelops the whole of the Christian life. In the East, even more than in the West, the Church is, in this period, a fact more than a doctrine. A fact which asserts itself as having the same absolute value as that of salvation, that is to say, the divine life acquired in Jesus Christ and communicated by his Holy Spirit; a fact which is lived, and which is the very reality in, by, and according to which one is a Christian and in communion with God.

'A fact which is lived' rather than theologized and dogmatized. Orthodox writers produced nothing comparable to the fairly frequent treatises *De Ecclesia* of western theologians in the Middle Ages, and we look in vain among Orthodox documents for authoritative definitions of the Church such as we find in the confessions of many of the Reformed churches.

THE CHURCH AS 'MYSTERY' AND THE IMAGE OF GOD, THE COSMOS, AND MAN

What we do find, however, in Orthodox writing throughout the centuries are many works which, with an abundant wealth of imagery, treat of the Church as a divine-human mystery. Among these are the 'Mystagogies'[12] (mystical interpretations of the Church and sacraments), commentaries on the liturgy, and descriptions of the Church as a building which draw out the symbolism of its various parts and ornaments. These works make clear that Orthodox ecclesiology holds the earthly and spiritual aspects of the Church closely together. Any sharp distinction between the Church militant and the Church triumphant is foreign to its thought. The Church 'is both *visible* and *invisible*, both *divine* and *human* . . . a single and continuous reality'.[13] On earth the Church is the *eikon* (image) of the heavenly, and Orthodox theology explicates this in terms of the communion of its members in the one faith, its liturgy, and the building in which its members gather for the celebration of the liturgy.

With a rather different nuance Orthodoxy also thinks of the Church as the image of God the Holy Trinity, of the *kosmos* (universe), and of man.

The *Mystagogy* of Maximus the Confessor[14] (c. 580–662) is an early, typical, and important example of this literature. The first seven chapters expound the symbolism of the Church as building and the following sixteen explain the meaning of the eucharist and its ceremonies. 'The idea of the Church which stands out', writes Yves Congar, 'is that of a mystery of unity.'[15] The Church is an image of God who is all in all and holds all things together in unity, in that it unites within a single body men of every age, condition, and race. It does this by the grace and power which the energy of God working within it generates.

The Church is also the image of the cosmos. Like the universe it unites things visible and invisible, the visible things of the Church's life (hierarchy, sacraments) being the symbols of invisible, spiritual realities. To illustrate the closeness of the union Maximus uses the figure of the wheels of the chariot of God in Ezekiel 1.16: 'their construction being as it were a wheel within a wheel'. The union of earthly and heavenly is imaged also in the Church as building, the nave representing the earthly and the sanctuary the heavenly, both brought together in the act of worship.

The Church, too, is an image of man as God intends him to be. The nave, the sanctuary, and the altar are the image of the body, soul, and mind (Greek, *nous*) of man who must approach God through his mind, which is represented by the altar.

Maximus also sees the nave and sanctuary as the image of the Old and New Testaments; and the later chapters of the *Mystagogia* interpret the liturgy as symbolically representing the whole saving work of Christ. The Church, then, and the building in which the faithful gather, are seen as what may be called all-embracing images of God the Holy Trinity in the totality of his work in creation, redemption, and sanctification.

This great wealth of imagery is again illustrated a little later in a work commonly, though perhaps mistakenly, attributed to Germanus (*c.* 634–733), Patriarch of Constantinople, and known as 'History of the Church and Mystical Contemplation' (Greek, *Historia ekklesiastikē kai mustikē theōria*).

> The Church is God's temple, a sacred enclosure, house of prayer, a gathering of the People, body of Christ, his Name, Bride of Christ, which calls the peoples to penitence and prayer; purified by the water of holy baptism and washed by his precious blood, adorned as a bride and sealed with the ointment of the Holy Spirit. . . . The Church is an earthly heaven wherein the heavenly God dwells and walks; it is an anti-type of the crucifixion, the burial and resurrection of Christ. . . . The Church is a divine house where the mystical living sacrifice is celebrated . . . and its

precious stones are the divine dogmas taught by the Lord to his disciples (*Historia Ekklesiastikē*, Intro.)[16]

That the Church is the terrestrial heaven is a frequent Orthodox theme. It follows from the concept of the Church (both as community and building) as the place where the visible and the invisible of the cosmos are brought together, and it is closely connected with the body of Christ image which we consider next. As in the incarnation there was a descent of the invisible into the visible, so in the Church the heavenly descends into the earthly. The idea is dramatically presented to the eye in the typical Byzantine church, in which the great central dome suggests the heavens descending upon the earth, and the huge mosaic of Christ the *Pantokrator*[17] which dominates the ceiling of the dome suggests the presence of him who is both merciful saviour and judge of the world.

THE MYSTICAL BODY

Orthodox theology gives great prominence to the idea of the Church as the body of Christ. The early Fathers who developed the doctrine of the mystical body, Cyril of Jerusalem, Cyril of Alexandria, and Augustine are often quoted, and the body of Christ idea is woven together with that of the deification of man in virtue of his participation in Christ.[18] Anastasius of Antioch (d. 599) provides a typical example:

> (God) assumed our whole race in a single individual, having become the first-fruits of our nature. Hence Christ is called 'the first-fruits' (1 Cor. 15.20, 23). For his purpose was to raise up in its totality what has fallen. Now what had fallen was our whole race. Therefore he mingled himself completely with Adam, Life itself with the dead, in order to save him. He penetrated into the totality of him to whom he was united, like the soul of a great body, vivifying it throughout, communicating life to it wholly in all its perceptive faculties. This is why mankind is called 'the body of Christ and his members in particular' (1 Cor. 12.27)—the body of the Christ who both diffuses himself equally in all together, and dwells individually in each one according to the measure of his faith (*De nostris dogmatibus veritatis, Oratio* III).[19]

The Church as the body of Christ is seen as the totality of those who believe in Jesus Christ as Son of God and Saviour, and are united with him, their Head, by participation in the sacraments. Therefore the

Church is, and can only be, one. Orthodoxy speaks of the Church as visible and invisible, but in doing so neither makes the western distinction between the Church militant and triumphant, nor the distinction between an invisible Church of the elect and a visible Church of saints mixed with sinners which the western Reformers took from Augustine and elaborated. It is rather a recognition that the one Church exists invisibly in the departed saints and faithful, *and* visibly in the worshipping community on earth. The distinction is made simply from the human point of view. There is but one Church, invisible and visible, heavenly and earthly: 'The Church, the Body of Christ, manifests forth and fulfils itself in time, without changing its essential unity or inward life of grace. And therefore, when we speak of "the Church visible and invisible", we so speak only in relation to man'.[20]

THE CHURCH AS THE EUCHARISTIC COMMUNITY

Ecclesiologies which present the Church as the mystical body of Christ place great emphasis on the eucharist.[21] So it is in Orthodox theology. Acts 2.42 which describes the life of the Church brought into being by the creative act of the Holy Spirit is an important text for Orthodox ecclesiology: 'They continued steadfastly in the apostles' teaching and fellowship [*koinōnia*], in the breaking of bread and the prayers.' It indicates that worship is essential to the Church's life.

The themes of the Church as body of Christ, as creation of the Holy Spirit, and as eucharistic community are closely integrated in Orthodox theology, as the following words of Professor N. A. Nissiotis[22] make clear:

> Orthodox worship is centred on the Christ event. The real presence of Christ in the midst of the worshipping community is the act of the Holy Spirit ... upon the invocation of the worshipping community to God the Father. The eucharistic *epiklēsis*[23] to the Father, 'send down thy Spirit on us and on these elements (the bread and wine) ...' is the climax and focus of all ecclesial worship which, following the biblical revelation, is an enactment of the energy of the Trinitarian God in history.
>
> The action of the Spirit—who is the Lord now in whom alone we can call Jesus Lord, who alone can lead us to the realization of the truth of Christ, who raised Christ from the dead, who set up the Church in history on the day of Pentecost, who gives us the earnest of the final victory of Christ over death according to the Scriptures—is absolutely decisive for Orthodox worship. Again and again, at the most decisive moments during

the Orthodox services, the Spirit is invoked, mentioned or prayed to as the Spirit creating the new situation in history, as the one through whom alone the reality of individual faith and the existence of the one community, the Ecclesia, becomes possible at all times and in all places. . . .

In this eucharistically centred worship, the Church is constantly recreated and recognized. Orthodox ecclesiology is directly affected by the liturgical-eucharistic event. Before the Church can be defined as a sacred institution in scholastic or ontological terms, or as a sociological organization for administering the Word and sacrament, she has to be understood as a charismatic community centred upon the real presence of Christ and enacted by the Spirit. That is why Orthodox ecclesiology emphasizes the 'mystery' aspect of the Church. 'Mystery' here does not signify an obscure and incomprehensible event, but it emphasizes the connection between the Head and the body as it is realized in Word and sacrament and points to the divine-human reality of the Church, as the people of God, united with Christ through the action of the Spirit.

Orthodox theology insists that in the eucharist the community, and each faithful member, is thankfully remembering Christ's work of redemption in the body of his flesh, celebrating his presence as the risen Christ, and anticipating his coming in final triumph as Lord of all. Past, present, and future are brought together in the one act of worship. Moreover, Orthodox obedience to Christ's command, 'do this', at the Last Supper has both an historical and an eschatological dimension; that is to say, the eye of Orthodox faith looks out to the world and its history, but also to the end which is God's purpose for the world beyond the world and its history. Christ is acknowledged as Lord of the Church and of the world, the Lord of history who is also Lord beyond the end of history.

This acknowledgement of the total lordship of Christ[24] makes it impossible for Orthodoxy to understand the sharp distinction which the Western Church and in particular the Protestant churches, have found it so easy to make between Church and world, sacred and secular. This is why the Eastern Church, from the time of Constantine and throughout the Byzantine period, conceived of Church and State (under a Christian ruler) as a single society, governed by two hierarchies, ecclesiastical and imperial, each autonomous, but acting in 'symphony'.[25] This is why Orthodoxy conceives Christian mission as the Church expressing itself in the life of the different regions of the world, committed to the conversion of the people within their own culture. This is why it is the concern of every faithful Orthodox pastor that the community under his care, which in the eucharistic liturgy acknowledges the world as the creation of God and Christ's total lordship over it, should bear active witness to this truth in its life, and the life of all its members. Liturgy as worship and liturgy as mission and service in the world are not to be separated.[26] The Orthodox understanding of the life of the Church in all its spheres, worship, mission, ministry to the needy, is based on the premiss that the Church is a community brought into being and sustained by the Holy Spirit in the eucharist which establishes the communion of the faithful with Christ crucified, risen, triumphant, and reigning Lord of all—the *Pantokrator*.

THE MARKS OF THE CHURCH

Orthodox ecclesiology follows in the main Augustine's interpretation of the credal marks of the Church,[27] but certain special emphases are to be noted. There is insistence that the unity of the Church is inclusive of diversity. This is an implication of the doctrine of the Church as the image of God the Holy Trinity, in whose essential unity are the distinctions of Father, Son, and Spirit. Unity is not conceived in any monolithic sense. Consequently, from the beginning, eastern Orthodoxy has opposed the idea of the supremacy of one ecclesiastical see over all others, has defended the autonomy of the patriarchates, and as its mission expanded[28] encouraged the creation of autocephalous churches creatively involved in the culture of the locality. Likewise, Orthodoxy sees the mystery of unity in diversity exemplified in councils, where under the guidance of the Holy Spirit the Church represented by bishops from many places seeks a common mind.

Catholicity is interpreted much as in the West, but less is made of the purely geographical sense of the word. This is perhaps because the Orthodox sees the local church as no less catholic than a church which is completely worldwide. Orthodox theologians lay great stress on the local church. The Church necessarily manifests itself locally. Appeal is made here to the earliest of the eastern Fathers, Ignatius of Antioch:

> Let that be considered a valid eucharist which is celebrated by the bishop or by one whom he appoints. Wherever the bishop appears let the congregation be present, just as wherever Jesus Christ is, there is the Catholic Church.[29]

Wherever faithful people are gathered round the bishop or his delegate for the celebration of the eucharist, there is the local Church *and* the Catholic Church. Ignatius' point, it is argued, is not that Christ and the bishop are to be equated in some way; rather it is that the local eucharistic community manifests, even explains, the nature of the whole Church of Christ. It is in the worshipping and working life of the local community of the faithful that the Catholic Church has its very being.

With regard to the note of holiness the Orthodox Church knows the tension which we have several times referred to:[30] the conviction that the Church, the body of Christ, is holy, and the knowledge that its members are imperfect and sinful.[31] The frequent litanies for the needs of the Church and the constantly repeated *kyrie eleison* (Lord, have mercy) eloquently dispel any suspicion that Orthodoxy conceives the members of the Church to be a society of perfect ones. Ephraim of Syria (*c.* 306–73) spoke of 'the Church of the penitents, the Church of those who perish'.[32] How can it be that members of the Church are sinners, but that the Church is the image of God, and the communion of saints? 'The mystery of the Church', writes Professor John Meyendorff, 'consists in the very fact that *together* sinners become *something different* from what they are as individuals; this "something different" is the Body of Christ'.[33]

The Orthodox interpretation of apostolicity will be discussed in the next section.

THE MINISTRY AND APOSTOLIC SUCCESSION

For the Orthodox Church 'apostolic succession' has a broader meaning than it bears, at least in the popular mind, in the West. Since the nature of the Church is both manifested in and sustained by the eucharist, continuity with the apostles lies in the succession of eucharistic communities. This is not to say that Orthodoxy minimizes the role of the bishop. It fully accepts the idea that the bishops have continuity with the apostles through their ordination.[34] But, as by Ignatius of Antioch and other early Fathers, the bishop's role as the chief celebrant of the liturgy is emphasized.

Ministry in the Church is Christ's ministry. He alone is truly bishop (1 Pet. 2.25), priest (Heb. 2.17), and deacon (Luke 22.27). The ministry of Christ is distributed in the Church by the Holy Spirit who apportions the gifts of God (1 Cor. 12.11). Bishop, priest, and deacon have their allotted functions in the life of the Church, and particularly in the eucharist wherein the life of the Church is sustained. The fact that the ordination of bishops, priests, and deacons takes place within the setting of the eucharist emphasizes that these are orders of ministry *within* a eucharistic community, and not above or apart from it. The eucharistic community is theologically prior to the bishop and the other orders of ministry. 'The documents at our disposal', writes Professor Meyendorff,[35] 'do not give us any certainty about the existence of a "monarchical episcopate" in all the Churches from the first century. . . . On the other hand, we can assert that there never was a Christian Church where the Lord's Supper was not celebrated.'

Episcopate, priesthood, and diaconate are *orders*. A hierarchy is implied, but not the spiritual superiority or greater importance of one over another. Nor is there implied a 'second-class citizenship' for laymen and laywomen. They are equally members of the eucharistic community. There can be no eucharistic liturgy without the presence of the laity.[36] Without the eucharistic community bishop, priest, and deacon would have no function.

Thus Orthodoxy insists that the Church is essentially the *people* of God, a eucharistic community:

> The apostolic succession has to be understood as a pentecostal event which first established the Church as a community and, within and by this community, the Spirit has appointed, through the apostles, deacons, presbyters, and bishops. It is, therefore, both an act of the community and a transmission of the apostolic ministry, but never an isolated line from Christ through the Twelve to the bishops as a separate divine order outside or above the laity. Apostolicity passes always through the eucharistic community and is recognized in him who presides over a eucharistic gathering. It is the people of God who precede the ministry in eucharistic practice and theological significance.[37]

THE CORPORATE EPISCOPATE

When Orthodoxy insists that the concept of hierarchy does not imply that the bishop has a spiritual superiority over other faithful members of the Church, it does not deny to the bishop a unique status. He succeeds the apostles as the guardian of the true faith.[38] He is the head on earth of the local eucharistic community. In these things the bishops have an essential equality.[39] The bishop's essential function is within the local church. Orthodoxy cannot conceive of a function for the bishop apart from the local church. Each local church is the Catholic Church in its completeness, and each bishop therefore exercises the fulness of episcopacy within it. The bishops together form a collegial body of which each member exercises the totality of episcopal authority within his own sphere. In this collegiate body none has an inherent juridical right over others. Orthodoxy has consistently rejected the idea of 'a bishop of bishops', even though it has admitted, with Cyprian, that the bishop of Rome has a primacy of honour comparable with that of Peter among the apostles. The Orthodox concept of collegiality is well expressed by a Greek, Athanasius, at a meeting held in Constantinople in 1357 at which the papal primacy was discussed. Against a Roman legate who maintained the necessity for a single head of the Church on earth, Athanasius said:

> I have said that the apostles are twelve, I know, but they are not twelve heads of the Church. Just as the faithful, despite their number, form one Church and the unique body of Christ because of identity of worship and religion, as we affirm, in the same way, I urge, you should think of the apostles, although twelve in number, as one sole head of the Church, because of identity of dignity and spiritual power. . . . [After citing John 17.11, 20–22 he proceeds]: you would not say that there are three Gods, for the three are perfectly one. How, then, in the case of those who have the same perfection, will you distinguish the inferior and the superior, or different heads? Should you not rather say that they are one and are the unique head of the Church of Christ? Assuredly, the pope is named first, and sits above the others, but this is only a matter of order,[40] and not because of any special dignity and spiritual power.[41]

The pope, then, is a bishop like any other—the bishop of a particular church. But as Nilus Cabasilas, uncle of the more famous Nicolas Cabasilas,[42] said, 'provided that the pope guards the order of the Church and remains in the truth, he retains the first place, which belongs to him by right'.[43]

Nevertheless, as we have already seen, Orthodoxy has accepted, on the authority of canons of early ecumenical councils, the principle that some sees may be acknowledged, for good historical reasons, as possessing a certain authority over other sees within the same region. Among such reasons were a strong tradition of apostolic foundation, the importance of the see city, the size of the community under the bishop's oversight, and the theological reputation of the see. The sees thus recognized were Rome, Alexandria, Antioch, Jerusalem, and Constantinople, and their bishops were accorded the title of 'patriarch'. From the time of the Council of Chalcedon (451) the five patriarchs were regarded as sharing between them the oversight and a measure of jurisdiction[44] over the whole of the known world (Greek *oikoumene*). This governmental system was known as the pentarchy (Greek *pentarchia*) or 'the rule of the five'. Justinian (Emperor 527–65) spoke of the five patriarchates as the five senses of the Empire. Orthodoxy insists that the pentarchy does not negate the principle of episcopal collegiality. On this Timothy Ware says:[45]

> The system of Patriarchs and Metropolitans is a matter of *ecclesiastical organization*. But if we look at the Church from the viewpoint not of ecclesiastical order but of *divine right*, then we must say that all bishops are essentially equal, however humble or exalted the city over which each presides. All bishops share equally in the apostolic succession, all have the same sacramental powers, all are divinely appointed teachers of the faith. If a dispute about doctrine arises, it is not enough for the Patriarchs to express their opinion: every diocesan bishop has the right to attend a General Council, to speak, and to cast his vote. The system of the Pentarchy does not impair the essential equality of all bishops, nor does it deprive each local community of the importance which Ignatius assigned to it.

AUTOCEPHALY

The patriarchate of Constantinople never claimed jurisdiction over other patriarchates as did the Church of Rome, but the historical circumstances of the submersion of the other eastern patriarchates under Moslem rulers, from the seventh century onwards, inevitably placed it in a position of responsibility for eastern Christendom. As Orthodoxy expanded towards the north through the remarkable missionary activity among the Slavic peoples, the principle of autocephaly[46] was developed, that is, the recognition of the right of a national church to elect its own metropolitan bishop,[47] and eventually to govern itself. This principle is normative in Orthodoxy to this day. It is valued as a true expression of the catholicity and unity of the Church in conformity with the spirit of the general councils. It is maintained that only the true autonomy of the Church within a region can give it the necessary flexibility to provide for the particular, and perhaps unique, needs of the people of that region.

Autocephaly, however, is not separation. The one Catholic Church is thought of as manifesting itself uniquely in each region, and the churches of all regions are bound in unity in the profession of the same faith, and in sacramental communion.

Autocephaly is the working out of a principle enunciated in the canons of early councils by which the Orthodox Church considers itself to be bound, the principle that there may not be more than one ecclesiastical jurisdiction in a single place. Canon 8 of the Council of Nicaea (325) declares 'there may not be two bishops in the city', and Canon 2 of the Council of Constantinople (381) says 'the synod of every province will administer the affairs of that particular province as was decreed in Nicaea'. Adherence to this principle is behind the Orthodox opposition to the papal claim to universal jurisdiction: 'The existence of one "vicar of Christ" for all the churches duplicates (if it does not suppress) the episcopal sacramental ministry of each particular local community.'[48] It places the centre of the ecclesiastical life of the local Christian community outside the community itself in a distant city.

Orthodoxy is uncomfortably aware that circumstances have led to a blurring of its witness to autocephaly and to the underlying principle that it is inadmissible to have different ecclesial communities in one place under different jurisdictions. Movements of population in the twentieth century have brought it about that in many cities of western Europe and North America Orthodox Christians in large numbers are to be found, not under the authority of a single bishop but, although in full communion with each other, under separate metropolitan jurisdictions, Greek, Russian, Serbian, and so on. This is an anomaly which Orthodox theology can only justify by the principle of 'economy'[49] for a limited period while every endeavour is made to restore canonical norms.

Part 4

THE REFORMATION PERIOD

12

Luther; Calvin; Separatism

1 MARTIN LUTHER (1483–1546)

'At the beginning of the sixteenth century everyone that mattered in the Western Church was crying out for reformation.'[1] It was set in motion in 1517, but not in the way, nor with the results, that the majority of those who had longed for it hoped. Western Europe was to be split into two religious camps, Catholic and Protestant, between which there was to be bitter hostility, and often open warfare, and few serious attempts at mutual understanding until late in the twentieth century. Moreover, to the dismay of many reformers, the movement produced splinter groups almost from the beginning, both because of the dissatisfaction of radicals with what they considered its cautious nature, and because of theological differences between the more conservative reformers.

Many factors contribute to explain the rise of the movement, political (rising nationalism in Europe) and social (the grievances of the German peasants) as well as moral and religious. But undoubtedly its immediate cause was the indulgence proclaimed by Pope Leo X to meet his desperate financial needs. The blatant methods of the Dominican friar Tetzel in promoting the indulgence[2] roused the indignation of a young Augustinian (or Austin) friar named Martin Luther. On 31 October 1517 Luther attached to the door of the Castle church in Wittenberg, where he was a university lecturer in Holy Scripture, 'Ninety-five Theses upon Indulgences'. Although outspoken on that subject, the theses were not particularly anti-papal. They assumed that if the Pope knew what was going on, he would disapprove; they called for a public discussion on indulgences, and declared Luther's readiness to defend his theses in such a debate. Little as he can have suspected it, Luther had launched a movement of vast significance for the history of Europe. Copies of the theses were printed, unknown to Luther, and circulated within a few weeks far and wide in Germany. They gained wide support, and gradually he found himself cast in the role of leader in a revolt against papal supremacy over the Church.

THE CHURCH AS THE CONGREGATION OF THE FAITHFUL

The central doctrine of the Luther reformation was that man is justified by faith alone, and not by works. This was a conviction which Luther had reached some years before the affair of the indulgence, as he had struggled with the consciousness that diligence in keeping the rule of the Austin friars and frequent confessions brought him no peace with God, no sense of being redeemed. His rejection of the idea that salvation can be earned by good works prompted his attack on indulgences. He saw them as a particularly odious symptom of the malaise of a Church which, in his view, had come to stand for the doctrine that man might win salvation by reliance on placatory acts performed on his behalf by a clerical hierarchy, in recognition of his pious works or money payments.

The doctrine of justification by faith alone has a direct influence on Luther's ecclesiology. With the acceptance of this doctrine as crucial it is natural to conceive of the Church as essentially the assembly of those who have the faith which justifies, the *congregatio fidelium*. And since those who have justifying faith are redeemed, the Church is defined as 'the congregation of saints'.[3]

THE CHURCH IS WHERE THE WORD OF GOD IS PREACHED AND THE SACRAMENTS ADMINISTERED

Unless the doctrine of justification by faith, however, is understood in a purely subjective way (and Luther did not so understand it), more than this must be said about the Church. Intimately related, in Luther's thought, with the doctrine of justification by faith (which more accurately is to be called the doctrine of justification *by grace* through faith) was the doctrine of the Atonement. This is the doctrine that, by the free gift or grace of God, his Son, Jesus Christ, has redeemed mankind through his life, sacrificial death, and resurrection. The Church of Christ, then, must be where God continues to offer his grace in Christ, and seeks the response which is the faith that justifies. Although Luther differed from Catholic theologians about the nature of grace, the place and importance of preaching, and in sacramental theology, he strongly held that God's grace is received by the preaching of the word of God and the administration of the sacraments. Consequently, while the Church may be described as 'the congregation of saints' one must add 'in which the Gospel is rightly taught and the sacraments are rightly administered'.[4] In *The Papacy at Rome* (1520), Luther writes:[5] 'Baptism, the sacrament, and the gospel are the signs by which the existence of the Church in the world can be noticed externally.'[6]

These signs or marks of the Church are the first three of seven[7] which he lists and treats more fully in a later work:

> First, the holy Christian people are recognized by their possession of the holy Word of God. ... Wherever you hear or see this word preached, believed, professed, and lived do not doubt that the true *ecclesia sancta catholica*, 'a Christian holy people', must be there, even though their number is very small. ...

> Second, God's people, or the Christian holy people are recognized by the holy sacrament of baptism, wherever it is taught, believed, and administered according to Christ's ordinance. ...

> Third, God's people, or Christian holy people, are recognized by the holy sacrament of the altar, wherever it is rightly administered, believed and received according to Christ's institution (*On the Councils and the Church* (1539)).[8]

THE INVISIBLE CHURCH

The true Church, or 'the Christian holy people' as Luther preferred to call it, is hidden or invisible, inasmuch as God alone knows who are the elect. He makes the distinction which we first found in Augustine between the invisible Church of the elect and the empirical 'mixed' Church of saints and sinners:

> Christianity is a spiritual assembly of souls in one faith ... no one is regarded as a Christian because of his body. Thus ... the natural, real, true, and essential Christendom exists in the Spirit and not in any external thing. ... This is the way Holy Scripture speaks of the holy Church and of Christendom. ...

> We shall call the two churches by two distinct names. The first, which is natural, basic, essential, and true, we shall call 'spiritual internal Christendom'. The second, which is man-made and external, we shall call 'physical, external Christendom' (*On the Papacy at Rome*).[9]

Luther goes further than Augustine when he speaks of the visible Church as man-made. J. S. Whale[10] comments that for Luther

> ecclesiastical institutions have not the divine character claimed for them: all are human, fallible, and alterable; he attaches relatively little importance to ecclesiastical forms as such. He therefore breaks with the specifically medieval conception that Christ's Kingdom is concretely and visibly manifested on earth as an institution hierarchically ordered; and governed, by divine authority, in terms of law. To the Church of history and law he opposes the Church of the Spirit which, ideally considered, has no need of a visible, corporate constitution to make it a reality in the world.

Luther likens the relationship between the 'internal' Christendom and the 'external' to that between soul and body. To the external Christendom belong 'all popes, cardinals, bishops, prelates, monks, nuns, and all those who are regarded as Christians according to externals, no matter whether they are true and real Christians or not'.[11] Some, he concedes, are true Christians, not because of their membership of the external Church ('the body does not keep the soul alive, but the soul does exist in the body as well as without the body'),[12] but because of their faith. Without faith they are 'outside the first community, are dead before God; they are hypocrites and are merely like images of true Christendom.'[13]

Luther's assertion in this context that the soul can exist 'without the body' suggests that he believed that the true Church can and should exist without embodiment in an historical institution and outward forms. In the light of experience, and under the influence of the scholarly and pacific Melanchthon, he came to recognize that this was too idealistic a view. In 1527 in a letter to his friend George Spalatin, the chaplain of the Elector Frederick of Saxony, he admitted that it had been vain to hope that men could be ruled by the gospel alone; men seemed to prefer constraint by law and sword. For, 'round Luther's cry for religious reformation gathered men who wanted other things besides religious reformation'.[14] The excesses of some of these, and the violence of the peasants' risings of 1524–5, led Luther to attach more importance to 'externals' like disciplinary measures and a regular ministry. When in 1539 he wrote the third part of *On the Councils and the Church* he was doing, J. S. Whale remarks,[15] 'very much what Calvin is doing in the second edition of the *Institutio* published that same year—namely coming down to "brass tacks", so to speak;

defining the primary and secondary signs of the Church visible'. In addition to the three signs mentioned above (p. 163), he enumerates the use of the 'keys' (i.e. public and private condemnation of sins); ministers, to whom alone are committed the duties of preaching, baptizing, absolving, and celebrating the eucharist; public prayer, thanksgiving, and praise; and a manner of life which is stamped with the cross of Christ in the face of persecution, temptation, and all adversity.

THE PRIESTHOOD OF ALL BELIEVERS

This is a constant theme with Luther, and 1 Peter 2.9, 'You are ... a royal priesthood' is the text by which he supports it.

> It is pure invention that pope, bishop, priests, and monks are called the spiritual estate while princes, lords, artisans, and farmers are called the temporal estate. This is indeed a piece of deceit and hypocrisy ... all Christians are truly of the spiritual estate, and there is no difference among them except that of office. ...

> We are all consecrated priests through baptism, as St Peter says ... 'You are a royal priesthood and a priestly realm'. ...

> There is no true, basic difference between laymen and priests, princes and bishops, between religious and secular, except for the sake of office and work, but not for the sake of status. ... All are truly priests, bishops, and popes (*To the Christian Nobility of the German Nation* (1520)).[16]

The same theme is pursued in *The Babylonian Captivity of the Church*, written also in 1520, in a passage in which he says that while all have the same power in respect of Word and sacraments, it is only by the consent of the community that it may be exercised. Luther was never, therefore, quite without a sense of the necessity of a regular ministry, but he repudiated the sharp distinction which the medieval Church had come to make between clergy as a privileged class and a passive, listening, and obedient laity.[17] He maintained that all believers share a common priesthood: they are called, each in his own sphere of life, to preach the gospel, to edify the neighbour in love and to use the 'power of the keys', that is, to rebuke sin, to proclaim forgiveness and salvation, and to reconcile. The essential meaning of apostolic succession is revealed when one Christian proclaims to another the reconciliation in Christ which he himself has heard from others.

It follows that it would be a grave mistake to accuse Luther of encouraging individualism. To him the Christian community was essential. Every individual Christian needs his brother, who is God's representative to him in two ways: it is through a brother that God assures each of his grace (the power of 'the keys' mentioned above); and secondly the brother 'is appointed by God to receive the sacrifices of love and service which God does not need',[18] namely, the good works in which the faith of the justified man is ceaselessly active. The Church as a company of believers exercising a common priesthood is necessary. It is of the Church so understood that Luther, echoing Cyprian, can say: 'Outside the Christian Church there is no truth, no Christ, no blessedness', and even declare that it is necessary to God himself.[19]

THE MINISTRY

Luther's often repeated and enthusiastic language about the priesthood of all believers is not, on the surface, easy to reconcile with any recognition of the necessity of a duly constituted ministry. Yet the mature Luther was clearly not content to sweep aside the ordained ministry with the epithet 'man-made' which he had used of the visible Church in 1520.[20] This can be substantiated by quoting the fifth of the seven signs of the Church in his *On the Councils and the Church* (1539):

> The Church is recognized externally by the fact that it consecrates or calls ministers or has offices that it is to administer. There must be bishops, pastors, or preachers who publicly and privately give, administer, and use the aforementioned four things or holy possessions, viz. Word, baptism, sacrament of the altar, keys, in behalf of and in the name of the Church, or rather *by reason of their institution by Christ* [italics mine], as St Paul states in Ephesians 4, 'He received gifts among men ...'—his gifts were that some should be apostles, some prophets, some evangelists, some teachers and governors, etc. The people as a whole cannot do these things but must entrust or have them entrusted to one person ... the others should be content with this arrangement and agree to it.[21]

The ordained ministry as such, then, is not to be described as a man-made contrivance; indeed it is instituted by Christ. What Luther does conceive to be man-made is the distinction of rank and status between ministers. From the interchangeability of the terms 'bishop' and 'presbyter' in the N.T. he argues for the parity of ministers or spiritual rulers. The distinctions between bishops, priests, chaplains, deans, and so on have been introduced 'by men's laws and regulations'. Long usage has led men to think that these distinctions are scriptural and of divine institution.[22] What is of divine institution, scriptural, and to be retained is the careful choice of men from among the faithful to be ministers of Word and sacrament:

> In previous times this matter was handled as follows, and this is the way it should still be done: since in every Christian town they were all equally priests, one of them—the oldest or rather the most learned and most godly—was elected to be their servant, official, caretaker, and guardian in regard to the gospel and the sacraments, just as a mayor is elected from among the common mass of citizens (*Answer to the Hyperchristian, Hyperspiritual, and Hyperlearned Book by Goat Emser* (1521)).[23]

The final words in the above quotation are a reminder that it is the responsibility of the whole body of the faithful to see that the right choice is made of those who are to represent them in the things of God.

THE PLACE OF THE CHRISTIAN PRINCE

In reviewing the development of the idea of the Church in the medieval period, we took note of the complicated questions which arose concerning the relationship of Church and State: the defining of the areas of autonomy of each, and of the rights and duties of each to the other. Such questions certainly belong to ecclesiology in the wide sense of the word, for the various answers which have been given to them have produced different concepts of the nature and the function of the Church. Adequate treatment of this aspect of ecclesiology would require a separate study, which would include an investigation of how the Christian understanding of the Church has been influenced according to whether the temporal ruler or government was hostile, Christian, or indifferent. In the western Europe of Luther's day it could still be taken for granted that emperor, kings, and magistrates were professing Christians. The idea of the Christian prince certainly influenced Luther's ecclesiology. The circumstances of the time ('sixteenth-century Germany was no Garden of Eden,' remarks J. S. Whale)[24] led him to accord to the ruler extensive coercive authority, and disorders within reformed churches[25] led him to demand of the Christian prince protection for the Church, and consequently to allow him a considerable measure of authority in ecclesiastical matters.

In 1523 Luther wrote *Temporal Authority: to what Extent it should be Obeyed*,[26] and dedicated it to the new Elector of Saxony, Duke John. J. S. Whale, who in his book *The Protestant Tradition* provides a thorough discussion of Luther's teaching on Church and State,[27] gives the following useful summary of this work:

> A Luther is at pains to establish two scriptural principles:
>
> (i) The divine sanction of civil government, and its independence of all clerical tutelage and control.
>
> (ii) The limits of this power, which may be exercised only over the bodies and goods of men, not in the domain of conscience, where man is answerable only to God.
>
> B ... The treatise fights on three fronts; it repudiates three distinct views of the proper relation between State and Church:
>
> (i) The medieval, Roman view. Luther denies that the State, as the 'secular arm' of the Church, has a duty to undertake religious persecution or coercion.
>
> (ii) The 'Machiavellian' view. He denies that Christian men may be persecuted as such by the civil power for reasons of State.
>
> (iii) The 'anarchist' view of Christian idealism and pacifism. He denies the 'anabaptist'[28] thesis that because the Gospel forbids resistance to evil, the Christian state may not use force in the name of law.
>
> C Luther distinguishes between
>
> (i) Natural society—which, because of sin, cannot subsist without the coercive sanctions of police force and sword.
>
> (ii) The religious sphere—where the Word is the only agency which may rightly be employed.[29]

Whale adds a comment of his own:

> D Luther thus anticipates some of the living issues of our own time. It is doubtful whether he also anticipates those erastian elements in historic Lutheranism which are now criticized and disavowed.[30]

'If all the world were composed of real Christians,' Luther wrote,[31] 'that is, true believers, there would be no need for or benefits from prince, king, lord, sword, or law.' But true Christians were, he admitted, unlikely ever to be numerous enough to make government 'in a Christian and evangelical manner'[32] feasible. And for the protection of the Church itself he called on the Duke of Saxony to conduct visitations of the churches, and began to provide for the government and discipline of the churches by a system of courts, or consistories, whose members were appointed by the prince.

Luther based his doctrine of the place of the Christian prince on that of the priesthood of all believers. All Christians, whatever their calling, were bound to serve the Church, using whatever talents and proper authority they possessed. The Christian who, by a divinely given right, is a ruler, is under obligation to use his authority, which includes the power to coerce, on behalf of the Church when this is necessary. The prince's authority is not, however, absolute. It does not extend to the sphere of conscience. Here Luther claimed the Christian man's right of passive resistance. Nor does that authority include the right to intervene in doctrinal matters. Yet it was admitted that the Christian ruler was obliged to protect the Church against heresy, and the distinction proved hard to draw between what was and what was not interference in purely spiritual matters. The Lutheran churches were to exist under something akin to State absolutism in things spiritual as well as temporal.

J. S. Whale concludes his discussion of Luther's doctrine of the Christian prince with the words:

> It seems that circumstances proved too strong for the author of *The Liberty of the Christian Man*. Not only Melanchthon and later German Lutherans, but the great Reformer himself began to swim with the political current which was everywhere bringing the absolute ruler to port, and to acquiesce in the political opportunism of his princely protectors. The prophet who began by proclaiming the priesthood of all believers at last found himself virtually exalting the temporal prince as *summus episcopus* [i.e. supreme bishop] or as *membrum praecipuum ecclesiae* [i.e. chief member of the Church].[33]

For Lutheranism the authority of pope and bishops had passed to the Christian prince.

2 JOHN CALVIN (1509–64)

The Reformation movement quickly swept from southern Germany to other places. By 1522 Zwingli was leading it in Zürich, by 1523 Martin Bucer in Strasbourg, and by 1530 William Farel in Neuchâtel. Farel, however, went to Geneva in 1535 to organize the reformation there. In 1536 he persuaded John Calvin, who was on a passing visit, to remain and help with the work, which was running into some difficulties. Opposition to some of the disciplinary measures they proposed led to the banishment of both in 1538. Calvin spent three years working with Bucer in Strasbourg. In 1541 he returned to

Geneva where he now met great success. The city rapidly became the favourite place of shelter for Protestant refugees from Catholic countries.[34] Calvin remained in Geneva for the rest of his life. His reputation as a biblical scholar, theologian, and ecclesiastical statesman was acknowledged far beyond the limits of the city of Geneva. He is rightly regarded as the father of those churches of the Reformation which have come to be known as 'The Reformed Churches', and which usually have a presbyterian system of government.

Calvin's *Institutio Christianae Religionis*[35] is one of the great Christian classics. It was first published in 1536, and was greatly expanded in subsequent editions in 1539, 1543, and 1559. It is in four books, the last of which deals with the Church. Much of what he has to say concerns the Church as a visible, organized institution. Keenly aware of the erratic individualism which the Reformation was engendering, and which caused so much concern to Luther, Calvin saw the need for strong churchmanship, and laboured to make Geneva a shining example of it. He is frequently spoken of as the Cyprian of the Reformation, and may with some justice be described as a 'high churchman'.[36]

THE CHURCH VISIBLE AND INVISIBLE

Calvin held a strict doctrine of predestination which would perhaps seem to leave little room for a doctrine of the visible Church. If, by God's eternal decree, some are elected to salvation and others are not, there would seem to be only a peripheral place for the Church as an historical institution: the provision of a ministry and discipline would appear to be unnecessary for the elect, and futile for the reprobate. But Calvin did not see the question in this way. On the contrary, for him the existence of the Church belongs to the mysterious eternal decrees of God. The Church visible is by God's provision the means by which, through the ministry of Word, sacraments, and discipline, he brings the elect to their salvation. Calvin's doctrine of the Church is thus closely linked to his predestinarianism.[37]

Calvin integrates the concepts of the invisible Church and the visible in a way which Luther never succeeded in achieving. There are not two Churches, but

> Holy Scripture speaks of the church in two ways. Sometimes ... it means that which is actually in God's presence into which no persons are received but those who are children of God by grace of adoption and true

members of Christ by sanctification of the Holy Spirit. . . . [It] includes not only the saints presently living on earth, but all the elect from the beginning of the world. Often however the name 'church' designates the whole multitude of men spread over the earth who profess to worship one God and Christ. By baptism we are initiated into faith in him; by partaking in the Lord's Supper we attest our unity in true doctrine and love; in the Word of the Lord we have agreement, and for the preaching of the Word the ministry instituted by Christ is preserved. In this church are mingled many hypocrites who have nothing of Christ but the name and outward appearance. . . . Just as we must believe, therefore, that the former church, invisible to us, is visible to the eyes of God alone, so we are commanded to revere and keep communion with the latter, which is called 'church' in respect to men (*Institutes* IV, i.7).[38]

Finding that Scripture speaks of the Church as at once visible and invisible, Calvin is content to argue the matter no further, but to devote the rest of the book to the marks of the Church visible, the means of grace which God has given it, and the forms of ministry and discipline which it needs.

TRADITIONAL CONCEPTS: BODY, MOTHER

The traditional images which Calvin most frequently uses are those of the Church as the body of Christ, and as mother. Membership of the body of Christ coincides completely with the invisible Church, but not with the Church visible, among whose membership are some who are not predestined to salvation. Yet because the invisible and visible are one Church and not two, Calvin can use the body image of the Church as institution; for Christ is its Head, and his spirit works within it, distributing varied gifts individually and pre-eminently the gift of love, ordering, unifying, and sanctifying its members.[39]

Calvin fully recognizes the Pauline tension between the 'now' and the 'not yet' of the Church. The Church visible *is* the body of Christ, but it is also in process of *becoming* his body. In a passage where, however, he is using the image of the bride, he says that while it is true that Jesus Christ has sanctified the Church, so that his bride is without wrinkle or blemish,

it is also no less true that the Lord is daily at work in smoothing out the wrinkles and cleansing the spots. From this it follows that the Church's holiness is not yet complete. The Church is holy, then, in the sense that it is daily advancing and is not yet perfect; it makes progress from day to day but has not yet reached its goal of holiness (*Institutes* IV, i.17).[40]

Like Cyprian and Augustine, Calvin boldly uses the mother image of the visible Church, and with them can say that apart from her there is no salvation:

> Because it is now our intention to discuss the visible church, let us learn even from the simple title 'mother' how useful, indeed how necessary, it is that we should know her. For there is no other way to enter into life unless this mother conceive us in her womb, give us birth, nourish us at her breast, and lastly, unless she keep us under her care and guidance until, putting off mortal flesh, we become like the angels ... away from her bosom one cannot hope for any forgiveness of sins or any salvation ... it is always disastrous to leave the Church (*Institutes* IV, i.4).

THE MARKS OF THE VISIBLE CHURCH

But what are the criteria for judging whether a group of people who claim to be Christians have Christ for their Head and are of his body? Calvin, as we have seen, was very conscious that the radicals of the reforming movement were separating themselves into small 'holiness' groups. Were they justified in doing so? Calvin believed that there are certain marks by which one may discern the Church. They are identical with the first three of the external marks which Luther listed:[41]

> Wherever we see the Word of God purely preached and heard, and the sacraments administered according to Christ's institution, there, it is not to be doubted, a Church of God exists (*Institutes* IV, i.9).

Wherever these marks are to be recognized, individuals do wrong to separate themselves. 'Let them ponder how much more important both the ministry of the Word and participation in the sacred mysteries are for the gathering of the church than the possibility that this whole power may be dissipated through the guilt of certain ungodly men.'[42] Calvin argues that differences in 'non-essential matters' do not justify schism: 'We must not thoughtlessly forsake the Church because of any petty dissensions.'[43]

Wendel notices[44] that, although Calvin attaches great importance to disciplinary provision, he did not include this in his marks of the Church. The explanation, he suggests, is that Calvin thought of discipline as belonging not to the definition of the Church, but to its organization as a 'measure of defence and a means of sanctification'. Be that as it may, Calvin certainly recognized the need for ecclesiastical discipline. The streak of puritanism and perfectionism in his own character contributed to the seriousness with which he viewed this matter. At Geneva he provided an elaborate machinery of discipline. The faithful were to be protected from bad example, and sinners prompted to repentance. In serious cases excommunication was to be used, but every effort was to be made to bring the excommunicated person back into fellowship. Calvin is careful to state that excommunication does not imply that the subject is not of the elect, for only God knows about this. The excommunicate are, however, 'assured of their everlasting condemnation unless they repent'. The purpose of excommunication is 'reconciliation and restoration to communion'.[45]

THE MINISTRY

J. S. Whale suggests[46] that Calvin must have been aware that his arguments against the Protestant separatists could equally be used by the Roman Church against Geneva. However, despite certain admissions[47] that some traces of the true Church remained in the Church of Rome of the sixteenth century, he was convinced of the necessity of separation from it. There the Word of God was not purely preached, he believed, nor were the sacraments administered according to the institution of Christ; and the papacy had usurped the headship of Christ.[48] He therefore sees no alternative to an outright rejection of Roman orders.[49]

This does not mean that Calvin rejected the concept of the distinction of ranks within the ministry. Distinctions such as that between patriarch, archbishop, and bishop in the early Church which were 'connected with the maintenance of discipline', are justified.[50] The term 'hierarchy', however, he does reject as 'improper, unscriptural, and likely to encourage ideas of lordship in the government of the Church which are contrary to the will of God'.[51] In his *Commentary on the Book of Numbers* he writes:

> Distinction of a political kind is not to be rejected, for common sense itself dictates it in order to remove confusion. But whatever has this end in view will be so arranged as neither to obscure the glory of Christ nor to minister to ambition or tyranny, nor to hinder all ministers from cultivating a mutual brotherliness among themselves with equal rights and liberties.[52]

His *Letter to the King of Poland*[53] makes clear that he has no fundamental objection to archbishops and bishops provided that they preach the Word of God, rightly administer the sacraments, and make no unjustified claims for status and privilege. The papal Church had failed in these respects. It had destroyed the true relationship between the faithful and Christ, the Head of the Church, and widespread corruption had ensued.

In the third edition of 1543 Calvin introduced into the *Institutes* a detailed account of the ministry by which he believed 'the Lord willed his Church to be governed'.[54] It is not necessary for our purpose to undertake a close examination of the fourfold ministry of pastors, teachers (or doctors), elders, and deacons.[55] It must be said that his attempt to find a scriptural basis for it is not more noticeably successful than that of the papist, episcopalian, or congregationalist endeavouring to provide scriptural justification for the ministry of his own tradition. The evidence is forced, and what does not fit into the preconceived scheme is explained away.

It is more important to notice that for Calvin, unlike the earlier, idealistic Luther, the ministry is no matter of human expediency and contrivance. It is ordained by God. This is implied by the Pauline concept of the body of Christ, not merely because of the obvious analogy between a human body and an institution, each of which possesses members who perform special functions for the benefit of the whole, but rather because Christ as the Head has, through his Spirit, imparted ministry to the Church, his body, as his gift. The Church's ministers 'represent his person'.[56] 'God himself appears in our midst, and, as Author of this order [namely, the ministry], would have men recognize him as present in his institution.'[57] 'No ecclesiology', says Geddes MacGregor, 'has ever more exalted the ministry, under Christ, than does Calvin's.'[58] The words 'under Christ' are important. The headship of Christ over the Church is constitutive of all that Calvin has to say about Church order. Any system which implied the usurpation of Christ's place as Head of the Church, whether by pope or people, was no Church order, but led inevitably to the chaos which Calvin saw both in the Church of Rome and in the anabaptist sects.

Calvin's high doctrine of the ministry is seen also in what he says about the choice and ordination of ministers.[59] Their selection from among those who are of sound doctrine and holy life is the responsibility of ministers who must instruct and examine them, and, if they are approved, present them to the people for their acceptance. At the ordination ministers preside and pray over the candidate. Calvin allows the ceremony of the laying on of hands,[60] although it was not the practice at Geneva in his time. He notes that it is a scriptural custom, observed by the apostles, and commends it accordingly, provided that it is not regarded superstitiously as an act which in itself confers the Holy Spirit. Ordination is accomplished by God through the Holy Spirit; the imposition of hands expresses it symbolically.[61]

Calvin is not unwilling to speak of ordination as a sacrament:

> As far as the true office of presbyter is concerned, which is commended to us by Christ's lips, I willingly accord that place [viz. as a sacrament] to it. ... However, I have not put it as number three among the sacraments because it is not ordinary or common with all believers, but is a special rite for a particular office (*Institutes* IV, xix. 28).[62]

CHURCH AND STATE

It remains to comment briefly on Calvin's teaching on the relationship between the Church's authority and that of rulers. It differs from the position which Luther reluctantly came to adopt, but, as F. Wendel remarks, is close to the latter's personal views. Spiritual and temporal jurisdictions are distinct. Calvin sets out the principle as follows:

> The Church does not have the right of the sword to punish or compel, not the authority to force; not imprisonment, nor the other punishments which the magistrate commonly inflicts. Then, it is not a question of punishing the sinner against his will, but of the sinner professing his repentance in a voluntary chastisement. The two conceptions are very different. The Church does not assume what is proper to the magistrate: nor can the magistrate execute what is carried out by the Church (*Institutes* IV, xi. 3).[63]

Civil government rightly exercises an authority which provides sanctions against crime and unsocial behaviour, and the Christian must acknowledge this. But the Church's concern is with men's consciences, and the purpose of its disciplinary measures is to expel notorious evildoers, to protect the community from bad example, and above all to lead offenders to repentance and restore them to communion.[64]

Many of the things which the Church does in a city or nation ought to cause a ruler to rejoice: the inculcation of honesty and industry, providence and thrift. As G. MacGregor puts it,[65] 'the least to be expected of the ruler and magistrates ... is that they should lend whatever authority and power they possess to the support of the Church through which the land has been so bountifully blessed'.

Calvin did expect it, and considered that the civil and ecclesiastical authorities should complement each other, and work in close collaboration. Calvin's Geneva was not a theocracy which subordinated the temporal to the spiritual power. That this has been so commonly assumed is a measure of the success he achieved (after much initial opposition) in securing the co-operation of the Genevan magistrates and the consistory. For Calvin the Church visible was more than an institution: it was an association, a community. He was not content that it should be a closed community walled off from the life of the population around it; it should embrace the whole people. Twentieth-century man may marvel that this should be so nearly achieved in the Geneva of Calvin's day. He will also probably have little liking for the strictness of the discipline which was exercised. But if the Church is the body of the Christ who came into the world to serve it and redeem it, Calvin's purpose was not at fault despite the faults which hindsight may discern in the relationship which he established between magistrates and Church at Geneva.

3 SEPARATISM

In our study up to this point we have met, broadly speaking, three types of thought about the Church visible. They are sometimes designated Catholic, Protestant, and Separatist; or hierarchical, evangelical, and pentecostal. Such labels, however, can be misleading, for no one of these types altogether excludes what is characteristic of the others. For example, it may not be said that the Catholic or hierarchical type excludes all consciousness of the need for protest and reform. We have come across a number of examples of such consciousness within the hierarchical Church of the Middle Ages. Nor may the great Catholic theologians justly be accused of unawareness of the demands of the gospel of Christ or the significance of the work of the Holy Spirit in the Church. Similar reservations are to be made for the other two types. Bearing this in mind, and also that summaries are certain to be inadequate, the three types are:

CATHOLIC (HIERARCHICAL)

The visible Church consists of all those who have been baptized and who participate in the grace of God given by Word and sacrament through episcopally ordained ministers. Spiritual discipline, worship, and government are ordered by the traditional hierarchy with, in Roman Catholic thought, the pope at its head. Stress is laid on the Church as an institution which is in continuity with the apostles, in that the hierarchy can trace its succession in orders back to the apostles.

PROTESTANT[66] (EVANGELICAL)

This type of Church idea has more in common with the first than is often acknowledged on either side. It sees the visible Church as con- sisting of the whole company of baptized faithful, nourished in their places of gathering by the preaching of the Word of God and the ad- ministration of the sacraments by ministers duly called and ordained. Spiritual discipline, worship, and government are ordered by properly constituted courts, consisting of ministers and laity, either at the local level as in Calvin's Geneva, or in a series of courts from the local to the national levels as in the Church of Scotland and the Lutheran state churches. Continuity with the apostles is conceived as preserved by the purity of the gospel preached rather than by a traceable succession in ministerial ordination.[67]

SEPARATIST (PENTECOSTAL)

We have already met certain of the characteristics of this type of thinking about the Church in the Montanists, the Novatianists, and the Donatists. The visible Church is the spirit-guided company of the holy, separated from the world and gathered together for the worship of God. No rule, discipline, or hierarchy external to the local group is acknowledged. The group itself is regarded as responsible to Christ for its own government. The Separatist church appoints and changes its ministers according to need. It tends to maintain a rigid separation from other Christians who cannot accept the standard of holiness which it sets up.

The Separatist idea was finding expression again in the wake of the Reformation, much to the consternation, as we have seen, of Luther and Calvin. It is true that religious fanatics and political extremists gravitated to the Separatist churches which sprang up in the sixteenth and seventeenth centuries. We are not here concerned with them (other Christian groups have had their share of these). Rather we are concerned with numbers of quiet godly people who almost from the beginning of the Reformation movement began to form themselves into separate local groups. They were motivated by the feeling that the Reformation leaders were not resolute enough and were retaining too much that smacked of the papal Church; by the conviction that religion is essentially a personal matter between God and the soul; that the gathering together of small groups for the breaking of bread and for prayers is the New Testament idea of the Church, and that personal holiness is to be attained by separating oneself from worldly enticements, and indeed from all worldly affairs so far as possible.

Both Luther and Calvin had no little sympathy with some of these convictions, and admiration for the courage of those who held them. But they opposed their separatism. This was destructive of the aim which Luther and Calvin were pursuing, each in his own way. Neither of them was, in intention, setting up a new or separate church. Each hoped for a reformation of the universal Church of Christ, whether city by city or nation by nation, which would be a true and inclusive *volkskirche* (church of the people).

The ecclesiology of the Separatists is well defined by the Englishman, Henry Barrow (executed in 1593):

> The true planted and rightly established Church of Christ is a company of faithful people, separated from the unbelievers and heathen of the land, gathered in the name of Christ, whom they truly worship and readily obey as their only King, Priest, and Prophet, and joined together as members of one body, ordered and governed by such offices and laws as Christ, in his last will and testament, hath thereunto ordained. . . . We hold all believers [to be] ecclesiastical and spiritual. . . . We know not what you mean by your old popish term of 'laymen' (*Discovery of the True Church*).[68]

No difference, then, is drawn between clergy and laity. Pastors are, however, appointed by the congregation. Discipline is the responsibility of 'ruling elders', also appointed by the congregation. The local congregation is thus autonomous, and in the words of a petition to James I of England in 1616 it has 'the right of spiritual administration and government in itself and over itself by the common and free consent of the people, independently and immediately under Christ'.[69]

Another characteristic of the Separatist churches was what is known as 'the voluntary principle'. It developed during the sixteenth century as it became clear that the power of the State was to be used to compel conformity in areas which were Lutheran, Calvinist, or Anglican no less than in countries which adhered to the papacy. Dissent was seen as tantamount to treason, and laws were passed to eradicate it. The voluntary principle was a protest against this Church-State totalitarianism. Its classical definition is given by Robert Browne (1550–1633) in a book with the expressive title, *A Treatise of Reformation without tarying for anie, and of the wickedness of those which will not reforme till the Magistrate command or compell them*[70] (1582):

> The Lord's people is of the willing sorte. It is conscience, not the power of man, that will drive us to seek the Lord's Kingdom. Therefore it belongeth not to the magistrate to compel religion, to plant churches by power, and to force a submission to ecclesiastical government by laws and penalties.

The Separatist groups which explicitly or implicitly adhered to these principles were many and varied.[71] They included the Hutterites of Moravia, the Mennonites of Holland, the English Independents, and many smaller groups. Agreed as they were in their main principles, there were important differences between them. Most, but not all, forbade the taking of civil office and were pacifists. Some practised community of goods. Some were apocalyptists in the sense that, like the second-century Montanists, they believed the Heavenly Jerusalem was soon to appear. Among these were the Melchiorites in Holland, and the violent group at Münster under John of Leyden. Many were pentecostalists in that they claimed for themselves a special guidance of the Holy Spirit. Henry Barrow, questioned in prison about his claim to possess 'a private spirit', answered that he had the spirit of the apostles 'in that measure that God hath imparted unto me, though not in that measure that the Apostles had, by any comparison. Yet the same Spirit. There is but one Spirit.'[72] Although not all these groups claimed special guidance of the Spirit, the name 'Spirituals' was often attached to the whole movement. 'Anabaptists' is another name often fastened on all Separatist groups, although all did not adopt the policy of rebaptizing their converts. Some, like the Quakers, the followers of George Fox (1624–91), dispensed with the sacraments altogether.[73]

J. S. Whale, to whom I have often referred in this chapter, himself a member of the Congregational Union of England and Wales, a union of groups which have their roots deep in the radical movement of the Reformation period, provides an illuminating study of it in Part III of his book *The Protestant Tradition*.[74] He points to its positive contributions to the history of Christianity. While he admits that the truth that religion is an intensely personal matter is complemented by the truth that it is also an intensely social matter, he holds that the radical reformers' insistence on the personal and voluntary principle came at a time when the totalitarian claims of both Catholic and Reformed states called for emphasis of the former truth. The persistence and courage with which the voluntary principle was held contributed much to the eventual achievement of religious toleration in most European countries. The claim to guidance by the Holy Spirit (the spiritual principle), open to question as it is if used to judge all others by the conscience of a small group or single individual, is nevertheless the proclamation, too often neglected in Christian thought and unrecognized in Christian experience, of the guiding work of the Spirit in the Church and its members.

On the other hand the fragmentation of Christian people into small separated sects can lead to disinterest in the unity of the Church; the claim to autonomy and the emphasis on the personal aspect of Christianity can lead to indifference to the note of catholicity; concentration on personal holiness can lead to a contempt for those who do not attain to the standard set by the group, and weakens that sense of missionary responsibility which is essential to apostolicity. These are the dangers of the Separatist ecclesiology. To place a disproportionate emphasis on one of the four credal notes of the Church has always endangered one or more of the others, and our study has revealed instances in which such over-emphasis has led to disaster. It is not being suggested that all churchmen of the Separatist type have succumbed to this danger. Mention of the name of the Baptist William Carey (1761–1834), often described as the father of modern Protestant missions, and of the role that many modern heirs of the sixteenth-century sectarians play in the ecumenical movement, is sufficient to refute any such insinuation.

13

Anglican Doctrine of
the Church

The Reformation took a different turn in England, despite the influence of Continental reformers like Martin Bucer and Peter Martyr
Vermigli, an Italian who was invited to England by Archbishop
Cranmer in the closing years of Henry VIII's reign. Its course ran
from its beginnings in the reign of the tyrannical but conservatively
Catholic Henry VIII (1509–47), through radical changes in a Protestant direction under the Protector Somerset in the short reign of the
boy king Edward VI (1547–53), reaction under Mary (1553–8), so
fanatically, if understandably, determined to restore papal authority,
and the long reign of Elizabeth I (1558–1603) who, with her
ecclesiastical and temporal advisers, attempted to unify the nation on
the basis of a moderate reformation of the Church. In this she met
with a large measure of success in the face both of numerous supporters of the papacy who received much help and encouragement
from Rome, France, and Spain, and of many who looked for a reformation closer to the Swiss pattern.

The Church in England, passing through this experience, and in the
seventeenth century through the struggle between episcopalians and
Puritans which came to its climax in the reign of Charles I (1625–49),
and through a period of radical remodelling on Puritan lines during
the Protectorate of Oliver Cromwell (1653–8) emerged after the
restoration of the monarchy in 1660 as a reformed Church unlike any
other in Europe, with the possible exception of Sweden. The Act of
Supremacy bound it to a recognition of the monarch as Supreme
Governor of the Church in England.[1] The Act of Uniformity of 1662
(succeeding those of 1549, 1552, and 1559) bound it to a Prayer Book
which was an attempt 'to mould the best of the old with the best of the
new',[2] and which its admirers claim 'as a ripe fruit of the Christian
centuries, bearing within itself the loveliness of a reformed and
Catholic devotion'.[3] Subscription to the Thirty-nine Articles of

Religion, which received their final form in 1571, was required of the clergy. While these Articles endorsed the main doctrinal emphases of the Reformation[4] they also maintained that the Nicene, Athanasian, and Apostles' creeds, long accepted by the Church in the West as authoritative, 'ought thoroughly to be received and believed' (Article VIII). The Church retained the threefold ministry of bishop, priest, and deacon in continuity with the medieval Church,[5] and the preface to its Ordinal declared the intention that these orders should be 'continued, and reverently used and esteemed'.

Our concern, however, is with the Anglican doctrine of the Church. English churchmen of the late sixteenth century and the seventeenth wrote a great deal on the subject,[6] and here I shall note the main trends of Anglican ecclesiology and illustrate them from the most prominent of these writers and from Anglican formularies.

THE CHURCH VISIBLE AND INVISIBLE

We have seen that the Reformers developed the idea of the invisible Church against the Roman claim that the visible hierarchical Church centred upon the papacy is the true Church. Anglican writers devoted much space to the meanings and relationships of such terms as 'invisible Church', 'the elect', 'body of Christ', 'mystical body of Christ', and 'visible Church'. H. F. Woodhouse's discussion shows that there is no unanimity among them on these matters, and that even in a single writer different answers seem to be given. He illustrates this from Richard Hooker (c. 1554–1600).

Hooker in a number of places clearly identifies the mystical body of Christ with the invisible Church whose members are known to God only.[7] It consists of 'none but only true Israelites, true sons of Abraham, true servants and saints of God'.[8] Hooker also speaks of the visible Church as having Christ for its Head, and as being a body.[9] Thirdly we find him using the phrase 'visible mystical body' in reference to the Church at worship:

> This holy and religious duty of service towards God concerneth us one way in that we are men, and another way in that we are joined as parts to that visible mystical body which is the Church.[10]

Woodhouse briefly discusses[11] whether Hooker is making a triple distinction: visible body, mystical body (invisible), and visible mystical body. He concludes that his distinction is basically between the visible Church and the mystical body. It is not a distinction between false and true, for the visible Church includes faithful and true Christians, although who these are none 'can pronounce, saving only the searcher of all men's hearts, who alone intuitively doth know in this kind who are His'.[12] This may well be the correct elucidation of Hooker's meaning. Woodhouse admits, however, that 'Hooker's qualifications and thought are not fully satisfactory'.[13] This is true, for Hooker gives the term 'mystical body' a meaning which it did not have prior to Wyclif; and since he identifies the mystical body with the invisible Church, his introduction of the phrase 'visible mystical body' can only be confusing.

It is not to be concluded that Hooker had no interest in the visible Church. The very title of *The Laws of Ecclesiastical Polity* proclaims his concern for the Church as an organized society, and of this, its membership, extension, divisions, ministry, sacraments, and life he has many wise things to say.

Richard Field (1561–1616) in his treatise *Of the Church* (1606) provides a clearer discussion in a passage where he seems to follow Calvin's reminder that Scripture speaks of the Church in two ways.[14] He maintains that it is more accurate to speak of different aspects of the one Church than of two churches, one visible and the other invisible:

> We say that there is a visible and invisible Church, not meaning to make two distinct Churches, as our adversaries falsely and maliciously charge us, though the form of words may serve to insinuate some such thing, but to distinguish the divers considerations of the same Church; which though it be visible in respect of the profession of supernatural verities revealed in Christ, use of holy Sacraments, order of Ministry, and due obedience yielded thereunto, and they discernible that do communicate therein; yet in respect of those most precious effects, and happy benefits of saving grace, wherein only the elect do communicate, it is invisible; and they that in so happy, gracious, and desirable things have communion among themselves are not discernible from others to whom this fellowship is denied, but are known only unto God. That Nathaniel was an Israelite all men knew; that he was 'a true Israelite, in whom was no guile', only Christ knew (*Of the Church* I, x).[15]

In the discussion which follows the above extract it is clear that Field firmly believes in the necessity of the Church visible and in its divine foundation. It is the locus within which men 'profess the saving truth of God, which all are bound to do that look for salvation'. He defends Luther and other early Reformers against the charge of denying the validity of the idea of the visible Church. They had, however, held (and Field agrees) that there were periods when 'errors and heresies so much prevail ... that the sincerity of religion is upholden and the truth of the profession of Christians defended and maintained but only by some few, and they molested, persecuted, and traduced, as ... enemies to the common peace of the Christian world'. This had been the case in the time of Athanasius, at the height of Arian ascendancy. They had believed also, though Field does not here mention it, that this point had been reached in the later medieval Church. But the great Reformers, and Anglican theologians like Field, did not believe that the Church visible had ceased to exist.[16] It was not the creation of a new Church for which they worked, but for the Church's reformation. Field goes on to say that Robert Bellarmine, the contemporary Roman Catholic apologist,[17] was wasting his time in 'proving that there is, and always hath been a visible Church', for this is not denied by Anglican theologians, although some hold that there have been times in its history when few have been faithful to the truth of God. Field concludes this discussion by declaring that 'touching the visibility and invisibility of the Church' one should say that 'the same Church is at the same time both visible and invisible in divers respects'.

THE VISIBLE CHURCH

A certain preoccupation with the question of the Church invisible, then, does not signify that Anglican theologians lacked interest in the Church visible. They use the Pauline concept of the body, and insist that Christ is its only Head, governing it and imparting to it life and order through the Holy Spirit, in contexts which leave no doubt that they are speaking of the visible Church. They are concerned with questions of the ministry, the preaching of the gospel, the administration of the sacraments, and discipline. Those of the Thirty-nine Articles which deal with the Church speak only of the visible Church. While the doctrine of predestination and election is set out in Article XVII, no attempt is made to link it with ecclesiology by means of a doctrine of the invisible Church.[18]

The articles, or paragraphs of articles, which speak of the Church are set out here, with some comments:

Article XIX, *Of the Church*:

The visible Church of Christ is a congregation of faithful men, in the which the pure Word of God is preached, and the sacraments be duly administered according to Christ's ordinance in all those things that of necessity are requisite to the same.

As the Church of *Jerusalem, Alexandria* and *Antioch* have erred, so also the Church of *Rome* hath erred, not only in their living and manner of Ceremonies, but also in matters of Faith.

It is noteworthy that, although the article is entitled *Of the Church*, its first words are 'The visible Church of Christ. . . .' To be noted also is the closeness of the definition in the first paragraph to that of the Lutheran Augsburg Confession.[19] The four churches mentioned in the second paragraph are the patriarchates of the early Church before the rise of Constantinople in the fourth century. There is no suggestion here that because of their errors they ceased to belong to the Church of Christ.

Article xx, *Of the Authority of the Church*, illustrates Anglican insistence on holy Scripture as the criterion in doctrine and forms of worship:

The Church hath power to decree Rites or Ceremonies, and authority in Controversies of Faith: And yet it is not lawful for the Church to ordain anything that is contrary to God's Word written ... besides the same ought it not to enforce anything to be believed for necessity of Salvation.

Article xxi, *Of the Authority of General Councils*, in declaring that 'General Councils may not be gathered together without the commandment and will of Princes' says something that was thoroughly understood and generally accepted in the Reformed churches of sixteenth-century Europe, but is not likely to be considered relevant in the twentieth. The article declares that general councils can err, and that their decisions on matters of faith are not binding unless it is clear that they are 'taken out of holy Scripture'.

Article xxiii, *Of Ministering in the Congregation*, rejects the radical claim that any man may preach and administer the sacraments. Only those may do so who are 'lawfully called, and sent ... by men who have public authority given unto them in the Congregation, to call and send Ministers into the Lord's vineyard'. Standing by itself, this might seem to legislate for the congregational type of church order advocated by the Separatists. But it must be read in conjunction with Article xxxvi (below, p. 186).

Article xxvi, *Of the Unworthiness of the Ministers, which hinders not the effect of the Sacrament*, is adequately summarized by its title.

It affirms that principle which was established at the Council of Arles in 314,[20] and was also to be affirmed in other Reformed doctrinal statements.[21] That this implies no condonation of wickedness in a minister is shown by the provision in the Article's second paragraph:

> that inquiry be made of evil Ministers, and that they be accused by those who have knowledge of their offences; and finally being found guilty, by just judgement be deposed.

Article xxxiv, *Of the Traditions of the Church*:

> It is not necessary that Traditions and Ceremonies be in all places one, and utterly like. ... Whosoever through his private judgement, willingly and purposely, doth openly break the traditions and ceremonies of the Church, which be not repugnant to the Word of God, and be ordained and approved by common authority, ought to be rebuked openly. ...
>
> Every particular or national Church hath authority to ordain, change, and abolish ceremonies or rites of the Church, ordained only by man's authority, so that all things be done to edifying.

The first paragraph is aimed at the English Puritans who held that nothing should be permitted in the worship and life of the Church which was not specifically commended in the Scriptures. The wording 'not repugnant to the Word of God' is, therefore, carefully chosen. The Puritans objected in particular to the use of the ring in marriage and to the sign of the cross in baptism.

The second paragraph anticipates the rejection in Article xxxvii of papal jurisdiction in England.

Article xxxvi, *Of Consecration of Bishops and Ministers*, affirms the adequacy of the Anglican Ordinal, first published in the reign of Edward VI, which provides forms for the consecration of bishops, the ordering of priests, and the making of deacons.[22] The preface of the Ordinal, as previously mentioned, declares the intention of the Church of England to continue the orders of bishop, priest, and deacon and to permit no one who has not had episcopal ordination to exercise ministerial functions in the Church. References to ministers elsewhere in the Thirty-nine Articles (e.g. xxiii) must, therefore, be interpreted in accordance with Article xxxvi.

The ministry of the Church of England is that of bishops, priests, and deacons. Nothing is said in the articles, or in the Ordinal, of a doctrine of apostolic succession, nor is it anywhere implied that churches which do not possess this threefold ministry have forfeited the name of Church.[23]

Article xxxvii, *Of the Civil Magistrates*:

> The King's Majesty hath the chief power in this Realm of England, and other his Dominions, unto whom the Chief Government of all Estates of this Realm, whether they be Ecclesiastical or Civil, in all causes doth appertain, and is not, nor ought to be, subject to any foreign jurisdiction.

Consequently in its third paragraph the Article states: 'The Bishop of Rome hath no jurisdiction in this Realm of England.' The second paragraph defines what is, and what is not, meant by the attribution to the monarch of the title of Supreme Governor in the Acts of Supremacy:

> We give not to our Princes the ministering either of God's Word, or of the Sacraments ... but that only prerogative, which we see to have been given always to godly Princes in holy Scriptures by God himself; that is, that they should rule all estates and degrees committed to their charge by God, whether they be Ecclesiastical or Temporal, and restrain with the civil sword the stubborn and evil-doers.

Dr Erik Routley notes[24] that this Article says nothing about the appointment of bishops by the Crown or parliamentary and royal assent to changes in the Book of Common Prayer: 'That all belongs to the British Constitution. . . . It is not stated in the Articles.' The Erastianism of these practices is greatly lessened by the consultation which now takes place regarding the appointment of bishops, and by powers now given to the Synod of the Church of England in the matter of forms of worship. The national churches and provinces of the Anglican Communion outside the established Church of England have autonomy in these matters.

Dr Routley, a Congregationalist, looks at the Thirty-nine Articles with mingled admiration and exasperation. He finds the articles on the Church to be indefinite and even evasive. Elements from different ecclesiologies are to be found: Catholic, in the implicit acceptance (Article viii) of the credal descriptions of the Church, and the continuance of the orders of bishop, priest, and deacon (Article xxxvi); Lutheran, in the dependence of Article xix on the Augsburg Confession; Calvinistic, in the use of the word 'visible' in Article xix, and in what is said about the authority and obligations of magistrates in Article xxxvii. He finds that 'without the other half of the Calvinist statement (concerning the Church invisible) Article xix is so vague as to include any doctrine whatever, since all depends on what is a congregation of faithful men and what, in the administration of Word and Sacrament, is deemed right'.[25]

On the other hand he writes:[26] 'It is the distinguishing quality of this document that alone of the sixteenth-century Confessions it seeks to accommodate diverse views rather than to separate its own from those of other bodies.' It may not have been remarkably successful in this, but the attempt had merit. In the ecumenical climate of the twentieth century it is being recognized that points of doctrine which sharply divided Christians 400 years ago are capable of a reconciliation which can enrich and strengthen the Church today, and that Catholic and Protestant have each preserved true insights which the other could not, or would not, recognize in a time of bitter conflict. This may be true of the doctrine of the Church.

THE BOOK OF COMMON PRAYER

Anglican thought and practice has been formed by the Book of Common Prayer at least as much as by the Thirty-nine Articles. In the Anglican Communion of autonomous churches and provinces which developed during the nineteenth and twentieth centuries, the Prayer Book of 1662, although revised by synodical action in many of them, is still regarded as a primary source of Anglican theology.

The book does not include any formal setting-out of a doctrine of the Church. It is to be noted, however, that the recital of one of the ancient creeds which contains the expression of belief in the Church under the marks of unity, holiness, catholicity, and apostolicity is prescribed at the principal acts of corporate worship. The Apostles' Creed is also made one of the bases of catechetical instruction.

Several of the collects prescribed for Sundays and festivals speak explicitly of the Church, and many more do so by implication. Biblical images are used: the household of God (Epiphany v and Trinity xxii), the body (Good Friday), and the temple (St Simon and St Jude). The Church is not a society contrived by men: it is God who built it 'upon the foundation of the Apostles and Prophets, Jesus Christ himself being the head corner-stone' (St Simon and St Jude); it is governed and sanctified by the Spirit of God (Good Friday); its various orders of ministry have been given by God (Ember Days). Several collects make clear that the historical, visible Church is in mind, and that this is 'a mixed society': it needs to pray that God will continually keep it in his true religion (Epiphany v); it acknowledges that the frailty of its members needs God's perpetual mercy (Trinity xv); it needs God's cleansing and defence (Trinity xvi and xxii); it is aware that its ministers may not always be faithful and true (St Matthias); it recognizes the need always to be nourished by the doctrine taught by the apostles and evangelists (collects for St John the Evangelist, St Mark, St Bartholomew, St Simon and St Jude).

There is one collect which introduces the idea of the Church as a society which extends beyond the empirical. The opening words of the collect for All Saints' Day are:

> O Almighty God, who hast knit together thine elect in one communion and fellowship, in the mystical body of thy Son Christ our Lord. ...

Is this to identify the mystical body of Christ with the invisible Church of the elect as Wyclif had done,[27] and as Hooker seems to do?[28] The sentence is not necessarily to be so interpreted. It certainly implies that the elect are members of Christ's mystical body, but not that all members of the mystical body are elect. Nothing here precludes the interpretation of the term 'mystical body' in its original sense of those who by Christian initiation have become members of Christ. The collect teaches that the saints of the past are still members of the Church, and that the faithful of every generation in following and holding them for an example are in the same fellowship with them:

> ... Grant us grace so to follow thy blessed saints in all virtuous and godly living, that we may come to those unspeakable joys, which thou hast prepared for them that unfeignedly love thee.

The phrase 'mystical body' occurs also in the prayer of thanksgiving after the communion in the Order for the Administration of the Lord's Supper:

> ... we most heartily thank thee ... that we are living members of his mystical body, which is the blessed company of all faithful people; and are also heirs through hope of thy everlasting kingdom. ...

Here the mystical body clearly includes the visible, worshipping community in which there are many who still need to pray:

> ... although we are unworthy, yet we beseech thee to accept this our bounden duty and service, not weighing our merits, but pardoning our offences; through Jesus Christ our Lord.

JOHN PEARSON ON THE CHURCH

One of the most influential Anglican theological works in the seventeenth century was *An Exposition of the Creed* by John Pearson (1612–86), Bishop of Chester. This commentary on the Apostles' Creed was published in 1659, had four further editions during Pearson's lifetime, and has been frequently reprinted. The section on the Church[29] deserves special notice here for its evidence of biblical and patristic scholarship, and because of its long continuing influence on Anglican theology.

He begins by stating that the Church is a society of 'the sons of men'. The Scriptures do not mention angels as members of the Church, nor can angels be said to be 'built upon the foundation of the apostles and prophets' (Eph. 2.20). He also excludes from his notion of the Church the people of Israel as such. He holds that all those who 'from the beginning pleased God' are saved through Christ; but because the catholicity of the Church 'must be understood in opposition to the legal singularity of the Jewish nation', the notion of the Church must be restricted to Christianity. Jesus spoke in the future tense to Peter: 'I will build my Church.' The Church, then, came into being at Pentecost by the gift of the Holy Spirit. Its first members were the apostles and other disciples of Jesus, about 120 in all, to whom were added those who were baptized in response to Peter's preaching, and who 'devoted themselves to the apostles' teaching and fellowship, to the breaking of bread and the prayers' (Acts 2.42).

THE UNITY OF THE CHURCH

This church in Jerusalem was one. Yet its members soon became members of several churches. How then can we speak of one Church? There follows an acute discussion of the N.T. use of the word *ekklesia* sometimes in the singular and sometimes in the plural. He finds that although there were several congregations or churches at Corinth (he cites 1 Cor. 14.34), Paul addresses his letter to 'the Church of God which is at Corinth'. A group of churches is properly spoken of as one Church because they are under one ruler or bishop. Similarly all churches in all cities and nations may be said to be one Church because all are under one supreme Governor, Jesus Christ, the bishop of our souls.

The unity of the churches in the one Church is sixfold. It is a unity of *origination* because Christ is their one foundation; of *faith* because they hold the doctrines taught by the apostles who received them from Christ; of the *sacraments* because they all acknowledge and receive baptism and the Lord's Supper; of *hope* because all are called, and this calling is in the hope of righteousness and eternal life, which are God's promises to those he calls; of *charity* because all 'endeavour to keep the unity of the spirit in the bond of peace' and heed Christ's words, 'by this shall all men know that ye are my disciples, if ye have love one to another'; and of *government and discipline* because they are united in having the same pastoral guides, appointed of God under the direction of the Spirit, to lead them in the same way of eternal salvation. 'As therefore there is no Church where there is no order, no ministry, so where the same order and ministry is there is the same Church.' By these six marks of unity 'millions of persons and multitudes of congregations are united into one body, and become one Church'.

THE CHURCH'S INDEFECTIBILITY

Pearson now asks whether this Church, which has had a continuous existence from the apostles to the present, will continue to the end of the world. In itself 'the Church is not of such a nature as would necessarily, once begun, preserve itself for ever'. Thousands have fallen away from it, and particular churches have disappeared. If this is possible of particular churches it is possible also of the universal Church. Nevertheless, the answer to the question is affirmative because, and only because, of the promises of God in Christ: 'The gates of hell shall not prevail against it'; 'lo, I am with you alway, even to the end of the world'.

THE CHURCH'S HOLINESS

The Church may properly be described as holy in several respects. Its members are called to holiness; the offices appointed and the powers exercised in the Church are holy 'by their institution and operation'; its members profess the holy name of Christ and are committed to holiness of life; God's purpose was to communicate sanctity through the Church so that men might become a 'holy and a precious people'.

But the unblemished holiness of which Paul speaks in Ephesians 5.21 ff clearly does not belong to the Church taken in the wide sense of all those who have been called and baptized. We have, then, to ask where, 'within the great complex body of the universal Church', may be found the Church to which this perfect holiness belongs. Pearson's answer is that it is beyond death. The Church of those who continue in this life is a mixed society of good and bad, as is taught in the parable of the wheat and tares and in similar parables.

> I conclude, therefore, as the ancient Catholics did against the Donatists, that within the Church, in the public profession and external communion thereof, are contained persons truly good and sanctified, and hereafter saved, and together with them other persons void of all saving grace, and hereafter to be damned; and that Church containing these of both kinds may well be called *holy*, as St Matthew called Jerusalem *the holy city* ... when we know there was in that city a general corruption in manners and worship.

The hypocrites and profane who have communicated with the rest of the Church while they lived are

> by death separated from the external communion of the Church, and having no true internal communion with the members and the head thereof, are totally and finally cut off from the Church of Christ.

Pearson, then, does not accept a distinction between the Church visible and invisible in any such way as to suggest that Christ founded two churches:

> Not that there are two Churches of Christ, one, in which good and bad are mingled together, another, in which there are good alone ... but one and the same Church, in relation to different times, admitteth or not admitteth the permixtion of the wicked, or the imperfection of the holy. ... The same Church is really holy in this world in relation to all godly persons contained in it, by a real infused sanctity; the same is farther yet at the same time perfectly holy in reference to the saints departed and admitted to the presence of God; and the same Church shall hereafter be more completely holy in the world to come, when all the members actually belonging to it shall be at once perfected in holiness and completed in happiness.

THE CHURCH'S CATHOLICITY

Pearson notes that the word 'catholic' is not scriptural, but came into early use among patristic writers. He discusses its various secular and ecclesiastical usages: a title for the emperor's chief revenue officer; to describe those epistles which are addressed to the Church in general; a title for Christian patriarchs. Most frequently, however, it was used for the Church as a whole. Its signification when so used is fourfold. First, it refers to the diffusiveness or extent of the Church as it fulfils

its commission to 'teach all nations'. Second, it refers to the whole-
ness of the Church's doctrine: it teaches all things 'necessary for a
Christian to know'. Third, it refers to the universal obedience which
the Church requires from all persons of all conditions to all the
precepts of the gospel. Finally, the Church is catholic because God
has provided in it all the necessary graces whereby men may become
perfect in Jesus Christ.[30]

NO SALVATION OUTSIDE THE CHURCH

Pearson holds as strongly as did Cyprian and Augustine that

> Christ hath appointed [the Church] as the only way unto eternal life. We
> read at the first, that 'the Lord added to them daily such as should be
> saved'; and what was then daily done hath been done since continually.
> Christ never appointed two ways to Heaven, nor did He build a Church to
> save some, and make another institution for other men's salvation.

Although the ark of Noah contained both good and bad, one had to
be in it to be saved from the flood. Pearson presents the doctrine of
extra ecclesiam nulla salus in all its starkness, showing no awareness
of any problem for theodicy in supposing that millions who have had
no opportunity of becoming members of the Church are damned.
'None shall ever escape the eternal wrath of God, which belong not to
the Church of God.' He therefore stresses the great danger of in-
curring excommunication and of falling into heresy or schism. Nor
must there be any complacent reliance on merely formal church
membership. The means of grace must not be neglected: 'It is
necessary that the persons abiding in the communion of (the Church)
should be really and effectually sanctified.'

THE CONTINUITY OF THE CHURCH

Pearson concludes this section of his book by maintaining that there
are no new Churches:

> (Since) the Church which is truly Catholic containeth within it all which
> are truly Churches, whosoever is not of the Catholic Church cannot be of
> the true Church. That Church alone which first began at Jerusalem on
> earth will bring us to the Jerusalem in Heaven; and that alone began there
> which always embraceth the 'faith once delivered to the saints'. What-
> soever Church pretendeth to a new beginning pretendeth at the same time

to a new Churchdom, and whatsoever is so new is none, so necessary it is to believe 'the Holy Catholic Church'.

Implicit here is the Anglican rejection of the suggestion that it is a new Church, founded in the sixteenth century.

14

Catholic Reformation and
Protestant Confessions

The Church of Rome's response to the reforming movement was a vigorous introduction of reforms which many of its adherents recognized to be necessary. Much was achieved in the areas of discipline, education, and pastoral care as a result both of a renewed devotion on the part of the clergy and the rise of new Orders founded by saintly men and guided by wise superiors. The most important of these were the Society of Jesus (Jesuits), founded by Ignatius Loyola and sanctioned in 1540, and the Congregation of the Oratory, founded by Philip Neri and sanctioned in 1575. This response is known as the Counter-Reformation,[1] and under this heading Church-history textbooks usually discuss the Council of Trent.

THE COUNCIL OF TRENT

The Emperor Charles V had long demanded a council which he hoped would address itself to the reform of the Church. Popes, while not refusing the demand outright, spoke much of the difficulties in the way, but at length a Council was summoned by Pope Paul III. It held twenty-five sessions between 1545 and 1563, at Trent (1547–9), at Bologna (1551–2), and again at Trent (1562–3) under Pius IV. An early decision that voting should be by individual bishops and not by nations ensured that the results of the Council would be conservative, since Italian pro-papal bishops far outnumbered those of any other nation. The Council examined many of the major theological issues raised by the Reformers. Much time was spent on the authority of the Scriptures, justification, predestination, and the theology of the sacraments, and the Reformers' views on these subjects were firmly rejected. In the areas of discipline and practice, however, the Council tacitly admitted the validity of many of the Reformers' protests. The

Council's 'Decrees of Reformation' called for significant reforms, among them a greater control over monasteries by diocesan bishops, stricter regulations for the issuing of indulgences, and provisions for raising the standards of holiness, learning, and competence of the clergy.

Our concern, however, is whether the Council contributes to the discussion of the nature of the Church. Since Article VII of the Augsburg Confession[2] had offered a definition of the Church, the Council might have been expected to formulate canons on this subject. Yet nowhere do we find any formal treatment of the doctrine of the Church. Yves Congar[3] opens a brief discussion of the Council with the words: 'Strange fact: this Council which had to give an answer to the Reformation did not deal with the ecclesiological problem.' Nor did it deal with the currently controversial topic of the papacy.[4]

Nevertheless, throughout the documents of the Council the papal and hierarchical conception of the Church is assumed. In the 'Bull of Indiction' which prefaces the decrees, Pope Paul III speaks of himself as one who has 'been called to guide and govern the bark of Peter'[5] in the troubles of the time and as exercising on earth the authority of the apostles Peter and Paul.[6] He does not fail to remind the archbishops, bishops, abbots, and all others who have the privilege of sitting in a general council, of the oath which they have taken 'to us and to this Holy See'.[7] At the close of the Council the decrees and canons were submitted for the confirmation of 'the most blessed Roman Pontiff'.[8] The hierarchical nature of the Church is asserted to be of divine ordinance in a canon which anathematizes whoever says 'that in the Catholic Church there is not a hierarchy instituted by divine ordination, consisting of bishops, priests, and ministers (deacons)'.[9]

THE CATECHISM OF THE COUNCIL OF TRENT

At the conclusion of the Council certain matters in connection with the implementation of its decrees were entrusted to the pope. Among these was the compilation of a catechism. Charles Borromeo was largely responsible for its drafting, and after revision by a committee it was published in 1566 by Pope Pius V. It is not strictly a catechism, but a theological exposition of the Apostles' Creed, the seven sacraments, the ten commandments, and prayer, intended for the edification of the clergy and for their use in preaching and teaching.

Part I, Chapter X deals with the credal article 'I believe the holy

Catholic Church' in twenty 'questions', and concludes with five questions on 'the Communion of Saints'. The questions treat in turn of the meaning of the word *ecclesia* (ii); other scriptural names and descriptions of the Church (iv); the distinction between the Church militant and the Church triumphant (v); the nature of the Church militant (vi–vii); what persons are excluded from it (viii); the use of the word 'church' for parts of the Church (ix); the Church's unity and the Roman pontiff as its visible head (x–xii); the Church as holy (xiii), catholic (xiv), and apostolic (xv); the inerrancy of the Church (xvi); the prefiguration of the Church in the O.T. (ark of Noah, city of Jerusalem) (xvii); why 'to believe the Church' is an article of faith (xviii–xix); the reason for the credal wording 'I believe the holy Catholic Church' (instead of 'I believe in . . .') (xx); the link between the articles on the Communion of Saints and the Church (xxi); communion in the fruit of the sacraments (xxii); co-operation in the body of the Church (xxiii); the use of graces for the common good (xxv).

The ecclesiology presented in this section of the catechism is traditional, and St Augustine is cited far more frequently than any other of the early Fathers. Here I shall mention points of particular interest.

1 The word ecclesia is defined in a way which most Reformers would have endorsed. It is noted that the N.T. ordinarily uses the word

> to designate the Christian commonwealth only, and the congregation of the faithful; that is, of those who were called by faith unto the light of truth and the knowledge of God. . . . 'The Church', says St Augustine, 'consists of the faithful, dispersed throughout the world' (part I, ch. x, q. ii).[10]

The Church differs from other societies of men in origin and end:

> [It rests] on the wisdom and counsel of God; for he called us by the inward inspiration of the Holy Ghost, who opens the hearts of men, and outwardly, through the labour and ministry of his pastors and preachers. . . . The Christian people are justly called a Church . . . because, despising earthly and mortal things, they pursue only things heavenly and eternal (q. iii).

That the Church is the body of Christ is noted in q. iv, but the concept of the Church as the mystical body is not developed. The nearest approach to such a development is in q. xxii where the communion of saints is interpreted as 'a communion of sacraments'. The sacraments 'unite us to God and render us partakers of him whose grace we receive'; and 'the word "communion" belongs in a more special manner to the Eucharist, which accomplishes this communion itself'. But in q. xxiii the body image, following 1 Cor. 12.14 ff, is used quite pragmatically to illustrate the contributions which each member of the Church makes to the health and welfare of the whole.

2   The Church triumphant and the Church militant. No reference is made to the doctrine of the invisible Church. The distinction which the catechism dwells on is that between the Church triumphant and the Church militant:[11.]

> The Church triumphant is the most glorious and happy assemblage of blessed spirits, and of those who have triumphed over the world, the flesh, and the devil, and who, now free and secure from the troubles of this life, enjoy everlasting bliss. But the Church militant is the society of all the faithful who still dwell on earth, and is called militant, because it wages eternal war with those most implacable enemies, the world, the flesh, and the devil (q. v).

They are not, however, two churches, but constituent parts of the one Church. The Church militant consists of both good and bad. The good 'are linked together not only by profession of the same faith, and the communion of the same sacraments, but also by the spirit of grace, and the bond of charity' (q. vi). None can know with certainty who belongs to this class. There then follows the sentence:

> Of this part of the Church, therefore, we are not to suppose Christ our Saviour to speak when he refers us to the Church, and commands us to obey her (Matt. 18.17); for, unknown as is that portion of the Church, how can anyone be certain to whose decision he should recur, whose authority obey? (q. vi).

Where, then, can authority within the Church be identified? The answer is not provided until q. ix in which we are told that Matthew 18.17 refers to the Church in the sense of 'the prelates and pastors', that is, 'the authorities of the Church'. Q. xi moreover makes plain that ultimate authority in the Church militant is exercised by the Roman pontiff.

The bad members of the Church are likened to the chaff which is mingled with the grain on the threshing-floor, and to 'dead members' which 'sometimes remain attached to a (living) body' (q. vii). Being still in the Church they may yet be 'assisted in recovering lost grace and life' by the faithful, and they 'enjoy those fruits which are ... denied to such as are utterly cut off from the Church' (q. xxiv). What these fruits are is not explained.

Three groups are excluded from the Church: unbelievers, who have never belonged to it; heretics and schismatics, who have quitted it, though these are still under the Church's power (*potestas*) and 'may be cited before her tribunal, punished and condemned by anathema'; and the excommunicated, who are excluded 'until they repent'.

> With regard to the rest, although shameful and wicked persons, there is no doubt that they still continue in the Church; and of this the faithful are frequently to be informed, in order that they may convince themselves, that, even were the lives of her ministers debased perchance by crime, they are still included within her pale, nor do they on that account lose any part of their power (*potestas*).[12]

3 The unity of the Church and the papacy. Papal primacy is discussed under the heading of the Church's unity.

> This Church has ... one ruler and one governor, the invisible one, Christ, whom the eternal Father 'hath made head over all the Church, which is his body' (Eph. 1.22); but the visible one is he, who, the legitimate successor of Peter, the Prince of the Apostles, occupies the See of Rome (q. x).

In q. xi the visible headship of the pope is supported by quotations from Jerome, Irenaeus, Cyprian, Optatus, Basil, and Ambrose.[13] No historical or theological arguments are adduced to support the claim of the bishop of Rome to be the legitimate successor of Peter, or to have universal jurisdiction over the Church. There is simply the assertion that

> as a visible Church requires a visible head, our Saviour appointed Peter head and pastor of all the faithful, when, in the most ample terms, he committed to his care the feeding of his sheep, so as that he wished his successor to have the very same power of ruling and governing the whole Church (q. xi).

There is no allusion to the temporal claims of the papacy.

4 Holiness. The Church is holy, even though it contains sinners, because, like the things called holy in the Scriptures (vessels, vestments, altars, the firstborn), it is dedicated to God. Similarly St

Paul calls the Corinthian Christians, grievous sinners though some of them were, 'sanctified and holy'. The Church is also holy because it is united to Christ, 'the fountain of all holiness'. Moreover,

> the Church alone has the legitimate worship of sacrifice, and the salutary use of the sacraments, by which, as by the efficacious instruments of divine grace, God effects true holiness, so that whosoever are really holy cannot be outside the Church (q. xiii).

5 Catholicity. The Church is catholic or universal because it is limited neither by territorial frontier, race, class, or sex, nor by time. All the faithful who have lived from the time of Adam and who shall live as long as the world exists are included.

> She is also called universal because, like those who entered the ark, lest they should perish in the flood, all who desire to attain eternal salvation must cling to and embrace her (q. xiv).

This last somewhat forced simile does not seem to illustrate very aptly the Church's catholicity.

6 Apostolicity. The true Church is to be recognized by its derivation from the apostles. Its doctrines are those which the apostles handed down. Moreover,

> the Holy Ghost, who presides over the Church, governs her by no other than apostolic ministers; and this Spirit was first imparted to the apostles, and has, by the supreme goodness of God, always remained in the Church (q. xv).

The apostolic succession is seen here as a tradition of doctrine, and a succession in ministry by the reception of the Holy Spirit.[14]

7 The Church's inerrancy.

> As this one Church, seeing it is governed by the Holy Ghost, cannot err in delivering the discipline of faith and morals, so all other societies which arrogate to themselves the name of Church, because guided by the spirit of the devil, are necessarily sunk in the most pernicious errors both of doctrine and morals (q. xvi).

8 The Church as an article of faith. Since the existence of the Church is a fact not doubted by any, why does the creed speak of the Church as an object of faith? The answer is that

> it is by the light of faith only, and not by any process of reasoning, that

the mind can comprehend those mysteries, which ... are contained in the holy Church of God ... the origin, privileges, and dignity of the Church (q. xviii).

The Church was not created by man, but by God. Its powers come not from man, but by a divine gift. Therefore

> by faith alone can we understand that with the Church are deposited the keys of the kingdom of heaven; that to her has been confided the power of remitting sins; of excommunicating; and of consecrating the real body of Christ; and that her children have not here a permanent dwelling, but look for one to come (q. xix).

9   The meaning of 'I believe the Church'. The catechism notices that whereas the clauses of the creed which speak of the three divine Persons are introduced by *Credo in* (I believe in), this clause begins simply with *Credo* (I believe the Church). The reason is

> that by this difference ... we may distinguish God, the author of all things, from the things he has created, and acknowledge ourselves indebted to the divine goodness for all those exalted benefits, which have been conferred on the Church (q. xx).

10   The communion of saints. This clause is said to provide an interpretation of the preceding article on the Church and to declare also 'what ought to be the use of the mysteries which are contained in the Creed':

> For all our researches and knowledge ought to be directed to one end, viz., to our admission into this so august and so blessed a society of the saints, and our most steady perseverance therein (q. xxi).

The communion of saints consists in communion in the fruits of the sacraments and communion in charity. The sacraments are divine gifts in the benefits of which all share.[15]

> Fruit of all the sacraments appertains to all the faithful (q. xxii).

> But there is also another communion in the Church which demands our attention; for every pious and holy action undertaken by one appertains to all, and becomes profitable to all, through charity, which 'seeketh not her own' (q. xxiii).

That the communion of saints is essentially a communion in charity is shown by Christ who 'taught us to say *our*, not *my*, bread, and other similar petitions, not looking to ourselves alone, but also to the general interests and salvation of all'. Paul's treatment of the aid which the members of the human body render to each other for the advantage of the whole body[16] teaches the same lesson. Nevertheless, the hierarchical structure of the Church is emphasized:

> To each member of this Church is also assigned his own peculiar office; for as some are appointed apostles, some teachers, but all for the public benefit, so to some it belongs to govern and to teach, to others, to be subject and to obey (ibid.).

Particular gifts which the faithful may possess are given to them 'for the public benefit, for the building up of the Church ... the gift of healing ... for the sake of him who is sick'. All must be ready to relieve the misery of the needy. He who is well supplied with this world's goods 'and seeth his brother in want, and will not assist him, is at once convicted of not having "the love of God within him"' (q. xxv).

During succeeding centuries the Roman Catholic Church has authorized innumerable catechisms in all languages. On all of them the Catechism of the Council of Trent was a major influence until the appearance of the Dutch Catechism, authorized by the bishops of the Netherlands in 1966.[17]

ROBERT BELLARMINE (1542–1621)

In the post-Reformation period the Roman Catholic Church paid much attention to the defence of its position, and many of its theologians concentrated on apologetics or controversial theology. Peter Canisius (1521–97) and Thomas Stapleton (1535–98) were notable amongst these, but the most influential was Robert Bellarmine, an Italian Jesuit. He became engaged in controversy at Louvain where he was professor of theology, 1569–76. In 1576 he was appointed to the *Collegium Romanum* in Rome to teach a course in controversial theology which had just been introduced. Bellarmine possessed ideal qualities as a controversialist. He was reasonable, temperate, and fair. He was ready to recognize the strengths of the Reformed theology as well as to probe its weaknesses. In 1599 he was made a cardinal, and devoted his last years to writing on the spiritual life.

His best known work is *Disputations against the Heretics of the present time on the Controversies regarding the Christian Faith*,[18] usually referred to as the *Controversies*. It was based on his lectures at the *Collegium Romanum*, and was published during 1586–93.

THE VISIBILITY OF THE CHURCH

Bellarmine's ecclesiology is marked by an insistence on the visibility of the Church. He minimizes the idea of the Church as existing from Abel or Adam, thus differing from Turrecremata[19] and others before him. Though it may be said that the Church in some sense had a beginning in Adam, its true existence is derived from Christ who founded a society and placed his vicar at its head. The Church is

> the congregation of men bound by the profession of the same Christian faith and by communion in the same sacraments under the rule of lawful pastors, and especially of the only vicar of Christ on earth, the Roman pontiff (*Controversies* IV, iii.2).

He emphasizes the visibility of the Church in startling fashion when he writes:

> For one to be said to be part of the Church in some degree, I do not consider any interior virtue is required, but only an exterior profession of faith and participation in the sacraments, things which our sense perception can confirm. For the Church is a congregation of men which is as visible and palpable as are the assembly of the people of Rome, or the Kingdom of Gaul, or the republic of Venice (ibid. IV, iii.10).

Bellarmine is not here asserting that no more is required of Church members than a formal profession of faith and attendance at worship which may or may not be willing and sincere. He is speaking of the Church as it appears to those outside. A little later he speaks of the inward graces which are characteristic of the soul of the Church. He is, in fact, making the distinction which some schoolmen of the thirteenth century had made between membership *numero* and membership *merito*.[20] It may be, as Congar says,[21] that the distinction intended is between two ways in which men belong to the Church which is at once a spiritual and a visible body. But Congar admits that 'the way in which Bellarmine expressed himself long encouraged the idea of a distinction *within the Church itself* between a body made of what is visible therein, and a soul made of the interior elements of grace'.

THE PAPACY

Bellarmine strongly supported the papal supremacy. The pope

represents Christ as head of the body. He inherits the universal authority given by Christ to Peter. This authority is transmissible, whereas that given to the other apostles was delegated and not transmissible (III, v. 23). Hence, the authority which bishops possess in their dioceses is received from the pope (III, iv. 24).

The *Controversies* narrowly escaped being placed on the Index of prohibited books by Pope Sixtus V on the ground that it attributed to the pope only indirect temporal power:

> The pontiff, as pontiff, does not directly and immediately possess any temporal power, but only spiritual; nevertheless in a spiritual way he does indirectly possess a power, and that the highest, in temporal matters (III, v. 4).

This was considered to put an unjustifiable restriction on the papal powers, even though Bellarmine himself could derive from his doctrine the papal right to forbid the implementation of any laws which denied the Church's rights and to depose heretical monarchs. Sixtus V died before his proposed action against Bellarmine could be effected, and his successor dropped the matter.

REFORMED CONFESSIONS

The development of the doctrine of the Church in the Reformed Churches during the immediate post-Reformation period can best be illustrated from some of the Confessions and other documents of those Churches from the mid-sixteenth to the mid-seventeenth centuries.[22]

THE FRENCH CONFESSION OF FAITH (1559)

was issued by the first National Synod of the Reformed Church of France. It is largely the work of Calvin. Articles xxv to xxxII deal with the Church and its ministers.

> The true Church ... is the company of the faithful who agree to follow (God's) Word, and the pure religion which it teaches. ... Among the faithful there may be hypocrites and reprobates, but their wickedness cannot destroy the title of the Church (xxvII).[23]

The Church, properly speaking, only exists where the Word of God is received, and submitted to, and the sacraments are administered according to Christ's institution. Papal assemblies are condemned 'as the pure Word of God is banished from them, their sacraments are corrupted ... and all superstitions and idolatries are in them'. Those who take part in them are separated from the body of Christ. Yet 'some trace of the Church is left in the papacy' and the efficacy of baptism in the papal church is admitted: 'Those baptized in it do not need a second baptism' (XXVIII).

Pastors, overseers, and deacons are needed for teaching, for the correction of errors, and for the care of the poor (XXIX). God is not 'bound to such aid and subordinate means' but it has pleased him to provide the Church with this order. 'Visionaries' who would like to destroy the ministry are denounced (XXV). All pastors have the same authority and power under the 'one only sovereign and universal bishop, Jesus Christ' (XXX). Thus the principle of parity of ministers is asserted.

'No person should undertake to govern the Church upon his own authority.' This should be by election. When the times demand, God may 'raise men in an extraordinary manner to restore the Church', but this rule must always be binding: 'that all pastors, overseers, and deacons should have evidence of being called to their office' (XXXI).

THE SCOTTISH CONFESSION OF FAITH (1560)

This was chiefly the work of John Knox, and was ratified by the Scottish Parliament in 1567. Chapters V and XVI–XVIII deal with the Church.

Chapter V on 'The Continuance, Increase, and Preservation of the Kirk' presents a brief summary of O.T. history in order to show that 'God preserved, instructed, multiplied, honoured, adorned, and called from death to life His Kirk in all ages since Adam until the coming of Christ Jesus in the flesh'.[24]

There has always been one Kirk, and always will be to the end of the world. It is catholic 'because it contains the chosen of all ages, of all realms, nations, and tongues'. It is the communion of saints, who have 'one God, one Lord Jesus, one faith and one baptism'. Outside it 'there is neither life nor eternal felicity'. It is invisible, known only to God, and includes the elect who are departed (the Kirk triumphant), and the elect who yet live or shall live (XVI).

The true Kirk is characterized by the notes of the true preaching of the Word of God, the right administration of the sacraments, and 'ecclesiastical discipline uprightly ministered'. It is contrasted with 'the

horrible harlot, the false Kirk'. 'Neither antiquity, usurped title, lineal
succession, appointed place, nor the numbers of men approving an
error' are notes by which the spotless bride of Christ may be known.
By the Word of God is meant the Scriptures of both Testaments,
whose interpreter is the Holy Spirit (XVIII). These Scriptures are
received from God, and it is blasphemous to say that they are received
through the Kirk. The true Kirk is obedient to them and does not
claim to control them.

THE BELGIC CONFESSION OF FAITH (1561)

This was drawn up by Guido de Brès. It is an expansion of the French
Confession. It received the approval of Geneva, was endorsed by
several synods in the Low Countries and declared authoritative by the
Synod of Dort (1619), since when it has been the doctrinal standard of
the Reformed Churches in Holland and Belgium and of the Dutch
Reformed Church in America. Articles XXVII–XXXII deal with the
Church.

This Confession, like the Scottish, adds Church discipline to the
pure teaching of the gospel and the administration of the sacraments
among the marks of the Church. Those who are members of the
Church

> may be known by the marks of Christians, namely, by faith; and when
> they have received Jesus Christ the only Saviour, they avoid sin, follow
> after righteousness, love the true God and their neighbour. . . . But this is
> not to be understood as if there did not remain in them great infirmities;
> but they fight against them through the Spirit . . . continually, taking their
> refuge in the blood, death, passion, and obedience of our Lord Jesus
> Christ (XXIX).[25]

The 'false Church', by which is meant the Church of Rome,
'ascribes more power and authority to herself and her ordinances than
to the Word of God . . . [and] relieth more upon men than upon
Christ' (ibid.). Neither the Belgic nor the French Confession mentions
the doctrine of the invisible Church,[26] though both teach the doctrine
of predestination.

> There must be ministers or pastors to preach the Word of God, and to ad-
> minister the Sacraments; also elders and deacons, who together with the
> pastors, form the Council of the Church (XXX).

These should be chosen by election. Parity of ministers of the Word is
asserted (XXXI).

THE SECOND HELVETIC CONFESSION (1566)

The First Helvetiç Confession, drawn up at Basel in 1536, was an attempt to provide a document which could unify Lutherans and the Swiss Reformed Churches. It failed in this purpose, but did unite the German-speaking Swiss Reformed Churches. The much longer Second Helvetic Confession (1566), was based upon it and was composed by Johann Heinrich Bullinger who had contributed to the former document. It was adopted by all the Swiss Reformed Churches except Basel, and remained authoritative until the mid-nineteenth century. Chapter XVII treats 'Of the Catholic and Holy Church of God and of the One Only Head of the Church', and XVIII 'Of the Ministers of the Church, their Institution and Duties'.

> Because God from the beginning would have men to be saved ... (1 Tim. 2.4), it is altogether necessary that there always should have been, and should be now, and to the end of the world, a Church (XVII).[27]

The Church is 'an assembly of the faithful called or gathered out of the world'; a communion of all saints, who by faith share in the benefits offered through Christ. It is called catholic because it is not limited to times and places: 'Therefore we condemn the Donatists who confined the Church to I know not what corners of Africa. Nor do we approve of the Roman clergy who have recently passed off only the Roman Church as catholic.' The Church militant on earth and the Church triumphant are parts of the same Church, each in fellowship with the other. The former has always had many particular churches because of the diversity of its members. The Church militant has been set up differently at different times, for example by the patriarchs, by Moses, and by Christ through the gospel. The claim is made 'that now the ceremonies being abolished, the light shines unto us more clearly, and blessings are given to us more abundantly, and a fuller liberty'.

The Church cannot err, provided it rests on Christ 'and upon the foundation of the prophets and apostles'. Christ is the sole Head. It needs no vicar of Christ. Christ does not need a substitute as though he were absent. To the charge that the Reformation brought confusion, dissension, and schism, the answer is given that the Roman Church had experienced much contention and division. Such things were not unknown in the early Church. Yet God uses dissensions to illuminate the truth and to test and strengthen those who are in the right.

Earlier Confessions are followed very closely in treating of the notes of the Church, and the marks of membership.

The principle that 'outside the Church of God there is no salvation' is asserted, but the interesting discussion which follows under this heading indicates unwillingness to apply it in a rigoristic manner. It is implied that it would be better to say 'outside Christ there is no salvation':

> For as there was no salvation outside Noah's ark when the world perished in the flood, so we believe that there is no certain salvation outside Christ, who offers himself to be enjoyed by the elect in the Church; and hence we teach that those who wish to live ought not to be separated from the true Church of Christ.

It is noted that 'God had some friends outside the commonwealth of Israel'. Biblical instances are cited. Not all those who do not participate in the sacraments, whose faith sometimes fails, or who are subject to imperfections and errors, are outside the Church. This is why the Church 'may be termed invisible ... because, being hidden from our eyes and known only to God, it often secretly escapes human judgement':

> Hence we must be very careful not to judge before the time, nor undertake to exclude, reject, or cut off those whom the Lord does not want to have excluded or rejected, and those whom we cannot eliminate without loss to the Church. On the other hand, we must be vigilant lest, while the pious snore the wicked gain ground and do harm to the Church.

The Confession also recognizes that not all who are in the number of the Church are living and true members. There are some who outwardly hear the Word, receive the sacraments, seem to pray and to exercise charity: 'They are not of the Church, just as traitors in a state are numbered among its citizens before they are discovered.'

The unity of the Church is said to consist not in outward rites and ceremonies but in the truth of the Catholic faith which is given by holy Scripture and summarized in the Apostles' Creed. Within this Catholic faith both a diversity of rites and a freedom is possible which does not dissolve the Church's unity.

Chapter xviii deals at considerable length with the ministry. 'The office of ministers is a most ancient arrangement of God himself' for the establishing, governing, and preservation of the Church. Ministers in the N.T. were called apostles, prophets, evangelists, bishops (overseers), elders, pastors, and teachers. In the course of time many other names for ministers were introduced:

> Some were appointed patriarchs, others archbishops, others suffragans; also metropolitans, archdeacons, deacons, subdeacons, acolytes, exorcists, cantors, porters, and I know not what others, as cardinals, provosts, and priors; greater and lesser fathers, greater and lesser orders. But we are not troubled about all these. . . . For us the apostolic doctrine concerning ministers is sufficient.

The Confession speaks of bishops, defined as 'the overseers and watchmen of the Church who administer the food and needs of the life of the Church', elders, pastors, and teachers as being sufficient for the times.

Ministers must be called and elected by the Church or by those delegated by the Church. They must be ordained by the elders with the laying on of hands. Those who set themselves up as ministers are condemned.

Emphasis is placed on the ministers of the Church as servants. They are not priests. Christ is 'the only priest for ever, and lest we derogate anything from him, we do not impart the name of priest to any minister'. The N.T. indeed speaks of all believers as priests, but this is because they are able to offer spiritual sacrifices to God through Christ, and not in respect of any office. Ministers are servants of Christ and stewards of the mysteries of God, called to preach the gospel and administer the sacraments:

> The apostle wants us to think of ministers as ministers. Now the apostle calls them *hupēretas* (1 Cor. 4.1), rowers, who have their eyes fixed on the coxswain, and so men who do not live for themselves, or according to their own will, but for others—namely, their masters, upon whose command they altogether depend.

Ministers are equal in power and authority. Yet the scriptural practice is admitted by which

> some one of the ministers called the assembly together, proposed matters to be laid before it, gathered the opinions of the others, in short, to the best of man's ability took precaution lest any confusion should arise.

So St Peter acted, according to the Acts of the Apostles, but 'was not on that account preferred to the others, nor endowed with greater authority than the rest'. Jerome is quoted[28] as a witness that the distinction between bishops and elders is not scriptural. The drift of the passage, however, is that, while some may rightly be chosen in the Church for a role of leadership, this is to be interpreted in terms of service.

The ancient principle that the efficacy of the Word and sacraments is not dependent on the worthiness of ministers[29] is affirmed. Yet there must be proper discipline among ministers, and the synods of the Church must have authority to depose.

THE WESTMINSTER CONFESSION (1647)

During the Civil War in England the 'Long Parliament' set up the Westminster Assembly to make recommendations for the reform of the Church of England. Although it included some Episcopalians and Independents the majority of its members were Calvinists who favoured a presbyterian form of government. The Assembly drew up a Confession of Faith, which was accepted by the General Assembly of the Church of Scotland in 1647, and approved by Parliament in 1648. It has become the standard of Presbyterian doctrine in the English-speaking world. Chapters xxv, xxvi, xxx, and xxxi deal with the Church.

The doctrine of the invisible Church in distinction from the visible Church is set out very clearly in Chapter xxv.

1 The catholic or universal Church, which is invisible, consists of the whole number of the elect, that have been, are, or shall be gathered into one, under Christ the head thereof; and is the spouse, the body, the fulness of him that filleth all in all.

2 The visible Church, which is also catholic or universal under the gospel (not confined to one nation as before under the law) consists of all those, throughout the world, that profess the true religion, and of their children; and is the kingdom of the Lord Jesus Christ, the house and family of God, out of which there is no ordinary possibility of salvation.

3 Unto this catholic visible Church Christ hath given the ministry, oracles, and ordinances of God, for the gathering and perfecting of the saints, in this life, to the end of the world: and doth by his own presence and spirit, according to his promise, make them effectual thereunto.

4 This catholic Church hath been sometimes more, sometimes less visible. And particular churches, which are members thereof, are more or less pure, according as the doctrine of the gospel is taught and embraced, ordinances administered, and public worship performed more or less purely in them.

5 The purest churches under heaven are subject both to mixture and error; and some have so degenerated as to become no churches of Christ, but synagogues of Satan. Nevertheless, there shall be always a Church on earth to worship God according to his will.

There is no other head of the Church but the Lord Jesus Christ.... (xxv).[30]

The communion of saints is the unity which men have with Christ by his spirit and by faith, and with one another by love. It involves community in service, edification, and works of charity. It is specifically stated that it does not imply community of goods (xxvi).

The Church's officers have 'the keys of the kingdom of heaven ... by virtue whereof they have power respectively to retain and remit sins'. They may admonish, censure, and excommunicate; and they may absolve the penitent and readmit to communion (xxx).

Synods are needed for the government of the Church. They may properly be called by civil rulers, but if these are enemies of the Church, the ministers may meet 'of themselves, by virtue of their office or ... upon delegation from their churches'. The decisions of synods must be in accordance with the Word of God. Synods may err, and their decisions 'are not to be made the rule of faith or practice, but to be used as a help in both'. They may not 'intermeddle with civil affairs', except by way of 'humble petition', or of advice if requested by the magistrate (xxxi).

The office of the civil magistrate is dealt with earlier in Chapter xxiii. His duty is to preserve peace and minister to the public good. He may not assume the administration of the Word and sacraments or exercise ecclesiastical discipline, but he has the responsibility of preserving order in the Church, suppressing blasphemies, and preventing corruptions.[31]

THE SAVOY DECLARATION (1658)

This Declaration was drawn up at a meeting of representatives of churches of the congregational type of government, held at the Chapel of the Savoy Palace in London. It was based on the Westminster Confession, but makes alterations in the chapters which concern the government of the Church, and civil magistrates.

The main points of difference are these:
(1) While 'the magistrate is bound to encourage, promote, and protect

the professors and profession of the gospel', and to prevent the publication of blasphemies and errors, he has no right to intervene in matters of doctrinal and liturgical dispute.

> In such differences about the doctrines of the gospel, or ways of the worship of God, as may befall men exercising a good conscience, manifesting it in their conversation, and holding the foundation, not disturbing others in their ways of worship that differ from them, there is no warrant for the magistrate under the gospel to abridge them of their liberty.[32]

Savoy is thus more explicit than Westminster in limiting the magistrate's powers.

(2) There is a greater emphasis on the invisible Church. Savoy omits Westminster's assertion that 'there is no ordinary possibility of salvation' outside the visible Church. Against Westminster XXV, 3, Savoy XXVI declares of the visible Catholic Church of Christ that 'as such it is not intrusted with the administration of any ordinances, or hath any officers to rule or govern in or over the whole body'.

(3) There is also emphasis on the autonomy of the local congregation in line with the Independent position. This appears in the 'Platform of Polity' which follows the Declaration of Faith and sets out the Church polity of Independency. The emphasis is on the local gathered Church, which possesses from Christ all the necessary power and authority to conduct worship and exercise discipline, and to choose and set apart by the laying on of hands pastors (or teachers, or elders) and deacons to minister in the congregation.

> Besides these particular Churches, there is not instituted by Christ any Church more extensive or Catholic intrusted with power for the administration of his Ordinances or the execution of any authority in his Name (Platform VI).

Chapter XXVI of the Platform, however, appears to jeopardize the principle of the completely autonomous local congregation in providing for a synod comprised of representatives of other congregations to meet when there are 'cases of difficulties or differences, either in point of doctrine or in administrations'. But it is declared that such a synod has no 'church power properly so called', cannot impose its decisions, and can only give advice.

THE CAMBRIDGE PLATFORM (1648)

This document, 'The Platform of Church Discipline',[33] was drawn up

at a synod held at Cambridge, Massachusetts, with the purpose of setting forth the principles of the churches founded in New England by
the Pilgrim Fathers. These were English Independents who had sailed
for America after a period of exile in Holland. The document, largely
the work of Richard Mather, consists of seventeen chapters and deals
throughout with the doctrine of the Church, its order and discipline.

The Catholic Church is declared to be the whole company of the
elect (II, 1), triumphant in heaven and militant on earth (II, 2).

> This Militant Church is to be considered as Invisible and Visible. Invisible,
> in respect of their relation wherein they stand to Christ, as a body unto the
> head, being united unto him, by the Spirit of God, and faith in their hearts:
> Visible, in respect of the profession of their faith, in their persons, and in
> particular Churches: and so there may be acknowledged a universal visi-
> ble Church (II, 3).

The next paragraph (II, 4) asserts that the members of the militant
visible Church are to be considered as those who 'walk according to
the church-order of the Gospel' (and II, 5 explains that this order is
congregational). 'Besides the spiritual union and communion common
to all believers, they enjoy moreover a union and communion
ecclesiastical-political: so we deny a universal visible church.' These
last words apparently contradict the last sentence of II, 3 above.
Williston Walker interprets this as meaning that although those who
profess the faith, wherever they may be, may be regarded as a universal visible Church, this is not in any corporate sense: 'There is no *corporate* union and communion of all the professed followers of Christ,
only an association of local churches.'[34] The text of the Platform at
this point, however, is far from clear. What is clear is that the document envisages the Church as being essentially the gathering together
of believers in particular places.

> A Congregational-church is by the institution of Christ a part of the
> Militant-visible-church, consisting of a company of saints by calling,
> united into one body, by a holy covenant, for the public worship of God,
> and the mutual edification one of another, in the Fellowship of the Lord
> Jesus (II, 6).

Particular churches are to be constituted by a covenant or voluntary agreement to meet regularly for worship and instruction, and to
accept church discipline. Such a covenant rather than 'faith in the
heart', a formal profession of faith, the fact of residing close at hand,
or even baptism, provides the true 'form' of a church, though the im-

portance of none of these things is denied. Emphasis is thus placed on a voluntary act of joining a particular congregation (IV).

Membership of a congregation should not be 'of greater number than may ordinarily meet together conveniently in one place: nor ordinarily fewer than may conveniently carry on Church-work' (III, 4). When a congregation grows too large, another church should be founded from it (xv, 4).

Authority resides in the congregation itself which receives it immediately from Christ and may exercise it immediately; and in the eldership which has the power of office. The ministers, however, possess their power through the congregation, and cannot, therefore, be said to exercise their power 'immediately' (v, 2). As the congregation has power to call, test, and ordain its officers, so it has power to depose them if they prove unworthy (VIII, 7).

The officers of the church are elders of whom 'some attend chiefly to the ministry of the word, as the Pastors and Teachers; others attend especially unto Rule, who are therefore called Ruling Elders' (VI, 4); and deacons whose office is 'limited unto the care of the temporal good things of the church' (VIII, 4). These church officers are to be freely elected by the congregation (VIII) and ordained by the laying on of hands by elders. If the congregation has no elder to perform this function, members of the congregation, duly chosen, may do so, or elders invited from another church (IX).

Chapter x sums up the concept of authority as the Platform perceives it:

> This Government of the church is a mixed Government. . . . In respect of Christ, the Head and King of the church, and the Sovereign power residing in him, and exercised by him, it is a Monarchy. In respect of the body, or Brotherhood of the church, and power from Christ granted unto them, it resembles a Democracy. In respect of the Presbytery (i.e. the Elders) and power committed to them, it is an Aristocracy (x, 3).

On the relation between the authority of the congregation and that of the elders it has this to say:

> This power of Government in the Elders doth not any wise prejudice the power of privilege in the brotherhood; as neither the power of privilege in the brethren doth prejudice the power of government in the Elders; but they may sweetly agree together, as we may see in the example of the Apostles, furnished with the greatest church power, who took in the concurrence and consent of the brethren in church administration (x, 10).

Chapter xv deals with 'the communion of churches one with another'. 'Although churches be distinct, and therefore have not dominion one over another' yet they are encouraged to care for each other's welfare, to consult and to admonish each other. The practice of worshipping occasionally at another church, especially to partake at the Lord's table, is commended. The calling of synods is provided for (xvi) when necessary 'to determine controversies of faith and cases of conscience'. Magistrates also may call synods 'to counsel and assist them in matters of religion', but it is made clear that 'the constituting of a synod is a church act' which is not dependent on the will of the magistrate.

It is lawful and necessary for Christians to form churches without the consent of magistrates, as happened in the early days of the Church (xvii, 1). Church government and civil government are not opposed. Each has its distinct jurisdiction, but each can help the other (xvii, 2). But it is unlawful for either to 'meddle' in the work proper to the other (xvii, 5). Magistrates have no power, therefore, to compel subjects to become church members or to reinstate members who have been excommunicated (xvii, 4), but they are called on to 'take care of matters of religion', to see that God's commandments are kept (xvii, 6), to restrain idolatry, blasphemy, and heresy (xvii, 8) and:

> If any church, one or more, shall grow schismatical, rending itself from the communion of other churches, or shall walk incorrigibly or obstinately in any corrupt way of their own, contrary to the rule of the Word; in such case, the Magistrate is to put forth his coercive power, as the matter shall require (xvii, 9).

The Cambridge Platform, says Dr Erik Routley,[35] 'expounds the Congregational doctrine of the Church more completely than any other English-speaking document'. It was intended, he points out, 'to lay down a polity for no dissenting minority, but for a Church whose universal hold over a whole country (as they then saw it) was more confidently to be hoped for than any Church which could have been founded at Savoy'. It envisaged also a situation in which the community and the congregation were almost identical, in which church members alone had voting rights and magistrates, therefore, would always be supporters, if not members, of the church.

The Cambridge Platform quickly won assent from a great number of congregations in New England, some of them of Anglican and Presbyterian ancestry. In 1651 the General Court at Boston legalized it as the polity of the church in Massachusetts, and so it remained until 1780. But long before this, the experiment had broken down. Men of strong independent views could not accept even the qualified powers given to the magistrates, and left Massachusetts to form or to join communities elsewhere. In Massachusetts itself difficulties quickly appeared. Not everybody shared the enthusiasm of the colony's founders. There were those in the community who, while well qualified for leadership, were not qualified for church membership. Others, being unwilling to accept the responsibilities of civic office, refrained from making the covenant. Church membership was dwindling. Assemblies held in 1657 and 1662 agreed upon a solution known as 'The Half-way Covenant'. This permitted those who were baptized, but had not made the covenant, to vote in civic elections and to accept office, but excluded them from the Lord's Supper and from any part in the deliberations of the congregation. That such a compromise departed from the principles of the Cambridge Platform is evident.[36]

The subject matter of this chapter bears witness to a certain tendency during the sixteenth and seventeenth centuries to define theological, and therefore ecclesiological, positions very closely. On the part of the Catholic Church there was determination to 'hold the fort', while the great concern of theologians of Protestant bodies was to define their doctrine of the Church not only against Rome, but against one another. The old orthodoxy and ecclesiology was challenged, but only to be replaced by various new orthodoxies and new ecclesiologies, strongly held, and often rigidly enforced in the differing Protestant churches. What we may call a hardening process was going on. But already in the seventeenth century new interests, scientific, cultural, and philosophical, had begun to engage men's minds. The changing image of the Church in relation to modern modes of thought will be the subject of our second volume.

Part 5

THE EIGHTEENTH AND NINETEENTH CENTURIES

15

The Age of Reason and
the Church

The middle of the seventeenth century was 'the beginning of a new era in western thought'.[1] It ushered in a period during which 'many of the important movements in modern Christianity have their rise, and many of the problems which distinguish the modern era first assume their familiar form'.[2] Many factors contributed to the new situation: the challenge of the Reformation to long-accepted authority; the establishment of more unified and powerful states in western Europe, and the rise of national spirit; the widening of world horizons by the discovery of the New World, its colonization, and the consequent development of trade and enrichment of the seafaring European powers; the enlargement of man's knowledge by striking advances in the physical sciences; weariness and disgust after decades of bitter, bloody, and often fratricidal fighting (the 'Religious Wars') which ended with the Peace of Westphalia in 1648, leaving central Europe exhausted economically, and engendering in many minds a scepticism concerning the truth and value of a religion which had plunged so many into such suffering. For all these reasons the Church found itself in a world which was loudly challenging the assumptions of seventeen hundred years.

THE AGE OF REASON

The eighteenth century is often called 'the age of Reason' or the 'Enlightenment' (German, *Aufklärung*; French, *l'illumination*). It is a true description, although it draws attention to but one, albeit very important, element in the thinking and culture of the time, namely, the emphasis on rationality. There were other strong elements: pietism in religion and, well before the end of the century, romanticism in reaction both to philosophical rationalism and to classicism in art and literature, each stressed the importance of the emotional side of man's nature.

The scientific successes of the late sixteenth and the seventeenth century were taken as tokens of what human reason could achieve. Isaac Newton (1643–1727) had unravelled the workings of the universe. John Locke (1632–1704) had discovered the workings of the mind. It began to be assumed that illimitable possibilities lay before man, provided that he took reason for his guide. The philosophical trends known as rationalism and empiricism received great impetus. Some thinkers noted that the success of science was closely related to mathematics, a discipline which demands a rigorous use of reason, and pursued their studies on the assumption that pure reason is capable of attaining truth. These were the rationalists (Descartes, 1596–1650; Spinoza, 1632–77; Leibniz, 1646–1716). Others, impressed by the scientific results of close attention to sense experience, adopted the view that knowledge is ultimately derived from sense experience. These were the empiricists (Locke; Bishop George Berkeley, 1685–1753; David Hume, 1711–76). The rationalism of this period was not usually atheistic. Those to whom the scientific advances of the time were due, like Robert Boyle, the chemist, Isaac Newton, the physicist, and John Ray, the naturalist, were convinced that they were making plain not only the existence of God but the workings of his laws. The philosophers also for the most part (Hume is an exception) found that reason led them to the conclusion that God exists. Locke in *An Essay Concerning Human Understanding* spoke of the existence of God as 'the most obvious truth that reason discovers' and one 'equal to mathematical certainty'. But the rationalists were sceptical about divine revelation: the competence of man's reason rendered it unnecessary. For them, God exists as the creator who has given to the universe the laws by which it runs, laws which human reason is fully capable of discovering, and he exists aloof in transcendent majesty. Man's responsibility is to discover and live by the laws which God has laid down for his human creation, and in proportion to his achievement rewards or punishments await him after death. This concept of God is known as Deism.

Close to the English Deists in some ways were the Latitudinarians, of whom Dr Samuel Clarke (1675–1729) is the best known representative. 'While continuing to conform with the Church of England they attached relatively little importance to matters of dogmatic truth, ecclesiastical organization, and liturgical practice.'[3] Like the Deists they held that the essence of religion could be expressed in rational yet simple terms. God is the wise and beneficent creator, and he requires of his children a like wisdom and kindliness. But whereas the Deists rejected the idea of revelation, the Latitudinarians defended it, contending that the Scriptures contained nothing contrary to reason.

The period is an important and fascinating one in many respects. Our concern, however, is with the doctrine of the nature of the Church. How was this affected by the movements of thought in the late seventeenth century and the eighteenth? The period produced no treatises on the Church of comparable influence with some which we have already studied and others which were to appear later. The ecclesiologies set forth in the catechisms, articles, and confessions which were discussed at the end of volume one, remained normative for Anglicans, Catholics, Congregationalists, Lutherans, and Presbyterians. But the spirit of the time did engender certain new ideas about the Church which, although not accepted into official formulae, have been very influential. These are the idea of the Church as an ethical society, and the concepts of toleration and the 'denomination'.

THE CHURCH AS AN ETHICAL SOCIETY

The philosopher John Locke, as we have seen, believed that the existence of God could be proved by reason. But unlike many other thinkers of the period, he also held that God had revealed his will to man through the Scriptures, and pre-eminently through the teachings of Jesus Christ. He sees Christ as primarily the teacher of an ethical code:

> Next to the knowledge of one God; maker of all things; a clear knowledge of their duty was wanting to mankind ... he that shall collect all the moral rules of the philosophers, and compare them with those contained in the new testament, will find them to come short of the morality delivered by Our Saviour. ... Such a body of Ethics, proved to be the law of nature, from principles of reason, and reaching all the duties of life, I think nobody will say the world had before Our Saviour's time (*The Reasonableness of Christianity* 241–2).[4]

The Reasonableness of Christianity abounds in phrases which describe the Christian life as 'sincere obedience to his law' (178), 'sincere obedience to the law and will of Christ' (179), 'a sincere endeavour after righteousness, in obeying his law' (181). What Christ expects from his followers, we are told, 'he has sufficiently declared as a Legislator' (220).[5]

> Our Saviour not only confirmed the moral law, and ... shewed the strictness, as well as obligations of its injunctions; but moreover ...

requires the obedience of his disciples to several of the commands he afresh lays upon them; with the enforcement of unspeakable rewards and punishments in another world, according to their obedience or disobedience (212).[6]

What is being proposed here is the idea of the followers of Christ as an ethical society of those who have voluntarily accepted a set of moral principles which is both advantageous to society and to themselves as individuals, and who endeavour to live in accordance with it. Such an idea was not unacceptable to the Latitudinarians. Benjamin Hoadly (1676–1761), successively Bishop of Bangor, Hereford, Salisbury, and Winchester, preached a sermon before George I in 1717 in which he made it clear that he had a negative view of the value of creeds, sacraments, and the ministry, and saw no need for the Church as a visible institution. The prevailing view among Latitudinarians was that Christianity is essentially a reasonable ethical code, that the *raison d'être* of the Church is to promote that code, and that therefore the Church is a useful institution deserving the support of the government in power. There were not lacking churchmen to oppose these ideas with considerable theological power, among whom William Law (1686–1761) and Joseph Butler (1692–1752), Bishop of Durham, are outstanding. But the interpretation of Christianity in moralistic terms, and the idea of the Church as primarily an institution for the improvement of moral standards has persisted to the present day, not least because churchmen have not infrequently used the idea as a valuable apologetic when the Church has come under attack and ridicule from the intelligentsia.

TOLERATION

In the wake of the Reformation came persecution of Protestants in Catholic lands and of Catholics in Protestant territory. There followed also the religious wars which devastated and impoverished large tracts of central Europe until the middle of the seventeenth century. By that time not only was Europe weary and sickened by bloodshed in the cause of religion, but the voice of reason was beginning to be heard. As early as 1554 Sebastian Castellio, who was converted to Protestantism by John Calvin and proved to be a somewhat unorthodox Calvinist, had argued in his *De Haereticis* that persecution could not be the will of Christ: 'If thou, O Christ, hast commanded these executions and tortures, what hast thou left for the devil to do?'[7] But such words fell on deaf ears for many decades.

At the Peace of Augsburg in 1555 the disputes between Catholics and Lutherans within the German empire had been settled by acceptance of the principle that the religion of the ruler determines the religion of the territory (*cuius regio, eius religio*). At the Peace of Westphalia, which in 1648 concluded the Thirty Years' War, the same principle was accepted, and extended to all the territories of the Holy Roman Empire and to include the Calvinists. But, despite provisions for the protection of minorities, toleration was as yet far from being achieved.

In England the question was vigorously debated, and Locke's *A Letter Concerning Toleration*[8] (1689) was widely read and most influential. Castellio's plea is again voiced, but in the more measured tones of the rationalist:

> If, like the Captain of our salvation, they [zealots] sincerely desired the good of souls, they would tread in the steps and follow the perfect example of the Prince of Peace, who sent out His soldiers to the subduing of nations, and gathering them into His Church, not armed with the sword or other instruments of force, but prepared with the Gospel of peace and with the exemplary holiness of their conversation. . . .

> The toleration of those that differ from others in matters of religion is so agreeable to the Gospel of Jesus Christ, and to the genuine reason of mankind, that it seems monstrous for men to be so blind as not to perceive the necessity and advantage of it in so clear a light.[9]

> It will be very difficult to persuade men of sense that he who with dry eyes and satisfaction of mind can deliver his brother to the executioner to be burned alive does sincerely and heartily concern himself to save that brother from the flames of hell in the world to come.[10]

Locke argues for 'the mutual toleration of private persons differing from one another in religion'; against the right of any person, church, or commonwealth 'to invade the civil rights and worldly goods of each other upon pretence of religion'; for the Christian duty of preaching peace, goodwill, and toleration; against religious compulsion by rulers or magistrates: 'Men cannot be forced to be saved whether they will or no'; and against the intervention of the magistrate *qua* magistrate in Church affairs unless there is any question of danger to the public good. And in respect of this proviso, 'the magistrate ought always to be very careful that he do not misuse his authority to the oppression of any church, under pretence of public good'.[11]

Locke would extend religious liberty widely, even to include idolaters,[12] but would withhold it from four groups. First, any whose opinions are contrary to the law and order of civil society;[13] second, such groups as are themselves intolerant;[14] third, the Roman Catholic Church:

> That church can have no right to be tolerated by the magistrate which is constituted upon such a bottom that all who enter into it do thereby *ipso facto* deliver themselves up to the protection and service of another prince.[15]

He gives as an instance one who professes to be 'a Mahometan only in his religion, but in everything else a faithful subject to a Christian magistrate, whilst at the same time he acknowledges himself bound to yield blind obedience to the Mufti of Constantinople'. There were few Muslims in England in the late seventeenth century. Locke was thinking of Roman Catholics. The fourth group is that of the atheists:

> Those are not at all to be tolerated who deny the being of a God. Promises, covenants, and oaths, which are the bonds of human society, can have no hold upon an atheist.[16]

In the same year that Locke published this letter the Toleration Act gave freedom of worship to dissenters, except Roman Catholics and Unitarians. They remained, however, under many civil disabilities most of which were removed in 1828. In 1829 the Roman Catholic Emancipation Act removed most of the disabilities from Roman Catholics.

DENOMINATIONALISM

The climate of opinion which promoted toleration also fostered the idea that the separated Christian bodies are all more or less acceptable categories of Christianity. The word 'denomination'[17] came to be used to describe them:

In *A Letter Concerning Toleration*, John Locke wrote:

> A church ... I take to be a voluntary society of men, joining themselves together of their own accord in order to the public worshipping of God in such manner as they judge acceptable to Him, and effectual to the salvation of their souls.[18]

This is reminiscent of the definitions of the Church which we found given by exponents of the congregational type of Church order. Locke, however, is speaking of all Christian groups, whether congregational, national, or transcending national boundaries. They are all voluntary, or in his opinion should be so regarded, in the sense that every man has liberty to join them or to dissociate himself from them.

They may differ from each other in respect of the doctrines which they consider essential, in forms of ministry, modes of worship, and rules of discipline, and therefore may be looked on as so many options open to a Christian person. As the spirit of toleration gained ground, they were increasingly looked on as tolerable options. That Christendom was divided into denominations came to be regarded as a natural, even desirable state of affairs. 'Denominationalism' denotes this position.[19] Concern for the unity of the body of Christ drops into the background.

The word 'denomination', which was not used by Locke, has passed into common currency. Those churches, however, which hold themselves to be representative of the one Church of Christ, or even to be *the* Church of Christ, tend not to use it of themselves, though they may do so of other Christian bodies. Nor is it much used by those Christians who, looking beyond a mere tolerance which leaves churches separated from, and even in competition with, one another, hope for a union of all Christian people on the basis of a common faith and order.

REACTION

During the period of the Enlightenment the talents of theologians were, for the most part, directed to the defence of the Christian faith against the most powerful and bitter attacks it had received since the *True Word* of Celsus in the second century, which drew forth Origen's apology, *Contra Celsum*, several decades later. At the official level, the intellectual resources of the churches were stretched to the utmost in the negative task of maintaining and justifying the status which the churches enjoyed in the various regions where they were recognized. This endeavour met with indifferent success. The papacy still asserted its full claims in those countries where its writ still ran. But, despite the zealous activity of the Jesuits, in almost every Catholic country those claims were ignored, and papal privileges were whittled away by 'enlightened' monarchs and their advisers. In France, for instance, the independent 'Gallican' spirit of French Catholics, which had frequently been expressed in previous centuries, renewed itself. Kings, the *parlements*, and the bishops each for their own reasons resisted the papal claims. In 1682 an assembly of the French clergy accepted four principles, known as the Four Gallican Articles, which had been drawn up by Jacques Bénigne Bousset, Bishop of Meaux. They asserted (1) the independence of kings from the pope in all things temporal; (2) the authority of general councils as superior to that of the pope, in accordance with the Council of Constance;[20] (3) that so far as France was concerned the pope must conform to the laws and customs of the French Church; (4) that, while in matters of faith the pope had the principal part, his decrees are not irreformable, unless the Church has given its consent. The ambitious and autocratic Louis XIV at once promulgated these articles, demanding their acceptance by all the clergy. They were revoked before the end of the century, and a compromise was worked out with the papacy. Gallicanism, however, has continued to be a potent force up to modern times.[21]

The Church of England, protected by its establishment, pursued a somewhat somnolent way, suspicious of all that savoured of enthusiasm, resisting change, and reluctant to see the lifting of the legal disabilities on dissenters. For several generations after the end of the Thirty Years' War, theologians of the Lutheran and Reformed Churches expended their energies in producing volumes of dogmatic theology. G. R. Cragg writes:[22] 'The intellect was in the ascendant, and in a particularly arid form, while vast and intricate dogmatic systems fortified the rival positions of Lutheran and Calvinist theologians. . . . Strict orthodoxy became an obsession.'

Reaction against formalism and sterile scholastic theology, whether Catholic or Protestant, prompted the most significant religious movements of the period. These were Pietism, Methodism, and Jansenism. Pietism flourished in Germany under the leadership of Philipp Spener (1635–1705)and August Francke(1663–1727),and in Bohemia under that of Count Nikolaus von Zinzendorf (1700–60) who in 1722 gave refuge to a group of exiled Moravian Brethren at Herrnhut on one of his estates. In England the revival of evangelism and spiritual life known as Methodism was pioneered by John Wesley (1703–91), his brother Charles (1707–88), and George Whitefield (1714–70). The movement was influential in America, and the preaching of Whitefield and Jonathan Edwards in New England in 1740–43 led to the widespread revival known as the Great Awakening. Within the Roman Catholic Church Jansenism, which takes its name from Cornelius Jansen (1585–1638), Bishop of Ypres, was a movement of a different kind. It began as a revival of St Augustine's doctrines of election and of grace as irresistible, giving rise to bitter theological controversies which do not directly concern us here. The Jansenists taught that man can only be saved by the predestinating love of God which creates faith. They stressed, therefore, man's need of personal conversion. They demanded a rigorous discipline, and opposed the principle of *probabilism*[23] taught by the Jesuits. Jansenism quickly spread from the Low Countries to France, and the Convent of Port-Royal became a centre of propaganda for the movement. In spite of official condemnation and persecution it remained a powerful influence on the French Church throughout the eighteenth century.

These movements in their different ways laid stress on the importance of an individual conversion experience, on a warm devotional life, and a strict, even puritanical discipline. Each sought to strengthen the Church by rekindling the fervour of the gospel where formalism in matters of doctrine and in worship was prevalent. In their early phases there was no thought of separation and the formation of a new 'denomination'. But in the event each movement led to the creation of a new church. After the condemnation of Jansenism in the papal Bull *Unigenitus* (1713), the Jansenists of the Netherlands rejected the papacy and in 1724 elected their own bishop of Utrecht. This was the first of the small national bodies now known as Old Catholic Churches, which have originated from groups that have seceded at different times from the Church of Rome. They exist also in Germany, Austria, and Switzerland. Their numbers were to be greatly increased by defections from the Roman Catholic Church after the promulgation of the dogma of the infallibility of the pope, at the First Vatican Council, in 1870.

A Methodist Church was organized in America in 1784. In England separation from the Church of England was a gradual process. It was effected after the death of the Wesley brothers, when in 1795 the 'Yearly Conference of the People Called Methodists' decided that preachers admitted by the Conference had authority to administer the sacraments without ordination.[24]

The Moravian Brethren of Herrnhut, under the inspiration and example of Count von Zinzendorf, showed from the beginning a remarkable missionary zeal in many countries both in Europe and the Americas. Separate communities have been established. In Europe they are known as the Moravian Brethren or the Moravian Church, and in North America, where they are far more numerous, as the Church of the Brethren.

These new churches developed no unique ecclesiologies. The Old Catholic Church represents a western Catholicism which rejects the claim of the pope to plenitude of ecclesiastical power over all dioceses, and the dogma of papal infallibility.[25]

The Methodist Church, in the words of a twentieth-century document,[26] 'claims and cherishes its place in the Holy Catholic Church which is the Body of Christ'. When, in the late eighteenth century, Methodists seceded from the Church of England, they needed an ecclesiology and a Church order. It may fairly be said that the Methodist ecclesiology is expressed by the definition of the Church in the Confession of Augsburg as 'the congregation of saints in which the Gospel is purely taught and the sacraments are rightly administered'.[27] The word 'saints' indicates not the morally perfect, but has the Pauline sense of those who have a living faith in God through Christ. While Methodism emphasizes the necessity for believers to persevere towards holiness and the perfection of love for God and man, it is not a Holiness Church of the Novatianist or Donatist type. It recognizes that the Church is a mixed society of good and bad. Much emphasis is placed on the priesthood of all believers, and abundant opportunities are provided at all levels, from the local 'society' to the Annual Conference, for lay participation in the Church's decisions and work. Ministers are trained, tested, and appointed to their pastorates by the authority of the Conference after ordination by prayer and the laying on of hands by ministers. In England the Methodist Church polity is most closely akin to the Presbyterian, though with a centralization of more authority in the Annual Conference than the Presbyterian Churches invest in their General Assemblies.

In the United States the size of the country has necessitated a different structure for the Methodist Church. The General Conference meets only every four years. Annual conferences are held on a regional basis, and these bodies elect representatives to six Jurisdictional Conferences. All these conferences consist of equal numbers of ministers and lay people. The Jurisdictional Conferences elect bishops. The bishops, who confer together in an annual Conference of Bishops, are charged with general oversight of the Church, the supervision of the Annual Conferences and the smaller District Conferences, and with the direction of evangelism at home and missions abroad. The Methodist Church makes no claim that its bishops are within the historic succession of bishops from apostolic times. Methodism sees its continuity with the Church of the past rather in the succession of believers from the days of the earliest disciples to the present:

> The true continuity with the Church of past ages which we cherish is to be found in the continuity of the Christian experience, the fellowship in the

gift of the one Spirit; in the continuity of the allegiance to one Lord, the continued proclamation of the message, the continued acceptance of the mission. .... The influence of one human personality on others is the chief means used by God for propagating the truth by which the Church lives. .... Behind each believer there stretches a long chain, each link a Christian man or woman, till we find ourselves, with the first disciples, in the company of the Lord Himself. ...

This is our doctrine of apostolic succession. It is our conviction, therefore, that the continuity of the Church does not depend on, and is not necessarily secured by, an official succession of ministers, whether bishops or presbyters, from apostolic times, but rather by fidelity to apostolic truth.[28]

The ecclesiology of the Church of the Brethren approaches more closely to the Holiness and Separatist type. The Church is seen as the fellowship of the saints, membership in which is based on faith in Christ as Saviour, repentance of sin, and baptism which is administered by immersion after a confession of faith. Church polity is of the congregationalist type. Elders, ministers, and deacons are elected by each congregation, and inducted into their office by the laying on of hands. Only in the case of elders is this called ordination. Traditionally the Church of the Brethren has stood aloof from the State and from other Christian bodies. It has insisted on the complete separation of the Church from the State, believing that the latter has its own autonomous function in the material sphere, and has refused to participate in political affairs even to the extent of advising its members against voting. At the same time it has tended to isolate itself in a close community life from the rest of the Christian world. In recent decades there are many signs that the Brethren are emerging from this isolationism by a more positive attitude to civic responsibility and to co-operation with other Christian groups.[29]

ROMANTICISM

As the eighteenth century progressed, the reign of reason was increasingly challenged, aside from the pietistic reaction within the churches, by what is known as the Romantic Movement. It marked an awareness that there was another ingredient in human nature besides rationality and common sense which could introduce man to reality and meaning. This was man's emotional side, his *sensibilité*, his feeling. The claim that scientific rationalism alone could provide a full and satisfying life and set mankind on the way to a golden age was rejected. 'Mystery and wonder, beauty and spontaneity asserted their right to a place in any adequate conception of a satisfying life.'[30] Romanticism touched almost every field of human activity, philosophy, ethics, politics, art and literature, the crafts. Jean-Jacques Rousseau (1712–78) is usually spoken of as 'the father of the Romantic Movement'. Influential in Germany were the poets J. W. Goethe (1749–1832), J. C. F. Schiller (1759–1805), and F. W. J. von Schelling (1775–1854), whose idealistic philosophy was in strong contrast with the systems of the rationalists.

The challenge to the omnicompetence of human reason, and the rehabilitation of a sense of wonder and of emotion as having a vital place in human affairs encouraged a religious attitude, but this did not necessarily lead men to Christian faith. It is true that reaction from the arid rationalism of the age engendered in some Romantics a wistful longing for things medieval, and a number of them espoused Catholicism. Usually they did not remain long within it: their individualism was neither comfortable nor congenial there. The Romantics for the most part found God in the emotions of the human heart; and since strong emotions could be called forth by the beauty, wonder, and might of nature, God was there too, conceived as immanent within the universe. With some this was close to a primitive nature-worship. Even in theologians influenced by the Romantic Movement there is a discernible tendency towards pantheism. This is true of Friedrich Schleiermacher (1768–1834) and of Samuel Taylor Coleridge (1772–1834).

'In the closing years of the eighteenth century,' writes G. R. Cragg,[31] 'the German people were awaiting a prophet who could relate with authority a living message to their sense of need. Frederick Schleiermacher proved to be that prophet. In a unique degree he possessed the gifts necessary for reinterpreting the Christian faith to a generation weary of rationalism and disillusioned by the course which the French Revolution had taken.' In chapter 16 we shall consider the doctrine of the Church of this German theologian who is frequently spoken of as the father of modern Protestantism.

THE CHURCH OF ROME AND THE AGE OF REASON

The Roman Catholic Church was not untouched by the movements of thought which ushered in the modern era. The rationalism of the eighteenth century, the Romantic reaction, and growing nationalism all had their effect.

French nationalism gave rise to a certain independent attitude towards papal claims. This was the Gallicanism which I have already mentioned.[32] A similar movement, known as Febronianism, occurred in Germany. Febronius was the pseudonym of Johann von Hontheim (1701–90), Bishop of Trier. Encouraged by the German archbishops, he conducted a lengthy historical research into the status of the papacy, and in 1763 published his findings in his book, *On the Present State of the Church and the Legitimate Power of the Roman Pontiff.* The Gallican principles appear again, but in a German setting. The Cyprianic concept of the corporate episcopate is asserted. The pope has only an honorific primacy, and, moreover, it is the responsibility of the civil ruler to hear appeals and check abuse. The book was immediately placed on the Index of Prohibited Books, but the views it expressed were widely disseminated, and accepted by many of the German bishops and clergy.

In Austria, Joseph II, Holy Roman Emperor from 1765 to 1790, introduced an attempt at ecclesiastical reform, known as Josephinism, which sprang directly from the 'enlightened' principle that, in so far as it has any place at all, religion must be rational, useful, and beneficial to the State. Religious toleration was granted, but the ruler's right to regulate ecclesiastical affairs was strongly asserted. So far as the Roman Catholic Church was concerned, the pope's authority was strictly spiritual, and his decisions must have the consent of the ruler. The bishops in each state were considered to have equal authority, but within limits imposed by the ruler. On the Emperor's death, Josephinism also died in those parts where it had been introduced: Austria, Hungary, the Netherlands, and Tuscany. As with Gallicanism and Febronianism, the ideas behind it, however, remained influential.

ROMANTICISM AND THE ROMAN CATHOLIC CHURCH

The Romantic reaction to the Enlightenment also influenced Roman Catholic ecclesiology, especially in Germany. While Romanticism emphasized the importance of the individual, it also fostered a sense of the community of man in and with nature. Yves Congar considers that 'the most common characteristic of the complex phenomenon of German Romanticism is the idea of life as a total movement uniting diversity in unity'.[33] Moreover, the renewed interest of the Romantics in the Middle Ages led churchmen back to the conception of the Church as the mystical body of Christ rather than as primarily a structured institution. These themes can be discerned in the ecclesiology of a group of German theologians, several of whom were members of the

Catholic Faculty of Theology which was opened at Tübingen in 1817. J. M. Sailer (1751–1832) saw the Church as 'the living mediation of an interior and living Christianity'.[34] J. S. Drey (d. 1853) conceived of the Church as, within the context of God's plan, 'the manifestation of the Kingdom of God, the instrument of his revelation, an organism vitalized from within by the Spirit'.[35]

More influential has been Johann Adam Möhler (1796–1838) of Tübingen. Möhler, a patristic and medieval scholar, cherished the hope of the reunion of the churches, and acquainted himself thoroughly with the Protestant thought of his day. He was particularly attracted by the idealism of Schelling and the mystical immanentism of Schleiermacher, whom he knew. Their influence is especially apparent in his early work, *Die Einheit in der Kirche*, 'Unity in the Church' (1825), in which he asserts that the Church as hierarchy and institution is 'an effect of Christian faith, the result of the living love of the faithful who have been united by the Holy Spirit', the answer to a human need first stirred up by God. But even so, Möhler does not deny the necessity of the hierarchy and external forms of the Church. They too are of the Holy Spirit, and the faithful can only draw their life from the visible community which the Spirit creates.

In his later works it is clear that he had come to realize that a predominantly pneumatological ecclesiology carried the danger of excessive subjectivism, and might be construed as the acceptance of the idea that the Church is essentially invisible. His study of the life and work of St Athanasius in preparation for his *Athanasius der Grosse* (1827) enabled him to see the importance of Christology and the doctrine of redemption, and to appreciate the role of the papacy.[36] Consequently, in his *Symbolik* ('Symbolism')[37] of 1832 he provides a more christological and objective view of the Church:

> By the Church on earth, Catholics understand the visible community of all believers, founded by Christ, in which the activity he exercised during his earthly life for the reconciliation and sanctification of mankind is continued to the end of the world, by means of an apostolate of uninterrupted continuity which was instituted by him; and into it in the course of time all peoples are to be led back to God. ... The Church ... is not a purely human institution. ... As in Christ divinity and humanity, although distinct, are closely united, so in his undivided wholeness he abides in his Church. The Church, his continuing manifestation, is at once both divine and human. ... It is he who, hidden in human forms, continues to act in it; and it necessarily has both a divine and human side.[38]

The ecclesiology of Möhler is still highly regarded by Roman

Catholic theologians. 'His equanimity and genius have proved an inspiration for modern scholars who find him a guide to the problems raised by the ecumenical movement of today.'[39]

ULTRAMONTANISM

Even in the countries most affected by the Gallican and similar movements, many remained loyal to the papacy and supported its universal claims. These were the Ultramontanes, so called from the Latin *ultra montes*, 'beyond the mountains'. The mountains were the Alps, beyond which lay Rome. Ultramontanism is the position which supports the centralization of ecclesiastical authority and administration in the bishop of Rome and the papal curia, and regards the pope as the sole judge of the orthodoxy of doctrine. The excesses of the French Revolution were seen as the inevitable product of the rationalism tinged with emotionalism of the preceding decades, and when the 'Terror' had subsided, the forces of conservatism reasserted themselves. Within the Roman Catholic Church, Ultramontanism now gained ascendancy. The Jesuit Order, always a strong support of the papacy but which had been suppressed in 1773 under pressure from European monarchs, was restored by Pope Pius VII in 1814. Pope Gregory XVI (1831–46), who in 1799 had published a treatise, *The Triumph of the Holy See*, in support of papal infallibility, condemned the liberalism of the French priest, Hugues Lamennais, although the latter had fondly supposed that the pope would endorse his crusade for freedom and his concept of the Church as authoritative in matters of faith but not of politics.

PIUS IX AND THE FIRST VATICAN COUNCIL

Gregory XVI was succeeded by Pope Pius IX (1846–78). His pontificate, in which the temporal power of the papacy was at its weakest, was marked by a considerable increase of authority in spiritual matters. The Roman Catholic hierarchy was established in England in 1850; he defined the doctrine of the Immaculate Conception of the Blessed Virgin Mary in the papal Bull, *Ineffabilis Deus*, in 1854; in 1864 he issued an encyclical, *Quanta Cura*, together with the *Syllabus Errorum*, a series of theses which condemned rationalism, socialism, and various contemporary philosophical trends; and in 1867 he convoked a General Council which was to meet at the Vatican in 1869.

The First Vatican Council was preceded by vigorous debate on the question of infallibility. Henri Maret, Dean of the Sorbonne, in *On the*

Ecumenical Council and Religious Peace (1869) advocated a moderate Gallican view: 'Neither the papacy nor the episcopate, but the papacy *and* the episcopate are the depositaries of infallibility.' In England, Henry Manning, the former Anglican, and now Archbishop of Westminster, and the layman W. G. Ward pressed for the definition of papal infallibility. Professor J. J. I. Döllinger (1799–1890) of Munich strongly opposed the doctrine, and found an equally doughty opponent in Professor Matthias Scheeben (1835–88) of Cologne. There were also those who held that a definition of infallibility was inopportune, in view of possible political repercussions and further alienation of the Orthodox and Protestants.

When the Council, which comprised some 700 bishops, met on 8 December 1869, the infallibility question was not on the agenda. A schema 'On Faith' first occupied the Council, and this, in revised form, was promulgated on 24 April 1870, as the constitution *Dei Filius*. It reaffirmed many of the theses of the *Syllabus*. The Council then proceeded to what was to be its most important business, the doctrine of the Church. A preparatory commission had proposed two schemata. One was in two parts, dealing with the Church itself, and Church and State relations. The subject of the second was *De Romano Pontifici*, 'On the Roman Pontiff', but no discussion of infallibility was proposed. But a majority of the bishops had petitioned for the inclusion of the infallibility question. This was successful, and, moreover, it was agreed to deal with the schema *De Romano Pontifici* first. Procedural matters occupied some weeks but the constitution *Pastor Aeternus*, which defined the infallibility of the pope, was passed on 18 July with 533 votes in favour, two against, and about sixty abstentions.[40] The Constitution states:

> We, with the approval of the sacred council, teach and define that it is a divinely revealed dogma: that the Roman Pontiff when he speaks *ex cathedra*, that is, when, acting in the offices of shepherd and teacher of all Christians, he defines, by virtue of his supreme apostolic authority, doctrine concerning faith or morals to be held by the universal Church, possesses through the divine assistance promised to him in blessed Peter the infallibility with which the divine Redeemer willed his Church to be endowed in defining faith or morals; and that such definitions of the Roman Pontiff are therefore irreformable of themselves, but not because of the agreement of the Church.[41]

On the next day the Franco-Prussian War broke out, and because of the political turmoil the Council was suspended without having completed its agenda. Thus, the Council had defined the magisterium of the pope without relating it to the authority of the bishops or of general councils. The Council was never formally closed, however, and it is possible, therefore, to regard the Second Vatican Council of 1963–5 as a continuation of the First to deal with its unfinished business. But at the time Vatican I seemed to mark the final failure of what Conciliarists and Gallicans had striven for, and the triumph of Ultramontanism. There were secessions from the Roman Church, notably that of Döllinger, resulting in the formation of a new section of the Old Catholic Church which received episcopal succession from the Jansenist Bishop of Deventer.

THE MODERNIST CRISIS

The denunciations in *Quanta Cura* and in Vatican I's constitution *Dei Filius* of a great deal of contemporary intellectual endeavour, posed problems of conscience for Roman Catholic scholars who took seriously the critical study of the Scriptures, or were aware that the new concept of historical process, closely associated with evolutionary theory, demanded a rethinking of scholastic theology, or believed that the philosophers of the day might have something to say to the Church. Liberal thinking gained momentum towards the end of the nineteenth century, and provoked the so-called Modernist crisis in the first decade of the twentieth. Here we trespass a little beyond the proper bounds of our Part 5.

Among, the leaders of the movement were Alfred Loisy (1857–1940), Maurice Blondel (1861–1949), Lucien Laberthonnière (1860 –1932), George Tyrrell (1861–1909), and Friedrich von Hügel (1852–1925). Their major interests ranged from biblical criticism and the study of Christian origins to contemporary trends in philosophy such as the pragmatism of William James and the intuitionism of Henri Bergson. But as Yves Congar says, their views cannot be reduced to a single uniform position.[42] The more radical were sceptical about the foundation of the Church by Jesus, but nevertheless held it to be a legitimate development from his teaching, and valued it as the setting in which the spiritual and moral life may best be fostered. Even if they were not convinced that the sacraments were instituted by Christ, they valued them, and in particular the Mass, as nourishing this spirituality.

The well-known phrase of Loisy in his *The Gospel and the Church* (1902): 'Jesus announced the Kingdom, and it is the Church which

came', may suggest the Modernists' scepticism about the Church's
origin. His argument, against Harnack, that the essence of the Church
is to be discerned in the form which it developed under the guidance of
the Holy Spirit illustrates their interest in evolutionism. He later
became more radical, and was prepared to accord little historical
worth to the Gospels. Tyrrell, a Jesuit, had a strong interest in the
devotional life of the Church, and wrote much on the subject. But he
came to interpret the devotional life as an immanental *élan vital* in the
human conscience, and to see the sole task of the Church and its
hierarchy as the protection of the open-endedness of this interior drive
which must not be restricted by the imposition of unalterable dogma.
In his posthumous book, *Christianity at the Crossroads* (1909),
Tyrrell suggested that Christianity was not final, but was to develop
into a more perfect and universal religion.

Seeing in the movement a threat to the Church as an historical institution, and to the objective truth of its affirmations of the faith, Pope
Pius X (1903–14) condemned Modernism in 1907 in the decree
Lamentabili and the encyclical *Pascendi* which asserted strongly that
the Church was not merely the expression of religious experience, nor
a phase in the evolution of another and truer institution. Loisy,
Tyrrell, and others were excommunicated. Others again were
prohibited from teaching and publishing.

The Baron Friedrich von Hügel, son of an Austrian father and a
Scottish mother, and whose home was in London, exercised a
moderating influence among the Modernists, with many of whom,
both in England and on the Continent, he was on close terms of
friendship. Well abreast of the state of biblical and historical criticism,
he was convinced that these were valuable scholarly tools which only
cast doubt on Christian origins if those who used them brought to
their work purely rationalistic presuppositions which excluded the
transcendent. And he argues cogently against the position of Modernists who taught that 'Christianity and Catholicism are essentially a
system of principles and laws ... [which] would remain true, even if
every one of the alleged happenings and historical facts [viz., those
recorded in the N.T.] turned out to be pure creations of the
imagination'.[43]

He shared Tyrrell's emphasis on the mystical, but for him the life of
devotion was not the subjective experience of a principle immanent in
human nature, but the converse of the soul with the transcendent God.
For von Hügel there was a 'fundamental and decisive difference ...

between religion conceived as a purely intra-human phenomenon, for which no evidence is to be found beyond the aspirations of humanity, and a religion conceived as having a basis in evidence and metaphysics; as the effect on us of something greater than ourselves—of something greater than any purely human facts and ideas'.[44]

Von Hügel was greatly distressed by the excommunications of Loisy and Tyrrell. He had exercised his considerable influence to prevent them. But he believed religious individualism to be a deviation. The religious life demands a social framework, an institution, and for him this was the Roman Catholic Church, to which, despite his acknowledgement of its weaknesses,[45] he remained completely loyal.

He believed the Church to have its origin in the explicitly declared will of Jesus Christ who gave it a hierarchy with Peter at its head. So he interprets Matthew 16.13–20.[46] The Church is not a static institution, but an organic reality manifesting a living energy which has developed from the original revelation. It works towards the universal goal of the transformation of society and the conversion of souls. Its unity is incarnated in a visible authority which must have a hierarchy and a supreme head. The Church, however, does not exist for itself, but to bring the world to the God who became incarnate in Christ. The Church itself incarnates spiritual realities within the temporal. The sacraments, which von Hügel associates intimately with the incarnation, are essential to its life, for in them Christ is present and active. But Christ died upon the cross. The element of tragedy is therefore to be expected in the Church. 'Von Hügel clung to the Church of Rome partly because he knew it was a Church in which he would have to suffer.'[47] And this, he believed, called for patience, courage, humility, and, moreover, a toleration and sympathy for the consciences of others.[48]

16

Schleiermacher and Ritschl

FRIEDRICH SCHLEIERMACHER, 1768–1834

Friedrich Schleiermacher was born in Breslau, the son of an army chaplain of the German Reformed Church. His parents were converted to the Moravian Brethren, and he received his early education at a Moravian school and seminary. He found Moravian teaching too restrictive for his independent mind, and his speculations led to his expulsion from the seminary. He always retained, however, much of what he had learned there, in particular a warm devotion and love of Christ. In 1787 he went to the University of Halle, was ordained in the Reformed Church in 1794 and appointed as preacher at the Charity Hospital in Berlin. In Berlin he came under the influence of the Romantic Movement, and in 1799 published the first edition of his *On Religion: Speeches to its Cultured Despisers*, which Rudolf Otto describes[1] as 'a veritable manifesto of the Romantics in its view of nature and history; its struggle against rationalist culture and the Philistinism of rationalism in the state, church, school, and society', Schleiermacher was appointed professor of theology at Halle in 1804, but returned to Berlin three years later to become preacher at Trinity Church, and in 1810 dean of the Faculty of Theology of the new Berlin University.

J. M. Creed says[2] that Schleiermacher was 'the first great Protestant theologian since the classical age of the Reformation to lay a primary doctrinal emphasis upon the idea of the Church'. This may seem surprising since he was brought up in a pietistic home, is known as the theologian of Romanticism, held the proper sphere of religion to be feeling, and defined theology as the expounding of one's self-consciousness of relationship with God. All these things suggest an individualism in which a doctrine of the Church would seem to have little place. Yet Creed is right. In both Schleiermacher's major works, the *Speeches* and *The Christian Faith* (1821–2), the Church receives much attention.

1 ON RELIGION: SPEECHES TO ITS CULTURED DESPISERS

The *Speeches*, as the full title makes plain, are addressed by Schleier-macher to his educated contemporaries for whom religion did not merit the consideration of a cultured person:

> In your ornamented dwellings, the only sacred things to be met with are the sage maxims of our wise men, and the splendid compositions of our poets. Suavity and sociability, art and science have so fully taken possession of your minds, that no room remains for the eternal and holy Being that lies beyond the world. I know how well you have succeeded in making your earthly life so rich and varied, that you no longer stand in need of an eternity. Having made a universe for yourselves, you are above the need of thinking of the Universe that made you (*On Religion*, pp. 3–4).

It is in the fourth speech, 'Association in Religion, or Church and Priesthood', that he deals directly with the Church. He notes that 'opposition to every institution meant for the communication of religion is always more violent than ... opposition to religion itself'.[3] He asks his readers to consider that 'if there is religion at all, it must be social, for that is the nature of man, and it is quite peculiarly the nature of religion'. Man has an impulse to communicate all that is in him. It would be unnatural and morbid to fail to do so. Therefore, 'if a religious view become clear to him, or a pious feeling stir his soul, it is rather his first endeavour to direct others to the same subject and if possible transmit the impulse'.[4] Moreover, realizing his own limitations, man needs association with others in order that his own understanding of religion may be filled out by theirs.[5] Conversational groups are neither adequate nor suitable to fulfil these impulses and needs: 'There must be a higher style and another kind of society entirely consecrated to religion.'[6] There follows a rhetorical description of a congregation assembled for worship. Here the preacher 'presents to the sympathetic contemplation of others his own heart as stirred by God'; here 'are sacred mysteries discovered and solemnized that are not mere insignificant emblems'; here 'in sacred hymns and choruses ... are breathed out things that definite speech cannot grasp. The melodies of thought and feeling interchange and give mutual support, till all is satiated and full of the sacred and the infinite.'[7]

THE PRIESTHOOD OF THE PEOPLE

Schleiermacher now turns to the distinction between priests and laity which the despisers, he says, believe to be the source of many evils. He asserts that they are mistaken:

You have been deluded; this is no distinction of persons, but only of office and function. Every man is a priest, in so far as he draws others to himself in the field he has made his own and can show himself master in; every man is a layman, in so far as he follows the skill and direction of another in the religious matters with which he is less familiar. That tyrannical aristocracy which you describe as so hateful does not exist, but this society is a priestly nation, a complete republic, where each in turn is leader and people, following in others the same power that he feels in himself and uses for governing others (ibid., p. 153).

In his explanation of this passage,[8] Schleiermacher says that if Christianity had attained its goal of being a royal priesthood (1 Pet. 2.9) 'so that there was no more need to awake religion in others', there would have been no need for a distinct priesthood. With the spread of Christianity the need arose 'to organize the more advanced for more effective operation on the rest'. But the distinction between priest and laity, teacher and taught, is not an original and essential difference. The more the function of the special priesthood succeeds, 'the more superfluous this organization will become'. The disappearance of the distinction is not to be expected quickly, but meanwhile its validity 'must ever more and more be limited to the sphere in which finally alone it can have a reason', that is, the training of the community to be a royal priesthood.

NO SALVATION OUTSIDE THE CHURCH

Schleiermacher condemns, as much as do the cultured despisers, 'the wild mania for converting to single definite forms of religion ... and the awful watchword, "No salvation save with us".'[9] Such a watchword is not to be used by one religious association against another. Nevertheless:

> The maxim *nulla salus* ... has for the great communion of the pious an absolute verity, for without any piety it can acknowledge no salvation. Only in so far as one religious party utters it against another, does it work destructively, which is to say, in so far as a universal communion is denied (ibid., p. 188).

Schleiermacher here asserts the existence of a universal religious communion, 'the great communion of the pious'. It is a graduated communion made up of 'different pious communions', Christian and non-Christian, of different historical origin, arising in different cultures, or representing different stages of development. Between these there should be no 'wild mania for proselytizing'. Yet he draws a distinction between 'that wild irreligious mania which easily degenerates into persecution' and 'a praiseworthy zeal for conversion' which, following the example of St Paul at Athens, finds a connecting link with the piety of others and seeks to build it up.[10] Moreover, 'the spread of our own form of religion is a natural and permissible private business of the individual';[11] and Schleiermacher is prepared to allow that 'individual' here need not be interpreted 'with too painful accuracy', and that such 'mild proselytizing' may rightly be the work of associations of individuals.[12]

THE INVISIBLE CHURCH

Schleiermacher proceeds to discuss the distinction between the visible Church and the invisible Church which he calls the true Church.[13] He departs from traditional usage in speaking of the true Church also as the Church triumphant. The Church militant is 'the Church that fights against what the age and the state of man place in its way', and the Church triumphant is 'the Church that has vanquished all opposition, whose training is completed'.[14] The visible Church comprises the great mass of people who 'wish to receive . . . but of reaction on others they do not so much as think. . . . They exercise no reaction because they are capable of none; and they can only be incapable because they have no religion.' Using 'a figure from science', Schleiermacher says that

> they are negatively religious, and press in great crowds to the few points [i.e. the religious associations or denominations] where they suspect the positive principle of religion. Having been charged, however, they again fail in capacity to retain. . . . They then go about in a certain feeling of emptiness, till longing awakens once more, and they gradually become again electrified. . . . Being without knowledge or guess of true religion . . . they repeat a thousand times the same endeavour, and yet remain where and what they were.[15]

It is a contemptuous description which in his later 'explanation'[16] he modifies considerably.

On the other hand, the true Church consists of those who 'have reached consciousness with their piety, and in whom the religious view of life is dominant'. They are 'men of some culture and much power', few in number and never to be found all together where 'many hundreds . . . are assembled in great temples'. They form a true religious society in which all communication is mutual, and they know 'how to estimate the Church, commonly so called, at about its true value, which is to say, not particularly high'.[17]

Yet Schleiermacher does not wish for the dissolution of the visible Church, nor that those who are of the true Church should stand aloof from it:

> In comparison with the more glorious association which, in my view, is the only true Church, I have spoken of this larger and widely extended association very disparagingly, as of something common and mean. This follows from the nature of the case, and I could not conceal my mind on the subject. I guard myself, however, most solemnly against any assumption you may cherish, that I agree with the growing wish that this institution should be utterly destroyed. Though the true Church is always to stand open only to those who have already ripened to a piety of their own, there must be some bond of union with those who are still seeking. As that is what this institution should be, it ought, from the nature of the case, to take its leaders and priests from the true Church (ibid., p. 161).

There needs to be a relationship between the true Church and the visible institution: 'Were persons of more individual emotion now to withdraw from those common forms of presentation, both parties would suffer loss.'[18] The visible Church, 'this institution for pupils in religion, must take its priests only from the members of the true Church'.[19] These latter must compassionately go to the help of those who are as yet beginners.[20] They themselves, too, need this sphere of activity, for 'if the true Church nowhere shows itself in actuality, nothing remains for (them) but an isolated, separatist existence, always decaying for want of a larger circulation'.[21]

Because of the unfavourable circumstances of the time, Schleiermacher sees this relationship between members of the true Church and the actually existing religious associations as yielding only 'scanty fruit'.[22] No more can be expected, he intimates, than 'the peaceful cosmopolitan union of all existing communions, each being as perfect as possible after its own manner'.[23]

CHURCH AND STATE

In the last part of this fourth speech on 'Association in Religion', Schleiermacher eloquently expresses his opposition to the domination of the Church by the State. A few extracts will illustrate his point of view:

> Listen to what may possibly seem an unholy wish that I can hardly suppress. Would that the most distant presentiment of religion had for ever

remained unknown to all heads of states, to all successful and skilful politicians! (ibid., pp. 166–7).

As soon as a prince declared a church to be a community with special privileges, a distinguished member of the civil world, the corruption of that church was begun and almost irrevocably decided (ibid., p. 167).

The members of the true church the visible church may contain ... are not in a position to do for it even the little that might still be done. ... There are worldly things now to order and manage, and privileges to maintain and make good (ibid., p. 168).

If it is the interest of the proud, the ambitious, the covetous, the intriguing to press into the church, where otherwise they would have felt only the bitterest *ennui*, and if they begin to pretend interest and intelligence in holy things to gain the earthly reward, how can the truly religious escape subjection? (ibid.).

[The State] treats the church as an institution of its own appointment and invention ... and it alone presumes to decide who is fit to come forward in this society as exemplar and priest (ibid., p. 169).

It is very apparent that a society to which such a thing can happen which with false humility accepts favours that can profit it nothing and with cringing readiness takes on burdens that send it headlong to destruction; which allows itself to be abused by an alien power, and parts with the liberty and independence which are its birthright, for a delusion; which abandons its own high and noble aim to follow things which lie quite outside of its path, cannot be a society of men who have a definite aim and know exactly what they wish. This glance at the history of ecclesiastical society is, I think, the best proof that it is not strictly a society of religious men. At most it appears that some particles of such a society are mixed in it and are overlaid with foreign ingredients (ibid., pp. 170–71).

The state may be satisfied, if it so pleases, with a religious morality, but religion rejects consciously and individually every prophet and priest that moralizes from this point of view. Whosoever would proclaim religion must do it unadulterated (ibid., p. 173).

Away then with every such union between church and state! That remains my Cato's utterance to the end, or till I see the union actually destroyed (ibid., p. 174).

In his later 'explanations' Schleiermacher puts forward his views about the relation between Church and State in such matters as marriage, law and education. He stands firm on the principle of separation, but adds, in words which echo John Locke:

Yet it is impossible that the church should be without any union with the state. That appears even where the church is freest. The least is that the state treat the religious societies like any other private society. As a general principle of association it takes knowledge of them and puts itself in a position to interfere in case they should cherish anything prejudicial to the common freedom and safety. With this least, however, it is seldom possible to escape, as appears even in North America where the church is freest. The freer the churches are, the easier it happens that some dissolve and some combine ... [in which case] there are difficulties of settlement in which the state is the natural arranger and umpire (ibid., p. 205).

2 THE CHRISTIAN FAITH

Schleiermacher's *The Christian Faith* is a systematic presentation of Christian theology. 'In the opinion of competent thinkers (it) is, with the exception of Calvin's *Institutes*, the most important work covering the whole field of doctrine to which Protestant theology can point.'[24] It is a work of dogmatic theology, and since dogmatics is the systematization of the teachings of the Christian Church, Schleiermacher holds that he 'must begin with a conception of the Christian Church, in order to define in accordance therewith what Dogmatics should be and should do within that Church'.[25] In his Introduction, therefore, he puts forward certain propositions about the Church, derived not from biblical or dogmatic sources, but from other disciplines, ethics primarily, but also philosophy of religion and apologetics: 'The general concept of "Church", if there really is to be such a concept, must be derived principally from Ethics, since in every case the "Church" is a society which originates only through free human action and which can only through such continue to exist.'[26] The first proposition derived from ethics is:

The piety which forms the basis of all ecclesiastical communions is, considered purely in itself, neither a Knowing nor a Doing, but a modification of Feeling, or of immediate self-consciousness (*The Christian Faith*, p. 5).

The words immediately following show that for Schleiermacher a church is essentially an association of those who share substantially the same kind of religious feeling:

That a Church is nothing but a communion of association relating to religion or piety, is beyond all doubt for us Evangelical (Protestant) Christians, since we regard it as equivalent to degeneration in a Church when it begins to occupy itself with other matters as well, whether the affairs of science or of outward organization; just as we also always oppose any attempt on the part of the leaders of State or of science, as such, to order the affairs of religion.[27]

The second and third propositions derived from ethics are:

> The common element in all howsoever diverse expressions of piety, by which these are conjointly distinguished from all other feelings, or, in other words, the self-identical essence of piety, is this: the consciousness of being absolutely dependent, or, which is the same thing, of being in relation with God (ibid., p. 12).

> The religious self-consciousness, like every essential element in human nature, leads necessarily in its development to fellowship or communion; a communion which, on the one hand, is variable and fluid, and, on the other hand, has definite limits, i.e. is a Church (ibid., p. 26).

Up to this point Schleiermacher is giving the word 'Church' a wide sense which includes all religious groups. The propositions which he now borrows from the philosophy of religion lead him to develop ideas which he had touched on in the *Speeches*: that the various religious communions are related to each other as different stages of development and as different kinds;[28] that monotheistic forms of piety are on the highest level;[29] and that those which 'subordinate the natural in human conditions to the moral' are superior to those which 'subordinate the moral to the natural'.[30]

From apologetics he derives a proposition which defines the peculiar essence of Christianity:

> Christianity is a monotheistic faith ... and is essentially distinguished from other such faiths by the fact that in it everything is related to the redemption accomplished by Jesus of Nazareth (ibid., p. 52).

Christianity, however, 'takes a greater variety of forms than other faiths and is split up into a multiplicity of smaller communions or churches'.[31] Schleiermacher concludes that 'Dogmatic Theology is the science which systematizes the doctrine prevalent in a Christian Church at a given time'.[32] However,

> Limitation to the doctrine of one particular Church is not a characteristic universally valid, for Christendom has not always been divided into a number of communions definitely separated by diversity of doctrine. But for the present this characteristic is indispensable; for, to speak only of the Western Church, a presentation suitable for Protestantism cannot possibly be suitable for Catholics, there being no systematic connection between the doctrines of the one and those of the other. A dogmatic presentation which aimed at avoiding contradiction from either of these

two parties would lack ecclesiastical value for both in almost every proposition (ibid., p. 89).[33]

Schleiermacher, therefore, undertakes to present the doctrine of one communion only, that of the Evangelical (Protestant) Church. Of this, he says, there are two principal branches, the Reformed and the Lutheran, whose 'original relation was such that, notwithstanding their different starting points, they might just as well have grown together into an outward unity as they have come to separate from each other'.[34] A union of the Lutheran and Reformed Churches had been effected in Prussia in 1817, and Schleiermacher was a member of this united Church. He feels able to proceed to his systematic presentation of doctrine with 'the assumption that the separation of the two has lacked sufficient grounds, inasmuch as the differences in doctrine are in no sense traceable to a difference in the religious affections themselves'.[35]

Schleiermacher's major treatment of the Church is found in the second part of his system, which is the 'Explication of the Facts of the Religious Self-Consciousness, as they are determined by the Antithesis of Sin and Grace'.

THE CHURCH AS A DIVINELY EFFECTED CORPORATE LIFE

In the Introduction to the 'Second Aspect of the Antithesis: Explication of the Consciousness of Grace'[36] he presents a doctrine which is close to the idea of the Church as the mystical body of Christ.[37] The religious consciousness which is specifically Christian is consciousness of the need of redemption and that redemption is made available by Jesus Christ. It is not a consciousness which is achieved by Christians as individuals, but is given in the experience of the Christian corporate life.

> We are conscious of all approximations to the state of blessedness which occur in the Christian life as being grounded in a new, divinely effected corporate life, which works in opposition to the corporate life of sin and the misery which develops in it (ibid., p. 358).

Schleiermacher is insistent that the blessedness (i.e. essentially the consciousness of redemption) which develops in the Christian fellowship proceeds directly from Christ himself:

> To regard our corporate life as divinely created, and to derive it from Christ as a divinely given One, are the same thing; just so, at that time [i.e. the lifetime of Christ], to believe that the Kingdom of God (that is, the new corporate life which was to be created by God) had come, were the

same thing. Consequently, all developing blessedness had its ground in this corporate life (ibid., p. 360).

While these propositions may apply to very different conceptions of Christianity, he maintains that they exclude two things:

> First, the idea that one can share in the redemption and be made blessed through Christ outside the corporate life which He instituted, as if a Christian could dispense with the latter and be with Christ, as it were, alone (ibid.).

And, second:

> the supposition that, without the introduction of any new factor, and within the corporate life of sin itself, the better individuals could attain to such an approximation to blessedness as would remove the misery (ibid., pp. 360–61).

Thus, the principle that Christianity is essentially corporate is strongly affirmed, and the idea of self-salvation by works is firmly rejected. These things are summed up in a further proposition:

> In this corporate life which goes back to the influence of Jesus, redemption is effected by Him through the communication of His sinless perfection (ibid., p. 361).

The sinless perfection which Jesus possessed is communicated in the fellowship which he founded. It was not, and is not faith that makes Jesus the Redeemer. He is Redeemer by his own work, 'constraining us to the new corporate life'.[38] In summary Schleiermacher says:

> We posit, on the one side, an initial divine activity which is supernatural but at the same time a vital human receptivity in virtue of which alone that supernatural can become a natural fact of history (ibid., p. 365).

Jesus Christ is the Second Adam, 'the beginner and originator of the more perfect human life, or the completion of the creation'.[39] The community which has its origin in him is the 'new creation' of 2 Corinthians 5.17.

Schleiermacher's more detailed exposition of the doctrine of the Church is contained in the second section[40] of his 'Explication of the Consciousness of Grace'. He includes here his discussion of holy Scripture, the ministry of the Word of God, baptism, the Lord's Supper, the power of the keys, and prayer in the name of Christ, all of which are 'essential and invariable features of the Church'.[41] We shall limit ourselves to his treatment of the origin of the Church, with which he closely associates the doctrines of election and the Holy Spirit,[42] of the Church visible and invisible,[43] and of the consummation of the Church.[44]

THE ORIGIN OF THE CHURCH

Schleiermacher begins by noting that fellowship may be understood in a narrower or wider sense. Within the one fellowship of believers or the Church an outer and an inner fellowship may be distinguished, each belonging to the Church 'though obviously in a different sense'.

> The new life of each individual springs from that of the community, while the life of the community springs from no other individual life than that of the Redeemer. We must therefore hold that the totality of those who live in the state of sanctification is the inner fellowship; the totality of those on whom preparatory grace is at work is the outer fellowship, from which by regeneration members pass to the inner, and then keep helping to extend the wider circle (ibid., p. 525).

At first, 'the power of the inner circle was entirely confined to Christ'.[45] Then, from among those who awaited the fulfilment of the messianic hope, some (the first disciples) recognized Jesus as the Christ, came under his redemptive influence, and at the same time began to exercise an influence upon others who had not yet attained to the recognition of Christ. 'These latter thus formed the outer circle, receiving from the first the preparatory operations of grace, in contrast to the inner circle from which the operations proceeded.'[46] Thus 'the Christian fellowship gradually expands as individuals and masses are incorporated into association with Christ'.[47]

The origin of the Church, then, is no different from what happens daily: redeeming activity reaches out from the community to lead the unconverted to conversion. It is a movement outward towards the world from the fellowship of believers, and a movement from the world to the Church. The corporate Christian consciousness, Schleiermacher says, is that the Church 'confronts us as something growing out of the world and gradually, of itself, expelling the world'.[48]

ELECTION

Schleiermacher sees the doctrine of election as intimately connected with the doctrine of the Church in that those who are to form the Church must be separated out from the world,[49] and this is a matter of divine government, a divine ordinance, or election, which rests in the divine good-pleasure.[50]

He does not hold a doctrine of election to damnation. This would be incompatible with the Christian self-consciousness of God.[51] There is a 'single divine fore-ordination to blessedness, by which the origin of the Church is ordered'.[52] 'Each man, when his time is fully come, is regenerated.'[53] The difficult theological question, then, is why some are regenerated later than others. This is similar to the question why the incarnation of Christ occurred when it did and not earlier. The answer can only be that it is 'when the fullness of time was come', which rests on the divine good-pleasure and knowledge of what is truly the best for every individual and group. In his postscript to this doctrine Schleiermacher says that 'it is an essential of our faith that every nation will sooner or later become Christian'.[54]

THE COMMUNICATION OF THE HOLY SPIRIT

All who are living in the state of sanctification feel an inward impulse to become more and more one in their common co-operative activity and reciprocal influence, and are conscious of this as the common Spirit of the new corporate life founded by Christ (ibid., p. 560).

This common Spirit is the Holy Spirit of whom Scripture speaks:

He is promised to the whole community, and where an original communication of the Spirit is spoken of, it comes by a single act to a multitude of people (John 20.22–3; Acts 2.4), who *eo ipso* become an organic whole (ibid., p. 562).

This common Spirit is the Spirit of Christ. This affirmation is based on the Christian self-consciousness:

For everyone is conscious of the communication of the Spirit as being connected in the closest fashion with the rise of faith in him, and everyone recognizes that the same is true for all the others. For faith only comes by preaching and always goes back to Christ's commission and is therefore derived from Him. And as in Christ Himself everything proceeds from the Divine within Him, so also does this communication, which becomes in everyone the power of the new life, a power not different in each, but the same in all (ibid., pp. 563–4).

After his departure from earth Christ fully communicated his Spirit to his followers,[55] and among them prolongs his 'fellowship-forming activity'.[56]

Every regenerate person partakes of the Holy Spirit, so that there is no living fellowship with Christ without an indwelling of the Holy Spirit, and *vice versa* (ibid., p. 574).

THE CHURCH VISIBLE AND INVISIBLE[57]

> Regeneration is not a sudden transformation; even though delight in God's will has become man's proper self, there remains in him everywhere an activity of the flesh striving against the Spirit; and thus even in those who taken together compose the Church, there is always something that belongs to the world (ibid., p. 676).

Only if it were possible to 'isolate and collect the effects of the divine Spirit' in the members of the Church, should we be able to see the Church in its purity.[58] A distinction between the Church visible and invisible is therefore necessary, but Schleiermacher prefers to use the antithesis he has already employed[59] between the Church's outer and inner circles:

> By the Invisible Church is commonly understood the whole body of those who are regenerate and really have a place within the state of sanctification; by the Visible Church, all those besides who have heard the gospel and therefore are called, and who confess themselves outwardly members of the Church, or who (as we should prefer to express it) form the outer circle of the Church, inasmuch as they receive preparatory gracious influences through the medium of an externally constituted relationship (ibid., p. 677).

The visible Church is divided and subject to error; the invisible is an undivided unity and infallible in the sense of possessing the whole truth of redemption.[60] The separations of the visible Church are not to be condoned. There must be 'endeavour to unite the separates',[61] and 'the complete suspension of fellowship between different parts of the Visible Church is un-Christian'.[62]

THE CONSUMMATION OF THE CHURCH

> We ... cherish the hope that the expansion of Christianity will be accelerated in proportion as the glory of the Redeemer is ever more clearly reflected in the Church itself. It is an undeniable possibility that this might take place in the course of human history; yet we cannot forget that during all that time the propagation of the species goes on, and that sin develops anew in each generation. ... The Church is thus ever anew admitting worldly elements ... and hence is never perfected. In this state it is usually designated the 'Church militant' because it has not only to stand on the defensive against the world but must seek to conquer the world. Just for that reason, as conceived in the state of consummation it is called the 'Church triumphant', because all that in this sense was worldly has

now been wholly absorbed in it, and no longer exists as its opposite (ibid., pp. 696–7).

But this takes us into the doctrine of 'the Last Things', and the 'Christian consciousness has absolutely nothing to say regarding a condition so entirely outside our ken'.[63] In Schleiermacher's view, therefore, this is a very uncertain part of Dogmatics. Nevertheless the Church's doctrines about personal immortality and the consummation have their source in the prophetic teaching of Christ. Consequently,

> this idea of the consummation of the Church is rooted in our Christian consciousness as representing the unbroken fellowship of human nature with Christ under conditions wholly unknown and only faintly imaginable, but the only fellowship which can be conceived as wholly free from all that springs from the conflict of flesh and spirit (ibid., pp. 697–8).

It is the Christian consciousness as hope and 'as a pattern to which we have to approximate'.[64]

ALBRECHT RITSCHL, 1822–89

The most influential theologian in Germany in the latter part of the nineteenth century was Albrecht Ritschl, the son of a Lutheran pastor. He became Professor of Theology at the University of Bonn in 1859, after more than a dozen years there as a lecturer. In 1864 he was appointed Professor of Theology at Göttingen where he remained until his death. His main publication was *The Christian Doctrine of Justification and Reconciliation* in three volumes (1870–74), the first presenting the history of the doctrine, the second its biblical basis, and the third Ritschl's own systematic theology.[65] His theology reacts sharply from the position of Schleiermacher, for whom theology was the explication of the Christian self-consciousness. It reacts equally sharply from the philosophical idealism of Hegel and his disciples. For Ritschl neither man's feelings nor intellectual speculation provided a firm foundation for theology. His starting-point is the revelation of God in Christ.[66] He regards all attempts to establish, for example, the divinity of Christ by philosophical methods as mistakes:

> Luther's warning against teachers who would determine the things of God *a priori*, from above downwards, previous to all definite Divine revelation, holds good (*Justification and Reconciliation*, p. 399).

Since Christ is received by the Christian as 'the Bearer of the final revelation of God'[67] the task of theology is to provide 'an orderly reproduction of the thought of Christ and the apostles'.[68] Ritschl believed he was rescuing Protestant theology from both the subjectivism of Schleiermacher[69] and the intellectualizing of the Hegelian school, and returning to the theological principles of Luther and to the firm basis of God's revelation in Christ.

A paragraph from his Introduction to volume 3 in which he defines 'Christianity', reveals the special characteristics of Ritschl's theology:

> Christianity, then, is the monotheistic, completely spiritual, and ethical religion, which, based on the life of its Author as Redeemer and as Founder of the Kingdom of God, consists in the freedom of the children of God, involves the impulse to conduct from the motive of love, aims at the moral organization of mankind, and grounds blessedness on the relation of sonship to God, as well as on the Kingdom of God (ibid., p. 13).

He bases his theology on the historical facts of Christ's life. It is practical, not speculative, concerned with man's will rather than with his feelings, and therefore has a strong ethical emphasis with both personal and social implications.

THE NECESSITY OF THE CHURCH

On the first page of the Introduction Ritschl speaks of Jesus as the Founder of the Christian Church and of the apostles as its earliest representatives. At once he goes on to assert the essential place which the Christian community (he prefers this term to 'Church') has in the purposes of God. The significance of Jesus' teachings about Redemption

> becomes completely intelligible only when we see how they are reflected in the consciousness of those who believe in Him, and how the members of the Christian community trace back their consciousness of pardon to the Person and the action and passion of Jesus (ibid., p. 1).

Only those who imagine themselves competent to discover 'the religion of Jesus' by themselves, or who conceive of him only as the originator of a new moral code, or as one who has contributed to the picture of an ideal humanity, can ignore the necessity of the Church and of membership of it.[70]

> Authentic and complete knowledge of Jesus' religious significance—His significance, that is, as a Founder of religion—depends, then, on one's reckoning oneself part of the community which He founded, and this precisely in so far as it believes itself to have received the forgiveness of sins as His peculiar gift.... We can discover the full compass of His

historical actuality solely from the faith of the Christian community. Not even His purpose to found the community can be quite understood historically save by one who, as a member of it, subordinates himself to His Person (ibid., pp. 2–3).

The idea of the Church as the essential *locus* where man in history comes to know and can appropriate the redemption offered in Christ occurs in several places. Thus:

Even the Evangelical Christian's right relation to Christ is both historically and logically conditioned by the fellowship of believers; historically, because a man always finds the community already existing when he arrives at faith, nor does he attain this end without the action of the community upon him; logically, because no action of Christ upon men can be conceived except in accordance with the standard of Christ's antecedent purpose to found a community (ibid., p. 549).[71]

There is much in common with Schleiermacher here,[72] but whereas for the latter the sharing of the God-consciousness of Jesus is primarily distinctive of the community, Ritschl places the emphasis on the acceptance of the moral standards and teaching of Christ.

THE CHURCH DISTINGUISHED FROM THE KINGDOM OF GOD

Ritschl affirms that the Christian religion has two focal points: redemption through Christ and the Kingdom of God. Protestant theology generally has taken the concept of redemption through Christ as the single centre from which all Christian faith and practice flow. 'But', says Ritschl, 'Christianity, so to speak, resembles not a circle described from a single centre, but an ellipse which is determined by two *foci*.'[73] In Christianity everything is related to redemption through Christ, but everything is related also to 'the moral organization of humanity through love-prompted action'. The former is 'the private end of each individual Christian'; the latter is the setting-up of the Kingdom of God—'the final end of all'.

The Church has a close relationship to the Kingdom of God, but is not to be identified with it. Ritschl rejects such an identification, which he believes to be characteristic of western Catholicism. He rejects also the view, which he attributes to Luther, Melanchthon, and Calvin, that the Kingdom is 'the inward union between Christ and believers through grace and its operations'.[74] Both views assume that the Kingdom is already fully in being. For Ritschl the Kingdom of God is a teleological concept, and its characteristics have a greater ethical content than either western Catholicism or the early Reformers allowed:

> In Christianity, the Kingdom of God is represented as the common end of God and the elect community, in such a way that it rises above the natural limits of nationality and becomes the moral society of nations .... Christ made the universal moral Kingdom of God His end, and thus He came to know and decide for that kind of redemption which He achieved through the maintenance of fidelity in His calling and of His blessed fellowship with God through suffering unto death ... a correct spiritual interpretation of redemption and justification through Christ tends to keep more decisively to the front the truth that the Kingdom of God is the final end (ibid., p. 10).[75]

Ritschl is prepared to describe the Church as 'the fellowship of believers',[76] and to affirm that its unity is 'essentially bound up with the pure preaching of the Gospel and the proper administration of the two sacraments'.[77] The distinction between the Church, so understood, and the Kingdom of God is the distinction between acts of devotion or worship and moral activity:

> Those who believe in Christ ... constitute a Church in so far as they express in prayer their faith in God the Father, or present themselves to God as men who through Christ are well-pleasing to Him. The same believers in Christ constitute the Kingdom of God in so far as, forgetting distinctions of sex, rank, or nationality, they act reciprocally from love, and thus call into existence that fellowship of moral disposition and moral blessings which extends through all possible gradations, to the limits of the human race (ibid., p. 285).

Ritschl justified this distinction on the ground that worship and devotional acts are ends in themselves in that a devotional act 'never can be at the same time a means to an act of the same kind', whereas a moral act is both an end and a means to other possible moral acts. Christians engaged in the first are the Church, while Christians engaged in moral action are the Kingdom of God.[78]

He goes on to say:

> The fellowship of Christians for the purpose of religious worship manifests itself in the sphere of sense, and therefore betrays its peculiar nature to every observer. On the other hand the moral Kingdom of God, even while it manifests itself sensibly in action, as a whole reveals its peculiar nature to Christian faith alone. Moreover, the fellowship of Christians for worship gives rise to legal ordinances which it requires for its own sake; but the Kingdom of God, while not injuriously affected by the fact that

moral action under certain circumstances assumes the garb of legal forms, does not in the least depend on them for its continued existence (ibid., p. 285).

Ritschl's distinction between Church and Kingdom appears, therefore, to bear a resemblance to that of the Reformers between the Church visible and invisible. The resemblance, however, is only superficial. The latter distinction does not fit into his theological framework, and he nowhere discusses it. Although Luther and Calvin broke with the idea that the Kingdom of God is the historical Catholic Church (which Ritschl takes to be Augustine's teaching),[79] he argues that they erred in identifying the Kingdom of God with the 'inward union between believers and the Mediator',[80] conceived of as purely spiritual. 'This conception of the Kingdom of Christ is very far indeed from expressing the fellowship of moral action prompted by love.'[81] Moreover, the Reformers involved themselves in contradictions by according to the State the function of preserving true religion by means of laws and government,[82] and by including preaching ('a legal institution') in their conception of the Kingdom of Christ.[83]

The distinction which Ritschl wishes to make is of a different kind. It is that between the Christian community constituted and organized for the conduct of worship (the Church), and the Christian community as engaged in common action inspired by love (the Kingdom of God):

A legally constituted Church, be it Catholic or Lutheran, is not the Kingdom of God or the Kingdom of Christ, for the simple reason that the Church is not the Kingdom of God. Activity of the most important kind for the service of the Church may be of no value whatever for the Kingdom of God. Nor is devotion to the Church a virtue which could in any way compensate for the absence of conscientiousness, justice, truthfulness, uprightness, tolerance. While we must at present put up with a great deal which contradicts this principle, I have always counted what Christ says in Matthew 7.21–3[84] as part of the consolations of the Gospel.

According to the canons of the New Testament, then, we find that the self-same subject, namely, the community drawn together by Christ, constitutes the Church in so far as its members unite in the same religious worship, and, further, create for this purpose a legal constitution; while on the other hand it constitutes the Kingdom of God in so far as the members of the community give themselves to the interchange of action prompted by love. These two modes of activity, however, are not unrelated to one another. They rather condition one another reciprocally. For Christians must get to know one another as such in the exercise of Divine worship, if they are to make sure of occasions to combine together in mutual action from love. On the other hand, the whole range of this loving activity serves to support the maintenance and extension of fellowship in Divine worship. For there is nothing from which the latter suffers more than from slackness in discharging the tasks of the Kingdom of God (ibid., pp. 289–90).

Ritschl's teaching on the distinction and relation between Church and Kingdom has been criticized on several scores. His conception of the Church as an external organization for the purpose of worship and as a preliminary school for moral action bears little relation to the fullness of the N.T. idea of Church. Nor in the N.T. does the Kingdom of God connote the moral endeavour of man, but rather the act of God in judgement and the inauguration of his reign on earth.

THE HOLY SPIRIT AND THE CHURCH

Ritschl regrets the neglect of the doctrine of the Holy Spirit by theology, and that his own book allows him no space to make good this lack.[85] He does, however, engage in several brief discussions in each of which the Holy Spirit is related to the community.[86] He is reluctant to enter into the question of the eternal relations within the Godhead: 'Our time-conditioned view of things'[87] makes this hazardous. Scripture, he asserts, uses the name of God always as 'a compendious description of his revelation', which is imparted through his Son, Jesus Christ, a process which is only completed when the revelation is accepted by the community under the influence of the Spirit:

> The name God has the same sense when used of Father, Son, and Holy Spirit (Matt. 28.19). For the name denotes God in so far as he reveals Himself, while the Holy Spirit is the power of God which enables the community to appropriate His self-revelation as the Father through His Son (1 Cor. 2.12). That the revelation of God through His Son, however, embraces the community which acknowledges His Son as her Lord, and how it does so, is explained by saying that God manifests Himself to the Son and to the community as *loving will* (ibid., p. 273).

Although 'for us, as pre-existent, Christ is hidden',[88] our estimate of him, based on the revelation of God in Christ, is that he is 'the eternally beloved Son of God', the 'object of the Divine mind and will'.[89] So also we may hold that

> the spirit of God is the knowledge God has of Himself, as of His own self-end. The Holy Spirit denotes in the New Testament the Spirit of God, in so far as the latter is the ground of that knowledge of God and that specific moral and religious life which exist in the Christian community. Since the community has for its conscious purpose the realization of the

Kingdom of God as the Divine self-end, it is correct to say that the practical knowledge of God in this community which is dependent upon God, is identical with the knowledge which God has of Himself even as the love of God is perfected in the fact that within the community love is practised towards the brethren. But if in His Son God loves eternally the community that is like His Son, in other words, if the community is *eo ipso* the eternal object of God's will of love, then also it is God's eternal will that His Spirit should be the Holy Spirit in the community of the Kingdom of God. In the form of this eternal purpose, the Spirit of God proceeds from God, inasmuch, namely, as He is destined to enter into the community which enjoys the perfect knowledge of God (ibid., pp. 471–2).

Ritschl presents the same doctrine of the Holy Spirit in the community in a later passage, more briefly:

The Spirit of God or the Holy Spirit, Who in relation to God Himself is the knowledge which God has of Himself, is at the same time an attribute of the Christian community, because the latter, in accordance with the completed revelation of God through Christ, has that knowledge of God and of His counsel for men in the world which harmonizes with God's self-knowledge (ibid., p. 605).

The Christian community, because it shares in God's knowledge of himself through his self-revelation in Christ, shares in God's Spirit. Ritschl goes on to assert that the Holy Spirit is at the same time the motive-power of the life of all Christians, directing that life to the common end of the Kingdom of God. Consequently, he argues, 'it is not permissible for any man to determine his relation to the Holy Spirit by observation of himself in which he isolates himself from all others'.[90]

Regarding the justification and regeneration of the individual, then, nothing further can be objectively taught than that it takes place within the community of believers as a result of the propagation of the Gospel and the specific continuous action of Christ's personal character in His community, through the awakening in the individual of faith in Christ as trust in God as Father and of the sense of union rooted in the Holy Spirit (ibid., p. 607).

'Rules for the objective operation of Divine Grace upon individuals are not to be found, the less so as the relations between men and God always manifest themselves in experience solely in the form of subjective self-consciousness.'[91] Claims about individual experiences of the Spirit, therefore, while open to psychological inquiry, are not subject-matter for dogmatic theology. Ritschl is suspicious of such claims in that 'sectarian or half-sectarian practice customarily appeals to the

Holy Spirit just in so far as thereby justification is supposed to be found for passionate zeal, or pathological experiences or forced, vague, aimless efforts to reach passive assurance of salvation'.[92] Here his antipathy towards subjectivism, enthusiasm, and pietism generally is apparent. At the same time his limiting of the activity of the Holy Spirit to the Christian community fails to do full justice to the biblical doctrine of the Spirit who is likened in John 3.8 to the wind which blows where it wills.

Ritschl's theology was very influential in Germany in the last quarter of the nineteenth century and the first quarter of the twentieth. Its chief exponents were W. Herrmann (1846–1922), J. Kaftan (1848–1926), A. Harnack (1851–1930), F. Loofs (1858–1928), and E. Troeltsch (1865–1923). In Harnack's widely read *Das Wesen des Christentums* (1900)[93] the Ritschlian interpretation of the Kingdom and ethical emphasis are very prominent. A question mark against the assumptions of the Ritschlian theology was, however, placed by two books. These were Johann Weiss's *Die Predigt Jesu vom Reiche Gottes*[94] (1893) and Albert Schweitzer's *Von Reimarus zu Wrede* ('From Reimarus to Wrede')[95] (1906), which made clear that, although the conception of the Kingdom of God as the gradual ethical development of mankind under Christian influence was thoroughly in accord with the prevalent optimism about historical progress, it bore little relation to the Kingdom of God which Jesus preached. Between the two world wars the Ritschlian school was greatly weakened under the impact of the 'Crisis theology' of Karl Barth and Emil Brunner.

Ritschlian influence was strong also in America. The Social Gospel Movement, of which Walter Rauschenbusch (1861–1916) was the most able theological exponent, owed much to Ritschl's doctrine of the Kingdom of God.

17

The Church of England
Its Parties

The nineteenth century brought great changes to the churches in Britain. The repeal of the Test and Corporation Acts in 1828 meant that the non-conformist churches, among which were the now rapidly increasing Wesleyans, were free of the most serious civil restrictions which had been laid on them for over 150 years. The Catholic Emancipation Bill of 1829 likewise lifted these disabilities from Roman Catholics. In 1850 a Roman Catholic hierarchy was set up in England with the appointment as Archbishop of Westminster of Cardinal N. P. S. Wiseman. At once the Roman Catholic Church made great strides, increasing in membership, building churches and schools, and reintroducing monastic communities. But as the century proceeded, no church was more markedly transformed than the established Church of England. When the century opened, three parties may be discerned within the Church of England: Evangelicals, Liberals or Broad Churchmen, and High Churchmen.

THE EVANGELICALS

Many who shared the Methodist concern for personal conversion to Christ, and the conviction that the sole work of a Christian minister is to convince hearers that justification is by faith alone in the efficacy of Christ's atoning sacrifice, remained within the Church of England. The formalism and suspicion of 'enthusiasm' of the Church sorely tempted these Evangelicals to secede. Much pressure was brought also upon bishops to discipline clergy who engaged in itinerant preaching or set up meeting places outside their own parishes.

Some leading Evangelical clergymen had done these things. Henry Venn (1725–97) had left Huddersfield in 1771 because of ill-health for the less demanding parish of Yelling in Huntingdonshire. Fearing that his successor at Huddersfield would not continue the 'gospel preaching', he encouraged the building of a chapel within the parish for those who were dissatisfied with their new incumbent. The tragedy of this was that when, two years later, another Evangelical was appointed, few seceders returned to the Church, and another permanent dissenting body was thus created.[1] As Rector of Yelling Venn still practised itinerancy, preaching in houses and barns in neighbouring parishes, and also visiting London regularly to preach at the Surrey Chapel[2] even after it had been registered as a dissenting chapel. John Berridge (1716–93), whose extraordinarily powerful preaching as incumbent of Everton in Cambridgeshire marked the beginning of the Evangelical Movement in that county, also did not hesitate to engage in preaching in the fields as well as in chapels of the Countess of Huntingdon's Connexion.

It is generally agreed that it was principally the influence of Charles Simeon (1759–1836) which held Evangelicals within the established Church. A Fellow of King's College, Cambridge, in 1783 he was appointed Vicar of Holy Trinity Church, Cambridge, where he remained until his death. He held that the object of Evangelical preaching is 'To humble the sinner. To exalt the Saviour. To promote holiness'.[3] This he determined to do in the spheres which had been assigned to him by ecclesiastical authority, his parish, and his College. He encountered not only the derision of Fellows and undergraduates of his College, but also opposition from his churchwardens and parishioners who had hoped for the appointment of their afternoon lecturer as vicar. They made the church as inaccessible to Simeon as possible. They locked their rented pews, leaving only the side aisles for any who attended. They refused his visits. Simeon's friends, Henry Venn among them, counselled patience and humility, and he heeded their advice. His quandary, however, led him to one irregularity which his enemies might have used against him, but oddly did not. When, after a few months, a few parishioners began to attend church, he felt the need to give them further instruction. His church being barred against him for this purpose, he hired a room in his parish and, as their numbers grew, a larger room in an adjoining parish. His dilemma (and that of other Evangelicals) is well expressed in his own Memoir: 'I was sensible that it would be regarded by many as irregular, but what was to be done? I could not instruct them in my church; and I must of necessity have them all drawn away by the dissenters, if I did not meet them myself; I therefore committed the matter to God in earnest prayer.'[4]

Early in his ministry (*c.*1785) Simeon also preached several times in a barn within another parish. Henry Venn, who had frequently preached in the same place, remonstrated with him on this. It is likely that the older man, ready himself to accept the opprobrium and penalties which itinerancy might bring, saw in Simeon a man who could bring the established Church to a recognition of the value of Evangelical principles. In later life, being reminded of his preaching in the barn, Simeon replied: 'O spare me! Spare me! I was a young man then.'

The history of Simeon's overcoming of opposition in his parish and in the University is told by his successor at Holy Trinity, William Carus, in his *Memoirs of the Life of the Rev. Charles Simeon, M.A.*[5] His incumbency, which lasted fifty-four years, was a remarkable instance of devoted pastoral work which sought to humble his people (and himself) and to exalt Christ.

We do not find in the writings of Simeon or other Evangelicals of the early nineteenth century any systematic exposition of the doctrine of the Church. It may safely be said that they held the Augustinian and Calvinistic doctrine of the Church Invisible. But they were also convinced that the Church of England embodied a divinely sanctioned Church order, and that it was there that they were called by God to serve. They were well aware of its faults. They would have subscribed to the view that the Church regarded as institution is a mixed society. Speaking of baptism in his University Sermons of 1811, 'On the Excellency of the Liturgy', Simeon said:

> We must distinguish between a change of state and a change of nature. Baptism is a change of state: for by it we become entitled to all the blessings of the new covenant. ... A change of nature may be communicated at the time that the ordinance is administered; but the ordinance itself does not communicate it. ... Simon Magus was baptized; and yet remained in the gall of bitterness.[6]

The idea of the 'mixed Church' is implicit here.

The common assumption that the Evangelicals saw the Church simply as a gathering of individual believers is not true. As for Simeon, it is belied both by his use of corporate terms in speaking of the Christian community ('fold of Christ', 'one family', even 'mystical body') and by his pastoral policy. He was a pioneer in encouraging the laity of his parish to realize that they were members of a body, and to show this by taking their part in pastoral care of the sick, needy, and troubled.

Simeon had a great regard for liturgical worship. In the series of sermons mentioned above he declared that if an objective comparison of the extemporary prayers offered in dissenting chapels over a period of time could be made with those of the Book of Common Prayer, 'there is scarcely a man in the Kingdom that would not fall down on his knees and bless God for the Liturgy of the Established Church'.[7] Elsewhere he wrote: 'The finest sight short of heaven would be a whole congregation using the prayers of the Liturgy in the true spirit of them.'[8] He was meticulously loyal to his bishop, and Charles Smyth notes[9] also 'his feeling that the Priestly benediction was more than a prayer . . . his recognition of the priestly power of Absolution'.

To many enthusiastic Evangelicals Simeon seemed 'more of a churchman than a gospel man'. As Smyth says,[10] Simeon had learned from his contact with John Berridge that 'although the Kingdom of Heaven is indeed taken by violence, it is not to be held by indiscipline'. This lesson he passed to those who came under his influence at the University, many of whom were to be the Evangelical leaders of the next generation. 'Do not attempt to act in a parish with which you have no connection,' he wrote to a young clergyman in 1817.[11]

However, an urgent problem faced the Evangelicals. How were Evangelicals to be placed in a sufficient number of parishes thus securing the continuity of 'gospel-preaching' in England without the formation of new dissenting groups, which too often was the result of preaching in fields, barns, and private houses? The solution was found in the purchasing of advowsons,[12] initiated by John Thornton, a wealthy layman, and enthusiastically adopted by Simeon, who devoted a great deal of his own money to it, and collected much more. The Simeon Trust, which administered the money and controlled the appointments, was constituted in 1817. This well-meant policy (Simeon was convinced that it was for the advancement of the established Church and the Kingdom of God) had unforeseen and unfortunate results. Other groups which did not share Evangelical principles adopted the practice of buying advowsons, and this did much to exacerbate party strife within the Church of England until well into the twentieth century.

Of much more positive value to the Church of England was the Evangelicals' zeal for overseas missions and social reform. Simeon was a co-founder in 1799 of the Church Missionary Society, which supplied a steady stream of missionaries first to India and other parts of the East, and later to Africa. From the Evangelical ranks came many of the nation's leaders in the campaigns for the abolition of the slave trade in British dominions (finally achieved in 1833), for the introduction of legislation to improve the inhuman conditions in factories and mills, and for educational reform. William Wilberforce, Hannah More, and Anthony Ashley Cooper, the seventh Earl of Shaftesbury, were all Evangelicals.

Later in the nineteenth century many Evangelicals took a course which their predecessors would hardly have approved. In violent reaction to the Oxford Movement (see pp. 51 ff), prompted by an irrational fear of the Church of Rome, they formed a strange alliance with the Liberal successors of the Latitudinarians. Virulent anti-Romanism became their chief preoccupation, and often the theme of their preaching rather than the gospel of Christ's love for souls. Simeon's charitable attitude to dissenters and Roman Catholics ('the clergyman ought to visit them all, visiting even their Ministers ... treating them with gentleness and delicacy, and making himself felt as their friend'),[13] and Wilberforce's defence of the Catholic Emancipation Bill were forgotten. Happily, this phase of their history has passed, and Anglican Evangelicals are to be found among those engaging in the ecumenical dialogues with Roman Catholics which are a feature of the post-Vatican II era.

THE LIBERALS

The Liberals were the successors of the Latitudinarians. They disliked dogmatic definition in theology, saw the maintenance and inculcation of a high moral standard in accordance with the teachings of Christ as the main significance of the Church's existence, and opposed the limitation of Church membership by rigid theories of Church order and ecclesiastical regulations.

Dr Thomas Arnold (1795–1842), the famous headmaster of Rugby School, would doubtless not have agreed that he was 'a party man', but it may certainly be said that his *Principles of Church Reform*[14] (1833) sets out an ecclesiology representative of the Broad Church party, or Liberals. It is often remarked that he took what he had been able to achieve at Rugby as a model for his proposals for a reformed national Church.[15] At Rugby, with great single-mindedness and courage he had brought into being, out of something akin to anarchy, a community for the good order and common purpose of which each member accepted responsibility: headmaster, masters, seniors, and even the newest boys. This was based on acknowledgement of faith in

Christ and the acceptance of Christian moral standards. Arnold envisaged a Christian state in which, just as at Rugby School, the Christian religion was related to all activities, whether in classroom, house, or on the sports field. Christianity would penetrate very aspect of the national life. To this end there should be one national Church in which the great majority of sincere Christians could unite.

In his Preface Arnold declares the following principles:

> that a Church Establishment is essential to the well-being of the nation; that the existence of Dissent impairs the usefulness of an Establishment always, and now, from peculiar circumstances, threatens its destruction: and that to extinguish Dissent by persecution being both wicked and impossible, there remains the true but hitherto untried way, to extinguish it by comprehension (*Principles of Church Reform*, p. 87).

Arnold was convinced that Church reform was impossible unless the problem of sectarianism, 'that worst reproach of the Christian name',[16] were boldly tackled, and he devoted several pages to a consideration of sectarianism in England. It arose, in his opinion, because the Establishment mistakenly identified unity with unanimity of opinion. Divisions among Christians are indeed evil, but 'whoever is acquainted with Christianity, must see that differences of opinion are absolutely unavoidable'.[17] The Establishment also made the mistake of assuming that dissent could be prevented by setting up a statement of doctrine and appointing a form of worship to which men were obliged to conform under the threat of severe legal penalties. 'But [our fathers] forgot that while requiring this agreement, they had themselves disclaimed, what alone could justify them in enforcing it—the possession of infallibility.'[18] The 'vindictive oppression' of the Clarendon Code[19] was replaced by the Toleration Act of 1689—'a strange measure by which the nation sanctioned the non-observance of its own institutions',[20] but there was no determined effort to effect a union with the non-conformists. 'The Church and the Dissenters lived in peace; but their separation became daily more confirmed.'[21] That separation was now widened in that dissenters, to their credit, exercised a great influence among the poorer classes, while the Establishment, confined by its prescribed forms of worship and operating from centres and buildings which were unstrategically placed for effective work in the new industrial areas, had little influence outside the upper and middle classes. The situation, moreover, was exacerbated by rivalry, jealousy, and recrimination, the established Church and dissenters each accusing the other of the sin of schism.[22]

Is it not, then, worth while to try a different system? And since disunion is something so contrary to the spirit of Christianity, and differences of opinion a thing so inevitable to human nature, might it not be possible to escape the former without the folly of attempting to get rid of the latter; to constitute a Church thoroughly national, thoroughly united, thoroughly Christian, which should allow great varieties of opinion, and of ceremonies, and forms of worship, according to the various knowledge, and habits, and tempers of its members, while it truly held one common faith, and trusted in one common Saviour and worshipped one common God? (ibid., pp. 107–8).

As a basis for such a national Church, Arnold proposes the following points, on which all Christians, he holds, are agreed: belief in God as creator and sustainer; belief in Jesus Christ, the Son of God, and in his atoning death and resurrection; belief that the Old and New Testaments uniquely contain the revelation of God's will to men; acceptance of Christian moral standards, 'that pride and sensuality are amongst the worst sins; that self-denial, humility, devotion, and charity, are amongst the highest virtues ... that our first great duty is to love God; our second, to love our neighbour'.[23] It is not unreasonable that those who are united in these principles should be content to live as members of the same religious society. Leaving aside different opinions on Church government, Arnold argues that no differences on the important points of pure doctrine need prevent Presbyterians, Methodists, Independents, Baptists, and Moravians from entering, with the established Church, into a united national Church. Of the Quakers, Roman Catholics, and Unitarians, however, he says that 'so long as these sects preserve exactly their present character, it would seem impracticable to comprehend them in any national Christian church; the epithet "national" excluding the two former, and the epithet "Christian" rendering alike impossible the admission of the latter'.[24] He proceeds to discuss what changes would be necessary in these bodies, and how a national Church, given these changes, might make it possible for them to unite by framing articles, creeds, and prayers for public use not to serve as tests for latent error, but 'to provoke the least possible disagreement, without sacrificing, in our own practical worship, the expression of such feelings as are essential to our own edification'.[25]

Arnold next considers the kind of 'government and administration' which this national Church will need. Its ministers are to be drawn from all classes of society: 'As all classes of society require the services of ministers of religion, the ministry should contain persons taken from all',[26] even from the poorest. The laity are to have a large share in the government of the Church at all levels. In the parishes a social organization must be built up which will involve the parishioners as a body. The lack of it compels passivity: 'The love of self-government, one of the best instincts in our nature, and one most opposite to the spirit of lawlessness, finds no place for its exercise.'[27]

As for the government of the Church, 'Episcopalians require that this should be *episcopal*; the Dissenters of almost every denomination would insist that it should not be *prelatical*. But it may be the first without being the last.'[28] Dioceses must be smaller. Each diocese is to have a council consisting of clergy and lay members, appointed partly by the bishop and partly by the clergy and laity of the diocese. The bishop must not act without his council. This would 'destroy that most mischievous notion ... that the Church is synonymous with the clergy'.[29]

Arnold advocates a part-time ministry, where need warrants it, of men who, having another profession or trade, would not be wholly dependent on the ministry for support.[30] He requires a radical revision of the patronage and appointments systems of the established Church.[31] He strongly defends the membership of bishops in the House of Lords, and argues that representative clergy should sit in the House of Commons: 'They are wanted in the national assembly of a professedly Christian nation.' He indignantly rejects the suggestion that they should be there only to vote on ecclesiastical matters.[32] He would wish the liturgy of the Church of England to be used once on every Sunday and great festival, but there should also be at other times of the day and week other services of a freer kind, even at the risk of 'some insipidity and some extravagance'.[33]

The commuting of tithes, the equalizing of the incomes of bishops and of clergy, the evils of pluralism and absentee incumbents, the exclusion of dissenters from the universities all come briefly under his review[34] before he turns to the question by what power the national Church should be brought into being. It would be by legislative enactment of the government. This would be prepared for by a commission charged with the revision of the Thirty-nine Articles. Arnold is insistent that any such commission should not consist of clergymen alone. It would also be necessary to draw up in detail the proposed constitution of the national Church. The body charged with this task would necessarily seek 'information on many points ... from persons locally or professionally qualified to furnish it'.[35]

Arnold concludes with an appeal to his fellow-members of the established Church:

> that they would regard those thousands and ten thousands of their countrymen, who are excluded from [the Church of England's] benefit; that they would consider the wrong done to our common country by these unnatural divisions amongst her children.... For the sake, then, of our country, and to save her from the greatest possible evils—from evils far worse than any loss of territory, or decline of trade—from the sure moral and intellectual degradation which will accompany the unchristianizing of the nation, that is, the destroying of its national religious establishment, is it too much to ask of good men, that they should consent to unite themselves with other good men, without requiring them to subscribe to their own opinions, or to conform to their own ceremonies? They are not asked to surrender or compromise the smallest portion of their own faith, but simply to forbear imposing it upon their neighbours. They are not called upon to give up their own forms of worship, but to allow the addition of others; not for themselves to join in it, if they do not like to do so, but simply to be celebrated in the same church, and by ministers, whom they shall acknowledge to be their brethren, and members no less than themselves of the National Establishment (ibid., p. 148).

On the last few pages of the book Arnold discusses some of the objections which he foresees to his proposals. The book won little assent. His proposals were not taken up by the Liberals. The Evangelicals saw the conversion of individuals as the nation's greatest need, and, as J. R. H. Moorman remarks, 'the High Church party, now on the eve of its great revival, had other ideas of what the Church should be'.[36]

THE HIGH CHURCH PARTY AND THE OXFORD MOVEMENT

The smallest of the three 'parties', the High Churchmen, were the successors of the seventeenth-century divines like Andrewes, Cosin, Bramhall, and Pearson to whom they looked with great veneration. In their ecclesiology they upheld the view, against both Roman Catholics and Protestant dissenters, that the Church of England was the successor in England of the primitive Church. They placed great emphasis on apostolic succession, and on the authority of the creeds and conciliar decisions of the patristic period. They greatly desired the renewal of the much neglected sacramental life of the established Church and the restoration of a stricter discipline. They were opposed to the authority over the Church which Parliament had come to exercise. It was against State control as much as against dissenters that they stressed the doctrine of apostolic succession, inasmuch as implicit in that doctrine is the concept that authority over the Church resides in the bishops who have received it in succession from the apostles and from Christ.[37]

During the eighteen-thirties the High Church party gained vigour under the leadership of a remarkable group of Oxford dons, chief among whom were John Keble (1792–1866), E. B. Pusey (1800–82), R. H. Froude (1803–36), and John Henry Newman (1801–90). With them began the Oxford Movement, whose supporters were variously named Tractarians, Puseyites, and, at a later stage, Ritualists and Anglo-Catholics.

In July 1833, Keble preached a sermon on 'National Apostasy' before the judges assembled for the Assizes in Oxford. It was directed against parliamentary legislation which proposed the suppression of a number of Irish bishoprics. This proposal was not without justification, in view of the small Anglican population of Ireland and the expense of maintaining an unnecessarily large number of sees. To High Churchmen, however, it was a glaring instance of State interference in ecclesiastical affairs, and Keble called on the nation to recognize that the Church was more than a mere creation of the State.[38] Shortly afterwards the Oxford High Churchmen met to discuss a campaign for the promotion of High Church principles and the defence of the Church against Erastianism. They decided to issue a series of *Tracts for the Times*,[39] twenty of which were issued in the same year. The ecclesiological interests of the Tractarians are prominent throughout the tracts, and often evident from their titles alone.

1 APOSTOLIC SUCCESSION

Several deal with apostolic succession and episcopacy. Tract 1, 'Thoughts on the Ministerial Commission', argues that even if the government should cast off the Church, the real ground of the authority of the Church's ministry would remain—'our apostolical descent'.[40] Tract 4 is entitled 'Adherence to the Apostolical Succession the Safest Course', and Tract 7, 'The Episcopal Church Apostolical'. Tract 12, 'On Bishops, Priests, and Deacons', argues that the threefold order of ministry is implicit in the N.T. and supported by the Apostolic Fathers: Clement of Rome, Polycarp, and Ignatius. Tract 15 is entitled 'On the Apostolical Succession in the English Church', and Tract 19 'On Arguing concerning Apostolical Succession'. Tract 74 cites at length support for the doctrine from post-Reformation English divines.

2 THE IDEAL OF THE PRIMITIVE CHURCH

Several tracts urge a return to the primitive practice of the Church in general (Tract 6, 'The Present Obligation of Primitive Practice') and in particular ways such as fasting (Tracts 18 and 66, two learned tracts by Pusey), and frequent communion (Tract 26). Tract 36 pleads for a greater appreciation of the value of primitive rites and customs in connection with Christian initiation and the celebration of the eucharist.

3 THE BRANCH THEORY

What has been called 'the Branch Theory' of the Church is implicit in several tracts. This is the notion that those Christian communions which have maintained the doctrinal standards of the early creeds and general councils are to be deemed true branches of the Church even though they are not in communion with one another. Tract 5, 'On the Nature and Constitution of the Church of Christ, and of the Branch of it established in England', claims that the Church of England is 'a pure and apostolic branch of Christ's holy Church'.[41] Tract 71, 'On the Controversy with the Romanists', speaks of the Church of England as 'that particular branch of the Church Catholic through which God made us Christians. . . . The only conceivable reasons for leaving its communion are . . . first, that it is involved in some damnable heresy, or second, that it is not in possession of the sacraments.'[42] It is admitted that the Church of Rome is 'a branch of Christ's Church', and that its orders are valid. Nevertheless its errors are such that the English churchman must resist the argument that it is 'safer' to unite with Rome, despite the imperfections of the English Church which the tract readily admits.[43] The Branch Theory was expounded at length in a *Treatise on the Church of Christ* (1838) by William Palmer, an early supporter of the Oxford Movement.

4 ANTI-ROMANISM

The Tractarians were consciously in controversy on several fronts: against State control, liberalism, dissent, but also against 'the Papists'. Several tracts deal with grievances against Rome. Tract 71 specifies the denial of the cup to the laity, insistence that the validity of sacraments depends on the priest's intention, compulsory auricular confession, unwarranted anathemas, the doctrine of Purgatory, the invocation of saints, the worship of images.[44] Tracts 27 and 28 reprint Bishop Cosin's *History of Popish Transubstantiation*. Tract 30, 'Christian Liberty; or Why should we belong to the Church of England?', rejects the pope's claim 'to control all the branches of the Church on earth'. The bishops of the Church of England rightly rejected the claim, and the conclusion is drawn that papists in England and Ireland are to be regarded as schismatic.[45]

5 THE CHURCH OF ENGLAND AS THE VIA MEDIA

Tracts 38 and 41, written by Newman and entitled 'Via Media', present the idea that the Church of England holds the middle path, *via media*, between the errors and exaggerations of Rome on the one hand, and Protestantism on the other.

> The glory of the English Church is, that it has taken the *via media*, as it has been called. It lies *between* the (so-called) Reformers and the Romanists (*Tracts for the Times*, p. 277).

> In the seventeenth century the theology of the divines of the English Church was substantially the same as ours is [i.e. the Tractarians]; and it experienced the full hostility of the Papacy. It was the true Via Media; Rome sought to block up that way as fiercely as the Puritans (ibid., p. 281).

Newman then adds a list of the errors of Rome. To those mentioned in the Anti-Romanism section, above, he adds: that it is unscriptural to say that 'we are justified by inherent righteousness', or that 'the good works of a man justified do truly merit eternal life'; that the sacrifice of masses as practised in the Roman Church is unscriptural and blasphemous; that indulgences are a gross and monstrous invention; that to celebrate divine service in an unknown tongue is a corruption; that there are not seven sacraments; that the Roman doctrine of tradition is unscriptural.[46]

In Tract 41 he discusses the catholic elements in the Book of Common Prayer. He acknowledges that in practice the established Church has neglected many of them, and suggests the need for another reformation:

> I would do what our Reformers in the sixteenth century did: they did not touch the existing documents of doctrine—there was no occasion; they kept the creeds as they were; but they *added* protests against the corruptions of faith, worship, and discipline, which had grown up round them. I would have the Church do the same thing now, if I could: she should not

change the Articles, she should add to them: add protests against the
Erastianism and Latitudinarianism which have incrusted them. I would
have her append to the Catechism a section on the power of the Church
(ibid., p. 299).

J. H. NEWMAN

At this time Newman, it is clear, was convinced that the Church of
Rome had in many respects declined from the doctrines and practices
of the primitive Church. In the next few years, however, certain influences were to alter his attitude to Rome. J. R. H. Moorman[47]
describes these:

> In 1839 N. P. S. Wiseman, a half-Irish and half-Spanish fanatical Roman
> Catholic priest, was sent to England and began publishing articles on the
> Donatist schism, suggesting that the Church of England was schismatic in
> just the same way that the Donatists had been pronounced schismatic in
> the fourth century. Newman was deeply impressed by this line of thought.
> Then again a small group of radical thinkers among the Tractarians, in-
> cluding W. G. Ward and F. W. Faber were becoming attracted, not, like
> Froude, to medieval Rome, the Church out of which the Anglican Church
> had emerged, but to the Rome of the Counter-Reformation and to post-
> Tridentine theology and practice. Newman was not, at first, impressed by
> this. The Church of Rome, he was convinced, had wandered far from the
> customs of the Primitive Church and, in so doing, had erred from catholic
> simplicity. But at this point he was introduced to the doctrine of
> 'Development'. Christ had promised that the Holy Spirit should guide the
> Church into all truth. The Primitive Church did not know the whole truth;
> this was revealed only slowly in the course of history. It was not the
> Primitive Church that should be taken as the model, but that Church
> which showed most signs of holiness, of being the true Body of Christ.
> From that moment Newman began to look on Rome with new eyes. What
> if her wandering had led her not away from catholic simplicity but on into
> wider fields of divine truth?

In February 1841 Newman's famous Tract 90 appeared, entitled
'Remarks on Certain Passages in the Thirty-nine Articles'.[48] It sought
to show that the Anglican Articles are capable of being interpreted in
harmony with the decrees of the Council of Trent. It occasioned
violent opposition. For many it confirmed what they had long
suspected, that the Tractarian aim was to Romanize the Church of
England and undo the work of the Reformation. It was condemned by
the heads of the Oxford Colleges, and Bishop Bagot of Oxford forbade the publication of more tracts. Newman resigned his benefice in

1843, and in 1845 was received into the Roman Catholic Church. Later in the same year his *Essay on the Development of Christian Doctrine* appeared, on which he had been working for some time.[49] The principle of development enabled Newman now to see the Roman Catholic Church of his day as one with the Church of the Nicene era and the Church which was founded by Christ. It was 'a sort of test which the Anglican [teaching] could not exhibit, that modern Rome was in truth ancient Antioch, Alexandria, and Constantinople, just as a mathematical curve has its own law and expression'.[50] He can therefore say of the Church of Rome in the *Essay on Development*:

> When we consider the succession of ages during which the Catholic system has endured, the severity of the trials it has undergone, the sudden and wonderful changes without and within which have befallen it, the incessant mental activity and the intellectual gifts of its maintainers, the enthusiasm which it has kindled, the fury of the controversies which have been carried on among its professors, the impetuosity of the assaults made upon it, the ever increasing responsibilities to which it has been committed by the continuous development of its dogmas, it is quite inconceivable that it should not have been broken up and lost, were it a corruption of Christianity. Yet it is still living, if there be a living religion or philosophy in the world; vigorous, energetic, persuasive, progressive; *vires acquirit eundo*;[51] it grows and is not overgrown; it spreads out, yet is not enfeebled; it is ever germinating, yet ever consistent with itself. . . . That its long series of developments should be corruptions would be an instance of sustained error, so novel, so unaccountable, so preternatural, as to be little short of a miracle, and to rival those manifestations of Divine Power which constitute the evidence of Christianity (*Essay on Development*, pp. 437–8).

Newman's reasons for concluding that the Church of Rome *alone* can be identified with the primitive Church are given in the following typical[52] passage:

> On the whole, then, we have reason to say, that if there be a form of Christianity at this day distinguished for its careful organization, and its consequent power; if it is spread all over the world; if it is conspicuous for zealous maintenance of its own creed; if it is intolerant towards what it considers error; if it is engaged in ceaseless war with all other bodies called Christian; if it, and it alone, is called 'catholic' by the world, nay, by those very bodies, and if it makes much of the title; if it names them heretics, and warns them of coming woe, and calls on them one by one, to come over to itself, overlooking every other tie; and if they, on the other hand, call it seducer, harlot, apostate, Antichrist, devil; if, however much

they differ one with another, they consider it their common enemy; if they strive to unite together against it, and cannot; if they are but local; if they continually subdivide, and it remains one; if they fall one after another, and make way for new sects, and it remains the same; such a religious communion is not unlike historical Christianity, as it comes before us at the Nicene Era (ibid., pp. 272–3).

In the years that followed there were other secessions to Rome. Pusey and Keble stood fast to the Tractarian principles. The Oxford Movement went on, gaining more support even as it aroused opposition both from within and outside the established Church. To the Tractarians and the 'Anglo-Catholics', as their later successors were called, the whole Anglican Communion owes a great debt, whether acknowledged or not. The renewal of the Church's sacramental life, greater appreciation of beauty in worship, the founding of many schools and colleges, a new impetus in missionary work abroad and in the slums of England, the reintroduction of religious communities all spring from the Tractarian conviction of the essential catholicity of the Church of England.

18

F. D. Maurice;
The Lambeth Conferences

F. D. Maurice was a theologian of original and independent mind. Although he had affinities with Evangelicals, Liberals, and High Churchmen, he abhorred party spirit, and stood aloof from them all. Since his lifetime, hardly a decade has passed without the appearance of a book or major article on his thought, and interest in him has increased by the recognition that certain principles, now commonly taken as guidelines in discussions on Christian unity and often assumed to be the invention of twentieth-century ecumenists, were expounded by Maurice over a century before. In many respects he 'was a hundred years in advance of his time'.[1] This is true of his ecclesiology, although it must be added that in other respects it is dated.

Maurice, who had a Unitarian upbringing, became a member of the Church of England in 1830 and was ordained in 1834. His best known book, which chiefly concerns us here, is *The Kingdom of Christ* (1838). It was first published under the title *Letters to a Member of the Society of Friends* in 1837, and a revised and enlarged edition appeared in 1842. Its themes recur in many of his other writings, especially *The Lord's Prayer* (1848), *The Gospel of the Kingdom of Heaven* (1864), and *The Commandments considered as Instruments of National Reformation* (1866). His ecclesiology is summarized here in the order he himself presents it in *The Kingdom of Christ*, and under four headings.

1 THERE EXISTS IN THE WORLD A UNIVERSAL AND SPIRITUAL KINGDOM FOR MAN

Maurice begins from the Quaker assertion that spiritual principles imply the rejection of outward ordinances. The Society of Friends sought to establish a spiritual kingdom in the world; but, Maurice asks, 'Did not such a Kingdom exist already, and were not these ordinances the expression of it?'[2]

> There rose up before me the idea of a Church Universal, not built upon human inventions or human faith, but upon the very nature of God Himself, and upon the union which He has formed with His creatures: a Church revealed to man as a fixed and eternal reality by means which infinite wisdom had itself devised (*Kingdom of Christ*, Dedication, vol. 2, p. 363).[3]

Maurice is convinced that if such a Church is a reality, 'apprehensions of the different sides and aspects of it' must be found in 'the different schemes which express human thought and feeling', apprehensions which will find their highest meaning in the 'Universal Society' which God has created. His method, therefore, in the early part of the book is to examine the most prominent of these 'different schemes', to distinguish the fundamental principles of each from the systems which have often distorted them, and to inquire whether the fundamental principles of each may be reconciled with those of the others, and so point, by way of agreement, to the reality of a universal society grounded in God. It is his belief that

> all sects and factions, religious, political or philosophical, were bearing testimonies, sometimes mute, sometimes noisy, occasionally hopeful, oftener reluctant, to the presence of that Church Universal, which is at once to justify their truths, explain the causes of their opposition, and destroy their existence (ibid., Introductory Dialogue).[4]

In turn there come under his review Quakerism, Protestantism both in its Lutheran[5] and Calvinist forms, Unitarianism, Methodism, the Irvingites (or Catholic Apostolic Church), the philosophical thought of the eighteenth and early nineteenth centuries, the political movements which inspired the American and French revolutions, the teachings of Jeremy Bentham, and the socialism of Robert Owen. Maurice's comprehensive review suggests that he was attempting to do for the early nineteenth century what Augustine did for the fifth in his *City of God*.

He argues that the positive principles of each of the post-Reformation religious bodies are valid, or at least contain the element of truth: the Quaker principles that there is in all men an inward light or an indwelling word of God, and that Jesus Christ came to establish a spiritual kingdom and to encourage men to lead a spiritual life; the Protestant principles of justification by faith, election, the Bible as the witness to these doctrines addressed to and intended to be heard by every man in his own language, the authority of the national sovereign, the importance of the individual man and at the same time the importance of national distinctness; the Unitarian principle of 'the deep primary truth' of the unity of God, the assertion of his absolute and unqualified love, and 'a benignant view of things' in general.

Maurice presents the objections to these various principles made by other religious bodies and schools of thought. Out of this dialectic, he holds, the truth in the principles stands more clearly revealed. It is the systems to which they have given rise which are at fault. The principles become distorted when they are used as weapons in controversy. The resulting ecclesiastical systems or organizations never exemplify the principles in a credible way. In its systematic working-out, Protestantism, for example, began to advance propositions about justification, illustrated them from the working of the law-courts and from the practices of common life, became involved in scholastic debate, and tended more and more to ethicize and rationalize its Christianity.

> What I wish the reader to observe here, is, how little the body which took justification by faith as its motto and principle, has been able, in any stage of its history, to assert that doctrine; how constantly the system, whether interpreted by earnest believers or stiff dogmatists, by orthodox doctors or mere moralists, has been labouring to strangle the principle to which it owes its existence (ibid., vol. 1, p. 115).

Similarly, he argues, the Quaker and Unitarian systems have introduced ambiguities, even contradictions which conceal the witness of the former to the existence of a universal kingdom, and of the latter to the concept of God as a universal and loving Father.

Maurice sees philosophical movements of thought as each contending for a true principle, but as losing sight of those principles as their systems harden. The principle of the Romantics, that 'the perfection of a man is to be in harmony with nature',[6] and the Kantian principle that there is a region which lies beyond human experience and that man possesses a faculty by which that region is cognizable,[7] each testify to a conviction that there exist bonds between man and the universe which 'do not depend for their reality upon our consciousness of them',[8] but are there antecedent to man's experience of them. Such insights, he believes, are capable of being reconciled, and in a universal and spiritual society which already exists:

> If reason affirm a truth which must have always been; if the communion with nature be something implied in our constitution, and therefore im-

plied in the constitution of those who lived a thousand years ago; if humanity be essentially spiritual, the reconciling method may already exist, and ... the work of our age may not be to create it afresh, but to discover its meaning and realize its necessity (ibid., p. 182).

In political movements and the reactions to them Maurice also discerns the expression of principles which can only find their true embodiment in a universal and spiritual society. Revolutionary movements beginning with the assertion of individual rights moved towards concepts of fellowship and even of a universal society. In Bentham's 'greatest happiness of the greatest number', Saint-Simon's recognition of the importance of the family and his principle of 'each according to his capacity', and Robert Owen's idea of co-operation, there is enshrined the feeling that 'a universal society is needful to man'.[9]

At the beginning of Part 2 Maurice recapitulates. The principles asserted by the religious societies formed since the Reformation are 'solid and imperishable', but 'the systems in which those principles have been embodied were faulty in their origin, have been found less and less to fulfil their purpose as they have grown older, and are now exhibiting the most manifest indications of approaching dissolution'.[10] The philosophers of the eighteenth century first rejected the idea of a spiritual kingdom, assuming that men possessed no faculties by which they could take cognizance of any such thing. In opposition to Christianity the idea of a comprehensive *world*, including all nations, systems, and even religions, knit together by benevolent philanthropy, became prevalent.

Yet a religious awakening occurred, born of a conviction that a spiritual influence is at work among men. Personal religion was emphasized, as was the need to co-operate in promoting spiritual objects. Among philosophers also there was a growing tendency to think of man as essentially a spiritual creature whose highest acts are of a spiritual kind, and to acknowledge the existence of a region for their exercise. Some would go no further than to identify this region with the universe of sight and sound into the understanding of which only a few gifted poets and sages had entry. Yet others were driven to recognize 'the existence of something which man did not create himself, but to which he must in some sort refer all his acts and thoughts, and which must be assumed as the ground of them'.[11] Men were searching for a universal constitution into which all men as men might enter. But each attempt to construct it was defeated by men's determination to assert their own wills. Maurice declares that a true universal society must not ignore these wills, for they are the very principle and explanation of its existence. He also says that 'it is equally impossible for men to be content with a spiritual society which is not universal, and with a universal society which is not spiritual'.[12]

He now asks again whether such a society, which he believes to be implied by the human constitution itself, has not been made known to men in the course of history. Are there traces of it in the early ages? Do the Scriptures, to which many of the religious groups he has examined have appealed, provide any evidence?

He sees the first indication that there is a spiritual constitution for mankind in the fact that men live in families, 'a state which is designed for a voluntary creature; which is his, whether he approve it or no'.[13] That man is inclined to rebel against it shows not that the bonds of the family are unnatural, but that man is meant also for other relationships, not necessarily incompatible with the family. History records the development of the national community. To be able to say 'I am a brother' reveals man's true nature as more than a self-contained unit; but to be able to say 'I am a citizen' is an onward step. Ancient history tells of the awakening of the desire for even a larger and more comprehensive constitution. The empire of Alexander the Great, however, was short-lived. That of Rome eventually perished. Maurice sees the cause of its break-up in its failure to maintain the health of family and national life. If there is to be a universal *Church*, he says, it must not set aside family or national life, but rather justify their existence and reconcile them to itself.[14]

He now turns to the Bible. The O.T. speaks of a covenant of God with a family, that of Abraham. Abraham recognized, and this is the essence of his faith, that there is a God who is related to men, and made known to them through their human relations. He may therefore rightly be called 'the beginner of the Church on earth'.[15] Despite rebellion against God and his laws Abraham's family was to become a nation. The national polity of the Jews, like that of other nations, ancient and modern, was exclusive. But among them were prophets who proclaimed God as the God of all nations and had a vision of a king who should reign in righteousness and whom all nations would own.

The N.T. speaks of the coming of one who is a son of David and of Abraham to establish a kingdom. All the words and acts of Jesus relate to this kingdom and the whole N.T. affirms him to be its king. Although this kingdom is not to be observed with the outward eye and is not of this world (Luke 17.20–21; John 18.36), it extends to all men and over all nature. At the last supper Jesus declared that his followers were united with him, and through him with his Father, and that his spirit would be with them, witnessing to him and cementing this union. He translated these words into acts by his sacrificial death and resurrection. He still communes with them, and they recognize that the union between heaven and earth is 'no longer a word, it is a fact'.[16] He bids his disciples go out, testify to it, and adopt men into a society based on its accomplishment, a society continuous with the past (being 'the child which the Jewish polity had for many ages been carrying in its womb'),[17] but containing a principle of expansion in its freedom from all national exclusions.

Although this universal society historically grew out of the Jewish family and nation, it is theologically prior. Aristotle's dictum, 'that which is first as cause is last in discovery', is caught up in the Epistle to the Ephesians which speaks of members of the Church as created by God before all worlds, and of God's 'transcendent economy as being gradually revealed to the apostles and prophets by the Spirit.... The mystery of the true constitution of humanity in Christ is revealed.'[18]

2 THE PRESENT SIGNS OF A SPIRITUAL SOCIETY

There are two possible kinds of universal society, 'one of which is destructive of the family and national principle, the other the expansion of them'.[19] Scripture calls the first 'this world', the latter 'the Church'. If the latter exists it must be a *distinct* body, and to say this does not negate its universality. Are there, Maurice now asks, any signs of the spiritual and universal society, that is to say, of the Catholic Church, upon the earth? He sees six such signs: baptism, the creeds, forms of worship, the eucharist, the episcopal ministry, and the Scriptures. His discussion of these and of the objections to them or views upon them of the Quakers, the Protestant Churches, philosophers, and the Roman Catholics of his day occupies most of Part 2 of the work. Into these dialogues we cannot follow him here, but must summarize.

Baptism is 'the sign of admission into Christ's spiritual and universal kingdom', and consequently every person receiving that sign is '*ipso facto* a member of that kingdom'.[20] Baptism announces to a man what his position is and the conditions by which he is to live. Conflicts lie in front, temptations and hindrances in the way of his entering into the blessing which has been obtained for him. But he is and remains a son of God, a member of Christ. 'We do not ... cease to be children because we are disobedient children.'[21] There will be constant need of repentance for living the lie that denies our baptismal status.

The creeds are documents, closely connected with baptism, which declare the name into which men are adopted by baptism. They are not digests of doctrine, but a man's declaration of belief in a Father and Creator, his Son who became incarnate to be man's redeemer, and his Holy Spirit who has established a holy universal Church. They are acts of allegiance. They affirm 'belief in a name and not in notions'.[22] They are signs of a spiritual and universal society, and a protection of the meaning of the Scriptures against the tendency of the learned to mangle them.[23]

Forms of worship have persisted through all the vicissitudes of Christian history. They vary according to time, locality, and culture, but have an underlying unity not only in the remarkable persistence of certain ancient forms, but in their purpose, which is 'the adoration of the one living and true God'.[24] Forms of worship have sometimes been made badges of distinction and instruments of controversy, but their preservation through so many generations is a sign of the existence of 'a community which the distinction of tongues and the succession of ages cannot break'.[25]

The eucharist is the service of worship which interprets all other acts of worship. In instituting this sacrament Christ meant that his disciples

> should have the fullest participation of that sacrifice with which God had declared himself well pleased, that they should really enter into that Presence, into which the Forerunner had for them entered, that they should really receive in that communion all the spiritual blessings which, through the union of the Godhead with human flesh, the heirs of this flesh might inherit. ... The new life which they had claimed for themselves, as members of Christ's body, was here to be attained through the communication of his life (ibid., vol. 2, p. 62).

The eucharist is misinterpreted if it is conceived of individualistically as a means of communion with a Lord who is somehow made present by a man's faith. A presence which is not a presence until we make it so is a strange conceit. In the eucharist men enter into the presence of Christ *where he is*. It is a continuing witness 'that the Son of man is set down at the right hand of the throne of God, and that those who believe in him, and suffer with him, are meant to live and reign with him there'.[26] It is a sign of the existence of a universal and spiritual kingdom.

The ministry The foregoing signs imply the agency of men. The universal society is 'not a kingdom ... if it have not certain magistrates or officers',[27] and such there are.

> It has been believed, as a necessary consequence of the importance attached to the Eucharist, that an order of men must exist in the Christian Church corresponding to the priests of the old dispensation, with the difference that the sacrifice in the one case was anticipatory, in the other commemorative (ibid., p. 99).

Priesthood has commonly been held to imply dominion over men's minds. In the Christian Church, however, it is *ministry*. From the Bishop of Rome to the founder of the latest sect the name of 'minister' is acknowledged. The minister's characteristic function is to absolve or set free. There are differences within Christendom about the nature of this power and the method of its exercise, but not about its existence.

The most conspicuous order of ministers, the episcopate, has assumed a universal character. Bishops have felt themselves to be 'the bonds of communication between different parts of the earth'.[28] Episcopacy has been preserved in the Orthodox churches of the East and in western Europe, and has developed in the New World. Christ came to minister, to absolve, and to bind men into a kingdom. He called and commissioned the apostles to the same ministry and to announce the same kingdom. They, not supposing that the kingdom was to die with them, appointed successors 'to bring before men the fact that they are subject to an invisible and universal Ruler'.[29] Consequently, 'those nations which have preserved the episcopal institution have a right to believe that they have preserved one of the appointed and indispensable signs of a spiritual and universal society'.

The view that it is a secret call of God that makes a man a minister runs into the danger of confounding man's spiritual faculty with the Holy Spirit. Moreover, there needs to be a formal, public, and open endowment of authority so that all may understand the extent and derivation of an office which is claimed. This was the practice of the N.T. Church.[30] Maurice opposes also the view that episcopal succession is the transmission of some part of the effect of Christ's ordination of the apostles. Rather, the episcopate receives the functions committed to the apostles (administering the sacraments, absolving, preaching, ministering) and the authority to exercise them directly from Christ; and the bishops' connection with previous ages and the apostles is maintained as a witness to the permanent constitution of the Church and to the continued presence of Christ.[31]

Maurice also opposes a doctrine of vicarial priesthood: that 'ministers are deputed by our Lord to do that work now which he did himself while he was upon earth'—as though Christ were absent. He holds that in baptism and the other signs there is 'a direct, real, and practical union between men and their Lord',[32] and therefore the priest is not Christ's *vicar*, as though the veil between men and God was not yet withdrawn, but his representative, commissioned with authority to absolve, set free, and bid men be what they are—members of Christ and his kingdom.

The Scriptures are also a continuing sign of the existence of a spiritual and universal kingdom. They declare a divine constitution for man, revealed first to a family, then to a nation, and through them to mankind. 'They make us conscious of the existence of two societies, one formed in accordance with the order of God, the other based upon self-will.'[33] Their object 'is to withdraw us from outward sensual impressions of the divine majesty, to make us feel the reality of the relation between him and his creatures, to make us understand that it is a spiritual relation, and that, therefore, it can manifest itself in outward words and acts'.[34] Consequently, it was a grievous mistake to attempt to conceal the Bible from men in order to exalt the Church.

Although Maurice discusses at length different views about these signs, he is chiefly concerned, as A. M. Ramsey remarks,[35] to emphasize the *fact* of each sign as a witness to the existence of a universal Church.

3 THE IDEA OF A CATHOLIC CHURCH DOES NOT EXCLUDE NATIONAL CHURCHES

Maurice is convinced that the universal and spiritual society must express itself in national societies. The O.T. is the story of a family which acknowledges God as Father, and a nation which acknowledges God as King. The principles of this kingdom which the ten commandments lay down are spiritual, but they also concern man as a mundane creature, in a particular place, with a defined circle of human relationships. They deal with such matters as family, sexual, and neighbourhood relations; property, tribunals, and oaths. Jewish history contains the 'divine specimen of a national life'.[36] The N.T. develops the principles of a universal society, but without superseding those of a true national society. The ten commandments are not abrogated, but shown to be basic not for one nation only, but for all nations, and in their deepest meaning for the universal society which is the Church of God.

In a historical survey[37] Maurice traces the relationship of the Church to empires and nations. The alliance, initiated by Constantine, between a 'superannuated despotism' based upon mere power with a body which recognized a King who rules in righteousness and whose strength is in weakness was a dispensation of God, but was not intended to last. The Roman, Carolingian, and Byzantine empires perished. As the Church penetrated barbarian lands, the bishops, had they been able, would have 'reduced Europe into one great society, having a common language, scarcely acknowledging any territorial or political distinctions'. This might have seemed appropriate to the idea of a divine commonwealth. In the event, the bishops were the main instruments in creating distinct national organizations, different from, though acting in concert with the ecclesiastical organization. Distinctions in character and institutions between the original tribes were slight, but in the course of time, by Christian nurture and education, the latent peculiarities and gifts of each were brought out. It would seem that in Europe the form of the national society was brought into existence by that very society which might have been supposed to displace it. Maurice sees here 'a higher will, another power at work, crossing human calculations'.[38] The universal society negates neither the family nor the nation.

In the early stages of European nationhood a spiritual element was found to be necessary to uphold a legal society. Maurice contends also that 'a legal element, a body expressing the sacredness and majesty of law, is shown to be necessary in order to fulfil the objects for which the spiritual and universal society exists'.[39] There is mutual benefit from the relationship of Church and nation. Many answers have been given to questions about the authority and function of each in relation to the other, and many experiments made. Some are now anachronistic, such as any claim of the legal power to use compulsion to enforce ecclesiastical conformity. That relationship took many forms, some of them gravely distorted but Maurice is in no doubt that two powers, one of which wishes to set men free, and the other to have a free intelligent people 'must be meant continually to act and react upon each other, and to learn better, by each new error they commit, their distinct functions, their perfect harmony'.[40] For its part the Church must acknowledge

> that she is not meant to have an independent existence; that she is not meant to be extra-national; that she has no commission or powers which dispense with the necessity of positive, formal law and with outward government; that her highest honour is to be the life-giving energy to every body in the midst of which she dwells (ibid., p. 254).

But can one Catholic Church be recognized under the distinctions and limitations of national bodies? Must it not inevitably lose the features which constitute its identity? Maurice distinguishes between 'certain ordinances in which the character and universality of the Church are expressed' and 'everything which is but accidentally connected with them'.[41] The ordinances are the six signs which he has discussed; the accidents are modes of treating the ordinances, such as particular modes of administering baptism and the eucharist or particular rules about the jurisdiction of bishops. There has been an unfortunate tendency to efface this distinction by identifying particular decrees and ceremonies with the very being of the Church, both by the papacy and by the Church within each nation. A national Church must learn that its substance is the ordinances which it shares with Christians everywhere and the powers it has in common with other parts of the body. Its convocations and synods are to be used with the purpose

> of determining those ceremonies which to a people of a particular climate, character, and constitution best express the great ideas of the Church, of more effectually establishing and directing discipline and education, of promoting fellowship with national Churches which are willing to acknowledge themselves as part of a great Catholic body (ibid., p. 262).

Maurice's diagnosis of the condition of Christendom since the Reformation is that two principles have been struggling for supremacy: one, 'embodied in Protestantism, resisting the claims of the spiritual power to any extra-national domination, and always tending to set at naught spiritual authority altogether'; the other, 'embodied in Romanism, resisting the attempts of the particular states to divide their own subjects from the rest of Christendom, continually striving to uphold the Church as a separate Power, and to set at naught the existence of each particular nation'.[42] He believes that it is

God's purpose to reconcile these principles and eliminate what is contrary to his will in each, so that 'the unity of the Church shall be demonstrated to be that ground upon which all unity in nations and in the heart of man is resting'.[43]

Eschatology Maurice is aware that his conception of the Kingdom of Christ as already established is open to the criticism that it ignores the eschatological element in the N.T. and sets aside the doctrine of the second coming of Christ. He defends himself against this charge. The Church has reason to live in expectation of the appearance and triumph of its Head. Scripture, however, gives no hint that this will be the beginning of a *new* order and constitution of things. Rather it will be 'the appearance of a light which shall show things as they are ... the day of judgement and distinction, the gathering of all together into one, the restoration of all things ... the full evidence and demonstration of that which *is now*',[44] the clearing away of all that hides from view the existence now of a kingdom, constitution, order which men have been trying to deny, but under which nevertheless they have been living, and which will then be shown to be the only one under which they can live.

Christ's second appearance will also make clear that his dominion is 'not merely over the heart and spirit of man ... but over all his human relations, his earthly associations, over the policy of rulers, over nature and over art',[45] all of which is as much the truth now as it ever can be in any future period. The principle of his book, Maurice contends, is not inconsistent with a sound apprehension of the second coming, but only with any system that leads men to think that present responsibilities may be taken lightly, and that God's providence means nothing much now and is leading only to something hereafter.

4 THE CHURCH OF ENGLAND IS AN EMBODIMENT OF THE UNIVERSAL AND SPIRITUAL ORDER

In Part 3 of *The Kingdom of Christ* Maurice applies his criteria to his own church. While he has much to criticize in it, he is convinced that it preserves the signs of a universal and spiritual constitution which again he enumerates, and now discusses in relation to the Church of England.[46] In a brief analysis of the Thirty-nine Articles,[47] he claims that they assert the *positive principles* of all the post-Reformation religious bodies and repudiate the *systems* which they have 'grafted' on them. Likewise the Articles repudiate the Roman Catholic system 'in every point wherein it is opposed to the distinct affirmations of the Reformers'.

In the English Church 'ecclesiastical and civil institutions are united'.[48] History is silent about the origin of this union. From the very beginning the relationship was presupposed. Maurice agrees that the Reformation in England originated with the sovereign, but it was not a purely political movement. For several centuries not only rebellious, but also most orthodox kings had attempted to break the relationship with Rome. 'The difference in the reign of Henry VIII was ... that a large body of the bishops and clergy had been led by their religious feelings to desire that this correspondence should be broken off.'[49]

Since the Reformation a number of sects had grown up in the country. He describes the attempts to coerce them into union with the national Church as stupid. That these various religious bodies still exist in England does not 'destroy a union which has cemented itself by no human contrivances, and which exists in the very nature of things'.[50]

In a most interesting section[51] on the particular characteristics of Englishmen, Maurice asserts that they are politicians at heart, and inclined, whether they would be artists, philosophers, or even mystics, to link thought with action. This political bias has had the beneficial result that it has led Englishmen to think of the Church as a kingdom rather than a system. Yet there was too great a tendency to forget that the Church is 'the type of all kingdoms, and is not moulded after the maxims of any',[52] and too ready an assumption that what is expedient for the ruling class must determine ecclesiastical matters. The English Church in the eighteenth century became identified with the aristocracy who regarded it as the upholder of the *status quo* in matters of property and privilege. It neglected the rising class of industrial workers and showed little sympathy with the Methodists who endeavoured to evangelize them. Maurice admits all this with shame, but believes that this kind of State churchmanship belonged to 'the spirit of an age of our national Church, not of the Church itself'.[53]

In Maurice's own day young and active churchmen were seeking alternatives to 'the dreariness of political Anglicanism'. Within the Church, parties were forming: the Liberals, the Evangelicals, and the High Church party.[54] Under the pressure of controversy there was a tendency to systematize in each of them. What he said in Part 1 about the various post-Reformation religious bodies he now says of these parties: that there is likely to be in each of them something which ought not to be rejected. It may be 'that there is a divine harmony, of which the living principle in each of these systems forms one note, of which the systems themselves are a disturbance and a violation'.[55] The Liberal contention that 'the Church is meant to comprehend and not to exclude', the Evangelical insistence on the power of the gospel, and the Catholic idea of a Church which God himself has established, possessing powers which the State neither gave nor can take away, are important. But when hardened into a *system* in opposition to other systems, each leads to error: Liberalism to the denial that anything is given to man in revelation; Evangelicalism to the denial of the idea of Church fellowship and unity; and the catholicism of the High Church party to the denial of the distinction of national Churches.[56]

Speaking again of the various religious systems, Maurice says: 'These systems, Protestant, Romish, English, seem to me each to bear witness of the existence of a *divine order*; each to be a miserable, partial, human substitute for it. In every country, therefore, I should desire to see men emancipated from the chains which they have made for themselves, and entering into the freedom of God's Church.'[57] He desires the acknowledgement of one Church, the universal and spiritual society, in which Christians of each nation, as a national Church, may claim their rightful place. He believes that in England, more clearly than elsewhere, there is an indication how this may be effected, for, although the English political bent does tend towards the creation of parties, 'system-building is not natural' to the English. Churchmen, and especially the younger ones, must seek for *principles* and grounds of action. The various systems and Church parties have made known certain principles, none of which may be disregarded; there is need of them all.[58] But the way forward is not to identify oneself with a party. That is to become involved in unfairness, libel, name-calling, polemics, and to merit judgement.

Much of the opposition to the national Church by sectarians and dissatisfaction with it by adherents of the parties is because 'it has put itself forth merely as an English church. Its character as a Catholic body, as a kingdom set up in the world for all nations, has been kept out of sight. Secondly ... it has taken a negative, that is a sectarian, form.'[59] It has accused those who have separated from it of wickedness, regarded its episcopacy and sacraments as excluding those who do not possess them, and made little attempt to show that the institutions which it requires others to accept are of a spiritual character and belong intrinsically to the divine kingdom. But those who are convinced that the English Church has the signs of the universal society must 'not despair of seeing all the true hearty dissenters gradually receiving them also'.[60] There must be patience, no forcing of ideas on others, concern that they should preserve the true principles and the faith which they already have, and the wish 'to make them integral members of the body from which they fancy that it is the object of our pride and selfishness to exclude them'.[61] The results of such a method are in God's hands. Other methods have been tried without success. This one has not been tried.

The final pages of *The Kingdom of Christ* show that Maurice finds much to criticize in the national English Church of his day: its identification with the aristocracy; neglect of the industrial districts; the subservience of churchmen in Ireland to English interests; the setting-up of episcopacy in Scotland 'as if it were an English thing', and the continued failure to understand the needs and aspirations of the Scots.[62]

Its experience in Ireland, Scotland, and North America has, he suggests, clear lessons for the English nation in its colonial policy and the English Church in its missionary policy elsewhere:

> See that you do not merely establish an English kingdom in those soils; if you do, that kingdom will not be a blessing to the colonists, to the natives, or to the mother country. See that you do not merely send forth preachers in your ships to tell the people that all they have believed hitherto—if they have believed anything—is false, and that we hold a doctrine which sets it all aside (ibid., p. 341).

The need is rather to raise up a kingdom which the inhabitants know to be 'as real as the one which is presented to them in the persons of governors and judges'; a kingdom which claims both settlers and natives for its citizens, does justice to both alike and extends its privileges to all,

> a kingdom which comes to subvert nothing, but to restore that which is decayed and fallen; to adopt into itself every fragment of existing faith and feeling; to purify it and exalt it; to cut off from it only that which the conscience of the native confesses to be inconsistent with it; to testify that wherever there is a creature having human limbs and features, there is one of that race for which Christ died, one whom he is not ashamed to call a brother (ibid., pp. 341–2).

Nearly a hundred years were to pass before Christian missionary strategists began to speak in similar terms.

As for its relationship with foreign churches, Roman or Protestant, Maurice says that the English Church has no cause to call itself better than they; in many respects it is worse. However, it holds an advantageous position. Its faith, represented in its liturgy and articles, is that of a Church, not a system; nor is it derived eclectically from elements taken from other systems. English churchmen, he claims, are better able than others to understand the difference between a church and a system.[63] It must seek to unite with foreign churches not 'on the ground of any one of their systems', but 'on the grounds of the universal Church'. Maurice, then, sees possession of the signs of the universal and spiritual society which he has described in Part 2 as the basis for the coming together of separated national churches. The nations will still be distinct, for the bonds which unite the churches of the nations themselves imply the peculiar characteristics and independence of national life.

If sects within the nation are to be reconciled, if the Church is rightly to be planted in the mission fields, and if a proper relationship with foreign churches is to be set up, there is need for discipline, study, and a spirit far different from the spirit of party and selfishness. National confession and reformation are needed, and the clergy must be foremost in both.

Maurice's final paragraph reiterates his detestation of systems, parties, and schools which attempt to amalgamate the doctrines of other schools:

> I do pray earnestly that, if any such schools should arise, they may come to naught; and that, if what I have written in this book should tend even in the least degree to favour the establishment of them, it may come to naught (ibid., pp. 346–7).

I have given much space to Maurice's conception of the Church because of its relevance to the Church of the late twentieth century. What many modern ecclesiologists and ecumenists contend for was already expounded eloquently in the pages of *The Kingdom of Christ*.

In the final section of this chapter I note the growth of the Anglican Communion, and the institution of the Lambeth Conferences which were to have an important influence on the ecumenical movement.

LAMBETH CONFERENCES

The nineteenth century saw the growth of the Anglican Communion.

In 1800, apart from the United States which then had several diocesan bishops, there were only two dioceses outside the British Isles: Nova Scotia and Newfoundland. Increasing emigration to the various parts of the British Empire, and the intensification of missionary work led to the expansion of the English Church on all continents and to the creation of dioceses which in some countries were organized into provinces, and eventually into national churches. There were seventy-two bishops overseas in 1882, the year of the death of A. C. Tait, Archbishop of Canterbury, who had done much to encourage this growth.

In these new lands the Church of England found itself faced with many unfamiliar problems. Among these were questions of organization and of relation to the mother church of England, questions not unlike those which in the twentieth century confront the Eastern Orthodox communities which have sprung up in new lands.[64] The bishops of the Church of England in Canada proposed in 1865 that a council should be held in England at which all Anglican bishops might discuss their common problems, and the first of a series of such meetings, known as the Lambeth Conferences, took place in 1867.

These conferences, usually at intervals of ten years, have been held at Lambeth Palace, the London residence of the Archbishop of Canterbury, and under his chairmanship. The Lambeth Conference has no legislative authority; its resolutions may or may not be ratified by the synods of the autonomous Anglican churches. Its influence, however, is strong. From the first, Christian unity was high on its agenda, and in this we may see the concern of bishops from parts of the world where Christian disunity was more clearly recognized as a scandalous hindrance to the gospel than it was in England.

The third Lambeth Conference in 1888 had before it reports from several committees which had been considering Anglican relations with other churches. It adopted in a revised form four basic conditions for the restoration of Christian unity which had been drawn up by the General Convention of the Protestant Episcopal Church in the United States at Chicago in 1886 (The Chicago Quadrilateral).[65] The form in which the 1888 Lambeth Conference Committee on Home Reunion accepted them is as follows:

a The Holy Scriptures of the Old and New Testaments as 'containing all things necessary **to** salvation', and as being the rule and ultimate standard of faith.

b The Apostles' Creed, as the Baptismal Symbol; and the Nicene Creed, as the sufficient statement of the Christian Faith.

c The two Sacraments ordained by Christ Himself—Baptism and the Supper of the Lord—ministered with unfailing use of Christ's words of institution and of the elements ordained by Him.

d The Historic Episcopate, locally adapted in the methods of its administration to the varying needs of the nations and people called of God into the unity of His Church.[66]

Succeeding Lambeth Conferences reaffirmed the Quadrilateral. It was the fourth point which received the greatest criticism from Protestant churches. It was felt to be inviting Nonconformists to reunion on condition that they should surrender one of the main points for which they had contended.[67] It was reframed in the 'Appeal to All Christian People',[68] sent out by the 252 Anglican bishops who attended the Lambeth Conference of 1920, to read:

> A ministry acknowledged by every part of the Church as possessing not only the inward call of the Spirit, but also the commission of Christ and the authority of the whole body.

The Appeal continued:

> May we not reasonably claim that the Episcopate is the one means of providing such a ministry? It is not that we call in question for a moment the spiritual reality of the ministries of those communions which do not possess the Episcopate. On the contrary, we thankfully acknowledge that these ministries have been manifestly blessed and owned by the Holy Spirit as effective means of grace. But we submit that considerations alike of history and of present experience justify the claim which we make on behalf of the Episcopate. Moreover, we would urge that it is now and will prove to be in the future the best instrument for maintaining the unity and the continuity of the Church.

If the desired end is the union of all Christian people, the claim is a reasonable one, for the churches of at least four-fifths of Christendom possess episcopacy, and value it as much more than merely an accidental inheritance and a convenient form of administration. It is to be noted that the Quadrilateral leaves open the questions of the theology of episcopacy and the form which it might take in a united Church. 'The Anglican Communion has never officially endorsed any one particular theory of the origin of the historic episcopate, its exact relation to the apostolate, and the sense in which it should be thought of as God-given, and in fact tolerates a wide variety of views on these points.'[69] Anglicans also are aware that in the past, both in England and elsewhere, the historic episcopate has taken many different forms,[70] and make no claim that their own form represents an ideal pattern.

The Lambeth Quadrilateral, made more widely known through the 'Appeal to All Christian People' which was sent to the heads of all churches throughout the world, stirred up wide interest, and has been an influential factor in the ecumenical movement of the twentieth century. The acceptance of episcopacy in some constitutional form has, in fact, been part of all plans for union which have advanced any distance between churches which have the historic episcopate and those which have not.

Part 6

THE TWENTIETH CENTURY

19

The Ecumenical Movement

In entering upon a study of the developments in ecclesiology during the twentieth century, the writer becomes aware that here a new volume should begin. Never before has such close attention been paid to the question of the nature of the Church. The number of books, major articles, and reports of conferences on the subject is immense. In this final section two things will be attempted: first, to discern the factors which have led to this close study of our subject; and second, to present the ecclesiology of some influential, but widely differing, twentieth-century theologians.

The factors which have brought the doctrine of the Church into the foreground arise partly from the life and activity of the churches themselves (the subject of this and the next chapter), and partly from the vastly changed, and swiftly changing, world in which the churches are situated (chapter 21).

THE CHURCH'S MISSION, AND CHRISTIAN DISUNITY

The nineteenth century saw a great expansion of missionary endeavour. Missionary societies were formed in many European and North American churches, from which dedicated men and women went out to evangelize in all the continents of the world. In large and increasing numbers nationals accepted the Christian faith, and churches were established. Before long these young churches began to see the divisions between the churches, largely regarded as normal in the 'home' countries, in their true light—as a shameful contradiction of the nature of the Church of the one Lord. Differences and rivalries which originated centuries before in the ecclesiastical and political history of Europe were being perpetuated among new Christians who could have had little understanding of them. Such divisions were a stumbling-block to the advance of the Christian mission. Divided

Christians were unconvincing messengers of the Prince of peace and the Spirit of fellowship.

In many places the churches and missionary societies tried to mitigate the damage in the situation. 'Comity' agreements were made by which a territory was regarded as exclusively the field of a particular denomination. Elsewhere there was co-operation in education and social work, and sometimes in joint worship. But many felt the need for a more radical solution.

In Europe and North America national organizations were formed to provide representatives of the various missionary societies with a forum for the discussion of missionary problems. International gatherings also began to be organized, at intervals of about ten years, in London (1878 and 1888), New York (1900), and Edinburgh (1910). The World Missionary Conference in Edinburgh was in many ways a turning-point in what has come to be known as 'the ecumenical movement'.[1] Its main concern, however, was with the evangelism of non-Christian peoples. It aimed at providing means by which the missionary agencies of the churches could continue to take counsel and plan together, conscious of a common task to be performed in the name of Christ. One of the Conference's eight commissions was designated to study co-operation and the promotion of unity. Questions of faith and Church order, however, were felt to be outside the competence of a missionary conference. But Bishop Charles Brent of the Protestant Episcopal Church of the United States of America voiced the feeling of delegates when he said that Christians could not be content with arrangements for co-operation, and that there was need of a forum in which the churches could study the causes of Christian divisions with the purpose of removing them. He was to be the chief instrument in bringing into being the Faith and Order Movement.

The Edinburgh Conference was strengthened by the presence of members of the young churches of Africa and Asia. Its weakness was the absence of Roman Catholic and Orthodox representation. More than one speech alluded to this. Dr R. Woodlaw Thompson, a Free Churchman and officer of the London Missionary Society said, 'I long for the time when we shall see another Conference, and when men of the Greek Church and the Roman Church shall talk things over with us in the service of Christ'.[2]

The Conference unanimously voted for the creation of a standing International Missionary Council. Preparations for its establishment were hindered by the 1914–18 war, but it came into existence in 1921 under the chairmanship of John R. Mott. Its functions were to foster and co-ordinate the work of the various missionary societies, and to promote co-operative or united action wherever this was seen as desirable. Study of the doctrinal issues between the churches was not seen as part of its work.

BIBLICAL SCHOLARSHIP AND THE CHURCH'S UNITY

An important contributing factor in creating a favourable atmosphere for a renewed examination of the question of the Church's unity was the increasing collaboration of Christian scholars across denominational lines. The scientific theories of the nineteenth century and the application of literary and historical criticism to the Scriptures posed challenges to some of the fundamental tenets of the Christian religion—the doctrine of creation, the uniqueness of man, the integrity of the Scriptures—and in answering them scholars were increasingly drawn together across confessional lines, and this century has witnessed a fruitful collaboration between them. The denominational barriers behind which many theological schools had previously worked were being lowered. For example, the abolition of religious tests at the English universities in 1871 opened the way to the holding of theological chairs by non-Anglicans in the twentieth century. Endowed lectureships, often the closely guarded prerogatives of scholars of a particular church, were now opened to others. Academic eminence was beginning to transcend denominational lines. This cross-fertilization was greatly expedited by more rapid means of communication and travel, and by a quicker pace in translating important theological works. These ecumenical exchanges brought to light two facts which had been hitherto ignored, or unsuspected: that doctrinal differences which had been thought of as distinguishing features between churches were often present within a single church; and that misunderstanding of the other's position was at the bottom of some important theological differences. The possibility of removing at least some of the root causes of disagreement through dialogue began to appear.

Collaboration in the field of biblical scholarship has been especially significant. In 1870 the Convocation of Canterbury resolved upon a revision of the Authorized (King James) Version of the English Bible (eventually published in 1881). The work was to be undertaken by members of its own body, but they were to be 'at liberty to invite the co-operation of any eminent for scholarship, to whatever nation or religious body they may belong'.[3] This liberty was taken. The American Standard Version (1885) and the American Revised Standard Version (1952) were the work of scholars of several American churches. Roman Catholic scholars have increasingly collaborated with others, both in biblical studies and translation, since the encyclical of Pope Pius XII, *Divino Afflatu Spiritus* of 1943 gave a large measure of encouragement to the use of modern critical methods of biblical study and to the production of new vernacular translations.[4] There is today a lively commerce between Catholic and Protestant scholars in the exchange of papers, at conferences on biblical studies, and by mutual consultation in the production of new translations. Roman Catholic observers sat with the commission which produced the New English Bible.[5]

THE QUICKENING OF THE ECUMENICAL MOVEMENT: FAITH AND ORDER

The desire for Christian unity so strongly expressed in mission fields and the greater freedom of discussion among theologians together gave impetus to the ecumenical movement. Its history is intricate, and the reader is referred for fuller details to the standard work on the subject, the two volumes of *A History of the Ecumenical Movement*.[6]

At Edinburgh in 1910, Bishop Brent announced his intention of working to establish an interchurch and international forum in which the doctrinal causes of Christian disunion could be examined. Under his leadership the Protestant Episcopal Church of the United States took the initiative, sending letters and deputations to other churches, proposing the setting-up of a commission to prepare for a world conference. A meeting in New York in 1913, at which fifteen churches were represented by commissions, set out three principles. First, a world conference should provide opportunity for the study not only of points of difference, but also of the values of the beliefs characteristic of the various churches. Second, 'that while organic unity is the ideal which all Christians should have in their thoughts and prayers, yet the business of the Commissions is not to force any particular scheme of unity'. Third, that the questions to be considered by a world conference should be formulated in advance by committees of competent representatives of the churches.[7]

The First World War interrupted these plans, but in 1919 a deputation from the Protestant Episcopal Church travelled widely in Europe and the Near East, visiting heads of churches to propose the plan for a world conference. A favourable response was received from several Orthodox churches. The deputation was received in audience, with great friendliness, by Pope Benedict XV, but on its departure received the following statement which summarizes succinctly the attitude of the Roman Catholic Church of the day towards the kind of conference proposed:

> The Holy Father, after having thanked them for their visit, stated that as successor of St Peter and Vicar of Christ he had no greater desire than that there should be one fold and one Shepherd. His Holiness added that the teaching and practice of the Roman Catholic Church regarding the unity of the visible Church of Christ was well known to everybody and therefore it would not be possible for the Catholic Church to take part in such a Congress as the one proposed. His Holiness, however, by no means wishes to disapprove of the Congress in question for those who are not in union with the Chair of Peter; on the contrary, he earnestly desires and prays that, if the Congress is practicable, those who take part in it may, by the Grace of God, see the light and become reunited to the visible Head of the Church, by whom they will be received with open arms.[8]

The First World Conference on Faith and Order was held at Lausanne in 1927, attended by 387 delegates of 108 churches from many countries, representing Anglican, Baptist, Congregational, Disciples of Christ, Lutheran, Methodist, Old Catholic, Orthodox, and Reformed Church traditions. The Conference was divided into sections in order to discuss topics such as the meaning of Christian unity, the nature of the Church, the ministry and the sacraments, and to produce draft reports. These reports were then discussed and revised by the whole Conference with a view to commending them to the churches. The Orthodox delegation, which took a full part in discussion, refrained from voting on most of the reports, but voted in support of that on the Church's Message to the World.

The problems and difficulties experienced by many in a conference of this kind are well summarized by Dr Tissington Tatlow in an account of the proceedings of section 4 on 'The Church's Common Confession of Faith'.

> Some vigorously worded opinions were heard during the first meeting and a good deal of heat was generated. 'We must declare our loyalty to the Nicene Creed,' said an Orthodox, to which a Congregationalist replied,

'Well, I think we should clear all that old lumber out of the way.' Many differences were expressed on the authority attaching to the Scriptures, the creeds, tradition, and various confessions of the Reformation period. During an interval one member approached another and asked, 'Can you tell me of any volume in which I could read one of these old creeds they have been talking about?' He was delighted at the immediate loan of a Book of Common Prayer.[9]

There were also misapprehensions about the purpose of the Conference. Some feared that its aim was to suggest a union of churches on the basis of no more than collaboration in mission and service with scant attention to unity in faith and order. Others assumed, while yet others feared, that the intention was to produce a blueprint for a universal united Church, something which was manifestly impossible in the absence of a Roman Catholic delegation. Bishop Brent and others endeavoured to clarify matters: the Conference did not aim at complete agreement, still less at a united Church, but was an occasion on which 'both agreements and disagreements were to be carefully noted'.[10] The Faith and Order Movement, like the World Council of Churches later, has always maintained that although the world conferences and committees can do much to provide opportunities for discussion, clarify issues, and identify misunderstandings, it is only the churches themselves that can unite.

At Lausanne a Faith and Order Continuation Committee was appointed to promote joint study groups to prepare material for another conference. The subjects proposed were (1) The Grace of our Lord Jesus Christ, (2) The Church of Christ and the Word of God, (3) The Church of Christ: Ministry and Sacraments, (4) The Church's Unity in Life and Worship. The Second World Conference on Faith and Order met in Edinburgh in 1937 under the presidency of William Temple, then Archbishop of York. It was attended by 344 delegates, representing 123 churches. Three points in the proceedings of the Conference must be noted here:

First, the report of the section on 'The Grace of our Lord Jesus Christ' began with the words: 'There is in connection with this subject no ground for maintaining division between churches.'[11] The Conference agreed.

Second, the report of the section on 'The Ministry and Sacraments' showed, as was expected, great differences between the delegates. Yet Professor Donald M. Baillie (Church of Scotland), in presenting it, could say: 'We have come to discover our nearness to one another, and agreements were reached, not by compromise, but by genuine rapprochement. ... If it can happen on this ground of ministry and sacraments, it can happen on any ground; and if it can happen in a conference such as this, it can happen also in the churches themselves.'[12] Succeeding decades, however, have proved that this does not quickly happen. The disagreements identified in the conference in Edinburgh, on the nature of the Church, on authority, and on the ministry, are still the major areas of dissension wherever conversations on Church union take place.

Third, the Conference approved, without dissentients,[13] a statement which called on all Christians 'to co-operate in the concerns of the Kingdom of God', to learn from one another and seek to remove the obstacles to the furtherance of the gospel which are caused by Christian divisions. It was recognized that these divisions were rooted in different understanding of Christ's will for the Church. Nevertheless, they are contrary to his will. It asserted an awareness of 'a unity deeper than our divisions', a unity based on the common acknowledgement of one Lord, Jesus Christ, and of the one Spirit, a unity in that all are 'the objects of the love and grace of God, and called by Him to witness in all the world to His glorious gospel'. It declared also the conviction 'that our unity of spirit and aim must be embodied in a way that will make it manifest to the world, though we do not yet clearly see what outward form it should take'.[14] The difficulty of envisaging the outward form of the one Church of Christ has increased rather than diminished since 1937, as we shall see.

LIFE AND WORK

Contemporaneously with the Faith and Order Movement there proceeded the Life and Work Movement, for which Nathan Söderblom, the Lutheran Archbishop of Uppsala provided the same kind of leadership as had Bishop Brent for Faith and Order. Its purpose was to relate the Christian faith to social, political, and economic problems. After a preparatory conference at Geneva in 1920, the first Universal Conference on Life and Work took place at Stockholm in 1925, and the second in 1937 at Oxford. The Oxford Conference was concerned with the Church and its function in society and its relation to the community, the State, and the economic order. Throughout, its reports showed awareness that the primary duty of the Church to the State is to be the Church, namely to witness for God, to preach His Word, to confess the faith before men, to teach both young and old to observe the divine Commandments, and to serve the nation and the State by proclaiming the Will of God as the supreme standard to which all human wills must be subject and all human conduct must conform. These functions of worship, preaching, teaching, and ministry the Church cannot renounce, whether the State consent or not.[15]

'Let the Church be the Church' has been said to be the essential message of the Conference.

THE WORLD COUNCIL OF CHURCHES

Within both the Faith and Order and the Life and Work Movements an awareness grew that the concerns of each were so intimately related that they needed to be brought together in a single council. The Oxford and Edinburgh Conferences of 1937 both passed resolutions recommending the uniting of the two movements in a World Council of Churches. This, however, was not to be achieved until after the Second World War. That it could take place as early as 1948 testifies to the devotion of those who continued to work for this end despite the difficulty of communication during the war years. At Amsterdam in 1948 the World Council of Churches[16] was inaugurated as 'a fellowship of churches which accept our Lord Jesus Christ as God and Saviour';[17] 351 delegates were present, representing 145 churches. A representative central committee was set up to meet annually, and with power to appoint an executive committee. Geneva was chosen as the headquarters of the Central Committee, and a secretariat was set up there. The Second World Assembly was held at Evanston, U.S.A., in 1954; the third at New Delhi, 1961; and the fourth at Uppsala in 1968. At Uppsala 704 delegates represented 235 churches, and 14 Roman Catholic observers were present.

The work of the F. and O. and Life and Work Movements has been incorporated with that of the W.C.C., and the integration of the International Missionary Council was effected at the New Delhi Assembly in 1961. The work of F. and O. is conducted by a commission which has initiated studies, produced reports, and continued to arrange world conferences, the third being held at Lund in 1952, and the fourth at Montreal in 1963. The social, economic, and political concerns of Life and Work have been prominent on the agenda of the

Central Committee and of the World Assemblies. After the Second World War acute problems for the churches arose from the rapid social changes being experienced in most parts of the world, the persistence of racialism, the emergence from colonial status of some countries, and revolutionary situations in others. The W.C.C. has incurred much criticism in conservative quarters for its involvement in such matters. Its condemnation of the South African policy of apartheid in 1960 occasioned the withdrawal from membership of three Dutch Reformed Churches of South Africa.

THE W.C.C. AND ECCLESIOLOGY

From the outset the W.C.C. has stated that it 'is not and must never become a Super-Church'.[18] Membership does not call for acceptance of a particular ecclesiology. That churches are members of the W.C.C. implies recognition 'that the membership of the Church is more inclusive than the membership of their own church body'. They may or may not regard other member churches as churches in the full sense of the word, but they recognize them as serving the same Lord and as possessing 'elements of the true Church'. The W.C.C. sees itself as instrumental to the union of the churches, enabling them to speak and act together, hoping to provide conditions in which they may move towards a unity which is both inward and outward. Union between particular churches can only be initiated from within the churches themselves. The W.C.C. recognizes that its own existence is strictly anomalous.

Study of the doctrine of the Church and the nature of unity has been the special task of the F. and O. Commission. In preparation for the Lund Conference it produced a volume entitled *The Nature of the Church*,[19] edited by R. Newton Flew. This is an informative collection of essays by representatives of different churches setting out what each considered essential in its ecclesiology. Its effect was to make clear that visible unity was unlikely to be achieved by 'ecclesiastical joinery'. The Lund Conference (1952) admitted: 'We have seen clearly that we can make no real advance towards unity if we only compare our several conceptions of the nature of the Church and the traditions in which they are embodied.'[20] But it also asserted that the unity of the Church must find visible expression,[21] and this was reiterated by the Third World Assembly in New Delhi (1961) in the following words:

We believe that the unity which is both God's will and his gift to his Church is being made visible as all in each place who are baptized into Jesus Christ and confess him as Lord and Saviour are brought by the Holy Spirit into one fully committed fellowship, holding the one apostolic faith, preaching the one Gospel, breaking the one bread, joining in common prayer, and having a corporate life reaching out in witness and service to all and who at the same time are united with the whole Christian fellowship in all places and all ages in such wise that ministry and members are accepted by all, and that all can act and speak together as occasion requires for the tasks to which God calls his people.

It is for such unity that we believe we must pray and work.[22]

The statement was well received, but it was pointed out that it gave no indication of the way in which such unity might be found, and was silent about the marks by which 'the whole Christian fellowship in all places and all ages' may be recognized.

It was beginning to be thought that the way of advance might be found through a study of the Church in relation to the purpose of God in creation and redemption.[23] The Montreal Conference (1963), which had a strong Orthodox delegation, and in which Roman Catholic observers shared in the discussion, devoted one section to the subject of 'The Church in the Purpose of God'. From the outset, however, dissatisfaction with the prepared papers was expressed, and disagreement developed in several areas: on the relationship of the Church to creation and redemption, on the proper balance between emphasis on the death of Christ (*theologia crucis*) and on the resurrection (*theologia gloriae*), and on the relationship of the authority of Scripture to that of tradition. The report of the Conference[24] speaks of 'elements of tension which we neither minimize nor disguise', and describes the Conference as 'promising chaos'. It was now recognized that comparative study of the differing conceptions of the nature of the Church could by no means be neglected, but the Conference recommended further study of the Church in the light of God's creative and redemptive purpose, in response to which the F. and O. Commission undertook a study of 'Creation, New Creation, and the Unity of the Church'.[25]

It has generally been recognized that among the factors which divide the churches are those which are not strictly theological, but have to do with sociological and cultural influences. In different places and times the Church necessarily and rightly adopts institutions suitable for those places and times. F. and O. published a report on this subject in 1961.[26] Outward institutions, it asserted, are implied by the incarnational nature of the Church, but it recognized that institutions created strong attachments, sometimes of a sentimental kind, and sometimes arising from vested interest. It acknowledged also the difficulty of distinguishing in all cases between 'constitutive and permanent and, on the other hand, derivative and historically variable features'.[27] Is, for example, a particular form of ministerial order of the essence of the Church, or is the form of the Church's ministry something which may and should be varied in response to the needs of the Church in a particular place or time? This has proved to be one of the thorniest questions encountered in Church union conversations.

In undertaking this study F. and O. found itself entering the field of the comparatively new science of sociology. The post-Second World War years have produced a number of essays in applying sociological principles to the 'phenomenon' of the Church, a method which was pioneered by Ernst Troeltsch[28] early in the century. Since the Church is a society which claims to have a mission to the world, the study of the relationship between the Church and the society in which it finds itself is by no means to be regarded as irrelevant to ecclesiology.

The Fourth World Assembly of the W.C.C. at Uppsala in 1968 assigned to its first section the subject of 'The Holy Spirit and the Catholicity of the Church'. The section took firm hold of a question which had always been beneath the surface in ecumenical encounter: is there hope of union, or even of sincere co-operation between churches so widely different as Roman Catholic, Orthodox, and Anglican on one hand, and Evangelical and Pentecostal on the other? Can the one Church be both Catholic, and all that this word has come to stand for—time-honoured institutions, continuity with the past, appointed channels of grace—and at the same time be the creation of the Spirit who, as the wind, blows where he wills?[29] A preliminary document[30] provided a useful study of the issues involved, clarifying the term 'catholicity', exploring the doctrine of the Holy Spirit as the source of the Church's catholicity, defining the relation between the local church and the universal Church, examining the meaning of continuity, the problem of apparent discontinuity and the concept of unity in diversity. The final report of the Assembly insists that unity is not synonymous with uniformity, that a diversity in love may enhance unity, that apparent discontinuity may be, and has in the past been, the way in which the Holy Spirit leads the Church to a truer continuity with the one Christ who is over all; that 'catholicity' and the Holy Spirit must not be set in opposition, as they are not in the New

Testament: 'The Church is faced by the twin demands of continuity in the one Holy Spirit and of renewal in response to the call of the Spirit amid the changes of human history.'[31] Renewal and the preservation of essential continuity are each functions of the Holy Spirit in the Church as in the world.

The Assembly also faced the question, which it knew to be in the minds of many, whether 'the struggle for Christian unity in its present form is irrelevant to the immediate crisis of our times'. Should not the Church 'seek its unity through solidarity with ... forces in modern life, such as the struggle for social equality, and ... give up its concern with patching up its own internal disputes?'[32] The Assembly indeed saw the Holy Spirit at work in civil rights movements and protests against discrimination, and the Christian as called to bear his witness in these contexts. But the urgency of this should not entail the neglect of the other (Matt. 23.23).

> The purpose of Christ is to bring people of all times, of all races, of all conditions, into an organic and living unity in Christ by the Holy Spirit under the universal fatherhood of God.[33]

The overcoming of division in the Church is not irrelevant to that.

THE CHURCHES AND UNION

Officials, committees, and assemblies of the W.C.C. have constantly declared that the initiative in effecting union between separated Christian groups must be taken by the churches themselves. Such initiative has not been lacking. The twentieth century has seen the coming together of many churches and groups by incorporation or organic union, or, more loosely, by federation, or by establishing concordats. A list of those which occurred between 1910 and 1952 is given by Rouse and Neill in *A History of the Ecumenical Movement*.[34] Examples of organic union are that between the Presbyterian Church in the United States of America and the Welsh Calvinistic Methodist Church in the U.S.A. (1920), retaining the name of the former; and that in England of the Wesleyan Methodist Church, the United Methodist Church, and the Primitive Methodist Church to form the Methodist Church (1931); the formation in France (1938) of the Reformed Church of France from the Union of Reformed Churches, the Union of Reformed Evangelical Churches, the Evangelical Methodist Church, and the Union of Evangelical Free Churches; and in Canada (1925) the Union of Presbyterians, Methodists, and Congregationalists to form the United Church of Canada.

Examples of federations, in which the contracting churches retain their own structure, are the Federation of Swiss Protestant Churches (1920) which includes the Reformed Churches of the cantons and the Methodist Church in Switzerland; and the Evangelical Church in Germany (1948) comprising twenty-seven autonomous regional churches of both Lutheran and Reformed tradition.

Examples of the concordat are that between the Old Catholic churches of Holland, Germany, Austria, and Switzerland and the Church of England (1931); and that between the Protestant Episcopal Church of the U.S.A. and the Polish National Catholic Church (1946). These concordats established terms of full intercommunion, and Anglican churches in other countries have entered into them since.

Along a different line there has been another ecumenical movement, namely the drawing together of Protestant churches of the same 'family' or confession, but existing in different countries, into World Alliances.[35] These alliances have provided opportunities for the member churches to take counsel together in periodic world conferences, and through their representative permanent staffs. The larger federations are the World Alliance of Reformed Churches (the first to be founded, in 1875), the Baptist World Alliance, the International Congregational Council, the World Convention of the Churches of Christ (Disciples), the Mennonite World Conference, and the Friends' World Committee for Consultation.

Both before and immediately after the creation of the W.C.C. in 1948 fears were expressed that the continued existence of these worldwide confessional organizations might discourage the local churches of the confessions from co-operation and seeking union with other churches. At Amsterdam it was decided that membership of the W.C.C. should be on the basis of churches, not of confessions, seats however being allotted with a view to adequate confessional and geographical representation. The importance of the confessional groups to the ecumenical movement was recognized in that they provided means for the churches of the confessions better to understand their own traditions. Many of these world federations have set up headquarters in Geneva, and since 1957 there have been regular meetings between their staffs and that of the W.C.C.

THE CHURCH OF SOUTH INDIA

The unions, concordats, and world alliances which I have been describing have provided no example of agreement between episcopal churches and those whose order of ministry is presbyteral or congregational. The first such instance was the union effected in 1947 between certain dioceses of the (Anglican) Church of India, Burma, and Ceylon, the South India United Church (itself a union of Presbyterians, Congregationalists, and the Basel Evangelical Mission) and the Methodist Church of South India, to form the Church of South India.[36] This union provided a model from which both positive and negative lessons have been drawn by those who have since been engaged in conversations between episcopal and non-episcopal churches.

Standards of faith were agreed upon without great difficulty: the Scriptures as the supreme authority for faith, the Nicene Creed as the authoritative summary of Christian teaching, and the sacraments of baptism and the eucharist as sacraments of the gospel. The question of ministry was not so easily settled. Anglicans, many of whom held that the episcopate within the historical succession belongs to the essence of the Church, and therefore that non-episcopal ministries lacked validity, were unwilling that there should be no more than a mutual acceptance of one another's ministers. Non-Anglicans were unable to accept the suggestion that their ministers should agree to episcopal ordination or conditional ordination, for this would either have denied, or thrown doubt upon, the reality of the ministry which they had previously exercised. Anglicans and non-Anglicans alike were unhappy with the proposal that all should receive supplemental ordination. The solution reached was a compromise, namely that from the inauguration of the Church of South India all new ministers should be episcopally ordained, but that all who were ministers at the time of inauguration should be accepted with equal rights and status without further commissioning or conditional ordination. It was expected that within about thirty years all ministries within the Church of South India would have been episcopally ordained. Meanwhile, this has meant that episcopally and non-episcopally ordained ministers have been working side by side. This is undoubtedly an anomaly, but, it is claimed, not so serious an anomaly as that of separate and competing churches attempting to present the gospel of the one Lord to a hostile or apathetic world.[37]

THE PROBLEM OF MINISTRY IN UNION CONVERSATIONS

The South India scheme throws into prominence the difficult problems which are encountered when episcopal and non-episcopal churches enter into negotiations.

On the one hand are those who are convinced that episcopacy is essential to the Church, and that the bishops who have received consecration in the historic line of succession from the apostles have the oversight (*episkope*) of the Church and are its ordaining ministers. From this position it follows that the ministry of those who are not episcopally ordained is invalid.

On the other hand are those who, while agreeing that *episkope*, in the sense of properly constituted oversight, is necessary to the church and in accordance with the will of Christ, claim that particular forms of *episkope* must be adapted to the needs of the Church and its mission. There have been and may be situations in which by the guidance of the Holy Spirit it is necessary to discover new forms. The condition of the Church on the eve of the Reformation was one such situation. The ministries of the Reformed Churches were constituted by the Spirit, have been blessed by God, and have borne the fruit of countless devoted Christian lives.

The two positions are diametrically opposed. Yet there are indications of willingness to overcome the opposition. Many who hold the first position admit gladly that the ministries of non-episcopal churches are effective in the sense that God has used them to impart grace to the lives of their members. Yet because those ministries must be deemed to be invalid—or, at the least, irregular—they invite those churches to embrace episcopacy, and their ministers to accept the laying on of hands by bishops. It should be noted that those who adopt this position raise for themselves some difficult questions. If a ministry and sacraments are *effective* without validity, what meaning does the word 'validity' have in this context? If a ministry and sacraments which are irregular are *effective*, may not the irregularity be justified?

It is a remarkable witness to the deep desire for Christian unity on the part of many non-episcopal churches now engaging in conversations that they are prepared to accept episcopacy 'in some constitutional form'.[38] But they are unwilling that the inauguration of a union with an episcopal church should include any rite which could be interpreted as casting doubt on the reality of the ministry which they have already exercised.

In the dialogue between these various positions, questions both of an historical and a theological nature arise, of which the following are examples:

1 What is the strength of the evidence that episcopacy in the same sense that Roman Catholics, Orthodox, and Anglicans understand it today was universally the ministerial order of the Church between N.T. times and the middle of the second century?

2 What is the significance of the fact that episcopacy was undoubtedly universally accepted by the beginning of the third century, and that today the great majority of Christians recognize the episcopal order of the Church?

3 Does apostolic succession mean only ministerial continuity conveyed by bishops, in succession from the apostles, consecrating other bishops in each generation? Are there not other senses of the words which are equally, perhaps more, important: an apostolic succession in faith and true doctrine, in fellowship and service? Should not the phrase properly refer to the continuity of the whole Church in the apostolic vocation and mission?

4 It being granted that due order, and the exercise of oversight are Christ's will for the Church, is it an unsurmountable cause of division that in some places and times oversight has been exercised by a body of presbyters while elsewhere it has been vested in the bishop alone? Is *no* rapprochement possible here?

These and similar questions continue to be discussed. In them are implicit some of the most obstinate barriers to union between episcopal and non-episcopal churches. It is by no means impossible, indeed there are some signs to suggest, that a way through may be pioneered by that church which has most lately entered the ecumenical movement: the Roman Catholic Church. To its relationship towards other Christian bodies, and to movements such as F. and O. and the W.C.C., I now turn.

20

The Roman Catholic Church
Vatican II and its Significance

In the first half of the twentieth century there was little to suggest that the Church of Rome had in any way moved from its position that the 'problem' of Christian divisions can only (but very simply) be solved by submission to the papacy, since the Roman Catholic Church is identical with the One Holy Catholic Church. Other Christian communions, confessions, and groups (with the sole exception of the Orthodox Churches) were officially referred to as societies, not churches. Pope Leo XIII in the Bull *Apostolicae Curae* (1896) had declared Anglican ordinations to be invalid, the implication being that the Church of England and its sister churches of the Anglican Communion are not part of the true Church of Christ. The polite but firm rebuff of Pope Benedict XV in 1919 to the invitation to the Roman Catholic Church to participate in a world conference on problems of faith and order made it clear that for him the unity of the Church meant the acceptance of the papacy.[1]

POPE PIUS XII

The encyclical *Mystici Corporis* (1943) of Pius XII was equally firm. It affirms that the doctrine of the mystical body is implicit in the very idea of the Church. It rejects all vague senses of the phrase. 'Mystical body' denotes the visible hierarchical body whose head is Christ, whose soul is the Spirit, and whose members may be saints or sinners. It signifies a unity which is not physical nor, on the other hand, merely metaphorical. It is a real unity which is constituted by regeneration in the waters of baptism, profession of the true faith, and adherence to the structure of the body. That structure is identified with the Roman Catholic Church and its hierarchy, since Christ rules on earth through his vicar, the Roman pontiff. Its members alone are effectively members of the mystical body. Of others, however, whether baptized or not, it is said that they may be ordained[2] to the mystical body 'by a kind of unconscious desire and will'. This opens the way for an interpretation of 'no salvation outside the Church' less rigid than was traditional.

A later encyclical, *Humani Generis* (1950), sharply attacked certain tendencies among liberal Roman Catholics, including that of distinguishing between the mystical body and the Church of Rome. In 1950 Pius XII took the step of defining *ex cathedra*, and therefore infallibly, the doctrine of the bodily assumption of the Blessed Virgin Mary, a doctrine which, though popularly accepted by Roman Catholics, was admitted by many theologians not to be contained in holy Scripture. This action was interpreted by many as an intentional closing of the door to any dialogue with other churches. Even the Orthodox were to receive a sharp reminder of their schismatic condition. Pius XII's encyclical *Sempiternus Rex* (1951) contains the words:

> Let those who, because of the inequity of the time, especially in Eastern lands, are separated from the bosom and unity of the Church, follow the teaching and example of their forefathers and not hesitate to render duly reverent homage to the Primacy of the Roman Pontiff.[3]

A brake was thus applied to ecumenical dialogue which had been undertaken by Roman Catholic theologians here and there.

POPE JOHN XXIII AND THE SECOND VATICAN COUNCIL

The accession of John XXIII in 1958 quickly brought a change of climate. The summoning in January 1959 of an Ecumenical Council,[4] the first since Vatican I of 1869–70, was unexpected even in circles close to the papacy. It quickly became clear that the doctrine of the Church was likely to be the main subject of the Council. The brake applied by Pius XII was felt to be eased, alike by non-Roman Catholics and by those within the Roman Catholic Church who believed that the way to Christian unity lay in the renewal of the Church and through dialogue rather than by a demand for submission. In the months following, many articles and books were written by Roman Catholic theologians on Church renewal and new possibilities of dialogue among the churches. During this period the Pope established a Secretariat for Promoting Christian Unity with Cardinal Augustin Bea as its first president. It saw its immediate task as to keep non-Roman churches informed about the Council. At the same time the relations with the W.C.C. were improved. A constructive meeting took place between Cardinal Bea and the General Secretary of the W.C.C., Dr W. A. Visser 't Hooft. Five Roman Catholic observers attended the Third Assembly of the W.C.C. at New Delhi in 1961. Moreover, some months before the Council met, it was decided that observers from other churches should be invited: Orthodox, Anglican, and the churches with world confessional organizations, as well as representatives of the W.C.C. About 150 observers in fact attended the Council for longer or shorter periods.

The Council assembled on 12 October 1962. There were four sessions, concluding on 8 December 1964, the last three sessions being presided over by Pope Paul VI after the death of John XXIII in 1963. Sixteen documents were promulgated. The doctrine of the Church is involved in all of them, but three in particular clearly reveal what the Church of Rome was moved to say at a time of unprecedented expectation on the part of Roman Catholic clergy and laity for renewal, and on the part of other Christians for an ecumenical gesture. These are the 'Dogmatic Constitution on the Church', the 'Pastoral Constitution on the Church in the Modern World', and the 'Decree on Ecumenism'.

VATICAN II: THE DOGMATIC CONSTITUTION ON THE CHURCH[5]

This Constitution, known as *Lumen Gentium* ('Light of All Nations') from its first words in Latin, begins by describing the Church as 'a kind of sacrament or sign of intimate union with God, and of the unity of all mankind',[6] and proceeds to speak of its divine foundation:

> [The Eternal Father] planned to assemble in the holy Church all those who would believe in Christ. Already from the beginning of the world, the foreshadowing of the Church took place. She was prepared for in a remarkable way throughout the history of the people of Israel and by means of the Old Covenant. Established in the present era of time, the Church was made manifest by the outpouring of the Spirit. At the end of time she will achieve her glorious fulfilment. ...
>
> The Son, therefore, came on mission from His Father. It was in Him, before the foundation of the world, that the Father chose us to become adopted sons. ... Christ inaugurated the kingdom of heaven on earth and revealed to us the mystery of the Father. By His obedience He brought about redemption. The Church, or, in other words, the kingdom of Christ now present in mystery, grows visibly in the world through the power of

God ('Dogmatic Constitution on the Church' i, 2–3; Abbott, op. cit., pp. 15–16).

The work of our redemption is carried on, and the growth of the Church in the unity of the one body of Christ is nourished by the constant celebration, in the eucharist, of Christ's sacrifice on the cross.

Chapter i goes on, with constant reference to biblical passages, to speak of the Holy Spirit's work of sanctifying, guiding, and renewing the Church, and to draw out briefly the significance of the various N.T. images of the Church: flock, vineyard, household, temple, spouse, and body of Christ.[7]

Christ established the Church as a visible structure through which he communicates grace to all. It is a single, visible structure:

> The society furnished with hierarchical agencies and the Mystical Body of Christ are not to be considered as two realities, nor are the visible assembly and the spiritual community, nor the earthly Church and the Church enriched with heavenly things. Rather, they form one interlocked reality which is comprised of a divine and a human element. For this reason, by an excellent analogy, this reality is compared to the mystery of the incarnate Word. ...
>
> This Church ... subsists in the Catholic Church, which is governed by the successor of Peter and by the bishops in union with that successor, although many elements of sanctification and of truth can be found outside her visible structure. These elements, however, as gifts properly belonging to the Church of Christ, possess an inner dynamism towards Catholic unity (ibid. i, 8; op. cit., pp. 22–3).

This is the Constitution's first reference to non-Roman Catholic Christians.

That Chapter ii is devoted wholly to a consideration of the Church as the people of God is said by Father Avery Dulles[8] to have 'met a profound desire of the Council to put greater emphasis on the human and communal side of the Church'. The Church is not to be equated with the hierarchy. Nevertheless, we are reminded that the people of God which as a whole exercises a priestly, prophetic, and kingly function, includes the hierarchical ministry whose priesthood differs from that of the whole people 'in essence and not only in degree'.[9]

Some passages which are reminiscent of F. D. Maurice[10] occur in a section which speaks of all men being called to belong to the new people of God:

> Among all the nations of earth there is but one People of God, which takes its citizens from every race, making them citizens of a kingdom

which is of a heavenly and not an earthly nature. . . . The Church or People of God takes nothing away from the temporal welfare of any people by establishing the kingdom. Rather does she foster and take to herself, in so far as they are good, the ability, resources, and customs of each people. Taking them to herself she purifies, strengthens, and ennobles them (ii, 13, p. 31).

Maurice might also have written: 'Within the Church particular Churches hold a rightful place',[11] but the words following show that the Constitution does not relax the claim to papal primacy: 'These Churches retain their own tradition without in any way lessening the primacy of the Chair of Peter.' Consequently,

they are fully incorporated into the society of the Church who, possessing the Spirit of Christ, accept her entire system and all the means of salvation given to her, and through union with her visible structure are joined to Christ, who rules her through the Supreme Pontiff and the bishops (ii, 14, p. 33).

What, then, of other Christians, those of whom the Constitution says that 'they do not profess the faith in its entirety, or do not preserve unity of communion with the successor of Peter'? With them, it is said, the Church is linked in many ways. They honour the Scriptures, believe in God and in Christ, are consecrated by baptism which unites them with Christ, recognize and receive other sacraments in 'their own Churches or ecclesial communities'.[12]

Likewise we can say that in some real way they are joined with us, in the Holy Spirit, for to them also He gives His gifts and graces, and is thereby operative among them with His sanctifying power (ii, 15, p. 34).

It is to be noted that this constitutes a rejection of the view advanced by Augustine during his controversy with Donatists,[13] that in Christian groups separated from the Catholic Church the Holy Spirit does not operate, so that their sacraments have no efficacy and their lives are bereft of grace—an opinion which has been widespread among Roman Catholics until very recent times.[14]

We have here, then, a declaration that 'in some real way' other Christians are joined to the one Church of Christ. The strong desire of all sincere Christians 'to be peacefully united in the manner determined by Christ'[15] is noted. While it is not here actually stated that the manner determined by Christ is to 'render duly reverent homage to the Primacy of the Roman Pontiff', this is clearly expected of all who would 'be fully incorporated into the society of the Church'. *Lumen*

Gentium offers little reason for the non-Roman Catholic Christian to hope for a change of mind on this point on the part of the Church of Rome.

Chapter III, 'The Hierarchical Structure of the Church, with Special Reference to the Episcopate', takes up the work which the First Vatican Council had left undone. That Council, having defined the papal primacy and infallibility, was interrupted by the political upheavals of 1870 before it could consider the authority of the bishops in relation to the pope. This chapter now enunciates the principle of episcopal collegiality. The Lord called the apostles, whom 'He formed after the manner of a college or fixed group, over which He placed Peter'.[16] The apostles 'took care to appoint successors in this hierarchically structured society',[17] among whom 'the chief place belongs to the office of those who, appointed to the episcopate in a sequence running back to the beginning, are the ones who pass on the apostolic seed'.[18] The account here given of the emergence of the episcopate is very sketchy, and many ambiguities in the early history of the development of Christian ministry are passed over.

As St Peter and the other apostles formed one apostolic college, so do the Roman pontiff and the bishops. This collegiality has found expression in the linkage of the bishops with one another all over the world and with the bishop of Rome, by 'bonds of unity, charity, and peace', in the decisions of conciliar assemblies, and ecumenical councils, and is marked by the practice by which several bishops take part in the consecration of a new bishop.[19] It is stressed that the word 'college' in this context is not to be understood as 'a group of equals who entrust their powers to their president'.[20] Hence:

> The college or body of bishops has no authority unless it is simultaneously conceived of in terms of its head, the Roman Pontiff, Peter's successor, and without any lessening of his power of primacy over all. . . . For in virtue of his office, that is, as Vicar of Christ and pastor of the whole Church, the Roman Pontiff has full, supreme, and universal power over the Church. And he can always exercise this power freely (iii, 22, p. 43).

The difference between this understanding of collegiality and that of Cyprian in the third century[21] should be noted. *Lumen Gentium's* definition, and the ways in which it can be made practically effective, are matters of sharp debate within the Roman Church.

Chapter III then discusses the prophetic, priestly, and kingly functions of the bishops (paras. 25–7) in relation to the ministries of priests and deacons (paras. 28–9).

Christ ... through His apostles, made their successors, the bishops, partakers of His consecration and His mission. These in their turn have legitimately handed on to different individuals in the Church various degrees of participation in this ministry. Thus the divinely established ecclesiastical ministry is exercised on different levels by those who from antiquity have been called bishops, priests, and deacons (iii, 28, pp. 52–3).

Professor Hans Küng notes[22] that the claim is not here made that these three orders of ministry have existed from the apostles' time. The phrase used is 'from antiquity' (*ab antiquo*), not 'from the beginning' (*ab initio*). Yet the suggestion that there was everywhere a smooth devolution of authority from apostles to bishops and then to ministers of a lower order 'who do not possess the highest degree of priesthood'[23] is again too simplistic a description of the early development of the Christian ministry, and begs several historical questions.

Chapter iv, 'The Laity', ascribes to the laity a positive ministry in the Church and to the world in virtue of their calling and commissioning through baptism and confirmation. This ministry is described as a share in the prophetic, priestly, and kingly work of Christ and of the whole people of God. The subject of Chapter v is 'The Call of the Whole Church to Holiness', and Chapter vi, entitled 'Religious', deals with the particular call to holiness of those who enter the religious Orders.

Chapter vii, 'The Eschatological Nature of the Pilgrim Church and her Union with the Heavenly Church' presents the Church in a new perspective. In Chapter iii, despite some hints of a greater openness to non-Roman Catholic Christians and to the non-Christian world, we were given much the same picture of the Church as had been painted in the Catholic West for centuries: the hierarchical structure, itself containing the whole of Christian truth, inerrant, majestic, triumphant, unshakably stable, presented almost as a statuesque image of perfection. In Chapter vii, however, although the Church is 'the universal sacrament of salvation', it is depicted as in progress on a pilgrim way. The restoration of all things is promised, and has indeed begun in Christ, so that on this earth the Church is marked with a genuine holiness. But it is an 'imperfect holiness'; it 'takes on the appearance of this passing world'. The note of triumphalism is muted; that of the need for renewal rises in crescendo. Joined with Christ in the Church its members are truly sons of God but 'have not yet appeared with Christ in the state of glory'. There is need, therefore, 'to live more for Him, who died for us and rose again', to strive 'to please the Lord in all things', to put on God's armour as a protection against evil.[24] Such words call forth an affirmative response from those of other churches in a way which the earlier chapters of the Constitution do not.

THE PASTORAL CONSTITUTION
ON THE CHURCH IN THE MODERN WORLD

This Constitution,[25] known also as *Gaudium et Spes* ('Joy and Hope') from its first words in Latin, is, significantly, the longest of the documents of Vatican II. It deserves, and is receiving, close attention. Here the Fathers of the Council show themselves to be fully aware that the Church is now in the twentieth century, a century which confronts a world with problems different from and more difficult than those of the past. And they declare the Church to be in, for, and open to the world, not above, against, and closed to it. More than any other Council document *Gaudium et Spes* has promoted renewal in the Roman Catholic Church—and involved it in the risks and tensions between the old and the new which inevitably accompany a determined effort at reformation. It is not possible here even to summarize how the Council Fathers draw out in detail the relation of a Church which sees itself as 'truly and intimately linked with mankind and its history'[26] to modern society in its cultural, economic, and political dimensions. I shall content myself with a quotation from an introduction to the Constitution by Father D. R. Campion, S.J., and some reference to comments of Dr Robert McAfee Brown.

Father Campion reminds us[27] that the preparatory commissions had not envisaged any document on the Church and the modern world. *Gaudium et Spes* was prompted by an intervention from the floor towards the close of the first session by the Belgian primate, Cardinal Suenens. He suggested that the Council should do more than concern itself with internal reform and should address itself to a question which the world was asking: Church of Christ, what do you say of yourself? Any answer to that must include an account of how the Church sees its relation to the contemporary world. The Pastoral Constitution is the Council's answer to the question. Father Campion holds that

> the most distinctive note sounded in the text ... is that of the Church putting itself consciously at the service of the family of man. It may well be that in generations to come men will read this as a highly significant step towards a rethinking of conventional ecclesiological images, e.g. that of

the Church viewed as a 'perfect society' standing over against the perfect society of the *Civitas*.[28]

Robert McAfee Brown, an American Protestant commentator, declares[29] that it is 'highly significant' that the Council, besides concerning itself with internal affairs, 'turned outward to examine the ways in which a Church subject to "reform and renewal" should relate to those beyond its walls'. The Constitution, he says, 'is an immeasurably important first word on a subject to which Catholicism has given far too little attention in the past'. He particularly welcomes its positive attitude to 'the world' in contrast with the negativism, sometimes perilously close to a denial of the goodness of creation, which has been characteristic of much Christian thought, both Catholic and Protestant. Recognition and understanding of the world, readiness to learn from it and to co-operate with all men, within and outside the Church—even with its avowed enemies—for the betterment of the human lot are corollaries of the new positive attitude which the Constitution itself draws out.[30]

He also sees as important the admission that the Church bears part of the responsibility for the present plight of the world, and the recognition that 'rather than striving to rule in the affairs of men, the Church must offer herself as a servant to men'. The Constitution's statement that the right of religious freedom is due to the dignity of the human person; the stress on lay activity and even initiative in the work of the Church; and the recognition of the social nature of man which 'renders untenable the frequent attempt to describe Christian ethical responsibility in purely individual terms' and calls for 'corporate human action on a large scale' are also singled out as encouraging signs of new and outward-looking attitudes on the part of the Roman Catholic Church.[31]

In the first stages of the implementation of 'The Pastoral Constitution on the Church in the Modern World', the Roman Catholic Church has not only engaged itself in conversations and in some measure of co-operation with other Christian bodies, but also has made contacts with representatives of other religions and with Marxists.

THE DECREE ON ECUMENISM[32]

Chapter I is entitled 'Catholic Principles of Ecumenism'. Prior to the final draft it had been headed 'Principles of Catholic Ecumenism'.

Father W. M. Abbott's note on this[33] explains that 'the change implies that the Council recognizes ecumenism as one movement for all Churches and Communities. The goal for all is the same, unity in the Christian faith, but the way of conceiving that unity and faith may vary, and so one may speak of a Church having its own principles of ecumenism'. The chapter begins by stating the beliefs which Roman Catholics bring to the ecumenical dialogue, summarizing what has been said in *Lumen Gentium*.

From the beginning rifts arose in the one and only Church. In later centuries large communities have separated from full communion with the Catholic Church. Often there was blame on both sides. Those who are born into separated communities cannot have the sin of separation imputed to them:

> The Catholic Church accepts them with respect and affection as brothers. For men who believe in Christ and have been properly baptized are brought into a certain, though imperfect, communion with the Catholic Church. Undoubtedly, the differences that exist ... do indeed create many and sometimes serious obstacles to full ecclesiastical communion. These the ecumenical movement is striving to overcome. Nevertheless, all those justified by faith through baptism are incorporated into Christ. They therefore have a right to be honoured by the title of Christian, and are properly regarded as brothers in the Lord by the sons of the Catholic Church ('Decree on Ecumenism' i, 3, p. 345).

As in *Lumen Gentium*[34] it is admitted that within the separated churches there are many elements of true Catholic faith and practice. Many of their sacred actions engender the life of grace, and can truly be described as 'capable of providing access to the community of salvation'.[35] But these churches do not have that unity which Christ wishes to bestow upon the faithful, a unity which is found in the Catholic Church alone.

Roman Catholics are exhorted to participate in ecumenism intelligently. There should be dialogue in which each side presents its position fully, avoiding provocative statements and actions. This is intended to lead to a greater appreciation of the teaching and religious life of each communion, to co-operation where conscience allows, to common prayer 'where this is permitted', to an examination of their own faithfulness to Christ, and to the undertaking of renewal and reform wherever necessary.[36]

Chapter ii, 'The Practice of Ecumenism', lays down further guidelines for ecumenism. These are often cautious, as the warning that common worship is not an instrument to achieve unity, but rather signifies a unity already present.[37] Chapter III, 'Churches and Ecclesial Communities separated from the Roman Apostolic See', examines the relationship of the Roman Catholic Church and other churches under two headings: 'The Special Position of the Eastern Churches', and 'The Separated Churches and Ecclesial Communities in the West'. The conviction that the unity of the Church demands the return of the separated churches to papal obedience is never far below the surface. Yet at the same time there shows through a new openness both towards these other churches and to the guidance of God. It is expressed in the admission that sins against unity are not all on the side of 'the separated brethren':

> Thus, in humble prayer, we beg pardon of God and of our separated brethren, just as we forgive those who trespass against us (ii, 7, p. 351).

And the Decree concludes with the words:

> This most sacred Synod urgently desires that the initiatives of the sons of the Catholic Church, joined with those of the separated brethren, go forward without obstructing the ways of divine Providence and without pre-judging the future inspiration of the Holy Spirit. Further this Synod declares its realization that the holy task of reconciling all Christians in the unity of the one and only Church of Christ transcends human energies and abilities. It therefore places its hope entirely in the prayer of Christ for the Church, in the love of the Father for us, and in the power of the Holy Spirit. 'And hope does not disappoint, because the charity of God is poured forth in our hearts by the Holy Spirit who has been given to us' (iii, 24, pp. 365–6).

AFTER THE SECOND VATICAN COUNCIL

The years since the close of the Council in 1965 have been difficult for the Roman Catholic Church. The period of the Council had been a time of self-examination, of expression of dissatisfaction with many features of the Church's life, of questioning even the nature of the Church's authority expressed through the magisterium, both on the part of the Church at large and in the Council itself. Many of the decisions of the Council arose out of this heart-searching and questioning. The question now, writes Dr Lukas Vischer, was: 'Would it be possible to restore an order comparable with that of the pre-conciliar period? Or would the questioning and seeking which had marked the sessions of the Council henceforth be a feature of the life of the Church as a whole?' He goes on:

> The Council had given rise to a new image of the Church. The very fact that for several years vital questions had been discussed openly before the whole Church, indeed before the whole world, had clearly demonstrated that the Church is most alive when it is moving forward, when it proclaims the gospel while at the same time asking itself questions about the gospel. Had not the Council itself planned with this movement in mind? Had it not continually stressed the Church's readiness for dialogue with the world? But could the Church face the problems of the modern world without also continuing its questioning and seeking?[38]

It is too early to answer the main question here, which is whether the Church of Rome will return to the self-understanding which prevailed from the time of Bellarmine to the accession of John XXIII. But in the years since the Council the questioning and seeking have continued.

Much has been done to implement the intention of the Council concerning ecumenism. The Secretariat for Unity has been continued in being, and through it official dialogue has been established with a number of churches. Discussion with the Lutheran World Federation began in 1965, with the Anglican Communion in 1966, and with the World Methodist Council in 1967. The practice has been to set up joint committees of theologians to study particular theological subjects and to prepare agreed statements for referral to the churches concerned. The Anglican Roman Catholic International Commission has issued statements on the eucharist, ministry, and authority in the Church which have been well received both by the Anglican and Roman Catholic Churches, and by others. They have not, however, been officially endorsed. The conferences of Roman Catholic bishops in several countries have set up ecumenical committees and centres which are fostering dialogue with other churches on the national level. By 1973 in the United States, for instance, conversations were being sponsored with the American Baptist Convention, the Christian Church (Disciples of Christ), the Episcopal Church (Anglican), Southern Baptists, Orthodox, Lutherans, Methodists, and Presbyterians.

Relations with the W.C.C. are closer. The Joint Working Group of the Roman Catholic Church and the W.C.C., established in 1965, has met twice a year for periods of several days. Its main task has been to discover whether a common understanding of the meaning of ecumenism can be reached, and to discuss possibilities of co-operation. The underlying question, whether the Roman Catholic Church may become a member of the World Council, is still unresolved. Fourteen Roman Catholic observers attended the Uppsala Assembly of the W.C.C. in 1968, and in the same year permission was given for Roman Catholic theologians to become full members of the Faith and Order Commission.

During these years the Roman Catholic Church has begun to experience difficulties which other Christian churches, with the exception of the newest evangelistic and pentecostal groups, have encountered for decades, and which have their roots in the materialistic, pluralistic, and anti-authoritarian society which has emerged with quickening pace as the century has advanced. There is declining membership in many places, and a shortage of clergy caused both by resignation of orders and by absence of vocation on the part of younger men (and for similar reasons a great reduction in membership of religious Orders, both of men and women). Many large buildings, monasteries, and seminaries stand empty. The Roman Catholic Church is reacting positively to these exigencies. For instance, the Synod of Bishops is currently addressing itself to the question of evangelization. A document[39] issued from the Vatican in 1973 calls on the conferences of bishops in the different countries to co-operate in this study and to help establish practical guidelines for evangelization. It abounds in questions. They are open-ended questions on which the corporate wisdom of the bishops is sought; and they are based on frank recognition of the world as it is:

> The world of today is in full evolution. Individuals and communities by their own activity are constructing their individual and social lives; a new way of life is coming into being, as a consequence of industrialization, urbanization, the independence of new nations, etc., indeed the very judgement and scale of values in men's consciences are undergoing change.[40]

Certain elements in the situation are seen as favouring evangelization. This part of the document deserves to be quoted in full:

a People are seeking a new life style, freedom from all types of servitude, and the development and promotion of the whole man.

b In human society individuals as well are seeking the meaning of life and are daily becoming more involved in the discussion of the matter.

c Dissatisfaction springs not only from lack of progress; it also increases with the advent of progress itself.

d The Church has become progressively less identified with society's political structures, and is able to manifest her religious nature more clearly.

e There is an evident reaction against conformism and immutable traditions. This reaction manifests itself in the questioning of structures imposed from without.

f New community forms of every kind arising everywhere demonstrate people's urge to foster mutual solidarity.

g There is an increase in the sense of personal responsibility.

h The less elevated forms of religious practice are coming to be recognized as lacking in substance and are being either rejected or corrected. A more genuine religious experience is prized and sought after.

i The various religious and world ideologies are coming together in the quest for peace and justice.[41]

A list of possible hindrances to evangelization follows: 'possible', because it is asked whether they are all to be regarded as obstacles, and not rather as providing fruitful ground for evangelization. The list includes: concepts of man and interpretations of human life which are not open to the gospel, and which are assumed as axiomatic in some currents of psychological, sociological, and anthropological thought and often accepted by the masses; the prevalence of atheism; the secularization of schools and hospitals; rapidly changing social conditions through urbanization and migration; the speedy dissemination of news by modern means of communication; the challenge to traditional values, e.g. of the family, and the questioning of ethical principles long held to be absolute. Under the heading 'Obstacles within the Church' are mentioned the shakiness of faith of many Christians; 'certain currents of thought, which find expression in the "death of God" and "religionless Christianity" theories' which gained much prominence in the 1960s; uncertainty about 'central teachings of the Gospel (Christ's identity, his true divinity, the Resurrection ...)'. With reference to the Roman Catholic Church itself are mentioned disagreements about moral standards in relation to the individual, the family, and the State; the difficulty of communicating the faith 'in a language understood by our contemporaries'; the accusation that the Church co-operates 'with certain organs of economic and political power which are perhaps unjust' for the sake of material support; a certain emphasis on plurality within the Church which tends towards 'diversity in customs, discipline, liturgy, and sometimes even in the way the faith is formulated'.[42]

How evangelism may be promoted in these circumstances is the question which this paper asks the conferences of bishops. The document is significant in various ways. It is part of the implementation of the doctrine of episcopal collegiality as defined by the Second Vatican Council. It is significant of a Church, fully aware of the kind of world in which men now live, which urgently seeks renewal in the light of this understanding. It reveals also that the Church is undergoing 'a crisis in authority'; 'disagreement concerning the interpretation of the moral demands made by the gospel' can only mean that the magisterium is being challenged. That this is so became clear when Pope Paul VI's encyclical, *Humanae Vitae* ('Of Human Life'), was published in 1968.

The Church of Rome no longer presents a monolithic image to the world.[43] The conservative-liberal tension is felt perhaps more strongly than in any other church. Objections to the introduction of the new and simplified liturgy in the vernacular in accordance with Vatican II's 'Constitution on the Sacred Liturgy' are as vehemently outspoken as the protests against the official adherence to traditional teaching on birth control in *Humanae Vitae*.[44] In ecclesiology a vigorous debate goes on. The nature of the Church is receiving much attention from a number of Roman Catholic scholars, all independent thinkers, and some of whom (Hans Küng and Rosemary Ruether perhaps) are more radical than others.[45] Chapter 24 will discuss Küng's ecclesiology. Here I shall briefly mention some of the others.

SACRAMENTUM MUNDI: THE CHURCH AS SERVANT

In these contemporary Roman Catholic ecclesiologists two themes are constant, both inspired by the documents of Vatican II. One is the idea of the Church as *Sacramentum mundi*, the Sacrament of the world; the other is the concept of the Servant Church. The phrase *Sacramentum mundi* is not found in the Vatican II documents, but *Lumen Gentium*'s first paragraph contains the words:

By her relationship with Christ, the Church is a kind of sacrament or sign of intimate union with God, and of the unity of all mankind. She is also an instrument for the achievement of such union and unity ('Dogmatic Constitution on the Church' i, 1, p. 15).

In Chapter VIII, 48, also, the Church is said to be the 'universal sacrament' of salvation. The Constitution did not develop these ideas, but here is the seed for a fruitful doctrine of the Church, and one which, although using different terminology, is very close to the doctrine of the mystical body.

A sacrament is a gift of God: something earthly is set aside for holy use, a sign and representative of what all things earthly are meant to be, and an instrument of sanctification of all that is earthly. In the idea of the Church as the sacrament of the world, then, we have the concept of a society instituted by God which is itself in microcosm what the world must be, and which exists to enable it to be that which itself is, the body of Christ. Thomas O'Dea in a recent article[46] explores what such a concept implies for the Church's structures and activity in the world of today. In the light of the technological revolution, the unsolved social problems it has created, and the consequent 'worldwide destructuration of traditional forms and the often chaotic search for new forms and structures of thought and relationship', O'Dea believes that the Church which has stood 'aloof and defensive for several centuries now becomes part of the quest of modern men, now as a "Pilgrim Church" takes its position in the ranks of evolving humanity', and asks: 'How shall it be a sacramental sign and a facilitating means in these circumstances?'[47] This article, with others in the same volume, 'The Church: Sign and Instrument of Unity' by Richard McBrien,[48] and 'Structures of the Church's Presence in the World of Today—through the Church's own Institutions' by Robert Rodes, attempts to suggest what the 'restructuration' of the Church demands in terms of canon law, diocesan and parochial organization (the question whether the territorial parish is outdated is raised), relationship to the State, education, and social service.

Edward Schillebeeckx, a Dutch theologian, also develops the idea of the Church as the sacrament of the world.[49] Taking up another hint from *Gaudium et Spes*,[50] he relates this aspect of the Church to the dialogue which he sees as a newly understood and accepted 'principle', 'basic attitude', and 'inner demand':[51]

> The Church's new understanding of herself and her new understanding of the world, form the basis of the Church's change from monologue to dialogue. The whole of this fundamental change of emphasis can be sum-

marized in the key-idea which inspired this change, even though it was not so used in any of the documents of the Council. This is the idea of the Church as the *Sacramentum mundi*. *Mundus* ('world') in this context means the confraternity, or other-orientated existence, of men in the world—man's mode of existence in dialogue with his fellow-men. The Church must, according to the Council, really be the sacrament of this brotherhood: ... the Church is 'the sign of that fraternity which permits and strengthens sincere dialogue'.[52] As such the Church really fulfils the 'ministry of communication' in the world. Wherever there are impediments to communication, the Church must lead the way in overcoming them. As Gibson Winter has said so succinctly, the Church 'has the task of re-opening communication'.[53] He went even further, saying that 'the ministry of reconciliation of the Servant Church is the restoration of communication to society'[54]. . . . The Church is the sacrament of dialogue, of communication between men (*God the Future of Man*, pp. 123–4).

This does not, he maintains, necessitate abandoning the Church's 'claim to exclusiveness', which previously seemed to make dialogue impossible. On the contrary, dialogue demands that the truth which each has should be brought into relation with the truth of others. Moreover, Schillebeeckx claims, however it has appeared in history, the Church does not claim to possess all truth and to be always right:

> The Church has a religious mission in the world and *thus*, in this mission, also a humanizing task. But for the task of humanizing the world as it is she receives from divine revelation no light other than that of all men and their experiences, and she has therefore to search tentatively for solutions. Furthermore, her *religious* claim, her 'claim to exclusiveness' on the basis of Christ's promise, is made relative by the fact that she is eschatologically orientated—still on the way, in history, towards the kingdom of God and not yet identical with the kingdom of God (ibid., pp. 124–5).

Whether this is consonant with the still official doctrine of the infallibility of the Church and of the pope is debatable. But on this basis Schillebeeckx is convinced that the Roman Catholic Church can, and must, as *Sacramentum mundi* enter into dialogue with the world, as a church which is a servant church[55] and one which 'will always need reform and purification'.[56]

Professor Gregory Baum of St Michael's College, Toronto, and editor of *The Ecumenist*, is a theologian who, both by his writing and by taking many opportunities of interchurch and interfaith dialogue, shows himself in agreement with Schillebeeckx's contention that the Roman Catholic Church has a mission to the world which must now manifest itself in dialogue.[57] He too is concerned to interpret the position of the Church of Rome in a way which will not stifle dialogue from the start. Its claims can, he admits, no longer be based on the traditional argument about identity through continuity with the Church of the New Testament,[58] nor on the argument that it alone manifests in any fullness the four credal 'marks' of the Church: 'Remembering the four marks of the Church, we discover in how many ways we are *not* united, *not* universal, *not* holy, and *not* faithful to the original gift.'[59]

The uniqueness of the Roman Catholic Church, Gregory Baum believes, rests rather on the fact that it is the only church which has maintained the tension between local and universal unity, and the tension between past and present. The former tension is built into the structure of the Church: 'Episcopacy affirms the unity and relative autonomy of the local community and the papacy affirms the unity of the universal Church, in which the local communities participate.'[60] Because the tension is maintained, 'the Catholic Church is able to come to consensus on the meaning of her own life of faith, which is acknowledged as authoritative by the faithful'.[61] The tension between past and present is that between belief 'that everything God has done for the salvation of man has happened in Jesus Christ and hence lies in the past' and the belief 'that the divine work of redemption, revealed in Christ, is still going on and hence is present to us'.[62] 'The Catholic Church, because of its concept of "tradition", is capable of retaining the two poles of this tension between past and present'[63] without falling into primitivism on the one hand or modernism on the other. Tradition is 'a process in which the Spirit is creatively involved'. Knowing this, the Church is not bound to the past, but open in the present and to the future, and is able to reinterpret its teaching 'in obedience to God's Word in the present',[64] or, to put it another way, it is able 'to refocus' the gospel upon the spiritual-cultural situation of today and of every day.[65] To summarize: the Roman Catholic Church, according to Baum, because of its papal-episcopal structure and its grasp of the true meaning of tradition, is able to arrive at doctrinal agreement and to make the gospel relevant to the contemporary world. In this it is unique, and in these terms its exclusive claims must be made. This is the contribution it must make to the Ecumenical Movement.[66]

But it has to be asked whether the bases for the claim to uniqueness which Baum expounds bear any more weight than the criteria he has rejected. The papal-episcopal hierarchy simply has not reached a consensus 'received as normal' by the Church's members, for example on infallibility and birth control: different matters indeed, but both of great relevance to the church-world relation. Moreover, it is not self-evident that the Roman Catholic Church alone has grasped the concept of the Holy Spirit as interpreter of the gospel and Christian tradition to every age.

Rosemary Radford Ruether appears to be the most radical of recent Roman Catholic writers on the Church. The phrase 'appears to be' is used advisedly since she herself in the Introduction to her book, *The Church Against Itself*, warns the reader against shock and tells us that it was written to test the spirit of openness to the world and the future which has been claimed for Vatican II.[67] She reacted, moreover, very sharply to a critical review by another Roman Catholic woman theologian, claiming that the reviewer had not understood the dialectical nature of her argument and consequently had attributed to her inconsistencies where none existed.[68] The book contains a trenchant criticism of institutionalism in the Church, and indeed in all churches, and asserts that it is only by discontinuity with its own past that the Church can keep continuity with the gospel, and therefore be true to the gospel in the present. Its institutional forms (the Scriptures, the episcopal succession, the sacraments are included) are means by which the Church has maintained itself in history. They were not instituted by Christ, or by the apostles, for they expected the near approach of the End, but by history: 'Only the Church as an eschatological community is "from Christ".'[69] The institutional office of the Church 'can put itself back into a positive relationship with the Spirit when it understands that it was *not* instituted by Christ, but was instituted by history',[70] and 'the Holy Spirit does not underwrite any finalized historical structures or dogmas, but rather breaks apart and brings to an end such history'.[71] Mrs Ruether, it seems, does not share Gregory Baum's confidence in the institution of pope and bishops. Not that she wishes to sweep all ecclesiastical institutions away, but 'all this is a secondary reality, not without its usefulness if properly understood, but which distorts and even betrays the inner nature of the Church when it is given a hypostatic reality of its own'.[72] The following paragraph brings out clearly the important point she is making:

> The role of the external institution is both indispensable and limited in power. For the institutional church to accept this limit to itself is at the

same time to keep itself in that open situation whereby the eschatological reality of the Church can again and again become real in history for the Christian community. Therefore, in order for Church office to fulfil its task authentically, it must know its own conditioned and relative nature. Its polity is always given by the political and social forms of the times, not appointed by God and invested with absolute validity in itself. It can truly be a fertile bed for the seed sown by the divine sower, or a rocky patch which withers and destroys it, depending on whether it takes an open and self-abnegating, or a closed and self-absolutizing, view of itself (*The Church Against Itself*, pp. 139–40).

Rosemary Ruether, then, is convinced that the Church must be recognized to be an eschatological community. 'To be in the Church is to be already, in principle, within that kingdom of the Christ, that new creation of God which brings this "evil aeon" to an end. ... We need to recover that vivid sense of the Church as an eschatological community that was so characteristic of primitive Christianity.'[73] But the *koinonia*, whose true mode of being is future, has allowed itself to become naturalized in history and has claimed ultimate significance for its historically induced institutions.[74]

Yet this *koinonia* is also an everyday mode of being for man here and now.[75] *Koinonia* and *diakonia*, therefore, belong together. Chapter 10, 'Christian Ministry as Encounter', is a compelling exposition of the nature of ministry:

> We are not called to play church games, but to put our whole existence on the line, to lay down our whole selves for our fellow-man in a way that leaves no aspect of our person untouched and which penetrates into every corner of human and cosmic reality (ibid., p. 193).

In the writings of all these contemporary Roman Catholic authors the second theme which we mentioned as inspired by Vatican II is prominent, namely that of the Church as servant. This is apparent in the case of Rosemary Ruether from the quotation immediately above. Edward Schillebeeckx declares that service in and to the world is implicit in the Church's nature as a sacrament of dialogue:

> The Church ... is certainly not present in the world for her own sake, but is there to give Christ's Good News of the kingdom of God which is to come. That is why the Church's dialogue must not be self-centred—it is rather a ministry or service of the Church. ... It is, moreover, an essential aspect of sincere dialogue that one is not thinking of oneself, but of the other. ... In this dialogue, the Church is *omnium bono serviens*, serving the well-being of all (*God the Future of Man*, pp. 127–8).

He goes on to describe the content of such a dialogue: 'It may take the form of encouragement and confirmation, help, collaboration, or the taking of initiatives. It may also consist of criticism and protest.'[76] There are 'experiences which evoke the protest "No! it can't go on like this; we won't stand for it any longer!"' and which compel the Church to 'protest against war, various forms of social injustice, racial discrimination, large landholding, colonialism'.[77] The Church's dialogue is not primarily 'a reflexive dialogue, but rather the existential involvement of Christians in the world'.[78]

Gregory Baum proposes[79] a sociological model for the institutional life of the Church which he believes corresponds to the new understanding of an 'open Church' whose mission is to unify and reconcile the whole human family. The model is 'the outer-oriented movement'. He sees the Church as a movement which 'wants to involve the whole of society in conversation . . . is in solidarity with the human community in which it lives . . . wants to bear the burden with others . . . wants to help solve the problems from which people suffer'.[80] He envisages cities in which there are various centres of Christian life, where worship is celebrated, and educative and active programmes are arranged, centres whose influence will be such that the social conscience of the city will be awakened, programmes of reform initiated, and people generally made 'more sensitive to what is precious and important in life'. Catholics will 'become more dedicated members of the secular society in which they live', and men will be drawn 'more deeply into the mystery of redemption present in human life'.[81]

> The Church as movement makes people conscious of what community means in the lives of men. At the institutional centre of the Church, Christians learn the mystery of community in the eucharist and in the teaching of Christ; they learn this, not to form a closed community about the visible centres but, rather, to become community-creators themselves and move into society, the places where they live and work, to form community with people there (*The Credibility of the Church Today*, p. 209).

Baum believes that in the cities in Roman Catholic Church is already being transformed into such an 'outer-oriented movement', a Church which both serves its Lord and serves the community in which it is situated.

We shall see (Chapter 24) Professor Hans Küng also placing emphasis on the servant aspect of the Church, on the ground that *diakonia* is intrinsic to the idea of the Church in the New Testament.

21

The Twentieth Century
Church and World

Since the work of Max Weber (1864–1920) and Ernst Troeltsch (1865–1923) it has been recognized that Christianity, the Church and the churches, whatever else must be said of them, are sociological phenomena, and can be studied as such. Weber distinguished two forms in which Christianity has manifested itself in history: the Church-type and the sect-type. Troeltsch added a third, the mystical-type.

Troeltsch distinguishes the first two types in this way:

> The Church is that type of organization which is overwhelmingly conservative, which to a certain extent accepts the secular order, and dominates the masses; in principle, therefore, it is universal, i.e. it desires to cover the whole life of humanity. The sects, on the other hand, are comparatively small groups; they aspire after personal inward perfection and they aim at a direct personal fellowship between the members of each group. From the very beginning, therefore, they are forced to organize themselves in small groups, and to renounce the idea of dominating the world. Their attitude towards the world, the State, and Society may be indifferent, tolerant, or hostile, since they have no desire to control and incorporate these forms of social life; on the contrary, they tend to avoid them; their aim is usually either to tolerate their presence alongside of their own body, or even to replace these social institutions by their own society. Further, both types are in close connection with the actual situation and with the development of Society. The fully developed Church, however, utilizes the State and the ruling classes, and weaves these elements into her own life; she then becomes an integral part of the existing social order; from this standpoint, then, the Church both stabilizes and determines the social order; in so doing, however, she becomes dependent upon the upper classes, and upon their development. The sects, on the other hand, are connected with the lower classes, or at least with those elements in Society which are opposed to the State and to Society; they work upwards from below, and not downwards from above (*The Social Teaching of the Christian Churches*, vol. i, p. 331).[1]

Examples of the church-type are the medieval western Church, the Russian Orthodox Church of pre-Revolution days, the Lutheran churches of Europe, the Church of England, the Reformed Church of Geneva, the Church of Scotland. Although the precise relationship with the State differs, in each case it is implied that Church membership and citizenship are two sides of the same coin.

Examples of the sect-type are the Waldensians, the 'Spiritual' Franciscans, the Lollards and the Hussites prior to the Reformation, the English Independents of the seventeenth century, the Congregational churches, and many modern Pentecostal churches. These differ greatly from each other in doctrine and practice, but are one in their rejection of the world and its culture and in their desire to form a 'gathered' church of voluntary believers, providing for their own leadership and discipline, and acknowledging no authority outside the congregation itself but Christ.

Earlier in this work I have treated of these two types and of most of the examples mentioned. It should, however, be noted that in the post-Reformation period there has occurred a combination of the two.[2] Many North American denominations have emerged as 'free churches' in which 'the church-type has become joined to the voluntarist principle'.[3] Both types and the combined type have deeply influenced society, whether it be by acquiescence and adoption, or by resistance and rejection. They have all, conversely, been moulded to a considerable degree by the society and culture in which they have emerged. Troeltsch's monumental historical survey makes this abundantly clear. Few can disagree that between the Church, in its various manifestations, and society a mutual interaction, a shaping and being shaped, has continuously been at work. Not even the most rigidly exclusive of sect-type churches have in fact succeeded in insulating themselves completely from the world.

Brief reference must be made to Troeltsch's third type, which he refers to as mysticism and spiritual idealism.[4] It is, he says, 'a very difficult matter to distinguish between this type of mysticism and the sect-movement'.[5] It has roots in primitive and medieval Christianity, but 'is far more closely connected with Luther's original main ideas, and is therefore still more strongly rooted within Protestantism'.[6] It is marked by 'insistence upon a direct inward and present religious experience', and either a reaction against 'the objective forms of religious life in worship, ritual, myth, and dogma', or an attempt to supplement them 'by means of a personal and living stimulus'.[7] He cites as examples of this third type, among others, Thomas Münzer, Karlstadt, Sebastian Franck, and Jacob Böhme, and notes that its characteristics appear in movements like the Quakers, Methodism, and Pietism. But the type itself, as Troeltsch describes it, seems essentially to be that of the sincerely religious individual, mystically inclined, who cannot easily or for long find fulfilment within a structured group.[8]

Towards the close of a discussion of the 'penetrating and comprehensive' social influence in western Europe and America of what he calls Ascetic Protestantism or Puritan Calvinism, Troeltsch writes:

> To what extent they [i.e. Puritan Calvinism and the 'purified' communities of the sects] will be able to dominate the modern civilized world permanently in a Christian manner is another question. This school of thought is still a power in world history. But it is clear on all hands that to a great extent the State, Society, and economic life will no longer allow themselves to be dominated by it, and in their present position cannot possibly be dominated by it any longer (ibid., vol. ii, p. 816).

This was written in 1911. Nearly seven decades later it must be said that those last words have been proved true. Even in the few remaining countries where there is a close relationship between Church and State, the question of the Church's domination of society no longer arises. The question rather is whether the Church now exercises, or can exercise, any effective influence upon modern society.

The process of secularization, whose pace quickened in the eighteenth century, now advances at a gallop. Men's minds are oriented to this world, this present age (*saeculum*). Modern society, having become increasingly pluralistic, acknowledges no divine right of kings or rulers, no divinely promulgated laws, relates everything to man himself. The process has kept pace with the scientific and technological advances which made possible the industrial revolution which began in the late eighteenth century and whose momentum is now changing the face of the earth. The aeroplane is now a more familiar sight than the horse. 'Agrarian' or 'mercantile' are no longer appropriate descriptions of any western state. Agriculture and trade still go on, to be sure, but these activities are being transformed by highly efficient agricultural machines and computers. Technology reaches even to those countries which western nations have come to call undeveloped, or underdeveloped, for it is from them that, to a very considerable extent, the raw materials are drawn which are necessary to sustain the higher standards of living which the technological revolution has engendered.

The pace of all this has been such that the world suddenly finds itself confronted with new problems. Technology has created urban populations so vast that it proves increasingly difficult to provide for essential services or for law and order. Technology has made it possible to utilize raw materials so rapidly that supplies for future generations are in jeopardy. Only recently has there dawned a general awareness of the problems of ecology: the atmosphere and the waters of the world are becoming so polluted by the waste products of industry that a threat is posed alike to plant, animal, and human life. The population of the world, nevertheless, increases rapidly, while the area of arable land is encroached on by sprawling cities, wide arterial roads, airports, industrial plants, and mining operations. Technology, moreover, has given to man instruments of destruction which, if touched off, could result in the destruction of the human race.

Although it is difficult to compare one age with another in matters of ethical behaviour, it can confidently be said that twentieth-century man is no less prone to acts of violence and to defiance of authority than were his ancestors. It is unsafe to walk alone at night in an increasing number of cities. Despite the factors which might be expected to foster mutual understanding and co-operation between nations (improved communications, greater knowledge of the needs and aspirations of others, cultural exchanges) national rivalry has scarcely abated. There are wars, and where there are not, peace is uneasy.

Technology has advanced in the name of progress and development. Yet many people, not unappreciative of very much that has been achieved, are asking the questions: progress towards what? Development of what, and for whom?

The subjects briefly touched on above (technology, urbanization, ecology, pollution) need no further elaboration here. The literature on them is enormous. Every issue of a daily newspaper illuminates some aspect of them. Obviously mankind faces a whole set of problems which, if not all new in kind, are new in the urgency they now assume, and in that they have arisen not singly, but simultaneously. Man seems to be standing at one of the crossroads of his history, and he wonders whether any of the possible turnings is anything but a cul-de-sac.

It would be deplorable if, in this situation, Christian thinkers and writers were not asking the question of the Church's *raison d'être*.

What significance has the Church, what possible function has it in the crisis of today's world? What *is* the Church? Will former answers to this question suffice? Does the secularization of the age prove the Church's failure? Has it become an anachronism, useful in its day, but now no more than an archaeological curiosity?

Dietrich Bonhoeffer, one of the first theologians to express awareness of the fact, and the challenge, of secularization, began to ask these questions.[9] In a letter written from prison to a friend, Eberhard Bethge, he said:

> What is bothering me incessantly is the question what Christianity really is, or indeed who Christ really is, for us today.... We are moving towards a completely religionless time; people as they are now simply cannot be religious any more. ...
>
> The questions to be answered would surely be: What do a church, a community, a sermon, a liturgy, a Christian life mean in a religionless world? ... How do we speak (or perhaps we cannot now even 'speak' as we used to) in a 'secular' way about 'God'? In what way are we 'religionless–secular' Christians, in what way are we the *ek-klesia*, those who are called forth, not regarding ourselves from a religious point of view as specially favoured, but rather as belonging wholly to the world? (*Letters and Papers from Prison* 30 April 1944).

In this letter Bonhoeffer first introduces several theological 'seed-thoughts' which have since become influential.[10] He recognizes the fact of the secularization of the western world, and *welcomes* it. He speaks of it as the world coming of age:

> The movement that began about the thirteenth century ... towards the autonomy of man (in which I should include the discovery of the laws by which the world lives and deals with itself in science, social and political matters, art, ethics, and religion) has in our time reached an undoubted completion. Man has learned to deal with himself in all questions of importance without recourse to the 'working hypothesis' called 'God' (ibid., 8 June 1944; op. cit., p. 325).

It is not to be supposed that Bonhoeffer himself had found it impossible or unnecessary to believe in God. His argument is that man has always tended to 'use' God as the explanation of what he himself cannot yet explain, as a solver of problems or a crutch in times of distress. As science and technology have solved more and more problems, God has been 'increasingly pushed out of the world that has come of age'.[11] Bonhoeffer's complaint is that the Church has accommodated itself to this development by a feverish attempt to find gaps in man's knowledge where God is still needed as an explanation, and to prove that in the inner areas of man's life (his guilt feelings and fears, for instance) God is also needed: 'There still remain the so-called "ultimate questions"—death, guilt—to which only "God" can give an answer, and because of which we need God, the church, and the pastor.'[12]

Bonhoeffer believes that such an apologetic is an attack on the adulthood of the world 'which is pointless, ignoble and un-Christian'.[13] Such tactics involve two theological errors: 'First, it is thought that a man can be addressed as a sinner only after his weakness and meannesses have been spied out.'[14] He speaks of 'clerical snuffing-around-after-people's-sins in order to catch them out'; and in an earlier letter he had written about the efforts of existential philosophers and psychotherapists 'who demonstrate to secure, contented, and happy mankind that it is really unhappy and desperate and simply unwilling to admit that it is in a predicament about which it knows nothing'.[15] This was not Jesus' way: 'When Jesus blessed sinners, they were real sinners, but Jesus did not make everyone a sinner first. He called them away from their sin, not into their sin.'[16]

Second, it is thought that a man's essential nature consists of his inmost and most intimate background ... his 'inner life', and it is precisely in those secret human places that God is to have his domain![17] But, Bonhoeffer points out, the Bible does not make this distinction between the outward and the inward. It is concerned with the whole man.[18]

Bonhoeffer believes that the Church should address modern man in a very different way:

> I therefore want to start from the premise that God shouldn't be smuggled into some last secret place, but that we should frankly recognize that the world, and people, have come of age, that we shouldn't run man down in his worldliness, but confront him with God at his strongest point (ibid., 8 July 1944, p. 346).

In the letter of 30 April 1944, he had written similarly:

> I should like to speak of God not on the boundaries, but at the centre, not in weaknesses but in strength; and not in death and guilt but in man's life and goodness (ibid., p. 282).

Not enough time was to be allowed to Bonhoeffer to develop the answer to his question about the meaning of the Church in his day. A few phrases only give us hints of how he might have done so. 'Jesus claims for himself and the kingdom of God the whole of life in all its manifestations.'[19] Consequently, the Church receives the vocation of claiming 'the whole of life in all its manifestations' for Christ. 'The Church stands, not at the boundaries where human powers give out, but in the middle of the village.'[20] 'The Church must come out of its stagnation. We must move out again into the open air of intellectual discussion with the world, and risk saying controversial things, if we are to get down to the serious problems of life.'[21]

In the 'Outline for a Book' which he sketched in August 1944, he includes a condensed criticism of the German Protestant churches, among them the 'Confessing Church', which had stood boldly against Hitler's domination of the Church in the pre-war years:

> The Protestant church: Pietism as a last attempt to maintain evangelical Christianity as a religion; Lutheran orthodoxy, the attempt to rescue the Church as an institution for salvation; the Confessing Church; the theology of revelation; a *dos moi pou sto* ['give me a place to stand'] over against the world, involving a 'factual' interest in Christianity; art and science searching for their origin. Generally in the Confessing Church: standing up for the Church's 'cause', but little personal faith in Christ. 'Jesus' is disappearing from sight. Sociologically: no effect on the masses—interest confined to the upper and lower middle classes. A heavy incubus of difficult traditional ideas. The decisive factor: the Church on the defensive. No taking risks for others (ibid., p. 381).

The outline for the third chapter tells us what kind of risks he means:

> The Church is the Church only when it exists for others. To make a start, it should give away all its property to those in need. The clergy must live solely on the free-will offerings of their congregations, or possibly engage in some secular calling. The Church must share in the secular problems of ordinary human life, not dominating but helping and serving. It must tell men of every calling what it means to live in Christ, to exist for others. . . . It must not underestimate the importance of human example . . . it is not abstract argument, but example, that gives its word emphasis and power . . . it is something that we have almost entirely forgotten (ibid., pp. 381–2).

Bonhoeffer is insistent that it is the Christian's vocation to suffer. God came in Christ to address men in their vigour and strength, but he also came in weakness and to suffer. So it must be with Christ's follower, because the world *is* godless:

> He must therefore really live in the godless world, without attempting to

gloss over or explain its ungodliness in some religious way or other. He must live a 'secular' life, and thereby share in God's sufferings. He *may* live a 'secular' life (as one who has been freed from false religious obligations and inhibitions). To be a Christian does not mean to be religious in a particular way ... on the basis of some method or other, but to be a man—not a type of man, but the man Christ creates in us. It is not the religious act that makes the Christian, but participation in the sufferings of God in the secular life (ibid., 18 July 1944, p. 361).

Three days later he writes:

By this-worldliness I mean living unreservedly in life's duties, problems, successes and failures, experiences and perplexities. In so doing we throw ourselves completely into the arms of God, taking seriously not our own sufferings, but those of God in the world—watching with Christ in Gethsemane. That, I think, is faith; that is *metanoia* [repentance] (ibid., 21 July 1944, p. 370).

He adds: 'I think you see what I mean, even though I put it so briefly.' Perhaps we do not completely grasp his meaning. His letters provide us with very little guidance about *how* one may live as a Christian in the world in a 'religionless way'. He seems not to mean that the Church and the Christian must refrain from speaking of God and Christ. He tells us that he found it easier to speak openly and naturally of God with those who have no religion[22] than with religious people. Nor does he envisage the neglect of prayer, worship, the sacraments. The letters reveal Bonhoeffer as one who prayed and read the Bible daily, who hummed remembered hymns, who kept track of the holy days of the Christian year. It does seem, however, that in the Church's situation in a godless world, he saw this kind of observance as a vital source of strength for Christians, but as not to be prominent in the Church's address to the world. Perhaps he feared that men would be encouraged again to believe that such observances were means of self-salvation—one aspect of the 'religion' which Bonhoeffer criticizes. Men must know God to be at the centre of their lives, and then they would see the need for prayer, worship, and sacrament. But Bonhoeffer is certain that he himself, and the faithful Christian, must not let go of prayer, worship, the study of the Bible, and the observance of traditions. This seems to be the thrust of the phrase 'secret discipline' (*disciplina arcani*) which he uses in the letter of 30 April: 'What is the place of worship and prayer in a religionless situation? Does the secret discipline ... take on a new importance here?' And in the letter of 5 May he writes: 'A secret discipline must be restored by which the mysteries of the Christian faith are protected against profanation.'[23]

We may not be far from the truth in suggesting that Bonhoeffer saw the situation of the Church in his day as close in many respects to that of the Church in its earliest days in the world of the Roman Empire, an environment of superstition mixed with scepticism. The same options were open. They included a policy of retreating from the world into small enclosed groups for the cultivation of holiness, an option which was taken by some in the early centuries, and again by some in the crises of the Renaissance and the Reformation. It is being taken by some today.

Bonhoeffer presents another option: 'The Church is the Church only when it exists for others.'[24] The Church must live on the one hand courageously and joyfully, but without triumphalism, in the world; and on the other, in the spirit of the man for others, agonize with him in the world's suffering. For this the Church and its faithful need to be enabled by holding fast to the truths and practices of Christian faith, endeavouring without any ostentation to make them understandable and relevant to others, and always ready, humbly and thankfully, to receive those others into the fellowship of faith.

RENEWAL

Bonhoeffer's last writings make frequent reference to the shortcomings of the Church. The need for repentance and renewal on the part of the Church is a note frequently struck in recent ecclesiology. *Gaudium et Spes* of Vatican II recognizes that Christians themselves have much to do with the rise of modern atheism,[25] that too many Christians have been content with 'a merely individualistic morality',[26] and that the social conscience of the Church needs strengthening.[27] Moreover: 'It does not escape the Church how great a distance lies between the message she offers and the human failing of those to whom the gospel is entrusted.'[28]

Among Protestant churches there is a similar recognition that their own attitudes have helped to produce the modern situation and its problems.[29] Liberal Protestantism gave its blessing to the 'progress' and 'development' which were the outcome of the prevailing scientific and humanistic spirit as the twentieth century dawned, as if they were signs of the coming of the Kingdom of God. The major Protestant churches have come to recognize that they have identified themselves too closely with the middle-class values of success in business and respectability, and have lost touch with the great mass of industrial workers.

This note of repentance is accompanied by a realization that the Church's organization and methods of ministry are now outdated. The geographical parish system, appropriate for rural areas and towns of moderate size, and the congregational system which assumes a settled population within easy distance of the church building and within reach of the personal ministrations of the pastor, are anachronistic in relation to the vast metropolitan areas of today and to a society which is increasingly mobile. Difficulties arise for the parish priest and minister of a congregation from the facts that the wage-earner of a family rarely works, the housekeeper rarely shops, and the children rarely go to school where they live; that a higher standard of living and the availability of transport make it easy for families to spend weekends away from home; that the business and industrial world is such that families are with increasing frequency uprooted in order to follow the wage-earners where employers send them. Rare nowadays are instances of people being baptized, married, seeing their children marry, and their grandchildren grow up within the same community. Yet the parochial and congregational organization of the churches and their forms of ministry are based on the assumption that this is the norm. How, then, can the Church be the Church, and how can it minister effectively in the world today? There is increasing sensitivity to the need to take cognizance of social realities, of the nature of industrialized and technological society, of the unlikelihood of decrease in the size of metropolitan areas, and of the highly mobile state both of the metropolitan and rural population.

In recent years many studies have been published relating to the problems of the Church in the modern situation. Here I shall speak of two of the best known: Professor Gibson Winter's *The Suburban Captivity of the Churches* (1962),[30] and Professor Harvey Cox's *The Secular City* (1965).[31]

GIBSON WINTER: THE SUBURBAN
CAPTIVITY OF THE CHURCHES

Gibson Winter begins with a sociological study of the development of the modern city and of the movements of population within the growing metropolitan areas. He writes of the North American city, but his analysis applies to many cities elsewhere. Industrial plants, railway stations and yards, and centres of all kinds of business were first established in or close to the centre of the city. Owners, managers, and workers lived close at hand. As the city prospered and became more crowded, wealthier citizens moved out from the centre, establishing new residential areas. As soon as they could afford to do so, the middle classes and those workers who had advanced themselves began to do the same. Thus the city becomes encircled by 'residential rings' for the upper and middle classes and skilled workers. Unskilled workers remain in the centre, living in the deteriorating dwelling-houses of former generations. Meanwhile, successful industrialization creates a demand for more workers which is met by immigration from rural areas, other countries and, in the United States especially, of blacks. These different groups tend naturally to live in close proximity, and thus ghettos are created. Such cities have become divided into separate areas whose residents are 'homogeneous'. The suburban dwellers find their personal fulfilment in their families and among friends in their neighbourhood, and do their utmost to protect the homogeneity of their suburb from the encroachments of others. The city centre becomes more crowded and less able to provide the services to make life tolerable. The resources of the wealthy are now primarily used to preserve their own communities, and the cost of providing adequate services in the city centre is beyond the means of those who live there.

Winter maintains that the churches (and he writes principally of the Protestant churches) have failed to adapt to the new situation. The situation is that in the metropolitan areas, instead of heterogeneous parishes or pastoral charges in which people of every social class live and work in close proximity, there now exists a conglomeration of homogeneous residential areas, ranging from the ghettos of the centre to the rich neighbourhoods of the outer ring. In those wealthy suburbs exclusiveness is carefully guarded, and relationships outside the community are on a strictly impersonal level.

> Since churches have traditionally anchored their communal life in residential areas, they inevitably become victims of the pathology that assails neighbourhood life.... How can an inclusive message be mediated through an exclusive group, when the principle of exclusiveness is social-class identity rather than a gift of faith which is open to all? (*The Suburban Captivity*, pp. 32–3).

Winter deplores the fact that the churches' leaders, 'confronted with a dilemma between organizational expansion and responsibility for the central city',[32] have too often concentrated on the middle-class suburbs:

> Denominational leaders have watched the new residential areas surrounding the central cities with greedy eyes. These are largely middle- and upper-class residential areas; they have adequate resources for constructing church buildings; their residents are responsive to religious programs; in fact, denominational leaders call these 'high potential areas'.... In recent decades almost exclusive attention has been given to establishing churches in suburban areas (ibid., p. 35).[33]

Although there are notable exceptions, ministry in central city areas has been left to a diminishing number of the churches of the main denominations, understaffed and with steadily decreasing congregations as members 'better' themselves and move out, and to small sectarian churches. The churches have been concerned about survival rather than ministry.[34] Yet by identifying themselves with the middle classes and failure to minister to the whole metropolitan area, they have cut themselves off from a much larger membership.[35]

Thus the social inclusiveness of the early church has been exchanged for the exclusive church of the metropolis.[36] Society has established a pattern by which 'residential association is ... built almost exclusively around similarity in economic rank', and churches which 'organize their congregations or parishes primarily around residential neighborhoods' inevitably find that their congregations are 'a cluster of people of like social and economic position'.[37]

> A new image of the Church is emerging in the contemporary world, an image created by the domination of contemporary life by economic activities. The Church is now a reflection of the economic ladder (ibid., pp. 76–7).

Congregations have become primarily economic peer groups, and only secondarily believing and worshipping communities.[38] Inclusiveness, which is an important aspect of catholicity and therefore intrinsic to the nature of the Church, is forgotten.[39] The organizational activity of the suburban church is so closely geared to the maintenance of the exclusive residential group that the concept of mission and reconciliation reaching to the whole metropolis is lost.[40] The suburban church becomes introverted:

> The introverted church is one which puts its own survival before its mission, its own identity before its task, its internal concerns before its

apostolate, its rituals before its ministry ... [it] stresses the Church as structure at the expense of the mission and task of the Church. ... Undue emphasis on the static structure of the Church has led to the disappearance of a significant lay ministry in denominational Protestantism. Loss of dynamic form and surrender of mission undercut the lay ministry, for it is the Church as mission which rests its case upon the laity and their outreach to the world. The more introverted the Church, the more it becomes subject to priestcraft and routinized activities. The introverted Church substitutes celebrations of its own unity for witness in the metropolis. An introverted church is an apostate body, for it denies the essential quality of Church—the testimony of reconciliation in the world (ibid., pp. 120–21).

In the middle-class areas which are distant from the place of work of the residents, the churches' ministry is almost entirely confined to the family concerns and leisure interests of their members. In allowing their ministry to be circumscribed in this way, the churches withdrew from the context of public accountability.[41] It is not that pastoral concern for people's private and family lives is wrong; but exclusive identification of ministry with the private sphere encourages the widespread idea that Christianity is irrelevant to all other areas of man's life and activity. The churches need a new vision of the metropolis and of their mission to it.

'To be the Church is to be involved in mission. To be the Church in the metropolis is to be rooted in the missionary task to inner city and suburb as an interdependent process.'[42] Ministry to fragments of society,.and those the most comfortably placed, is to ignore that 'there is strong warrant in Scriptures for beginning with the areas of greatest personal, physical, and social need—the poor of the earth—as the decisive point for estimating the form appropriate to the task' of ministry.[43]

Winter is convinced that the Church must minister to the whole metropolis. He sees certain experimental ministries which are often of an ecumenical nature, and which cut across parochial boundaries and transcend traditional congregational concerns as pointing a way forward. But his main suggestion[44] is that, so far as metropolitan areas are concerned, the basic unit of ministry should be not the parish or congregation as we have known it, but a sector of the city stretching from its heart to the outer edges, 'from blight to suburb, Negro to White, blue collar to white collar, down-and-out to privilege'.[45] A council of representatives drawn from the whole area would make the decisions about use of money and buildings, and the kind of ministries to be engaged in, according to developing needs. Some such development of organic interdependence between neighbourhoods and ministries he sees as a way in which the Church may be renewed. It would provide opportunities and a challenge to lay men and women to engage in a ministry much more Christian than the round of activities which are invented for the consolidation and perpetuation of an exclusive suburban enclave.

> Until men and women are drawn into the missionary enterprise of the Church, they do not discover the meaning of their baptism. . . . The sector ministry, or any other interdependent form of Christian community, is essential as a context of ministry and Christian experience; everyone who joins the Christian Church should have an opportunity to serve in the lay ministry, when he can answer for the faith that is in him and discover his true identity in Christ through sharing in His reconciling work. The breakthrough from a local enclave to a public platform of ministry and worship is essential for the renewal of the churches and for the recovery of the lay apostolate (ibid., pp. 179–80).

The parish and the congregation *as units for the Church's ministry* represent, Winter contends, 'an arrested form of development'. In most cases they do not provide an opportunity for people to become both a receiving and a giving community, a ministering and missionary fellowship. Evolution, therefore, must be towards an organically interdependent ministry which transcends the social barriers of life in the city, whatever may be the structural details necessary to bring this about in different places. 'The Church is deformed by the struggle to survive and reformed only as ministry and mission.'[46]

Although his book concentrates on the Church's ministry to the modern city, Winter is not unmindful of the Godward life of the Church, expressed in faith and worship. The Church has many privileges and graces bestowed upon it by the Holy Spirit. But they are given to it on behalf of the world. Ministry is obedience to Christ, so that, in demonstrating the meaning of community to the metropolis, the Church is no mere servant of the world, but the servant of Christ and his Spirit.[47]

HARVEY COX: THE SECULAR CITY

Professor Harvey Cox's *The Secular City* has two sub-titles: 'Secularization and Urbanization in Theological Perspective' on the inside title page, and 'A Celebration of its Liberties and an Invitation to its Discipline' on the cover. The latter indicates that Professor Cox welcomes the evolution of the secular city, that same metropolitan area about which Winter writes. Some readers[48] have felt that, although he distinguishes between the kingdom of God and the secular city, the two are very close together in Cox's thought. 'The idea of the secular city supplies us with the most promising image, by which *both* to understand what the New Testament writers called "the kingdom of God" *and* to develop a viable theology of revolutionary social change.'[49] He sees in the secular city 'a present-day sign of the kingdom of God'.[50] The anonymity of the city, its opportunities for mobility and its technology offer the citizen privacy, freedom, and happy leisure respectively, and these things he regards as good and the will of God.[51] The same sub-title shows that Cox, however, knows that the secular city calls for discipline. All is not well with the secular city. There are 'urban fractures'. There is a crisis, a challenge which man must accept.

With Bonhoeffer he regards secularization[52] as a maturing process in the history of man, and as 'basically a liberating development'.[53] The process, he suggests, stems from the biblical literature. The Hebrew doctrine of creation desacralizes nature; the exodus from Egypt, being a revolt against a duly constituted monarch, points to the desacralizing of politics ('no one rules by divine right in secular society');[54] the prohibition of 'graven images' in the Sinai Covenant desacralizes and relativizes all human values ('for the ancients, gods and value systems were the same thing').[55] Under biblical and Christian influence, though slowly and with many hesitations, secularization has proceeded to the point at which the technopolis, made possible by modern technology, has emerged:

> Our task should be to nourish the secularization process, to prevent it hardening into a rigid world-view (viz., secularism). Furthermore, we should be constantly on the lookout for movements which attempt to thwart and reverse the liberating irritant of secularization (*The Secular City*, p. 36).

The few years which have elapsed since Cox wrote have made it clear that there are indeed such threats. The anonymity which he regards as a liberating characteristic is also a cloak for crime. Statistics show a rapid increase of serious crime in most big cities. Mobility is the last word which would occur to a commuter in any large city of the western world between 4.0 and 6.0 pm. Despite technology some public services have deteriorated, notably postal services and street-cleaning. The opinion grows that the particular expression of technological advance which Cox calls 'technopolis' is a mistake. Be that as it may, our concern is with Cox's doctrine of the Church.

THE CHURCH AS GOD'S *AVANT-GARDE*

'The starting-point for any theology of the Church today', Cox writes, 'must be a theology of social change. The Church is first of all a responding community, a people whose task it is to discern the action of God in the world and to join in His work.'[56] But the Church which should, therefore, be responding to social change is still working with definitions of itself which belong to the past. A Church which recognizes the significance and challenge of the process of secularization must be prepared to be reshaped continuously by God's action. It must be God's *avant-garde*.

The Church is the people of God. God in Christ went, and goes, before the Church into the world, and the Church must follow him where the action is. The action, Cox is convinced, is in the secular city, the sign of the coming kingdom of God, of the new régime. Only when Christian people recognize where God is at work, and discern what their function must be, can their institutional forms be decided. In fact, he suggests, 'a doctrine of the Church is a secondary and derivative aspect of theology which comes *after* a discussion of God's action in calling man to co-operation in the bringing of the kingdom'.[57] The institutional forms must be such as to enable the people of God to locate and participate in the mission of God, to continue the ministry of Jesus as he described it in his reply to John the Baptist (Luke 4.18–19). In traditional terms it is a ministry of *kerygma* (proclamation), *diakonia* (reconciliation, healing, service) and *koinonia* (fellowship).

'Because the new régime breaks in at different points and in different ways, it is not possible to forecast in advance just what appearance the Church will have.'[58] Nor, because cities differ, is it possible to describe a missionary strategy appropriate for all places. But everywhere the task must be *kerygmatic*, *diakonic* and *koinoniac*: to proclaim 'that a revolution is under way and that the pivotal battle has already taken place'.[59]

The *kerygma* is the message that 'God has defeated the

"principalities and powers" by Jesus and has made it possible for man to become the "heir", the master of the created world'.[60] The 'principalities and powers' of this age of the secular city are those forces which still cripple and corrupt human freedom. Cox cites as examples the concepts of the *id*, of the collective unconscious, of the dialectic of history, of statistical probability and economic pressures. These were not meant to control man. God's action, made known in Jesus, calls man to freedom from the 'principalities and powers' and to responsibility in controlling them. Men must accept responsibility in and for the city of man.

The Church's diakonic ministry is best defined as healing or reconciling, and must be directed to the 'urban fractures', the cleavage between city centre and suburbs, rich and poor, racial groups and political parties. Like Gibson Winter, Cox regards the desertion of the city centre by the Protestant churches as shameful, and not to be rectified by planting mission churches or patronizing incursions from outside. It is rather a matter of Christian suburbanites participating in a revolution aimed at decreasing the power of the suburbs in relation to the less privileged sections. To work for changed banking practices, new zoning laws, more equitable school financing and tax structures calls for sacrifice on the part of suburbanites. But it is *diakonia*.[61]

The Church's koinoniac function is to make visible 'a kind of living picture of the character and composition of the true city of man'. The Church is already what Rudolf Bultmann calls the eschatological community, and what Karl Barth describes as 'God's providential demonstration of his intention for all humanity'. The Church 'occurs' where its three functions occur, and where 'a new inclusive human community emerges'.[62] It must include 'all the elements of the heterogeneous metropolis'. If it is divided along ethnic, racial, or denominational lines it is not performing its koinoniac function. It is not a Church at all, but a group of antichurches, unable to break out of the past. The true eschatological nature of the Church will be shown when it is recognized that

> [Jesus Christ] is always ahead of the Church, beckoning it to get up to date, never behind it waiting to be refurbished. Canon and tradition function not as sources of revelation but as precedents by which present events can be checked out as the possible *loci* of God's action (ibid., p. 148).

THE CHURCH AS CULTURAL EXORCIST

Cox believes that the three functions of the Church come together in its role as 'cultural exorcist'. The casting out of demons was central in Jesus' ministry. The N.T. demoniacs really believed that they were possessed by demons. The culture and society which surrounded them persuaded them of it. Modern man is no less prone to irrationalities caused by his own repressions or by the projection of others on to him. Modern society, even in the secular city, is riddled by attitudes, prejudices, and norms which belong to the past. Exorcism in the twentieth century is 'that process by which the stubborn deposits of town and tribal pasts are scraped from the social consciousness of man'.[63] To set men free to see things as they really are 'was what Jesus was always doing, and it represents an indispensable element of the Church's function in the secular city'.[64]

> The ministry of exorcism in the secular city requires a community of persons who, individually and collectively, are not burdened by the constriction of an archaic heritage. It requires a community which, if not fully liberated, is in the process of liberation from compulsive patterns of behavior based on mistaken images of the world. In performing its function the Church should be such a community and should be sensitive to those currents in modern life which bear the same exorcizing power. The Church should be ready to expose the fallaciousness of the social myths by which the injustices of a society are perpetuated and to suggest ways of action which demonstrate the wrongness of such fantasies (ibid., p. 155).

Such an idea of the Church is seen by many as an intolerable threat to the forms of Church life which they have known. It is Cox's opinion that the real ecumenical crisis today is not between Catholic and Protestant, but between those who are ready to explore new structures and modes of Church life and those who are not.[65] The structural changes and new forms of ministry which he goes on to suggest are along lines similar to those proposed by Gibson Winter; and in Part Three of his book he discusses the work of the Church as cultural exorcist in the contexts of work and leisure, sexual relations, and the secular university.

As we have seen, Cox's delineation of the Church and its functions is largely drawn from the realm of political action. He is, however, convinced that his conception rests on biblical foundations.

It is important to remind ourselves of another important feature of the biblical view of the Church [i.e. other than the description of the Church as *avant-garde* and exorcist]: *only faith can discern the Church of Jesus Christ*. It is not an entity which can be empirically detected and located by a bulletin board or a sociological survey. Only God knows the name of His saints. Furthermore, the Greek word for church, *ecclesia*, is a word of motion. It refers to those on the way, responding to the herald's announcement. The Church is what such diverse theologians as Karl Barth, Rudolf Bultmann, and Gerhard Ebeling have called 'an event'. It *happens*. It occurs where the reconciling actuality of God's work in human history comes to fulfilment and is brought to human speech. ... The Church is the word-event by which reconciliation across the divisive lines of race, nation, belief, sex, age, and social status occurs, and men live, if only provisionally, in the new age (ibid., pp. 225–6).

To say that the Church is an object of faith is not to say that it is invisible. Yet it is 'not a building, a budget, a program, an organization. It is a people in motion, an "eventful movement" in which barriers are being struck down and a radically new community ... is emerging'.[66]

22

The Ecclesiology of Karl Barth

There is little doubt that Karl Barth (1886–1968) was the most out-standing Protestant theologian of the first two-thirds of the twentieth century. Born in Berne, Switzerland, he studied there and in Germany, and following twelve years in pastoral ministry became a professor successively at Göttingen (1921), Münster (1925), and Bonn (1930). When Hitler came to power in 1933, Barth was among the foremost of those who resisted the attempt to subjugate the Evangelical Church to National Socialism, and was the principal draftsman of the courageous Barmen Declaration (1934). On refusing to take an oath of allegiance to Hitler, he was deprived of his chair at Bonn in 1935, and returned to Switzerland, becoming Professor of Theology at Basel, a post which he held until he retired in 1962. His greatest work was the four huge volumes of *Church Dogmatics (Die Kirkliche Dogmatik)* begun in 1932, which occupied him for well over twenty years.[1]

Barth's Commentary on the Epistle to the Romans (*Der Römer-brief*), published in 1919 with an enlarged edition in 1921,[2] first gained him prominence. It was a sharp rejection of the liberal theology which had dominated German Protestantism since the time of Schleier-macher. His study of Romans convinced him that liberal theology had neglected the great themes of N.T. theology. With an optimistic es-timate of man and reliance on the capability of human reason, it had brushed aside the Pauline insistence on the sovereignty and righteousness of God, the sinfulness of man, and God's initiative in man's salvation through revelation and by grace. Barth utterly rejects 'natural theology'. If man searches for God by the light of his reason he will find only an idol of his own creation, and not the God who can only be known as he reveals himself. God is not an object of man's search. There is an 'infinite qualitative difference' between God and man—a phrase which Barth takes from Kierkegaard. God is transcendent, wholly other, always Subject and never Object.

Students of Barth have noted development in his theology, something not unlikely during a writing career of some fifty years. Barth himself readily admitted in an address delivered in 1956[3] that there were certain exaggerations in his early theology, but maintained that its forthrightness was necessary in the decade following the First World War. He had not retreated from his earlier basic affirmations of the otherness, priority, and freedom of God and his graciousness in revelation. It was rather a question of revision, 'a new beginning and attack in which what previously has been said is to be said more than ever, but now even better'.[4] Barth by then had ceased to use terms like 'the infinite qualitative difference' between God and man. The address mentioned above was, indeed, on 'The Humanity of God', which 'rightly understood,' he says, 'is bound to mean God's relation to and turning towards man'.[5] This is not to deny God's sovereignty, for it is in his divine freedom that he wills to be the God of man, to be for man, entering into history and into dialogue with man. 'It is precisely God's *deity* which, if rightly understood, includes his *humanity*.'[6] We know this through his revelation, his Word, in Jesus Christ. The theme (although the phrase 'the humanity of God' does not appear) is worked out at length in *Church Dogmatics*, volume iv, 'The Doctrine of Reconciliation', part 1, published in 1953.

Some have discerned also a development in Barth's doctrine of the Church. Emilien Lamirande, a Roman Catholic scholar, distinguishes four periods in its evolution:[7] the period of the commentary on Romans, characterized by a very negative attitude to the Church; an intermediate period of some ten years to the beginning of the *Church Dogmatics* (1932), which he describes as 'the period of the Word of God and of the Church as pure event'; third, the period of the *Church Dogmatics* 'which brings out more explicitly the link between the Church and the Incarnate Word'; and finally a period inaugurated by the 1956 lecture on 'The Humanity of God'.

Lamirande says that in the first period Barth 'envisages the Church as an attempt to humanize the divine, to comprehend it, to secularize it. ... The Church was seen as a form of the religion of the world, a form of sin, in opposition to revelation, but also as a way to the gospel, in this sense at least, that she reveals what we are: sinners and darkness'.[8] H. R. Mackintosh in his *Types of Modern Theology* (1937)[9] notes some of the more radical things which Barth says in the *Römerbrief*: 'The work of the Church is the work of men: it can never be God's work'; 'In the Church the hostility of man against God is brought to a head; for there human indifference, misunderstanding, and opposition attain their most sublime and also their most naive form.' But Mackintosh, like Lamirande, notes that Barth declares that the Church is not to be forsaken: 'It would never enter our heads to think of leaving the Church. For in describing the Church we are describing ourselves.'[10] At this stage Barth lays stress on the Church as an institution, subject to the weaknesses of every human organization. Yet it is the community of justified sinners, 'the place of fruitful and hopeful repentance'[11] and an instrument of God for man's salvation.

THE CHURCH AS 'EVENT'

Lamirande denotes the second period of Barth's ecclesiology as that of the Church as 'pure event'. But this is a concept which endures in Barth's thought, being closely linked to his unswerving insistence on the sovereignty and free grace of God. It has been called his 'actualism'. Man as such is and possesses nothing that is not God's gift. His life as man, the Word of revelation, his faith, his communityness in the Church are God's continuing gifts. Man has these things only *in actu*, by an act of God, an event. It is a dynamic as opposed to a static concept of the relationship between God and man. The faith of a Christian, then, is an event.[12] So is the existence of the Church. The Word given to the Church to be proclaimed must continually be received and proclaimed. Otherwise whatever word the Church spoke would not be the Word of God and the Church would not be the Church. The Word is always an act of God, an event. The Church, therefore, which exists to proclaim the Word of God, is also an act of God, an event.[13] To some this has suggested an idea of the Church as fluctuating between existence and non-existence according as it does or does not proclaim the Word of God. Thus Lamirande writes:

> Barth persistently insisted that the Church is pure event, that she has nothing of her own, that her very being is the being of God and of Christ. The Church appeared as the transient, discontinuous, the event which occurs in the institution and is thus made visible to the eyes of faith. Through God's sovereign action, the Church is at every moment actualized, she is a totally dynamic event. Thus Barth apparently failed to acknowledge her objective permanent reality. To the eyes of a Roman Catholic, his position was still, in this period, radical actualism, tantamount to a mere negation of the Church.[14]

There seems to be inconsistency in this paragraph, for how can the Church be both 'transient, discontinuous' and 'at every moment actualized'? But Lamirande is voicing a criticism which others[15] have raised against Barth's actualism and his consequent denial that there is a *state* of being a Christian and that the Church is a *static* entity. But, as Dr Herbert Hartwell has pointed out,[16]

> Barth's actualism does not mean ... that his theology leaves no room for the idea of a 'state' of things. It only denotes that there can be no 'state' which does not arise out of God's constant giving. ... Act and being are linked up in Barth's theology in such a way that there is no 'being' apart from God's continued action, and this action takes place in the freedom of the divine grace.

Barth's actualism is another way of insisting on the principle of 'grace alone' and of rejecting triumphalism in the Church or in the Christian individual.

BARTH'S DEVELOPED ECCLESIOLOGY

Lamirande speaks of the third period in the development of Barth's ecclesiology as that of the *Church Dogmatics*. This is somewhat misleading, since the two halves of volume iv, part 3, were not published in Switzerland until 1959, three years after the lecture which he suggests inaugurates the fourth period! Lamirande probably means to indicate the period from 1932 to 1955, the date of publication of *CD* iv, 2, after which four years elapsed before the appearance of iv, 3. Just as we noted[17] that there is reason to doubt whether a distinction can properly be made between a second and a third period in Barth's ecclesiology (at least in quite the way Lamirande wishes to make it), so we may doubt whether the lecture on 'The Humanity of God' marks a new development in his doctrine of the Church. However this may be, although the Church is discussed in many contexts in the earlier volumes of *CD*, it is in volume iv, 'The Doctrine of Reconciliation', that we find Barth's fullest treatment. Part 1, published in 1953, has a section on 'The Holy Spirit and the Gathering of the Christian Community', and part 3, second half (1959) has a section on 'The Holy Spirit and the Sending of the Christian Community'. To these sections I now turn.

THE HOLY SPIRIT AND THE GATHERING OF
THE CHRISTIAN COMMUNITY

Barth prefaces this section with a summary:

> The Holy Spirit is the awakening power in which Jesus Christ has formed and continually renews His body, i.e. His own earthly-historical form of existence, the one holy, catholic, and apostolic Church. This is Christendom, i.e. the gathering of the community of those whom already before all others He has made willing and ready for life under the divine verdict executed in His death and revealed in His resurrection from the dead. It is therefore the provisional representation of the whole world of humanity justified in Him (*CD* iv, 1, p. 643).

The Church has its being in the divine *actus* of God in the Word of his revelation in Jesus Christ. It is the true Church only as Jesus Christ, the risen Lord, is present and acting in and through its members. This he does through the power of the Holy Spirit.

> It is still God Himself in this work, in the strict sense in which the same must be said of the work of creation and the objective realization of the work of Atonement in Jesus Christ (ibid., pp. 645–6).

> In everything that we have to say concerning the Christian community and Christian faith we can move only within the circle that they are founded by the Holy Spirit and therefore that they must be continually refounded by Him, but that the necessary refounding by the Holy Spirit can consist only in a renewal of the founding which He has already accomplished (ibid., p. 647).

> . Fundamentally and in general practice we cannot say more of the Holy Spirit and His work than that He is the Power in which Jesus Christ attests Himself effectively, creating in man response and obedience (ibid., p. 648).

The Church, then, has its being in a new and continuous creative work of God. In describing its being, Barth says that we must abandon the usual distinctions between being and act, status and dynamic, essence and existence:

> Its act is its being, its status its dynamic, its essence its existence. The Church *is* when it takes place that God lets certain men live as His servants, His friends, His children, the witnesses of the reconciliation of the world with himself as it has taken place in Jesus Christ, the preachers of the victory which has been won in Him over sin and suffering, the heralds of His future revelation in which the glory of the Creator will be declared

to all creation as that of His love and faithfulness and mercy (ibid., pp. 650–51).[18]

Barth insists on the visibility of the Church ('no sect, however spiritual, can completely escape it'[19]). A doctrine that the Church is invisible is an ecclesiastical docetism which is as impossible as a Christological docetism. God is for the world, and His Church is for the world. Christ was the incarnate Word of God in the world, and His Church is in the world. 'The Christian community as such cannot exist as an ideal commune or universum but—also in time and space—only in the relationship of its individual members as they are fused together by the common action of the Word which they have heard into a definite human fellowship; in concrete form, therefore, and visible to everyone.'[20] There is, indeed, an 'invisible aspect which is the secret of the visible',[21] and this is that 'the community is the earthly-historical form of existence of Jesus Christ Himself'.[22] Knowing this, the Church cannot but be involved visibly in the conflicts and dangers of history.

Barth then discusses[23] the Pauline doctrine of the Church as the body of Christ which he takes to be neither symbolic nor metaphysical, but a statement of the reality that the Christian community is the earthly-historical form of Christ's existence. He then turns to the four credal notes of the Church: 'I believe one holy, catholic, and apostolic Church.' The principle of interpretation is that these marks belong to the Church in so far as it is the earthly-historical form of existence of the one living Lord, and that they can only be recognized by faith. Barth's discussion is lengthy, and I shall here refer to his main points, and as much as possible, through quotation, allow him to speak for himself.

THE CHURCH IS ONE

The Church in its visible and invisible aspects is one: 'The one is the form and the other the mystery of one and the self-same Church.'[24] Likewise the Church militant and the Church triumphant are one. The people of Israel both before and after Christ and the Christian Church initiated on the day of Pentecost are two forms and aspects of the one inseparable community.[25] Barth speaks of the existence of a Judaism which does not believe in Jesus Christ as something which makes even the Church's own existence problematical, 'an ontological impossibility', 'a gaping hole in the body of Christ, something which is quite intolerable'. The Jewish question, if Paul is right in Romans 9–11, is the Christian question.[26]

The existence of Christian communities in different places does not damage the unity of the Church, but the existence of different and opposing churches does:

> It is an impossible situation that whole groups of Christian communities should exhibit a certain external and internal unity among themselves and yet stand in relation to other groups of equally Christian communities in an attitude more or less of exclusion (ibid., p. 676).

Recognizing that separate churches sincerely claim Jesus Christ for themselves, each believing that his real presence is among them, Barth's plea is that they should act upon their belief that he really is the present, living, and speaking Lord,[27] and listen to him:

> In the realization of faith in the one Church in face of its disunity, the decisive step is that the divided churches should honestly and seriously try to hear and perhaps hear the voice of the Lord by them and for them, and then try to hear, and perhaps actually hear, the voice of others. Where a church does this, in its own place, and without leaving it, it is on the way to the one Church. It is clear that in so doing it has already abandoned its claim to be identical with the one Church in contrast to the others, and in this sense to be the only Church. The claim has been dashed out of its hand by the One who is the unity of the Church ... and if it lets Him open the question of its individual existence, then it will automatically be open to the other churches in the sense that it will be willing and ready to let them say something to it, thus renouncing, in fact, its isolation as the only Church, its exclusion of all other churches (ibid., p. 684).

THE CHURCH IS HOLY

> Holy means set apart, marked off, and therefore differentiated, singled out, taken (and set) on one side as a being which has its own origin and nature and meaning and direction—and all this with a final definitiveness, decisively, inviolably and unalterably, because it is God who does it. The term indicates the contradistinction of the Christian community ... to the other gatherings and societies which exist in the world (ibid., p. 685).

'It is God who does it', and God does it by the calling of his Word and the gathering of his Holy Spirit:

> What else can the holiness of the Church be but the reflection of the holiness of Jesus Christ as its heavenly Head, falling upon it as He enters

into and remains in fellowship with it by His Holy Spirit? ... In the existence of the community we have to do with the earthly-historical form of His existence. As it is gathered and built up and commissioned by the Holy Spirit it becomes and is this particular part of the creaturely world, acquiring a part of His holiness, although of and in itself it is not holy, it is nothing out of the ordinary, indeed as His community within Adamic humanity it is just as unholy as that humanity, sharing its sin and guilt and standing absolutely in need of its justification (ibid., pp. 686–7).

The Church is holy only as the body of Christ, because He, the Head is holy; holy only in its community with Him, gathered to Him by the Holy Spirit. It is not a question of an individual acquiring holiness and *therefore* becoming a member of the Church. In the N.T. the 'partner' of Jesus Christ is the community. 'The community lives in Christians, Christians live in the community, and in this way Jesus Christ lives in the world. In this way they are holy in Him and with Him.'[28] Barth remarks that this is to say something very like *extra ecclesiam nulla salus*. Yet he will not restrict the freedom of God to save outside the Church. It must, however, be said that outside the Church there is no revelation, no faith, no knowledge of salvation, and no holiness. 'There is no legitimate private Christianity', for the Holy Spirit leads the individual 'directly into the community and not into a private relationship with Christ.'[29]

Barth in no way avoids the fact that the holy community, indestructible because it is the body of Christ and possesses his promise (Matt. 16.18), has constantly failed and fallen into error: 'When has it been the case that men could simply see the good works of Christians and had to glorify their Father which is in heaven?'[30] The Church is always in need of reformation, always needs to pray 'forgive us our trespasses'.

The Creed says 'I believe one holy, catholic Church', not 'I believe *in* ...'. We can only believe *in* God, Father, Son, and Holy Spirit. We believe the existence of the holy Church because of the promise of the Holy God. It is a matter of the perception of faith, and therefore: 'We all do well to begin with the question how it is with ourselves', with a readiness to allow to count in favour of others what we believe to be in our own favour, which, stripped to its essential basis, is that 'the Holy One of his free grace has called us into his Holy community'.[31]

THE CHURCH IS CATHOLIC

'Catholic' means general, comprehensive. Applied to the Church it speaks of 'a character in virtue of which it is always and everywhere the same and always and everywhere recognizable in this sameness, to the preservation of which it is committed'.[32] The term 'catholic' implicitly raises the question of a Church which is false, heretical, even apostate. *Credo catholicam ecclesiam* means 'I believe in the existence of a community which in the essence which makes it a Christian community is unalterable in spite of all its changes of form, which in this essence never has altered and never can or will alter. And negatively, I do not believe that a community which is different in essence is the Christian community'.[33]

Catholicity is not negated by geographical and cultural variety: 'In essence the Church is the same in all races, languages, cultures, and classes, in all forms of State and society',[34] and it must not accept any kind of dependence on any other society. Every church must always seriously ask whether it is merely a respectable expression of local culture; whether it is an instrument of the ruling class; whether it is simply tolerated because its moral stance is considered useful for the State. In short it must ask: 'Does it exist of its essence and in faithfulness to its essence? We must never think that we can arrive at a position where we will not be disturbed by this question' (ibid., pp. 703–4).

'Catholic' also indicates a temporal dimension for the Church. It exists in history: 'It is in a way which is surrounded by a continually changing landscape and in which it is itself subject to change—but in which it can never be anything other than itself.'[35] Barth here criticizes both 'ecclesiastical romanticism' and 'flirtation with the new'. The Church is the true and catholic Church, 'only to the extent that in its own age it participates in the essence of the one Church, being faithful to it and knowing how to do it justice in its visible expression'.[36] What counts is not progress—a highly doubtful idea as applied to the Church—but continual reformation.

The Church is also catholic, general, and comprehensive, in its relationship to individual members. Again Barth insists that 'the Christian is first a member of the Christian community and only then, and as such, this individual Christian in his particular Christian being and nature and presence'.[37] He insists strongly on the priority of the Church over its members, something which, he says, has been flagrantly neglected in modern Protestantism. He devotes a long note[38] to the 'depressing phenomena' of churches which, even in official documents, assume that individuals first become Christians and *then*, out of community of interest, join themselves into a church.

He concludes his treatment of catholicity by acknowledging that too frequently the Church has failed to maintain it: 'There is hardly a church which in this respect has not been seriously, perhaps very seriously, damaged.'[39] In particular, 'where a church thinks that it cannot and should not merely believe its catholicity but should be able—in its own form—to see and maintain it, then in its arrogance and unreadiness to repent, this church shows itself to be a-catholic'.[40]

As with its unity and holiness, so with its catholicity, the Church has no control over it. The Church is the earthly-historical form of the existence of Christ, and its catholicity is grounded in him as its Head. The community is catholic only as he lives, speaks, and acts within it and as it listens and is obedient. The mark of catholicity is only to be recognized and realized by an active faith in Jesus Christ as its Head.[41]

THE CHURCH IS APOSTOLIC

Barth contends that 'apostolic', introduced in the creed of the Council of Constantinople in 381, does not add anything new to the three other predicates, but does provide the criterion by which a judgement can be made whether 'in this or that case we have or have not to do with the one holy, catholic Church'. This criterion is spiritual (to be understood only, like the Church's oneness, holiness, and catholicity, by faith in the Head of the Church),[42] but it is also concrete:

> Apostolic means in the discipleship, in the school, under the normative authority, instruction, and direction of the apostles, in agreement with them and accepting their message. The Church is the true Church and therefore the one holy Church in the fact and to the extent that it is apostolic in this sense, and by this fact it can and should be distinguished from the false Church (ibid., p. 714).

Apostolicity especially emphasizes the being of the Christian community as an event. A relationship to the apostles can only take place in a history between the community and the apostles. He who wishes to recognize the community as apostolic must himself take part in this history:

> He cannot be a neutral and decide its apostolicity from outside. He must be a living member, and as such must know its basis in the apostles, himself standing in their discipleship, in their school, under their authority and direction, himself hearing their witness, himself being taught and

questioned by them. He must be put by them in a definite movement, in the movement in which they found themselves, in which they still find themselves today—for in the New Testament they are still before us in living speech and action. To be in the community of Jesus Christ means to take part in this movement (ibid., pp. 714–15).

Barth rejects the idea that the Church's apostolicity can be sought on historical and juridical grounds. He refers to the claim that historical proof can support the notion that apostolic authority and office is transmitted successively to supreme office-bearers in the Church, 'e.g. from a bishop to his successor, and from this successor to the inferior ministers who will be ordained by him'.[43] This kind of apostolic succession may be as a 'welcome adornment' of the institution of a church. To prove the possession of it is a matter of historico-critical examination of a list of names—which has little to do with the Holy Spirit, or with faith. It does not, however, guarantee apostolicity[44] as Barth understands it. It seems, moreover, to involve an unscriptural doctrine which asserts that the Holy Spirit can be controlled, and his presence and action confined:

How can apostolic authority, and power and mission, how can the Holy Spirit be transferred, when obviously apostolicity is His work and gift?—as though the Holy Spirit were a legal or technical or symbolical It (ibid., p. 717).

Barth maintains that the apostolicity of the Church belongs with its character as the earthly-historical form of the existence of Jesus Christ in which he gives himself to be known to the community and through it to the world. The earthly-historical medium of his self-manifestation is those who knew him as the Word made flesh in the form of a servant and then in his glory—namely, the apostles. These he chose, called, ordained, and sent out as his direct witnesses. They are the rock on which he builds his Church. They do not build his community. He is the builder, they his servants. It is in this serving that their normative significance lies, and that they are the holy apostles. He speaks through them. He who hears them hears him. He himself and the awakening power of his Holy Spirit have no other earthly-historical form than the apostles' witnessing power. Only when their witness is proclaimed, received, accepted, and reproduced is the community present.[45]

Thus the existence of His community is always its history in its encounter with this witness—the history in which it is faithful or unfaithful to it in its exposition and application. There is, therefore, a legitimate apostolic succession, the existence of a Church in the following of the apostles, only when it takes place in this history that the apostolic witness finds in a community discipleship, hearing, obedience, respect, and observance. But it is in the fact that they serve that the apostles follow the Lord Himself and precede the community. It would, therefore, be very strange if the community for its part tried to follow them in any other authority, power, and mission than that of their service (ibid., p. 719).

There is but one true apostolic succession, and it is a succession of service, of the *ministerium verbi*, not of *dominium*.

Barth points out that this interpretation of apostolicity is identical in substance with a term used, in a different context, 'to describe the authority of the Bible as the source and norm of the existence and doctrine and order of the Church—the "Scripture-principle" '.[46] The apostles are the original disciples of the evangelical records, the eyewitnesses of the Messiah of Israel. Consequently, the apostolic Church is that which bears the apostolic witness of the N.T., which reads the Scriptures as the direct witness to Jesus Christ alive yesterday and today, which is constantly in encounter with the biblical witness, which allows the Holy Spirit to direct it to look in the direction in which Scripture looks, to the living Jesus Christ:

> As Scripture stirs up and invites and summons and impels the Church to look in this same direction, there takes place the work of the Spirit of Scripture who is the Holy Spirit. Scripture then works in the service of its Lord, and the Church becomes and is apostolic and therefore the true Church (ibid., p. 723).

THE CHURCH AS SERVANT

In his treatment of apostolicity, Barth has emphasized the note of service which we have seen to be prominent in twentieth-century ecclesiology. In the second half of *CD* iv, 3 he devotes a section to this subject under the heading 'The Holy Spirit and the Sending of the Christian Community'.[47] There are four sub-headings: (1) The People of God in World-Occurrence; (2) The Community for the World; (3) The Task of the Community; (4) The Ministry of the Community. It is a long section of 220 pages in which he frequently reintroduces former themes. Here I shall draw attention to the new material.

THE PEOPLE OF GOD IN WORLD-OCCURRENCE

Here Barth is at his most profound, and his most difficult:

> [Jesus Christ] is the man in whose person God has ... elected and loved from all eternity the wider circle of humanity as a whole, but also, with a view to this wider circle, the narrower circle of a special race, of His own community within humanity (*CD* iv, 3 (second half), p. 682).

Thus the Church is in the world and must know that its Lord is Lord also of the world. 'The community would be guilty of a lack of faith and discernment if it were to see and understand world history as secular or profane history.'[48]

Barth recognizes that the world is ruled *hominum confusione* (by man's confusion); but it is also ruled *Dei providentia* (by God's providence). He faces frankly the grim results of man's confusion, even the possibility of world destruction (atomic sin). But God has decided for mankind, and 'the community of those to whom Jesus Christ has entrusted the word of reconciliation ... cannot possibly accept either human confusion or a cosmic confusion ... as the final meaning of world-occurrence'.[49] The world is also the theatre of the glory of God 'in all its explored and unexplored dimensions, with all its known and as yet unknown or only suspected possibilities and powers, with a nature God Himself has given no less than in the case of men'.[50] Barth acknowledges the mystery of the relationship between man's confusion and God's providence. But he is certain that it is not to be explained in the manner of Hegel as a matter of thesis and antithesis which are one day to be brought together in a synthesis, for this would be an eventual justification of man's rebellious confusion:

> What does the people of God see in world-occurrence around it? To be sure, up above it sees first and last the glorious spectacle of its God, the Creator of the world and man, who as such is the Lord and Ruler of this occurrence. To be sure, down below it sees the dreadful spectacle of the man who has fallen away from God and fallen out with his neighbour and himself. To be sure, it sees the contradiction, the conflict, the *diastasis*, the riddle of this occurrence. And accordingly, to be sure, it sees no real synthesis resolving the riddle, no harmony between above and below, no relation between the positive will of God and the confusion of man, no possibility of understanding the one as the basis of the other, or the other as grounded in it. It accepts the twofold view. But it also sees that there is more to be said (ibid., p. 708).

This additional thing to be said is 'a new thing' which the community knows on the basis of its own existence. The 'new thing' is that God has revealed himself as for the world, and has spoken his Word to it. 'The new thing which the people of God perceives in world-occurrence is the new unique person, Jesus Christ. It is the grace of God addressed to the world in Him.'[51] The community knows that it is entrusted with the task of attesting this new thing to the world. It is therefore 'concerned not only with God but also directly with humanity ... with the very impure, historical, and sinful humanity which has fallen away from God and fallen out with itself, with the "flesh of sin" (Rom. 8.13), and therefore with the subject of the great confusion of world history'.[52] Since God in Jesus Christ has decided for men, the Church can only be for men. If the community truly believes in the living Christ, it accepts this role 'in the resoluteness of a definite hope for world-occurrence':[53]

> It is a resolute confidence even in relation to the future, to the goal of the totality of world history. The Christian community dares to hope for the world. It waits for Him who came once and for all yesterday, and who is and lives always and therefore tomorrow. In relation to Him it knows that the form of the world which now confronts it cannot last but will one day perish and be seen no more, and that its new reality will then appear and alone be seen by itself and all men—the world reconciled to God, the covenant fulfilled by Him, the order reconstituted by Him. It waits for Jesus Christ. It waits for Him to emerge from His concealment in world-occurrence and to show Himself to it and to the men of every age and place as the One He already is as its Lord. It yearns for this. It rejoices in it (ibid., p. 720).

World history for the people of God is the sphere in which it has to live with this resoluteness. It is the time between Easter and the final coming of Christ.[54] It is the time of which Barth said in a series of lectures given in 1946:

> In the resurrection of Jesus Christ the claim is made, according to the New Testament, that God's victory in man's favour in the person of His Son has already been won. Easter is indeed the great pledge of our hope, but simultaneously this future is already present in the Easter message. It is the proclamation of a victory already won. The war is at an end—even though here and there troops are still shooting, because they have not heard anything yet about the capitulation. The game is won, even though the player can still play a few further moves. Actually he is already mated. ... It is in this interim time that we are living: the old is past; behold, it has

all become new. The Easter message tells us that our enemies sin, the curse and death, are beaten. Ultimately they can no longer start mischief. They still behave as though the game were not decided, the battle not fought. We must still reckon with them but fundamentally we must cease to fear them any more ... one thing still holds ... that Jesus is the Victor ... we are invited and summoned to take seriously the victory of God's glory in this man Jesus and to be joyful in Him (*Dogmatics in Outline*).[55]

This interim time is given to the world as a time for human response, a time for the community to proclaim the gospel of reconciliation in Christ and to elicit faith.

Therefore the Christian community exists in the world as an empirical phenomenon, in the sphere of visibility, even in a sense, as Bellarmine said, 'like the kingdom of France or the republic of Venice'.[56] Again Barth rejects a doctrine of the Church as solely invisible as 'ecclesiastical docetism'.[57] Like its Lord, Jesus Christ, the Word who became flesh, the Church must be directed *ad extra* (towards the outside world), visible, like the world and in solidarity with it. But at once it must be said that like its Lord who is visibly true man and invisibly true God, the Christian community too is not merely visible as one group among others, but invisible as the people of Jesus Christ, called by God. 'It is both visible and invisible in the one essence.'[58] The Church is invisible, i.e. not plainly seen by all, because it is the community of Jesus Christ and the people of God in world-occurrence. Indeed, without God's calling and election it would not exist at all, even visibly. But by the power of the divine decision the Church exists, not only visibly, but also 'from within, uniquely and therefore invisibly, i.e. in a way which is visible to some, though not all'.[59] They who perceive its invisible aspect are those who know that the community is grounded in the being of Jesus Christ, and that 'what it is from within is what calls for expression *ad extra*. What it is invisibly wills as such to become generally visible, and has the promise that one day it will do so.'[60]

> Its being, then, is invisible, but its impulse is from within outwards, from invisibility to visibility, from particularity to universality. Even as visible, it bears the promise of invisibility within it. This means, however, that, even though it is like the world and in world-occurrence, yet it is distinct from the world and different, individual and unique in relation to it, being set over against and in confrontation with world-occurrence. The existence of the Christian community thus corresponds to the existence of Jesus Christ to the extent that He first came in the flesh, so that in His

human nature He is the eternal Son of God, and as such different from the world in spite of His solidarity with it, confronting world-occurrence unequivocally as its Lord even while He inconspicuously integrates Himself into it. His community follows Him as it must understand and therefore express its own being as one which is wholly worldly and yet also as a being in encounter with world-occurrence (*CD* iv, 3, p. 728).

THE COMMUNITY FOR THE WORLD

The community of Jesus Christ is for the world, i.e. for each and every man. ... In this way it also exists for God. ... First and supremely it is God who exists for the world. And since the community of Jesus Christ exists first and supremely for God, it has no option but in its own manner and place to exist for the world. How else could it exist for God? (ibid., p. 762).

Barth finds that there is a gap at this point in the patristic, scholastic, Reformation, and post-Reformation doctrine of the Church. No answer, or at the most an unsatisfactory answer, is given to the question concerning the meaning and purpose of the existence of the Christian community. The impression is given that the Church is 'an end in itself in its existence as the community and institution of salvation'.[61] 'What', he asks, 'has become of the decisive New Testament saying in 2 Corinthians 5.19 that it was the world which God reconciled to Himself in Jesus Christ?'[62]

The community exists for the world. It is the fellowship in which it is given to, man to know the world as it is, to know man as he is, seeing, addressing, and treating him in the light and on the basis of God's covenant with all men, concluded in Jesus Christ. It is the society in which it is given to men to know and practise their solidarity with the world (which does not imply conformity), and to be under obligation to the world. It is not given to it to rule the world (that is God's work), but it is called to co-operate with God in his work.[63]

It is not a matter of any activity in the world, but of that which is required, of that which corresponds to its commission, of that for which it is empowered by the One who gives it. In no circumstances, however, may it or should it try to evade this task. In discharging it, it will always need the forgiveness of the sins which it commits, and therefore correction, and therefore constant self-criticism. But even the most stringent self-criticism must never be a reason or occasion for prudently doing nothing. Better something doubtful or over bold and therefore in need of correction and forgiveness than nothing at all! If even in the most holy reserve and modesty and prudence it prefers to fold its hands and therefore to rest itself, it is certainly not the true Church. The true Church may sometimes engage in tactical withdrawal, but never in strategic. It can never cease wholly or basically from activity in the world (ibid., pp. 779–80).

THE TASK OF THE COMMUNITY

The community's task is very definite. It is to exist for the world: 'If it had not been given it, it would not have come into being.'[64] The content of the task is to confess Jesus Christ: 'To use the simplest and biblical formulation: "Ye shall be witnesses unto me" (Acts 1.8).'[65] 'Jesus Christ signifies God Himself become man's Neighbour and Brother, akin and alongside in order in his stead to redeem his ruined cause.'[66] Therefore: 'Man cannot be omitted either for a single instant or in a single respect from the content of the message entrusted to the community.'[67]

Although there are differences in the vocation of members of the community, and various kinds of service,

> there are no differences within the community and in the execution of its task which can possibly throw doubt on the unity and totality of its content, i.e. of that which is at issue in it, the Gospel. ... Its concern will be with the total content and therefore unconditionally with Jesus Christ, with the great Yes, with the goodness of God, and with man ennobled by God's goodness (ibid., p. 801).

The man who is addressed in this task is not man as understood by any particular anthropology or analysis of 'modern' man (which may or may not be relevant), but man as he is known and addressed by God Himself acting and revealed in Jesus Christ.[68]

> We have to distinguish between what the Gospel sees man to be in himself in virtue of his ignorance, and what it also sees him to be in virtue of the work of God and the Word of God addressed to his ignorance ... this ignorant and suffering and unloving and loveless man in all the historical forms, in all the twists and turns, in which he tries to be rid of his need and anxiety, is the man whom God loves as His creature, whom He has elected in His Son ... and whom He has called once and for all in His incarnate Word to Himself, to fellowship with His life, to eternal life (ibid., p. 809).

The Church does justice to its task only if it addresses every man as 'one who will be within even though he is now without', as one who is called to the service of God and is open to this future. It does not do justice to its task if it gives up one whom God does not give up.[69]

Barth proceeds to discuss the ways in which the community may fail, and has in the past failed in its task. He speaks of the temptation and danger of distorting the gospel into 'general timeless truth' which men are invited to consider favourably in comparison with competing theories of world-occurrence; of failing to recognize that God has a concrete and decisive Word for every time and situation; of the temptation and danger of falsifying the gospel by dressing it in the philosophical and ethical notions of the age (which is to treat the gospel as an object over which the community has control); of neglecting those for whom the community exists (with the excuse, perhaps, that there are so many tasks to be done for the 'inner circle'); or, on the other hand, of patronizing them, which means to treat them as so much material for one's own benevolence, ability, or superior knowledge. In all these ways the community fails in its task and negates its *raison d'être*.[70]

THE MINISTRY OF THE COMMUNITY

The ministry of the community is concretely defined as 'a ministry to God and man by its institution and ordination as such in the discipleship of Jesus Christ'.[71] It is a ministry of witness to the Word and reconciling work of God, spoken and accomplished in Jesus Christ, the primary Witness, the Mediator between God and man. This ministry is sustained, as it needs to be because the community shares the weakness of humanity, by the promise of God that its ministry is fulfilled in Jesus Christ.[72]

The *nature* of the ministry is the declaration of the gospel, its explanation or explication, and 'evangelical address', i.e. the application of the gospel to the situation in time and place of those who are addressed. Whatever forms the ministry may take, this is its essential nature.[73]

The *forms* of ministry are multiple: 'The Holy Spirit does not enforce a flat uniformity';[74] the community is one body, but has many members, and these are called by the Spirit to special forms of ministry and endowed for them by grace. On the basis of texts like Mark 6.12–13 and Luke 9.6, 'preaching the gospel and healing everywhere', Barth makes a distinction, though not a division, between ministries of speech and action:

> There can be no doubt that in the light of its origin, of the Giver of its task who is also its content, [the community's] ministry and witness have always to move along these two lines ... no less along the one than the other, but with equal seriousness and emphasis along both. ... There is a work of the lips and also of the hands. There is speech and also action, proclamation, and also healing; though it must be remembered, of course, that the direction given by Jesus to His disciples displays a clear sequence, the speech always preceding the action (ibid., p. 863).

Paul, who placed prophecy, the word of wisdom and knowledge, and the ministry of apostles and prophets first in his lists of various ministries (Rom. 12.6; 1 Cor. 12.8; Eph. 4.11), also evidently regarded the bearers of the ministry of the Word as the principal members of the whole body.[75]

The *'speech' forms of ministry* are described by Barth as (within the community): (1) to praise God; (2) the proclamation of the gospel in the assembly; (3) instruction of the community; and (directed outwards to the world): (4) evangelization in the immediate surroundings of the community; (5) mission to non-Christian lands. He adds also (6) the ministry of theology.[76]

ACTION FORMS OF MINISTRY

Forms of ministry which are predominantly action are (7) prayer; (8) the cure of souls; (9) personal example of Christian living; (10) diaconate in the sense of bringing relief to the needy in and outside the community; (11) prophetic action, by which Barth means action based on perception into the meaning of the current situation both of the community and of the world, and apprehension of what the Word of God has to say in this situation; and (12) the establishment of fellowship between nations, races, cultures, and economic classes.[77]

Baptism and the Lord's Supper are the community's significatory actions which establish fellowship:

> In baptism we have the once-for-all and conscious entry and reception, manifested in the sign of purification, of the individual man into membership of the people of those who are called by God in free grace to be His witnesses, to participate in the work of His witness. And in the Lord's Supper we have the repeated and conscious unification of this people, manifested in the sign of common eating and drinking, in new seeking

and reception of the free grace which it constantly needs and is constantly given in its work of witness. There is more to be said concerning baptism and the Lord's Supper. But it certainly has to be said concerning them that they are significatory actions in which men, instead of being merely alongside or even apart, both come and are together. They are thus actions which establish fellowship. In baptism and the Lord's Supper an invisible action of God—the fellowship of the Father and the Son in the Holy Ghost, the fellowship of God and man in Jesus Christ, the fellowship of Jesus Christ the Head with His body and its members, and finally the fellowship of God with the world created by Him and reconciled to Him—is the prototype, the meaning and the power of the visible and significatory action of the community and therefore of the unification of men therein attested. But on this basis and as likenesses of this original, baptism and the Lord's Supper are not empty signs. On the contrary, they are full of meaning and power. They are thus the simplest, and yet in their very simplicity the most eloquent, elements in the witness which the community owes to the world, namely the witness of peace on earth among the men in whom God is well-pleased (ibid., p. 901).

Throughout his long description of the forms of ministry Barth is insistent that each form of ministry is laid upon the whole community. We find here no discussion of the ordained ministry. The nearest Barth comes to this subject is the assertion, in respect of those who are called to particular forms of ministry, that

> in virtue of their origin in God, in Christ and in the Holy Spirit, it is made impossible that any one of them ... shall break loose and swallow the others, finally making itself out to be the one ministry, or the one fellowship of ministry, and acting as such. All of them, i.e. of the few or many Christians who find themselves commonly called to this special action and equipped for it, have to serve together 'the edifying of the body of Christ' (Eph. 4.12) and have thus to be modest in their mutual relations.[78]

There is no indication that he has modified his earlier rejection of a hierarchy of office in the Church and of a distinction between clergy and laity, office-bearers and others: 'Strictly, no one has an office; all can and should and may serve; none is ever "off duty".'[79]

It was noted above[80] that some have discerned the beginning of a new development in Barth's ecclesiology in his address on 'The Humanity of God' in 1956. It has to be remembered that by this date *CD* iv, Parts 1 and 2 were already published, and the writing of iv, 3, published in 1959, must have been well advanced. In the few pages devoted to the Church at the end of the lecture he certainly admits that in 1920 he viewed the Church in an exaggeratedly negative way.[81]

He does not withdraw, however, his early teaching that God's judgement rests upon the Church, nor the concept that the Church is *event* before it is institution.[82]

He does now say very clearly that the Church is prior to the individual: 'Jesus Christ is the Head of His body and only so is He also the Head of its members.'[83] He does declare that 'what Jesus Christ is for God and for us, on earth and in time, He is as Lord of this community, as king of this people, as Head of this body and all its members'.[84] Despite the sins and failures of this 'strange communion of these strange saints', the Church is not too mean a thing for Jesus Christ, 'but, for better or for worse, sufficiently precious and worthy in His eyes to be entrusted with His witnessing and thus His affairs in the world—yes, even Himself. So great is God's loving-kindness!'[85] We have here a 'high', christologically grounded doctrine of the Church. But Barth had said most, if not all, of these things in the earlier *CD* iv, 1.

I have tried to let Barth speak for himself in this chapter, and it may fittingly close with the concluding words of this address:

> Our 'I believe in the Holy Spirit' would be empty if it did not also include in a concrete, practical, and obligatory way, the 'I believe one Holy, Catholic, and Apostolic Church'. We believe the Church as the place where the crown of humanity, namely, man's fellow-humanity, may become visible in Christocratic brotherhood. Moreover, we believe it as the place where God's glory wills to dwell upon earth, that is, where humanity—the humanity of God—wills to assume tangible form in time and here upon earth. Here we recognize the humanity of God. Here we delight in it. Here we celebrate and witness to it. Here we glory in the Immanuel, just as He did who, as He looked at the world, would not cast away the burden of the Church but rather chose to take it upon Himself and bear it in the name of all its members. 'If God is for us, who is against us?' (*The Humanity of God*).[86]

23

The Ecclesiology of
Paul Tillich

Paul Tillich (1886–1965) was deprived of his chair of Philosophy at
the University of Frankfurt because of his opposition to the Hitler
régime, and sailed for the United States in 1933. He became Professor
of Philosophical Theology at Union Theological Seminary, New York,
and later University Professor at Harvard (1955). He was one of the
most influential theologians in the English-speaking world during the
middle years of the century. His intimate acquaintance with
philosophy, psychiatry, and many branches of the arts and sciences
won him a respectful readership in and beyond the circle of
professional theologians, and he was 'one of the most widely read and
widely debated thinkers of his time'.[1]

SOME MAIN THEMES IN TILLICH'S THEOLOGY

His ecclesiology is developed in the third volume of his *Systematic
Theology*.[2] In order to put his doctrine of the Church in its proper context, it is necessary to describe certain of his main themes. For Tillich,
the function of theology is to declare and interpret the Christian
message for each generation. It must elucidate the crucial questions
which man asks in his situation in existence, and then show how the
revelation of the New Being in Jesus as the Christ answers those
questions. It must be an 'answering' or apologetic theology. Tillich
calls this 'the method of 'correlation'; it 'explains the contents of the
Christian faith through existential questions and theological answers
in mutual interdependence'.[3] In his theological method, therefore, as in
many other ways, Tillich's theology is in sharp contrast with that of
his great contemporary, Karl Barth.

In pursuance of his aim, Tillich offers an acute analysis of man's
situation. Man in existence is in 'a state of estrangement from his essential nature';[4] he 'is not what he essentially is and ought to be'.[5] He

has fallen from his essence by actualizing the finite freedom which belongs to him, and which he had possessed in 'dreaming innocence' in union with the ground of his being—God. This is symbolized in the garden of Eden story of Genesis 2–3. This fall was the transition from essence to existence.[6] Man in existence is finite being, subject to the categories of time, space, causality, and substance, all of which threaten him with the possibility of his *not* being—not being somewhen, somewhere, somehow, somebody. He is anxious; he asks how he can continue to be, what basis there is for 'the courage to be' in his present. The answer of theology is the doctrine of God, which Tillich expounds in *Systematic Theology*, volume 1. The being of God is being itself. He is the ground of all being, and 'he is the power of being in everything and above everything'.[7] This power is the power of infinite love which desires the union of the estranged, and the fulfilment of all being.

But man in his existential situation has other urgent questions. There is not only the question of courage in the face of the threat of not being. Aware that his being is estranged from its essence and involved in inextricable contradictions, man asks about the possibility of salvation, the possibility of new being in which his essential being may be regained.

Being has a structure which, Tillich holds, has been disrupted for man in finite existence. Basically it is a subject–object structure. Every being is an individual, confronted by an environment, and man experiences this as a self-world relationship. Tillich analyses[8] the basic self-world structure of being into three elements, which are polarities: individualization and participation; dynamics and form; and freedom and destiny. Man who is a self participates in all other being (physical, biological, personal). But how can he do so without losing his individuality? Man as self has potentialities (*dynamis*) which must take some form, must in some way be actualized. But how can man employ his potentialities without on the one hand embarking on a chaotic life ('everything by starts and nothing long'), or, on the other hand, arriving at some rigid form which crushes all potentialities but one? Man as self has freedom, but his freedom is interdependent with his destiny, by which Tillich means that which a man is at any given moment, i.e. as formed by all the influences which have made an impact on him, ancestral and environmental, and by his own decisions. But how can man preserve his freedom without defying his destiny, so losing the meaning and direction of his life, and how can he preserve his destiny without losing his freedom?

Man in existence tends to assert his individuality, potentialities, and freedom against their opposite poles. On the other hand, stress on the other poles carries the danger of collectivization, rigidity, and loss of freedom. In either case the structure of man's being is thrown out of equilibrium. Tillich uses the word 'estrangement' to denote man's situation—estrangement from the ground of his being (God), from other beings, and from his essential self. Estrangement is, however, to use biblical terms, 'sin' (unbelief, *hubris* or self-elevation, and concupiscence) and a state of 'guilt'.[9]

Man's attempts at self-salvation must fail, because he can only act within the resources of his estranged being, and these are not sufficient to overcome the ambiguities of his estrangement and restore unity with his essential being. He therefore asks, and must ask, about the possibility of new being. Here, as elsewhere, Tillich upholds what he calls 'the Protestant principle'; the distance between God and man cannot be bridged by man; all is of God. The answer to this question of man is given in the appearance of the New Being in Jesus as the Christ. It is in *ST* 2 that Tillich expounds this theological answer. In Jesus as the Christ, essential being in 'undisrupted unity' with God appears under the conditions of finite existence. He preserves this unity while taking upon himself the self-destruction implicit in man's existence,[10] and thus conquers the gap between essence and existence. In him the power of the New Being is manifested. It grasped the disciples of Jesus, who, in the receiving act which every revelation needs, themselves grasped the New Being in their acceptance of him as the Christ. And in accepting him as the Christ they accepted that he had accepted them. That man must accept that he is accepted is another nuance of the 'Protestant principle'.

THE SPIRITUAL PRESENCE

Man's life, even the life of the man who has accepted that he is accepted, needs to be transformed (or, in more traditional language, salvation, initiated in justification by grace through faith, is a process which continues in sanctification). His life is still a 'mixture' of essence and existence, still has to come to terms with the polarities of individualization and participation, dynamics and form, freedom and destiny, and is still ambiguous. In *ST* 3 Tillich again analyses the ambiguities which confront man, this time in connection with the basic functions of life, namely self-integration, self-creativity, and self-transcendence.[11] These are the functions of human life which man expresses in morality, culture, and religion. In each of them the ambiguities and problems inherent in the self-world structure of being become apparent. Goodness, beauty, truth, holiness lie beyond man's grasp because he cannot bridge the gap between subject and object or overcome his estrangement from his essential being. What, then, can bring about for man the transcendent unity of life, union with his essential being and with God, unambiguous life? The answer that theology gives is the Spiritual Presence, i.e. 'the presence of the divine Spirit within creaturely life'.[12]

The Spiritual Presence was fully manifested in Jesus as the Christ:

> The divine Spirit was present in Jesus as the Christ without distortion. In him the New Being appeared as the criterion of all Spiritual experiences in past and future. Though subject to individual and social conditions his human spirit was entirely grasped by the Spiritual Presence; his spirit was 'possessed' by the divine Spirit, or, to use another figure, 'God was in him'. This makes him the Christ, the decisive embodiment of the New Being for historical mankind (*Systematic Theology*, vol. 3, p. 144).[13]

THE SPIRITUAL COMMUNITY

'Jesus, the Christ, is the keystone in the arch of Spiritual manifestations in history.'[14] His appearance is the central revelatory event. But revelation must be *received*, or there is no revelation:

> The Christ would not be the Christ without those who receive him as the Christ. He could not have brought the new reality without those who have accepted the new reality in him and from him (ibid., p. 149).

Two New Testament stories in particular illustrate the nature of the revelation of the Christ to those who have received him as such:

> The first one, which is most significant for the meaning of 'Christ', is also most significant for the relation of Christ to the Spiritual Community. It is the story of Peter's confession to Jesus that he is the Christ at Caesarea Philippi and Jesus' answer that the recognition of him as the Christ is a work of God; this recognition is the result not of an ordinary experience but of the impact of the Spiritual Presence. It is the Spirit grasping Peter that enables his spirit to recognize the Spirit in Jesus which makes him the Christ. This recognition is the basis of the Spiritual Community against which the demonic powers are powerless and which Peter and the other

disciples represent. Therefore we can say: As the Christ is not the Christ without those who receive him as the Christ, so the Spiritual Community is not spiritual unless it is founded on the New Being as it has appeared in the Christ (ibid., p. 150).

The second is the story of Pentecost and its immediate sequel (Acts 2–4) which reveal the ecstatic character[15] of the Spiritual Community, its grounding in a faith which had almost been destroyed by the crucifixion, its expression in love and service and its drive towards unity and universality.[16] Thus is constituted a community, grasped by the New Being, and responding to it, a community wherein the New Being may continue to manifest itself.

THE SPIRITUAL COMMUNITY IN ITS LATENT AND MANIFEST STAGES

The Spiritual Presence was present fully and without distortion in Jesus as the Christ. But throughout history mankind has been under the impact of the Spiritual Presence:

> Mankind is never left alone. The Spiritual Presence acts upon it in every moment and breaks into it in some great moments, which are the historical *kairoi* (ibid., p. 140).[17]

Wherever and whenever men have been open to the divine Spirit, there is the Church latent. The distinction between the Church latent and manifest is not to be confused with the classical distinction between the Church visible and invisible. Nor is it merely the temporal distinction between before and after Christ. Tillich is not simply repeating what many others have said, that there is a sense in which the Church existed before Christ. Rather, he is speaking of contemporary individuals and groups who have responded to the Spiritual Presence. He lists the communities of the world religions. 'Not even Communism', he says, 'could live if it were devoid of all elements of the Spiritual Community.'[18] In all these, and in many other religious and humanist movements 'there are elements of faith in the sense of being grasped by an ultimate concern, and there are elements of love in the sense of a transcendent reunion of the separated'.[19] But in so far as they have not yet accepted the New Being in Jesus as the Christ as the ultimate criterion of the Spiritual Presence, the Spiritual Community is still latent in them. The distinction, then, between the Church latent and manifest points to stages in the history of the Spiritual Community—before and after encounter with and acceptance of the New

Being in Christ. The Church latent and the Church manifest may and do exist contemporaneously:

> It is most important for the practice of the Christian ministry, especially in its missionary activities towards those both within and without the Christian culture, to consider pagans, humanists, and Jews as members of the latent Spiritual Community and not as complete strangers who are invited into the Spiritual Community from outside. This insight serves as a powerful weapon against ecclesiastical and hierarchical arrogance (ibid., p. 155).

The manifest Church is the Spiritual Community of those who have found themselves grasped by the Spiritual Presence of Jesus as the Christ, the one who has conquered existential estrangement, and whose lives express this central revelatory experience. In them is initiated a movement which Tillich describes as 'ecstatic', in which man's spirit is driven out of itself towards the overcoming of the ambiguities of the functions of life (morality, culture, and religion) and towards transcendent unity. Faith and love are the content of this ecstatic movement, being the marks of the Spirit which was supremely manifested in Jesus.[20] The faith and love of the Spiritual Community drive towards its unity and universality under the impact of the Spiritual Presence:

> The unity and universality of the Spiritual Community follow from its character as a community of faith and love. Its unity expresses the fact that the tension between the indefinite variety of the conditions of faith does not lead to a break with the faith of the community. The Spiritual Community can stand the diversities of psychological and sociological structures, of historical development, and of preferences as to symbols and devotional and doctrinal forms. This unity is not without tensions, but it is without break. It is fragmentary and anticipatory because of the limits of time and space, but it is unambiguous and, as such, the criterion for the unity of the religious groups, the churches of which the Spiritual Community is the invisible Spiritual essence (ibid., p. 156).

The Spiritual Presence drives towards universality:

> The immense diversity of beings with regard to sex, age, race, nation, tradition, and character—typological as well as individual—does not prevent their participation in the Spiritual Community. The figurative statement that all men are children of the same father, is not incorrect, but it has a hollow sound, because it suggests mere potentiality. The real question is whether, in spite of the existential estrangement of the children of God from God and from each other, participation in a transcendent union

is possible. This question is answered in the Spiritual Community and by the working of *agape* [love] as a manifestation of the Spirit in it (ibid., p. 157).

In the Spiritual Community, the Spiritual Presence, operating through faith and love, restores the unity of morality, culture, and religion. These functions of life, united in man's essential nature, have been separated under the conditions of existence. The Spiritual Community realizes their unity in that, when the Spirit is present, 'every act is an act of self-transcendence',[21] and the false separation between what is moral, cultural, and religious disappears: 'Culture is the form of religion, and religion the substance of culture',[22] and both are expressions of acceptance of the moral imperative which is implicit in 'the personal–communal character in which the New Being appears',[23] i.e. in the Spiritual Community itself.

Tillich constantly insists that the overcoming of ambiguities and the achievement of unity is only fragmentary, for while the churches participate in the unambiguous life of the Spiritual Community they also participate in the ambiguities of life in general. The life of the Spiritual Community is a process whose principles are an increasing awareness both of the ambiguities of life and of the power of the Spiritual Presence which can overcome them, increasing freedom, increasing relatedness to others, and increasing self-transcendence in the direction of the ultimate, i.e. participation in the holy.[24]

> How these principles will unite in a new type of life under the Spiritual Presence cannot be described before it happens, but elements of such a life can be seen in individuals and groups who anticipated what may possibly lie in the future (ibid., p. 231).

> The Christian life never reaches the stage of perfection—it always remains an up-and-down course—but in spite of its mutable character it contains a movement towards maturity, however fragmentary the mature state may be (ibid., p. 237).

THE SPIRITUAL COMMUNITY, THE CHURCH, AND THE CHURCHES

Tillich, as will have been noticed, prefers the term 'Spiritual Community' to Church. He explains:

> The term 'Spiritual Community' has been used to characterize sharply that element in the concept of the Church which is called the 'body of

Christ' by the New Testament and the 'church invisible or Spiritual' by the Reformation. In the previous discussion[25] this element has sometimes been called 'the invisible essence of the religious communities'. Such a statement implies that the Spiritual Community is not a group existing beside other groups but rather a power and a structure inherent and effective in such groups, that is, in religious communities. If they are consciously based on the appearance of the New Being in Jesus as the Christ, these groups are called churches. If they have other foundations they are called synagogues, temple congregations, mystery groups, monastic groups, cult groups, movements. In so far as they are determined by an ultimate concern, the Spiritual Community is effective in its hidden power and structures in all such groups. In the language of the New Testament, the manifestation of the Spiritual Community in the Christian church is described in the following way: the Church in New Testament Greek is *ecclesia*, the assembly of those who are called out of all nations by the *apostoloi*, the messengers of the Christ, to the congregation of the *eleutheroi*, those who have become free citizens of the 'Kingdom of the Heavens'. There is a 'church', an 'assembly of God' (or the Christ), in every town in which the message has been successful and a Christian *koinonia*, or communion, has come into being. But there is also the overall unity of these local assemblies in the Church universal, by virtue of which the particular groups become churches (local, provincial, national, or after the split of the Church universal, denominational). The Church universal, as well as the particular churches included in it, is seen in a double aspect as the 'body of Christ', on the one hand—a Spiritual reality—and as a social group of individual Christians on the other. In the first sense, they show all the characteristics which we have attributed to the Spiritual Community...; in the second sense, all the ambiguities of religion, culture, and morality that were already discussed in connection with the ambiguities of life in general are present (ibid., pp. 162–3).

Tillich does not, however, advocate giving up the word 'Church' to denote the body of Christ. He believes, however, that his own terminology avoids some of the confusion which has surrounded it in connection with the distinctions between Church and churches, and Church invisible and Church visible. The Spiritual Community, he explains, is not something existing beside the churches. It is their spiritual essence. It is not an ideal constructed out of the positive elements in the life of the churches; nor is it an assembly of spiritual beings, angels, saints, and the saved from all ages. Rather, the Spiritual Community is to be interpreted 'essentialistically': it is the essential, which gives power and direction to the existential churches and 'is the source of everything which makes them churches'.[26] In scriptural terms it is the New Creation.

The churches exist in a paradoxical manner since they participate both in the unambiguous life of the Spiritual Community, which is their essential being, and in the ambiguities of their historical existence. Their paradoxical character is evident when one considers how the credal marks of the Church can be applied to the churches. The churches are holy, united, and universal (catholic) because of the holiness, unity, and universality of their foundation. These marks can be attributed to the churches as they exist historically only with the addition of an 'in spite of'.[27]

The same must be said of the faith and love of the churches. The Spiritual Community is the community of faith and love. It is the dynamic essence which makes the churches communities of faith and love. But in the churches the ambiguities of religion are not eliminated. They are conquered 'in principle', which Tillich, in accordance with the strict meaning of the Latin *principium*, interprets as 'the power of beginning, which remains the controlling power in a whole process'.[28] The ambiguities are conquered in the life of churches only in so far as they embody the New Being. Faith and love have often failed in the churches and their members, but in so far as they are truly grasped by the Spiritual Presence, and constantly refer to the original revelatory event of Jesus as the Christ, they possess faith and love unambiguously even while they struggle against the failures of faith and lack of love within and between their particular communities. Nevertheless, the victories, under the conditions of finite existence, can only be fragmentary.

CHURCH AND WORLD: THE FUNCTIONS OF THE CHURCHES

For Tillich, then, the Spiritual Community or the Church is the community of those who have received the revelation of the New Being in Jesus as the Christ, and have been grasped by the divine Spirit which was present without distortion in Jesus. This is the essential nature of the Church, and what imparts its essential character to each of the particular existential communities (churches) which are consciously based on the New Being in Christ. This essential nature is necessarily expressed in a number of functions, which Tillich categorizes as constitutive, expanding, constructing, and relating.

1 **The constitutive functions of the churches**[29] are concerned with the reception and mediation of the message which constitutes the Church—the message of the New Being in Jesus as the Christ. Receiving and mediating must go on continuously. Tillich includes pastoral care and counselling, worship, prayer, and contemplation among the churches' constitutive functions.

The mediation of the message implies the preservation of tradition (or the message would be lost); it also entails the application of the message to every new situation, and therefore readiness for reformation. In this the churches experience the tension between 'conservative' and 'liberal'.

2 **The expanding functions of the churches**[30] are mission, education, and apologetics as they strive to enlarge the borders of the Spiritual Community. Here arises the question to what extent the culture of those to whom the message is addressed is relevant to the way in which the message is given. Tension is experienced between those who hold that the integrity of the message must be preserved by insulating it from the culture of human groups, and those who hold that its integrity is precisely manifested in its ability to speak to men in and through their culture.

3 **The constructing functions of the churches**[31] have to do with the building of the life of the churches under the influence of the Spiritual Presence. In this they clearly cannot insulate themselves from human culture:

> The church can never be without the functions of construction and, therefore, cannot forgo the use of cultural creations in all basic directions. Those who indulge in contrasts of the divine Spirit with the human spirit in terms of exclusiveness cannot avoid contradicting themselves: in the very act of expressing this rejection of any contact between cultural creativity and Spiritual creativity, they use the whole apparatus of man's cognitive mind, even if they do it by quoting biblical passages, for the words used in the Bible are creatures of man's cultural development. One can reject culture only by using it as a tool of such rejection. This is the inconsistency of ... the radical separation of the religious from the cultural sphere (ibid., pp. 196–7).

Tillich analyses the constructive functions into the aesthetic and cognitive (which belong to the realm of theory) and the communal and personal functions (which belong to the realm of practice). He discusses the use of art forms, painting, architecture, music, dance, and drama; the use of the discursive element of cognition in theology; the relation of the churches to social and political structures; and the relationship between asceticism, or Christian self-discipline, and humanity.

In the performance of all these constructive functions, the churches and individual Christians encounter dangers, tensions, and ambiguities. The questions must constantly be faced: 'How can the human spirit be prevented from replacing the impact of the Spiritual Presence by self-creative acts of its own? How can the life of the churches be prevented from falling under the sway of the profane element in the ambiguities of religion?'[32]

4   The relating functions of the churches[33] arise from the fact that the churches are sociological realities in continuous encounter with other social groups. Tillich discusses three ways in which this may happen. The first is silent penetration, 'the continuous radiation of the Spiritual essence of the churches into all groups of the society in which they live'.[34] But the churches must realize that the influence is mutual; they receive their forms from the surrounding society.

The second is the way of critical judgement, 'prophetic criticism of the negativities in ... society up to the point of martyrdom'.[35] Again, the churches must know that 'there is, on the part of society, a criticism directed towards the churches ... as justified as the churches' prophetic criticism of society. It is the criticism of "holy injustice" and "saintly inhumanity" within the churches and in their relation to the society in which they live.'[36]

The third way is that of political establishment. One task of church leaders is to gain from other social groups the acknowledgement of the right of the Church to exist and to exercise its functions. There are many ways in which this can be, and has in the past been, secured. But if churches have to act politically, they must do so in the name of the Spiritual Community, rejecting all means which contradict its spiritual character (force, false propaganda, trickery, the arousing of fanaticism):

> The character of the church as expression of the Spiritual Community must remain manifest. This is first endangered if the symbol of the royal office of the Christ and through him of the church, is understood as a theocratic–political system of totalitarian control over all realms of life. On the other hand, if the church is forced to assume the role of an obedient servant of the state, as if it were another department or agency,

this means the end of its royal office altogether and a humiliation of the church which is not the humility of the Crucified but the weakness of the disciples who fled the Cross (ibid., p. 215).

In all these functions the churches find themselves in paradoxical situations. They act in the name of the Spiritual Community which is founded on the New Being in Jesus as the Christ, but they inevitably act also as sociological groups subject to the ambiguities of life. Tillich holds strongly, however, that the churches cannot be separated from the world: that world into which the Church is sent 'is not simply not-church but has in itself elements of the Spiritual Community in its latency which work towards a theonomous culture'.[37] The world is open to the Spiritual Presence. 'The divine Spirit is not bound to the media it has created, the churches.'[38] The divine Spirit is present in all human culture, morality, and religion. Within the various cultures there arise prophetic individuals and groups who see the need of the union of the secular and the holy, and point towards man's ultimate concern. This creates the latent church. The function of the Spiritual Community which is the manifest church is, in the power of the Spiritual Presence, to overcome the ambiguities which inhere in all culture, morality, and religion, and, by love, which is the creation of the Spiritual Presence, to unite all life and being in transcendent unity. This transcendent unity has appeared in the New Being in Jesus as the Christ. It appears, although fragmentarily, wherever the divine Spirit creates the Spiritual Community.

THE CHURCH AND THE KINGDOM OF GOD

Tillich's ecclesiology is similarly developed in the course of his treatment of the Kingdom of God.[39] There are, he asserts, three main symbols for the theological answers to the questions raised by the ambiguities of life. These symbols of unambiguous life are: Spirit of God (or Spiritual Presence), Kingdom of God, and Eternal Life.[40] Of these, he says, Kingdom of God is the most inclusive symbol for salvation. It includes both the vision of the Hebrew prophets of this-worldly, inner-historical renewal, and the other-worldly, trans-historical reference which the later Jewish apocalyptists emphasized.[41] Moreover, 'the New Testament adds a new element to these visions: the inner-historical appearance of Jesus as the Christ and the foundation of the church in the midst of the ambiguities of history'.[42] The symbol, 'Kingdom of God', therefore has both an immanent and a transcendent reference, and may be said to include both the symbols of the Spiritual Presence and Eternal Life.

There can be no identification of the Church, still less of the churches, with the Kingdom of God. The churches, and the Spiritual Community itself in its historical dimension, are in a situation of finitude. The finite must not be elevated to infinite value and meaning. 'This self-elevating claim to ultimacy is the definition of the demonic.'[43] The claim of any church to have brought into being 'the ultimate towards which history runs',[44] or to be the Kingdom of God, is demonic. But the churches do represent the Kingdom of God, although this representation is as ambiguous as their embodiment of the Spiritual Community in that they both reveal and hide the holy. Despite this ambiguity, the churches remain churches:

> Just as man, the bearer of spirit, cannot cease to be such, so the churches, which represent the Kingdom of God in history, cannot forfeit this function even if they exercise it in contradiction to the Kingdom of God. Distorted spirit is still spirit; distorted holiness is still holiness (ibid., p. 375).

Tillich acknowledges here, as elsewhere, that in many places and times the churches have failed grievously.

In this section, Tillich again introduces[45] the distinction between the manifest and the latent Church. The manifest Church exists wherever there is successful struggle against demonization (i.e. the elevation of the finite to ultimate significance) and against profanization (i.e. contentment with a world and its affairs dissociated from the holy). This struggle is conducted in the consciousness of the power of the Spirit and of the reality of the New Being in Jesus as the Christ. It leads to reformation movements within the churches themselves, and gives them 'the right to consider themselves vehicles of the Kingdom of God'.[46] But the Spirit's presence and activity is not restricted to the manifest Church. The power of the Kingdom of God is expressed also, in a preparatory way, in those individuals and groups in which, despite the fact that they are outside the churches, elements of faith and love are discernible. This consideration calls the churches to humility.

In words which are as close to a definition of the Church as anything we find in Tillich, he declares that 'where there are churches confessing their foundation in the Christ as the central manifestation of the Kingdom of God in history, there the church is'.[47] The history of the churches, however, though they are never without some manifestations of the Kingdom of God, is not to be identified with the history of the Kingdom of God. Church history falsifies any such claim. The churches—all churches—in their historical existence, being subject to ambiguity, both reveal and hide saving history. They reveal it when they are faithful to the criterion of the New Being. They hide it in that they are confined to particular sections of mankind,[48] in their many contradictory interpretations of the saving event on which their history is based,[49] and the recurring profanization of the holy of which church history records so many examples. No more can be said than that the churches are the representatives of the Kingdom of God in history, and that in them the Kingdom struggles for victory. Victories are achieved, even though they are fragmentary.

When these victories occur, answers begin to appear to the questions which arise out of the threefold function of life, self-integration, self-creativity, and self-transcendence.[50] Where the Kingdom of God is manifested, there is a power which controls but does not obliterate individuality. The ambiguities of self-integration are conquered.[51] Where the Kingdom of God is manifested, there it is recognized that 'revolution is being built into tradition in such a way that, in spite of the tensions in every concrete situation and in relation to every particular problem, a creative solution in the direction of the ultimate aim of history is found'.[52] The ambiguities of self-creativity (the conflict between the old and the new, between tradition and change) are conquered. Where the Kingdom of God is manifested, concern for social transformation is not allowed to obscure the truth that salvation lies beyond history. Utopianism is inevitably the seed-bed of cynicism.[53] The Kingdom of God requires emphasis both on the horizontal line of active social transformation and the vertical line of salvation. It is the task of the churches as representatives of the Kingdom of God 'to keep alive the tension between the consciousness of presence and expectation of the coming'.[54] Thereby the ambiguities of self-transcendence are conquered.

All these answers to the ambiguities of the functions of life represent but partial and fragmentary conquests, since they are given through finite institutions within history. The final answer to man's existential questions is given at the end of history, in eternal life. Tillich concludes his system[55] with a discussion of eternal life as the exclusion of all that is negative in history and in man's life, and the raising of the positive into unity with God who is being-itself.

SOME COMMENTS ON TILLICH'S ECCLESIOLOGY

It is obvious that Tillich's ecclesiology departs considerably from traditional lines. It might be said that it provides an example of that reconciling of tradition and revolution which he has noted as a sign of the overcoming of the ambiguities of self-creativity. I note here briefly first the traditional elements, and then those which, if not altogether revolutionary, are new in relating ecclesiology to the situation, questions, and needs of contemporary man.

TRADITIONAL ELEMENTS

He is emphatic that the Church is the creation of the Holy Spirit who builds up the Spiritual Community on the foundation of Jesus Christ. The Spiritual Community is no man-made association of persons. This is completely in accord with N.T. teaching.

Certain elements of ecclesiology which have been stressed in Catholic and Protestant theology are taken up by Tillich who frequently insists on adherence to the 'Protestant principle' and the preservation of 'Catholic substance'.[56] By the former he means essentially the principle that man's salvation and all that relates to it is from God, 'the principle of justification by grace through faith'.[57] By Catholic substance he means 'the concrete embodiment of the Spiritual Presence',[58] and in particular the concept of the sacraments as powerful symbols which mediate the New Being in Jesus as the Christ.[59] In the Introduction to *ST* 3 Tillich writes:

> Although my system is very outspoken in its emphasis on 'the Protestant principle', it has not ignored the demand that the 'Catholic substance' be united with it, as the section on the church ... shows (ibid., p. 6).

Tillich has a wide-reaching doctrine of sacraments. He holds that the Spiritual Presence always manifests itself through word and sacrament: 'Reality is communicated either by the silent presence of the object as object or by the vocal self-expression of a subject to a subject.'[60] The sacraments of the Church are symbols grounded in the New Being which have inherent power to actualize and nourish the Spiritual Community. They are neither to be distorted into magical means of manipulating the divine (naive Catholicism) nor reduced to mere outward marks of faith (Zwinglianism). Moreover, there must be emphasis on the sacramental presence of the divine if a church is to represent the Kingdom of God in the struggle against profanization:

Strongly sacramental churches, such as the Greek Orthodox, have a profound understanding for the participation of life under all dimensions in the ultimate aim of history. The sacramental consecration of elements of all life shows the presence of the ultimately sublime in everything and points to the unity of everything in its creative ground and its final fulfilment. It is one of the shortcomings of the churches of the 'word', especially in their legalistic and exclusively personalistic form, that they exclude, along with the sacramental element, the universe outside man from consecration and fulfilment (ibid., p. 377).

While the details of Tillich's sacramental theology do not concern us here, it supports the contention that his ecclesiology is, despite some appearances to the contrary, 'built into tradition'.

NEW ELEMENTS

I turn to those elements which are, or have the appearance of being new. In accordance with his method of correlation, by which he seeks to show how revelation answers vital questions which are raised by man's existence, Tillich's ecclesiology is directly related to the contemporary situation of man in his world. He provides the groundwork for this by a searching analysis of man's situation in existence. His analysis of the functions of life reveals their inherent ambiguities, and raises the questions to which he believes the doctrines of the Spiritual Presence and the Spiritual Community provide the answers. He is not content with any academic definition of the Church, however theologically balanced. The Church is the gift of God in the world and for the world, and therefore must be seen by men to be relevant to the world's situation.

Tillich rejects triumphalism. 'The claim to have or to bring the ultimate towards which history runs'[61] by a church or by any group is demonic. Moreover, he insists constantly that the victories of the Spiritual Community over life's ambiguities, though real, are and must be fragmentary. Only at the end of history in eternal life are the ambiguities of life fully resolved, and the estrangement of man from his essential self, from others, and from God completely overcome.

The recognition of the tension between the imperfection of the Church and the holiness of its calling and purpose is, of course, not new. We have seen the problem faced, and attempts made to solve it by distinctions between the empirical Church and the heavenly, between the Church visible and invisible. But a triumphalism is often hidden beneath these distinctions: the claim that there does exist in history, in this or that group, the perfect Church of Christ, a Church of the impeccably orthodox, of the spiritual ones or the saints. What is fresh in Tillich's ecclesiology is his cogent presentation of the reasons why any such claim is, and must be false. The Spiritual Community manifests itself in the churches *under the conditions of finite existence.* That there is healing and victory over estrangement Tillich does not deny, but it is fragmentary and partial. He speaks of the churches as the representatives of the Kingdom of God,[62] but in history the Kingdom of God does not manifest itself as a static, structurally perfect entity, composed of perfect human beings. It is engaged in a struggle, and 'the struggle of the Kingdom of God in history is, above all, this struggle within the life of its own representatives, the churches'.[63] 'Struggle', 'conflict', 'fight' are words which Tillich frequently uses of the life of the Spiritual Community. Here on earth it is most truly the Church militant.

The distinction between the latent and manifest church also has the appearance of a new element in ecclesiology. It certainly breaks down the sharp distinction between Church and world which is characteristic of much traditional ecclesiology. Yet it is no more than an acknowledgement of what modern comparative study of religion has made plain to many students, namely that the non-Christian religions cannot be regarded as totally in error and lacking any sign of what Tillich calls the Spiritual Presence. This acknowledgement is implicit in the changed strategy of modern Christian mission. No longer does the Christian missionary hold that the religion and culture which he finds in his mission field must be demolished root and branch so that the Christian Church may be planted there (and all too often after a western model). He knows that the Spiritual Presence has been manifested there long before his arrival. He has the lengthier and more difficult task of helping a latent church respond anew to the Spiritual Presence and root itself in the New Being in Jesus as the Christ, in whom the Spiritual Presence is fully manifested.

Tillich included humanism among his examples of the latent church.[64] It is a striking witness to the increasing acceptance of something very close to his concept of the latent church that Bishop B. C. Butler, the Roman Catholic author of a somewhat conservative book entitled *The Idea of the Church,*[65] published in 1962, could nine years later publicly express the hope[66] for a wider scope not only for Christian ecumenism, but also for dialogue and co-operation between religious believers and non-believers, and in the European context could call upon Christians, Jews, and humanists to promote jointly the values which they share. It is a confession that the activity of the Holy Spirit is not restricted, despite St Augustine, to the confines of the Catholic Church.

It must not be supposed that Tillich advocates complacence in a state of things in which members of the manifest church are greatly outnumbered by those of the latent church. Receptive encounter with the New Being in Christ (repentance and faith) is the boundary point between the two. It is the work of the Spiritual Community to invite and help the latent community to engage in this encounter so that the Spiritual Presence may be the more widely experienced in love and unifying power.

24

The Ecclesiology of
Hans Küng

Hans Küng, of the Catholic Theological Faculty of the University of Tübingen, has written two major works on ecclesiology, *Structures of the Church*[1] and *The Church*.[2] In his Foreword to the latter Dr Küng says that *Structures* is to be understood as a *prolegomenon*. *Structures* was written after the announcement of Pope John XXIII convoking an ecumenical council (Vatican II).[3] The announcement was surprising because, both within and outside the Roman Catholic Church, it was widely assumed that the authority of the pope as defined in the First Vatican Council in 1870 rendered a council unnecessary. Küng sets out to suggest a theology of ecumenical councils, and to show how the Church's structures, the laity, ecclesiastical offices, and the Petrine office relate to councils.

The Church was published two years after the conclusion of Vatican II. In *Structures* Küng had outlined the theological re-examination and reforms which he hoped the Church would undertake. These, he recognized, were matters requiring time. But in the Preface to *The Church* he speaks of the Council as achieving 'a powerful breakthrough in terms of freedom, openness, and flexibility on behalf of the Catholic Church' and as 'evidence of a new lease of life breaking through after centuries of reserve and isolationism'.[4] He is convinced that the Church is on the right path. To be on the right path does not merely mean that it is adapting itself to the present, which would content some, nor that it is holding fast to the past, which would content others. Rather it means reform and renewal in accordance with its origins, 'the events which gave it life'. He now undertakes a systematic theology of the Church, based on biblical themes, 'so that the original Church may light the way once more for the Church of today'.[5] The two books together provide a thorough treatment of the doctrine of the Church which I shall here summarize under headings which Küng himself suggests: the Nature of the

Church; the Marks (or dimensions) of the Church; its Structures.

THE NATURE OF THE CHURCH

Throughout these two books Küng's preference for the N.T. concept of the Church as the people of God (though he by no means denies the theological value of the other biblical images), and his recognition that the idea of the Church as the *congregatio fidelium* (assembly of believers) is basic, constantly appear. 'In the history of theology', he writes, 'the Church as assembled community of the faithful has been too often neglected in favour of the Church as institution.'[6] This underlies the description of the Church (Küng would be chary of using the word 'definition') which he gives at the beginning of *Structures*. After an examination of the biblical use of the word *ekklesia*, during which he notes that the Latin *concilium* (council) has the same root meaning,[7] he declares that 'the Church is an ecumenical council by divine convocation'.[8]

> The Church presents and constantly renews herself as the council of believers convoked by God through Christ in the Spirit: in the proclamation of the Word as appointed by Christ through the apostolic office and in the celebration of the sacraments; in the profession of the common faith; in the exercise of an all-uniting love; in the hopeful expectation of the Second Coming of the Lord. The Church manifests herself most intensively during the act of worship, and in the common participation in the sacrament of the Eucharist (*Structures*, p. 15).

ESSENCE AND FORM

Küng believes that the old controversy about the visibility and invisibility of the Church is long out of date.[9] A real Church whose members are real people cannot possibly be invisible. There are, however, hidden and invisible aspects which it would be disastrous for the Church to neglect: the activity of the Spirit, the operation of grace, the inward response of faith. These are its vital elements. In truth, 'the one Church, in its essential nature and in its external forms alike, is always at once visible and invisible'.[10] The Church is 'first and foremost a happening, a fact, an historical event. The real essence of the real Church is expressed in historical form.'[11] That is to say, its essence *must* take historical form. Essence and form, though not to be separated, are nevertheless not identical. No form of the Church, even that of the N.T., embodies its essence perfectly and completely. The

essence of the Church, permanent but not immutable, is given in its
origins in the gospel of Christ. It is the gospel, and not the earliest
form of the Church, which is the criterion by which any subsequent
form of the Church is to be judged. It is mistaken, therefore, to advocate a return to the first century in an attempt to imitate the N.T.
community:

> The New Testament Church is not a model which we can follow slavishly
> without any regard to the lapse of time and our constantly changing situa-
> tion. ... On the other hand ... the New Testament Church ... beginning
> with its origins in Jesus Christ, is already the Church in the fullness of its
> nature, is therefore the original design; we cannot copy it today, but we
> can and must translate it into modern terms (*Church*, p. 24).

THE CHURCH AND THE KINGDOM (REIGN) OF GOD

Jesus' message was that 'the time is fulfilled, and the kingdom of God
is at hand; repent, and believe in the gospel' (Mark 1.15). By the reign
of God (Küng prefers to translate the Greek *basileia* by 'reign' rather
than 'kingdom' because of the misleading associations of the latter
word) Jesus 'means the eschatological, that is the fully realized, final,
and absolute reign of God at the end of time'[12] which he says is now at
hand. It is not to be brought about by man, but appears as a sovereign
act of God. It is not an earthly, religio-political theocracy, but is purely religious: God's rule, God's salvation offered to all men under the
one condition of repentance and belief in the gospel. Küng believes
that Jesus announced the reign of God both as something to come and
as something now present, Jesus himself and his work being the signs
that it has already begun. He agrees with Bultmann that 'the decisive
element of Jesus' message lies not in an imminent end, but in the
challenge to decide here and now for the reign of God'.[13] But the
futurist perspective of the biblical teaching about the kingdom is not to
be pushed aside. The reign of God will be perfected. Christian
existence, therefore, is in the interim period.

But what, Küng asks, has all this to do with a Church? Did Jesus
intend a Church at all? 'To the very last, despite all his lack of success,
Jesus addressed himself to *all* the ancient people of God.'[14] 'The
Gospels do not report any public announcement by Jesus of his intention to found a Church or a new Covenant or any programmatic call
to join a community of the elect.'[15] 'Not until Jesus is risen from the
dead do the first Christians speak of a "Church". The Church (and in

this sense the new people of God) is therefore a post-Easter phenomenon.'[16] But '*in the pre-Easter period*, Jesus, by his preaching and ministry, *laid the foundations* for the emergence of a post-resurrection Church'.[17] 'As soon as men gathered together in faith in the resurrection of the crucified Jesus of Nazareth and in expectation of the coming consummation of the reign of God and the return of the risen Christ in glory, the Church came into existence.'[18] The Church's origins, therefore, lie in the entire action of God in Christ, his birth, ministry, his calling of the disciples, his death, resurrection, and the sending of his Spirit to the witnesses of his resurrection.

The Church is neither to be identified with the Kingdom of God, nor dissociated from it. It is not the perfected Kingdom which is to come, but it is already under the reign of God which has begun; it 'lives and waits and makes its pilgrim journey under the reign of Christ, which is at the same time, in Christ, the beginning of the reign of God'.[19] It can be termed 'the fellowship of aspirants to the Kingdom of God'.[20] Its function is to *serve* the Kingdom of God. The same divine demands which Jesus preached under the heading 'the reign of God', the Church preaches under the heading 'Jesus the Lord'. The preaching of the reign of God as the decisive, future, and final act of God, as purely religious, as a saving event for sinners, and as demanding a radical decision now for God has become, Küng asserts, an ecclesiological imperative.

Throughout this section[21] Küng's abhorrence of ecclesiastical triumphalism, so often expressed in these two books, comes out clearly. The Church 'should not pretend to be an end in itself or appear to claim for itself the glory which rightly belongs to God. . . . It must not give the impression that the *Church* itself is the end and consummation of world history . . . that man exists for the Church, rather than the Church for mankind, and hence for the reign of God.'[22]

THE NEW TESTAMENT DOCTRINE OF THE CHURCH

1 THE PEOPLE OF GOD

We mentioned previously Küng's stress on the biblical concept of the people of God. This is, he says, 'the oldest and most fundamental concept underlying the self-interpretation of the *ekklesia*. Images such as those of the body of Christ, the temple and so on, are secondary.'[23] He supports this statement with a wealth of biblical evidence. Here another characteristic of Küng's ecclesiology appears—his opposition to clericalization in the Church.

The Church is always the whole people of God. Everyone belongs to the chosen race, the royal priesthood, the holy nation. 'This fundamental parity is much more important than the distinctions which exist in the people of God and which it would be foolish to deny.'[24] The word *laos* in the N.T. means the whole people of God, not 'the laity' in the sense of uneducated members incapable of holding office. Not before the third century did the distinction between 'clerics' and 'laymen' appear, a distinction which later led to the characterization and treatment of the 'laity' as second-class members.

2 THE CREATION OF THE SPIRIT

Küng examines thoroughly the biblical basis of this concept. The Spirit is the Spirit of God acting in Christ who 'opens up for the believer the way to the saving action of God in Christ'[25] and who creates the unity of the body of believers, imparting charisms (gifts) in great variety to all. 'The Church owes to the Spirit its origin, existence, and continued life, and in this sense the Church is a creation of the Spirit.'[26]

But the Church is not to be in any way identified with the Spirit. Those who would make such an identification fall into a triumphalism which ignores the fact that 'the real Church ... is not only a Church composed of people, but of sinful people'.[27] The Church is subordinate to the Spirit, and it must know that the Spirit works where and when he wills:

> The Spirit of God cannot be restricted in his operation by the Church; he is at work not only in the offices of the Church, but where he wills: in the whole people of God. He is at work not only in the 'holy city', but where he wills: in all the churches of the one Church. He is at work not only in the Catholic Church, but where he wills: in Christianity as a whole. And finally he is at work not only in Christianity, but where he wills: in the whole world (*Church*, p. 176).[28]

Küng sees that this poses certain questions for Catholic sacramental theology, which has been reluctant to recognize the validity of the sacraments of other churches. He suggests that, if the starting-point of Catholic judgements were the freedom of the Holy Spirit, this 'in nearly all cases would make a definite *negative* judgement impossible' (ibid., p. 178).

Citing 1 Corinthians 7.7, 12.7 and 1 Peter 4.10, he shows that the

N.T. speaks of the gifts of the Spirit as distributed to all believers, and not limited to the ordained: 'Each Christian has his *charism*. Each Christian is a charismatic.'[29] While the Pastoral Epistles speak of charisms given through the laying on of hands in ordination, the early and authentic letters of Paul, which have much to say about charisms, make no reference to ordination even though gifts of leadership, teaching, and preaching are included (1 Cor. 12.28). The charisms are not simply natural talents (though these may become charisms); they are calls to service. Any state of life or situation is for the Christian a potential charism. Küng regrets that Catholic ecclesiology has too often, until recently, been based on the Pastoral Epistles, and has neglected the charismatic structure of the whole Church which is so clearly stressed in the authentic Pauline epistles. As we shall see,[30] he holds that the development of ecclesiastical offices within the Church, to which the Pastoral Epistles and the Acts of the Apostles bear witness, was legitimate. But he is emphatic that there should be no neglect of 'the fundamental truth about the ordering of the Christian Church',

> namely that *all* members of the Church are inspired by the Spirit, *all* members of the Church have their charism, their special call and their personal ministry, and that pastoral ministries are not the only ones in the Church (ibid., p. 432).

In his view the emergence of a clerical class regarded as set over the 'laity' in a relationship of teacher to learner, director to passive recipient, has disastrously weakened and disrupted the Church.

3 THE BODY OF CHRIST

Küng provides a penetrating examination[31] of the biblical passages which relate to the 'body' concept, including those on baptism and the eucharist. He sees the concept 'body of Christ' as describing very fittingly the unique nature of the new people of God. The two concepts, people of God and body of Christ, are closely linked both in Paul's thinking and through their Jewish roots.[32] The meaning of the doctrine of the body of Christ is that Christ is present in the Church as the risen Lord. He is for the Church not only an event in the past—or in the future—but is present in its life and work. 'Christ is above all present and active in the *worship of the congregation* to which he called us in his Gospel, and into which we were taken up in baptism, in which we celebrate the Lord's Supper and from which we are sent again to our work of service in the world.'[33] Not that Christ is wholly contained in the Church. The N.T. references to the body and head, especially in Colossians and Ephesians 'are concerned not so much with the Church as the body, but with Christ as the head of the Church'[34] who gives it unity through his Spirit. Although he is continually present with his Church, Christ is its Lord.

It is misleading, therefore, to use language which implies the identity of the Church with Christ, such as to speak of the Church as 'a divine–human reality' or 'the extension of the incarnation'.[35] He adds a note which must disconcert not a few theologians, both Roman Catholic and others:

> To talk of the 'mystical body' of Christ is misleading, since the word is very often taken in the sense of what we nowadays understand by mysticism; this gives rise to a view of the Church as united with the divinity in a way that overlooks human creatureliness and sinfulness, and suggests a direct relationship with Christ, an identity with Christ, which is quite wrong.[36]

There is indeed a union between Christ and the Church, but it is one in which the personal differences between them are maintained. The Church remains the fellowship of believers *in Christ*. It is composed of sinful men: 'With good reason it says its *Confiteor* and repeats "Lord I am not worthy".'[37] Its growth is not an organic or automatic process. It takes place only in obedience to Christ, and when Christ through the activity of the Church in history penetrates the world, outwards through missions, or inwards through men of faith and love revealing the reign of God.

The claim that the Church as body of Christ is identified with Christ or possesses him wholly is triumphalism. It leads to the assumption that the Church is only responsible to itself: 'Its all too human directives are given out as the directives of Christ, human commandments are turned into divine commandments. Such a Church is a caricature of itself. Is there such a Church? ... Such a Church always exists, at least as a powerful temptation.'[38] Küng indeed recognizes that it is of this that the Catholic Church is often accused.[39] But as Christ is Head of the Church, so his word is over the Church: 'The teaching authority of the Church can never lie in its own first-hand teaching; it must always be derived from Christ and his word.'[40] Küng keeps this principle in clear view in his discussions of the Petrine office and papal infallibility.[41]

THE MARKS (DIMENSIONS) OF THE CHURCH

Both in *Structures* and *The Church* Küng devotes long sections to the credal 'marks' or 'notes' of the Church: one, holy, catholic, apostolic. These are not 'static labels'; he prefers to speak of them as dimensions which 'dynamically penetrate each other at every point'.[42] They are definitive, essential features of the Church, but all of them are only imperfectly realized on earth. They are divine gifts to the Church by virtue of its foundation in Christ, but they are also tasks to be carried out. The effectiveness of the Church's work in the world ('that the world may believe')

> depends entirely upon whether the Church presents her unity, catholicity, and apostolicity credibly. ... Credible here does not mean without any shadows; this is impossible in the Church composed of human beings and indeed sinful human beings. Credible does mean, however, that the light must be so bright and strong that darkness appears as something secondary, inessential, not as the authentic nature but as the dark flecks on the luminous essence of the Church during the time of pilgrimage (*Structures*, p. 63).

This is a passage which invites comparison with Barth's reminder that the Church exists 'within Adamic humanity', and with Tillich's insistence that in the situation of existence there can only be fragmentary and partial victories over estrangement.[43]

In his treatment of the four 'dimensions' Küng naturally covers ground which many theologians before him had traversed. I shall therefore note here only his own emphases and new contributions under each head.

One The Church's unity does not imply 'a centralized egalitarian or totalitarian monolith'.[44] Unity is not a synonym for uniformity. It has room for churches coexisting with different rites and forms of devotion, even with different theologies and styles of thought, different laws, customs, and administrative systems. Unity is broken when churches coexist without co-operation but in hostile confrontation. Divisions can arise from honest convictions and cannot always be described in terms of 'Church' and 'heresy'; they seem more like the breaking-up of the one great Church. Küng sees two major schisms of this kind, that between the western and eastern Churches, and that between the western Church and the Church of the Reformation. This is, he says, a state of things 'so abnormal, so contradictory, and so hopeless that it is easy to understand how ways have been sought to justify the unjustifiable'.[45] One such way is to place all emphasis upon an invisible, ideal Church; another is to assert that the divisions are divinely intended, and to be reconciled in the eschatological fulfilment; another (popular with Anglicans) is to regard the different churches as branches of the one Church; another is the claim that only one empirical church is identical with the Church of Christ, and that the others are no part of it. Küng is aware that the Roman Catholic Church has been accused of such 'pharisaical self-conceit, self-righteousness, and impenitence' but believes that 'although there are still some ambiguities, Vatican II largely clarified the attitude of the Catholic Church to the other Christian churches'.[46]

All these are evasions. There can be no justification for Church divisions, for they are sinful. 'The first step in healing the breach must be an admission of guilt and a plea for forgiveness addressed both to God, the Lord of the Church, and to our brothers.'[47] Küng formulates five theological principles for the ecumenical journey of all the churches.[48]

1   The recognition of the *existing* common ecclesiastical reality: one Lord, one Spirit, one Father, one gospel, one baptism, one Supper of the Lord.
2   Prayer: for deliverance from the evil of divisions; of churches for one another. Action: churches listening to and learning from one another; working together to witness to Christ before the world.
3   Discovery of the true nature of one's own church; attention to what F. D. Maurice[49] had called 'the positive principles' of other churches.
4   The rediscovery of truth. Churches must make sacrifices, but not that of truth. There are irreformable constants of truth given by God's revelation. The dogmas and articles in which they have been formulated are not irreformable. The constants have to be 'prised out of their historical setting' so that they can be understood more fully.
5   Acceptance of the gospel of Jesus Christ, taken as a whole, as the standard for unity. Reunion will come in sight by the conversion of all the churches to Christ.

Holy   The Church is not holy because its members make it so by their own moral endeavours. On the contrary, the Church is a 'communion of sinners', totally in need of justification and sanctification.

The Church is holy because it is called by God to be the 'communion of saints', and 'by virtue of the sanctifying Spirit who continually establishes and animates the Church anew, and preserves, illuminates, guides, and sanctifies'.[50] The Church is both a communion of sinners and a communion of saints. Holiness is at once God's gift to it, and a challenge, a dimension into the depths of which it must grow. Many theologians have interpreted the holiness of the Church in a similar way, but Küng brings the subject down to earth by the reminder[51] that the Holy Spirit is not the captive of the Church, and that until the Church is 'open to the Holy Spirit which bloweth where it listeth, within or without any institution'[52] its own holiness will not be credible, and by the statement that the Church's holiness is not credibly represented by magnificence, pomp, or splendour, but rather in making clear its purpose to serve the world in humility.

Catholic   After a discussion of the different senses in which the phrase 'Catholic Church' has been used, Küng affirms that originally and basically it means the whole, universal Church.[53] A local church, however, is properly called catholic in that it represents the entire Church in a particular place.

But spatial extension alone does not make a church catholic; nor do numerical quantity, cultural variety, and temporal continuity. A church possessing all these characteristics may yet have become unfaithful to its nature.

> It is an all-embracing identity which at bottom makes a Church catholic, the fact that despite all the constant and necessary changes of the times and of varying forms, and despite its blemishes and weaknesses, the Church in every place and in every age remains unchanged in its essence (*Church*, p. 302).

'Identity' here indicates no kind of 'ecclesiastical narcissism'. The Church does not exist for itself, but for mankind as a whole, the world. By its very origin and nature the Church must be and act with reference to the whole inhabited earth (Greek, *oikumene*). 'Ecumenical' and 'catholic' are closely related words.

Küng maintains that a manifold variety is as necessary to the Church's true catholicity as it is to its unity: 'The Church must show herself as the Church which respects all languages, traditions and spiritual experiences in the forms peculiar to each of the different nations.'[54] He counsels a realism about the unlikelihood of Asiatic and African peoples accepting a 'centrally directed Western, Latin, unified

Church', and recognizes that it is 'untenable theologically' for the Roman Catholic Church to demand that Orthodox and Protestant Christians who have experienced a development of autonomous Christianity for centuries should surrender their own sound Christian values.[55]

During his discussion of catholicity in *The Church* Küng deals with two questions which have long bedevilled Church relations. The first is the claim to be the one Church by that church which is commonly referred to by its own members and by others as 'the Catholic Church'.[56] The churches of the East and of the Reformation, however they explain their relationship with the Church of the Apostles, were once, directly or indirectly, linked with this so-called Catholic Church. Might not their relationship to it, he cautiously asks, be thought of as that between mother and daughters who, for what they sincerely believe to be good reasons, 'could no longer live with mother'. The analogy is worked out in an illuminating way, and Küng concludes that neither the Catholic Church nor the other churches will achieve the necessary unity and catholicity of the Church without 'working out' their relationship with one another and mutually making peace.

The second question relates to the dictum, 'No salvation outside the Church'.[57] Küng rejects the 'theological sleight of hand' which attempts to include within the Church non-Christians of upright life. An explicit belief in Christ is fundamental to the concept of the Church. Those who make no such profession and might not even wish to do so cannot be silently claimed as members. He would probably doubt the usefulness of Tillich's idea of 'the latent Church'.

Küng believes that the negative and exclusive formula was dubious from the beginning, is open to misunderstanding, and damaging to the Church's mission. He would prefer the positive formulation 'salvation inside the Church', which does not imply that there is no salvation outside. The whole world is in God's hand, and the Church can lay no exclusive claim to certainty of salvation.

Apostolic   The apostolicity of the Church is its possession of and faithfulness to the apostolic commission. The apostolic office is 'unique and unrepeatable',[58] for the apostles were the original witnesses to Christ and their preaching is the original, fundamental testimony to him. But the apostolic *commission* and task remain. There is still an apostolic ministry, and it is the Church, 'the whole Church, not just a few individuals',[59] which succeeds to it. The Church's real link with the apostles, its apostolicity, resides in its preservation of agreement with the witness of the apostles and of a vital continuity with their ministry. Moreover, 'to be itself, the Church must follow the apostles in continually recognizing and demonstrating that it has been sent out into the world'.[60]

Like the other three marks of the Church, apostolicity is not a static attribute, but a dimension which has constantly to be fulfilled anew in history. Küng dares to express the opinion[61] that agreement by the Christian churches on these four fundamental dimensions of the Church is not an impossible hope: not an agreement which would exclude differences in theological interpretation, but one which would overcome the divisions in the one holy, catholic, and apostolic Church.

THE EXTERNAL STRUCTURE OF THE CHURCH

Küng is well aware that disagreement about external structure and about the place of ecclesiastical office is a most—perhaps the most—cogent cause of the Church's continuing disunity. To these subjects he allots a great deal of space both in *Structures* and *The Church*.

THE LAITY[62]

The basic structure of the Church is its standing as the people called by God. Küng maintains that the doctrine of the universal priesthood of all believers is a fundamental truth of Catholic ecclesiology, and he regrets that so often, until recently, Catholic theology has treated ecclesiology as a hierarchology, as though ecclesiastical offices constituted the basic structure of the Church.[63] He notes that the N.T. nowhere speaks of the ordained minister of the gospel as a priest. Christ is the High Priest, who has 'fulfilled definitively the truth of the priestly idea',[64] and is the representative of mankind before God, the Mediator. But the N.T. does speak of all believers as 'a royal priesthood'.[65] Through Christ's universal priesthood all who believe in him have a priestly function. They have direct access to God; they are to offer sacrifices, not of atonement since as sinners they can add nothing to Christ's sufficient sacrifice, but of praise, thanksgiving, and above all the humble and penitent offering of themselves wholly to God; they are 'called to preach the gospel in the sense of their personal Christian witness, without being all called to preach in the narrow sense of the word or to be theologians';[66] they have an essential role in the administering of baptism, the Lord's Supper and forgiveness of sins; they have a mediatory function between the world and God by devoting themselves to their fellow-men in service and by praying for them. Does then every member of the Church have the right and responsibility to do all things in the Church? Is there need for any kind of ecclesiastical office?

ECCLESIASTICAL OFFICE

Martin Luther had interpreted the priesthood of all believers as meaning that any baptized person 'may claim that he has already been consecrated as a priest, bishop, or pope, although it is not seemly for any one person to exercise this authority arbitrarily',[67] and that the Christian community has the right to call and appoint office-bearers, and to depose them. Küng concedes that Luther believed the situation in his day presented an emergency in which there was no alternative to reformation without the bishops, and that he believed this with some reason: 'The Reformation would have taken a different turn if the bishops (and the pope) had taken a different, an *apostolic* attitude ... if they had espoused a serious Church reform.'[68] But he considers that Luther failed to provide a theological foundation for ecclesiastical office. He tended to regard it as little more than a matter of convenience, and to neglect the scriptural doctrine (1 Tim. 4.14; 2 Tim. 1.6) that in ordination a grace is bestowed and not only ratified. On the other hand he notes with approval Luther's great emphasis on vocation, and his later willingness to distinguish between induction into a pastoral charge, and ordination which does not have to be repeated. Küng reveals his own conviction when he asks whether spiritual and ecclesiastical office in the Church is not

> something that emanates from the apostolic attestation of Scripture, namely succession in the apostolic *office*? Not, of course, in an ecclesiastical office for the exercise of power, or in an office for self-glorification, but in an office of service, of service in the apostolic spirit for the maintenance, defence, and expansion of the apostolic faith and the apostolic confession? And yet an office that is not merely an ecclesiastical officialdom delegated by men, but an authority established and legitimatized from above within the royal and priestly community, as a

special authority derived from a grace-dispensing apostolic vocation, blessing and commission? (*Structures*, p. 107).

Küng insists that ecclesiastical office is essentially diaconal.[69] The word chosen in the N.T. to describe the place and function of the Church officer 'carried no overtones of authority, officialdom, rule, dignity, or power: the word *diakonia*, service'.[70] Commenting on the frequency of the word 'serve' and its synonyms in the recorded teaching of Jesus, he says: 'In contrast to all the concepts of office in existence at the time, Jesus chose and emphasized this new conception of service.'[71] The Church is a fellowship of gifts of the Spirit (charisms). Charisms are calls to service. This is the very basis of Christian discipleship. The whole Church has, therefore, both a charismatic and a diaconal structure, and those who have received the gift of office stand within this structure.

Küng gives close attention to the evidence of the N.T. about the development of ecclesiastical office in the Church.[72] The ministries of which the New Testament speaks are many and varied. Some are exercised publicly and regularly, others are more private and occasional. Some have endured, others have disappeared. All are based on charisms, gifts of the Spirit, recognized and used in the service of the community.

Küng notes again that in the Christian communities founded by Paul there were no formal ministerial appointments. Those responsible for the various ministries derived their authority from their charisms and their call, 'not from the community and not from the apostle, not even from their own decision'.[73] There were no presbyters, no monarchical episcopate, no ordination by laying on of hands,[74] even though Paul's lists of charisms include administrators and overseers (*episkopoi*).

The office of presbyter, or elder, originated in Jewish–Christian communities, as did ordination by laying on of hands, following Jewish tradition. Küng suggests[75] that the two types of ministry, one charismatic and the other more institutional, influenced one another, and began to interlock at the end of the Pauline period. For example, the titles 'presbyter' and *episkopos* came to be used interchangeably. Within a generation or two the Palestinian form of constitution obscured the Pauline, and in the Pastoral Epistles we see the beginning of the monarchical episcopate. Yet the apostle Paul would have resisted the suggestion that the churches he founded were lacking in any essential because they had no monarchical *episkopoi* and the laying on of hands was not practised.

Küng believes that the rise of the threefold ministry was justifiable, but regrets that it led to 'a loss of the general *charismatic structure* of the Church and ... the forgetting of the particular diaconal structure of *all* ministries'.[76] The later forms of ministry and Church order, which took on a canonical force, were the realization of certain possibilities among many, and should not be mistaken for dogmatic necessities.[77] Following a discussion in *Structures* which covers much the same ground, he is prepared to say that in the new situation of ecumenical encounter between the Catholic Church and other Christian bodies questions such as that of the recognition of other means of reaching ecclesiastical office than by the imposition of episcopal hands deserve thorough theological examination.[78] Other questions ripe for renewed study are the relationship between the offices and functions of the *episkopos*, the *presbyteros* and the *diakonos*, and the spiritual and ecclesiastical acts which may be performed by any Christian as one who participates in the priesthood of all believers.[79]

However such questions may be decided in his own Church, Küng is insistent that those who are ordained to the pastoral ministry are not 'a separate caste of consecrated priests, as they often are in primitive religions. ... In the Church of Jesus Christ, who is the only high priest and mediator, all the faithful are priests and clergy.'[80] This priesthood of all believers, however, does not exclude a particular ministry of pastors whose authority is not simply by delegation from the community: 'It is the glorified Lord who creates them through his gifts, encouraging each to make a contribution to the community through his ministry (Eph. 4.12).'[81]

ECCLESIASTICAL OFFICE AND APOSTOLIC SUCCESSION

Küng notes and welcomes the increasing attention being given to the doctrines of ecclesiastical office and episcopacy by the Reformed Churches. Of the important 'Declaration concerning the Apostolic Succession', published by the United Evangelical Church of Germany in 1957, he says that 'many ambiguities in Luther's theology of office ... were cleared up ... and *several Catholic desiderata were fulfilled*'.[82] Points on which the Catholic can agree with the Declaration are:[83]

(a) All believers are called to the royal priesthood.

(b) The office of the apostles precedes all other ministries. It is unique, but standard-setting.

(c) Ecclesiastical office, while it is to be distinguished from that of the apostles, continues their function of leadership. Holders of pastoral office are subordinate to Christ and constantly in need of the grace of the Holy Spirit. They are subject also to the apostles, as being bound by the authority of the apostles' witness. Their office excludes neither other special ministries nor the priesthood of all believers.

(d) The basic apostolic succession is that of the whole Church. It is manifested in the continuous process of baptizing and being baptized, in the transmission and reception of the faith, in the Church's worship and work.

(e) Within the apostolic succession of the Church there is a succession of office, entry into which 'occurs with the co-operation ... of the office-holders and the congregation'. The holder of pastoral office is not set in an exclusive position; he needs the co-operation of the priesthood of all believers which is itself an expression of the apostolic succession.

In the protest of the 'Declaration' against 'papalistic formalization of the succession' Küng sees misunderstanding of the Catholic doctrine. He defends the Catholic doctrine against the charge of mechanical formalism by the following points:[84] Apostolic succession is not an arbitrary human invention, but a work of the Spirit of Christ. The imposition of hands is its sacramental sign. Ordination is an *opus operatum* (a work worked) not of the ordaining minister, but of the Spirit:

> The power of ordination is not handed down on a horizontal level from the past, although in the temporal dimension the man who received his ordination from his predecessors in turn ordains his successor. Rather, the power of ordination is passed down in the vertical dimension, from the Spirit, transcending time and space (*Structures*, p. 166).

The consecration of a bishop is not the mechanical succession of an individual to a predecessor, but entrance into a community, the corporate body, or college of bishops which as a whole succeeds the college of the apostles. Apostolic succession does not contradict the Word of God, but serves it. The Word is not only to be read, but preached, and therefore needs a succession of preachers with a commission and continuity which goes back to the apostles. The doctrine of apostolic succession presupposes faith awakened by God's grace in the person to be ordained. Without this 'all that occurs is sacrilege'. The office bestowed imposes the obligation of faithfulness to the Lord, and service of the Church in an apostolic spirit. Such a doctrine, Küng maintains, is unjustly described as formalistic, mechanical, and dangerous.

At the close of a similar summary of the meaning of apostolic succession in *The Church*,[85] Küng writes:

> In the light of the Pauline or Gentile Christian view of the Church, other ways of entry into the pastorate and into the apostolic succession of the pastors must remain open. The other view of the Church, the presbyterial and episcopal view, which rightly became established in the Church in practice, must still be basically open to other and different possibilities, such as existed in the New Testament church (*Church*, p. 442).

In view of the theological and ecumenical implications of this question there is, he says, 'serious need for them to come under urgent discussion'.[86]

THE PAPACY

Both the books which we have considered include a discussion of the relationship of the papacy to the structure of the Church.[87] As we have seen, Küng has been able to note an increasingly positive attitude to episcopacy on the part of the Reformed churches. He is aware that there is no similar attitude towards the papacy. He attempts 'to present the Petrine office credibly',[88] and his treatment is explanatory and more patently apologetic. To summarize his main points:

a Christ founded the Church on the rock of the Petrine office. Küng adds in brackets 'and also the apostolic office'.[89]

b The Petrine office has the task of representing and guaranteeing unity, of strengthening faith, and of pastoral care.[90] It is a ministry, and only as such is it an authority in (not over) the Church.[91]

c Canon 218 gives to the pope 'supreme and juridical power over the universal Church', and Canon 1156 declares that 'the first See is under judgement of nobody'. The First Vatican Council in 1870 elaborated this papal status and authority in great detail. But Küng reminds us that this Council was interrupted by war before it could discuss the episcopate. There are, he maintains, limitations to papal authority both by natural and divine law.[92] Among these are the existence of the episcopate, and the orderly exercise of office by the bishops which the pope may not disturb; the *aim* of the pope's exercise of power, which must share the diaconal character of every ecclesiastical office; the *mode* of the papal exercise of power, which must be through the self-administration of individual churches with very rare interventions. Moreover, the Church has a legal defence against an unworthy pope through an ecumenical council.

d Canon 228 declares 'an ecumenical council holds supreme power over the universal Church'. This assertion can be supported from the Council of Constance, the binding character of whose decrees cannot be evaded.[93] That Council defines a distinct kind of superiority of ecumenical councils, namely their function as a 'control authority', not only for the emergency of the fifteenth century, but 'on the premise that a possible future pope might again lapse into heresy, schism, or the like'.[94] Küng suggests that the relationship of the supreme authority of the ecumenical council (Canon 228) to that of the pope (Canon 218) 'is not to be understood as a relationship of super-ordination and subordination, but as a reciprocal ministerial relationship in the service of the Church under the one and only Lord'.[95]

e Küng disagrees with Canon 222 which accords to the pope the exclusive right to convoke councils. He argues that this Canon does not base itself on a divine law. In times of crisis 'one could not dispute, *ex iure divino*, even the right of lay persons to convoke a council for the welfare of the Church',[96] granted that they have the support of the whole Church. Constantine and other emperors convoked councils, some of which are reckoned ecumenical, without consulting the popes, and even promulgated their decrees prior to papal confirmation.

f He welcomes certain ways in which Vatican II corrected and modified Vatican I's definition of the papacy.[97] The Petrine ministry is emphasized as a ministry, and not a dominion. The pope is referred to as 'the pastor of the whole Church' instead of 'the head of the Church'. Bishops are said to receive their full authority by episcopal consecration, and not by papal appointment, and pope and bishops together are to share a collegial responsibility for the government of the whole Church. The council also called for a reform of the centralized papal system by the setting-up of national and regional conferences, by representing the whole episcopate in Rome by a synod of bishops, and by making the Roman curia more international.

g Küng recognizes the stumbling-block which the doctrine of papal infallibility, defined by Vatican I, raises for the Reformed Churches. On the principle that no human formulation is ultimate, and that doctrine develops and should develop, provided that it is in keeping with revelation, and bearing in mind that 'dogmas are no more and no less than emergency measures which the Church was forced to adopt because of heresies',[98] he sees reason to suggest that the questions of the infallibility of the Church and of the pope merit further study in the light of criticism made since Vatican I, for example by Karl Barth.[99] He himself undertakes a contribution to such a study.[100] It is to be understood that a papal definition is not a new revelation, but an authoritative bearing of witness to the revelation which has occurred, 'not a divine word but only a human utterance about the Word of God'.[101] Vatican I defined limits to the pope's infallibility. It is operative only when he speaks as chief pastor and teacher (*ex cathedra*) and when he intends to define a matter of faith and morals; and his infallibility is that 'with which the divine Redeemer willed his Church to be endowed'. This phrase from the Vatican I definition must be given full weight. Papal infallibility is not separate from that of the Church. Vatican I's declaration that papal definitions do not depend on the *consensus* (agreement) of the Church does not mean that a pope can define a dogma *against* the *consensus* of the Church. This would incur the charge of schism, if not of heresy. He is under obligation to consult in order to obtain the *sensus* (mind) of the Church.[102] Küng puts these considerations forward to enable ecumenical discussion on the subject to proceed with fewer misunderstandings.

h Küng realizes, however, that many Christians call into question the very existence of the papacy. He frankly faces the theological and historical difficulties of this question. He expresses sorrow that the Petrine ministry has so often appeared to men to be a Petrine dominion. But he does not believe that the concept of the primacy is in opposition to Scripture. He sees in Pope John XXIII one who 'inaugurated a new epoch of hope for the whole of Christendom and for the Petrine ministry itself'.[103] He pleads for a voluntary renunciation of spiritual power on the part of the papacy, and 'a way back, or rather a way forward to the original idea of a primacy of service'[104] which serves the whole Church in evangelical humility, simplicity, and brotherliness, and which furthers evangelical freedom.[105]

In summary, for Hans Küng the Church is the people of God called into being by the Spirit of God through Christ, the community of those who believe in God through Christ, with whom Christ is present as their risen Lord. It is a worshipping and serving people; it is called to preserve and to perfect its essential marks of oneness, holiness, catholicity, and apostolicity. Its structures are: first and basically, the whole body of the faithful as a priestly community; second, the ecclesiastical offices in the succession of the apostles; and third, the Petrine office or papacy, succeeding to the Apostle Peter's position among the apostles. These three are not set apart from each other. They exist in a communion of reciprocal ministries, and have a common ministry to the world.

Postscript

Every book, if the author hopes for its publication, must come to an end. But every book which deals with a subject historically comes to an end which must be unsatisfying. In dealing with the past the writer has to omit much that is relevant in one way or another. He has to be selective, thus opening himself to the charge that his selection is prejudiced. Moreover, the end of an historical study has to be unsatisfactory, because, as the last sentence is written, history goes on, history which, as Tillich says, is characterized by 'the production of new and unique embodiments of meaning'.[1]

What is often described as the Church's first history book, the Acts of the Apostles of St Luke, ends in a way which many find abrupt. It concludes with the information that Paul spent two years in Rome, 'preaching the kingdom of God and teaching about the Lord Jesus Christ quite openly and unhindered'.

Readers down the centuries have regretted that Luke has told us nothing of the activities of the other apostles during the period in which the Acts concentrated on the story of Paul. So of this book it is possible to ask why no mention is made of the ecclesiology of such men as Karl Rahner, the most eminent of contemporary Roman Catholic theologians; of the studies of the biblical doctrine of the Church of the Anglican Lionel Thornton of the Community of the Resurrection; and of the missionary's viewpoint on ecclesiology of Lesslie Newbigin, formerly a bishop in the Church of South India.[2] The author is aware of many such gaps, and not only in his treatment of the twentieth century. He can only plead his inability to master all the relevant material, and the consideration of space.

Readers of the Acts have also regretted that Luke did not take his account a few years further. Writing, as most scholars assume, some twenty years after Paul's arrival in Rome, he must have been in a position to tell us more about the early history of the Church in Rome, of its growth and its struggles, of the persecution under the Emperor Nero in 64 when, according to tradition, the apostles Peter and Paul were martyred. It may be, as some suggest, that Luke's purpose was not so much to write a detailed history as to describe the passage of the gospel of Christ from Jerusalem to the capital of the ancient world, and that therefore he felt that his work had a satisfactory completeness.

I have attempted to bring my account of the ways in which Christians have understood the nature of the Church as close as possible to the date of publication. It has been seen how, in different ways, recent theologians have brought into prominence the image of the Church as servant—servant of the world, because servant of God and because this is God's world. This recovered insight must surely be retained. It needs to be deepened, for it is not yet fully recognized at what we now call 'the grass roots level', nor by many a Church leader, and still less by parish and congregational finance committees. Too often the unbiblical saying 'charity begins at home' is in mind, and it is forgotten that, according to the Scriptures, it is judgement which begins at the household of God (1 Pet. 4.17).

For the future, who can prophesy? There are signs that in many ways the future belongs to the Third World. Western industrialized nations have recently begun to realize that what they have been pleased to speak of as undeveloped nations can no longer be regarded as a source of cheap raw materials and labour in return for some paternalistic gestures. In many of these countries the Church has become indigenous, and in some of them is having to struggle for its very existence—the situation of the early Church. Perhaps we must now look to these Christians whose history, culturally, socially, economically, and politically, has differed greatly from that of those whose writings *de ecclesia* have been considered in this book, to help us to understand what God means his people, the body of Christ, and the communion of the Holy Spirit to be in the years which lie ahead of us.

Notes

CHAPTER 1

[1] Some have argued that it was written later, from Ephesus, on Paul's third missionary journey, but the earlier date of A.D. 50, from Athens, gains the widest acceptance.

[2] Each appears well over a hundred times. Hebrew has several other words with similar meanings, but these occur rarely. Both words are translated in the English versions by 'assembly', 'congregation', and less frequently by 'company' and 'council'.

[3] *Ēdhah* appears with great frequency in Exodus, Leviticus, Numbers, and Joshua. Occurrences in later books are rare.

[4] In these three instances *qāhāl* is the word used. The meanings of *qāhāl* and *ēdhah* are clearly set out by George Johnston, *The Doctrine of the Church in the New Testament* (Cambridge 1943), p. 36, n. 2 and p. 37, n. 2.

[5] See H. B. Swete, *Introduction to the Old Testament in Greek* (Cambridge 1902), p. 317; K. L. Schmidt, article 'Ekklesia', in G. Kittel, *Theological Dictionary of the New Testament,* vol iii (Grand Rapids, Michigan 1965), pp. 528–9.

[6] Swete, op. cit., p. 315.

[7] Schmidt, op. cit., p. 528. George Johnston in his article 'The Doctrine of the Church in the New Testament' in *Peake's Commentary on the Bible,* ed. M. Black and H. H. Rowley (London 1962) makes the new suggestion that the Hebrew *yahadh* (community or union) may lie behind the N.T. use of *ekklesia* in view of its frequent use in the Qumrân literature. In the 'Manual of Discipline', e.g., it is used 'for the Qumrân brotherhood or that community to which the Qumrân "camp" belonged. It is not distinct from Israel, but embodies the true Israel' (p. 719).

[8] Schmidt, op. cit., pp. 516–17.

[9] There are eight occurrences of *sunagoge* in Josephus, six of which refer to the synagogue building.

[10] Schmidt, op. cit., p. 517, suggests this as a reason why LXX translators preferred *ekklesia* as a translation for *qāhāl*.

[11] G. Johnston, op. cit., pp. 43–4.

[12] Cf. also Romans 16.5 and 1 Corinthians 16.19.

[13] See Schmidt, op. cit., p. 505.

[14] The singular *ekklesia* is a better manuscript reading than the plural which is reproduced in the Authorized (King James) Version.

[15] This is clear in the case of Luke, because of his frequent use of *ekklesia* in the Acts of the Apostles.

[16] Schmidt, op. cit., pp. 525–6. Schmidt argues (pp. 519–25) that Matthew 16.18 is an authentic saying of Jesus. He does not discuss the papal interpretation of the verse.

[17] See G. Johnston, op. cit., p. 49.

[18] Ibid., p. 58.

[19] See Schmidt, op. cit., p. 531, n. 92 for other suggestions which have been made.

CHAPTER 2

[1] The most complete discussion in English of the N.T. images of the Church is Paul S. Minear, *Images of the Church in the New Testament* (Philadelphia 1950). See also A. Richardson, *Introduction to the Theology of the New Testament* (London 1958), pp. 242–90.

[2] G. Johnston, op. cit., p. 43, n. 2.

[3] Cf. Paul's argument in the Epistle to the Romans, especially ch. 9.

[4] T. W. Manson, *The Teaching of Jesus* (Cambridge 1931). See ch. 9, the argument of which he sums up on pp. 234–6. Another influential book, published in the same year, E. C. Hoskyns and F. N. Davey, *The Riddle of the New Testament* (London 1931), likewise insists that the significance of the life and death of Jesus and the question of the origin of the Church are to be elucidated as do the Synoptic Gospels and the other N.T. books, i.e. in the context of the O.T. Scriptures. See especially ch. 4.

[5] Hoskyns and Davey, op. cit., pp. 82–4.

[6] G. Henton Davies, article 'Remnant', in A. Richardson, ed., *A Theological Word Book of the Bible* (London 1950), p. 191.

[7] Ibid.

[8] Note the references to numbers in Acts 1.15; 2.41, 47; 4.4; 6.1, 7.

[9] This German word, meaning 'salvation history', is used here in the sense of an interpretation of certain historical events as being specially significant of the working-out of a divine purpose for man's salvation.

[10] E. Best, *One Body in Christ* (London 1955), has a full exegetical discussion of these phrases.

[11] Ibid., p. 184.

[12] Note the 'all' of 1 Corinthians 15.22 (and cf. v. 28), and the 'for all men' of Romans 5.18.

[13] J. A. T. Robinson, *The Body* (London 1952), p. 9. The whole Introduction to this book (pp. 7–10) is illuminating on Paul's solidarity doctrine.

[14] E. Best, op. cit., pp. 98–101.

[15] Ibid., p. 184.

[16] Ephesians 1.3–10.

[17] Cf. G. Johnston, op. cit., p. 92: 'Whether or not the apostle Paul wrote (Ephesians), it offers nothing which is untrue to his thought.'

[18] For commentary on the passage see, e.g., E. Best, op. cit., pp. 139 ff: J. A. T. Robinson, op. cit., pp. 65 ff. Note the translations suggested in text and notes of the New English Bible.

[19] A. E. J. Rawlinson, 'Corpus Christi', in G. Bell and A. Deissmann, eds., *Mysterium Christi* (London 1930), pp. 223 ff.

[20] Note that the context of Paul's main discussion of the eucharist (1 Cor. 11.17–34) is a strong protest against the divisions, even schisms, of the Corinthian Christians which were manifest even in their gatherings for the Lord's Supper.

[21] G. Johnston, op. cit., pp. 98–9.

[22] The theme of Christ as the bridegroom of the Church is also found in John 3.27–30 and in several passages in Revelation, most clearly in 19.6–9; 21.2; 22.17.

[23] Consult 'holiness of the C.' in Index of Subjects, p. 248.

[24] R. J. McKelvey, *The New Temple* (Oxford 1969), provides a thorough examination of the many passages in which the temple theme is to be detected. See also E. Best, op. cit., ch. ix, 'The Building in Christ'.

[25] 1 Corinthians 14.12; 2 Corinthians 10.8; 12.19; 13.10.

[26] Most recently, R. J. McKelvey, op. cit., pp. 114, 195–204.

[27] E.g. J. Jeremias, article '*Akrogoniaios*', in G. Kittel, *Theological Dictionary of the New Testament*, vol. 1 (1964), pp. 792–3; E. Best, op. cit., pp. 165–6.

414

28 Op. cit., pp. 182–3.
29 G. Johnston, op. cit., p. 99.
30 Ibid., p. 74. Cf. Galatians 5.22–3; 2 Corinthians 6.16.
31 Matthew 18.21 ff; John 13.34; 1 Corinthians 1.10; Galatians 6.1 ff, 10; Philippians 2.1 ff; Hebrews 13.1 ff; 1 Peter 3.8 ff; 1 John 2.7 ff are a few of many instances.
32 Similarly the phrase 'love of God', also in 2 Corinthians 13.14, includes the idea both of God's love for us, and our love for God.
33 Cf. John 14.16–17, 26; 15.26; 16.7, 13.
34 G. Aulén, The Faith of the Christian Church (London 1954), pp. 329, 333.
35 G. Johnston, op. cit., p. 100.
36 Ibid., p. 101, n. 2.
37 J. A. T. Robinson, op. cit., p. 79.

CHAPTER 3

1 See below, pp. 69–71.
2 Smyrnaeans VIII, 2. English translation (E.T.) of the 'Apostolic Fathers' is from Kirsopp Lake, The Apostolic Fathers (London 1959).
3 The Martyrdom of Polycarp VIII.
4 E. T. of J. N. D. Kelly, Early Christian Doctrines (London 1958), p. 192.
5 There is no reason to doubt the early tradition which attaches the name of Clement to this Letter.
6 If this be doubted, compare Acts 20.17 (presbuteroi) with 20.28 (episkopoi); and in 1 Timothy note that in 3.5 it is the bishop (episkopos) who is said to have the care of God's Church, while in 5.17 it is the elders (presbuteroi) who rule. Chapter 3, which describes the qualifications and responsibilities of ministers, mentions bishops and deacons, but not presbyters. Clearly episkopos and presbuteros are alternative words for the same ministerial office.
7 'Monarchical' in this connection has no overtone of despotism. It simply describes the bishop as the one who has the authority to rule in a given Christian community.
8 The address of the letter is: 'The Church of God which sojourns in Rome to the Church of God which sojourns in Corinth'.
9 H. Bettenson, The Early Christian Fathers (Oxford 1956), p. 47, is surely right in denying that Clement intends an equation between High Priest, priests, and Levites and bishop, priests, and deacons.
10 Note the words 'with the consent of the whole Church' in 1 Clement XLIV, quoted above, p. 32. Cyprian of Carthage (see below, p. 71) constantly makes the same point. On the significance and history of the distinction between 'layman' and 'cleric', see Hans Küng, The Church (New York 1967), pp. 363–87.
11 The council certainly consisted of the presbyters. Ignatius does not make clear whether or not deacons and any non-officeholders were included.
12 Instances of this are very numerous, e.g. Eph. II, V, XX; Magn. IV, VI, XIII; Trall. II; Phil. VII; Smyrn. VIII; Polycarp VI.
13 Kirsopp Lake's translation is the ambiguous 'to refresh the bishop'. The Greek verb used literally means 'to lift up the soul'.
14 E.g. Justin Martyr, Apology LXVII; Hippolytus, The Apostolic Tradition I, 9.
15 The Greek texts have eis topon, 'in the place', but Syriac and Armenian versions suggest that the original Greek may have been eis tupon, 'as a type'. Cf. the excerpt from Trall..III which follows on p. 37.
16 Evidence is lacking that in Ignatius' day the office of bishop as he understood it existed outside Syria and Asia Minor.

[17] B. H. Streeter, *The Primitive Church* (London 1929). For a different estimate of Ignatius' motives, character, and temperament see Virginia Corwin, *St Ignatius and Christianity in Antioch* (New Haven, Connecticut 1960).

[18] 'Monepiscopacy', 'monepiscopate', 'monarchical episcopate' are all terms used of the form of Church government in which a single bishop exercises oversight (*episkope*) and is the centre of authority in a local Christian community.

[19] Discovered in the eighteenth century by Ludovico Muratori. It is a Latin translation of an eighth-century manuscript of a list of early Christian writings. Its Greek original is thought to date from the later second century.

[20] Examples, each however with its own emphasis, are Montanism, Novatianism, Donatism, and a number of medieval and post-Reformation sects.

[21] See p. 30 above.

[22] '|God| chose us in him |Jesus Christ| before the foundation of the world, that we should be holy and blameless before him.'

[23] See pp. 60 and 63 below.

[24] *Kathedra*, usually translated 'throne', does not necessarily mean an elaborate piece of furniture like the bishop's throne in medieval and modern cathedral churches. It does, however, denote a seat of authority. The teacher in ancient Greek schools lectured sitting on a *kathedra*. Its adoption in Christian usage was probably in order to emphasize the bishop's teaching authority. The throne, therefore, is a symbol of the bishop's responsibility to teach the pure doctrine of Christ rather than of exaltation over other members of the Church. Those churches where the bishop's *kathedra* was placed were later known as cathedral churches. Note that the English term 'episcopal see (seat)' refers primarily to the bishop's throne.

[25] Justin came to Rome from Ephesus where, if Ignatius' teaching was still heeded, the *episkopos* or his delegate was the celebrant of the eucharist.

[26] See below, pp. 44–6.

[27] See below, p. 56.

[28] But Harnack dates it in the third century.

[29] *Adversus Haereses* was written in Greek, but apart from fragments it has come down to us in a Latin translation.

[30] Irenaeus' work is one of our chief sources of information about the details of Gnostic systems.

[31] The Gnostic presupposition that the Supreme Being can have no contact with the physical world precludes, however, any doctrine of incarnation.

[32] The E.T. of passages from Irenaeus is from A. Roberts and J. Donaldson eds., The Ante-Nicene Christian Library (ANCL), vol. 1 (Edinburgh 1864 ff); published also in New York under the title *The Ante-Nicene Fathers*.

[33] Tertullian, *De Praescriptione Haereticorum* 13.

[34] Origen, *De Principiis*, Preface.

[35] The significance of this passage as an early acknowledgement of the primacy of the bishop of Rome does not concern us here. For a brief discussion, see J. N. D. Kelly, op. cit., pp. 192–3.

[36] See above, pp. 31–3.

[37] See below, p. 88.

[38] Jerome, *On the Epistle to Titus* I, 6–7. The passage is quoted below on p. 93.

CHAPTER 4

[1] *Apologeticus* xxxix.

[2] *Contra Marcionem* IV, xi; *De Pudicitia* I.

[3] *Ad Martyres* I.

[4] The E.T. of passages from Tertullian is from The Ante-Nicene Christian Library, vols. iii and iv.

[5] *De Praescriptione* xx.

[6] Ibid. xxxvi.

[7] Tertullian also gives a shorter version which he attributes to the Church of Rome in *De Virginibus Velandis* i.

[8] See p. 44 above.

[9] *Early Christian Doctrines*, p. 41.

[10] Marcion, who taught in Rome c. 140–50, e.g. rejected the whole of the O.T., and retained only a reduced version of Luke's Gospel and ten epistles of Paul in his canon of Scripture.

[11] Note, e.g., the many scriptural references in *De Carne Christi* where Tertullian is defending the Church's belief in both the divinity and the humanity of Christ.

[12] Kelly, op. cit., p. 41.

[13] Tertullian, *De Fuga* ix.

[14] *De Anima* ix.

[15] *Adversus Praxean* xxx.

[16] *De Pudicitia* xxi. This short work begins with a trenchant condemnation of a bishop who had recently admitted to communion some who had committed adultery. It is usually assumed that the bishop was Zephyrinus of Rome (d. 217) or his successor Callistus. But it may have been an African bishop.

[17] I.e. 'gathers together'.

[18] R. C. Moberly, *Ministerial Priesthood* (New York 1916), pp. 48 ff.

[19] *Adversus Marcionem* iv, v.

[20] *De Exhortatione Castitatis* vii. The ambiguity in Tertullian's later (Montanist) attitude to the episcopal system is discussed by R. F. Evans in a chapter on Tertullian in his *One and Holy* (London 1972), pp. 27–35. He tends to agree with Moberly: 'The motto "No bishop, no Church" is at the farthest point removed from Tertullian's late thought' (p. 33).

[21] The E.T. is that of Gregory Dix in *The Apostolic Tradition of St Hippolytus* (London 1937). Words in brackets are either introduced by Dix to assist the sense in English, or are judged by him not to have belonged to the original Greek (which is not extant), although having support in the versions.

[22] I hold that it is most probable that in the early decades in many places the council of presbyters ordained one of their number to the office of bishop. No principle of apostolic succession is thereby contradicted, provided that apostles or apostolic men appointed these collegial bodies of presbyters and authorized them so to act. See C. Gore, *The Church and the Ministry* (London 1893), pp. 73–6. But evidence is lacking about any such explicit commission from the apostles to the presbyteral colleges.

[23] See p. 34 above, and p. 75, n. 9.

[24] *Summus sacerdos* and *sacerdos* are the Latin for the Greek *archiereus* and *hiereus*, High Priest and priest. In the N.T. these terms are never used of a Christian minister. Christ is the High Priest; the Church is a priestly community, a kingdom of priests (Rev. 1.6).

[25] Note the words 'propitiate Thy countenance' in the passage quoted above, p. 57.

[26] See, e.g., Romans 3.25; 1 John 2.2; 4.10, and the whole argument of Hebrews, 7–10.

[27] E.g. *summus sacerdos* (High Priest), *sacerdos* (priest), *sacerdotalis* (priestly), *sacerdotium* (priesthood).

[28] From Justin Martyr we learn that the deacon also had liturgical functions which included the distribution of the eucharist to those present, and those absent through age or infirmity. In his function of distributing the Church's alms to the needy, the deacon was closely attached to the bishop.

[29] *Protreptikos* (An Exhortation to the Greeks); *Paidagogos* (The Tutor); and *Stromateis* (Miscellanies).

[30] *Paidagogos* I, vi. The E.T. of passages from Clement is from ANCL, vol. ii.

[31] The Greek phrase is *he kuriōs ekklesia*, which can be translated 'that which is properly the Church'.

[32] E.T. of Origen is my own except where otherwise stated.

[33] See p. 44 above.

[34] *Homilies on Leviticus* VI, 3.

[35] *Commentary on Matthew* XII, 14.

[36] *Contra Celsum* III, 51. Cf. also *Hom. on Numbers* XX, 4.

[37] *Hom. on Leviticus* IX, 1.

[38] Ibid. IX, 9.

[39] Cf. also *Hom. on Ezekiel* I, 11.

[40] *Hom. on Joshua* XXI, 1.

[41] *Hom. on Ezekiel* VI, 5; *Hom. on Numbers* III, 1; *Comm. on John* VII, 17.

[42] *On Prayer* XX, 1; commenting on Ephesians 5·27.

[43] The theme is constant in Origen's mystical treatment of the Song of Solomon in his *Commentary on the Song of Songs*; e.g. in I, 1.

[44] *Hom. on Exodus* IX, 3.

[45] E.T. of R. P. Lawson in *Origen: The Song of Songs, Commentary and Homilies*, vol. 26 in the 'Ancient Christian Writers' series (London; and Westminster, Maryland 1957).

[46] Origen places Adam among the prophets in view of Genesis 2.24, taken as a prophecy concerning the Church.

[47] See below, pp. 88–9.

[48] *Hom. on Joshua* III, 5.

[49] *Hom. on Jeremiah* XX, 3. It is a passage in which he interprets the scarlet cord in Rahab's window (Josh. 2) allegorically as the redemptive blood of Christ, and her house as the place of salvation.

[50] *Hom. on Psalm 36* II, 1.

[51] *De Principiis* I, vi. 1–2.

CHAPTER 5

[1] See R. F. Evans, op. cit., p. 64.

[2] See above, pp. 55–6.

[3] Cyprian, *Epistles* L, 3 (LIII]. The numbering of Cyprian's *Epistles* followed here is that in ANCL, vol. v. Many edns use the numbering of the Oxford edn of 1682: I place this in square brackets when it differs from ANCL.

[4] The full title is *De Catholicae Ecclesiae Unitate*, 'On the Unity of the Catholic Church'. E.T. of passages from Cyprian is that of Ernest Wallace in ANCL, vol. v.

[5] *Epistles* LXXV, 3 (LXIX].

[6] This passage strongly implies that Peter and the other apostles were the first bishops. 'Cyprian took a crucial step in the history of thought about the episcopate: the Apostles themselves were the first bishops of the Church' (R. F. Evans, op. cit., p. 49). Cf. also *Epp.* LXIV, 3 [III]; LXVIII, 4 [LXCI]; and LXXIV, 16 (LXXV].

[7] Cyprian frequently speaks of bishops as *sacerdotes*, a word which he also uses to denote the presbyters. The context usually makes clear what the word signifies.

[8] *Ep.* LXXII, 21 [LXXIII].

[9] *Ep.* LXXIII, 8 (LXXIV).

[10] *Ep.* LXXI [LXXII].

[11] Some later sects of the 'Holiness' type have not observed it. And it is to be noted

that both Novationists and the Donatists of the fourth century rebaptized their 'converts'.

[12] 'On the Unity of the Catholic Church', c. 251, referred to hereafter as *De Unitate.*

[13] *De Unitate* 3.

[14] Another version of this section of *De Unitate* is extant, usually known as the Papal or Primacy Text. See below, p. 70.

[15] Ibid. 5.

[16] E.g. in *Ep.* LI, 21 [LV]; LXVIII, 8 [LXVI], quoted above, p. 000.

[17] Kelly, op. cit., p. 205.

[18] R. H. Bettenson, op. cit., p. 363.

[19] *Ep.* LIV, 5 [LIX).

[20] *Ep.* LXVIII, 1 [LXVI].

[21] *Ep.* LXVII, 3.

[22] See above, p. 57.

[23] The English word 'priest' (French *prêtre*, German *priester*) derives from the Greek *presbyteros*, and in itself has no sacerdotal connotation. As the presbyter came rapidly to be regarded as having the right to celebrate the eucharist in virtue of his ordination, and not solely by delegation from the bishop, we find the word *sacerdos* increasingly used of the presbyter.

[24] *De Unitate* 5.

[25] Ibid. 6.

[26] Ibid.

[27] E.g. by those who urge that divided Christendom should be seen as a state of schism *within* the Church, and that the notion that among the historic churches there is any one which is the true Church in relation to which all others are in schism should be abandoned. See the last paragraphs of Oliver C. Quick, *Doctrines of the Creed* (London 1963).

[28] See below, pp. 87.

CHAPTER 6

[1] Diocletian (Emperor, 284–305) created the administrative structure of the empire which Constantine inherited. The empire was divided into twelve dioceses (Greek *dioikesis*) or 'exarchies' (Greek *exarchia*). Each diocese consisted of a number of provinces or eparchies (Greek *eparchia*). The smallest, Britain, had four and the largest, the East (*Oriens*) had sixteen.

[2] Although ecclesiastical districts coincided closely with civil boundaries, there was no such close correspondence in nomenclature. This is a somewhat confusing matter since terms were often used interchangeably. Generally speaking, in the East *dioikesis* described the area of jurisdiction of a metropolitan bishop, and 'eparchy' or *paroikia* that of other bishops. In the West the area of a bishop was denoted either by *dioecesis* or by *parochia* (Latinizations of *dioikesis* and *paroikia*). Much later *paroikia* and *parochia* came to be used of a smaller unit, the 'parish' of today.

[3] Pontus and Asia comprised the northern and western parts of Asia Minor.

[4] There are twenty-three Lectures. The last five were delivered on the days immediately following the Easter baptism.

[5] E.T. of Cyril of Jerusalem from The Nicene and Post-Nicene Fathers (NPNF), 2nd ser., vol. 7, ed. P. Schaff and H. Wace (New York; London 1894).

[6] See above, pp. 13–17.

[7] *Cat.* XIX, 1.

[8] Ibid. XX, 3.

[9] From the Greek *chrisma*, consecrated oil. *Christos* (Christ) literally means 'the anointed one'.

[10] Ibid. XXI, 1.
[11] Ibid. XXI, 2.
[12] Ibid. XXI, 5.
[13] Ibid. XXII, 1.
[14] Athanasius, *De Incarnatione* 54.
[15] Gregory of Nyssa, *Oratio Catechetica* 25 ('The Great Catechism').
[16] *In illud 'Tunc Ipse'*, a short treatise which expounds 1 Corinthians 15.28. Greek text in *PG*, vol. 44, column 1317.
[17] The Greek *musterion*, mystery, is also the Greek word for 'sacrament'. The reference here is doubtless both to the mystery of the incarnation and to the eucharist.
[18] Hilary, *De Trinitate* VIII, 7. E.T. of passages from Hilary are from NPNF, 2nd ser., vol. ix.
[19] The 'gradation and sequence' is 'you' (Christians), I (Christ), and the Father. Hilary's point seems to be that a 'unity of will' or mutual agreement is an arrangement between equals. The unity of the Church is not of that kind; it is given to the Church by God through Christ in virtue of Christ's participation in the nature of God and the Christian's participation in the nature of Christ who took flesh. Hence it is a union of natures, or a 'natural unity'. But Hilary would not deny that it may also be said to be supernatural, since it comes by the grace of God.
[20] Ibid. VIII, 7.
[21] From the Latin *trado*, to hand over. The English 'traitor' is derived from *traditor*.
[22] J. N. D. Kelly, op. cit., p. 411.
[23] See above, p. 68.
[24] E.g. Thomas Aquinas, *De Articulis Fidei et Sacramentis Ecclesiae* 2.
[25] The passages in which Optatus refers to Peter, and Peter's chair (*De Schism. Donat.* I, 10; II, 2; VII, 3) have sometimes been supposed to support the idea of papal supremacy. Optatus' argument, following Cyprian, is that Christ provided for the unity of the Church by giving first to Peter authority which was later to be communicated to all the apostles. The see of Rome, whose first bishop was Peter, is then to be regarded as the centre of unity, and it is a schismatic act to set up a chair (or see) in opposition to it. The passages support the idea of the primacy of the see of Rome, but certainly not the later claims for papal supremacy. J. N. D. Kelly (op. cit., p. 419) says 'we should note that he laid almost equal stress on the desirability of communion with the Oriental Churches' (*De Schism. Donat.* II, 6; VI, 3). The text of Optatus' work may be found in *Corpus Scriptorum Ecclesiasticorum Latinorum,* vol. xxvi (Prague; Vienna; Leipzig 1893).

CHAPTER 7

[1] Hippo Regius was about 100 miles west of Carthage on the coast of modern Algeria.
[2] *Sermon* 341.
[3] E.g., ibid. 341.10.
[4] *Homilies on 1 John* VI, 10.
[5] *Sermon* 341.9.
[6] See Yves Congar, *L'Eglise de Saint Augustin à l'époque moderne* (Paris 1970), p. 12; S. J. Grabowski *The Church: an Introduction to the Theology of St Augustine* (London; St Louis, Missouri 1957), pp. 18–19; J. N. D. Kelly, op. cit., p. 413.
[7] Early liturgists insist that at the conclusion of the eucharistic prayer the 'amen' should be unanimously and audibly said. See Justin Martyr, *Apology* 65, 67.
[8] E.T. of passages from St Augustine is from The Nicene and Post-Nicene Fathers (NPNF), 1st ser., ed. P. Schaff (New York 1886–9) where available. Elsewhere it is the author's translation.

[9] *Sermon* 267.4.

[10] See *On the Trinity* VI, 7; XV, 29, 38.

[11] The reference to the Spirit's gift of languages (Acts 2.4 ff) is directed against the Donatists, whose sect was confined to North Africa and therefore to its languages.

[12] *On Baptism* IV, 17 (25).

[13] Cyprian, *De Unitate Ecclesiae* 7. Cyprian's language, however, is not consistent. In the same passage he speaks of the Church being rent and divided.

[14] E.g. in *Letters* XLIII, 21.

[15] Acceptance of the notion that there may be schisms *within* the Church has been urged as a promising approach to modern problems of Church unity, e.g. by O. C. Quick, *Doctrines of the Creed*, op. cit., pp. 338–9; S. L. Greenslade, *Schism in the Early Church* (London 1953), pp. 212 ff; B. C. Butler in *The Idea of the Church* (London 1962) reacts against the suggestion.

[16] *On Baptism* VI, 1. The distinction is usually spoken of as that between validity and efficacy.

[17] See above p. 82.

[18] See above, pp. 59–60 and 62–3.

[19] *On Baptism* V, 27 (38).

[20] Ibid.

[21] Op. cit., p. 417.

[22] *Letters* XLIX, 3.

[23] *Expositions on the Psalms* LVI, 13; *Contra Faustum* XXVIII, 2; *Letters* XCIII, 7.23.

[24] *Expositions on the Psalms* LVI, 1.

[25] See Yves Congar, op. cit., p. 12.

[26] See H. R. T. Brandreth, *Episcopi Vagantes* (London 1947).

[27] *Against Petilian* III, 10.

[28] *On Baptism* I, 10 (13) to 17 (26).

[29] Ibid. I, 15 (23).

[30] Ibid. I, 10 (14).

[31] Ibid. I, 17 (26).

[32] See, e.g., 'Dogmatic Constitution on the Church', 64, in *The Documents of Vatican II*, ed. W. M. Abbott (New York 1966), pp. 92–3.

[33] As is recognized in 'The Decree on the Ministry and Life of Priests', ibid., p. 546.

[34] E.g. *Sermons* 191, 2–3; 192, 2; *On Virginity* VI, 6.

[35] *De Civ. Dei* XIV, 28.

[36] Augustine makes the identification also in *De Civ. Dei* XIII, 16.

[37] S. J. Grabowski, op. cit., pp. 532–7, gives a full account of these.

[38] *De Civ. Dei* XI, 9.

[39] *Encheiridion* LXVI.

[40] Ibid.

[41] R. W. Battenhouse in *A Companion to the Study of St Augustine*, ed. Battenhouse (New York; Oxford 1955), p. 54.

[42] Cf. *Epistle* CXLVI, 1 (Letter to Evangelus): 'What, apart from ordaining, does a bishop do which a presbyter does not do?'

[43] Acts 20.17, 28; Philippians 1.2.

[44] The evidence is set out by W. Telfer, 'Episcopal Succession in Egypt', in *The Journal of Ecclesiastical History*, vol. 3, no. 1, April 1952.

CHAPTER 8

[1] See above, pp. 45, 70–1, 75, 83, 94

[2] Op. cit., pp. 419–20.

[3] The exegesis on which this statement is based is tenuous.

[4] Migne, *Patrologia Latina* (hereafter cited as *PL*), vol. 54, 671.

[5] *PL* 59, 42.

[6] R. C. Petry, *A History of the Christian Church* (Englewood Cliffs, New Jersey 1962), p. 181.

[7] R. W. Southern, *Western Society and the Church in the Middle Ages* (Harmondsworth 1970), p. 94.

[8] Yves Congar, op. cit., pp. 47–8.

[9] See above, p. 98.

[10] Einhard, *Vita Karoli Magni* 24. E.T. in A. J. Grant, *Early Lives of Charlemagne* (London 1905).

[11] R. W. Southern, op. cit., p. 92.

[12] Ibid., p. 93.

[13] See above, p. 41.

[14] Petry, op. cit., pp. 221–30 provides material for such a debate.

[15] *PL* 117, 564.

[16] See above, pp. 69–70.

[17] See Congar, op. cit., pp. 58–60, 65–6.

[18] Ibid., p. 65.

[19] The works of Hincmar are contained in *PL* 125 and 126.

[20] Congar, op. cit., p. 57.

[21] Florus, *Capitula*, *PL* 119, 421c.

[22] John VIII, *Epistles* 5. Its authorship is doubtful, though of this period.

[23] See below, pp. 144–5.

[24] Southern, op. cit., p. 100.

[25] Congar, op. cit., p. 97.

[26] O. J. Thatcher and E. H. McNeal, *A Source Book for Medieval History* (New York 1905) gives the full text in E.T., pp. 136–8.

[27] Ibid., p. 156.

[28] Liemar of Bremen, in a letter written in 1075.

[29] Thatcher and McNeal, op. cit., pp. 153–5.

[30] E.g. Ivo of Chartres (d. 1116).

[31] See above, p. 98.

[32] Congar, op. cit., pp. 116–18.

[33] Canticle xxix, 7 (*PL* 183, 932).

[34] *De Consideratione* iv, 3, 6 (*PL* 182, 776). Bernard addressed the five books of *De Consideratione*, 'On Meditation' and the ascetic life, to Pope Eugenius III.

[35] Ibid. i, 1–2 (*PL* 182, 727–31).

[36] See above, p. 98.

[37] *De Consideratione* iii, 4, 14 (*PL* 182, 766–7).

[38] Canticle lxxxiii, 4 (*PL* 182, 1183).

[39] Corrupt attempts of Roman noble families to influence papal elections had long been scandalous. These had been made more difficult, by a papal decree in 1159 giving the cardinals the exclusive right to elect, and by the Third Lateran Council, (1179), which decided that all cardinals had an equal vote, and that a two-thirds majority was necessary.

[40] For the full text of Canon 1 see Petry, op. cit., pp. 322–3.

[41] Canon 21; ibid., p. 323.

[42] Ibid.

[43] Petry, op. cit., pp. 319–21 gives the text of Innocent's letter to John to which John's submission is attached. (E.T. of C. R. Cheney and W. H. Semple, *Selected Letters of Pope Innocent III concerning England* (Edinburgh 1953).

[44] *PL* 214, 292.

[45] The full text is given in Thatcher and McNeal, op. cit., pp. 314–17.
[46] Boniface's exegesis of Psalm 22.20 is not altogether clear. He seems to identify the 'darling' of the psalm both with the body of Christ and with the bride of Christ of John 3.29, and so with the Church (cf. Eph. 5.22 ff). As there is one Bridegroom, so there is but one Church.
[47] The exegesis of the 'two swords' text had occupied theologians and canonists for a long time. The question at issue was whether the two swords (spiritual and temporal power) were given into the hands of distinct and autonomous authorities (pope and emperor), or into the hands of the pope alone. There is no doubt about Boniface's answer.
[48] Again, Boniface's argument is not crystal-clear, since Peter presumably was wielding only one sword in Gethsemane.
[49] The reference is to a writer of about 500 who used the pseudonym of Dionysius the Areopagite (Acts 17.34). Among his works were treatises on the celestial hierarchy and the ecclesiastical hierarchy.
[50] E.g. it is not clear whether Boniface saw himself as the vicar of Peter or the vicar of Christ.

CHAPTER 9

[1] Congar, op. cit., p. 217.
[2] Hans Küng, *Structures of the Church* (Notre Dame 1968), p. 260.
[3] *De Sacramentis* i, 12. i (*PL* 176, 347–9).
[4] Ibid. (*PL* 176, 415 D).
[5] Ibid. (*PL* 176, 417 A).
[6] Congar, op. cit., p. 164.
[7] Ibid.
[8] See above, p. 93.
[9] *Glossa in* iv *Sent.* d. 24, n. 3.
[10] 'Faith' here means assent. The 'faith which has been formed' (*fides formata*) is much closer to Paul's 'faith working through love' (Gal. 5.6), and to what Luther meant by faith.
[11] *Summa* ii. ii. *in qu.* 2.
[12] *Opera* ii, p. 709 (*S. Bonaventurae Opera Omnia*, 10 vols., Quaracchi, 1882–1907).
[13] Ibid. iv, p. 203.
[14] Congar, op. cit., p. 222.
[15] *Opera* viii, p. 375.
[16] *Opera* v, p. 198b.
[17] Ibid. viii, p. 235a.
[18] The works (*opera*) of Albertus were edited by A. Borgnet in 38 vols. (Paris 1890–99).
[19] *Opera* xxxviii, pp. 64–5.
[20] Congar, op. cit., p. 231.
[21] *Opera* xxix, p. 440.
[22] Ibid. xxxviii, pp. 104–6.
[23] Ibid. xxiii, p. 685.
[24] *Summa Theologica* iiia, 8, 1.
[25] Ibid. iiia 8, 3. E.T. from *The Summa Theologica of St Thomas Aquinas,* tr. Fathers of the English Dominicans (London 1920 ff).
[26] See above, p. 115.
[27] *Summa Theologica* ia, 92, 3; cf. also iiia, 64, 2 *ad* 3.

[28] But in *Summa* IIIa, 8, 1 *ad* 3 Thomas likens the Holy Spirit to the heart which quickens the body.

[29] E.T. of passages from the *Exposition* is from T. Gilby, *St Thomas Aquinas: Theological Texts* (Oxford 1955), pp. 340–43.

[30] Ibid.

[31] *Summa* IIa–IIae, 183, 3 *ad* 3; cf. *Compendium Theologiae* I, 147.

[32] Congar, op. cit., pp. 234–5.

[33] 'Habitual grace' is 'the gift of God inhering in the soul, by which men are enabled to perform righteous acts. It is held to be normally conveyed in the Sacraments' (F. L. Cross, ed., *Oxford Dictionary of the Christian Church* (Oxford 1957), p. 577).

[34] *Summa* IIIa, 8, 3 *ad* 2.

[35] Hans Küng, *Structures of the Church*, pp. 13, 260. In addition to the passage under discussion Küng lists seven other occurrences. See also Congar, op. cit., p. 233.

[36] See below, p. 136.

[37] See below, pp. 136–7.

[38] This image, frequent in medieval ecclesiology, is used by Boniface VIII in *Unam Sanctam*; see above, p. 110.

[39] E.g. in Jerome; see above, p. 94.

[40] No patristic or scholastic writer has provided a systematic treatment of the Trinitarian nature of the Church as at once the People of God, the Body of Christ, and the Fellowship of the Spirit (the three basic N.T. themes of the Church).

[41] We have here the well-known threefold division of the Church as militant, expectant, and triumphant. Augustine had spoken of the Church on earth as *perigrans*, 'on a journey' (e.g. *Encheiridion* LVI). The expression 'Church militant' appeared about the middle of the twelfth century, perhaps with reference to the crusades against the Turks and the struggle against heresy. Departed souls who are being purged of their sins and awaiting the resurrection of the body are the Church expectant.

[42] This notion is derived from Augustine, *De Civ. Dei* XV, 1; *On the Psalms* LXIV, 2. It is taken up by Gregory the Great. 'From righteous Abel to the last elect' is a frequent description of the membership of the true Church; see list of occurrences in Y. Congar, *L'Ecclésiologie du haut Moyen-Age* (Paris 1968), p. 68, n. 43.

[43] IV *Quodlibets* VIII, 13. E.T., Gilby, op. cit., p. 398.

[44] See below. pp. 136–8.

[45] E.T., Gilby, op. cit., pp. 399–400.

[46] Ibid., p. 399.

CHAPTER 10

[1] Some representative documents both from Albigensian and Catharist sources are gathered together in Petry, op. cit., pp. 342–50.

[2] This catechism was long accepted as an early Waldensian document. Recent examination, however, has shown its dependence on the writings of Martin Bucer, the sixteenth-century reformer. See G. MacGregor, *Corpus Christi* (Philadelphia 1958), pp. 37–8. But there is no doubt that the Waldensians anticipated Reformation teaching in some important respects.

[3] Tr. R. C. Petry, op. cit., p. 353 from A. Monastier, *Histoire de l'Eglise vaudoise* (Paris 1847), II, pp. 301 ff.

[4] Petry, op. cit., p. 334 gives some excerpts, quoted from F. S. Stevenson, *Robert Grosseteste, Bishop of Lincoln* (London 1899), pp. 286–8.

[5] *De potestate regia et papali*, ed. J. LeClercq (Paris 1942).

[6] Many of his works suffered destruction on account of his condemnation. Extant ser-

mons, treatises, and fragments have been edited by G. Thery and R. Klibansky, *Opera Latina* (Leipzig 1934 ff).

[7] Text ed. C. W. Previté-Orton (Cambridge 1928). Petry, op. cit., pp. 510–13 provides some extracts in E.T. including the 'Conclusions' in the E.T. of Thatcher and McNeal.

[8] Erastianism is so called after Thomas Erastus (1524–83). It signifies the complete submission of the Church to State control. Erastus himself did not, however, teach so sweeping a doctrine. He opposed excommunication by Church authorities without permission of the lay ruler.

[9] See Thatcher and McNeal, op. cit., pp. 317–24, or Petry, op. cit., pp. 511–13.

[10] Marsilius distinguishes between the inseparable (essential) and separable (inessential) functions of the clergy. The inseparable functions are the power to administer the sacraments. The separable functions are the control of one priest over others (e.g. as archbishop or bishop), and the administration of the sacraments in a particular place or to a particular group.

[11] *Conclusions* 17 and 18.

[12] *Dialogus* I, 1, 4. (Edn of text in M. Goldast, *Monarchia S. Romani Imperii*, vol. 2 (Hanover 1612).

[13] *Opera Politica*, vol. iii, p. 191, ed. J. G. Sikes *et al* (Manchester 1940).

[14] Congar, *L'Eglise*, pp. 294–5.

[15] *De Imperatorum et Pontificum Potestate*, ed. C. K. Brampton (Oxford 1927).

[16] Quoted in Petry, op. cit., p. 515 from the E.T. of Ewart Lewis, *Medieval Political Ideas* (New York 1954), vol. ii, p. 608.

[17] I.e. a priest who is not a member of a religious Order.

[18] Among these are *De Dominio Divino* ('On Divine Lordship'), *De Civili Dominio* ('On Civil Lordship'), *De Ecclesia* ('On the Church'), *De Eucharistia* ('On the Eucharist'), *De Ecclesia et Membris eius* ('On the Church and its Members'), *De Officio Regis* ('On the Office of the King'), *De Potestate Papae* ('On the Authority of the Pope'). His *Trialogus* (1382) restates his main theses in sharper fashion. Most of these have been published by the Wyclif Society: *Wyclif's Latin Works* (London 1884 ff).

[19] *Trialogus* IV, 22. The *Trialogus* is ed. G. V. Kechner (Oxford 1869).

[20] See above, pp. 120, 228, n. 41.

[21] G. Macgregor, op. cit., pp. 34–7.

[22] *Tractatus de Ecclesia*, ed. J. Loserth, Wyclif Society (London 1886): pp. 17, 22, 57, 132–3.

[23] Ibid., pp. 298–328.

[24] *Tractatus de Officio Regis*, ed. A. W. Pollard and C. Sayle, Wyclif Society (London 1887): pp. 13, 137.

[25] Matthew Spinka, *John Hus' Concept of the Church* (Princeton 1966).

[26] See below, pp. 136–8.

[27] See G. Macgregor, op. cit., pp. 25–8.

[28] Ibid., pp. 23–4.

[29] See Petry, op. cit., pp. 526–7. He quotes the whole document from Francis Oakley, 'The *Propositiones Utiles* of Pierre d'Ailly: an Epitome of Conciliar Theory', in *Church History* XXIX, 4 (December 1960), pp. 399–402.

[30] Cf. William of Ockham, above, p. 131.

[31] This Council first met at Ferrara, was transferred to Florence in 1439 and to Rome in 1442.

[32] See below, pp. 146–7.

[33] Küng, *Structures of the Church*, p. 242.

[34] Thatcher and McNeal, op. cit., pp. 328–9.

[35] G. Macgregor, op. cit., p. 40.

[36] *Summa de Ecclesia* I, 21.

[37] Ibid., especially I, 67–8.
[38] Ibid. I, 22.
[39] Ibid. I, 6.
[40] Ibid. II, 32–4.
[41] Turrecremata's understanding of astronomy may, of course, be ignored.
[42] Ibid. II, 54. For Latin text see Congar, *L'Eglise*, p. 342, n. 7.
[43] Küng, *Structures of the Church*, pp. 271–5.
[44] *Summa de Ecclesia* II, 93, 102; IV, 18.
[45] It is noticeable that Turrecremata interprets the 'rock' of Matthew 16.18 not as the person of Peter, but as faith in Christ.
[46] See Küng, *Structures*, pp. 256–7.
[47] *Summa de Ecclesia* III, 16.
[48] Ibid. III, 64.

CHAPTER 11

[1] For brief accounts of the history see Timothy Ware, *The Orthodox Church* (Harmondsworth 1963), chs. 1–3; R. W. Southern, op. cit., ch. 3.
[2] See above, pp. 75–6.
[3] Quoted from Southern, op. cit., p. 71.
[4] See above, p. 104.
[5] Hans Küng, *The Church*, p. 446.
[6] Southern, op. cit., p. 74.
[7] Ibid., p. 75.
[8] Ibid., p. 82. A twentieth-century example is A. Harnack's treatment of eastern Christianity in his popular *What is Christianity?*
[9] John Meyendorff, *Orthodoxy and Catholicity* (New York 1966), p. 88.
[10] Yves Congar, *L'Ecclésiologie du Haut Moyen-Age*, pp. 324–5.
[11] John of Damascus, *c.* 675–*c.* 749, one of the most influential of Greek theologians. His *De Fide Orthodoxa* is a systematic treatment of the main articles of Christian faith.
[12] Greek, *mustagogia*, literally, 'introduction to the mysteries'.
[13] T. Ware, op. cit., p. 247.
[14] *PG*, vol. 91, 658–718.
[15] Congar, op. cit., p. 327.
[16] *PG* 98, 383f.
[17] Greek, 'all-sovereign'. Whether or not in the central dome, an ikon of Christ the *Pantokrator* is prominent in every Orthodox church.
[18] See above, p. 78. For a brief discussion of the modern Orthodox understanding of the deification of man, see T. Ware, op. cit., pp. 240–42.
[19] 'On our Strict Doctrines of Truth', *PG* 89, 1340.
[20] Alexis Khomiakov, *The Church is One*, section 9, quoted in T. Ware, op. cit., p. 247.
[21] For St Paul, see above, pp. 17–18; Cyril of Jerusalem, p. 78; Cyril of Alexandria, p. 79; Augustine, p. 85.
[22] In a preparatory document for the seminar on Orthodox Theology and Worship held at the Ecumenical Institute, Bossey, Switzerland in April 1971.
[23] Literally, 'calling upon'.
[24] It is expressed in the title *Pantokrator*. See above, p. 150.
[25] See T. Ware, op. cit., p. 49; J. Meyendorff, *The Orthodox Church* (London 1962), pp. 20 ff.
[26] The Greek *leitourgia* means 'service'. Orthodox theology does not (and no theology

should) make a sharp distinction between the service of God in worship and the service of God in work.

[27] See above, pp. 86–90.

[28] A common western misconception is that the Church of the East has been inactive in mission. The Slavonic missions from the ninth century on, and Orthodox activity in eastern Asia in the eighteenth century alone are sufficient to disprove this charge.

[29] Ignatius, *Smyrn.* VIII; see above, pp. 35–6.

[30] E.g. above, pp. 16–17, 20, 88.

[31] T. Ware, op. cit., p. 248, briefly discusses this tension.

[32] Quoted by T. Ware, ibid.

[33] J. Meyendorff, 'What Holds the Church Together?' in *Ecumenical Review*, vol. xii (1960), p. 298.

[34] Orthodoxy is quite clear that bishops are not to be equated with apostles. See J. Meyendorff, *Orthodoxy and Catholicity*, p. 12 where he quotes from Nilus Cabasilas' (d. 1363) *On the Primacy of the Pope*: 'The apostles did not ordain other apostles, but pastors and teachers.'

[35] J. Meyendorff, ibid., p. 5.

[36] The western practice of 'private masses' with a single layman present as server is foreign to Orthodoxy.

[37] N. A. Nissiotis in the document mentioned in n. 22 above.

[38] Orthodox theologians often appeal to the authority of Irenaeus on this point.

[39] On this point Orthodox theologians appeal to the authority of Cyprian. See J. Meyendorff, *Orthodoxy and Catholicity*, pp. 158–9.

[40] The Greek word is *taxis*, 'order' in the sense of 'placing'.

[41] E.T. of quotation by Y. Congar, *L'Eglise*, p. 265, from J. Darrouzès, 'Conférence sur la Primauté du Pape à Constantinople en 1357' in *Revue des Etudes Byzantines*, 19 (1961).

[42] Nicolas Cabasilas, *c.* 1320–*c.* 1370, author of *The Life of Christ* and *Interpretation of the Divine Liturgy*.

[43] Nilus Cabasilas, *On the Primacy of the Pope*, PG 149, 728–9.

[44] This jurisdiction included the right to hear appeals, to judge disputed cases in the eparchies of the patriarchate, to confirm elections to metropolitan sees. Larger claims by the patriarch of Rome were resisted in the East.

[45] T. Ware, op. cit., p. 35.

[46] From the Greek *autos* (self), and *kephalē* (head).

[47] The title of patriarch has been accorded to the metropolitan bishops of some autocephalous churches, e.g. Russia, Serbia, Rumania, Bulgaria.

[48] J. Meyendorff, *Orthodoxy and Catholicity*, p. 115.

[49] J. Meyendorff, ibid., p. 117, defines 'economy' as 'a conscious relaxation by the ecclesiastical authorities of the letter of the canons in cases when a strict legalistic observance would do more harm than good to the entire body of the Church'.

CHAPTER 12

[1] Owen Chadwick, *The Reformation* (Harmondsworth 1964), vol. 3 in 'The Pelican History of the Church', p. 11.

[2] There is no reason to doubt that Tetzel used words like 'the moment the money tinkles in the box a soul flies out of purgatory'.

[3] So in the Augsburg Confession, Article VII, which was largely drawn up by Luther's friend and colleague, Melanchthon.

[4] Ibid. 7.

[5] E.T. of quotations from Luther is from *Luther's Works*, 55 vols. (St Louis, Missouri;

Philadelphia 1955 ff). General eds. Jaroslav Pelikan and H. T. Lehmann. This is designated *LW.*

[6] *LW,* vol. 39, p. 75.

[7] For the other four marks see below, p. 165.

[8] *LW* 41, pp. 148–52.

[9] *LW* 39, pp. 69–70.

[10] *The Protestant Tradition* (Cambridge 1955), p. 110.

[11] *The Papacy at Rome; LW* 39, p. 70.

[12] Ibid.

[13] Ibid.

[14] Owen Chadwick, op. cit., p. 61.

[15] Whale, op. cit., pp. 112–13.

[16] *LW* 44, pp. 127–9.

[17] See R. W. Southern, op. cit., pp. 37–8 for a brief comment on the medieval demotion of the laity. See also Hans Küng, *The Church,* pp. 363–87, for a modern Roman Catholic discussion of the N.T. usage of the words 'priest' and *clerus* (Greek *kleros*) in relation to 'people' (*laos*). Of Luther, Küng says (ibid., p. 280): 'He helped to revive original N.T. perspectives (the primacy of grace, the priesthood of all believers, ecclesiastical office as ministry, the importance of the Word, the opposition between the law and the Gospel, the ethos of everyday life and work, etc.) and ... made an important contribution to the reform of the Church—indirectly to the reform of the Catholic Church too.'

[18] J. S. Whale, op. cit., p. 98.

[19] Ibid., p. 111.

[20] See above, p. 164.

[21] *LW* 41, p. 154.

[22] *Answer to the Hyperchristian, Hyperspiritual, and Hyperlearned Book by Goat Emser, LW* 39, p. 155.

[23] Ibid.

[24] Whale, op. cit., p. 301.

[25] An early example is the radical activity, including incitement to riot of Carlstadt and others in Wittenberg as early as 1522. A later example is the attempt of John of Leyden to make Münster the New Jerusalem in 1534–5, entailing the banishment or slaughter of opponents, and the institution of communism not only in goods, but in wives.

[26] *LW* 45, pp. 81–129.

[27] Ch. 18, 'The Crown Rights of the Redeemer', pp. 288–305.

[28] 'Anabaptist' (Greek, *anabaptistes,* rebaptizer) describes those groups of reformers who rejected infant baptism and baptized their 'converts' again. They condemned the use of force, courts of law, and taking oaths. The word later became a label for all radical reformers, many of whom were only too ready to use force themselves.

[29] Whale, op. cit., p. 290.

[30] Ibid., p. 291.

[31] *Temporal Authority; LW* 45, p. 89.

[32] Ibid., p. 91.

[33] Whale, op. cit., pp. 303–4.

[34] John Knox, who was one of them, said of Calvin's Geneva that it was 'the most perfect school of Christ that ever was'.

[35] Literally, 'Instruction in the Christian Religion'. The plural *Institutiones* was sometimes used in edns after Calvin's death. It is usually known in English as *The Institutes.*

[36] A North American professor, teaching a course on the doctrine of the Church, was accustomed to read to his students a paragraph or two from the beginning of

Institutes IV, and to ask them to name the writer. Thomas Aquinas was the most frequent response.

[37] For a discussion of this, and a criticism of Calvin on this point, see G. MacGregor op. cit., pp. 48–50. Calvin did not arrive at his mature doctrine of the Church quickly. F. Wendel, *Calvin* (E.T., London 1965), p. 294, says that in 1536 Calvin had hardly considered the Church except under its invisible aspect. J. S. Whale, op. cit., pp. 146–62 traces the development of Calvin's ecclesiology in the succeeding editions of the *Institutes*.

[38] E.T. of passages from the *Institutes* is from the translation of F. L. Battles in the edn of J. T. McNeill in vols. xx and xxi of the 'Library of Christian Classics' (London; Philadelphia 1961) entitled *Calvin: Institutes of the Christian Religion*.

[39] *Institutes* IV, i. 2–3.

[40] See also ibid. IV, i. 13.

[41] See above, p. 163.

[42] *Institutes* IV, i. 16.

[43] Ibid. IV, i. 12.

[44] Wendel, op. cit., pp. 300–301.

[45] *Institutes* IV, xii. 10.

[46] Whale, op. cit., p. 155.

[47] E.g. *Institutes* IV, ii. 11–12.

[48] *Institutes* IV, vi. 9.

[49] For a discussion of this, see Benjamin C. Milner, *Calvin's Doctrine of the Church* (Leiden 1970), pp. 150–57.

[50] *Institutes* IV, iv. 4.

[51] Ibid.

[52] *Commentary on Numbers* III, 5: *Ioannis Calvini Opera quae supersunt omnia*, ed. G. Baum *et al.*, in 'Corpus Reformatorum', (Brunswick 1863–1900; reprinted, New York and London 1964), vol. 52 (vol. 24 of Calvin's works), pp. 444–5.

[53] 'Corpus Reformatorum', vol. 43 (vol. 15 of Calvin's works), pp. 329–36. Students of Calvin differ on the question whether he was prepared to accept episcopacy in the sense of a distinct order of ministry. See the brief discussion in B. C. Milner, op. cit., pp. 147–8 and footnotes. Milner's view is that Calvin admitted distinction of ministry for practical purposes ('distinction of a political kind'), but that he strongly held that 'the office of bishop ... cannot be different from that of the pastor'.

[54] *Institutes* IV, iii. 1.

[55] It is described also in the *Draft Ecclesiastical Ordinances* of 1541, drawn up by Calvin and his colleagues. See J. K. S. Reid, ed., *Calvin, Theological Treatises* in 'The Library of Christian Classics', vol xxii (1954), pp. 58 ff.

[56] *Institutes* IV, iii. 1.

[57] Ibid. IV, i. 5.

[58] G. MacGregor, op. cit., p. 57.

[59] *Institutes* IV, iii. 10–16.

[60] Ibid. IV, iii. 16; IV, xix. 31.

[61] *Comm. Acts* 6.6; *Comm. 1 Tim.* 4.14; *Comm. 2 Tim.* 1.6. The relevant passages are quoted in B. C. Milner, op. cit., p. 143.

[62] Cf. *Institutes* IV, xix. 31, 'I concede that it [the laying on of hands] is a sacrament in true and lawful ordinations.'

[63] Cf. also III, xix. 15; IV, xx. 1–2.

[64] Ibid. IV, xii. 5.

[65] MacGregor, op. cit., p. 107.

[66] The word 'Protestant' has a positive as well as the negative connotation which it is usually given. The Latin *protestor* means literally 'bear witness for'. The Reformers, while protesting against what they held to be abuses in the medieval Church, were at

the same time bearing witness for principles which they believed to have been submerged. 'Protestant' came into use as a term to describe a reformer after the Diet of Speyer (1529), at which a reforming minority made a formal *Protestatio* in defence of the rights of minority groups.

[67] The Lutheran Church of Sweden, however, retained the office of bishop in succession from the pre-Reformation bishops, and values this aspect of continuity with the apostolic Church. There are also Presbyterians who claim 'a succession of presbyters both by office and by ordination in direct descent from the days of the apostles': see R. Newton Flew, ed., *The Nature of the Church* (London 1952), p. 114.

[68] Quoted from J. S. Whale, op. cit., pp. 186–7. Barrow's works are contained in Leland H. Carson, ed., *The Writings of Henry Barrow, 1587–90* (Elizabethan Nonconformist Texts, vol. iii, London 1962).

[69] Quoted from J. S. Whale, op. cit., p. 193. It was drawn up by John Robinson, author of *Justification of Separation from the Church of England* (1610), who was to sail in the *Mayflower* as one of the Pilgrim Fathers in 1620.

[70] Browne's book is regarded as a foundation document of modern Congregationalists: see R. N. Flew, op. cit., p. 169. Browne, however, recanted in 1585 and conformed to the Church of England.

[71] See Owen Chadwick, op. cit., ch. 6, for a brief account of the Separatists of the sixteenth century and the early seventeenth.

[72] Quoted from J. S. Whale, op. cit., pp. 215–16.

[73] See chs. 14 and 15 of Robert Barclay, *Apology for the True Christian Religion, as the same is set forth and preached by the People called in Scorn 'Quakers'* (London 1701).

[74] See also J. S. Whale, *Christian Doctrine* (London 1957), pp. 130 ff.

CHAPTER 13

[1] Henry VIII had insisted on the words 'Supreme Head'.

[2] Owen Chadwick, op. cit., p. 119.

[3] Ibid., p. 215.

[4] E.g. the prevenience of grace (x), justification by faith alone (xi), predestination (xvii), the sufficiency of holy Scripture for salvation (vi).

[5] This claim has been disputed by Roman Catholic theologians. The adverse judgement on the validity of Anglican Orders by Pope Leo XI in the Bull *Apostolicae Curae* (1896) is still the Church of Rome's last official word on the subject.

[6] See H. F. Woodhouse, *The Doctrine of the Church in Anglican Theology, 1547–1603* (London 1954), published for the Church Historical Society, for an account of those of the sixteenth century; and P. E. More and F. L. Cross, eds., *Anglicanism* (London 1957), for biographies and extracts from the works of those of the seventeenth century on ecclesiology, as well as other major theological topics.

[7] *The Laws of Ecclesiastical Polity* iii, i. 3, 8; v, lvi. 7, 11; *Sermon* ii (*Of Justification, Works, and how the Foundation of Faith is overthrown*) 23, where the 'body mystical' is said to be a 'building undiscernible by mortal eyes'.

[8] *LEP* iii, i. 8.

[9] Ibid. viii, iv. 5, 7.

[10] Ibid. v, xxiv. 1.

[11] Woodhouse, op. cit., pp. 50–51.

[12] *LEP* iii, i. 2.

[13] Op. cit., p. 51.

[14] See above, p. 170. Richard Hooker makes the same point, though with less clarity, in *LEP* iii, i. 3: 'And as those everlasting promises [viz., in the Scriptures] of love,

mercy, and blessedness belong to the mystical Church; even so on the other side when we read [i.e. in the Scriptures] of any duty which the Church of God is bound unto, the Church whom this doth concern is a sensibly known company.'

[15] P. E. More and F. L. Cross, op. cit., p. 41. Hooker also uses the illustration of Jesus' knowledge of Nathaniel in *LEP* III, i. 2.

[16] For the views of sixteenth-century Anglican writers on whether the Church of Rome had ceased to be part of the Church of Christ, see ch. 10 in Woodhouse, op. cit. For the views of selected seventeenth-century Anglican writers, see More and Cross, op. cit., pp. 53–72. The views expressed have a wide range. John Bradford condemns Rome as a 'strumpet-church' and the spouse of the Antichrist. From men like Hooker, John Cosin, and Isaac Barrow we have reasoned and scholarly examinations of Roman claims in the light of Scripture and the writings of the Fathers.

[17] Bellarmine's *De Ecclesia Militante* (a section of his *Controversies*) was published in 1586. See below, pp. 202–4.

[18] The words 'we must receive God's promises in such wise, as they be generally set forth to us in holy Scripture' in the final paragraph of Article XVII may readily be interpreted as implying that the elect will be found within the visible Church.

[19] See above, pp. 163 and 231, nn. 3, 4.

[20] See above, p. 82.

[21] E.g., the Second Helvetic Confession (1566), Article XVIII; The Westminster Confession (1647), Article XXVII.

[22] The Ordinal, or 'The Form and Manner of Making, Ordaining, and Consecrating of Bishops, Priests, and Deacons' is printed with the Book of Common Prayer, although, like the Thirty-nine Articles, it is a separate document.

[23] Anglicans have differed on these matters. For the views of Richard Hooker and seventeenth-century Anglican theologians, see More and Cross, op. cit., pp. 345–403.

[24] Erik Routley, *Creeds and Confessions* (London 1962), p. 112.

[25] Ibid., p. 111.

[26] Ibid., p. 108.

[27] See above, p. 133.

[28] See above, pp. 182–3.

[29] The text of this may be read in More and Cross, op. cit., pp. 23–9, from which quotations here are taken. More and Cross use the 1864 Oxford edn of Edward Burton which was first published in 1833.

[30] Cf. Cyril of Jerusalem on catholicity; above, pp. 76–7.

CHAPTER 14

[1] Roman Catholics prefer to use the terms 'Catholic Reformation' or 'Catholic Renewal' which lay less stress on these reforms as a mere response to the Protestant Reformation; see Y. Congar, *L'Eglise*, pp. 380–81.

[2] See above, pp. 163 and 231, nn. 3, 4.

[3] Y. Congar, op. cit., p. 364.

[4] See H. Küng, *The Church*, p. 11.

[5] *The Canons and Decrees of the Council of Trent*, translated by T. A. Buckley (London 1851), p. 2.

[6] Ibid., p. 9.

[7] Ibid., p. 10.

[8] Ibid., p. 255.

[9] Hans Küng, op. cit., pp. 418–19 discusses this sentence, and remarks: 'The Tridentine proposition, if strictly interpreted, does not agree with historical realities.' There is no dominical ordinance concerning distinctions in office between bishops, priests, and

deacons. The distinctions emerged later than the N.T. period. He notes that Vatican II is more in accordance with recent exegetical and historical research in saying: 'The divinely established ecclesiastical ministry is exercised on different levels by those who from antiquity (*ab antiquo*, not *ab initio*) have been called bishops, priests, and deacons' (*Constitution on the Church* III, 28).

[10] The E.T. used is that of T. A. Buckley, *The Catechism of the Council of Trent* (London 1852). The translation has been checked with the Latin in *Catechismus ex Decreto Concilii Tridentini* (Leipzig 1872).

[11] It is to be noted that there is no mention here of the Church expectant (in purgatory). However, the doctrine of purgatory is alluded to in Part II, ch. IV, q. lxxvi (Buckley, op. cit., p. 255), and in Part IV, ch. V, q. iv (ibid., p. 489).

[12] Cf. Article XXVI of the Thirty-nine Articles (see above, pp. 185–6).

[13] The passage from Ambrose (*Commentary on Luke*, Book IX, 9) is curiously omitted from some Latin editions, including the Leipzig edition mentioned in n. 10 above. It is not a particularly strong witness to the papal claims.

[14] The catechism treats of the sacrament of order in Part II, ch. VII (Buckley, op. cit., pp. 312–32).

[15] See above, pp. 197–8.

[16] See above, pp. 14–15.

[17] *A New Catechism: Catholic Faith for Adults* (New York 1967).

[18] *Disputationes de Controversiis Christianae Fidei adversus huius temporis Haereticos* (Ingolstadt 1586–93), in 3 vols. Modern edns in *Opera Omnia* (Naples 1856–62, 8 vols.; and Paris 1870–74, 12 vols.).

[19] See above, p. 140.

[20] See above, pp. 115–17.

[21] Congar, *L'Eglise*, p. 373.

[22] Texts are to be found in A. C. Cochrane, *Reformed Confessions of the 16th Century* (E.T., Philadelphia 1966); P. Schaff, *The Creeds of Christendom*, vol. 3, 'The Evangelical Protestant Creeds' (New York 1877); Williston Walker, *The Creeds and Platforms of Congregationalism* (New York 1893).

[23] E.T. from Cochrane, op. cit.

[24] E.T. from Cochrane, op. cit.

[25] E.T. from Cochrane, op. cit.

[26] See E. Routley, *Creeds and Confessions* (London 1962), p. 90.

[27] This and the following quotation from chs. xvii and xviii are from the E.T. of Cochrane, op. cit.

[28] See above, p. 93.

[29] See above, p. 82.

[30] Quotations are taken from Schaff, op. cit.

[31] This chapter was altered in the later American revision to bring it into line with the principle of the separation of Church and State and of the neutrality of the State in ecclesiastical matters.

[32] Quotations from Schaff, op. cit.

[33] The full text is given in Williston Walker, op. cit., from which quotations here are taken, the spelling, however, being modernized, and the punctuation sometimes altered.

[34] Williston Walker, op. cit., p. 205, n. 3; see also p. 204, n. 2.

[35] Routley, op. cit., p. 130.

[36] See G. R. Cragg, *The Church and the Age of Reason, 1648–1759* (Harmondsworth 1970), pp. 176–7. For an account of the 'Half-way Covenant' decisions of 1657 and 1662, and of the connected controversies, see Williston Walker, op. cit., pp. 238–339.

[1] G. R. Cragg, *The Church and the Age of Reason, 1648–1789* (Harmondsworth, 1970), p. 37.

[2] Ibid., p. 16.

[3] F. L. Cross, ed., *The Oxford Dictionary of the Christian Church* (London 1957), p. 789.

[4] I. T. Ramsey, ed., *John Locke, 'The Reasonableness of Christianity'* (California, Stanford University Press, 1958), pp. 60–62. This is an abridgement of the 1731 edn. Ramsey has numbered the *paragraphs* in this edn. Numbers here in brackets refer to these paragraphs.

[5] Ramsey, op. cit., pp. 45, 46, 50.

[6] Ibid., pp. 48–9.

[7] Quoted from Owen Chadwick, *The Reformation*, 'Pelican History of the Church', vol. 3 (Harmondsworth 1964), p. 402.

[8] Locke wrote three more letters on the subject, in answer to attacks on the first by Jonas Proast who argued that force was justified to promote true religion. Locke's fourth letter was only in draft form when he died.

[9] John Locke, *A Letter Concerning Toleration* (New York, The Liberal Arts Press, 1955), p. 16.

[10] Ibid., p. 29.

[11] Ibid., pp. 23–4, 27, 28, 35, 40.

[12] Ibid., p. 40.

[13] Ibid., p. 50.

[14] Ibid., pp. 50–51.

[15] Ibid., p. 51.

[16] Ibid., p. 52.

[17] 'Denomination' strictly means a designation by class; the naming of a particular category among entities which share the same characteristics. It is in this sense that we speak of banknotes as having denominations of one, five, ten, etc.

[18] Ibid., p. 20.

[19] More recently the word has been used to denote zealous partiality for *one* 'denomination' over others.

[20] See vol. 1, p. 139.

[21] Gallicanism took differing forms, some more radical than others. See Yves Congar, *L'Eglise de saint Augustin à l'époque moderne* (Paris 1970), pp. 392–412 *passim*, and for a brief account, G. R. Cragg, op. cit., pp. 21–5.

[22] Cragg, op. cit., p. 99.

[23] Probabilism was thus defined by Bartolomeo Medina (1527–80): 'If an opinion is probable it is permissible to follow it, even though the opposite be more probable.' The doctrine was vehemently attacked by Blaise Pascal in his *Provincial Letters* (1656).

[24] The Conference adopted a form of ordination with the laying on of hands, in 1836.

[25] The Augustinian doctrines of the early Jansenists are no longer emphasized.

[26] *The Deed of Union* (1932), drawn up when the separate Primitive Methodist, United Methodist, and Wesleyan Methodist Churches in England entered into union.

[27] See vol. 1, pp. 163 and 231 nn.

[28] 'The Methodists: Statement approved by the British Methodist Conference, Bradford, 1937' in R. Newton Flew, ed., *The Nature of the Church* (London 1952), pp. 207–8.

[29] See Warren W. Slabaugh, 'The Church of the Brethren', in Flew, op. cit., pp. 298–302.

[30] Cragg, op. cit., p. 283.

[31] Cragg, op. cit., p. 254.

[32] See above, p. 9.

[33] Congar, *L'Eglise*, p. 418.

[34] Ibid.
[35] Ibid., pp. 418–19.
[36] Ibid., p. 421.
[37] 'Symbolism' is used here in its theological sense of 'study of the creeds'. The Greek *symbolon* was the usual word for a creed in the early Church. The sub-title of Möhler's *Symbolik* is 'an account of the doctrinal differences of Catholics and Protestants according to their published confessions'.
[38] *Symbolik*, para. 36, quoted in Congar, op. cit., p. 422.
[39] R. H. Nientaltowski, 'Möhler', in *The New Catholic Encyclopedia* (New York, McGraw-Hill, 1967), vol. ix; see also Congar, op. cit., p. 423.
[40] These figures indicate that about a hundred bishops were not present for the voting.
[41] H. Denzinger, *Enchiridion Symbolorum, Definitionum et Declarationum de rebus fidei et morum* (Freiburg 1960), p. 1859, quoted in H. Küng, *Structures of the Church* (Notre Dame, U.S.A., 1968), p. 314.
[42] Congar, op. cit., p. 460.
[43] F. von Hügel, *Essays and Addresses on the Philosophy of Religion*, 2nd ser. (London 1930), p. 106.
[44] F. von Hügel, *Selected Letters, 1896–1924* (London 1927), p. 334.
[45] E.g. in *Eternal Life* (Edinburgh 1912), pp. 336 ff; *Essays and Addresses*, 1st ser. (London 1927), pp. 257–9, 267.
[46] In *Some Notes on the Petrine Claims* (London 1930), pp. 16–33. These notes were written in 1893.
[47] Maurice Nédoncelle, *Baron Friedrich von Hügel* (London 1937), p. 133.
[48] Von Hügel gives a striking example of what he means in *Essays and Addresses*, 1st ser., p. 285, citing the incident of the Jewish rabbi of Lyons, a chaplain in the First World War, 'holding up at a dying Catholic soldier's request, this soldier's crucifix before his eyes, and this amidst a hail of bullets and shrapnel'. For von Hügel's ecclesiology, *Essays and Addresses*, 1st ser., essays 8–11, pp. 227–98 are important.

CHAPTER 16

[1] In an introduction to a reprint in 1926 of the 1st edn; quoted here from Friedrich Schleiermacher, *On Religion: Speeches to its Cultured Despisers* (New York, Harper & Row, 1958), p. xi. This vol. gives the E. T. of John Oman of the 3rd edn of 1831, together with Schleiermacher's own 'Explanations' of certain passages. Quotations here from the *Speeches* are from this work.
[2] J. M. Creed, *The Divinity of Jesus Christ* (London 1964), p. 39.
[3] *Speeches*, p. 147.
[4] Ibid., p. 149.
[5] Ibid.
[6] Ibid., p. 151.
[7] Ibid., pp. 151–2.
[8] Ibid., pp. 185–6.
[9] Ibid., p. 155.
[10] Ibid., p. 188.
[11] Ibid., p. 187.
[12] Ibid., p. 188.
[13] Ibid., pp. 156–66.
[14] Ibid., p. 157.
[15] Ibid., pp. 158–9.
[16] Ibid., p. 190.
[17] Ibid., p. 157.

[18] Ibid., p. 190.
[19] Ibid., p. 163.
[20] Ibid., p. 166.
[21] Ibid., p. 191.
[22] Ibid., p. 166.
[23] Ibid., p. 191.
[24] Friedrich Schleiermacher, *The Christian Faith*, E. T. of the 2nd German edn, ed. H. R. Mackintosh and J. S. Stewart (Edinburgh 1960), p. v (Editors' Preface).
[25] Ibid., p. 3.
[26] Ibid.
[27] Ibid., pp. 5–6.
[28] Ibid., p. 31.
[29] Ibid., p. 34.
[30] Ibid., pp. 39–40.
[31] Ibid., p. 53.
[32] Ibid., p. 88.
[33] Many modern Catholic and Protestant theologians would disagree with the sharp distinction between Catholic and Protestant doctrine which Schleiermacher asserts here.
[34] Ibid., p. 107.
[35] Ibid.
[36] Ibid., pp. 355–70.
[37] Schleiermacher notes that the word 'mystical' is often used vaguely, but is prepared to admit its use in connection with his presentation of the redeeming activity of Christ (and therefore with his concept of the Church), provided that it is used in its original sense, which is decidedly less than 'magical', but decidedly more than 'empirical'. See ibid., pp. 428–31.
[38] Ibid., pp. 362–3.
[39] Ibid., p. 367.
[40] Ibid., pp. 525–722.
[41] Ibid., p. 586.
[42] Ibid., pp. 525–81.
[43] Ibid., pp. 676–95.
[44] Ibid., pp. 696–722.
[45] Ibid., p. 529.
[46] Ibid., p. 533.
[47] Ibid., p. 529.
[48] Ibid.
[49] Ibid., p. 533.
[50] Ibid., p. 538.
[51] Ibid., p. 544.
[52] Ibid., pp. 548–9.
[53] Ibid., p. 540.
[54] Ibid., p. 559.
[55] Ibid., p. 565.
[56] Ibid., p. 568.
[57] See also Schleiermacher's earlier treatment in the *Speeches*, above, pp. 25–6.
[58] Ibid., p. 676.
[59] See above, p. 32.
[60] Ibid., p. 678.
[61] Ibid., p. 681.
[62] Ibid., p. 683.
[63] Ibid., p. 697.

[64] Ibid., p. 696.

[65] An E.T. of vol. 3 was edited by H. R. Mackintosh and A. B. Macauley (*A. Ritschl: The Christian Doctrine of Justification and Sanctification*. Edinburgh 1900. References in this ch. are to this vol.

[66] Ritschl, op. cit., pp. 7, 202, 212, 238.

[67] Ibid., p. 388.

[68] Ibid., p. 8.

[69] Ritschl acknowledges many debts to Schleiermacher, although his references to the latter are often accompanied by a correction, and sometimes by the charge of inconsistency.

[70] Ibid., p. 2.

[71] Cf. also pp. 7, 546–7.

[72] See the discussion ibid., pp. 559–64.

[73] Ibid., p. 11.

[74] Ibid.

[75] Here Ritschl presents his view of the mutual relation of the two *foci*.

[76] E.g. ibid., pp. 130, 288, 590.

[77] Ibid., p. 109.

[78] Ibid., pp. 284–5.

[79] Ibid., p. 286.

[80] Ibid., p. 287.

[81] Ibid., p. 288.

[82] Ibid., p. 287.

[83] Ibid., p. 289.

[84] 'Not every one who says to me, "Lord, Lord," shall enter the kingdom of heaven, but he who does the will of my Father who is in heaven. . . .'

[85] Ibid., p. 553. See also p. 603.

[86] These are p. 273 (in ch. 4, 'The Doctrine of God'); pp. 471–2 (in ch. 6, 'The Doctrine of the Person and Life-work of Christ'); pp. 532–4 (in ch. 7, 'The Necessity of the Forgiveness of Sins or Justification in General'); and pp. 603–8 (in ch. 8, 'The Necessity of Basing the Forgiveness of Sins on the Work and Passion of Christ').

[87] Ibid., p. 471.

[88] Ibid.

[89] Ibid.

[90] Ibid., p. 606.

[91] Ibid., p. 607.

[92] Ibid., p. 603.

[93] An E.T. by T. B. Saunders under the title *What is Christianity?* was published in London in 1901, and has been many times reprinted.

[94] 'The Preaching of Jesus on the Kingdom of God'.

[95] An E.T. by W. Montgomery under the title *The Quest of the Historical Jesus* was published in 1910.

CHAPTER 17

[1] Charles Smyth, *Simeon and Church Order* (Cambridge 1940), pp. 240–43.

[2] The Surrey Chapel belonged to the Countess of Huntingdon's Connexion. She was a wealthy and influential woman who devoted herself and her resources to promoting Methodism among the upper classes. She favoured the Calvinistic Methodism of Whitefield. Her 'connexion' included a number of Church of England clergymen whom she took on herself to appoint as her chaplains in the meeting-houses which she founded. The Bishop of London's consistory court declared this to be uncanonical in

1779, whereupon the Countess registered the meeting-houses as dissenting conventicles under the Toleration Act of 1689.

[3] Quoted in Charles Smyth, *The Church and the Nation* (London 1962), p. 143.

[4] William Carus, *Memoirs of the Life of the Rev. Charles Simeon, M.A.* (New York, Robert Carter, 1847), p. 23.

[5] See also H. C. G. Moule, *Charles Simeon* (London 1892); and Charles Smyth, *Simeon and Church Order.*

[6] Quoted in Moule, op. cit, pp. 102–3.

[7] Carus, op. cit., p. 171.

[8] Quoted in Smyth, *The Church and the Nation*, p. 143.

[9] Smyth, *Simeon and Church Order*, p. 299.

[10] Ibid.

[11] Carus, op. cit., p. 272.

[12] An advowson is the right to present a clergyman to a bishop for institution and induction as incumbent of a parish. The holder of an advowson, or patron, may be an individual or a corporation, such as a college. The right of advowson, which is not peculiar to the English Church, goes back to feudal times. English law regards advowsons as property which may be given away or sold.

[13] Quoted in Smyth, *Simeon and Church Order*, p. 292.

[14] References here are to Thomas Arnold, *Principles of Church Reform*, with an introductory essay by M. J. Jackson and J. Rogan. London 1962.

[15] See, e.g., J. R. H. Moorman, *A History of the Church in England* (London 1953), pp. 331–2.

[16] Arnold, op. cit., p. 97.

[17] Ibid., p. 99.

[18] Ibid., p. 101.

[19] Ibid., p. 103.

[20] Ibid., p. 104.

[21] Ibid.

[22] Ibid., p. 105.

[23] Ibid., p. 110.

[24] Ibid., p. 111.

[25] Ibid., p. 115.

[26] Ibid., p. 118.

[27] Ibid., p. 122.

[28] Ibid., p. 123.

[29] Ibid., p. 124.

[30] Ibid., p. 125.

[31] Ibid., pp. 125–7.

[32] Ibid., pp. 128–34.

[33] Ibid., pp. 134–8.

[34] Ibid., pp. 141–5.

[35] Ibid., pp. 145–7.

[36] Moorman, op. cit., p. 332.

[37] See C. C. Richardson, *The Church through the Centuries* (New York, Scribner, 1938), pp. 217–18.

[38] The Irish Church Act is referred to in Tract 2, written by Newman.

[39] References here are to the American edn (2 vols.), *Tracts for the Times: by Members of the University of Oxford*. New York, Charles Henry, 1839–40.

[40] Op. cit., vol. 1, pp. 9–10.

[41] Ibid., p. 29.

[42] Ibid., vol. 2, p. 3.

[43] Ibid., p. 4.

[44] Ibid., pp. 8–11.

[45] Ibid., vol. 1, pp. 237–8.

[46] Ibid., pp. 281–2.

[47] Moorman, op. cit., pp. 344–5.

[48] Newman explains his motives in writing Tract 90 at the end of part iv of his *Apologia pro vita sua* (1864).

[49] J. H. Newman, *An Essay on the Development of Christian Doctrine*. New York, Longmans Green, 1927. References here are to this edn.

[50] Newman, *Apologia pro vita sua* (London 1930), p. 185.

[51] 'It takes on strength as it proceeds.'

[52] Typical, because he uses similar language in concluding arguments that the Roman Church is to be identified with the Church of the fifth and sixth centuries and with the Church of the first three centuries (op. cit., pp. 245–7, 321–2).

CHAPTER 18

[1] A. J. Hartley, 'The Way to Unity: Maurice's Exegesis for Society', *Canadian Journal of Theology*, vol. xvi, nos. 1 and 2 (1970), p. 95.

[2] Advertisement to the 1842 edn, F. D. Maurice, *The Kingdom of Christ*, ed. A. R. Vidler (London 1958), vol. 1, p. 25. References here are to this edn.

[3] The 1842 edn was dedicated to the Revd Derwent Coleridge, son of Samuel T. Coleridge.

[4] Vidler's edn gives only short extracts from the Introductory Dialogue. See the Everyman edn (London n.d.), p. 41.

[5] Maurice's treatment of Luther is sympathetic. He is 'one of the few exceptions to the almost complete failure of Anglican theologians to understand Luther' (A. M. Ramsey, *F. D. Maurice and the Conflicts of Modern Theology* (Cambridge 1951), p. 28).

[6] Maurice, *The Kingdom of Christ*, p. 163.

[7] Ibid., p. 170.

[8] Ibid., p. 175.

[9] Ibid., p. 201.

[10] Ibid., pp. 211–26.

[11] Ibid., p. 220.

[12] Ibid., pp. 220–21.

[13] Ibid., p. 229.

[14] Ibid., p. 235.

[15] Ibid., p. 238.

[16] Ibid., p. 251.

[17] Ibid., p. 253.

[18] Ibid., pp. 253–4.

[19] Ibid., p. 258.

[20] Ibid., p. 261.

[21] Ibid., p. 285.

[22] Ibid., vol. 2, p. 22.

[23] Ibid., p. 30.

[24] Ibid., p. 36.

[25] Ibid., p. 37.

[26] Ibid., p. 91.

[27] Ibid., p. 102.

[28] Ibid., p. 98.

[29] Ibid., p. 102.

[30] Ibid., pp. 106 ff.

[31] Ibid., pp. 139–40.

[32] Ibid., p. 146.

[33] Ibid., p. 151; cf. Augustine, *City of God* xiv, 28.

[34] Ibid., p. 164.

[35] Ramsey, op. cit., p. 30.

[36] Maurice, op. cit., vol. 2, p. 193.

[37] Ibid., pp. 197–204.

[38] Ibid., pp. 202–3.

[39] Ibid., p. 203.

[40] Ibid., pp. 203–4.

[41] Ibid., p. 259.

[42] Ibid., p. 263.

[43] Ibid.

[44] Ibid., p. 283.

[45] Ibid., p. 284.

[46] Ibid., pp. 293–300.

[47] Ibid., pp. 303–5.

[48] Ibid., p. 306.

[49] Ibid., p. 308.

[50] Ibid., p. 312.

[51] Ibid., pp. 313–19.

[52] Ibid., p. 315.

[53] Ibid., p. 319.

[54] See above, ch. 17.

[55] Ibid., p. 322.

[56] Ibid., p. 328.

[57] Ibid., pp. 328–9.

[58] Ibid., pp. 329–30.

[59] Ibid., p. 334.

[60] Ibid.

[61] Ibid.

[62] Ibid., p. 340.

[63] Maurice admits, however, that there have been periods, e.g. in the reign of Charles I, when 'the systematic tendency' became 'very prevalent' among English churchmen; see ibid., p. 316.

[64] See vol. 1, p. 158.

[65] See R. Rouse and S. C. Neill, eds., *A History of the Ecumenical Movement* (London 1954), pp. 264–5.

[66] Ibid., p. 265.

[67] Ibid., pp. 282–3.

[68] The text of this Appeal is given in G. K. A. Bell, ed., *Documents on Christian Unity, 1920–30: a Selection.* London 1955.

[69] *Report of the Anglican–Methodist Unity Commission: Part 2, The Scheme* (London 1968), p. 37.

[70] See Gregory Dix, 'The Ministry in the Early Church' in K. E. Kirk, ed., *The Apostolic Ministry* (London 1957), pp. 187–8, 297–8.

CHAPTER 19

[1] The Greek word *oikoumene* from which 'ecumenical' is derived means 'the inhabited world'. The New York gathering of 1900 was called the Ecumenical Missionary

Conference 'because the plan of campaign which it proposes covers the whole area of the inhabited world' (quoted from Rouse and Neill, op. cit., p. 354).

2 Rouse and Neill, op. cit., p. 362.

3 Revisers' Preface to the N.T.

4 This encouragement was welcomed and acted on by the Pontifical Biblical Institute under the rectorship of Cardinal Augustin Bea, and sustained by the Constitution 'On Divine Revelation' of Vatican II.

5 The N.T. was published in 1961, the O.T. and Apocrypha in 1970.

6 Vol. 1, ed. R. Rouse and S. C. Neill, takes the history to 1948. Vol. 2, *The Ecumenical Advance: A History of the Ecumenical Movement, 1948–1968*, ed. Harold E. Fey. London 1970.

7 See Rouse and Neill, op. cit., p. 411.

8 Quoted ibid., p. 416.

9 Ibid., p. 422.

10 Ibid., p. 423.

11 Ibid., p. 433.

12 Ibid.

13 Although, as at Lausanne, Orthodox representatives participated fully in the discussions, Archbishop Germanos of Thyateira had earlier explained that the Conference's statements were often worded in a way in which the Orthodox could not conscientiously vote for them.

14 Ibid., pp. 434–5.

15 *The Churches Survey Their Task*, The Report of the Oxford Conference on Church, Community, and State (London 1937), p. 82.

16 For brevity's sake I shall use the acronym W.C.C.; and for Faith and Order, F. and O.

17 In 1961 this basis was enlarged to 'a fellowship of churches which confess the Lord Jesus Christ as God and Saviour according to the Scriptures and therefore seek to fulfil together their common calling to the glory of the one God, Father, Son, and Holy Spirit'.

18 In 'The Toronto Statement', a document of the Central Committee issued in 1950.

19 London 1952.

20 *The Third World Conference on Faith and Order*, Oliver S. Tomkins (London 1953), p. 15.

21 Ibid., p. 33.

22 *The New Delhi Report: The Third Assembly of the World Council of Churches, 1961*, ed. W. A. Visser 't Hooft (New York, Association Press, 1962), p. 116.

23 Oliver S. Tomkins, later Bishop of Bristol, had already written *The Church in the Purpose of God*, London 1950, in preparation for Lund.

24 *The Fourth World Conference on Faith and Order, Montreal, 1963*, ed. P. C. Rodger and L. Vischer. London 1964.

25 See *New Directions in Faith and Order, Bristol, 1967* (F. and O. Papers, 50). Geneva 1968.

26 *The Old and the New in the Church* (F. and O. Papers, 34). London 1961.

27 Ibid., p. 78.

28 E. Troeltsch, *Die Soziallehren der Christlichen Kirchen und Gruppen* (1911); E. T., *The Social Teaching of the Christian Churches* (see p. 206, n. 1.).

29 Fey, op. cit., pp. 419–20.

30 *Drafts for Sections prepared for the Fourth Assembly of the World Council of Churches, Uppsala, 1968*. Geneva 1968.

31 *The Uppsala Report 1968: Official Report of the Fourth Assembly of the World Council of Churches* (Geneva 1968), p. 16.

32 Ibid., p. 12.

[33] Ibid., p. 13.

[34] Pp. 496–500.

[35] See Fey, op. cit., ch. 5, 'Confessional Families and the Ecumenical Movement'.

[36] See Rouse and Neill, op. cit., pp. 473–6. Also *The Constitution of the Church of South India* (Madras, Christian Literature Society for India 1952).

[37] Cf. the words of those who signed the report of the conversations between the Church of England and the Methodist Church: 'If it be said that the Scheme proposed is not free from anomalies, we reply that the present division of our Churches from each other, frustrating their work and running counter to the declared will of God, is an anomaly so great that all other anomalies taken together are insignificant beside it.' *Anglican–Methodist Unity: Part 2, The Scheme* (London 1968), p. 181.

[38] The words are from *The Principles of Union* (1965), a document accepted by the Anglican Church of Canada and the United Church of Canada, and later by the Christian Church (Disciples of Christ) in Canada as providing guidelines by which to prepare a plan of union. The whole context is instructive: 'The United Church of Canada has ... declared that, in view of the fact that episcopacy was accepted from early times and for many centuries and is still accepted by the greater part of Christendom, it should be continued and effectively maintained in some constitutional form both at the inauguration of a union with the Anglican Church and thereafter. We are therefore agreed in accepting the threefold ministry of Bishops, Presbyters, and Deacons in some constitutional form and with the same freedom of interpretation that is now permitted within the Anglican Church. By the term "constitutional" we intend to point to the concept of the episcopacy as one element in the life of the Church in which councils and congregations also have their place, the episcopate not being separated from the life of the whole Church but integrated with it and exercised in it. By the phrase "freedom of interpretation" we mean to indicate a safeguard against any interpretation which would require either Church to repudiate or condemn the work of God in its own history, but we do not mean to imply that no agreement on the meaning of ministry in general or episcopacy in particular is necessary for unity in the faith.'

A *Plan of Union* for the three churches named was published by the General Commission on Church Union, Toronto 1973, and was remitted to the churches for study. The Anglican Church of Canada withdrew from the negotiations in 1975.

CHAPTER 20

[1] See above, p. 83.

[2] The Latin is *ordinentur*, the precise meaning of which is difficult to grasp in the context. Y. Congar (*L'Eglise*, p. 471) describes the word as *mystérieux*.

[3] *Sempiternus Rex*, 4; quoted in Fey, op. cit., p. 318.

[4] 'Ecumenical Council' here means an assembly of all bishops of the Roman Catholic Church. In some circles it was mistakenly thought that John XXIII's intention was to summon a council representative of all churches throughout the world.

[5] Quotations here are from Walter M. Abbott, S. J., ed., *The Documents of Vatican II* (New York, Guild Press, 1966).

[6] Ch. i, 1, Abbott, op. cit., p. 15.

[7] i, 4–7, pp. 16–22.

[8] Ibid., p. 24, n. 27.

[9] ii, 10, p. 27.

[10] See above, pp. 59, 62, 66 ff.

[11] ii, 13, p. 32.

[12] ii, 15, pp. 33–4.

[13] See vol. 1, pp. 86–91.

[14] As recently as 1949 it was necessary for the Holy Office to write to Archbishop Cushing of Boston to explain that Catholic doctrine does not deny that non-Roman Catholics may receive grace to salvation.

[15] ii, 15, p. 34.

[16] iii, 19, p. 38.

[17] iii, 20, p. 39.

[18] Ibid.

[19] iii, 22, pp. 42–3.

[20] See 'Prefatory Note of Explanation', sent to the Council 'from a higher authority' before the vote was taken on the Constitution: ibid., pp. 98–9.

[21] See vol. 1, pp. 69–70.

[22] Hans Küng, *The Church*, p. 418.

[23] iii, 28, p. 53.

[24] vii, 48, pp. 79–80.

[25] Ibid., pp. 199–308.

[26] Preface, para. 1, p. 200.

[27] Ibid., p. 184.

[28] Ibid., pp. 185–6.

[29] In 'A Response', ibid., pp. 309–16.

[30] Ibid., pp. 310–11.

[31] Ibid., pp. 311–14.

[32] Ibid., pp. 341–66.

[33] Ibid., p. 343.

[34] See above, pp. 98–9.

[35] i, 3, p. 346.

[36] i, 4, p. 347.

[37] ii, 8, p. 352.

[38] Fey, op. cit., pp. 343 ff.

[39] *The Evangelization of the Modern World*, Vatican City 1973.

[40] Ibid., p. 5.

[41] Ibid., pp. 7–8.

[42] Ibid., pp. 9–10.

[43] But perhaps it has never been so monolithic a structure as Protestants generally, and even some Catholics, have managed to persuade themselves.

[44] The latter question is discussed by Harry J. McSorley, c.s.p. in an article 'The Right of Catholics to Dissent from *Humanae Vitae*' in *The Ecumenist* (New York, Paulist Press), vol. 8, no. 1 (November/December 1969), pp. 5–9.

[45] For an account of some of the more influential of these see Robert S. Paul, *The Church in Search of Itself* (Grand Rapids, Michigan, Eerdmans, 1972), ch. vii, 'Catholic Reform or Roman Rebellion', pp. 226–71.

[46] 'The Church as *Sacramentum Mundi*', in *Structures of the Church* (*Concilium*, vol. 58), ed. Jiménez Urresti. New York, Herder, 1970.

[47] Op. cit., pp. 39–40.

[48] Richard McBrien has also written *Do we need the Church?* (New York, Harper & Row, 1969) and *Church, the Continuing Quest* (New York, Newman Press, 1970).

[49] E.g. in *God and the Future of Man* (London 1969), ch. iv, 'The Church as the Sacrament of Dialogue'.

[50] v, 92, Abbott, op. cit., p. 120.

[51] Schillebeeckx, op. cit., p. 120.

[52] The reference is to *Gaudium et Spes*, ch. v, 92.

[53] Gibson Winter, *The New Creation as Metropolis* (New York, Macmillan, 1963), p. 130.

[54] Ibid., p. 121.
[55] Schillebeeckx, op. cit., p. 127.
[56] Ibid., p. 138.
[57] Gregory Baum, *The Credibility of the Church Today* (New York, Herder, 1968), pp. 88 ff.
[58] Ibid., pp. 106–13.
[59] Baum, *Faith and Doctrine* (New York, Newman Press, 1969), p. 93. See also *The Credibility of the Church Today*, pp. 113–20.
[60] Baum, *The Credibility of the Church Today*, p. 134.
[61] Ibid., p. 136.
[62] Ibid., p. 141.
[63] Ibid., p. 145.
[64] Ibid., p. 152.
[65] Ibid., pp. 152 ff.
[66] Ibid., p. 176.
[67] Rosemary Radford Ruether, *The Church Against Itself* (London 1967), p. 6.
[68] Ruether, 'Letter to the Editor', in *The Ecumenist*, vol. 6, no. 4 (May/June 1968), p. 160. The review was by Joanne Dewart in the same journal, vol. 6, no. 3 (March/April 1968), pp. 140–42.
[69] Ruether, *The Church Against Itself*, p. 138.
[70] Ibid.
[71] Ibid., p. 61.
[72] Ibid., pp. 159–60.
[73] Ibid., p. 163.
[74] Ibid., p. 173.
[75] Ibid.
[76] Schillebeeckx, op. cit., p. 134.
[77] Ibid., p. 136.
[78] Ibid., pp. 137–8.
[79] Baum, *The Credibility of the Church Today*, p. 196.
[80] Ibid., p. 197.
[81] Ibid., pp. 207–8.

CHAPTER 21

[1] Ernst Troeltsch, *The Social Teaching of the Christian Churches*, E.T. by Olive Wyon, 2 vols., London; New York, Macmillan, 1931. First published in 1911 under the title *Die Soziallehren der Christlichen Kirchen und Gruppen*.
[2] See J. C. McLelland, *Toward a Radical Church* (Toronto, Ryerson Press, 1967), pp. 62–3.
[3] J. C. McLelland, op. cit., p. 62.
[4] Troeltsch, op. cit., vol. ii, pp. 729 ff.
[5] Ibid., p. 730.
[6] Ibid.
[7] Ibid.
[8] For further elucidation of Troeltsch's conception of the third type, see ibid., pp. 816–17.
[9] Dietrich Bonhoeffer, *Letters and Papers from Prison*, ed. Eberhard Bethge (New York, Macmillan, 1972), letter of 30 April 1944, pp. 279–81.
[10] E.g. 'religionless Christianity', the idea of the world come of age, the concept that God has been edged out of the world, the error of treating God as a *deus ex machina*,

or stop-gap, and the suggestion that Christians must live 'as though God were not given'.

[11] Ibid., 30 June 1944, p. 341.
[12] Ibid., 8 June 1944, p. 326.
[13] Ibid., p. 327.
[14] Ibid., 8 July 1944, p. 345.
[15] Ibid., 8 June 1944, p. 326.
[16] Ibid., 30 June 1944, p. 341.
[17] Ibid., 8 July 1944, p. 345.
[18] Ibid.
[19] Ibid., 30 June 1944, p. 342.
[20] Ibid., 30 April 1944, p. 282.
[21] Ibid., 3 August 1944, p. 378.
[22] Ibid., 30 April 1944, p. 281.
[23] Ibid., pp. 281, 286.
[24] Ibid., p. 382.
[25] *The Documents of Vatican II: Gaudium et Spes*, ch. i, 19, p. 217.
[26] Ibid., ii, 30, p. 228.
[27] Ibid., ii, 30–32, pp. 228–31.
[28] Ibid., iv, 43, p. 245.
[29] See R. S. Paul, op. cit., pp. 184 ff.
[30] Gibson Winter, *The Suburban Captivity of the Churches* (New York, Macmillan, 1962).
[31] Harvey Cox, *The Secular City* (New York, Macmillan, 1965).
[32] Winter, op. cit., p. 34.
[33] The adequacy of the resources and the responsiveness have both diminished since Professor Winter wrote.
[34] Ibid., pp. 42, 55.
[35] Ibid., p. 63.
[36] Ibid., p. 67.
[37] Ibid., p. 76.
[38] Ibid., p. 82.
[39] Ibid., p. 90.
[40] Ibid., p. 120.
[41] Ibid., p. 159.
[42] Ibid., pp. 164–5.
[43] Ibid., p. 166.
[44] Ibid., pp. 166–78.
[45] Ibid., p. 171.
[46] Ibid., p. 207.
[47] Ibid., pp. 208–9.
[48] See R. S. Paul, op. cit., p. 215.
[49] Cox, op. cit., p. 110.
[50] Ibid., p. 112.
[51] Ibid., ch. 2.
[52] Cox provides an excellent discussion (pp. 18–21) on the important distinction between secularization and secularism. The latter is 'an ideology, a new closed world-view which functions very much like a new religion'.
[53] Ibid., p. 20.
[54] Ibid., p. 25.
[55] Ibid., p. 32.
[56] Ibid., p. 105.
[57] Ibid., p. 125.

[58] Ibid., p. 127.
[59] Ibid.
[60] Ibid., p. 128.
[61] Ibid., pp. 143–4.
[62] Ibid., p. 145.
[63] Ibid., p. 154.
[64] Ibid., p. 156.
[65] Ibid., p. 160.
[66] Ibid., p. 226. See R. S. Paul, op. cit., pp. 215–25, for a critique of *The Secular City*. The question whether Cox identifies the Church too closely with the secularized technopolis is discussed on pp. 224–5.

CHAPTER 22

[1] For a succinct account of Barth's theology see W. Nicholls, *Systematic and Philosophical Theology* (Harmondsworth 1969), pp. 75–149. References to the *Church Dogmatics* are to the E.T., ed. G. W. Bromiley and T. F. Torrance, *Karl Barth: Church Dogmatics*, Edinburgh. It is to be remembered that the date of each volume is about three years later than the Swiss edn.

[2] E.T. by E. C. Hoskyns, *Karl Barth: The Epistle to the Romans*, Oxford 1933.

[3] Karl Barth, *The Humanity of God* (Richmond, Virginia, John Knox Press, 1968), p. 62. The volume includes another lecture, delivered in 1957, on 'Evangelical Theology in the Nineteenth Century', in which he is much more generous in his estimate of its accomplishments than he had been thirty years earlier.

[4] Ibid., p. 42.

[5] Ibid., p. 37.

[6] Ibid., p. 46.

[7] E. Lamirande, O.M.I., 'Roman Catholic Reactions to Karl Barth's Ecclesiology', in *Canadian Journal of Theology*, vol. xiv, no. 1 (January 1968), pp. 28–42.

[8] Ibid., p. 33.

[9] H. R. Mackintosh, *Types of Modern Theology* (London 1937), pp. 309–13.

[10] Hoskyns, op. cit., pp. 353, 371, 418.

[11] Ibid., p. 418.

[12] This underlies the whole section 'Justification by Faith Alone' in *Church Dogmatics*, vol. iv, 1. See especially pp. 629–34. Cf. also in the *Römerbrief*, 'Faith cannot be a concrete thing that once began and then continued its course. Faith is the Beginning, the Miracle, the Creation in every moment of time' (Hoskyns, op. cit., p. 499).

[13] CD (*Church Dogmatics*), vol. iv, 1, pp. 650 ff.

[14] Lamirande, op. cit., p. 34.

[15] E.g., H. R. Mackintosh, op. cit., pp. 314–16.

[16] H. Hartwell, *The Theology of Karl Barth: an Introduction* (London 1964), pp. 36–7.

[17] See above, p. 137.

[18] The closeness to the idea of the Church as *Sacramentum mundi* (see above, pp. 109 ff) should be noted.

[19] CD iv, 1, p. 653.

[20] Ibid.

[21] Ibid., p. 654.

[22] Ibid., p. 661. It is possible to suggest that this phrase gives the essential meaning of the doctrine that the Church is the extension of the incarnation, favoured by some Anglican theologians, but usually rejected by Protestants on the ground that it iden-

tifies the Church with the risen Christ and that it is triumphalistic in assuming the Church to be a perfect society. Yet Barth himself sharply rejects this Anglican doctrine as 'not only out of place but even blasphemous' (*CD* iv, 3, 2nd half, p. 729).

23 *CD* iv, 1, pp. 661–8.
24 Ibid., p. 669.
25 Ibid., pp. 669–70.
26 Ibid., p. 671.
27 Ibid., pp. 681–2.
28 Ibid., p. 688. Cf. the Orthodox theologian, J. Meyendorff, quoted, in vol. 1, p. 154.
29 Ibid., pp. 688–9.
30 Ibid., p. 690.
31 Ibid., pp. 698–9. Cf. the treatment of this credal clause in the Catechism of the Council of Trent; see vol. 1, pp. 200–1.
32 Ibid., p. 701.
33 Ibid., p. 702.
34 Ibid., p. 703.
35 Ibid., p. 704.
36 Ibid.
37 Ibid., p. 705.
38 Ibid., pp. 706–7.
39 Ibid., p. 708.
40 Ibid.
41 Ibid., pp. 710–12.
42 Ibid., pp. 712–13.
43 Ibid., p. 715.
44 *CD* iv, 1, pp. 715–18 deserve the careful study of those who claim that apostolicity depends upon a traceable line of bishops from the present day to the apostles.
45 Ibid., pp. 718–19.
46 Ibid., p. 721.
47 *CD* iv, 3, 2nd half, pp. 681–901.
48 Ibid., p. 687.
49 Ibid., p. 693.
50 Ibid., p. 695.
51 Ibid., p. 710.
52 Ibid., p. 711.
53 Ibid., p. 720.
54 See also *CD* iv, 1, pp. 725–39, 'The Time of the Community'.
55 Karl Barth, *Dogmatics in Outline* (London 1949), pp. 122–3.
56 See vol. 1, p. 203.
57 *CD* iv, 3, p. 724.
58 Ibid., p. 726.
59 Ibid., p. 727.
60 Ibid., p. 728.
61 Ibid., p. 766.
62 Ibid., p. 767. Barth here cites also John 3.16, Colossians 1.16, and Hebrews 1.3.
63 Ibid., pp. 769–77.
64 Ibid., p. 796.
65 Ibid., p. 797.
66 Ibid., p. 798.
67 Ibid., p. 800.
68 Ibid., p. 803.
69 Ibid., p. 811.
70 Ibid., pp. 812–30.

[71] Ibid., p. 831.
[72] Ibid., pp. 838–43.
[73] Ibid., pp. 843–54.
[74] Ibid., p. 855.
[75] Ibid., p. 863.
[76] Ibid., pp. 865–82.
[77] Ibid., pp. 882–901.
[78] Ibid., p. 858.
[79] *CD* iii, 4, pp. 488–90.
[80] See above, p. 136.
[81] Karl Barth, *The Humanity of God*, p. 62.
[82] Ibid., p. 63.
[83] Ibid.
[84] Ibid., p. 64.
[85] Ibid.
[86] Ibid., p. 65.

CHAPTER 23

[1] R. T. Handy, 'Paul Tillich', in Alan Richardson, ed., *A Dictionary of Christian Theology* (London 1969), p. 340.
[2] Paul Tillich, *Systematic Theology* (London; Chicago, Chicago University Press, vol. 1, 1951; vol. 2, 1957; vol. 3, 1963). Hereafter designated as *ST*. Page references are to the Chicago edn.
[3] *ST* 1, p. 60.
[4] *ST* 2, p. 25.
[5] Ibid., p. 45.
[6] Many students of Tillich are baffled by his apparent equation of the fall with creation.
[7] *ST* 1, p. 261.
[8] Ibid., ch. 7.
[9] *ST* 2, pp. 46 ff.
[10] Ibid., p. 138.
[11] *ST* 3, pp. 30–110.
[12] Ibid., p. 107.
[13] Passages like this have incurred the charge that Tillich's Christology is adoptionist: see A. J. McKelway, *The Systematic Theology of Paul Tillich* (New York, Dell Publishing Co., 1964), pp. 166–8. It is my belief, however, that he can be strongly defended against the charge.
[14] *ST* 3, p. 147.
[15] Tillich uses the words 'ecstatic' and 'ecstasy' in the sense of the human spirit being lifted beyond itself but without loss of its rational character. It is not to be confused with 'enthusiasm'.
[16] Ibid., pp. 150–52.
[17] The Greek word *kairos* means 'time' in the sense of an opportune or particularly significant moment.
[18] Ibid., p. 155.
[19] Ibid., p. 154.
[20] Ibid., pp. 155–6.
[21] Ibid., p. 158.
[22] Ibid.
[23] Ibid., p. 159.
[24] Ibid., pp. 231–7.

[25] E.g., ibid., p. 157.
[26] Ibid., p. 165.
[27] Ibid., p. 167.
[28] Ibid., p. 173.
[29] Ibid., pp. 188–93.
[30] Ibid., pp. 193–6.
[31] Ibid., pp. 196–212.
[32] Ibid., p. 197.
[33] Ibid., pp. 212–16.
[34] Ibid., pp. 212–13.
[35] Ibid., p. 214.
[36] Ibid.
[37] Ibid., p. 216.
[38] Ibid., p. 246.
[39] See especially *ST* 3, pp. 374–82.
[40] Ibid., p. 107.
[41] Ibid., pp. 359–60.
[42] Ibid., p. 361.
[43] Ibid., p. 344.
[44] Ibid.
[45] Ibid., p. 376.
[46] Ibid., p. 377.
[47] Ibid., p. 378.
[48] Ibid.
[49] Ibid., p. 379.
[50] See above, pp. 159, 162.
[51] *ST* 3, pp. 385 ff.
[52] Ibid., p. 389.
[53] Ibid., p. 390.
[54] Ibid., p. 391.
[55] Ibid., pp. 394–423.
[56] E.g., *ST* 3, pp. 6, 245.
[57] Ibid., p. 223.
[58] Ibid., p. 245. Tillich does not deny that the Protestant principle is recognized by sound Catholic theology; nor that Catholic substance is present in many Protestant churches.
[59] Ibid., p. 122.
[60] Ibid., p. 120.
[61] Ibid., p. 344.
[62] Ibid., p. 375.
[63] Ibid., p. 381.
[64] Ibid., p. 155.
[65] Baltimore, Helicon Press; and London.
[66] Bishop Butler, in a letter to *The Times* of London, dated 21 August 1971, writing in his capacity as president of the Social Morality Council.

CHAPTER 24

[1] Original title, *Structuren der Kirche* (Freiburg, Herder, 1962), E.T., London 1964; and in paperback, Notre Dame, U.S.A., University of Notre Dame Press, 1968, from which citations here are made (referred to as *Structures*).

448

² Original title *Die Kirche* (Freiburg, Herder, 1967). E.T., London 1967; and New York, Sheed & Ward, 1968, from which citations here are made (referred to as *Church*).
³ See above, pp. 96 ff.
⁴ *Church*, p. ix.
⁵ Ibid., p. xiii.
⁶ *Structures*, p. 12, n. 8.
⁷ Ibid., p. 9: '*Con-cilium* is derived from *con-kal-ium*, or from *con-calare*. *Calare* is employed as a religious technical term for "to announce", "to summon".'
⁸ Ibid., p. 14.
⁹ *Church*, p. 34.
¹⁰ Ibid., p. 38. Cf. Richard Field, in vol. 1, pp. 183–4; and Karl Barth, above, p. 140.
¹¹ Ibid., p. 5. Cf. Barth on the Church as 'event', above, pp. 137–8.
¹² Ibid., p. 48.
¹³ Ibid., p. 62.
¹⁴ Ibid., p. 72.
¹⁵ Ibid., p. 73.
¹⁶ Ibid.
¹⁷ Ibid., p. 74.
¹⁸ Ibid., p. 75.
¹⁹ Ibid., p. 95.
²⁰ Ibid., pp. 95–6.
²¹ Ibid., pp. 88–104.
²² Ibid., p. 97.
²³ Ibid., pp. 119–20.
²⁴ Ibid., p. 125.
²⁵ Ibid., p. 167.
²⁶ Ibid., p. 172.
²⁷ Ibid., p. 174.
²⁸ Cf. Tillich: see above, pp. 160–61.
²⁹ *Church*, p. 187.
³⁰ See below, p. 188.
³¹ *Church*, pp. 203–41.
³² Ibid., pp. 224–5.
³³ Ibid., p. 235.
³⁴ Ibid., p. 236.
³⁵ Ibid., pp. 237, 239. Cf. Barth's rejection of this phrase, p. 209, n. 22.
³⁶ Küng's assertion in the same note (p. 237) that 'mystical' in this usage simply means 'mysterious' must be challenged. The word is connected with the Greek *mueomai*, 'to become an initiate', and the 'mystical body' basically means no more and no less than the company of those who have been baptized. See vol. 1, p. 77.
³⁷ Ibid., p. 237.
³⁸ Ibid., p. 239.
³⁹ Ibid., pp. 239–40.
⁴⁰ Ibid., p. 241.
⁴¹ *Structures*, ch. viii; *Church*, pp. 444–80.
⁴² *Structures*, p. 63.
⁴³ See above, pp. 142, 162–4.
⁴⁴ *Church*, p. 275.
⁴⁵ Ibid., p. 281.
⁴⁶ Ibid., p. 283.
⁴⁷ Ibid., p. 284.
⁴⁸ Ibid., pp. 285–96.

449

[49] See above, pp. 58–61.
[50] *Structures*, p. 48.
[51] Cf. above, p. 178.
[52] *Structures*, p. 48.
[53] *Church*, pp. 296–300.
[54] *Structures*, p. 40.
[55] Ibid., p. 39.
[56] *Church*, pp. 305–13.
[57] Ibid., 313–19.
[58] Ibid., p. 354.
[59] Ibid., p. 355.
[60] Ibid., p. 358.
[61] Ibid., p. 359.
[62] See also above, pp. 177–8, under 'The People of God'.
[63] As proof of the reversal of this trend in Catholic theology, he cites (*Structures*, pp. 86–7) numerous recent books and papal pronouncements on the laity.
[64] *Church*, p. 367.
[65] 1 Peter 2.4, 11; Revelation 1.5.
[66] *Church*, p. 377.
[67] *Structures*, p. 108. Quoted from M. Luther, *Werke* 6, 408 (Weimar, 1883 ff).
[68] Ibid., p. 120.
[69] *Church*, pp. 388 ff.
[70] Ibid., p. 389.
[71] Ibid., p. 391.
[72] Ibid., pp. 393–444. See also *Structures*, pp. 136–54.
[73] *Church*, p. 401.
[74] Acts 14.23 is anachronistic, Küng argues, in saying that Paul and Barnabas appointed elders.
[75] *Church*, p. 407.
[76] Ibid., p. 432.
[77] Ibid., p. 429.
[78] *Structures*, p. 184.
[79] Ibid., pp. 185–90.
[80] *Church*, p. 438.
[81] Ibid., pp. 438–9.
[82] *Structures*, p. 154. The italics are Küng's.
[83] Ibid., pp. 157–64.
[84] Ibid., pp. 165–8.
[85] *Church*, pp. 441–2.
[86] Ibid., p. 444.
[87] *Structures*, pp. 201–304; *Church*, pp. 444–80.
[88] *Structures*, p. 203.
[89] Ibid., p. 205.
[90] Ibid. This is based on the commission to Peter in Matthew 16.18–19; Luke 22.32; John 21.15–19.
[91] At this point the non-Catholic reader looks in vain for an attempt to provide an historical and theological link between the office of Peter and the holder of the see of Rome.
[92] Ibid., pp. 209–23.
[93] See vol. 1, p. 138. Küng writes: 'The legitimacy of the new pope (Martin V) depended on these decrees [i.e. of Constance] ... according to the usual view, it is in turn the premise of the legitimacy of the popes in the last five hundred years' (*Structures*, p. 254).

[94] Ibid., p. 255.
[95] Ibid., p. 258.
[96] Ibid., p. 295.
[97] *Church*, p. 451.
[98] *Structures*, p. 349.
[99] Karl Barth, *Church Dogmatics* i, 2, pp. 544–72. Küng discusses this long note of Barth's in *Structures*, pp. 314–26.
[100] *Structures*, ch. 8; *Church*, pp. 449–50. In his more recent book, *Infallible? An Inquiry* (New York, Doubleday, 1971), he subjects the concept to even more searching examination.
[101] *Structures*, p. 322.
[102] Ibid., p. 334.
[103] *Church*, p. 471.
[104] Ibid., p. 472.
[105] Ibid., pp. 477–8.

POSTSCRIPT

[1] Tillich, *Systematic Theology*, vol. 3, p. 304.
[2] Significant are: Karl Rahner (among his many works), 'Questions on the Theology of History', part ii in *Theological Investigations*, vol. v [Later Writings] London, and Baltimore, Helicon Press, 1966; *The Shape of the Church to Come*, London, and New York, Seabury, 1974; L. S. Thornton, *The Common Life in the Body of Christ*, London 1942; Christ and the Church, part iii of a treatise on 'The Form of a Servant', London 1956; Lesslie Newbigin, *The Household of God*, London 1953.

Bibliography
CHAPTERS 1–14

The dates given are those of the editions used in this volume, and do not necessarily indicate the dates of the original publications.

A. TEXTS OF COLLECTED OR SINGLE WORKS; TRANSLATIONS; SELECTIONS

Migne, J. P., ed., *Patrologia Graeca.* Paris 1857–66.

Migne, J. P., ed., *Patrologia Latina.* Paris 1844–55.

Roberts, A. and Donaldson, J., eds., The Ante-Nicene Christian Library, 9 vols. Edinburgh 1864 ff. Published also in New York under the title *The Ante-Nicene Fathers.*

Schaff, P., ed., The Nicene and Post-Nicene Fathers, 1st ser., 14 vols. New York 1886–9.

Schaff, P. and Wace, A., eds., The Nicene and Post-Nicene Fathers, 2nd ser., 28 vols. New York; London 1890–1900.

Lake, Kirsopp, ed., *The Apostolic Fathers,* 2 vols. Heinemann, The Loeb Classical Library 1959.

Bettenson, R. H., ed., *The Early Christian Fathers.* Oxford University Press 1956.

Bettenson, R. H., ed., *The Later Christian Fathers.* Oxford University Press 1970.

Dix, Gregory, ed., *The Apostolic Tradition of St Hippolytus.* SPCK 1937.

Lawson, R. P., ed., *Origen; The Song of Songs, Commentary and Homilies,* vol. 26 of 'Ancient Christian Writers'. Longmans Green; Westminster, Maryland, Newman Press, 1957.

Goldast, M., ed., *Monarchia Sancti Romani Imperii,* 3 vols. Hanover 1612.

S. Bonaventurae Opera Omnia, ed. Franciscan Brethren of Quaracchi, 10 vols. 1882–1907.

Albertus Magnus, *Opera,* ed. A. Borgnet, 38 vols. Paris 1890–99.

The Summa Theologica of St Thomas Aquinas, tr. Fathers of the English Dominican Province. Burns, Oates & Washbourne. 1914 ff.

Gilby, T., *St Thomas Aquinas: Theological Texts*. Oxford University Press 1955.

John of Paris, *De potestate regia et papali*, ed. J. LeClercq, in *Jean de Paris et l'ecclésiologie du xiiie siècle*. Paris 1942.

Meister Johann Eckhart, *Opera Latina*, ed. G. Thery and R. Klibansky. Leipzig 1934 ff.

Marsilius of Padua, *Defensor Fidei*, ed. C. W. Previté-Orton. Cambridge University Press 1928.

William of Ockham, *Opera Politica*, ed. J. G. Sikes *et al.* University of Manchester Publications 1940.

William of Ockham, *De Imperatorum et Pontificum Potestate*, ed. C. K. Brampton. Oxford University Press 1927.

John Wyclif, *Trialogus*, ed. G. V. Kechner. 1869.

Wyclif's Latin Works, published by the Wyclif Society. 1884 ff.

Johannes de Turrecremata (Torquemada), *Summa de Ecclesia*. Venice 1560.

Corpus Reformatorum. Brunswick 1863–1900; reprinted, New York and London, Johnson Reprint Corporation, 1969.

Luther's Works, 55 vols., ed. J. Pelikan and H. T. Lehmann. St Louis, Missouri, Concordia Publishing House; Philadelphia, Fortress Press, 1955 ff.

Calvin: Institutes of the Christian Religion, tr. F. L. Battles, ed. J. T. McNeill, vols. xx and xxi of 'The Library of Christian Classics'. SCM Press; Philadelphia, Westminster Press, 1961.

Calvin: Theological Treatises, ed. J. K. S. Reid, vol. xxii of 'The Library of Christian Classics'. SCM Press; Philadelphia, Westminster Press, 1954.

Anglicanism, ed. P. E. More and F. L. Cross. SPCK 1957.

The Works of that Learned and Judicious Divine, Mr Richard Hooker, ed. J. Keble 1836; rev. R. W. Church and F. Paget 1888.

Richard Hooker, *The Laws of Ecclesiastical Polity*. J. M. Dent, Everyman's Library 1907.

Richard Field, *Of the Church*, ed. Ecclesiastical History Society. 1847.

The Writings of Henry Barrow, 1587–90, ed. Leland H. Carson, Elizabethan Nonconformist Texts, vol. iii. Allen & Unwin 1962.

John Pearson, *An Exposition of the Creed*, ed. E. Burton. 1864.

Robert Barclay, *Apology for the True Christian Religion, as the same is set forth and presented by the People called in Scorn 'Quakers'*. 1701.

The Canons and Decrees of the Council of Trent, tr. T. A. Buckley. 1851.

The Catechism of the Council of Trent, tr. T. A. Buckley. 1852.

Robert Bellarmine, *Disputationes de Controversiis Christianae Fidei adversus huius temporis Haereticos,* 3 vols. Ingolstadt 1586–9. Modern edns in *Opera Omnia,* Naples 1856–62, 8 vols. and Paris 1870–74, 12 vols.

Reformed Confessions of the 16th Century, ed. A. C. Cochrane. Philadelphia, Westminster Press, 1966.

The Evangelical Protestant Creeds, ed. P. Schaff, vol. 3 of 'The Creeds of Christendom'. New York 1877.

The Creeds and Platforms of Congregationalism, ed. Williston Walker. New York 1893.

B. GENERAL WORKS

Aulén, Gustaf, *The Faith of the Christian Church*. SPCK 1954.

Battenhouse, R. W., *A Companion to the Study of St Augustine*. New York, Oxford University Press, 1955.

Best, Ernest, *One Body in Christ*. SPCK 1955.

Brandreth, H. R. T., *Episcopi Vagantes*. SPCK 1947.

Butler, B. C., *The Idea of the Church*. Darton, Longman & Todd 1962.

Chadwick, Owen, *The Reformation*, 'Pelican History of the Church', vol. 3. Penguin Books 1964.

Congar, Yves, *L'Ecclésiologie du haut Moyen-Age*. Paris, Les Editions du Cerf. 1968.

Congar, Yves, *L'Eglise de Saint Augustin à l'époque moderne*. Paris, Les Editions du Cerf, 1970.

Corwin, Virginia, *St Ignatius and Christianity in Antioch*. New Haven, Connecticut, Yale University Press, 1960.

Cragg, G. R., *The Church and the Age of Reason, 1648–1759*, 'Pelican History of the Church', vol. 4. Penguin Books 1970.

Cross, F. L., ed., *The Oxford Dictionary of the Christian Church*. Oxford University Press 1957.

Davies, G. Henton, 'Remnant', in A. Richardson, ed., *A Theological Word Book of the Bible*. SCM Press 1950.

Evans, R. F., *One and Holy*. SPCK 1972.

Flew, R. Newton, ed., *The Nature of the Church*. SCM Press 1952.

Gore, Charles, *The Church and the Ministry*. Longmans Green 1893.

454 *Bibliography*

Grabowski, S. J., *The Church: An Introduction to the Theology of St Augustine.* London; St Louis, Missouri, Herder, 1957.

Greenslade, S. L., *Schism in the Early Church.* SCM Press 1953.

Hoskyns, E. C. and Davey, F. N., *The Riddle of the New Testament.* Faber 1931.

Jeremias, J., 'Akrogoniaios', in G. Kittel, ed., *Theological Dictionary of the New Testament* (see below).

Johnston, George, *The Doctrine of the Church in the New Testament.* Cambridge University Press 1943.

Johnston, George, 'The Doctrine of the Church in the New Testament', in M. Black and H. H. Rowley, eds., *Peake's Commentary on the Bible.* Nelson 1962.

Kelly, J. N. D., *Early Christian Doctrines.* Black 1958.

Kittel, G., ed., *Theological Dictionary of the New Testament*, 9 vols. Grand Rapids, Michigan, Eerdmans, 1964 ff.

Küng, Hans, *The Church.* New York, Sheed & Ward, 1967.

Küng, Hans, *Structures of the Church.* Nelson 1964; Notre Dame, University of Notre Dame Press, 1968.

MacGregor, Geddes, *Corpus Christi.* Philadelphia, Westminster Press, 1958.

McKelvey, R. T., *The New Temple.* Oxford University Press 1969.

Manson, T. W., *The Teaching of Jesus.* Cambridge University Press 1931.

Meyendorff, John, *Orthodoxy and Catholicity.* New York, Sheed & Ward, 1966.

Meyendorff, John, *The Orthodox Church.* Darton, Longman & Todd 1962.

Meyendorff, John, 'What Holds the Church Together?', in *Ecumenical Review*, vol. xii. 1960.

Milner, B. C., *Calvin's Doctrine of the Church.* Leiden, E. J. Brill, 1970.

Minear, P. S., *Images of the Church in the New Testament.* Philadelphia, Westminster Press, 1950.

Moberly, R. C., *Ministerial Priesthood.* New York, Longmans Green, 1916.

Nissiotis, N. A., unpublished paper on 'Orthodox Theology and Worship'. 1971.

Petry, R. C., *A History of the Christian Church,* vol. 1. Englewood Cliffs, New Jersey, Prentice-Hall, 1962.

Quick, O. C., *Doctrines of the Creed.* Collins 1963.

CHAPTERS 15-24

Dates given are those of the editions used or referred to in this book, and do not always indicate the date of the first publication.

Barth, Karl, *Church Dogmatics* (E.T. ed. G. W. Bromiley and T. F. Torrance), 4 vols. each in several parts. Edinburgh, T. & T. Clark, 1936–62.

Barth, Karl, *Dogmatics in Outline*, SCM Press 1949.

Barth, Karl, *The Epistle to the Romans* (E.T. by E. C. Hoskyns). Oxford University Press 1933.

Barth, Karl, *The Humanity of God.* Richmond, Virginia, John Knox Press, 1968.

Baum, Gregory, *The Credibility of the Church Today.* New York, Herder & Herder, 1968.

Baum, Gregory, *Faith and Doctrine.* New York, Newman Press, 1969.

Bell, G. K. A., ed., *Documents on Christian Unity: a Selection, 1920–30.* Oxford University Press 1955.

Bonhoeffer, Dietrich, *Letters and Papers from Prison*, ed. Eberhard Bethge. New York, Macmillan, 1972.

Butler, B. C., *The Idea of the Church.* Darton, Longman & Todd; Baltimore, Helicon Press, 1962.

Carus, William, *Memoirs of the Life of the Rev. Charles Simeon,* M.A. New York, Robert Carter, 1847.

Chadwick, Owen, *The Reformation*, 'Pelican History of the Church', vol. 3. Penguin Books 1964.

Congar, Yves, *L'Eglise de saint Augustin à l'époque moderne.* Paris, Les Editions du Cerf, 1970.

Cox, Harvey, *The Secular City.* New York, Macmillan, 1965.

Cragg, G. R., *The Church and the Age of Reason, 1648–1789*, 'Pelican History of the Church', vol. 4. Penguin Books 1970.

Creed, J. M. *The Divinity of Jesus Christ.* Collins 1964.

Cross, F. L., ed., *The Oxford Dictionary of the Christian Church.* Oxford University Press 1957.

Denzinger, H., *Enchiridion Symbolorum, Definitionum et Declarationum de rebus fidei et morum.* Freiburg 1960.

Fey, Harold E., *The Ecumenical Advance: A History of the Ecumenical Movement, 1948–1968.* SPCK 1970.

Flew, R. Newton, ed., *The Nature of the Church.* SCM Press 1952.

Harnack, Adolf, *Das Wesen des Christentums,* 1900; E.T. by T. B. Saunders, *What is Christianity?* Williams & Norgate 1901.

Hartwell, H., *The Theology of Karl Barth: an Introduction.* Duckworth 1964.

Jackson, M. J. and Rogan, J., eds., *Thomas Arnold, Principles of Church Reform.* SPCK 1962.

Küng, Hans, *The Church.* Burns & Oates; New York, Sheed & Ward, 1967.

Küng, Hans, *Infallible? An Inquiry.* New York, Doubleday, 1971.

Küng, Hans, *Structures of the Church.* Nelson 1964; Notre Dame, University of Notre Dame Press, 1968.

Locke, John, *A Letter Concerning Toleration.* New York, The Liberal Arts Press, 1955.

Locke, John, *The Reasonableness of Christianity* (see under Ramsey, I. T., below).

Loisy, Alfred, *L'Evangile et l'Eglise.* Paris 1902; E.T. Christopher Howe, *The Gospel and the Church.* New York, Scribner, 1912.

McBrien, Richard, *Church, the Continuing Quest.* New York, Newman Press, 1970.

McBrien, Richard, *Do we need the Church?* New York, Harper & Row, 1969.

McKelway, A. J., *The Systematic Theology of Paul Tillich.* New York, Dell Publishing Co., 1964.

Mackintosh, H. R., *Types of Modern Theology.* Nisbet 1937.

McLelland, J. C., *Toward a Radical Church.* Toronto, Ryerson Press, 1967.

Maurice, F. D., *The Gospel of the Kingdom of Heaven.* Macmillan 1888.

Maurice, F. D., *The Lord's Prayer.* Macmillan 1861.

Maurice, F. D., *The Kingdom of Christ,* 2 vols., ed. A. R. Vidler. SCM Press 1958.

Möhler, Johann A., *Die Einheit in der Kirche* ('Unity in the Church'). Mainz 1825; ed. with commentary by J. R. Geiselmann.

Köln–Olten 1957; French tr., Collection Unam Sanctam 2. Paris, Les Editions du Cerf, 1938.

Möhler, Johann A., *Symbolik* ('Symbolism'). Mainz 1832; ed. J. R. Geiselmann. Köln–Olten 1958; French tr. F. Lachat. Besançon 1836.

Moorman, J. R. H., *A History of the Church in England*. A. & C. Black 1953.

Moule, H. C. G., *Charles Simeon*. Methuen 1892.

Nédoncelle, Maurice, *Baron Friedrich von Hügel*. Longmans Green 1937.

Newbigin, Lesslie, *The Household of God*. SCM Press 1953.

Newman, John Henry, *Apologia pro vita sua*. Dent 1930.

Newman, John Henry, *An Essay on the Development of Christian Doctrine*. New York, Longmans Green, 1927.

Nicholls, William, *Systematic and Philosophical Theology*. Penguin Books 1969.

Palmer, William, *Treatise on the Church of Christ*, 2 vols. Rivington 1839.

Paul, Robert S., *The Church in Search of Itself*. Grand Rapids, Michigan, Eerdmans, 1972.

Rahner, Karl, *The Shape of the Church to Come*. SPCK; New York, Seabury, 1974.

Rahner, Karl, *Theological Investigations*, vol. 5 (Later Writings). Darton, Longman & Todd; Baltimore, Helicon Press, 1966.

Ramsey, A. M., *F. D. Maurice and the Conflicts of Modern Theology*. Cambridge University Press 1951.

Ramsey, I. T., ed., *John Locke, 'The Reasonableness of Christianity'*. Stanford University Press, California, 1958.

Richardson, Cyril, *The Church through the Centuries*. New York, Scribner, 1938.

Ritschl, Albrecht, *The Christian Doctrine of Justification and Sanctification* (E.T. by H. R. Mackintosh and A. B. Macauley). Edinburgh, T. & T. Clark, 1900.

Rouse, R. and Neill, S. C., eds., *A History of the Ecumenical Movement, 1517–1948*. SPCK 1954.

Ruether, Rosemary Radford, *The Church Against Itself*. Sheed & Ward 1967.

Schillebeeckx, Edward, o.p., *God the Future of Man*. Sheed & Ward 1969.

Schleiermacher, Friedrich, *The Christian Faith* (E.T. by H. R.

Mackintosh and J. S. Stewart). Edinburgh, T. & T. Clark, 1960.

Schleiermacher, Friedrich, *On Religion: Speeches to its Cultured Despisers* (E.T. by John Oman). New York, Harper, 1958.

Schweitzer, Albert, *The Quest of the Historical Jesus* (E.T. by W. Montgomery). A. & C. Black 1956.

Smyth, Charles, *The Church and the Nation*. Hodder & Stoughton 1962.

Smyth, Charles, *Simeon and Church Order*. Cambridge University Press 1940.

Thornton, Lionel, c.r., *Christ and the Church*. Dacre Press 1956.

Thornton, Lionel, c.r., *The Common Life in the Body of Christ*. Dacre Press 1942.

Tillich, Paul, *Systematic Theology*, 3 vols. Nisbet; Chicago University Press, 1951–63.

Tomkins, Oliver S., *The Church in the Purpose of God*. SCM Press 1950.

Tracts for the Times: by Members of the University of Oxford, 2 vols. New York, Charles Henry, 1839–40.

Troeltsch, Ernst, *The Social Teaching of the Christian Churches* (E.T. by Olive Wyon of *Die Soziallehren des Christlichen Kirchen und Gruppen*, 1911), 2 vols. Allen & Unwin; New York, Macmillan, 1931.

Tyrrell, George, *Christianity at the Crossroads*. London and New York, Longmans Green, 1909.

von Hügel, Friedrich, *Essays and Addresses on the Philosophy of Religion*, 1st and 2nd ser. Dent 1927, 1930.

von Hügel, Friedrich, *Eternal Life*. Edinburgh, T. & T. Clark, 1912.

von Hügel, Friedrich, *Selected Letters, 1896–1924*. Dent 1927.

von Hügel, Friedrich, *Some Notes on the Petrine Claims*. Sheed & Ward 1930.

Winter, Gibson, *The New Creation as Metropolis*. New York, Macmillan, 1963.

Winter, Gibson, *The Suburban Captivity of the Churches*. New York, Macmillan, 1962.

ARTICLES IN JOURNALS; CHAPTERS IN BOOKS

Dix, Gregory, 'The Ministry in the Early Church', chapter in K. E. Kirk, ed., *The Apostolic Ministry*. Hodder & Stoughton 1957.

Handy, R. T., 'Paul Tillich', article in Alan Richardson, ed., *A Dictionary of Christian Theology*. SCM Press 1969.

Hartley, A. J., 'The Way to Unity: Maurice's Exegesis for Society', article in *Canadian Journal of Theology*, vol. xvi, nos. 1 and 2, 1970.

Lamirande, E., 'Roman Catholic Reactions to Karl Barth's Ecclesiology', article in *Canadian Journal of Theology*, vol. xiv, no. 1, 1968.

McBrien, Richard, 'The Church: Sign and Instrument of Unity', article in Jiménez Urresti, ed., *Structures of the Church (Concilium*, vol. 58). New York, Herder & Herder, 1970.

McSorley, Harry J., C.S.P., 'The Right of Catholics to dissent from *Humanae Vitae*', article in *The Ecumenist*, vol. viii, no. 1. New York, Paulist Press, 1969.

Nienaltowski, R. H., 'Möhler', article in *The New Catholic Encyclopedia*, vol. ix. New York, McGraw-Hill, 1967.

O'Dea, Thomas, 'The Church as *Sacramentum Mundi*', article in Jiménez Urresti, ed., *Structures of the Church (Concilium*, vol. 58). New York, Herder & Herder, 1970.

Rodes, Robert, 'Structures of the Church's Presence in the World of Today—through the Church's own Institutions', article in Jiménez Urresti, ed., *Structures of the Church (Concilium*, vol. 58). New York, Herder & Herder, 1970.

Ruether, Rosemary Radford, 'Letter to the Editor' in *The Ecumenist*, vol. vi, no. 4. New York, Paulist Press, 1968.

Slabaugh, Warren W., 'The Church of the Brethren', statement in R. Newton Flew, ed., *The Nature of the Church*. SCM Press 1952.

REPORTS OF COMMISSIONS, CONFERENCES, AND COUNCILS; AND OTHER DOCUMENTS

The Churches Survey Their Task, Report of the Oxford Conference on Church, Community, and State. George Allen & Unwin 1937.

The Third World Conference on Faith and Order, ed. Oliver S. Tomkins. SCM Press 1953.

The Fourth World Conference on Faith and Order, eds. P. C. Rodger and L. Vischer. SCM Press 1964.

The Old and the New in the Church, Faith and Order Papers, no. 34. SCM Press 1961.

New Directions in Faith and Order, Faith and Order Papers, no. 50.

Geneva, W.C.C., 1968.

The New Delhi Report: The Third Assembly of the World Council of Churches, 1961, ed. W. A. Visser 't Hooft. New York, Association Press, 1962.

The Uppsala Report, 1968: Official Report of the Fourth Assembly of the World Council of Churches. Geneva, W.C.C., 1968.

Drafts for Sections prepared for the Fourth Assembly of the World Council of Churches, Uppsala, 1968. Geneva, W.C.C., 1968.

The Documents of Vatican II, ed. Walter M. Abbott, s.J. New York, Guild Press, 1966.

The Evangelization of the Modern World (for the Use of the Episcopal Conferences). Vatican City 1973.

The Constitution of the Church of South India. Madras, Christian Literature Society for India, 1952.

Report of the Anglican–Methodist Unity Commission, Part 2, The Scheme. SPCK 1968.

The Principles of Union. Toronto, Anglican Church of Canada and The United Church of Canada, 1965.

Plan of Union. Toronto, General Commission on Church Union, 1973.

Index

Names

Abbott, W. M.   320, 421n
Abel   89, 120, 140, 203
Abraham   278
Adam   14, 63, 200, 203
Albertus Magnus   114, 116–17
Alexander of Hales   115, 117
Ambrose, Bp of Milan   91, 119
Anastasius, emperor   98, 100
Anastasius of Antioch   150
Andrews, Lancelot, Bp of Winchester
   267
Anselm, Abp of Canterbury   114
Aristotle   279
Arnold, Thomas   263–267
Athanasius, Bp of Alexandria   78, 81,
   184, 232
Athanasius the Greek   156
Athenagoras, Patriarch of Constanti-
   nople   145
Augustine, Bp of Hippo   18, 63, 69,
   73–4, 84–92, 97, 99, 114, 133, 140,
   150–1, 153, 163–4, 172, 193, 197, 226,
   255, 275, 315, 389, 418n

Bagot, Richard, Bp of Oxford   271
Baillie, Donald M.   300–1
Barnabas, Epistle of   30
Barrow, Henry   178–9
Barth, Karl   258, 350, ch.22, 372, 397,
   408, 428nn, 430n
Basil, Bp of Caesarea   199
Basilides   43
Battenhouse, R. W.   92
Baum, Gregory   327–29, 331
Bea, Augustin, Cardinal 312–13, 419n
Bede, the Venerable   99, 103
Bell, G.K.A., Bp of Chichester   419n
Bellarmine, Robert   141, 184, 202–4,
   322, 365
Benedict XV, pope   299, 311
Bentham, Jeremy   275, 277
Bergson, Henri   235
Berkeley, George, Bp of Cloyne   220
Bernard of Clairvaux   107, 125
Berridge, John   260, 262
Best, E.   14–15, 218nn

Bethge, Eberhard   336, 423n
Bettenson, R. H.   71, 219n
Blondel, Maurice   235
Böhme, Jacob   334
Bonaventure   92, 114, 116–17
Bonhoeffer, Dietrich   336–340, 346
Boniface, Abp of Mainz   100
Boniface VIII, pope   110–12, 117, 129
Borromeo, Charles   196
Bousset, Jacques Bénigne, Bp of Meaux
   225
Boyle, Robert   220
Bramhall, John, Abp of Armagh   267
Brent, Charles, Bp of Western New York
   296, 298, 300
Brown, Robert McAfee   318–19
Browne, Robert   179
Brunner, Emil   258
Bucer, Martin   169, 181
Bullinger, J. H.   207
Bultmann, Rudolf   350
Butler, B.C.   388
Butler, Joseph, Bp of Durham   222

Caecilian, Bp of Carthage   81–2
Callistus I, pope   55–6
Callistus II, pope   107
Calvin, John   92, 164, 169–176, 178,
   183, 204, 222, 244, 253, 255
Campion, D. R.   318–19
Canisius, Peter   202
Carey, William   180
Carus, William   261
Castellio, Sebastian   222
Celsus   225
Chadwick, Owen   412n
Charlemagne, emperor   92, 100–1, 143
Charles V, emperor   195
Clarke, Samuel   220
2 Clement   30, 39, 62
Clement IV, pope   145
Clement V, pope   112
Clement of Alexandria   39, 50, 58–60,
   62, 88
Clement of Rome   30–5, 45, 47–8, 53,
   57, 112, 268

Subjects

C. indicates Church

472